Color	Red	Green	
gainsboro	DC	DC	DC
ghostwhite	F8	F8	FF
gold	FF	D7	00
goldenrod	DA	A5	20
gray	80	80	80
green	00	80	00
greenyellow	AD	FF	2F
honeydew	F0	FF	F0
hotpink	FF	69	B4
indianred	CD	5C	5C
indigo	4B	00	82
ivory	FF	FF	F0
khaki	F0	E6	8C
lavender	E6	E6	FA
lavenderblush	FF	F0	F5
lawngreen	7C	FC	00
lemonchiffon	FF	FA	CD
lightblue	AD	D8	E6
lightcoral	F0	80	80
lightcyan	E0	FF	FF
lightgoldenrodyellow	FA	FA	D2
lightgreen	90	EE	90
lightgrey	D3	D3	D3
lightpink	FF	B6	C1
lightsalmon	FF	A0	7A
lightseagreen	20	B2	AA
lightskyblue	87	CE	FA
lightslategray	77	88	99
lightsteelblue	B0	C4	DE
lightyellow	FF	FF	E0
lime	00	FF	00
limegreen	32	CD	32
linen	FA	F0	E6
magenta	FF	00	FF
maroon	80	00	00
mediumaquamarine	66	CD	AA
mediumblue	00	00	CD
mediumorchid	BA	55	D3
mediumpurple	93	70	DB
mediumseagreen	3C	B3	71
mediumslateblue	7B	68	EE
mediumspringgreen	00	FA	9A
mediumturquoise	48	D1	CC
mediumvioletred	C7	15	85
midnightblue	19	19	70
mintcream	F5	FF	FA
mistyrose	FF	E4	E1

continues

JavaScript continued

Color	Red	Green	Blue
moccasin	FF	E4	B5
navajowhite	FF	DE	AD
navy	00	00	80
oldlace	FD	F5	E6
olive	80	80	00
olivedrab	6B	8E	23
orange	FF	A5	00
orangered	FF	45	00
orchid	DA	70	D6
palegoldenrod	EE	E8	AA
palegreen	98	FB	98
paleturquoise	AF	EE	EE
palevioletred	DB	70	93
papayawhip	FF	EF	D5
peachpuff	FF	DA	B9
peru	CD	85	3F
pink	FF	C0	CB
plum	DD	A0	DD
powderblue	B0	E0	E6
purple	80	00	80
red	FF	00	00
rosybrown	BC	8F	8F
royalblue	41	69	E1
saddlebrown	8B	45	13
salmon	FA	80	72
sandybrown	F4	A4	60
seagreen	2E	8B	57
seashell	FF	F5	EE
sienna	A0	52	2D
silver	C0	C0	C0
skyblue	87	CE	EB
slateblue	6A	5A	CD
slategray	70	80	90
snow	FF	FA	FA
springgreen	00	FF	7F
steelblue	46	82	B4
tan	D2	B4	8C
teal	00	80	80
thistle	D8	BF	D8
tomato	FF	63	47
turquoise	40	E0	D0
violet	EE	82	EE
wheat	F5	DE	B3
white	FF	FF	FF
whitesmoke	F5	F5	F5
yellow	FF	FF	00
yellowgreen	9A	CD	32

JavaScript™

Richard Wagner, et al.

sams
net

201 West 103rd Street
Indianapolis, IN 46290

UNLEASHED

Dedicated to Nicholas Andrew Clair Abraham

"There will come one day a personal and direct touch from God when every tear and perplexity, every suffering and pain, and every wrong and injustice will have a complete and ample and overwhelming explanation."

Copyright © 1996 by Sams.net Publishing

FIRST EDITION

International Standard Book Number: 1-57521-118-1

Library of Congress Catalog Card Number: 96-68239

99   98   97   96   4   3   2   1

Interpretation of the printing code: the rightmost double-digit number is the year of the book's printing; the rightmost single-digit, the number of the book's printing. For example, a printing code of 96-1 shows that the first printing of the book occurred in 1996.

Composed in Agaramond and MCPdigital by Macmillan Computer Publishing

Printed in the United States of America

Publisher, Sams Publishing   *Richard K. Swadley*

Publishing Manager   *Rosemarie Graham*

Managing Editor   *Cindy Morrow*

Director of Marketing   *John Pierce*

Assistant Marketing Managers   *Kristina Perry, Rachel Wolfe*

Acquisitions Editor
Corrine Wire

Development Editor
Michael Watson

Software Development Specialist
John Warriner

Production Editor
Mary Inderstrodt

Copy Editors
Brice Gosnell
Howard Jones
Kris Simmons

Technical Reviewers
Greg Guntle
John Nienart

Editorial Coordinator
Bill Whitmer

Technical Edit Coordinator
Lorraine Schaffer

Resource Coordinator
Deborah Frisby

Editorial Assistants
Carol Ackerman
Andi Richter
Rhonda Tinch-Mize

Cover Designer
Tim Amrhein

Book Designer
Gary Adair

Copy Writer
Peter Fuller

Production Team Supervisor
Brad Chinn

Production
Charlotte Clapp
Ayanna Lacey
Chris Livengood
Paula Lowell

Contents

Part VIII JavaScript Database Applications

Part IX Appendixes

Acknowledgments

Richard Wagner would like to express his deepest thanks to each of the people below, who in some way contributed to this book:

- Bruce Beck and Acadia Software, for your strong support throughout this project.
- Gary Griffin, Bill Chosiad, and Kim Daniels, for your interest in working on this book from the get-go.
- Corrine Wire, for your assistance in keeping me on schedule as well as your courteous and ever cheerful attitude.
- Michael Watson, for your excellent job of developing the book and your feedback to help hammer out a well-rounded outline.
- Rosemarie Graham and everyone at Sams.net, for your support and interest in this book.
- Chris Van Buren at Waterside Productions, for getting me involved in this project in the first place.
- Finally, Kimberly and the Js, for your tenacity and patience to see this project through to the end.

About the Authors

Richard Wagner is Chief Technology Officer of Acadia Software and is an experienced author in the computer industry. He has considerable development experience in both Web and client/server applications using JavaScript, Delphi, and a variety of other development tools.

In addition, Richard is Contributing Editor to *Delphi Informant* and regular contributor to *Web Informant*. In *Delphi Informant*, he has a monthly column in the magazine called *File\New*, which focuses on trends in software development. Richard is also a member of Team Borland, assisting Borland technical support on their CompuServe and Web forums.

Mr. Wagner is author of *Inside Paradox for Windows* (3 eds.), *CompuServe Internet Tour Guide*, and *Inside CompuServe* (3 eds.) and contributor to *Ultimate Windows 3.1*, *Inside Windows NT*, *Inside Microsoft Access*, *Inside dBASE for Windows*, and *Integrating Windows Applications*.

Finally, he has a Bachelor of Arts from Taylor University and pursued masters studies at American University. He welcomes your comments at rwagner@acadians.com or http://www.acadians.com.

Arman Danesh (armand@bwc.org) is the author of *Teach Yourself JavaScript in a Week* and coauthor of *JavaScript Developer's Guide*. He is the World Wide Web specialist for a large public information Web site, is fluent in several programming languages, and has experience managing large-scale production systems. He is also a technology reporter and columnist for several publications in the Far East. He can be reached by e-mail at armand@juxta.com.

Kim Daniels is a Senior Applications Developer with Acadia Software in Boxborough, MA. She specializes in Delphi client/server database application development as well as Internet development using Javascript and other Web development tools.

She received a BS in Management Information Systems from Rensselaer Polytechnic Institute in Troy, New York. Your comments are welcome at kdaniels@acadians.com.

Rick Darnell is a midwest native currently living with his wife and two daughters in Missoula, Montana. He began his career in print at a small weekly newspaper after graduating from Kansas State University with a degree in broadcasting. While spending time as a freelance journalist and writer, Rick has seen the full gamut of personal computers, since starting out with a Radio Shack Model I in the late 1970s. When not in front of his computer, he serves as a volunteer firefighter and member of a regional hazardous materials response team. Rick Darnell just recently contributed to *FrontPage Unleashed*. Rick may be contacted at darnell@montana.com.

Heather Downs is a software consultant specializing in compilers and various Internet technologies. She holds a degree in math from the Massachusetts Institute of Technology. In her spare time, Heather enjoys maintaining her Web site, http://www.bungalow.com/, and writing obfuscated C programs. She lives in Mountain View, California with her Significant Other and can be reached via e-mail at heather@bungalow.com.

Gary Griffin wrote Part II, "The JavaScript Language." He is an applications developer for Acadia Software specializing in Paradox, C++, Java, and JavaScript. His favorite bands include Stone Temple Pilots, Jane's Addiction, and Ned's Atomic Dustbin. Gary may be contacted with comments or suggestions at `ggriffin@acadians.com`.

Christopher Haddad is an equity partner and founder of Rock Creek Technologies. Chris manages development teams and designs, creates, and enhances proprietary application development frameworks. The associated Windows and DOS tools and utilities are being successfully used by development teams to produce end-user applications.

Michael Kmiec is an Applications Developer with PFN Incorporated in Cambridge, MA. With a background in C, C++ and philosophy, he uses JavaScript to fuel some of the functionality of a network publishing system.

Stephen Le Hunte is an independant software developer and freelance technical author specializing in HTML, WinHelp, Visual Basic, and C++. He is currently trying to finish his PhD at the University of Wales Swansea.

Michael G. Moncur is the owner of Starling Technologies, a consulting firm specializing in networking and the Internet. He is also a freelance Webmaster and author, and has worked with the Internet since 1989. He is the author of *Laura Lemay's Web Workshop: JavaScript,* also from Sams.net.

Jimmy Nasr is currently an Internet Program Manager at Aetna Inc., in Connecticut and was the founder of MJN Computer Consulting located there, specializing in Internet design, development, and security. He earned a BS in Computer Science from Coventry University in England and an MBA from the University of Connecticut. Jimmy is an avid soccer player and German Shepherd dog owner! He can be contacted at `jnasr@mjn.com`.

Claudia Piemont is a German freelance author and computer science journalist. She earned a BS in Computer Science from FH Darmstadt in Germany. She has a broad knowledge in both software development and consulting gained through practical experience in a major German corporation. Her special interests are object-oriented technology, the Internet, and multimedia.

Robert L. Platt (`http://www.realtime.net/~rlp`) has worked for AT&T Bell Laboratories and Tandem Computers as a software developer and as a project manager. He has worked on a variety of projects including advanced graphical user interfaces and speech recognition. His areas of interest include the Internet, graphical user interfaces, object-oriented programming, and financial analysis. Bob enjoys being the father of a five-year-old, travel, and science fiction. Robert may be contacted at `rlp@acm.org`.

Ed Smith is an Internet Consultant and Web Site Developer in York County, Pennsylvania. His own company, E.T. Smith Associates, develops, establishes, and maintains Internet sites for businesses and organizations specializing in highly interactive sites. A former armored cavalry officer, Ed worked in the electric utility industry as an engineer for 11 years before leaving to start his own Internet business.

Ed enjoys travel and motorcycle riding. He's ridden his Harley Softail through the U.S., to the top of the Colorado Rockies, and gone 2,000 miles in a couple of days to meet friends for a Thunder Run. However, he most enjoys time with his wife, two daughters, and his wife's pit bull Katie. (He's really good to the wife.)

Tell Us What You Think!

As a reader, you are the most important critic and commentator of our books. We value your opinion and want to know what we're doing right, what we could do better, what areas you'd like to see us publish in, and any other words of wisdom you're willing to pass our way. You can help us make strong books that meet your needs and give you the computer guidance you require.

Do you have access to CompuServe or the World Wide Web? Then check out our CompuServe forum by typing GO SAMS at any prompt. If you prefer the World Wide Web, check out our site at http://www.mcp.com.

> **NOTE**
>
> If you have a technical question about this book, call the technical support line at (800) 571-5840, ext. 3668.

As the team leader of the group that created this book, I welcome your comments. You can fax, e-mail, or write me directly to let me know what you did or didn't like about this book—as well as what we can do to make our books stronger. Here's the information:

Fax: 317/581-4669
E-mail: enterprise_mgr@sams.mcp.com
Mail: Rosemarie Graham
         Comments Department
         Sams Publishing
         201 W. 103rd Street
         Indianapolis, IN 46290

Introduction

JavaScript is quickly emerging as a significant tool for Web development, whether for simple enhancements to HTML pages or full-fledged Web-based applications. But because its *raison d'etre* is not as glamorous, JavaScript will perhaps never be as popular as Java, ActiveX, or even HTML. Having said that, JavaScript does something none of the others can do: make divergent technologies work seamlessly together. Indeed, the jack-of-all-trades nature of JavaScript is perhaps what gives this language staying power.

To date, most people probably see JavaScript as a client-side language. That it is—and much of this book focuses on how to embed JavaScript into HTML to run under a Netscape or Microsoft browser. However, JavaScript is also emerging as a server-side scripting language as well. Products such as Netscape's LiveWire Pro and Borland's IntraBuilder are the first of many that will use JavaScript as their Web scripting language. This book takes an in-depth look at each of those products.

STRONG VENDOR SUPPORT

The following software companies have announced they will use JavaScript as part of a forthcoming product:

America Online, Apple Computer, Architext Software, AT&T, Borland International, Brio Technology, Computer Associates, Digital, Hewlett-Packard, Iconovex Corporation, Illustra, Informix, Intuit, Macromedia, Metrowerks, Microsoft, Novell, Oracle, Paper Software, Precept Software, RAD Technologies, The Santa Cruz Operation, Silicon Graphics, Spider Technologies, Sybase, and Verity.

I am a developer by trade, and the more I use JavaScript, the more I see its wide ranging applicability in the applications my company develops. It is my hope that JavaScript's flexibility to handle a wide variety of tasks comes through the pages of this book. A few of the many questions we'll answer together include

- What is the relationship between JavaScript and HTML?
- How can you create *smart frames* with JavaScript?
- What is the JavaScript object model?
- How does JavaScript integrate with ActiveX controls, Netscape Plug-Ins, and Java applets?
- How does JavaScript compare to Java?
- How does JavaScript handle state maintenance?
- How can I use JavaScript on my Web server?
- How can I connect to my SQL database using JavaScript?

Who Should Read This Book?

Because of its status as the primary Web scripting language, JavaScript is used by all sorts of people for all sorts of things. These include

- Webmasters
- HTML authors and designers
- Java developers
- Database application developers
- Power users

I believe readers in each of these categories will appreciate this book. The book, however, does assume that the reader has basic Web and HTML knowledge. Also, no JavaScript experience is expected, but an assumption is that the reader has had some programming language experience in a scripting or full language. If you have never programmed before, this does not mean the book is not designed for you. But in *JavaScript Unleashed*, you will get less tutelage on beginner programming issues that are non-germane to JavaScript. Finally, for the advanced server- and database-related chapters, some server and database experience is required.

How This Book is Organized

JavaScript Unleashed provides a whole-hog look at JavaScript and related technologies. It is divided into nine sections, each of which are summarized in the following subsections.

Part I: Getting Started with JavaScript

In Part I, you will get a complete introduction to JavaScript. Chapter 1 takes a unique look at JavaScript, focusing on how and where it fits into the Web application development framework. You will also see how it relates to other Web technologies both on the client- and server-side. In Chapter 2, you will learn about the relationship between JavaScript and Hypertext Markup Language (HTML) and how the browser interprets your code at runtime. Chapter 3 looks at the software tools you need to develop in JavaScript.

Part II: The JavaScript Language

The second part presents a thorough look at the JavaScript language. In Chapters 4-7, you will learn about language basics, control structures, operators, and functions.

Part III: JavaScript Objects

Part three dives into the heart of JavaScript: objects. After an introduction to object-oriented concepts in Chapter 8, Chapter 9 looks at how you can handle user and system events. Chapter 10 then looks at the built-in JavaScript hierarchy and introduces you to each of the

Navigator and built-in language objects. Chapters 11-14 continue where the previous chapter left off by exploring in-depth each of the built-in JavaScript objects. Chapter 15 rounds out the discussion on objects, focusing on how you can create your own. It includes many innovative ideas related to custom object development within JavaScript.

Part IV: JavaScript Programming

The next section builds upon everything you learned up to that point to look at specific areas of interest to the JavaScript developer. Chapter 16 explores how you can enhance HTML forms with JavaScript, such as providing client-side data validation. Both Chapters 17-18 focus on frames and how you can use JavaScript in multiframe windows. I've found frame management to be perhaps the most common use of JavaScript on the Web. Chapter 19 looks at yet other key topics, cookies and other techniques for handling and maintaining state in the Web's stateless environment.

Part V: JavaScript on the Server

Parts I-IV focused on client-side JavaScript, and this section focuses on its server-side counterpart. Within Netscape's LiveWire and other products such as Borland's IntraBuilder, you can use JavaScript as a server-side scripting language. In doing so, you are free from writing CGI scripts and dealing with such languages as Perl. Chapter 20 looks at server-side JavaScript, focusing on LiveWire and IntraBuilder. Chapter 21 takes a look at the issue of how to architect client/server applications on the Web. Covered are many of the issues you will encounter as you plan such an application.

Part VI: Advanced JavaScript

Part VI explores five advanced subjects, many of which are emerging as key topics as JavaScript matures. Chapter 22 dives into error-handling and debugging JavaScript applications. Chapters 23-24 cover the hot topic of integrating JavaScript with Netscape Plug-Ins and ActiveX controls. Chapter 25 looks at integrating JavaScript with VRML and multimedia data. Chapter 26 closes the section by looking at a more conceptual topic: JavaScript security. The chapter not only looks at the key issues surrounding this subject but provides some helpful advice as you consider using JavaScript for your Web site.

Part VII: Java and JavaScript

JavaScript is an important tool to glue HTML and Java applets. This part looks at Java from a JavaScript perspective in Chapter 27 and shows how similar or different the language is for JavaScripters. Chapter 28 provides a good introduction on how to build a Java applet, and Chapter 29 is where the "rubber meets the road" when it focuses on integrating Java and JavaScript.

Part VIII: JavaScript Database Applications

Many corporations use the Web as a way to get at their data. As a result, how JavaScript can access data will be an increasingly important topic as the technology matures. This part shows how you can work with data both on the client-side and server-side. Chapter 30 introduces the notion of maintaining lookup tables on the client-side to lessen the need to access the server. Chapter 31 then gets into how you can use JavaScript to access server-side data. LiveWire and IntraBuilder will again be used in this context.

Part IX: Appendixes

The final part of this book provides some extra information that will assist you as you read the book. Appendixes A-B provide basic references on the JavaScript and HTML, respectively. Appendix C looks at how VBScript and JavaScript compare. Appendix D lists JavaScript resources that are available online.

System Requirements

In order to use JavaScript, you simply need a capable computer that has access to the Web. The authors primarily use Windows 95 and Windows NT, but the same JavaScript code will work on Netscape Navigator versions for Macintosh and UNIX.

Conventions Used in This Book

JavaScript Unleashed uses certain conventions to help make the book more readable and helpful to you.

The following style conventions are used:

- **Code**. JavaScript code listings, JavaScript method names, and screen messages or displays are shown in a `monospaced type font`.
- **New terms**. New terms that are introduced or defined are displayed in *italics*.
- **Multiline code lines**. Sometimes a line of JavaScript code is unable to fit on a single line within the dimensions of this book. If so, the line is separated and continued on the following line. The ➥ character denotes these multiline code lines.

In addition, this book uses special sidebars that are set apart from the rest of the text. The sidebars included are Notes, Tips, Cautions, and Resources.

PART

I

Getting Started with JavaScript

JavaScript and the World Wide Web

by Richard Wagner

IN THIS CHAPTER

CHAPTER 1

The popular adage of the day is that an Internet year is equal to three calendar months. With that in mind, I recommend fastening your seat belt and jumping into JavaScript head first. Before diving into the nuts and bolts of creating JavaScript code, it is important to look at the purpose of JavaScript within the context of the Web application framework. Just like other Web technologies, such as browser software, HTML, Java, CGI, and Netscape plug-ins, JavaScript by itself is rather limited in scope. JavaScript emerges as a powerful tool as you begin to use it with other technologies to provide effective and deliberate solutions.

In this chapter, I provide an overview of JavaScript and then look at JavaScript within the context of the Web application framework. Next, I look at the major uses of JavaScript today and then close with a look at current browsers' support for JavaScript.

Introducing JavaScript

Like everything else connected to the Web, JavaScript is a new technology—even newer than Java itself. JavaScript was initially developed by Netscape under the name of LiveScript. This scripting language was intended to extend the capabilities of basic HTML and provide an alternative to using CGI scripts. After Netscape saw Java, however, it began to work with Sun to provide a scripting language even more closely linked to Java itself—hence, the name change to JavaScript.

One of the motivations behind JavaScript was the recognition for logic to exist on the client, not simply on the server. With all logic on the server side, all processing is forced to go to the server, even for simple tasks such as data validation. In fact, with no logic on the front end, the Web environment falls into the outdated terminal-to-host architecture that was replaced with the PC revolution in the 1980s. Providing logic within the browser can empower the client and make the relationship a true client/server arrangement.

Java is a step in this direction, but it is implemented as an adjunct to HTML itself and not intended to be integrated from a language standpoint. Also, as a strongly typed language, Java is not optimal for gluing together divergent applets. Java also requires low-level programming skills, something that most HTML developers would rather not exercise just to provide some logic behind HTML form elements. A higher-level, client-side scripting language seemed like a natural missing piece in the Web development tool arena.

Since its roll out in December 1995, JavaScript has drawn support from the major industry vendors, including Apple, Borland, Sybase, Informix, Oracle, Digital, HP, and IBM. Although Microsoft is working on its own competitor to JavaScript called VBScript, it will support JavaScript in version 3.0 of its Internet Explorer.

JavaScript is likely to become established as the standard Web scripting language. As vendors produce Web development tools that require a scripting language, it is expected that JavaScript will often be used for that purpose. Netscape uses JavaScript as a server-side scripting language in its LiveWire environment, something you will dive into later in Chapter 20, "Server-Side JavaScript."

Another example from Borland International is IntraBuilder. It is a Web database development tool that uses JavaScript as its native language. However, as explored in Chapter 31, "Database Connectivity Using Server-Side JavaScript," IntraBuilder extends the JavaScript language for its own uses within the product. If other vendors continue to do the same, JavaScript will become ubiquitous for scripting on the World Wide Web.

RESOURCE

Visit Borland's home page at `http://www.borland.com` for the latest information and downloads on IntraBuilder and Latte.

Ten JavaScript Facts Every Scripter Should Know

Trying to learn a new tool such as JavaScript can be challenging because it can be difficult to understand how it is used and how it fits into the general picture. I have boiled down the basics of JavaScript to ten facts that will help you as you begin to work with it. Study these before you continue.

JavaScript Is Embedded into HTML

Perhaps the most important JavaScript fact is its marriage with HTML. If you deal with JavaScript, there is hardly any separation of the two. JavaScript code is usually housed within HTML documents and executed within them. Additionally, by itself, JavaScript has no user interface; it relies on HTML to provide its means of interaction with the user. Along this line, most of the JavaScript objects have HTML tags that they represent. If you have little background in HTML, you will discover that to be an effective JavaScript developer, you also need to learn the ins and outs of HTML.

JavaScript uses HTML as a means of jumping into the Web application framework. It also extends the normal capabilities of HTML by providing events to HTML tags and allowing event-driven code to execute within it.

Although I wait for future chapters to explain JavaScript, Listing 1.1 provides an example of how JavaScript code is embedded in HTML source code. The text in bold represents the JavaScript-specific code in the document. Everything else is plain HTML.

Listing 1.1. JavaScript embedded in an HTML file.

```html
<html>
<head>
<title>Status Bar</title>
<SCRIPT LANGUAGE="JavaScript">
<!--
    window.defaultStatus = "Welcome to the large URL page."

    function changeStatus() {
        window.status = "Click me to go to the Acadia Software
        home page."
    }

    function changeDefaultStatus() {
        window.defaultStatus = window.document.statusForm.messageList.
        options[window.document.statusForm.messageList.
        selectedIndex].text
    }
//-->
</SCRIPT>
</head>

<body>
<p> </p>
<p> </p>
<p align=center>
<font color="#008040">
<font size=7>
<strong>http://www.acadians.com</strong></font></font></p>
<p align=center>
<a href="http://www.acadians.com" onMouseOver="changeStatus()
    ;return true">Go...</a></p>

<form name="statusForm" method="POST">
<p><br>
<br>
<br>
<br>
</p>
<p align=center>
<font size=1>To change the default status bar message, select
a message from the list below and click the Change button. </font></p>
<p align=center><select
    name="messageList"
    size=1>
    <option selected>Welcome to the large URL page.</option>
    <option>On route to Acadia Software</option>
    <option>This page intentionally left (nearly) blank.</option>
    <option>An exciting example of changing status bar text.</option>
    </select>
<input
    type=button
    name="Change"
    value="Change"
    onClick="changeDefaultStatus()"></p>
</form>
</body>
</html>
```

JavaScript Is Browser Dependent

JavaScript is but a scripting language, not a tool in and of itself. The software that actually runs the JavaScript code you write is the Web browser—whether it's Netscape Navigator, Microsoft Internet Explorer, or whatever. JavaScript depends on the Web browser to support it. (See Figure 1.1.) If the browser does not support it, your code will be ignored. Even worse, if you do not account for unsupporting browsers, the JavaScript code itself is displayed as text on your page. (See Figure 1.2.) See Chapter 2, "How JavaScript and HTML Work Together," for details on how to prevent your code from being displayed.

FIGURE 1.1.

Microsoft Internet Explorer 3.0 supports JavaScript.

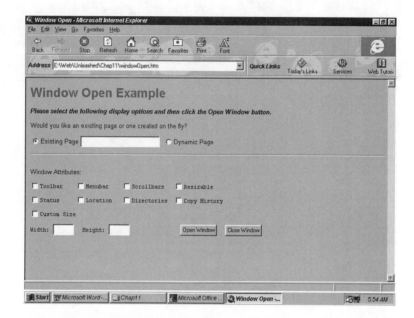

It is critical to remember this dependence as you decide when and where to use JavaScript in your application solution. Will you require a browser that supports JavaScript? If so, how should you notify users who use an unsupporting browser? Will you create a non-JavaScript solution as well? You need to answer all these questions as you develop your JavaScript applications.

NOTE

When first released, frames were an innovative solution but were viewable only to users with Netscape Navigator 2.0. HTML authors had to decide when to use frames and what to do when a browser did not support them. With the continued popularity of Netscape, and Microsoft's support for them in Internet Explorer 3.0, frames are becoming more common on Web sites. In fact, the unspoken assumption of many is that if you are "with it," you already have a browser that supports frames.

Fortunately for JavaScript developers, it is likely that the same will hold true for JavaScript support. Netscape Navigator 2.x and above and Microsoft Internet Explorer 3.0—the browsers with some 90 percent of the market—do provide JavaScript support. If these trends continue, browser dependence will become less of an issue.

FIGURE 1.2.

Spry Mosaic does not support JavaScript.

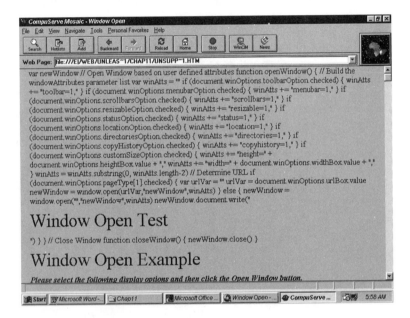

JavaScript Is an Interpreted Language

As with most scripting languages, JavaScript is interpreted at runtime by the browser before it is executed. JavaScript is not compiled into an actual program—like an .EXE file—but remains part of the HTML document to which it is attached. The disadvantage of an interpreted language is that it takes longer for the code to execute because the browser compiles the instructions at runtime just before executing them. However, the advantage is that it is much easier to update your source code. You do not have to worry about old versions of a JavaScript script hanging around because if you change it in your source HTML file, the new code is executed the next time the user accesses the document.

JavaScript Is a Loosely Typed Language

JavaScript is far different from strong-typed languages such as Java or Delphi, in which you must declare all variables of a certain type before using them. In contrast, JavaScript is much more flexible. You can declare variables of a specific type, but you do not need to. You can also work with a variable when you might not know the specific type before run time. A short code snippet can demonstrate this. Suppose you want to declare a variable called `myVal`, assign a string value to it, and then display it in a message box. You could use the following code:

```
function flexible() {
   var myVal    // declare variable myVal
   mVal = "Pi"  // assign value to myVal
   alert(myVal) // use it
}
```

Although it is generally a good practice to declare your variables explicitly, you are not required to do so. The following code, perfectly valid in JavaScript, would be unthinkable in a strongly typed language:

```
function flexible() {
   mVal = "Pi"  // assign value to an undeclared variable myVal
   alert(myVal) // use it
}
```

To further illustrate JavaScript's flexibility, you can change the type of value the variable represents as well. For example, the `myVal` variable changes from a string to a number value during the course of the function's execution:

```
function flexible() {
   var myVal = "Pi"
   alert(myVal)
   myVal = 3.14159
   alert(myVal)
}
```

JavaScript Is an Object-Based Language

You might see JavaScript referred to as an object-oriented programming (OOP) language by Netscape and others, but this is actually a stretch of the true meaning of OOP. As you will learn in Chapter 8, "Fundamentals of Object Orientation," JavaScript is really an *object-based* language.

You do work with objects that encapsulate data (properties) and behavior (methods). (If you have used dot notation—whether in Visual Basic, Java, or Delphi—you will find JavaScript quick to pick up.) However, although you can work with objects, you cannot subclass them. The JavaScript object model is instance-based, not inheritance-based.

JavaScript Is Event-Driven

Much of the JavaScript code you write will be in response to events generated by the user or the system. The JavaScript language itself is equipped to handle events. HTML objects, such as buttons or text fields, are enhanced to support event handlers. If you are coming from a Java or Visual Basic background, this event-driven environment is second nature. If you come from a procedural, top-down language environment, the event-driven nature of JavaScript might require some study. Chapter 9, "Handling Events," provides a complete look at JavaScript events.

JavaScript Is Not Java

As you surf the Web, you will see a common phrase on JavaScript-related Web sites: *JavaScript is not Java*. As discussed previously, Java and JavaScript were created by two different companies, and the primary reason for the name similarity is purely for marketing purposes. I save the in-depth comparison between JavaScript and Java for Chapter 27, "Java from a JavaScripter Perspective," but it might be helpful to briefly mention some of the differences (and similarities) that exist between them in this context as well.

First, although JavaScript is tightly integrated into HTML, a Java applet is simply connected to an HTML document through the <APPLET> tag. The applet itself is stored in another file, which is downloaded from the server.

Second, with strong-typing, true object-orientation, and a compiler, Java is a more robust and complete language. Keep in mind, Java is for applets or complete applications; JavaScript is primarily for scripts.

If you look at the language itself, JavaScript's syntax does resemble Java. If you get used to the JavaScript control structures, you could use that as a head start to learning Java itself.

> **NOTE**
>
> For anecdotal evidence on the confusion between JavaScript and Java, I offer my own personal story as I wrote this book. When I told people about writing a JavaScript book, all but the most informed ignored the "script" and responded, "Oh, I've heard a lot about Java recently."

JavaScript Is Multifunctional

JavaScript is multifaceted and can be used in a variety of contexts to provide a solution to a Web-based problem. Later in this chapter in the section "JavaScript's Role in Web Application Development," I discuss the variety of uses for JavaScript. Some of the primary purposes include the following:

- Enhance and liven static HTML pages.
- Develop client-side applications.
- Serve as a building block for client/server Web applications.
- Serve as client-side glue between HTML objects, Java applets, ActiveX controls, and Netscape plug-ins.
- Serve as an extension to a Web server.
- Provide database connectivity without using CGI.

JavaScript Is Evolving

Earlier in the chapter, I discussed how new JavaScript is as a technology. If you add that fact to the rapid rate of change on the Web, it is easy to recognize that JavaScript itself continues to evolve as a language. As you develop JavaScript applications, not only do you need to consider whether the browser supports JavaScript, but also consider which iteration of JavaScript it supports. Netscape Navigator 3.0 has several bug fixes and new features that are unavailable in version 2.*x*. Also, Microsoft Internet Explorer 3.0 provides general support for JavaScript, but the beta version I was using at the time of writing did not implement everything.

> **RESOURCE**
>
> Visit Netscape's home page at `http://home.netscape.com` for information on future enhancements to JavaScript.

The JavaScript Language Spans Contexts

To repeat something mentioned earlier in this chapter: JavaScript is a language, not a tool. As a Web scripting language, it can be useful in a variety of contexts. Much of the focus on JavaScript by Web developers (and this book) is for client-side scripting. However, you can also use it on the server-side in the Netscape LiveWire Pro environment and Microsoft's ActiveX Server framework. It is also used as the native language for Web development tools, such as Borland's IntraBuilder, mentioned earlier in the chapter. When you think of JavaScript, do not think of it exclusively as a client-side scripting language.

Four Phases of the World Wide Web

The revolutionary changes in Web technology over the past six years make the Web a constantly moving target. Before I discuss Web applications, it is helpful to review the evolution of the Web from its humble beginnings as an extension of the Internet into a culture that is changing technology today. You can view this transformation as four distinct phases of the Web.

Phase I: Character-Based Hypertext

Originally, the Web was a text-based hypertext system when it started in 1989. This limitation was primarily because the computers that accessed the Web had no good way of displaying graphics. In the Web's early days, users were forced to type in a number representing the page they wanted to access. In time, you could select highlighted text and then move to the associated page. For the Web's scientific and academic uses, the hypertext nature of the Web was revolutionary.

Phase II: Graphical-Based Static HTML Documents

The second phase of the Web began in 1993 with the release of the first graphical Web browser called NCSA Mosaic. Mosaic was developed by undergraduate student Marc Andreessen for the National Center for Supercomputing Applications (NCSA). Although the concept of the Web was already proving useful for the scientific and academic communities, a graphical browser suddenly harnessed the raw power of the Internet and made it easy to navigate. At the same time, graphical environments were becoming more popular than character-based systems on the desktop. Microsoft was winning the desktop war with Windows 3.1.

Adding a graphical browser on top of the graphical desktop environment proved to be the "killer" application that the media looked for. In just a matter of months, a frenzy of activity emerged from the media, computer companies, and corporations racing to provide content or services on the Web.

At this time, the Web itself remained static (see Figure 1.3). Its content consisted of text or graphic documents and little else. Perhaps a page contained a sound or video file, but you would typically download the file and then play it using an external application.

FIGURE 1.3.
Static HTML page.

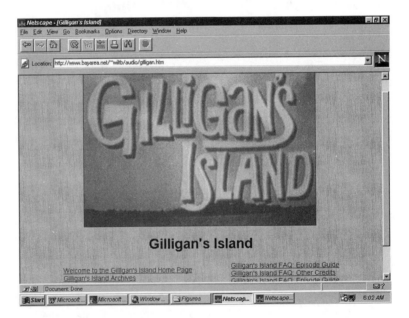

Phase III: Dynamic HTML Documents

During Phases I and II, Web pages were created using an HTML text editor and placed on a Web server. Once they were placed on the server, most pages remained static until the author modified them. Static pages are satisfactory for some Web uses but not for others. To meet the need for dynamically generated HTML documents, Web developers started using Common Gateway Interface (CGI) scripts on the Web server to generate HTML documents on the fly.

This provided the first level of interaction with the user on the Web. With this enhancement, the Web could be the platform for hypertext documents but also serve as a distinct application environment. The FedEx Web site, shown in Figure 1.4, proved to be one of the first Web applications that demonstrated the power of the Web.

FIGURE 1.4.

FedEx offered one of the first compelling Web applications.

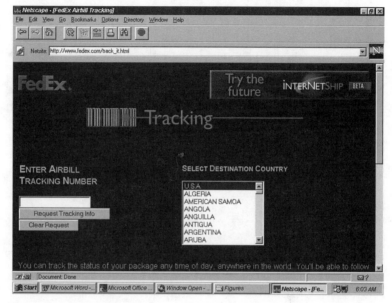

Phase IV: Active HTML Documents

The fourth phase of the Web began slowly in 1995 with the use of plug-ins in Netscape Navigator but rose to prominence with the release of Java later that year. The major focus of this phase has been to empower the client and not rely exclusively on the server to either run the application or process information entered by the user.

The hype surrounding Java is due primarily to the fact that the Web is no longer simply a collection of HTML documents but can be a true client/server environment in which the client has some independence from the server. This is where JavaScript fits in. With JavaScript, Java, ActiveX, and other client extensions, the browser can become a powerful operating environment in which to run Web applications.

Web Application Framework

Using the Web as a development environment is a relatively new phenomenon. With the advent of Java, JavaScript, ActiveX, and other technologies, the idea of developing Web-centric applications has many attractive qualities.

The Web as a development environment can seem rather confusing. Because of the distributed nature of the Web, a Web application can be composed of many parts, using a variety of technologies. In a typical LAN-based client/server architecture, you might have a client-based application attached to a database server on the network. You would often develop the client application using a single tool such as Delphi or Visual Basic. The server side of the application is typically developed and maintained using a SQL server's administrative tools.

In contrast, a Web application can have many parts to it. Figure 1.5 shows a list of the various parts that make up the application framework. This section examines each of those parts.

Figure 1.5.

Web application framework.

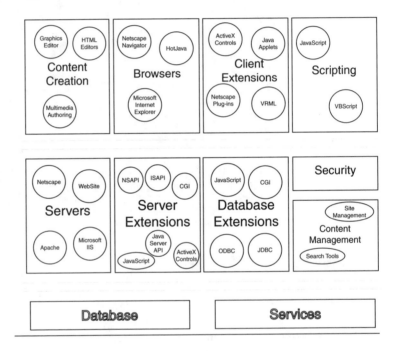

The Web development framework is truly an example of the sum being greater than the parts. By themselves, each of these technologies is limited and rather narrow in scope. When combined into cohesive applications, they provide a convincing means of developing Internet and intranet solutions.

Client Side

The client side of the Web application framework consists of four building blocks:

- Web browser
- HTML (Hypertext Markup Language)
- Client-side extensions (Java applets, ActiveX controls, and Netscape plug-ins)
- Scripting languages (JavaScript and VBScript)

This section examines each of these technologies and how they work together. Figure 1.6 shows their interrelationships.

FIGURE 1.6.

Client-side framework.

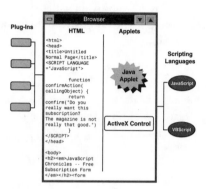

Browsers

Undoubtedly, the most important component of a Web application is the browser itself. The browser alone is the window to the Web for the user and serves as the user interface for your application. Browser technology is relatively simple (reading HTML and displaying it appropriately on screen), but the advent of nonstandard enhancements, such as Netscape frames and JavaScript, has made the selection of your browser software a critical one as you determine a Web development platform.

If you are creating an intranet application, you can probably ensure that all users are using a standard Web browser. You can then make certain assumptions when you develop your application. However, if you are creating an Internet application that the world will use, your application design decisions become more complicated, continuously weighing features against compatibility.

Table 1.1 highlights the two major browsers today and notes the versions that support the specified client-side technologies.

Table 1.1. Browser support of client-side technologies.

Support	Netscape Navigator	Microsoft Internet Explorer
JavaScript support	2.0 and above	3.0
Java support	2.0 and above	3.0
ActiveX support	3.0 (plug-in)	3.0
Netscape plug-ins	2.0 and above	3.0
VBScript support	Unannounced	3.0

HTML

HTML is obviously one of the primary technologies upon which the Web is built. HTML is a markup language that is used to provide structure and formatting to a plain text file. As a "technology," it is rather mundane—some would say, outdated. Nonetheless, the commonness of the language gives it its power.

Although the browser provides the window for displaying Web-based content to the user, the content itself comes in the form of HTML text. It does not matter if you are presenting static documents, returning a query result, providing a feedback form, or displaying a JavaScript-based application. Regardless of the means of obtaining this data, it is ultimately converted into HTML tags for presentation.

Client Extensions

As the need for active Web pages increased, simply beefing up Web browsers was not considered the best solution. Some extensions are mere third party add-ons to the browser software to make it more powerful. However, there was also the need to work with "executable content" within the browser. Although the browser needs to support the technology, it need not be tied to the browser to run. What is emerging today is three separate client-side extensions. Each have similarities, but they also have their distinct identity.

Java Applets

If you have never heard of the Java programming language, one could call you Rip Van Winkle. After all, Java has been hyped like no other programming language before. I want to back up and discuss it within the context of the Web application framework.

> **RESOURCE**
>
> For information on Java, go to the main Java site at Sun at http://java.sun.com/.

Java is a multiplatform programming language developed by Sun Microsystems. The reason for all the hype is the capability to create executable content—called a Java applet—that can be executed on a multitude of platforms.

The applet is linked via an <APPLET> tag in the HTML document and can be downloaded onto the client computer. The applet comes to the browser in *bytecodes*. If a browser supports Java, it interprets these bytecodes and executes them on the client machine. The Java applet reference is ignored in browsers that are not Java-enabled.

Java applets have several uses, and as the language itself matures, the uses grow more convincing as well. Figures 1.7 and 1.8 provide two examples of uses of Java.

FIGURE 1.7.

A Java applet moves the plane across the screen.

FIGURE 1.8.

Interactive Java map.

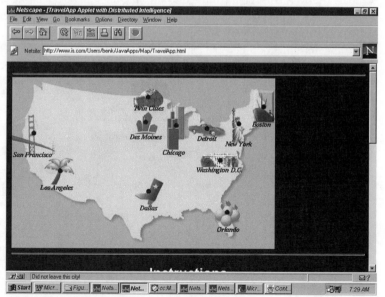

ActiveX Controls

Formerly known as OCXs, ActiveX controls are Microsoft's answer to Java applets. They are similar to Java applets in that you can use ActiveX controls as a means of providing executable content across the Web. (See Figure 1.9.) Unlike Java, ActiveX controls are limited to the Microsoft Windows operating environments.

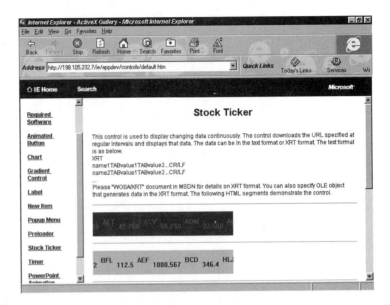

Although ActiveX controls are limited to running on a single operating environment, they are not necessarily limited to Web applications. For example, you can use the same ActiveX control in a Web application with an ActiveX-enabled browser (see Figure 1.10) and with a Windows programming tool such as Delphi or Visual Basic. (See Figure 1.11.)

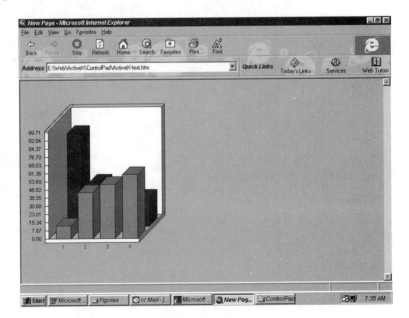

FIGURE 1.11.

The same ActiveX control used in a Delphi application.

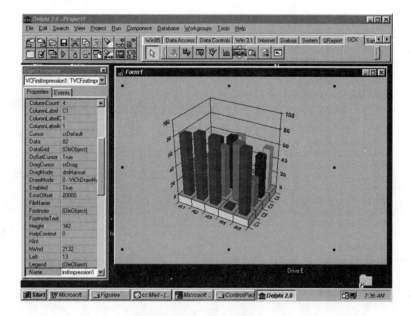

The jury is still out on whether Java or ActiveX will become the applet standard as the Web development environment matures. Both have strengths and weaknesses. Fortunately for you as a JavaScript developer, your programs can interact with both of these applet technologies. Chapter 24, "ActiveX Scripting with JavaScript," discusses how JavaScript and ActiveX controls work together.

RESOURCE

For information on ActiveX, go to Microsoft's Internet Center at `http://www.microsoft.com/internet/`.

Netscape Plug-Ins

Plug-ins are a slightly different technology, but they're still a client-side extension of the Web browser. Plug-ins essentially extend the normal capabilities of the Netscape Navigator browser to provide support for additional data types and other features. Specifically, you use a plug-in to display a specific MIME (Multipart Internet Mail Extension) type file.

When you start Netscape, it looks in its `program\plugins` folder for any plug-ins to register. Netscape then calls a plug-in on an as-needed basis when it comes across a matching MIME file type.

Plug-ins become added modules onto the browser and do not require any user interaction to start once installed. They are proving especially useful for multimedia data, such as sound, video, and graphics. Figure 1.12 demonstrates the use of a plug-in that enables you to view Adobe Acrobat files within Netscape.

FIGURE 1.12.

Viewing a .PDF file using a plug-in.

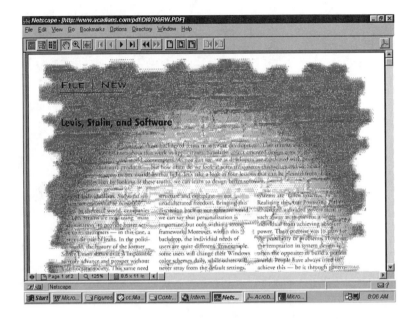

You can use JavaScript to communicate with plug-ins. Chapter 23, "Working with Netscape Plug-Ins," explores this subject in detail.

Client Scripting Languages

The final pieces of the puzzle on the client side are the client scripting languages. JavaScript is the leading scripting language today, but Microsoft is now promoting VBScript as an alternative. Because of the millions of Visual Basic developers, it is likely that VBScript will also prove popular for this community. Appendix D, "JavaScript Resources on the Internet," compares and contrasts JavaScript and VBScript.

Server Side

The server side of the Web application framework consists of the Web server itself along with extensions to the server software. As you will learn, these extensions can take various forms and be employed using a variety of technologies. Figure 1.13 displays the interrelationships of the server-side framework.

FIGURE 1.13.
Server-side framework.

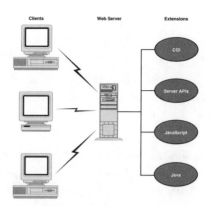

Servers

The Web server is charged with handling requests for HTML documents from the client and returning them for viewing. The server software is an application that runs on a TCP/IP-enabled machine. Popular servers today include Netscape Commerce Server, Microsoft Internet Information Server (IIS), Apache, and WebSite.

Server Extensions

By itself, the Web server provides static HTML pages to the client when requested and performs a variety of other functions. However, several extensions to servers are being developed to provide capabilities that the server itself does not support. These include CGI, server APIs, JavaScript, and Java.

CGI

CGI (Common Gateway Interface) is the *de facto* standard means of interfacing external programs with Web servers. Using CGI, you can execute CGI programs or scripts on the server to generate dynamically created content for displaying to the user. A typical scenario is that a request is generated from an HTML form and sent to the server. The request runs the CGI program or script, which is located in a special directory on the server. The CGI program processes the request and then returns an HTML document with the result.

You can write a CGI program using any programming language—such as Delphi, C++, Visual Basic, or FORTRAN—as long as it can be executed on the Web server. Common in the UNIX world is writing CGI scripts in scripting languages such as PERL or a UNIX shell.

Server APIs

Another means of integration with the server is through its native application programming interface (API). Two of the most commonly used Web server APIs are the Netscape Server

API (NSAPI) and the Microsoft Internet Server API (ISAPI). Using the APIs provides tighter integration with the server. For example, in the Windows world, you would create a DLL that is accessed by the server, not a separate EXE.

The advantage to using these server APIs is that the processes are much more efficient than CGI programs. CGI requires that a separate instance of the program is executed for each client request or submittal. Not only is this more expensive, but it also limits the amount of data sharing that can be performed.

The disadvantage to using a proprietary server API is that your solution is specific to that single server. Your ISAPI DLL will not work with a Netscape server. If you are working primarily with one of these servers, then the negative aspect of this limitation is minimized.

Server-Side JavaScript

Much of the attention shown to JavaScript to date has been to its capabilities on the client side. However, you can use JavaScript as a server-side scripting tool as well. The first such environment out the door is, as you would expect, Netscape.

Netscape's LiveWire environment allows you to use JavaScript scripts to extend the capabilities of a Netscape server. LiveWire has several server-side extensions to the JavaScript language that provide the additional capabilities of generating dynamic HTML, communicating with the client, accessing external files on the server, and connecting to SQL databases. LiveWire also enables you to compile JavaScript scripts for greater server-side performance.

Additionally, Microsoft has said that its ActiveX Server framework will support JavaScript as a server-side scripting language.

Java

As the technology matures, Java will also be used as a programming tool to develop server-side programs to extend the Web server.

JavaScript's Role in Web Application Development

Now that you have surveyed the technologies that make up Web applications, you can look at the role that client-side JavaScript can play in developing Web applications.

Client-Side Applications

You can use JavaScript to develop entire client-side applications. Although JavaScript is not an all-encompassing language like Java, it does provide rather substantial capabilities when it comes

1

to working with HTML tags and associated objects. One of the best known JavaScript applications is hIdaho Design's ColorCenter (`http://www.hidaho.com/c3/`), as shown in Figure 1.14. You can use this JavaScript application to select browser-related colors and preview them in a separate frame. Trying to design such an application using Java would be much more complex because of the interaction that is required with HTML. For certain cases, JavaScript provides the ideal programming backbone on which to develop the application.

FIGURE 1.14.

*hIdaho Design's
ColorCenter.*

NOTE

I have seen JavaScript applications referred to by some as *Weblications*. It is this author's hope that the term will die a quick death and not catch on.

Smart Frame Support

Multiframe windows are proving to be a powerful means of presentation for Web developers. Displaying multiple frames within the browser provides you much more control over the user interface of the application. When dealing with multiframe windows, JavaScript proves its worth as providing a powerful means for control. Netscape's home page (shown in Figure 1.15) shows us an example of using JavaScript with smart frames.

FIGURE 1.15.

*Netscape's home page
employs JavaScript.*

Data Validation

JavaScript gives you, as a Web developer, a basic means of validating data from the user without hitting the server. Within your JavaScript code, you can determine whether values entered by the user are valid or fit the correct format. (See Figure 1.16.) JavaScript becomes a much more efficient validation method than throwing unqualified values to a server process. Not only is the process more efficient for the user entering the data, but it's better for the server as well. By the time data is transferred to the server for processing, you can be assured the data has been qualified in a proper state for submission.

Creating Interactive Forms

Another common use of JavaScript is livening up HTML forms. Part of this task might include validating data, which is discussed in the last section. It can also include additional features that are unavailable with straight HTML, such as providing information to the user on the status bar, opening a second browser window for help information, and so on. Figure 1.17 shows an example of a JavaScript-enabled form.

Client-Side Lookup Tables

Besides including data validation, another means of minimizing the need to access the server is to employ JavaScript to generate and maintain client-side lookup tables. The data must be embedded in the HTML document itself, however, so you will want to limit your use of lookup tables to small, read-only databases of information.

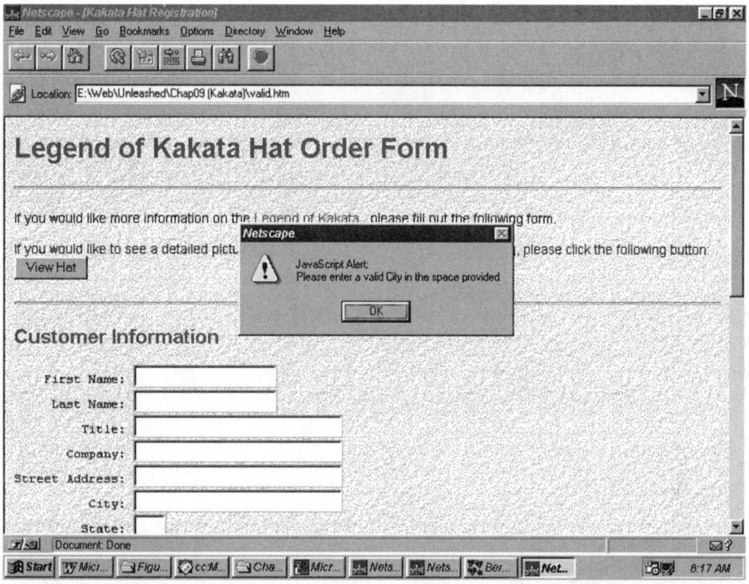

FIGURE 1.16.
Using JavaScript to validate data.

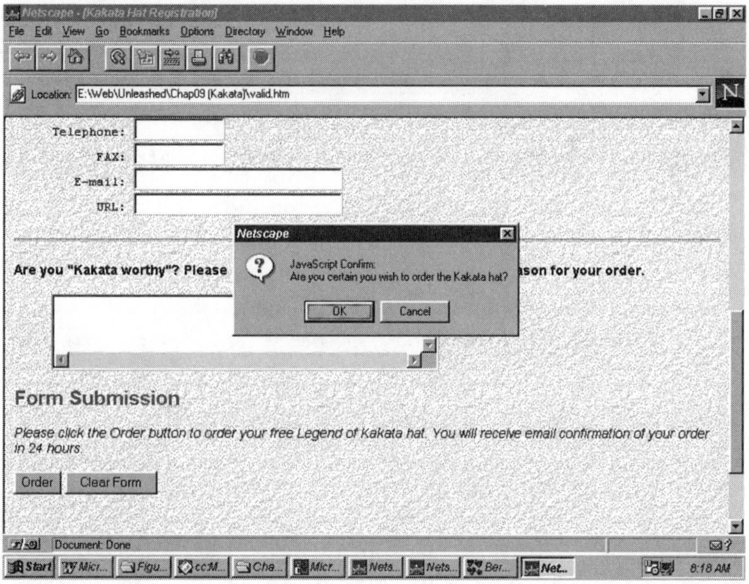

FIGURE 1.17.
Interactive HTML form.

State Maintenance

In the stateless environment of the Web, you can use JavaScript to help maintain the state between exchanges between the client and the server. The most use of state maintenance is with cookies (information stored by the browser on the client's PC). JavaScript provides a means for you to store and retrieve cookies on the client's PC. Figure 1.18 shows an example of using a cookie to display information specific to the current user. See Chapter 19, "Cookies and State Maintenance," for more information on working with cookies in JavaScript.

FIGURE 1.18.

Using cookies in JavaScript.

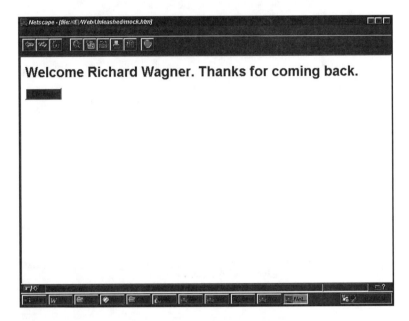

Work with Java Applets, ActiveX Controls, and Plug-Ins

As the JavaScript language is enhanced, it continues to have increased capabilities in working with client-side extensions, including Java applets, ActiveX controls, and Netscape plug-ins. You can access a Java or ActiveX object's properties and execute its methods. You can also determine whether a plug-in is installed. As this capability is enhanced, JavaScript will be considered an essential glue that holds together HTML, applets, and client-side extensions.

Browser Support for JavaScript

Compared to other applications you use, browsers are relatively simple pieces of software, but they are evolving into more powerful applications as Web technology matures. A browser is your window into the Web; therefore, no matter the potential for JavaScript, it does no good if a browser does not support it. This section examines the browsers available today and their support for JavaScript.

Because JavaScript is an interpreted language and embedded in HTML documents, it is entirely dependent on the browser software to work. If you use an old browser, it will not know what to do with the code and will ignore it.

Netscape Navigator

During the mid 1990s, Netscape became perhaps the single most important player in the Web industry. Not only was it the first to market many important technological breakthroughs, but it also teamed up with other industry leaders—such as Sun—to push the technology envelope on many fronts on the Web.

Although the emergence of Microsoft as a Web powerhouse could change the scene, it is likely that Netscape will continue to dominate the browser market for some time.

Obviously, because Netscape developed JavaScript, you would expect its phenomenally successful Navigator browser to support the scripting language. Navigator 2.0 was the first browser to support JavaScript. Later versions provide important enhancements to the language itself. Figure 1.19 shows the Netscape Navigator 3.0 window.

FIGURE 1.19.

*Netscape
Navigator 3.0.*

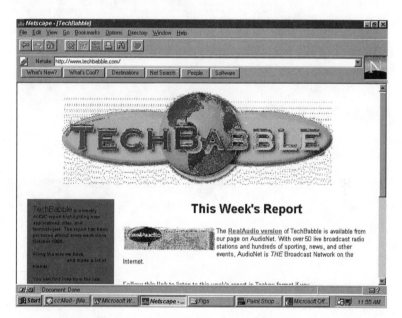

Microsoft Internet Explorer

Microsoft Internet Explorer 3.0 is the first non-Netscape browser to support JavaScript (see Figure 1.20). Microsoft's support of JavaScript in the Internet Explorer makes its chance of long-term viability much greater. Older versions of the Internet Explorer (that is, versions 1.0 and 2.0) do not support JavaScript.

Figure 1.20.

Microsoft Internet Explorer 3.0.

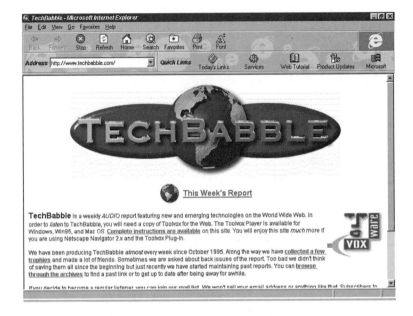

Other Browsers

At the time of writing, no other browsers provide support for JavaScript. Sun's HotJava browser is expected to provide support in the future.

> **NOTE**
>
> The current versions of ActiveX control browsers do not provide JavaScript support.

Summary

This chapter looked at the Web application framework, and how each of the pieces of Web technology fit together. JavaScript is an important tool in a Web developer's toolkit. As you learned in this chapter, JavaScript serves many important functions within the Web application framework, and it is becoming more of a standard in the Web development marketplace. Because JavaScript is a language and not a tool itself, it is dependent on browser software in order to execute. Although Netscape Navigator and Microsoft Internet Explorer are the only browsers that currently provide JavaScript support, these two browsers own the lion's share of the marketplace, making JavaScript support fairly dependable.

Now that we have a solid foundation on which to look at JavaScript, we can begin to look in the next chapter at the details of how JavaScript interacts with HTML.

How JavaScript and HTML Work Together

by Kim Daniels

IN THIS CHAPTER

HTML gives you the capability to create remarkable static Web pages. Although these documents have been creative, interesting, and by all means useful, JavaScript gives you the capability to make these extensive static pages interactive and more responsive to user actions and input. Extending your HTML pages with JavaScript puts more power to your page and gives you more flexibility with what your HTML can do. JavaScript cannot stand alone but is always tied to your HTML page and the browser. JavaScript is an interpreted language that is processed by the browser when the page loads.

JavaScript enables the Web developer to create more dynamic pages by embedding a scripting language in the existing HTML structure. You can now put processes behind buttons, run calculations on form-entered data, or perform actions when the user moves the mouse over an HTML object. In general, you get more bang for your HTML buck.

JavaScript offers advantages over client-based interactive documents such as CGI because JavaScript-based documents are less dependent on client-side processing, so they are quicker to respond to user interactions and requests.

Embedding JavaScript in Your HTML

JavaScript scripts are integrated into HTML using the HTML <SCRIPT> and </SCRIPT> tags. Both the start and end tags are required for <SCRIPT>, and at the current time, the language attribute and source attribute are the only attributes currently available. Language is used to specify the scripting language in which the script is written, and source (SRC) is used to specify the filename of the JavaScript statements, if they are stored in a separate file.

> **WARNING**
>
> Once future language extensions are available, JavaScript will no longer be the "assumed" language. It is more stable to specifically define your language as JavaScript so it will not conflict in future revisions of browsers and HTML.

```
<SCRIPT LANGUAGE="JavaScript">
</SCRIPT>
```

You have two options when integrating JavaScript statements into your HTML document. The method that you choose depends on your requirements when viewing and modifying code. The first option allows you to view all your codes simultaneously and involves writing JavaScript statements directly into your HTML document. All your statements are embedded in your HTML page between the script tags. The other option, only available in Netscape 3.0 and higher, is to write your JavaScript into a separate file and save the file with the extension .js. You can then call this file from your HTML on the first script tag line. The examples that follow demonstrate the two options in embedding JavaScript in your HTML:

```
<SCRIPT LANGUAGE="JavaScript">
function options() {
document.write("embedding the code")
}
</SCRIPT>
```

The following segment shows the other option:

```
<SCRIPT SRC="myscript.js">
</SCRIPT>
```

In the second option, you will create a file called `myscript.js`, which will have one line of code:

```
document.write("calling from a separate file")
```

When you load the script from another file, the `Language` attribute is not necessary as long as you use the correct `.js` extension. Using this methodology, you have the capability to modify your JavaScript code without ever opening and risking unwanted changes to your HTML pages. The downside to this method is that you might have to modify two sets of code depending on your JavaScript changes. For example, if you change the name of a function in your JavaScript code, you will also have to remember to change the name in the function call in the HTML code.

> **WARNING**
>
> The above option is available in Netscape 3.0 and later.

Viewing JavaScript Code

Because you can write JavaScript code inline with your HTML code, you can easily view and edit it. JavaScript code can be viewed with any HTML editor as well as from your Web browser. You should be familiar with the Document Source menu choice that is available in your browser (in Netscape, it's under the View menu) to view the source of an HTML page. When you view the source of the document, you can also view the JavaScript code that is included in the document. (See Figure 2.1.) (This is obviously not the case when your JavaScript statements are called from the `.js` file instead of written into the document. All you will see is the call to the `.js` file in the script tag.) JavaScript doesn't need a special viewer, and because it is just interpreted code and not compiled, it appears in your document source by default.

FIGURE 2.2.

The alert dialog called directly from JavaScript.

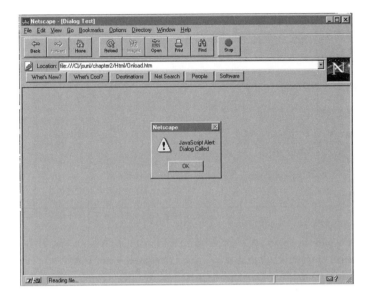

User Action

The second process by which JavaScript statements are executed is though function calls. Any statement contained within a function will not be executed until a JavaScript event calls the function. JavaScript events can be triggered in numerous ways on an HTML page, including user action and explicit event calls from within the script itself. User actions upon your document might trigger JavaScript events in many instances when you are unaware that they could happen. Be sure to fully test your JavaScript statements to be sure that user interaction with your page doesn't cause unnecessary or unwanted events to occur.

Chapter 9, "Handling Events," provides a more detailed explanation of JavaScript events and how they are implemented and incorporated into your HTML.

In Listing 2.3, the dialog is presented when the pushbutton is clicked.

Listing 2.3. Calling a function to display the alert dialog.

```
<!DOCTYPE HTML PUBLIC "-//W3C//DTD HTML 3.2//EN">
<HTML>
<HEAD>
<TITLE>Dialog from function call</TITLE>
<SCRIPT LANGUAGE="JavaScript">
<!--
function opendoc()
{
alert("Dialog called by Push Button")
}
// -->
</SCRIPT>
</HEAD>
```

```
<BODY>
<B>Test page of function called from Push Button</B>
<FORM METHOD="POST">
<P>
<INPUT TYPE="Button" NAME="BUTTON1" VALUE="PUSH" onclick="opendoc()">

</P>
</FORM>
</BODY>
</HTML>
```

Figure 2.3 shows the results of the function call.

FIGURE 2.3.

The alert dialog called from the submit event handler.

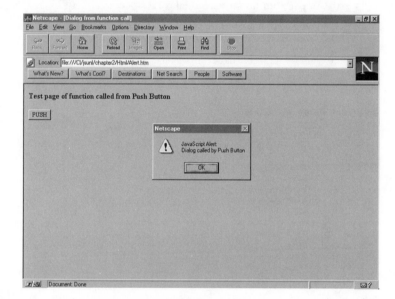

User action or explicit event calls are the more frequent methods by which JavaScript is executed. One key advantage of JavaScript is that it can increase the amount of user interaction with your HTML document by providing you with a means to process and evaluate user input in a timely manner.

Accommodating Unsupported Browsers

The fast-moving pace of changes in HTML and JavaScript makes it necessary to be wary of browsers that do not support the documents you are creating. Not all browsers will be current with the newest HTML enhancements, and you, as the programmer, must make your documents as user-friendly as possible to all browsers and environments.

> **TIP**
>
> Testing your HTML and JavaScript in as many browser environments as possible will give your documents better stability and usability.

Although using JavaScript can enable you to provide HTML enhancements to your users, you must always remember that many older browsers might not be able to make full use of the JavaScript that you have written. By surrounding all statements that are inside the <SCRIPT> and </SCRIPT> tags with HTML comment tags, you will allow users with the older browsers to still view your page but not process the JavaScript code. They will not get the full effect of your page, but at least they will not see unwanted text in the browser. Note the use of the following two HTML comment statements in Listing 2.4:

```
<!-- hide your code from older browsers
// stop JavaScript code hiding -->
```

Listing 2.4. Hiding scripts from older browsers.

```
<!DOCTYPE HTML PUBLIC "-//W3C//DTD HTML 3.2//EN">
<HTML>
<HEAD>
<TITLE>Hide From Browser</TITLE>
<SCRIPT LANGUAGE="JavaScript">
<!-- hide your code from older browsers
document.write("I can view JavaScript code")
// stop JavaScript code hiding -->
</HEAD>
<BODY>
</BODY>
</HTML>
```

The use of the JavaScript comments tag, //, in the last HTML comment line keeps JavaScript from interpreting this statement during processing. Without these comment markers, JavaScript will attempt to process the statement, and you will receive a JavaScript error upon evaluation.

Using Netscape HTML Enhancements

The ever changing world of the Internet always has room for improvement in the current technology. This, of course, holds true for Netscape and HTML.

Netscape continues to improve its Web browser to keep up with the changes to HTML standards. This section provides an overview of some of the new enhancements, but to remain completely up-to-date on the newest additions and changes to HTML and Netscape, you can keep an eye on the following sites.

RESOURCE

You can find HTML enhancements as well as the current HTML 3.2 standards document at `http://www.w3.org`.

Netscape enhancements are covered at `http://home.netscape.com`.

Because of the increasing interest in Java, JavaScript, and the user interactivity in HTML, developers are focusing quite a bit of the enhancement effort in these areas. As a JavaScript programmer, you should stay aware of strategic changes to keep ahead of the game.

The issues surrounding the use of JavaScript with unsupported (not JavaScript enabled) browsers applies also, in principle, to HTML and Netscape enhancements (discussed later in this chapter), and the use of older browsers. Netscape is watching the continuing stream of technology changes and releasing new versions to stay current. Keep in mind that not all browsers will be able to handle some of the newer tags, scripting, Java, and other enhancements. If your Web pages rely heavily on some of the new technology, it is wise to also provide an option to a simpler version. Otherwise, those users viewing your pages with older browsers will probably find your HTML documents of little or no use.

NOTE

The methodology for accommodating browsers that do not support JavaScript is similar to the methodology that you have probably seen on many Web sites that use frames. The user is provided with the option of loading the document with or without frames. Functionality may be lost without frames, but at least the document is viewable.

Overview of HTML 3.2 and Netscape Enhancements

A new feature to Netscape puts much more power behind JavaScript and HTML development. JavaScript evaluation allows your HTML documents to become more dynamic. You can now define the attributes of the right-hand side of an HTML object to be JavaScript expressions or function calls. Information from one tag or a function calculation can drive the attributes of another tag. Listing 2.5 demonstrates using JavaScript evaluation to change the width of an image based on the current time in seconds.

Listing 2.5. JavaScript evaluation.

```
<!DOCTYPE HTML PUBLIC "-//W3C//DTD HTML 3.2//EN">
<HTML>
<HEAD>
```

continues

Listing 2.5. continued

```
<TITLE>Javascript Evaluation Test</TITLE>
</HEAD>
<SCRIPT LANGUAGE="JavaScript">
<!--
function getSeconds()
{
        var temp = new Date();
         return(temp.getSeconds());
}
//-->
</SCRIPT>
<BODY>
<IMG SRC="mypict.gif" HEIGHT="36" WIDTH="&{getSeconds() * 10};">
</BODY>
</HTML>
```

Additional non-JavaScript–specific enhancements will not directly affect your JavaScript development but will increase your overall development capabilities with Netscape. Netscape 3.0 has added the following additional capabilities:

■ Better image control. Change GIF and JPEG images automatically, either at specified intervals or with user input from a button.

■ Enhanced image capabilities. Select an image in an HTML document (with a right click) and make it a Windows desktop wallpaper.

■ Enhanced plug-in capabilities. Detect plug-ins for a page and react correctly to them. If the correct plug-ins are not detected, you can make plug-in substitutions to keep the look of the page as designed.

■ Increased performance of JavaScript scripts.

■ Reduced JavaScript memory usage.

HTML Enhancements

The current standard set for HTML is HTML 3.2. The previously written set of standards for HTML 3.0 is no longer being maintained and has been replaced by the new HTML 3.2 standards. The new standard incorporates the majority of HTML 3.0 features and adds other significant features. This document will continue to evolve as features are added and modified.

The following new text-related attributes enhance text formatting on HTML pages (see Figure 2.4 for in-document examples):

<S> strikes out text in a document. Netscape version 2.0 also supported strike-out text but used the <STRIKE> tag. Both the <S> and <STRIKE> tags are supported in Netscape browsers.

<U> underlines text on the page.

`<BIG>` displays text in a bigger font size than normal text.

`<SMALL>` displays text in a smaller font size than normal text.

`<SUB>` displays text as a subscript to other text on the page. Subscript text is also in a smaller font than normal text.

`<SUP>` displays text as a superscript to other text and uses a smaller font than normal text.

`<P>` defines paragraph breaks in the HTML document. (This tag doesn't require the corresponding `</P>`.)

`<DIV>` defines a logical division block in the body of the text. This tag has no formatting value except to end the previous paragraph tag. Nested `<DIV>` tags can organize the document. `<DIV>` takes a few attributes; the main one is the `Class`, which specifies the type of division block. You can use division blocks to put restrictions on certain sections of an HTML page.

FIGURE 2.4.

New text features.

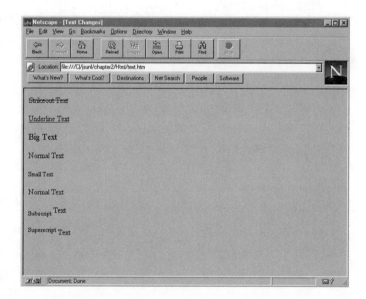

The HTML 3.2 standard states that all HTML documents should begin with the `<!DOCTYPE>` tag. This standard was present in previous HTML versions but is becoming increasingly more critical as HTML evolves. This tag helps browsers distinguish the version of HTML in which a document was created. Currently, it specifically differentiates the HTML 3.2 version from all others. This tag is not required but will help, in the future, to distinguish which version of HTML a document was written in.

```
<!DOCTYPE HTML PUBLIC "-//W3C//DTD HTML 3.2//EN">
```

<FORM> Enhancements

The form attribute of ACTION specifies the URL to which the document input is submitted. In the following code sample, the form input—that is, the file—is sent to www.acadians.com. (See the next section for more information on the <INPUT> type of file.)

The form attribute of ENCTYPE gives the specifications for the MIME content type of encryption to use when sending file information as input.

```
<FORM ACTION="http://www.acadians.com"
METHOD=POST ENCTYPE="APPLICATION/X-WWW-FORM-URLENCODED">
Send this File to me:
<INPUT NAME="KimsFile" TYPE="FILE" VALUE=" MyFile">
<HR><HR>
<INPUT TYPE="SUBMIT" VALUE="Send File">
</FORM>
```

See Figure 2.5 for use of File as an input type.

FIGURE 2.5.

*Using <ENCTYPE> and
input of type* "FILE".

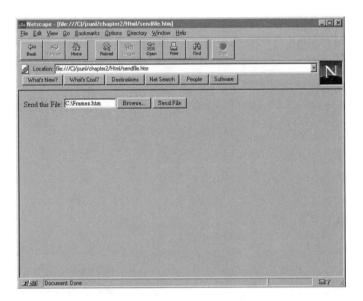

<INPUT> Type Additions and Enhancements

The new RANGE input type is displayed in the document as a slider bar. The start and end values of the slider are specified by the values defined in the MIN and MAX attributes. (RANGE is currently the only input type to use MIN and MAX values.)

The SCRIBBLE input type is a graphical scratch pad. The "scratch pad," or image onto which the user can scribble, is defined in the SRC attribute. This attribute is required for this input type to define the image. To accommodate browsers where SCRIBBLE is not supported, be sure to put text in the VALUE attribute of the input. In browsers where SCRIBBLE is not supported,

HTML will display a text box with text from the VALUE attribute. (SCRIBBLE is not yet supported in Netscape 3.0.)

```
<!DOCTYPE HTML PUBLIC "-//W3C//DTD HTML 3.2//EN">
<HEAD>
<BODY>
<FORM>
<INPUT NAME="MyScribble" TYPE="SCRIBBLE"
SRC="C:\CSERVE\MOSIAC\CIM.GIF"  VALUE="no scribbling">
</FORM>
</BODY>
</HEAD>
```

The input type of FILE enables the user to enter a filename as Web page input. The ACCEPT attribute allows you to specify file type restrictions and thus limit the file types to accept.

SUBMIT and RESET have been enhanced to accept the SRC attribute in their tag definitions. SRC contains the name of an image file to use instead of the button object. The "image" button behaves identically to the "button" SUBMIT and RESET input types.

<INPUT> Attribute Enhancements

Several attributes that were added to the <INPUT> tag will increase the flexibility the developers have when accepting user input.

DISABLED allows you to disable the input element on the document. Enabling and disabling input fields through JavaScript opens up programming possibilities to make certain elements active only in specific instances. HTML 2.0 browsers ignore this attribute, and the element is displayed as usual.

ERROR gives the developer the opportunity to inform the user when the content of field is in error. The error "reason" is found in the VALUE of the error attribute. It is up to you, the programmer, to display the error reason to the user when an error is triggered during JavaScript execution.

The attributes of MIN and MAX define minimum and maximum values for the new RANGE input type (discussed earlier in this chapter in the section "<INPUT> Type Additions and Enhancements").

The ALIGN attribute is now available for image object input types. These include SCRIBBLE, IMAGE, and SUBMIT and RESET when SRC is used to define the image. This attribute enables you to align the image in relation to surrounding text.

Frames

Frames are important development tools when you're writing JavaScript and HTML pages. Frames let you have multiple independent windows on your page that can interact with each other. JavaScript scripts can react to events in one frame and apply them in another frame. Frames expand the capabilities available to you as your HTML code and JavaScript become more complex.

As with browsers that do not support JavaScript, you must also account for browsers that do not support frames. An important tag to remember when using frames in your JavaScript script is the <NOFRAMES> tag. This tag pair, <NOFRAMES></NOFRAMES>, goes inside your initial <FRAMESET> tag. You should place some descriptive text inside these tags to inform the users that they will not be seeing the full effect of your Web document because their browsers do not support frames. The text inside these tags will only display if the browser does not support frames.

JavaScript enables you to update certain "windows," frames of your document, based on input into other frames. This is possible because frames are completely independent so the entire page doesn't have to change every time.

The following example uses a main document window, defined in Listing 2.6, and two separate frame documents, HTML pages defined in Listings 2.7 and 2.8. This is a basic example of how you can use JavaScript in conjunction with basic HTML when using frames. Clicking the submit button in frame2.htm redisplays the number from the input text box in the result text box and also rebuilds the document in frame1.htm to include the input number.

Listing 2.6. frames.htm.

```
<HTML>
<HEAD>
<TITLE>Main Frame</TITLE>
<FRAMESET Rows="34%,*">
<FRAME SRC=FRAME1.HTM NAME="frame1" SCROLLING="yes">
<FRAME SRC=FRAME2.HTM NAME="frame2" SCROLLING="yes">
<NOFRAMES>
</NOFRAMES>
</FRAMESET>
</HEAD>
<BODY>
</BODY>
</HTML>
```

Listing 2.7. frame1.htm.

```
<HTML>
<HEAD>
<TITLE>Frame 1</TITLE>
</HEAD>
<BODY>
<B>This is the original text in Frame 1<B>
<P>
<B>It will be replaced on button click in frame #2 <B>
</BODY>
</HTML>
```

Listing 2.8. frame2.htm.

```
<HTML>
<HEAD>
<TITLE>Frame 3</TITLE>
<SCRIPT LANGUAGE="JavaScript">
function printtoframe(form)
{
if (confirm("Do you want to update the top frame?"))
{
form.result.value = eval(form.input.value);
parent.frame1.document.open();
parent.frame1.document.open();
parent.frame1.document.write("<HTML>");
parent.frame1.document.write("<BODY>");
parent.frame1.document.write(eval(form.input.value));
parent.frame1.document.write("</BODY>");
parent.frame1.document.write("</HTML>");
parent.frame1.document.close();
}
else
alert("Please come back again")
}
</SCRIPT>
</HEAD>
<BODY>
<FORM>
Enter a number to evaluate:
<INPUT TYPE="text" NAME="input" SIZE=15>
<INPUT TYPE="submit" VALUE="pushbutton" ONCLICK="printtoframe(this.form)">
<BR>
Print it here again:
<BR>
<INPUT TYPE="text" NAME="result" SIZE=15>
<BR>
<B> And notice it has printed in frame above also <B>
</FORM>
</BODY>
</HTML>
```

Figures 2.6 and 2.7 show the changes.

Netscape 3.0 enhancements offer two new areas of added functionality to frame design and frame navigation. Netscape improved the navigation capabilities within frames. The Netscape toolbar Back button now functions more accurately in relation to frames. The Back button returns your document to the previous frame state, and the Forward button moves one frame state ahead. This behavior is similar to that of the Back and Forward buttons on pages, which are used to go back on page "state."

Another new feature is the addition of three attributes to both the FRAME and FRAMESET tags. These enhancements give you better control over your frame design. The FRAMEBORDER attribute enables you to turn frame borders on and off, whereas BORDER allows you to specify the thickness of the border around your frames, and BORDERCOLOR lets you define the specific color of your border.

2

HOW JAVASCRIPT
AND HTML
WORK TOGETHER

Listing 2.9. Basic JavaScript document.

```
<!DOCTYPE HTML PUBLIC "-//W3C//DTD HTML 3.2//EN">
<HTML>
<HEAD>
<TITLE>My first HTML page</TITLE>
<SCRIPT LANGUAGE="JavaScript">
</SCRIPT>
</HEAD>
<BODY>
</BODY>
</HTML>
```

The beginning script tag should include the LANGUAGE attribute to identify that the script enclosed in the tags is in fact JavaScript.

Writing the Script

As in any other programming language, JavaScript statements can be implemented using various methodologies. I have found that the practice of defining JavaScript functions in the <HEAD> section and then calling these functions within the HTML body is the best way to take advantage of the object-based JavaScript language.

The JavaScript language itself is not difficult, and for developers with an object-based background, the hurdles are fewer. Once you grasp the concepts of object-based development, the creation of JavaScript functions becomes fairly straightforward. Note the following example:

```
document.write("I can view JavaScript code")
```

In plain English, this statement is, "On my document, write the following text."

> **NOTE**
>
> Although HTML statements are not case-sensitive, JavaScript statements are.

When beginning to write your code, keep the following items in mind:

- Code reuse
- Readability
- Ease of modification

You can use JavaScript tags in either the body or the head of a document. As recommended previously, placing the <SCRIPT> in the head rather than the body ensures that all statements will be evaluated (and executed, if necessary) before the user has any interaction with the document. The hazards of putting script statements in the body of the document are varied. Depending on the specific tags and the order of the document, you can never be positive that the user will not interact with the script in the wrong manner or react to the page before the script has fully loaded or executed. If any of these occur, the effect that you want for your page might not be seen. (After all your effort, who wants that?)

The practice of defining your JavaScript functions and then calling them from the body will ensure that all the functions are evaluated before the user can begin interaction with the page. Listing 2.10 shows an example of this practice, and Listing 2.11 shows the alternative.

Listing 2.10. Calling from a function.

```
<!DOCTYPE HTML PUBLIC "-//W3C//DTD HTML 3.2//EN">
<HTML>
<HEAD>
<TITLE>Page with Pushbutton</TITLE>
<SCRIPT LANGUAGE="JavaScript">
<!--
function pushbutton() {
alert("pushed")
}
// -->
</SCRIPT>
</HEAD>
<BODY>
<FORM>
<INPUT TYPE="SUBMIT" NAME="BUTTON1" VALUE="PUSH" onclick="pushbutton">
</FORM>
</BODY>
</HTML>
```

Listing 2.11. Putting script directly in `onclick`.

```
<!DOCTYPE HTML PUBLIC "-//W3C//DTD HTML 3.2//EN">
<HTML>
<HEAD>
<TITLE>Page with Pushbutton</TITLE>
</HEAD>
<BODY>
<FORM>
<INPUT TYPE="SUBMIT" NAME="BUTTON1" VALUE="PUSH" onclick="alert("pushed")">
</FORM>
</BODY>
</HTML>
```

Listing 2.11 demonstrates that it is possible to put JavaScript statements directly in your HTML tags. I can relate the drawbacks of this practice to the code-writing guidelines I mentioned previously. Modifying and reusing the code in tags is difficult. You must search for the tag and then cut and paste the code. Only then can it be reused or redefined in a function call.

You are also limiting readability and ease of modification for both you and subsequent developers when you do not place your JavaScript statements in functions in the head section. Endlessly searching for code that could have been easily segregated is tedious and unnecessary.

Styles are as important in JavaScript as they are in any programming language. Keeping your styles consistent, your variables defined, and your formatting neat will save future development time.

Creating your JavaScript scripts function by function, piece by piece, will build stable interactive documents that have the functionality you want. Because JavaScript is interpreted and not compiled, the debugging process is not always completely straightforward. Many issues, or bugs, will not be apparent until the document is rigorously tested. I recommend that someone other than the developer test the page to ensure that all situations are encountered when testing the document and integrated JavaScript. (You never know what checking a checkbox out of order might do to your script.)

Running the Script

As you probably realized, JavaScript scripts are as simple to load as HTML documents. You do not have to explicitly execute any code to run your scripts; because you place your code in the HTML document or call it explicitly in the first script line, your script will run when the page loads. Remember that not all the code will necessarily execute immediately upon loading. Code that is enclosed in a function call is only evaluated when the page loads but does not execute until the function is explicitly called from a JavaScript event. Code that is not enclosed in a function call runs after the page finishes loading but before the user has a chance to interact with the page.

Summary

It is apparent that although JavaScript is a separate scripting language from HTML, the two are very closely integrated when it comes to full-scale document design, development, and implementation. JavaScript can be written directly into HTML expanding the current capabilities of your web documents. It is also viewable and loadable right along with the HTML.

The enhancements that are continuously arising in HTML itself, as well as Netscape and Microsoft specific enhancements such as Frames, Tables, and Input options, are making it possible to add more functionality to your JavaScript code, thus expanding your documents to make them more interactive and user friendly.

Assembling Your JavaScript Toolkit

by Richard Wagner

IN THIS CHAPTER

CHAPTER 3

FIGURE 3.6.

Netscape Navigator Gold.

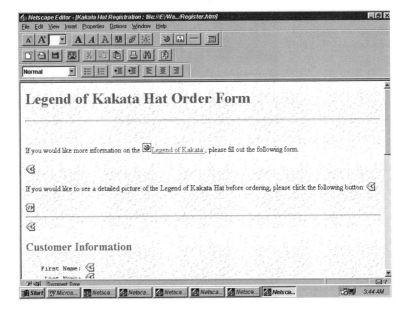

FIGURE 3.7.

Creating HTML pages visually using Microsoft FrontPage.

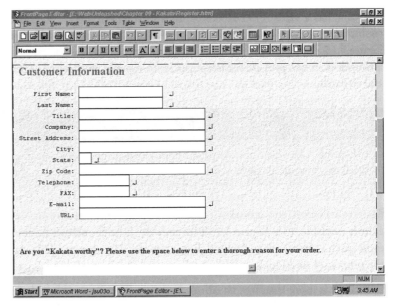

> **RESOURCE**
>
> Check the Microsoft home page at http://www.microsoft.com for the latest information on FrontPage. When Microsoft released FrontPage 1.1, it offered a public beta copy to try. Check back to see if they intend to provide a similar beta release in the future.

A current shortfall of visual HTML editors is the inability to go into a text-based mode and edit raw HTML. For both Gold and FrontPage, you need an external editor for doing that. Additionally, both of these editors hardly know what to do with JavaScript code, so do not even think of using either of these tools as a JavaScript editing environment. Nonetheless, when used in combination with an editor such as Netscript, these tools provide a quick head start to developing sophisticated Web pages.

> **CAUTION**
>
> If you intend to use FrontPage 1.1, be sure to surround your code with HTML comment tags (<!-- and -->). FrontPage 1.1 does not support the <SCRIPT> tag and will treat your code as if it were normal text.

Web Browser

The final component that you need to have is a Web browser that supports JavaScript. (See Figure 3.8.) Chapter 1, "JavaScript and the World Wide Web," discussed the various Web browsers and their support for JavaScript, so I do not need to dive into that discussion any further. However, because various versions of browsers provide different levels of JavaScript language support, you probably need to have many of these available during your testing phase.

The basic rule of thumb is to test your script using all the possible types of browsers that will access the page. For intranet applications, you might have only a single browser to test, but for public Internet applications, you need to consider that the following browsers might access your JavaScript-enabled site:

■ Latest Netscape Navigator (3.0 or above)

■ Earlier Netscape Navigator (2.0)

■ Latest Microsoft Internet Explorer (3.0 or above)

■ Non-supporting browser

Figure 3.8.

The quintessential JavaScript-enabled browser.

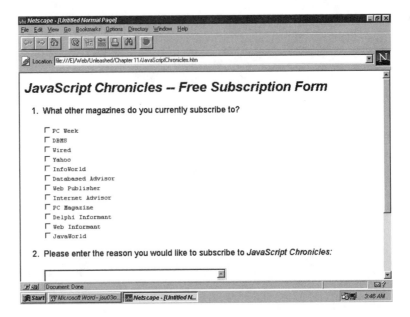

You do not necessarily have to support all browsers in your JavaScript application. For example, you might need to use a JavaScript feature that was added in Netscape Navigator 3.0 and then require that version of the browser (or a later one). However, having previous versions available for testing can be invaluable to providing the best application environment possible.

> **TIP**
>
> Because Netscape Navigator and Microsoft Internet Explorer are emerging as the most popular Web browsers, you will probably find it helpful to regularly test your code in both browser environments. Netscript allows quick access to both of these browsers within its editing environment.

JavaScript Development Process

Once you have your toolkit elements gathered, you need to assemble them into a workable development environment. Before you perform this process, it is helpful to understand how the JavaScript application development process is often structured. Figure 3.9 shows a typical scenario in which basic HTML page creation is followed by adding JavaScript code to the HTML document. The page is then tested iteratively in the Web browser of choice.

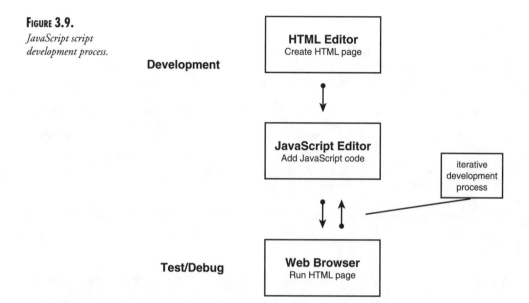

FIGURE 3.9.
JavaScript script development process.

Server-Side JavaScript Tools

JavaScript is featured as the scripting language for two server-side Web development tools. This section provides a brief overview of these tools, both of which are covered more completely in Chapter 20, "Server-Side JavaScript."

Netscape LiveWire

LiveWire (and the enhanced LiveWire Pro) is a suite of tools that works with a Netscape server to help you administer a Web site. LiveWire includes JavaScript as a native scripting language and provides some server-side language extensions for file and database access. You can use server-side JavaScript to develop custom scripts that run on the Netscape server, eliminating the need for CGI in your applications.

RESOURCE

Check the Netscape home page at `http://home.netscape.com` for the latest information on LiveWire.

3
ASSEMBLING YOUR JAVASCRIPT TOOLKIT

Borland IntraBuilder

Borland International's IntraBuilder is a Windows-based visual development environment designed to let you create, maintain, and administer Web database applications. If you have ever worked with a Windows visual development tool, you will feel at home with IntraBuilder.

RESOURCE

Check the Borland home page at http://www.borland.com for the latest technical and support information on IntraBuilder.

IntraBuilder's programming language is an extended version of JavaScript that supports true object-orientation (including inheritance) and database-related objects. Figure 3.10 shows the IntraBuilder integrated development environment (IDE).

FIGURE 3.10.

Creating Web applications using IntraBuilder.

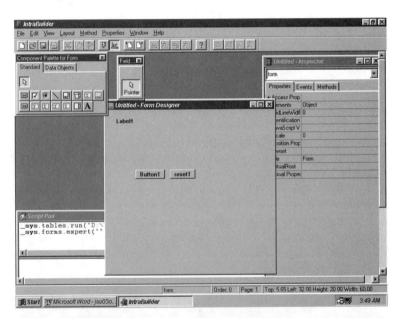

NOTE

No doubt about it, IntraBuilder has the look and feel of Borland's Visual dBASE.

Summary

Because JavaScript is so new in the marketplace, there are no all-in-one solutions for developing client-side JavaScript applications. As a result, you are constrained to working with a host of tools that can be combined to provide a comprehensive development platform. This chapter examined the basic building blocks needed by a JavaScript programmer: a JavaScript editor, HTML editor, and Web browser. I also introduced you to two server-side products—Netscape LiveWire and Borland IntraBuilder—that feature JavaScript as their native programming language.

PART

The JavaScript Language

Fundamentals of the JavaScript Language

by Gary Griffin

IN THIS CHAPTER

CHAPTER 4

JavaScript is a high-level, object-based language designed to enable Web authors and programmers to easily create interactive Web documents. It offers the basic characteristics of an object-oriented language without the complicated features that accompany other languages such as Java and C++. The relatively small vocabulary that makes up JavaScript is easy to understand but gives way to a number of new possibilities that were previously unavailable. In this chapter, I briefly explain how JavaScript relates to two well-known Web technologies and then provide you with the information that you need to create your own JavaScript scripts.

How JavaScript Relates to CGI and Netscape Plug-Ins

Some people might wonder what JavaScript has to offer that using a CGI program or plug-in software does not. Semi-interactive Web pages were around long before JavaScript was born, thanks to CGI programs and plug-in software. I'll define these different technologies so that you can understand how JavaScript adds even more to your Web authoring toolbox.

CGI Programming

CGI (Common Gateway Interface) is the standard for the way programs interface with a Web server. Using a programming language such as Perl, C/C++, AppleScript, or JavaScript and complying with the CGI standard, you can create programs that pass information from the client to the Web server. For example, developers have created many search utilities using CGI to help you locate your favorite sites on the Web. Typically, the user enters a word or phrase into an HTML text element and clicks a Search button. Doing this submits the text and starts a CGI program on the server. The program searches through a master database, finding only the sites that match the search criteria. Once the CGI program is finished with the search, the program creates a new HTML document that includes a list of the results and sends it back to the user's Web browser. You'll notice that all the hard work is done by the server. If you were limited to static Web pages that must be written ahead of time, you would have to consider every search combination possible. To create a Web document for each query would be impractical—a ridiculous way to emulate the type of searching function that users are accustomed to. This is one problem that CGI has solved to help the Web become more interactive.

RESOURCE

For all the information you need about CGI or even links to pre-made CGI scripts, point your Web browser to http://hoohoo.ncsa.uiuc.edu/cgi/overview.html.

Netscape Plug-Ins

Clicking a Web link essentially tells the browser to download a file. If the file is a text, HTML, or graphic file, it is output to the display. If the browser does not recognize the file, it asks you to save the file locally (on your hard disk). Using plug-in extensions, Netscape has increased the number of files that it recognizes. Plug-ins are extra program modules that you can add to deal with files that Netscape was not originally designed to understand. Such files might include audio, animation, Acrobat, and VRML files. For example, if you click a link that points to a .WAV file, Netscape looks for a plug-in module that is configured to deal with .WAV files. If it finds one, Netscape starts the plug-in module and begins playing the audio clip for you. The integration of the browser and audio player is practically seamless.

> **RESOURCE**
>
> There are plenty of Netscape Plug-Ins to enhance your browsing experience. You will find a large list to choose from by pointing your Web browser to `http://home.netscape.com/comprod/products/navigator/version_2.0/plugins/index.html`.

JavaScript

As I mentioned previously, you can use the JavaScript language, along with many others, to create CGI programs that run on the server side. What is unique about JavaScript is that you can also use it to write programs that run on the client side. Suppose you have created an HTML document to collect data from people visiting a particular Web page. You could start out with a form that includes three text elements for their name, company, and telephone number. At the bottom of the form, you included a submit button to send the data to a database on your Web server. You also decided to require that the user complete every field and include both the area code and a seven digit number for the telephone number. After the user clicks the submit button, all the data in the form is passed to a CGI program for processing. If the program notices that the user left out some information, it responds with a new HTML document, asking for the data to be re-entered. If the user then submits the form again with all the required data, the CGI program checks that the required data was given and then continues by posting the data to the database. Handling errors like these can add up to substantial delays, which are now avoidable with JavaScript. You can perform the data validation on the client side with JavaScript so that the Web server does not have to. This leaves only the necessary work of saving data to the server's processor. Data validation is one example of how JavaScript can complement a CGI program by offering a quicker response to errors and freeing up more resources on the server. Chapter 9, "Handling Events," presents an in-depth look into data validation.

Embedding a Script in an HTML Document

You can implement JavaScript in two ways: either embedded in an HTML document between a set of <SCRIPT> tags or inserted inside an HTML tag to respond to an event. Each time an HTML page is downloaded, JavaScript is interpreted by the client's browser. Depending on the actions of the user and other events that occur while the HTML document is being viewed, portions of the embedded script or scripts are executed.

Events

One of the key characteristics of JavaScript is its capability to catch a limited number of user actions, known to most programmers as *events*. Some HTML elements already react to events such as clicking the familiar link element that brings you to another HTML document. As you move your mouse pointer over the text or graphic that makes up the link, your pointer changes from an arrow to a small hand pointing a finger. Some browsers also respond by displaying the destination URL in the status bar. JavaScript calls this the MouseOver event and reacts whenever you move your mouse pointer over the element. If you click any part of the link, the browser responds by sending you to a different location on the Web or opening a new file. This action is cleverly called the Click event, which is triggered whenever you click the link. HTML catches these events, and the browser always reacts the same way.

With JavaScript, you can now create custom reactions to many events that can occur while the user views an HTML document. Chapter 9 shows you how to handle events more in depth.

Basic Syntax Issues

JavaScript is embedded into HTML documents by means of a beginning and ending script tag. The browser starts by finding the first script tag:

```
<SCRIPT LANGUAGE="JavaScript">
```

It then reads everything that follows until the ending script tag:

```
</SCRIPT>
```

JavaScript translates each line of code into instructions to perform in the same way, for example, that you might follow directions to a seminar on JavaScript. Just as you would read each instruction and act on it by turning or driving your car in the appropriate direction, JavaScript follows each of your instructions in order. On your way to the seminar, you might need to stop at a red light until the signal turns green or stop to pick up a friend. You can also emulate this with JavaScript if you want the computer to sit idle until something happens. Listing 4.1 shows how to embed JavaScript in the body section of an HTML document.

Listing 4.1. Embedding JavaScript inside an HTML document.

```
<HTML>
<HEAD>
<TITLE>JavaScript Unleashed</TITLE>
</HEAD>
<BODY>
<CENTER><H2>JavaScript brings the Web to life!</H2></CENTER>
<SCRIPT LANGUAGE = "JavaScript">
<!-- begin hiding from old browsers
document.write("Hello World Wide Web!")
// end hiding -->
</SCRIPT>
</BODY>
</HTML>
```

Figure 4.1 shows a basic HTML page that sets the title bar of your browser to "JavaScript Unleashed" and begins the page with the header "JavaScript brings the Web to life!" After the first script tag, you need to include HTML comment tags before and after the script. By surrounding the JavaScript code with these, you prevent it from showing up as plain text in older Web browsers that do not understand the <SCRIPT> tags.

The keywords, document and write, are recognized by JavaScript and used together to perform an action. To be more specific, the write() method places the greeting onto the HTML document before it is viewed by the client's browser. This is how you can actually create an entire HTML. You must use lowercase when typing the words write and document because JavaScript is case-sensitive. If you accidentally capitalize any letters, JavaScript will simply display an error. Hopefully you plan to test your scripts before letting others access them. That way you can easily correct the mistake and reload the HTML document into your browser. The extra blank lines and indentation within the script do not have any effect because JavaScript ignores white space. Thoughtfully using white space provides for easy reading as your scripts become longer. The sentence, Hello World Wide Web!, within the parentheses could be any phrase that you want to display, as well as a result from a calculation. The statement ends with a semicolon, which is not required. However, you could use a semicolon to separate statements that might need to appear on the same line. Otherwise, as long as you start a new line, JavaScript knows that you are starting a new set of statements.

4

FUNDAMENTALS OF THE JAVASCRIPT LANGUAGE

FIGURE 4.1.

A short sentence displayed using JavaScript.

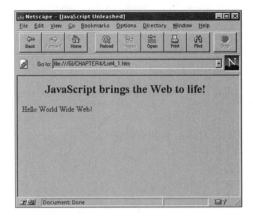

Tokens

Tokens are the smallest individual words, phrases, or characters that JavaScript can understand. When JavaScript is interpreted, the browser parses the script into these tokens while ignoring comments and white space. JavaScript tokens fit in five categories: identifiers, keywords, literals, operators, and separators. As with all computer languages, you have many ways to arrange these tokens to instruct a computer to perform a specific function. The *syntax* of a language is the set of rules and restrictions for the way you can combine tokens.

Identifiers

Identifiers are simply names that represent variables, methods, or objects. They consist of a combination of characters or a combination of characters and digits. Some names are already built into the JavaScript language and are therefore reserved (see the next section, "Keywords"). Aside from these keywords, you can define your own creative and meaningful identifiers. Of course, you have a couple of rules to follow. You must begin all identifiers with either a letter or underscore (_). You can then use letters, digits, or underscores for all subsequent characters. Letters include all uppercase characters, A through Z, and all lowercase characters, a through z. Digits include the characters 0 through 9. Table 4.1 shows some examples of valid and invalid identifiers.

Table 4.1. Examples of user-defined JavaScript identifiers.

Valid	*Invalid*
current_WebSite	current WebSite
numberOfHits	#ofIslands
n	2bOrNotToBe
N	return

Notice that current WebSite is invalid because it contains a space. JavaScript tries to interpret this as two identifiers instead of one. If a space is needed, it is standard practice to use an underscore in its place. #ofIslands is invalid because the pound sign is not included in the set of characters that are valid for identifiers. 2bOrNotToBe is not valid because it begins with a number. The return identifier is already used by JavaScript for another purpose. Attempting to use this as your own identifier will only confuse your browser and cause it to say terrible things to you. Also, both n and N are valid identifiers, not to mention different from each other. JavaScript is case sensitive and therefore considers identifiers with different case to be unique even though they may be spelled the same.

Keywords

Keywords are predefined identifiers that make up the core of a programming language. In JavaScript, they perform unique functions such as declaring new variables and functions, making decisions based on the present state of the computer, or starting a repetitive loop inside your application. Keywords, which are built into JavaScript, are always available for use by the programmer but must follow the correct syntax. The keyword var is the first that I describe in detail later in the chapter. As you need them, I show you how you can use other keywords to create more dynamic programs. The following list shows the available keywords:

```
break       if          this
continue    in          true
else        int         var
false       new         while
for         null        with
function    return
```

Reserved Words

Reserved words are identifiers that you might not use as names for JavaScript variables, functions, objects, or methods. This includes keywords (described in the previous section) along with identifiers that are set aside for possible future use. The following is a complete list of the reserved words for JavaScript:

Literals

Literals are data comprised of numbers or strings used to represent fixed values in JavaScript. They are values that do not change during the execution of your scripts. The following five sections contain descriptions and examples of the different types of literals that you can use.

Integer Literals

Integers can be expressed in either decimal (base 10), octal (base 8), or hexadecimal (base 16) format. An integer literal in decimal format can include any sequence of digits that does not begin with a 0 (zero). A zero in front of an integer literal designates octal form. The integer itself can include a sequence of the digits 0 through 7. To designate hexadecimal, 0x (or 0X) is used before the integer. Hexadecimal integers can include digits 0 through 9 along with the letters f through f or A through F. Some examples include

Decimal (base 10)	33, 2139
Octal (base 8)	071, 03664
Hexadecimal (base 16)	0x7b8, 0X395

Floating-Point Literals

Floating-point literals represent decimal numbers with fractional parts. They can be expressed in either standard or scientific notation. With scientific notation, use either e or E to designate the exponent. Both the decimal number and exponent can be either signed or unsigned (positive or negative) as shown in the examples:

3405.673

−1.958

8.3200e+11

8.3200e11

9.98E−12

Boolean Literals

JavaScript implements *Boolean data types* and therefore supports the two literals, `true` and `false`. They represent the Boolean values `1` and `0`, respectively. If you are new to programming, you will soon realize how often true and false values are needed. This is why JavaScript has built them into the language. The `true` and `false` keywords must appear in lowercase. As a result, the capitalized words TRUE and FALSE are left open to define as your own identifiers, but it is not recommended.

String Literals

A *string literal* is zero or more characters enclosed in double (") or single (') quotes. JavaScript gives you this option, but you must use the same type of quote to surround each string. The following are examples of string literals enclosed in quotes:

```
"virtual communities"
'virtual communities'
```

```
"#12-6"

"Look, up in the sky!"
```

The use of either type of quotation mark is handy if you have a preference for one or the other. When you learn about JavaScript's built-in methods in Chapter 10, "JavaScript Object Model," be careful to note the guidelines that you must follow when using string literals as parameters. In some instances, to use the method properly, you might have to use both types of quotations when enclosing a string literal inside another. This is different from "escaping" characters, which is described in the next section.

Special Characters

When writing scripts, you might sometimes need to tell the computer to use a special character or keystroke such as a tab or carriage return. To do this, use a backslash in front of one of the special characters as shown in the following list:

\b indicates a backspace

\f indicates a form feed

\n indicates a new-line character

\r indicates a carriage return

\t indicates a tab character

If you want to emulate a tab key to align two columns of data, you must use the tab character (\t). Listing 4.2 shows how to align text using tabs. The script itself can be harder to read after adding special characters, but as Figure 4.2 shows, the results look much better.

Listing 4.2. Using special characters in JavaScript.

```
<HTML>
<HEAD>
<TITLE>JavaScript Unleashed</TITLE>
</HEAD>
<BODY>
<PRE><!-- Notice: Special characters do not take effect unless
enclosed in a pre-formatted block -->
<SCRIPT LANGUAGE = "JavaScript">
<!-- begin hiding from old browsers
document.writeln("\tPersonnel")
document.writeln("Name\t\tAddress")
document.writeln("Jeff\t\tjeff@company.com")
document.writeln("Bill\t\tbill@company.com")
document.writeln("Kim\t\tkim@company.com")
// end hiding -->
</SCRIPT>
</PRE>
</BODY>
</HTML>
```

> **NOTE**
>
> Special characters only take effect when used in a formatted text block; therefore, your script must be within tags such as <PRE> and </PRE>.

FIGURE 4.2.

Aligning text using the tabs in JavaScript.

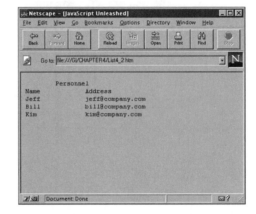

If you need to represent quotation marks within a string literal, precede them with a backslash, as shown in this example:

```
document.write("\"Imagination is more important than knowledge.\"")
```

```
document.write(", Albert Einstein")
```

The previous script would display the following line of text:

```
"Imagination is more important than knowledge.", Albert Einstein
```

Variables

A *variable* is the name given to a location in a computer's memory where data is stored. The first computer programmers spent much of their time translating data such as the "Hello World Wide Web" message into binary data. They would then find an empty area in the computer's memory to put all of the 1s and 0s while remembering where the data began and ended. By knowing this location (address), they were able to find, update, or retrieve the data as needed during the rest of the program. This basically meant keeping track of a lot of numbers! Variables have made this process of storing, updating, and retrieving information much easier for the modern day programmer. With variables, you can assign meaningful names to pieces of data that you want to store while the computer handles the rest.

Naming Variables

The name of a JavaScript variable comprises one or more letters, digits, or underscores but cannot begin with a digit. Digits include 0 through 9. Letters include all uppercase characters, A through Z, and all lowercase characters, a through z. JavaScript is case sensitive and therefore considers the following examples to be different variable names:

```
internetAddress
internetaddress
_lastName
n
number_2
```

Declaring Variables

To let JavaScript know you are going to use an identifier as a variable, you must first declare it. To declare variables in JavaScript, use the keyword var followed by the new variable name. This action reserves the name as a variable to be used as a storage area for whatever data you might want to hold with it. In the examples that follow, notice that you can also declare more than one variable at a time by using a comma between variable names:

```
var internetAddress
var n
var i, j, k
var isMouseOverLink, helloMessage
```

Once a variable is declared, it is then ready to be filled with its first value. This *initializing* is done with the assignment operator, =. You can initialize a variable at the same time it is declared or at any point thereafter in your script. Assigning a value when the variable is declared can help you remember what type of value you originally meant the variable to hold. The following shows the previous example rewritten to include all initializations:

```
var internetAddress = "name@company.com"
var n = 0.00
var i = 0, j = 0, k
var isMouseOverLink = false
var helloMessage = "Hello, thank you for coming!"
k = 0
```

Notice that all variables have been initialized and declared at the same time except for k, which is initialized soon after. JavaScript reads from the top down, stepping through each line of code and performing the instructions in order. Until the program reaches the initializing step, the variable is said to be *undefined*, and you cannot extract any value from it. Reading a value from a variable before it is initialized causes an error in your application when you execute it. JavaScript allows you to determine whether a variable has been assigned using the typeof operator. This is explained in Chapter 5, "Operators."

JavaScript offers one other way of declaring a variable and it is simply by initializing it without using the var keyword. By assigning a value to a new variable, JavaScript will automatically declare it for you. It is important to note that doing so will automatically declare the variable to be *global* in scope. Although this can be a shortcut, it is good programming practice to declare all variables specifically. Using the var keyword maintains the scope of the variable. Under special circumstances you can avoid using var to declare a variable to be global when it would otherwise be declared *local* in scope. This is covered in more detail in the section, "Scope of Variables."

Variable Types

When storing a piece of data (more commonly known as a *value*), JavaScript automatically categorizes it as one of the five JavaScript data types. Table 4.2 shows the different types of data that JavaScript uses.

Table 4.2. JavaScript data types.

Type	*Examples*
number	−19, 3.14159
Boolean	true, false
string	"Elementary, my dear Watson!", ""
function	unescape, write
object	window, document, null

A variable of the number type holds either an integer or a real number. A boolean variable holds either the value true or false. String variables can hold any string literal that is assigned to it. Functions are either user-defined or built-in. For example, the unescape function is built into JavaScript. You can learn how to create user-defined functions in Chapter 7, "Functions." Functions that belong to objects, called methods in JavaScript, are also classified under the function data type. Elements such as the window or document are of the object data type. Object variables, or simply "objects," can store another object. A variable that holds the null value is said to be of the object type. This is because JavaScript classifies the value null as an object. Initializing a variable with null is a great way to prevent errors if you're not sure whether the variable will be used.

Typically, programming languages require that you define the type of data a new variable will represent. Throughout your program, any value assigned to that variable is expected to be its defined data type. Furthermore, an error occurs when you make an attempt to assign a different data type to the variable. This does not happen with JavaScript, which is classified as a loosely typed language. You are not required to define data types, nor are you prevented from assigning different types of data to the same variable. JavaScript variables can accept a new type of data at any time, which in turn changes the type of variable they are. The following example shows valid uses of JavaScript variables:

```
var carLength
carLength = 4 + 5
document.writeln(carLength)
carLength = "9 feet"
document.writeln(carLength)
```

After you declare the variable, carLength is assigned the value of 4 + 5. JavaScript stores the number 9 as the number type. However, when you reassign carLength to "9 feet", JavaScript lets you store a new type of value, a string, in carLength. This eliminates the extra steps that are usually needed by other computer languages to let the computer know that you are switching data types.

Scope of Variables

The *scope* of a variable refers to the area or areas within a program where a variable can be referenced. Suppose you embed one script in the head of an HTML document and another script (using another set of script tags) in the body of the same HTML document. JavaScript considers the variables in either of these two areas as residing in the same area and having the same scope. These variables are considered *global*. Later in this chapter, I formally introduce functions, which are separate blocks of code. Variables declared within these blocks are considered *local*.

Local

A variable declared inside a function is local in scope. Only that function has access to the value that the variable holds. Each time the function is called, the variable is created. Likewise, each time the function ends, the variable is destroyed. Another function can also declare a variable with the same name, but JavaScript considers it a different variable and does not address the same block of memory.

Global

If you want more than one function to share a variable, you declare the variable outside of any functions (but, of course, inside the <SCRIPT> tags). With this method, any part of your application, including all functions, can share one instance of a variable. I recommend that you declare global variables in the head of an HTML page to ensure that they are loaded before any other part of your application. Listing 4.3 demonstrates how a global variable is declared and implemented. To show the difference between scopes, I included two functions in this program. You do not need to understand how functions work, but realize that they are like separate parts of a script enclosed by curly braces, {}. If you are not familiar with functions, you can find this listing on the CD-ROM that came with this book and load it into your browser. For more information on functions, refer to Chapter 7.

Listing 4.3. Global versus local scope of a variable.

```
<HTML>
<TITLE>JavaScript Unleashed</TITLE>
<HEAD>
<SCRIPT LANGUAGE = "JavaScript">
<!-- begin hiding from old browsers
//Global Variable
var globalString = "A"
//Functions
function changeToB() {
     document.outputForm.beforeB.value = globalString
     globalString = "B"
     document.outputForm.afterB.value = globalString
}

function changeToC() {
     document.outputForm.beforeC.value = globalString
     globalString = "C"
     document.outputForm.afterC.value = globalString
}
// end of hiding from old browsers -->
</SCRIPT>
</HEAD>
<BODY>

<SCRIPT LANGUAGE = "JavaScript">
<!-- begin hiding from old browsers
document.write("The initial value of globalString is \"" +
 globalString + "\".")
// end of hiding from old browsers -->
</SCRIPT>
<BR>
<FORM NAME="outputForm">
<INPUT
     NAME="changeButtonA"
     TYPE="button"
     VALUE="Change To B"
     onClick= "changeToB()">
<INPUT
     NAME="changeButtonB"
     TYPE="button"
     VALUE="Change To C"
     onClick= "changeToC()">
<BR> <BR>
Value of globalString<BR>
<BR>
<INPUT
     NAME="beforeB"
     TYPE="TEXT"
     SIZE=5,1>
Before clicking on "Change To B"<BR>
<INPUT
     NAME="afterB"
     TYPE="TEXT"
     SIZE=5,1>
After clicking on "Change To B"<BR>
```

```
<INPUT
     NAME="beforeC"
     TYPE="TEXT"
     SIZE=5,1>
Before clicking on "Change To C"<BR>
<INPUT
     NAME="afterC"
     TYPE="TEXT"
     SIZE=5,1>
After clicking on "Change To C"<BR>
</FORM>
</BODY>
</HTML>
```

In this example, the initial value of globalString is displayed first. This shows that even though the variable was declared in the <HEAD> block of the document, a script inside the <BODY> block of the document can use it. If you click on the Change to B button, the function changeToB() first displays the initial value of globalString, changes it to B, and then displays the new value that globalString holds. To demonstrate that all functions in the document can use the same variable, I added a second button to call a different function. Clicking on the Change to C button displays the current value of globalString, which is now B, and then changes globalString to C. Figure 4.3 shows the final output.

FIGURE 4.3.

Difference between local and global scopes.

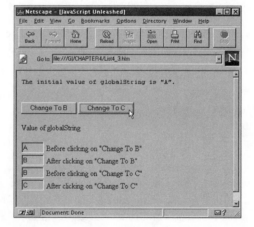

To Declare or Not to Declare?

So far, you have declared all your variables with the keyword var. JavaScript actually allows you to skip this step and create a variable by merely initializing it. I do not recommend skipping this step because it can have a different effect on the scope of the variable. When you skip or forget to declare a variable and begin by initializing it, JavaScript assumes that the variable is global regardless of whether it was initialized inside a function. This action is exactly the same as declaring the variable outside a function, except for one point—a global variable declared outside a function can be used by the whole application as soon as the document is loaded. A global variable initialized inside a function cannot be used by any part of the application until that function is actually called and executed.

Naming Conventions

When naming variables with a single word in JavaScript, it is common practice to use all lowercase letters. When using two or more words to name a variable, it is common to use lowercase letters for the first word and capitalize the first letter of all words thereafter.

I make it a practice to use two or more words when naming variables to give myself and others a better idea of what the variable was created to do. For example, suppose you need a variable to hold a boolean value (true or false) that will let you know if a visitor to your Web page is finished typing his name into a text field. If you chose a variable name such as finish, another programmer(or you, a couple of months down the road) could look at it and think, "Was this a flag that can be checked to find out if the visitor is done? Or was it a string stating what to write when the visitor was done, such as a thank-you message?" The variable name isDone would be a better choice in this case. By using the word is as a prefix, you can indicate that this variable is posing a yes-or-no question, which indicates that the variable will store a boolean value. If the visitor is done entering their name, isDone is assigned the value true—otherwise, false.

While the length of a JavaScript variable is only limited by a computer's memory, it is a good idea to keep variables to a practical length. I recommend between 1 and 20 characters or two to three words. Try to prevent running over the end of a line while writing your scripts. Large variable names make this easy to do and can ruin the look and structure of your code.

Some traditional one-word and even single-character variables represent program or mathematical values. The most common are n for any number; x, y, and z for coordinates; and i for a placeholder in a recursive function or a counter in a loop. Again, these methods for using variables are simply traditional, and you may use them for whatever purpose you see fit.

There is a good chance that at some point, especially in the professional environment, your code will need to be read by other people. Using consistent and meaningful naming conventions can be a big help to someone who is maintaining your scripts. Poorly thought out conventions cause big headaches and can significantly affect a company's bottom line.

Constants

JavaScript does not supply any built-in constants. You could call true and false constants, but Netscape really categorizes them as keywords. A constant holds the same value throughout an application so that you can be sure it always carries the same value. Netscape might find a need for constants in the future, but for now, it works fine without them.

User-Defined Constants

User-defined constants are variables whose values do not change. JavaScript does not support these in the traditional sense. Typically, a programming language that supports constants ensures that no other part of your application can change the value of a constant you defined. Attempting a change causes an error. Nevertheless, defining your own constants in an application can be useful. Even though JavaScript does not ensure that a variable you use as a constant will not be altered, you can still follow the traditional practice of using them. Constants are typically characterized by capitalized words and defined at the beginning of a program. They are great for holding values that you use repeatedly in a script. By replacing the multiple instances of a common value with a constant, you make it easier to update a script at a later time. All you have to do is change what the constant holds in the beginning of your program.

Colors

JavaScript supports the colors that are used in HTML. To specify a color in your application—for example, to change the color of a font—you can pick from the list of colors in Table 4.3. These values are string literals (not constants) that you can assign to specific object properties. Listing 4.4 shows how you can use these values to set the color of strings that are written to the display. Notice that you can use either the name of the color or its hexadecimal equivalent. The method might look somewhat strange, but it simply changes the `fontcolor` property of the string literal that is written to the display. You can learn more about changing this and other properties of a string in Chapter 14, "Built-In Language Objects." An invitation to the company picnic can be seen in Figure 4.4.

The hexadecimal string for each color is actually a combination of the RGB (Red/Green/Blue) values that are used to make up each color. For example, the hexadecimal value for aqua is #00FFFF. If the number sign is eliminated, you are left with 00 for the red value, FF for the green value and again, FF for the blue values. Two digits in hexadecimal allows for 256 degrees of each color. For the color aqua, the red is set to zero which means that there is no red included. As for the green and blue degrees, they are each turned up all the way. An equal amount of green and blue is combined to create the color aqua. With 256 combinations for red, green, and blue, there are over 16 million colors possible, but all are not supported by JavaScript. The full list of supported colors is shown in Table 4.3.

4

FUNDAMENTALS OF THE JAVASCRIPT LANGUAGE

Listing 4.4. Using colors in JavaScript.

```
<HTML>
<HEAD>
<TITLE>JavaScript Unleashed</TITLE>
</HEAD>
<BODY BGCOLOR = "WHITE">
<CENTER><PRE><H2>
<SCRIPT LANGUAGE = "JavaScript">
<!-- begin hiding from old browsers
```

continues

Listing 4.4. continued

```
document.writeln("Company Picnic!".fontcolor("crimson"))
// end hiding -->
</SCRIPT>
</H2><H4>
<SCRIPT LANGUAGE = "JavaScript">
<!-- begin hiding from old browsers
document.writeln("July 19th at 1pm".fontcolor("blue"))
document.writeln("Bring your family!".fontcolor("#008000"))
// end hiding -->
</SCRIPT>
</H4></PRE>
</CENTER>
</BODY>
</HTML>
```

FIGURE 4.4.

*Changing the color of
text in JavaScript.*

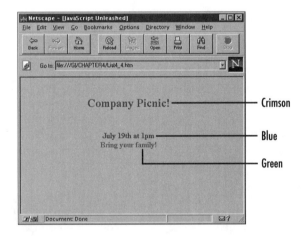

Table 4.3. Color values with hexadecimal equivalents.

Color	Red	Green	Blue	Color	Red	Green	Blue
aliceblue	F0	F8	FF	antiquewhite	FA	EB	D7
aqua	00	FF	FF	aquamarine	7F	FF	D4
azure	F0	FF	FF	beige	F5	F5	DC
bisque	FF	E4	C4	black	00	00	00
blanchedalmond	FF	EB	CD	blue	00	00	FF
blueviolet	8A	2B	E2	brown	A5	2A	2A
burlywood	DE	B8	87	cadetblue	5F	9E	A0
chartreuse	7F	FF	00	chocolate	D2	69	1E
coral	FF	7F	50	cornflowerblue	64	95	ED
cornsilk	FF	F8	DC	crimson	DC	14	3C

Color	Red	Green	Blue	Color	Red	Green	Blue
cyan	00	FF	FF	darkblue	00	00	8B
darkcyan	00	8B	8B	darkgoldenrod	B8	86	0B
darkgray	A9	A9	A9	darkgreen	00	64	00
darkkhaki	BD	B7	6B	darkmagenta	8B	00	8B
darkolivegreen	55	6B	2F	darkorange	FF	8C	00
darkorchid	99	32	CC	darkred	8B	00	00
darksalmon	E9	96	7A	darkseagreen	8F	BC	8F
darkslateblue	48	3D	8B	darkslategray	2F	4F	4F
darkturquoise	00	CE	D1	darkviolet	94	00	D3
deeppink	FF	14	93	deepskyblue	00	BF	FF
dimgray	69	69	69	dodgerblue	1E	90	FF
firebrick	B2	22	22	floralwhite	FF	FA	F0
forestgreen	22	8B	22	fuchsia	FF	00	FF
gainsboro	DC	DC	DC	ghostwhite	F8	F8	FF
gold	FF	D7	00	goldenrod	DA	A5	20
gray	80	80	80	green	00	80	00
greenyellow	AD	FF	2F	honeydew	F0	FF	F0
hotpink	FF	69	B4	indianred	CD	5C	5C
indigo	4B	00	82	ivory	FF	FF	F0
khaki	F0	E6	8C	lavender	E6	E6	FA
lavenderblush	FF	F0	F5	lawngreen	7C	FC	00
lemonchiffon	FF	FA	CD	lightblue	AD	D8	E6
lightcoral	F0	80	80	lightcyan	E0	FF	FF
lightgoldenrod-yellow	FA	FA	D2	lightgreen	90	EE	90
lightgrey	D3	D3	D3	lightpink	FF	B6	C1
lightsalmon	FF	A0	7A	lightseagreen	20	B2	AA
lightskyblue	87	CE	FA	lightslategray	77	88	99
lightsteelblue	B0	C4	DE	lightyellow	FF	FF	E0
lime	00	FF	00	limegreen	32	CD	32
linen	FA	F0	E6	magenta	FF	00	FF
maroon	80	00	00	medium-aquamarine	66	CD	AA

continues

Table 4.3. continued

Color	Red	Green	Blue	Color	Red	Green	Blue
mediumblue	00	00	CD	mediumorchid	BA	55	D3
mediumpurple	93	70	DB	medium-seagreen	3C	B3	71
mediumslateblue	7B	68	EE	medium-springgreen	00	FA	9A
medium-turquoise	48	D1	CC	medium-violetred	C7	15	85
midnightblue	19	19	70	mintcream	F5	FF	FA
mistyrose	FF	E4	E1	moccasin	FF	E4	B5
navajowhite	FF	DE	AD	navy	00	00	80
oldlace	FD	F5	E6	olive	80	80	00
olivedrab	6B	8E	23	orange	FF	A5	00
orangered	FF	45	00	orchid	DA	70	D6
palegoldenrod	EE	E8	AA	palegreen	98	FB	98
paleturquoise	AF	EE	EE	palevioletred	DB	70	93
papayawhip	FF	EF	D5	peachpuff	FF	DA	B9
peru	CD	85	3F	pink	FF	C0	CB
plum	DD	A0	DD	powderblue	B0	E0	E6
purple	80	00	80	red	FF	00	00
rosybrown	BC	8F	8F	royalblue	41	69	E1
saddlebrown	8B	45	13	salmon	FA	80	72
sandybrown	F4	A4	60	seagreen	2E	8B	57
seashell	FF	F5	EE	sienna	A0	52	2D
silver	C0	C0	C0	skyblue	87	CE	EB
slateblue	6A	5A	CD	slategray	70	80	90
snow	FF	FA	FA	springgreen	00	FF	7F
steelblue	46	82	B4	tan	D2	B4	8C
teal	00	80	80	thistle	D8	BF	D8
tomato	FF	63	47	turquoise	40	E0	D0
violet	EE	82	EE	wheat	F5	DE	B3
white	FF	FF	FF	whitesmoke	F5	F5	F5
yellow	FF	FF	00	yellowgreen	9A	CD	32

Data Types

Although I have already discussed the basic data types that you can assign to variables, functions and objects are special types of data. They offer interesting ways to store and act upon the data that your scripts deal with. You will learn how to take advantage of these aspects of the language in Chapter 7, which is dedicated to functions, and Part III, dedicated to "JavaScript Objects."

Expressions

Expressions are a set of statements that, as a group, evaluate to a single value. This resulting value is then categorized by JavaScript as one of the five data types: `number`, `string`, `logical`, `function`, or `object`.

An expression can be as simple as a number or variable by itself or can include many variables, keywords, and operators joined together. For example, the expression `x = 10` is a statement that assigns the value `10` to the variable `x`. The expression as a whole evaluates to 10, so using the expression in a line of code such as `document.writeln(x = 10)` is valid. JavaScript would rather take whatever is between the parentheses and display it, but in this case, it finds some work to do before moving on. It must first evaluate what is between the parentheses and then display the value. In this case, the number 10 is displayed.

Once the work is done to assign 10 to x, the following is also a valid expression: x. In this case, the only work that JavaScript needs to do is read the value from the computer's memory; JavaScript performs no assignment. In addition to the assignment operator, there are many other operators you can use to form an expression (see Chapter 5).

Comments

So far, I have used HTML comment tags for surrounding scripts, which ensures that old browsers do not read scripts that they cannot understand. The tags' main purpose is to hide text within a document that HTML will ignore. What if you want to place comments in your JavaScript code that JavaScript will ignore? The two solutions were borrowed from the C and C++ languages, and the syntax follows:

```
//comments
```

For larger blocks of comments, use the following:

```
/*multiple-lines
comments */
```

The two forward slashes (or division signs), //, hide text that follows it until the end of the current line. Whitespace is ignored so the following are also valid:

```
//       comments

/*         multiple lines

comments                */
```

Listing 4.5. Using JavaScript comment tags.

```
<HTML>
<HEAD>
<TITLE>JavaScript Unleashed</TITLE>
</HEAD>
<BODY>
<PRE>
<SCRIPT LANGUAGE = "JavaScript">
<!-- begin hiding from old browsers
//variables
var firstName = "Jon",
lastName = "Simpson",
internetAddress = "jsimpson@company.com"
/*Display the user's first and last name
along with their e-mail address */
document.writeln(firstName + " " + lastName) //combine three strings
document.writeln("e-mail address: " + internetAddress)
// end hiding -->
</SCRIPT>
</PRE>
</BODY>
</HTML>
```

The two forward slashes do not hide code from older browsers. To avoid giving old browsers a headache, continue to use <!-- and --> to surround all of your scripts. In Figure 4.5, anything that was commented is not output to the display.

FIGURE 4.5.

Comments are not displayed in the browser.

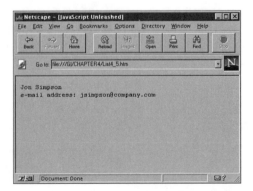

Being able to hide code from JavaScript gives you the ability to document your scripts. It is considered good programming practice to add design notes, friendly reminders, or warnings throughout your program. This can help you and others see what the different sections of your program were meant to do. Another use for comments is debugging your scripts. You can hide your code to track down problems and then easily replace it when you are done by simply removing comment identifiers. Doing this instead of deleting parts of your script helps save time.

Operators

Operators are symbols or identifiers that represent the way in which a combination of expressions is evaluated or manipulated. The most common operator you have used thus far is the assignment operator. In the example x = 10, both 10 by itself and the variable x are expressions. When JavaScript sees an assignment operator between two expressions, it acts according to the rules of the assignment operator. In this case, it takes the value from the expression on the right side and assigns it to the expression on the left side. Along with the common arithmetic operators, JavaScript supports over 30 others. I cover these more thoroughly in Chapter 5.

Functions

In its simplest form, a function is a script that you can call by name at any time. This enhances JavaScript in two ways. When an HTML document is read by a JavaScript-enabled Web browser, the browser will find any embedded scripts and execute the instructions step-by-step. This is fine unless you would rather have part or all of your program wait before executing. Writing this part of your program in a function and assigning it a name is a great way to set up a script to be run at a later time. When a specific event occurs, you can run this script by using the name that you gave to the function. Another advantage of functions is the capability to reuse scripts without typing in the same code over and over again. Instead, you can just use the name given to the function to execute the group of code contained within.

To see how JavaScript executes a function, see Listing 4.6. The first thing to notice is where the function is declared. Just as other variables need to be declared, so do functions. Be sure to enclose all function declarations within <SCRIPT> tags. I recommended declaring your functions in the <HEAD> block of the HTML document. Doing this ensures that the function is loaded by the browser before it is executed by the body. To use the function all that needs to be done is place the name of it anywhere in your program. The main program is placed within the body and is surrounded by its own set of <SCRIPT> tags.

Listing 4.6. Embedding a JavaScript function.

```
<HTML>
<HEAD>
<TITLE>JavaScript Unleashed</TITLE>
<SCRIPT LANGUAGE = "JavaScript">
function displayMessage() {
    document.write("JavaScript functions are easy to use!")
    document.write("<BR>")
}
<!-- begin hiding from old browsers
// end hiding -->
</SCRIPT>
</HEAD>
<BODY>
<PRE>
<SCRIPT LANGUAGE = "JavaScript">
<!-- begin hiding from old browsers
document.write("Calling a JavaScript function...<BR>")
displayMessage()
document.write("Done.<BR>")
// end hiding -->
</SCRIPT>
</PRE>
</BODY>
</HTML>
```

Starting with the main script, JavaScript executes the first line as always and then arrives at the `displayMessage()` function call. It looks up the function in memory and begins with the first line of `displayMessage()`. After writing `JavaScript functions are easy to use!`, a line break is displayed. The end of the function is reached and program execution returns to where it left off in the main script. As you can see in Figure 4.6, each line of text is displayed in this sequence. If you have a lengthy program that displays this message many times you can insert the function call in each place where you need it. If at a later time there was a need to update the message, you need only change the message in one place. Change it within the function declaration and your whole application is updated. You can learn more about functions and their advantages in Chapter 7.

Figure 4.6.

Calling a function in JavaScript.

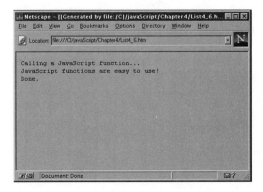

Summary

JavaScript is a great addition to the Web author's tool kit. It makes some things possible that CGI and plug-ins have not. It offers direct interaction with the user while an HTML document is being viewed.

Scripts are placed directly into HTML documents and surrounded by <SCRIPT> tags. Use the correct type of comments to have either the browser or JavaScript itself ignore particular sections of your scripts.

Starting from the first line of code, the script is read line by line by the JavaScript interpreter. *Tokens* are the smallest individual words, phrases, or characters that JavaScript can understand. Tokens can be either literals, identifiers or operators.

The different data types available include the number, Boolean, string, function and object types. Variables can store one of these data types at a time. To declare a variable, use the var keyword or simply initialize the variable. Initializing a variable without first declaring it will always create a global variable. Try to use meaningful names for variables to make your scripts easier to read.

Expressions are a set of statements that evaluate to a single value. The most common expressions are ones that assign values to variables. The assignment operator, =, is used to assign the value of its right operand to the variable which is its left operand. JavaScript supports all standard math operations either through operators or by using the built-in Math object.

Use comments to help document your scripts. This will keep it easy to maintain them by yourself and others.

Operators are symbols or identifiers that represent the way in which a combination of expressions is evaluated or manipulated. Operators are covered thoroughly in Chapter 5.

Functions are scripts that you can execute at any time before or after an HTML document is viewed by the user. With functions you can set aside a script to be executed at any time and as often as you like. Using functions can also make your scripts easier to maintain. Chapter 7 explains functions in greater detail.

In the next chapter, "Operators," I help you take a closer look at the built-in tools that JavaScript offers to handle and manipulate data. If you are familiar with C and C++ style operators, you could use Chapter 5 as a reference and move on to Chapter 6, "Control Structures and Looping," to find out how to make decisions with JavaScript.

4

FUNDAMENTALS OF THE JAVASCRIPT LANGUAGE

Operators

by Gary Griffin

IN THIS CHAPTER

The whole idea of writing a script is to input, evaluate, manipulate, or display data. Until now, you have concentrated on displaying data with JavaScript. To create more useful programs, you need to evaluate or even change the data that your scripts are dealing with. The tools for this job are called *operators*. They are the symbols and identifiers that represent either the way that the data is changed or the way a combination of expressions are evaluated. JavaScript supports both binary and unary operators. Binary operators require that there be two operands in the expression, such as 9 + x, whereas unary operators only need one operand. One example is x++.

Both of the examples used here are arithmetic operators, and their use will come naturally to those who understand basic math. Other types of JavaScript operators deal with strings and logical values. They do not act as intuitively, but are easy to learn and very handy when dealing with the enormous amounts of text on the Internet. I'll take a closer look at each type of JavaScript operator.

> **NOTE**
>
> Netscape offers a type-in mode that allows you to type in expressions and have their values displayed immediately. I have found it to be an excellent way to quickly check the value of an expression and an easy way to experiment. To enter this mode, choose File | Open Location and enter the following text in the location field:
>
> `JavaScript:`
>
> Press Enter again and your screen will be split into two sections. You may now type in just about any line of JavaScript. This includes declaring variables, functions, and objects along with evaluating expressions. I have shown an example of using this feature in Figure 5.1. I entered
>
> `12<<1`
>
> into the `typein` field and pressed Enter. The result was then displayed in the main browser window.

FIGURE 5.1.

Using the typein *feature of Netscape.*

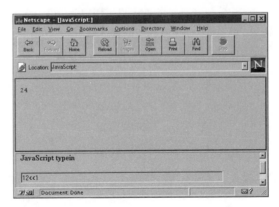

Assignment Operators

An operator you already know is the assignment operator. Its most basic function is assigning a value to a variable, thereby placing the value in memory. For example, the expression x = 20 assigns the value 20 to the variable x. When JavaScript encounters the assignment operator (=), it first looks to the right for a value. It then looks to the left and ensures that there is a place to store the number. If it finds a variable, it assigns the value to it. In this case, x holds the value of 20. It always works from right to left, so the expression 20 = x causes an error in JavaScript by trying to assign a new value to 20. This is not allowed, given the fact that 20 is not a variable, but an integer whose value cannot be changed.

JavaScript supports 11 other assignment operators that are really a combination of the assignment operator and either an arithmetic or bitwise operator. These shorthand versions follow:

Combination of Assignment and Arithmetic Operators

x += y is short for x = x + y

x -= y is short for x = x - y

x *= y is short for x = x * y

x /= y is short for x = x / y

x %= y is short for x = x % y

Combination of Assignment and Bitwise Operators

x <<= y is short for x = x << y

x >>= y is short for x = x >> y

x >>>= y is short for x = x >>> y

x &= y is short for x = x & y

x ^= y is short for x = x ^ y

x |= y is short for x = x | y

Arithmetic Operators

When working with numbers, you use arithmetic operators. The most basic operators of the group include the plus sign (+), to add two values; the minus sign (-), to subtract one value from another; the asterisk (*), to multiply two values together; and the forward slash (/), to divide one value by another. When JavaScript encounters one of these operators, it looks to the right and left sides of the operator to find the values to work on. In the example 7 + 9, JavaScript sees the plus operator and looks to either side of it to find 7 and 9. The plus operator then adds the two values together, resulting in the expression as a whole equating to 16. Using arithmetic operators with the assignment operator, you can assign a variable the value of an expression. The following assignment uses the expression from the last example.

5

OPERATORS

```
x = 7 + 9
```

x will now equal 16 and can be used again, even to give itself a new value!

```
x = x + 1
```

Follow the last two examples in order. x is first assigned the value 16. Next, x is reassigned to the sum of the present value of x (which at that moment is still 16) and 1. It is a very common operation to increment the value that a variable holds and reassign itself to that value. It is used so often in computer programs that some languages incorporate special shorthand operators to increment and decrement the values that variables hold more easily. JavaScript is one such language and uses ++ to increment and -- to decrement a value. Note the following syntax:

++i is the same as using i = i + 1

--i is the same as using i = i - 1

You can use these operators either as a prefix or a suffix. This way, you can change the order in which a value is returned by the expression and when the new value is assigned. Listing 5.1 demonstrates how increment and decrement operators work.

Listing 5.1. Examples of using increment and decrement operators.

```
<HTML>
<HEAD>
<TITLE>JavaScript Unleashed</TITLE>
</HEAD>
<BODY>
<PRE>
<SCRIPT LANGUAGE = "JavaScript">
<!-- begin hiding from old browsers
var i = 0,  result = 0
document.writeln("If i = 0,")
document.write("\t++i returns the value of i")
document.write(" after incrementing  : ")
result = ++i //increment prefix
document.writeln(result)

i = 0 //reset variable
document.write("\ti++ returns the value of i")
document.write(" before incrementing : ")
result = i++ //increment suffix
document.writeln(result)

i = 0 //reset variable
document.write("\t--i returns the value of i")
document.write(" after decrementing  : ")
result = --i //decrement prefix
document.writeln(result)

i = 0 //reset variable
document.write("\ti-- returns the value of i")
document.write(" before decrementing : ")
result = i-- //decrement suffix
```

```
document.writeln(result)
// end hiding -->
</SCRIPT>
</PRE>
</BODY>
</HTML>
```

The difference here is whether i is incremented before or after the expression is evaluated.

In the first example, result is set to the original value of i plus 1. In the second example, result is immediately set equal to the original value of i before i is incremented. The next two examples work the same way, but demonstrate the decrement operator. The results are shown in Figure 5.2. Although these might seem like unnecessary ways to allow the operator to be used, they can come in handy when writing scripts that repeat a part of the program. This is shown in Chapter 6, "Control Structures and Looping."

FIGURE 5.2

Increment and decrement operators. Display from Listing 5.1.

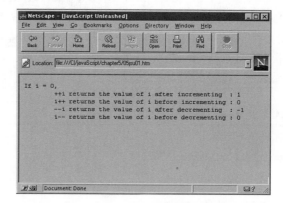

Another arithmetic operator is the unary negation operator (-). It is unary because it only operates on one operand. If, for example, you assign the value 5 to a variable x (x = 5) and then negate x and assign the value to y (y = -x), y will then equal -5. The opposite is also true when negating a negative number; the result will be positive. In both instances, the negation operator does not negate the value of x. The value of x remains unchanged.

The modulus operator is symbolized by the percent sign (%). To find the modulus of two operands is to find the remainder after dividing the first operand by the second. In the example x = 10 % 3, x is assigned the number 1 because 10 divided by 3 is equal to 3 with one third left over. With the modulus operator you can easily determine that one number is the multiple of another if the modulus of the two is equal to zero. This is not the case in the previous example, but would be for x = 25 % 5. 25 divided by 5 is equal to 5 with no remainder which leaves x equal to zero.

5

OPERATORS

CAUTION

In some cases, Netscape 2.0 returns an incorrect value when dealing with fractions. For example, 10/3 should return 3 1/3. Try using the `typein` feature of Netscape to evaluate 10/3 and you will see that the result is 3.3333333333333335. The small inaccuracy at the sixteenth decimal place occurs due to the way in which fractions are stored in a computer's memory. Microsoft's Internet Explorer uses a workaround to the problem by displaying only fourteen decimal places. Displaying the result of the same calculation shows 3.33333333333333.

Comparison Operators

Comparison operators are used for just that, comparing. Expressions that use comparison operators are essentially asking a question about two values. The answer can either be true or false.

Two equal signs together (==) make up the equal operator. When you use the equal operator in the middle of two operands, you are asking the question, "Are the values of these two operands equal?" Listing 5.2 shows how to display the result when asking if two variables are equal.

Listing 5.2. Using the equal operator.

```
<HTML>
<HEAD>
<TITLE>JavaScript Unleashed</TITLE>
</HEAD>
<BODY>
<PRE>
<SCRIPT LANGUAGE = "JavaScript">
<!-- begin hiding from old browsers
var x,y,z
x = 5
y = 5
z = 10
//output to display
document.writeln("x = "+x)
document.writeln("y = "+y)
document.writeln("z = "+z)
document.write("Is x equal to y,(x==y)? ")
document.writeln(x==y)
document.write("Is y equal to z,(y==z)? ")
document.writeln(y==z)
// end hiding -->
</SCRIPT>
</PRE>
</BODY>
</HTML>
```

Be sure to use the correct operator for the job. Again, the equal operator (==) tests to see whether two values are equal, but the assignment operator (=) sets a variable equal to a value. If you happen to make a mistake and use the wrong one, the JavaScript interpreter is good about letting you know! Figure 5.3 shows the display after executing Listing 5.2.

FIGURE 5.3.

The equal operator. Display from Listing 5.2.

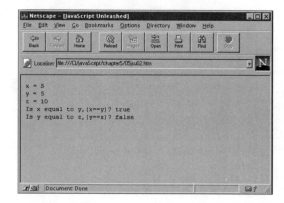

Here is a list of all comparison operators:

==   The equal operator returns true if both of its operands are equal.

!=   The not-equal operator returns true if both of its operands are not equal.

>   The greater-than operator returns true if its left operand is greater in value than its right operand.

>=   The greater-than-or-equal operator returns true if its left operand is greater than or equal to its right operand.

<   The less-than operator returns true if its left operand is less than the value of its right operand.

<=   The less-than-or-equal operator returns true if its left operand is less than or equal to its right operand.

Comparison operators are usually used in JavaScript for making decisions. You must ask the question, "What path in my script do I want to take?" Chapter 6 goes into detail on this topic.

Conditional Operators

JavaScript uses the set of two operators, ? and :, to form conditional expressions. Conditional expressions return one of two values based on the logical value of another expression. You might recognize this type of expression as an immediate if statement. For example, you can use the following conditional expression to alert the user if he is the millionth person to view the page:

5

OPERATORS

```
resultMsg = (numHits==1000000)?"You have won!" : "You lost. Try again!"
```

```
alert(resultMsg)
```

This expression returns the string "You have won!" if numHits is equal to 1000000; otherwise, it returns, "You lost. Try again!" To put this idea to work, the second line of the previous example displays the result to the user using the built-in alert() function. If numHits is equal to one million, an alert dialog box pops up to let the visitor know. Otherwise, the expression returns false and a sympathetic message is displayed.

A conditional expression can be used to return any data type such as a number or Boolean. The following expression returns either a string or a number depending on whether useString is true or false.

```
result = useString ? "seven" : 7
document.write(result)
```

String Operators

The set of string operators includes the concatenate operator (+), which is also used as the arithmetic operator for addition, and all comparison operators. Using the concatenate operator, you can easily attach strings together to make a larger one. (See Listing 5.3.)

Listing 5.3. Concatenating strings.

```
<HTML>
<HEAD>
<TITLE>JavaScript Unleashed</TITLE>
</HEAD>
<BODY>
<PRE>
<SCRIPT LANGUAGE = "JavaScript">
<!-- begin hiding from old browsers
var a, b, c, sumOfParts, address1, address2
a = "www"
b = "company"
c = "com"
document.writeln("Part a is equal to \""+a+"\".")
document.writeln("Part b is equal to \""+b+"\".")
document.writeln("Part c is equal to \""+c+"\".\n")
sumOfParts = a + "." + b + "." + c
address1 = "WWW.COMPANY.COM"
address2 = "www.company.com"
//output to display
document.write("Is sumOfParts equal to "+address1+"? ")
document.writeln(sumOfParts == address1)
document.write("Is sumOfParts equal to "+address2+"? ")
document.writeln(sumOfParts == address2)
document.write("Is sumOfParts greater than "+address1+"? ")
document.writeln(sumOfParts > address1)
// end hiding -->
</SCRIPT>
```

```
</PRE>
</BODY>
</HTML>
```

To begin, the script initializes three variables to hold three parts of an Internet Web address. Next, all three parts are added together, separated by the appropriate dots found in all Web addresses. To test if sumOfParts holds an actual Internet address, the script compares it to two possibilities. Figure 5.4 shows that when comparing strings, JavaScript is case sensitive and therefore only returns true when comparing addresses with the same case. JavaScript uses the ASCII character set when determining what value to give a string when comparing it to another. All uppercase letters have values less than their lowercase equivalents, which explains why the last comparison in Listing 5.3 returns true.

FIGURE 5.4.

Concatenating strings. Display from Listing 5.3.

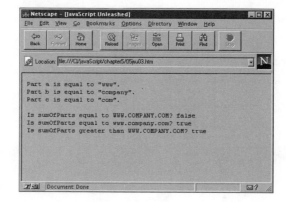

Boolean Operators

Boolean operators (also called logical operators) are used in conjunction with expressions that return logical values. The best way to understand these is to see them used with comparison operators. The following is a list of the three Boolean operators:

&&   The logical and operator returns true if both Expression1 and Expression2 are true. Otherwise, it returns false. Note the following examples:

    (1>0) && (2>1) returns true.

    (1>0) && (2<1) returns false.

¦¦   The logical or operator returns true if either Expression1 or Expression2 is true. If neither Expression1 nor Expression2 is true, then it returns false. Note the following examples:

    (1>0) ¦¦ (2<1) returns true.

    (1<0) ¦¦ (2<1) returns false.

5

OPERATORS

! The logical not operator is an unary operator that returns the opposite value of Expression. If Expression is true, it returns false; and if Expression is false, it returns true. This works in the same way as the arithmetic negation operator and will not permanently change the value of Expression. Note the following examples:

!(1>0) returns false.

!(1<0) returns true.

The typeof Operator

The typeof operator returns the type of data that its operand currently holds. This is especially useful for determining if a variable has been defined. Note the following examples:

typeof unescape returns the string "function".

typeof undefinedVariable returns the string "undefined".

typeof 33 returns the string "number".

typeof "A String" returns the string "string".

typeof true returns the string "boolean".

typeof null returns the string "object".

CAUTION

The typeof operator was added by Netscape in version 3.0 of their Navigator Web browser. This will not work with earlier versions.

Function Operators

Functions are first covered in Chapter 7, "Functions." There are two operators to be familiar with when dealing with functions. One is the call operator, which is symbolized by a set of parentheses and always follows the function name. For example, a function named displayName would be declared using the following syntax:

```
function displayName(){
    [statements]
}
```

The call operator is also used when calling the function from elsewhere in a script, and would look like this:

```
displayName()
```

The parentheses signify that a function is being used instead of any other user-defined identifier.

The comma operator is used with functions to separate multiple arguments that a function can accept. Arguments are always enclosed by the call operator. Modifying the `displayName()` function to accept two arguments would look like the following:

```
function displayName(argument1,argument2){
    [statements]
}
```

Data Structure Operators

The operators described in this section are first used in Part III, "JavaScript Objects."

Data structure operators is the name I have given to classify two operators that are needed when dealing with data structures. Data structures are frameworks that are set up to store one or more basic pieces of data in an orderly fashion. In JavaScript, objects are used to group pieces of data to serve a more specific purpose. An operator to be familiar with when dealing with objects is commonly referred to as the dot. Symbolized by a period, the dot is technically called the structure-member operator. It allows you to refer to a member (a variable, function, or object) belonging to the specified object. The syntax is as follows:

```
objectName.variableName
```

or

```
objectName.functionName()
```

or

```
objectName.anotherObject
```

This way of referring to a piece of data, usually called *dot notation,* returns the value of the rightmost variable, function, or object.

The member operator, also known as the array subscript operator, is used to access a piece of data from an array. Symbolized by a pair of square brackets, it allows you to refer to any one element of an array. Arrays are objects in JavaScript and are first introduced in Chapter 14, "Built-In Language Objects." The following shows the syntax for using the member operator:

```
arrayName[indexNumber]
```

The member operator encloses an integer, seen here as `indexNumber`, which specifies an index of `arrayName`.

Bitwise Operators

At the lowest level, integers (along with all data) are stored in memory as bits. They are stored using the binary number system, which can represent any integer using the symbols 0 and 1. Depending on placement, a bit set to 1 represents a value equal to 2 raised to n where n is the number of places from the right of the number. For example, the integer 12 can be represented by the binary number 1100 and takes 4 bits to store in memory. Starting from the right and moving left, 1100 can be calculated using the following expression:

$$0 \times 2^n + 0 \times 2^1 + 1 \times 2^2 + 1 \times 2^3 = 12$$

A larger number such as 237 in binary, 11101101, requires 8 bits of memory to be stored. 11101101 can also be calculated in the following way:

$$1 \times 2^0 + 0 \times 2^1 + 1 \times 2^2 + 1 \times 2^3 + 0 \times 2^4 + 1 \times 2^5 + 1 \times 2^6 + 1 \times 2^7 = 237$$

JavaScript sets aside 32 bits per integer when storing it in memory. Once in memory, 237 conceptually looks like 00000000000000000000000011101101, but is typically written as 11101101, excluding the leading zeros which are insignificant. You can enter an integer as a decimal, octal, or hexadecimal number, and JavaScript will store it in binary form. To accommodate for negative values, the left-most bit or highest bit represents a negative value equal to $-(2^{31})$. Using the highest bit, you can start with $-(2^{31})$ and add positive values to it (represented by the remaining 31 bits) to generate any negative number greater than or equal to $-(2^{31})$. Note the following examples:

```
10000000000000000000000000000001 = -2147483648 + 1 = -2147483647

10000000000000000000000000000011 = -2147483648 + 3 = -2147483645

11111111111111111111111111111111 = -2147483648 + 2147483647 = -1

11111111111111111111111111111110 = -2147483648 + 2147483646 = -2
```

JavaScript gives you access to an integer's binary representative through bitwise operators. The simplest of bitwise operators is the unary ones complement operator symbolized by the tilde character (~). Its job is to "flip" every bit of its operand. This is classified as a negation operator because it negates each bit. If a bit is a 1, it will become a 0. If a bit is a 0, it will become a 1. Finding the ones complement of the number 6 can be visualized in the following ways:

```
x = ~6

x = ~00000000000000000000000000000110

x =   11111111111111111111111111111001

x = -7
```

Bitwise Logical Operators

When you use bitwise logical operators, JavaScript pairs up each operand bit-by-bit. It then performs the operation on each pair of bits. For example, using the bitwise and operator on the numbers 01111 and 11011 results in the number 00011. Their binary equivalents are aligned from right to left to form five pairs of bits. The pairs are then operated on separately and a new number is generated. One way to visualize this is in the following way:

```
01111    & 10011

1        & 1 = 1

1        & 1 = 1

1        & 0 = 0

1        & 0 = 0

0        & 1 = 0
```

    &   The bitwise and operator returns a 1 if both operands are a 1. Otherwise, it returns a 0.

        Example: `15 & 27` returns 11 (`01111 & 11011` returns `01011`).

    ¦   The bitwise or operator returns a 1 if either operand is a 1. Otherwise, it returns a 0.

        Example: `15 ¦ 27` returns 31 (`01111 ¦ 11011` returns `11111`).

    ^   The bitwise exclusive or operator returns a 1 if one but not both operands are 1. Otherwise, it returns 0.

        Example: `15 ^ 27` returns 20 (`01111 ¦ 11011` returns `10100`).

Bitwise Shift Operators

All bitwise shift operators take two operands. The left operand is an integer whose bits are to be shifted. The right operand is the number of bits to shift the binary representation of the integer.

    <<   The left-shift operator returns the value of an integer if its bits were shifted a number of places to the left. All void rightmost bits are filled in with zeros. The following examples shift 15 to the left by one and then by two, respectively. Note that shifting a positive integer to the left n times is equivalent to multiplying the value by two, n times. In most cases a computer can perform a left-shift faster than multiplying by two. For this reason, it is common to see the bitwise left-shift chosen over its higher-level counterpart when having the computer perform many multiplications. Any small increase in efficiency could result in a noticeable advantage. Using the left-shift on a negative integer could result in either a negative or positive integer depending on the state of the highest bit after the left-shift has been performed.

15 << 1 returns 30 (1111 << 1 returns 11110).

15 << 2 returns 60 (1111 << 2 returns 111100).

>> The sign-propagating right-shift operator returns the value of an integer if its bits were shifted a number of places to the right. All void bits are filled in with a copy of the left-most bit (also called the sign bit). Copying the left-most bit ensures that the integer will stay either positive or negative. This is also a more efficient way to divide a positive, even integer by two, n times. In the case of a positive odd integer, a right-shift is the same as dividing by two, *n* times, but throws away remainders. Note the following examples:

15 >> 1 returns 7 (1111 >> 1 returns 0111).

-15 >> 1 returns -8 (11111111111111111111111111110001 >> 1 returns 11111111111111111111111111111000)

>>> The zero-fill right-shift operator returns the value of an integer if its bits were shifted a number of places to the right. All void high-order bits are filled in with zeros. When operating on positive integers, the zero-fill right-shift operator produces the same result as using the sign-propagating right-shift operator. This is due to the fact that the sign bit being copied is always zero for positive integers. As for negative integers, any zero-fill right-shift will change the highest bit from a one to a zero. The result will always be an integer that is greater than or equal to zero. Note the following examples:

15 >>> 1 returns 7 (1111 >>> 1 returns 0111).

-15 >>> 1 returns 2147483640 (11111111111111111111111111110001 >> 1 returns 01111111111111111111111111111000).

Why Mess with Bits?

The need to use bitwise operators is not needed in most scripts. It's possible that you may never have to deal with bits for your entire JavaScript career. However, there are special cases where dealing with data at its lowest level becomes practical or even necessary. An example of when bitwise operators are needed is when converting a number from base 10 (decimal) to base 16 (hexadecimal). This takes a little extra effort because JavaScript only allows you to display the decimal representation of a number stored in memory. There is no built-in way to display the number in an alternate base. Using bitwise operators, the solution to this obstacle is relatively easy. For instance, if you store the value 0xDC in a variable x, JavaScript converts it to binary. If you try and display x as in the following lines of code, the number is displayed in decimal as 220:

```
x = 0xDC
```

```
document.writeln(x)// will write "220" to the display
```

JavaScript does not offer a method to display 220 as its hexadecimal equivalent, DC. This is a useful function if you are performing operations on HTML color values which are in hexadecimal. The easiest way to accomplish this is to use the binary value of the integer and translate it into hexadecimal.

Hexadecimal values are easily represented in binary. Four bits of memory can store 16 values. Because hexadecimal uses 16 digits, it takes 4 bits to store the value of each hexadecimal digit. In a 32-bit integer, the right-most 4 bits of memory represent the right-most digit of a hexadecimal integer. The next 4 bits store the next digit, and so on. To convert a 32-bit integer into hexadecimal you can do this eight times matching each 4-bit value to its hexadecimal equivalent.

To read in only 4 bits at a time, use the & operator with a control value. The control value should have a 1 in each bit location that you would like to copy from the integer being converted. Because you want the value of the first 4 bits, the control value should have a 1 in its first 4 bits. All other bits should be set to 0. The control value in this case must equal 1111 (15 or 0xF). This operation conceptually appears as the following:

Control: 000000000000000000000000001111 &

Integer to convert: 00000000000000000000000011011100 =

Result: 00000000000000000000000000001100

The result is a copy of the first 4 bits of the integer you are converting. You can easily compare this to each of the 16 hexadecimal digits to find that it is equal to C. To find the next hexadecimal digit, copy the next 4 bits out of the integer. I have chosen to do this by shifting all the bits in the integer 4 bits to the right while using the same control. This will work as in the following:

Control: 000000000000000000000000001111 &

Integer to convert: 00000000000000000000000000001101 =

Result: 00000000000000000000000000001101

Again, you can use the result to match up against the second digit, D. If the original integer was larger, you could continue this process up to six more times.

Listing 5.4 shows this algorithm in action. Using only operators discussed up to this point, it can convert any 8-bit value into a string representing its hexadecimal equivalent. The value to be converted is first assigned to the variable intValue. I then display the value to show that JavaScript will only return the decimal value of DC, which is 220. The program proceeds to translate the binary form of 220 into hexadecimal and displays the result. The output can be seen in Figure 5.5.

Listing 5.4. Converting base 10 to base 16 using bitwise operators.

```
<HTML>
<HEAD>
<TITLE>JavaScript Unleashed</TITLE>
</HEAD>
<BODY>
<PRE>
<SCRIPT LANGUAGE = "JavaScript">
<!-- begin hiding from old browsers
var originalInt
var intValue = 0xDC //intValue can be any 8 bit value.
var controlValue = 0xF, fourBitValue
var hexChar = "", hexString = ""
document.writeln("When displaying integers from memory,")
document.writeln("JavaScript always uses their decimal ")
document.writeln("equivalent: " + intValue)
originalInt = intValue
fourBitValue =  controlValue & intValue
hexChar = (fourBitValue == 0x0) ? "0" : hexChar
hexChar = (fourBitValue == 0x1) ? "1" : hexChar
hexChar = (fourBitValue == 0x2) ? "2" : hexChar
hexChar = (fourBitValue == 0x3) ? "3" : hexChar
hexChar = (fourBitValue == 0x4) ? "4" : hexChar
hexChar = (fourBitValue == 0x5) ? "5" : hexChar
hexChar = (fourBitValue == 0x6) ? "6" : hexChar
hexChar = (fourBitValue == 0x7) ? "7" : hexChar
hexChar = (fourBitValue == 0x8) ? "8" : hexChar
hexChar = (fourBitValue == 0x9) ? "9" : hexChar
hexChar = (fourBitValue == 0xA) ? "A" : hexChar
hexChar = (fourBitValue == 0xB) ? "B" : hexChar
hexChar = (fourBitValue == 0xC) ? "C" : hexChar
hexChar = (fourBitValue == 0xD) ? "D" : hexChar
hexChar = (fourBitValue == 0xE) ? "E" : hexChar
hexChar = (fourBitValue == 0xF) ? "F" : hexChar
//build hexString placing digits from right to left
hexString = hexChar + hexString
//shift intValue four bits right
intValue = intValue >> 4
//extract the next four bit value
fourBitValue =  controlValue & intValue
//find the matching hex value and assign its string
//equivalent to hexChar.
hexChar = (fourBitValue == 0x0) ? "0" : hexChar
hexChar = (fourBitValue == 0x1) ? "1" : hexChar
hexChar = (fourBitValue == 0x2) ? "2" : hexChar
hexChar = (fourBitValue == 0x3) ? "3" : hexChar
hexChar = (fourBitValue == 0x4) ? "4" : hexChar
hexChar = (fourBitValue == 0x5) ? "5" : hexChar
hexChar = (fourBitValue == 0x6) ? "6" : hexChar
hexChar = (fourBitValue == 0x7) ? "7" : hexChar
hexChar = (fourBitValue == 0x8) ? "8" : hexChar
hexChar = (fourBitValue == 0x9) ? "9" : hexChar
hexChar = (fourBitValue == 0xA) ? "A" : hexChar
hexChar = (fourBitValue == 0xB) ? "B" : hexChar
hexChar = (fourBitValue == 0xC) ? "C" : hexChar
hexChar = (fourBitValue == 0xD) ? "D" : hexChar
hexChar = (fourBitValue == 0xE) ? "E" : hexChar
hexChar = (fourBitValue == 0xF) ? "F" : hexChar
```

```
hexString = hexChar + hexString
document.write(originalInt +" displayed in")
document.write(" hexadecimal :")
document.writeln(hexString)
// end hiding -->
</SCRIPT>
</PRE>
</BODY>
</HTML>
```

NOTE

The previous example uses multiple conditional expressions to find a match. More efficient ways to compare a range of numbers include using loops, which are discussed in Chapter 6.

FIGURE 5.5.

Converting base 10 to base 16. Display from Listing 5.4.

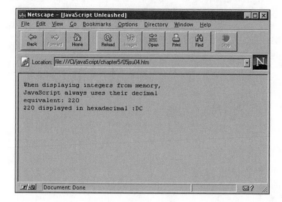

Notice from the previous discussion how many zeros are left unused when storing a relatively small number. This is another area where bitwise operators can prove useful. Using bitwise operators, you can conserve memory by storing data in the unused portion of any variable. For example, if your script uses a large group of positive integers less than or equal to 255, you could store four of them within one 32-bit word. Using a simple bitwise operation, you could then extract any number at will. With the amount of RAM most computers have today, it is usually not worth the extra coding effort. Although because JavaScript is designed to run on many platforms, you never know who will be running your script and who might run out of memory. Even still, you would have to be storing a lot of data in memory to begin worrying about this.

5

OPERATORS

Operator Precedence

When creating expressions that use more than one operator, you should be aware that JavaScript does not necessarily evaluate an expression from right to left or vice versa. Each part of an expression is evaluated in an order based on a predefined precedence for each operator. Note the following example:

```
x = a * b + c
```

a is multiplied by b; the result is added to c. The result of the addition is finally assigned to x. The multiplication operator has a higher precedence than the addition operator and therefore is evaluated first. If, however, you need the addition to be evaluated first, you can surround the expression with parentheses:

```
x = a * (b + c)
```

Parentheses are operators that boost the precedence of the expression that they enclose. When an expression has more than one operator of the same kind, JavaScript evaluates from left to right.

The following lists operators in order of their precedence from lowest to highest:

comma	,
assignment	= += -= *= /= %= <<= >>= >>>= &= ^= ¦=
conditional	? :
logical or	¦¦
logical and	&&
bitwise or	¦
bitwise xor	^
bitwise and	&
equality	== !=
comparison	< <= > >=
bitwise shift	<< >> >>>
addition/subtraction	+ -
multiply/divide	* / %
negation/increment	! ~ - ++ --
call, data structure	() [] .

One effect operator precedence can have is determining the type of value that is returned by an expression. This becomes apparent when trying to concatenate strings and numbers together. (See Listing 5.5.)

Listing 5.5. Operator precedence and different data types.

```
<HTML>
<HEAD>
<TITLE>JavaScript Unleashed</TITLE>
</HEAD>
<BODY>
<PRE>
<SCRIPT LANGUAGE = "JavaScript">
<!-- begin hiding from old browsers
carLength = 4 + 5
document.writeln(carLength)
carLength = 4 + 5 + " feet"
document.writeln(carLength)
carLength = "Length in feet: " + 4 + 5
document.writeln(carLength)
carLength = "Length in feet: " + (4 + 5)
document.writeln(carLength)
// end hiding-->
</SCRIPT>
</PRE>
</BODY>
</HTML>
```

When expressions have operators of the same precedence, JavaScript evaluates from left to right. The addition operator has the same precedence as the concatenate operator; therefore, JavaScript will evaluate all additions and concatenations from left to right throughout the statement. Notice in Figure 5.6 that the first two examples work as you would hope them to. The third example shows what can happen when JavaScript works as designed. With the first plus symbol, it converts the number 4 to a string and concatenates it to the end of "Length in feet: ". The result of this is the string "Length in feet: 4". It then does the same with the number 5 to produce "Length in feet: 45". If, however, you want to display the sum of 4 and 5 instead, you can use parentheses to increase the precedence of 4 + 5. In this case, both operands are numbers and JavaScript performs an addition rather than a string concatenation. Figure 5.6 shows this as the fourth example.

FIGURE 5.6.

Operator precedence and different data types. Display from Listing 5.5.

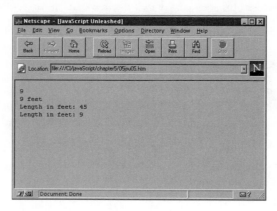

5

OPERATORS

Summary

Assignment operators assign values to variables. Along with the simple assignment operator, JavaScript supports 11 combination assignment operators that combine either arithmetic or bitwise operators with the simple assignment operator.

Arithmetic operators let you perform basic math operations in JavaScript. These include addition, subtraction, multiplication, division, and modulus. JavaScript also includes increment and decrement operators as shortcuts to two common math operations. More advanced math operations are also built into the JavaScript language, but must be accessed through the Math object. This is covered in Chapter 14.

Comparison operators compare two values and return a value of true or false. You can check to see if one value is equal to another, greater or less than another, or any combination of these.

The conditional operators let you return one of two values that you can define to be of any data type. The value returned is decided by the value of a logical expression that you also define.

String operators include the concatenation operator and all comparison operators. The concatenation operator is used to append one string onto another to form a new string. Comparison operators can be used with strings to compare their ASCII values. Starting with the left-most character of each string and moving right, a pair of characters are compared at a time. The returned value is either true or false.

Boolean operators are used with logical expressions to form another logical expression. The and operator returns true if both of its operands are true. Otherwise it returns false. The or operator returns true if at least one of its operands are true. Otherwise it returns false. The not operator returns true if its operand is false and it will return false if its operand is true.

The typeof operator was added in version 3.0 of Netscape's Navigator Web browser. It is now a built-in operator for JavaScript used to return a string representing the type of data that it operand holds. This is especially useful when determining if a variable has been defined yet.

Two operators are involved to declare and use JavaScript functions. The call operator always follows a function name and surrounds any arguments that the function might accept. The comma operator is used to separate arguments if the function accepts more than one.

When dealing with arrays and other objects, two operators are needed. The dot is used to reference a member of an object. This is the standard dot notation. The member operator is used to index one element of an array object. It follows the array name and encloses a integer that refers to the location of the element being accessed.

JavaScript allows access to the binary representation of any integer through its bitwise operators. The ones complement operator is used to flip each bit of an integer. Bitwise logical operators are included to compare two integers. The binary form of each operand is used to pair up the bits in each integer. The logical operation is then performed on each pair of bits to return the resulting integer. Bitwise shift operators shift the bits of an integer to the right or left *n* number of places. When shifting to the right, JavaScript allows you to specify either sign-propagating or zero-fill shifting.

When all operations in the expression are of the same precedence, JavaScript interprets from right to left when evaluating expressions Otherwise, the operation with the highest precedence is performed first and then the next highest, and so on. The precedence of each operator is predefined by JavaScript.

Control Structures and Looping

by Gary Griffin

IN THIS CHAPTER

CHAPTER **6**

Designing a script to make a decisions during runtime can be the most interesting part of JavaScript. When you have a script make a decision based on its present state, you are simply telling it to ask a question and then choose a path to take based on the answer. I think of my morning commute to work. I can take a couple of different routes, and I choose the one based on certain factors. I seldom cook, so the most important question I ask myself in the morning is whether I am hungry. If I am, I choose the route that passes by the bagel shop. By the time I have finished picking up my breakfast, I am usually running a little late. To make up for lost time, I drive directly to the highway where I can quickly accelerate to just under the speed limit, give or take a couple. On the other hand, if I am not hungry, which is hardly ever the case, I choose to drive past the bagel shop and continue onto work at a steady 10 miles per hour below the speed limit.

With the same idea, you can design your JavaScript programs to perform specific operations based on one or more factors. For example, in Chapter 5, "Operators," you learned how to test if a variable is equal to a particular value or even a range of values. Using control structures, you can now make your program take one or more different paths based on the result of such a test. This is the first topic I cover in this chapter.

As your programs become larger, one thing to watch for is the length of time it could take for the client to download them. One way to cut down on the amount of source code in a script is to use looping statements. In special situations, you can make your scripts perform many similar operations with only a few lines of code. This can help you shrink the size of your scripts and avoid typing in the same commands over and over again. Also in this chapter, I demonstrate ways to make your scripts more efficient.

Conditional

In Chapter 5, I covered two conditional operators, ? and :. With these operators, you can form an expression that first evaluates an expression to be either `true` or `false`. Based on the result, one of two values are returned. You can also use the keywords `if` and `else` to evaluate an expression. Instead of returning a value based on the result, the program takes one of two paths. With this ability, you can make JavaScript perform many different functions based on just about any information you have available.

If

You use the `if` statement in the following syntax:

```
if (condition) {
    statements
}
```

The `condition` can be any logical expression. If the result of condition is true, the `statements` enclosed in curly braces are executed and program execution continues. If the condition

Control Structures and Looping

Chapter 6

115

6

CONTROL
STRUCTURES AND
LOOPING

returns false, JavaScript ignores the block of code between the curly braces and continues thereafter. In Listing 6.1, I emulated the type of influence an overbearing marketing department might have on a company's Web site. The script begins by setting the value of visitorInterest to one of two values. I selected "Technical Support" for this example and commented out the alternate assignment. Next, the script reaches the first if statement, which checks whether the value of visitorInterest is equal to the string "New Products". The resulting value of this expression is false and the block of code immediately following the if statement is ignored. The script then reaches the second if statement and checks the value of visitorInterest against "Technical Support". The expression returns true and the code that is enclosed in curly braces is executed. Regardless of what value visitorInterest is equal to, the last statement always executes and Frank Zealous sends his sales pitch to the visitor. The entire display can be seen in Figure 6.1. Switch the value of visitorInterest and the output will change.

Listing 6.1. Using the if statement to make decisions.

```
<HTML>
<HEAD>
<TITLE>JavaScript Unleashed</TITLE>
</HEAD>
<BODY>
<IMG SRC="file:///C¦/javaScript/CHAPTER6/frank.gif" ALIGN=RIGHT>
<BR>
<PRE>
<SCRIPT LANGUAGE = "JavaScript">
<!-- begin hiding from old browsers
var visitorInterest
//visitorInterest = "New Products"
visitorInterest = "Technical Support"
document.writeln("Hello, my name is Frank Zealous!")
if (visitorInterest == "New Products") {
    document.writeln("Thank-you for inquiring about our products!")
}
if (visitorInterest == "Technical Support") {
    document.writeln("Technical support is now available.")
    document.write("But first, let me introduce you to our ")
    document.writeln("newest products!")
}
document.write("Our newest products will satisfy all of your ")
document.writeln("business needs!")
// end hiding -->
</SCRIPT>
</PRE>
</BODY>
</HTML>
```

It is common practice to indent the set of statements enclosed in curly braces. This helps keep a logical look to your scripts and proves especially helpful when you "nest" if statements. When you use an if statement within another if statement, it is said to be nested. Listing 6.2 demonstrates how you can use logical variables by themselves to determine the path a script can take. The first `if` statement evaluates the variable `needsInfo`. `needsInfo` was set to `true`, so JavaScript enters the first `if` block and continues by displaying, "Our products are used all over the world." Next, the second or "nested" `if` block is reached and `needsMoreInfo` is evaluated. Again, the value returned is `true` and the statements within the second block are executed. The end of the nested `if` block is completed and JavaScript picks up where it left off with the first block. Notice how the indentation helps distinguish the separate blocks of code that may or may not be executed. Figure 6.2 shows that JavaScript performed each line of code in sequence. By resetting the values of `needsInfo` and `needsMoreInfo`, you can create three different results. One important thing to realize is that if `needsInfo` is `false`, the second `if` block is never reached. In this case it does not matter if `needsMoreInfo` is set to `true` or `false` because it will never have a chance to be evaluated. Sorry Frank, but if they do not need information then they certainly don't need more information.

FIGURE 6.1.

Frank gives a customized sales pitch.

Listing 6.2. Nested `if` statements.

```
<HTML>
<HEAD>
<TITLE>JavaScript Unleashed</TITLE>
</HEAD>
<BODY>
<IMG SRC="file:///C¦/javaScript/CHAPTER6/frank.gif" ALIGN=RIGHT>
<BR>
<PRE>
<SCRIPT LANGUAGE = "JavaScript">
<!-- begin hiding from old browsers
var needsInfo, needsMoreInfo
//set either of the following to false and the output notice the change.
needsInfo = true
needsMoreInfo = true
document.writeln("I work for Best Products International!")
if (needsInfo) {
```

Control Structures and Looping

CHAPTER 6

117

6

CONTROL
STRUCTURES AND
LOOPING

```
        document.writeln("Our products are used all over the world.")
        if (needsMoreInfo) {
            document.write("I don't know how you have managed")
            document.writeln(" without them.")
        }
document.writeln("\nOrdering is easy using our on-line service.")
}
// end hiding -->
</SCRIPT>
</PRE>
</BODY>
</HTML>
```

FIGURE 6.2.

One of three possible outcomes.

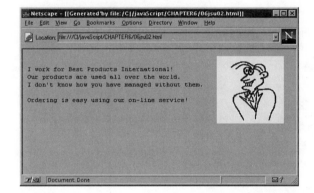

If...Else

Sometimes using the `if` statement alone is not enough. You can also reserve a set of statements to execute if the conditional expression returns false. This is done by adding an `else` block of statements immediately following the `if` block. The syntax follows:

```
if (condition) {
    statements
} else {
    statements
}
```

Nothing is worse than a nagging computer, but Listing 6.3 demonstrates how interactive a Web page can be with only a few lines of code. Again I have hard coded the key value, `purchaseAmount`, which determines the outcome of the script. To truly interact with the users of your script, you need to be able to receive input from them. This way `purchaseAmount` could end up being any value depending on what the customer orders. You can do this using JavaScript and standard HTML input objects such as checkbox and text objects. Chapter 13, "Form Objects," covers this topic in more detail.

For this example, the user has not spent enough money to satisfy Frank. The if statement evaluates to false and the else block is executed. Figure 6.3 shows how the user's purchase is questioned by a pushy salesman.

Listing 6.3. The else block responds to a false value.

```
<HTML>
<HEAD>
<TITLE>JavaScript Unleashed</TITLE>
</HEAD>
<BODY>
<IMG SRC="file:///C¦/javaScript/CHAPTER6/frank.gif" ALIGN=RIGHT>
<BR>
<PRE>
<SCRIPT LANGUAGE = "JavaScript">
<!-- begin hiding from old browsers
var purchaseAmount
purchaseAmount = 10.00
if (purchaseAmount > 500.00) {

    document.write("Thank-you for your purchase!")} else {
    document.writeln("Thank-you, but surely there is something ")
    document.writeln("else you would like to purchase.")

}
// end hiding -->
</SCRIPT>
</PRE>
</BODY>
</HTML>
```

FIGURE 6.3.

One of two possible outcomes.

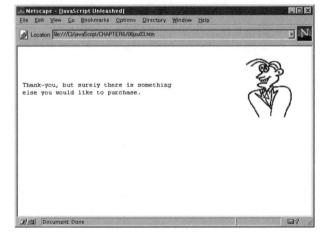

Looping

Creating a loop inside a script can serve many purposes. One simple but very common use of a loop is counting. For example, writing a program that displayed the numbers 0 through 9 is a quick and easy task. You could simply write ten commands to display each number:

```
document.writeln("0")
document.writeln("1")
...
document.writeln("9")
```

This works for counting from 0 to 9, but what if you needed to count to 1,000? You can do it in the same manner, but it takes much more time to write and significantly increases the time it takes to download. The best way to count to 1,000 or any number is to use the same display statement with a variable in place of the string literal. By counting like this, the only thing you need is a way to increment the variable and repeat the display statement. JavaScript supplies you with the tools to handle this and other looping operations.

for

You use the `for` statement to start a loop in a script. Before taking a detailed look at the `for` statement in Listing 6.4, note the following syntax:

```
for ([initializing_expr]; [condition_expr]; [loop_expr]) {
    statements
}
```

The three expressions enclosed in parentheses are optional, but if you omit one, the semicolons are still required. This keeps each expression in its appropriate place. You typically use the initializing expression to initialize and even declare a variable to use as a counter for the loop. Next, the condition expression must evaluate to true before each execution of the statements enclosed in curly braces. Finally, the loop expression typically increments or decrements the variable that is used as the counter for the loop.

Listing 6.4 demonstrates the use of a `for` statement to count from 0 to 99 while displaying each number. To fit the output on a standard page, I added a line break after each set of ten numbers. The output can be seen in Figure 6.4.

Listing 6.4. A `for` loop used to count from 0 to 99.

```
<HTML>
<HEAD>
<TITLE>JavaScript Unleashed</TITLE>
<BODY>
<PRE>
<SCRIPT LANGUAGE = "JavaScript">
<!-- begin hiding from old browsers
```

continues

Listing 6.4. continued

```
document.writeln("Numbers 0 through 99 : ")
for (var i = 0 ; i < 100; ++i) {
     if(i%10 == 0) {
          document.writeln()
     }
     document.write(i + " ")
}
document.writeln("\n\nAfter completing the loop, i equals : " + i)
// end hiding -->
</SCRIPT>
</PRE>
</BODY>
</HTML>
```

FIGURE 6.4.

Output after looping through the same code 100 times.

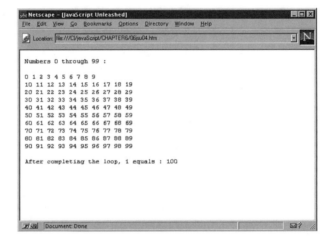

In Listing 6.4, the order of execution is as follows. The initializing expression declares the variable i and sets it equal to zero. The variable i is then tested to ensure that it is less than 100. Where i is still equal to zero, the condition expression returns true and the program executes the statements between the curly braces. Once the program executes all the statements and reaches the ending curly brace, it evaluates the loop expression, ++i. This increments i by one concluding the first full loop, and the process starts again from the top. This time JavaScript knows not to perform the initializing section of the for loop. Instead, the condition expression is evaluated again. Where i is still less than 100, another loop is allowed to occur. This continues, and the set of statements inside the for block is repeated until i reaches 100.

At 99 the condition expression returns true and the program executes the statements one last time. Once again, i is incremented and set equal to 100. When the condition expression is evaluated, it returns false and the loop breaks. Program execution picks up immediately after the ending curly brace. Because i was incremented to 100 before the loop was broken, 100 is the resulting value of i after the loop is finished. Notice also that the scope of i extends outside the for loop, obeying the rules of scope discussed in Chapter 4, "Fundamentals of the JavaScript Language."

> **NOTE**
>
> If the condition expression returns false on the first loop, the statements between the curly braces are never executed.

As with if statements, for loops can also be nested. Listing 6.5 shows how to step through each coordinate of a ten-by-ten grid. For each iteration of the first loop, there are ten iterations of the nested loop. The result is that the nested loop is executed one hundred times.

x is first assigned the value of 0. JavaScript reaches the nested loop and also assigns 0 to y. The nested loop displays the values of x and y and then increments y by one. The nested loop continues until y is no longer less than 10. At this point, there are 10 sets of coordinates generated. The nested loop breaks and control returns to the outer loop. x is incremented by one and again the nested loop starts. JavaScript knows that the nested loop is starting from the beginning and the initializing expression must be evaluated again. This resets y to 0, and the statements are run another 10 times. The entire process continues until x is no longer less than 10 and the outer loop finally breaks. This displays one hundred sets of coordinates as seen in Figure 6.5. You are not limited to a single nested loop so you can increase the number of coordinates to three or even four. You can also use this same method to visit each element of a multidimensional array.

Listing 6.5. Demonstration of a nested loop.

```
<HTML>
<HEAD>
<TITLE>JavaScript Unleashed</TITLE>
</HEAD>
<BODY>
<PRE>
<SCRIPT LANGUAGE = "JavaScript">
<!-- begin hiding from old browsers
document.writeln("All x,y coordinates between (0,0) and (9,9) :\n")
for (var x = 0; x < 10; ++x) {
    for (var y = 0; y < 10; ++y) {
        document.write("("+x + "," + y +") ")
    }
    document.writeln()
}
document.writeln("\nAfter completing the loop, x equals : " + x)
document.writeln("After completing the loop, y equals : " + y)
// end hiding -->
</SCRIPT>
</PRE>
</BODY>
</HTML>
```

FIGURE 6.5.

One hundred sets of coordinates generated by two loops.

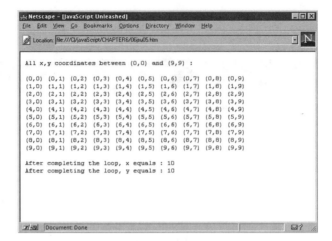

for...in

You need a basic understanding of JavaScript objects to use a `for...in` loop. After reading Chapter 8, "Fundamentals of Object Orientation," you should be able to use the `for...in` construct with ease.

You can use the `for...in` loop with any JavaScript object, regardless of whether it has properties. One iteration is executed for each property so if the object does not have any properties, no loops occur. The `for...in` loop also works with custom objects. A variable of a custom JavaScript object is considered a property and therefore executes a loop for each one. The syntax follows:

```
for (property in object) {
    statements
}
```

property is a string literal generated for you by JavaScript. For each loop, *property* is assigned the next property name contained in *object* until each one is used. Listing 6.6 uses this function to display each property name of the document object along with each of the property's values. (Also see Figure 6.6.)

CAUTION

The `for...in` loop only works correctly under Netscape's Navigator version 3.0. It does not work properly in older versions of Navigator nor Microsoft's Internet Explorer version 3.0 Beta 2.

Listing 6.6. Using a for...in loop in JavaScript.

```
<HTML>
<HEAD>
<TITLE>JavaScript Unleashed</TITLE>
</HEAD>
<BODY>
<PRE>
<SCRIPT LANGUAGE = "JavaScript">
<!-- begin hiding from old browsers
var anObject = document
var propertyInfo = ""
for (var propertyName in anObject) {
    propertyInfo = propertyName + " = " + anObject[propertyName]
    document.writeln(propertyInfo)
}
// end hiding -->
</SCRIPT>
</PRE>
</BODY>
</HTML>
```

FIGURE 6.6.

*Each property and its
value for the document
object.*

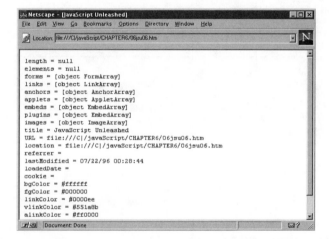

while

The statement while acts similarly to a for loop but does not include the function of initializing or incrementing variables in its declaration. You must declare variables beforehand and increment or decrement the variables within the *statements* block. The syntax follows:

```
while (condition_expr) {
    statements
}
```

Listing 6.7 shows how you can use a logical variable as a flag in determining whether to continue looping. The variable, status, is declared ahead of time and set to true. Once i is equal to 10, status is set to false and the loop breaks. The result of Listing 6.7 is the sum of the integers from 0 to 10 and is displayed in Figure 6.7.

Listing 6.7. Using the `while` loop in JavaScript.

```
<HTML>
<HEAD>
<TITLE>JavaScript Unleashed</TITLE>
</HEAD>
<BODY>
<PRE>
<SCRIPT LANGUAGE = "JavaScript">
<!-- begin hiding from old browsers
var i = 0,
    result = 0,
    status = true
document.write("0")
while (status) {
    result = result + ++i
    document.write(" + " + i)
    if(i == 10) {
        status = false
    }
}
document.writeln(" = " + result)
// end hiding -->
</SCRIPT>
</PRE>
</BODY>
</HTML>
```

FIGURE 6.7.

*Results of Listing 6.7.
Eleven iterations of a
`while` loop.*

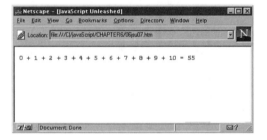

break and continue

A loop usually does not stop repeating itself until the specified condition returns false. Sometimes, you might want to exit the loop before the program reaches the ending curly brace. You can do this by adding either break or continue to the statements block of a loop. break terminates the loop altogether, whereas continue skips the remaining statements for the current loop, evaluates the loop expression (if one exists), and begins the next loop. You can see the difference between these two statements in Listing 6.8. This script takes a very basic approach to finding the approximate square root of a number, n. Starting with i set equal to 0, the for loop begins by displaying the value of i. Next, the script checks to ensure that n is not negative. If n is negative, the loop is broken and program execution starts again after the ending curly brace. If n is positive, i is multiplied by itself and the result is compared to n. If the result is less than n, i is stored as the highest number so far to be equal or less than the square root of n. The

Control Structures and Looping

CHAPTER 6

125

6

CONTROL
STRUCTURES AND
LOOPING

continue statement then skips the rest of the current loop and resumes from the top of the loop after incrementing i. As soon as i squared is greater than n, the script passes the continue statement and reaches the break statement, which stops the loop completely. The approximate square root of 175 is displayed in Figure 6.8.

Listing 6.8. Using the continue and break statements.

```
<HTML>
<HEAD>
<TITLE>JavaScript Unleashed</TITLE>
</HEAD>
<BODY>
<PRE>
<SCRIPT LANGUAGE = "JavaScript">
<!-- begin hiding from old browsers
var highestNum = 0
var n = 175 //any number will do.
for (var i = 0; i < n; ++i) {
    document.writeln(i)
    if (n < 0) {
        document.write("n cannot be negative.")
        break
    }
    if (i * i <= n) {
        highestNum = i
        continue
    }
    document.writeln("Finished!")
    break
}
document.write("The integer less than or equal to the Square Root")
document.writeln(" of " + n + " = " + highestNum)
// end hiding -->
</SCRIPT>
</PRE>
</BODY>
</HTML>
```

FIGURE 6.8.

The display after break *is reached and the loop stops.*

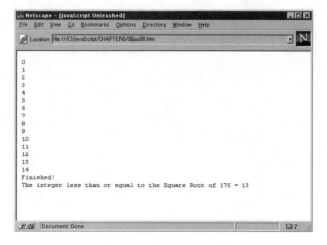

`with`

You use the `with` statement to avoid repeatedly specifying the object prefix when accessing properties or methods of that object. Any property or method in a `with` block that JavaScript does not recognize is associated with the object specified for that block. The syntax follows:

```
with (object) {
    statements
}
```

object specifies which object prefix to use in the absence of one in the *statements* block. This is quite useful when you're using advanced math functions that are only available through the math object. The math object is covered in Chapter 14, so I demonstrate the use of the `with` statement using the `document` object, which you are more familiar with. Each time I used the `write()` or `writeln()` methods associated with the `document` object, I included the prefix `document.` as in the following line:

```
document.writeln("Hello!")
```

When you're displaying a large amount of data using this technique, it is not uncommon to use the same statements, `document.writeln()`, many times over. To cut down on the amount of code needed, enclose all references to the `document` object within a `with` block as shown in Listing 6.9. This way you can eliminate the `document` prefix when using a document's method or property. Notice that `title` and `URL` are properties of the `document` object and would normally be written as `document.title` and `document.URL`, respectively. Using the `with` statement you need only reference the object once to produce the same results as typing each line out. Figure 6.9 shows the results.

CAUTION

Microsoft's Internet Explorer Version 3.0 Beta 2 does not support the `with` statement.

Listing 6.9. Using the `with` statement in JavaScript.

```
<HTML>
<HEAD>
<TITLE>JavaScript Unleashed</TITLE>
</HEAD>
<BODY>
<PRE>
<SCRIPT LANGUAGE = "JavaScript">
<!-- begin hiding from old browsers
with (document) {
    writeln("Hello!")
    writeln("The title of this document is, \"" + title + "\".")
    writeln("The URL for this document is: " + URL)
    writeln("Now you can avoid using the object's prefix each time!")
```

```
}
// end hiding -->
</SCRIPT>
</PRE>
</BODY>
</HTML>
```

FIGURE 6.9.

*Displaying information
using the* with
statement.

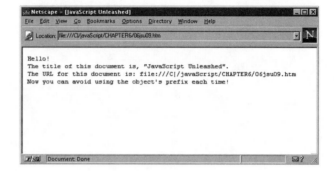

Summary

To make decisions in JavaScript, use the conditional statements if and else. You can use if by itself to execute a section of code based on the condition of an expression. If the expression returns true, the code will be executed; otherwise, it will not.

Use the else statement immediately after the if block to have JavaScript execute code when the expression from the if block returns false.

JavaScript allows you to nest if and if...else statements within each other. Using this, you can ask questions based on the answers to previous questions.

Use for loops to repeat a section of your script. You can initialize a variable to be used and how to change the variable each time a loop is finished. Based on the conditional expression of the for loop, you can specify the reason for a loop to stop.

Use the for...in loop to perform a set of operations for each property of an object. JavaScript automatically assigns the name of the property to a variable which you specify. Using this variable you can perform operations on that property.

Use the while loop to repeat a section of your script. You only need to specify a conditional expression that needs to return true before each loop is executed.

The break and continue statements are used to stop the execution of any loop. break stops the loop completely while continue only stops the current iteration of a loop and skips to the beginning of the next iteration.

The with statement is used in conjunction with JavaScript objects. It allows you to reference an object once rather than each time you access a property or method of the object. Inside the with block, you can use the property and method names of an object without their object reference prefix.

CHAPTER 7

Functions

by Gary Griffin

IN THIS CHAPTER

Performing a function, or many functions, is the purpose of all JavaScript programs. In its simplest form, a script can read or take in data, perform operations on a set of data, or display and send out data. As you have seen in previous examples, you can use a combination of these basic tools or merely one of them to serve an overall purpose. To entertain a casual browser, you might first inquire about his interests and then point him in the right direction. To welcome someone back to your Web page, you might let her know what is new and exciting. If you have products to sell, JavaScript can easily quote a price for any combination of items that interest the user while storing this data for your marketing department.

Accomplishing tasks such as these requires writing many lines of JavaScript code. Some sections of the script might need to execute immediately upon loading a Web page into the browser. Other parts of the script might be most useful if delayed until accepting data from the client. Sometimes, you might need parts of a script more than once or even an unlimited amount of times, and intermittently repeating a section of code could become necessary. These issues bring about the idea of splitting a script into smaller parts to serve an individual, specific purpose. A specific purpose might be to signal a "direct hit" during a game developed with JavaScript. Validating data entered in an HTML form is another task you might want a script to run more than once while someone is viewing your Web page.

It makes a lot of sense to logically split a script into sections that each serve a single purpose. When the time comes, one particular section of a script can be called to execute. JavaScript gives you this ability through a structure known as a *function*.

Understanding Functions

A JavaScript function is simply a script that is sectioned off as a separate piece of code and given a name. Using this name, a script can then call this separate script to execute at any time and as often as it needs. Many programming languages such as C and C++ also use functions, whereas others incorporate the same tools but call them procedures or subroutines. They all do basically the same thing, but they do have their differences.

Functions are meant to serve a single purpose to help split up the many tasks that one script is designed to do. You can think of it as telling JavaScript to "perform this list of related instructions and tell me when you're done!"

Functions can receive values from their calling statements, called *arguments*. You can then use the data that is received within the statement block as *variables*.

Creating Functions

The following segment shows the syntax for declaring a function:

```
function functionName ([argument1] [...,argumentN]) {
    [statements]
}
```

The keyword function is used to specify a name, *functionName*, which serves as the identifier for the set of statements between the curly braces. Enclosed in parentheses and separated by commas are the argument names that hold each value that a function receives. Technically, arguments are variables that are assigned to literal values, other variables, or objects that are passed to the function by the calling statement. If you do not specify any arguments, you must still include an empty set of parentheses to complete the declaration. The statements, which are the core of the function, are executed each time the function is called. For better readability, statements within the statement block are typically indented.

Where to Declare Functions

You can declare functions anywhere inside a <SCRIPT> block except within other functions or control structures. Keep in mind that just as different blocks of an HTML document are loaded ahead of others, so are any scripts that are embedded in these blocks. For this reason, it is recommended that you declare functions inside a script that is embedded in the <HEAD> block of a document. Declaring all your functions here ensures that the functions are available if another script needs to use them immediately.

Inside the <HEAD> Section

Listing 7.1 shows a function named defaultColors() declared inside of the <HEAD> block of an HTML document. The function is then called once within the <BODY> block of the document.

Listing 7.1. Declaring a function in the <HEAD> block.

```
<HTML>
<HEAD>
<TITLE>JavaScript Unleashed</TITLE>
<SCRIPT LANGUAGE = "JavaScript">
<!-- begin hiding from old browsers
function defaultColors() {
     document.fgColor = "black"
     document.bgColor = "white"
     document.writeln("Inside of defaultColors()")
}
// end hiding -->
</SCRIPT>
</HEAD>
<BODY>
<PRE>
<SCRIPT LANGUAGE = "JavaScript">
<!-- begin hiding from old browsers
document.writeln("Functions are scripts just waiting to run!")
defaultColors()
document.writeln("All done.")
// end hiding -->
</SCRIPT>
</PRE>
</BODY>
</HTML>
```

Calling Functions

Listing 7.1 shows how the function, `defaultColors()`, is called from the second script block. This is an example of calling a function that takes no arguments. When the HTML document is loaded, the function is loaded into memory and put "on hold." The function is not executed until the main script block calls it with the following statement:

```
defaultColors()
```

At this point, program execution jumps immediately to the first line of the `defaultColors` function. After executing all three lines of code, the program jumps back to where it left off and finishes what is left. This gives the same effect as if you had inserted all the function's statements directly into that position in your code. Now that there is a name assigned to this function, all you need to do to run the same statements is use its name again. You can view the results of this in Figure 7.1. Reusing code like this is the ideal way to use functions.

FIGURE 7.1.

Reusing code.

Working with Arguments

Setting up functions to accept arguments can be very useful. For example, you might want to create a function to be used many times throughout your program; however, you can encounter different issues when reusing the function. One of the values inside the function might need to change each time it is used. One way to solve this problem is to use global variables that can be modified both outside and inside the function. This can get confusing if you typically use the same variable names inside different functions. The best thing to do is set up the function to accept an argument for each value you want it to receive. Listing 7.2 shows a function that takes advantage of using arguments.

Listing 7.2. Using an argument with a JavaScript function.

```
<HTML>
<HEAD>
<TITLE>JavaScript Unleashed</TITLE>
<SCRIPT LANGUAGE = "JavaScript">
```

```
<!-- begin hiding from old browsers
function getBinary(anInteger) {
     var result = "" // full 32-bit result
     var shortResult = "" // without leading zeros
     for(var i=1; i <= 32; i++) {
          if(anInteger & 1 == 1) {
               result = "1" + result
               shortResult = result
          } else {
               result =  "0" + result
          }
          anInteger = anInteger >> 1
     }
     return(shortResult)
}
// end hiding -->
</SCRIPT>
</HEAD>
<BODY>
<PRE>
<SCRIPT LANGUAGE = "JavaScript">
<!-- begin hiding from old browsers
var binaryString = ""
x = 9
binaryString = getBinary(x)
document.write("The number " + x + " in binary form is : ")
document.writeln(binaryString)
x = 255
binaryString = getBinary(x)
document.write("The number " + x + " in binary form is : ")
document.writeln(binaryString)
document.writeln("The variable x is still equal to : " + x)
// end hiding -->
</SCRIPT>
</PRE>
</BODY>
</HTML>
```

When the function is called with the statement getBinary(x), the function receives a copy of the value that is stored in x. This is called passing by value. The value is then assigned to the variable, anInteger, which is local to the function. Notice that you do not need to declare anInteger using the var keyword. JavaScript automatically declares a new variable every time the function is called. You can then use the variable throughout the statement block as a local variable. If anInteger changes value while inside the function, it does not affect the value of the variable, x, that was passed as an argument, as shown in Figure 7.2.

The last statement given in the function is return(shortResult). Just as a function can receive a value, it can also return a value, as the previous example shows. Returning a value from a function works in the same way as returning a value from an expression. The following statement assigns the value returned by getBinary() to the variable binaryString:

```
binaryString = getBinary(x)
```

FIGURE 7.2.

Passing by value does not affect the original variable.

In this case, the final value of `shortResult` ends up assigned to `binaryString`.

You can use functions that return values anywhere you use a normal expression. This technique is demonstrated in Listing 7.3. The function call `isPhone(userInput)` is used as the condition expression of an `if` statement. Some functions return the result of a set of calculations, whereas some return a logical value just to let you know if everything went all right. The function `isPhone()` is a function that returns a logical value. The value returned lets the caller know if a phone number was entered in the correct format. This is useful for validating data that the user has entered in an HTML form. Figure 7.3 shows that the phone number is entered in correctly and an appropriate message is displayed. You can find more information about validating data entry in Chapter 16, "Enhancing Forms with JavaScript."

Listing 7.3. Functions that return values can be used in expressions.

```
<HTML>
<HEAD>
<TITLE>JavaScript Unleashed</TITLE>
<SCRIPT LANGUAGE = "JavaScript">
<!-- begin hiding from old browsers
function isPhone(aString) {
    var aChar = null
    var status = true
    if(aString.length != 13) {
        status = false
    } else {
        for(var i = 0; i <= 12; i++) {
            aChar = aString.charAt(i)
            if ( i == 0 && aChar == "(" )
                continue
            else
                if( i == 4 && aChar == ")" )
                    continue
                else
                    if( i == 8 && aChar == "-" )
                        continue
                    else
```

```
                                 if( parseInt(aChar,10) >= 0 &&
                                    parseInt(aChar,10) <= 9 )
                                        continue
                              else {
                                    status = false
                                    break
                              }
                      }
                 }
            return(status)
}
// end hiding -->
</SCRIPT>
</HEAD>
<BODY>
<PRE>
<SCRIPT LANGUAGE = "JavaScript">
<!-- begin hiding from old browsers
var userInput = "(508)937-5820"
if(isPhone(userInput)) {
      document.writeln("Thank you for your phone number.")
document.writeln("I will have a representative get you")
      document.writeln("more information.")
} else {
      document.writeln("Please re-enter your phone number")
      document.writeln("using the format (###)###-####")
}
// end hiding -->
</SCRIPT>
</PRE>
</BODY>
</HTML>
```

FIGURE 7.3.

Using a function as a conditional expression.

Varying the Number of Arguments

A function is set up to accept a certain number of arguments. Although it is good programming etiquette to pass the same number of arguments that were declared, it is practical on occasion to pass a different number of arguments. This is common when calling a function that usually uses the same parameter each time but is set up to handle exceptions. In this case, you might want to use a default value inside the function if no arguments are passed. This lets you use the function without arguments or allows you to specify a value other than the default. In Listing 7.4, I set up a function to display a very basic welcome message when a user arrives at a Web page.

Listing 7.4. Accepting either one or no arguments.

```
<HTML>
<HEAD>
<TITLE>JavaScript Unleashed</TITLE>
<SCRIPT LANGUAGE = "JavaScript">
<!-- begin hiding from old browsers
//userName is optional
function welcomeMessage(userName) {
     if (userName != null) {
          document.writeln("\"Hello again, " + userName + ".\"")
     } else {
          document.writeln("\"Welcome to our Web site!\"")
          document.write("\nIf a value is not passed to this ")
          document.writeln("function, displaying the")
          document.write("variable \"userName\" would show : ")
          document.writeln(userName)
     }
}
// end hiding -->
</SCRIPT>
</HEAD>
<BODY>
<PRE>
<SCRIPT LANGUAGE = "JavaScript">
<!-- begin hiding from old browsers
document.writeln("First call to welcomeMessage(),\n")
welcomeMessage("Mr. President")
document.writeln("<HR>\nSecond call to welcomeMessage(),\n")
welcomeMessage()
// end hiding -->
</SCRIPT>
</PRE>
</BODY>
</HTML>
```

Depending on whether it knows the visitor's name, the program displays one of two messages. To figure this out, it checks to see if the value sent is equal to null. If userName is not null, then the variable was defined. This is possible only if a value, such as "Mr. President," was passed to the function. If the function is equal to null, the program avoids using the variable altogether in the welcome message. Using it displays unwanted data, as shown in Figure 7.4. Depending on your Web browser, the unwanted data will be displayed as undefined or will be left blank.

Figure 7.4.

The results of passing either one or two arguments.

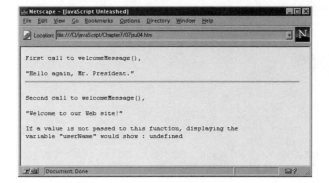

Another possibility is that a function gets passed more arguments than were specified in the declaration. The extra values are not lost but are stored in an array named `arguments`, which is a property of every function. All arguments stored in the array can be extracted within the statements block. For example, to get the first argument passed to the `welcomeMessage` function, you can use the following statement:

```
firstArg = welcomeMessage.arguments[0]
```

JavaScript arrays are indexed starting with the number 0. To find the second item in the array, you would use 1 and so on. To find the total number of arguments that were passed, you can use the following statement to find the length of the array:

```
numArgs = welcomeMessage.arguments.length
```

Using these features, I modified the `welcomeMessage()` function to accept a variable number of arguments and included it in Listing 7.5. The `welcomeMessage` function can therefore accept the following syntax:

```
welcomeMessage([userName] [,extraMessage1] [,extraMessage2]...)
```

Listing 7.5. A function can be set up to accept a variable number of arguments.

```
<HTML>
<HEAD>
<TITLE>JavaScript Unleashed</TITLE>
<SCRIPT LANGUAGE = "JavaScript">
<!-- begin hiding from old browsers
//Use this syntax for welcomeMessage function:
//welcomeMessage([userName] [,extraMessage1] [,extraMessage2]...)
function welcomeMessage(userName) {
    if (userName != null) {
        document.writeln("\"Hello again, " + userName + ".\"")
    } else {
        document.writeln("\"Welcome to our Web site!\"")
    }
    numArgs = welcomeMessage.arguments.length
    //If more arguments than the userName were sent,
//display each one.
    if (numArgs > 1) {
        for(var i = 1; i < numArgs; i++) {
            document.writeln("\""+welcomeMessage.arguments[i]+"\"")
        }
    }
}
// end hiding -->
</SCRIPT>
</HEAD>
<BODY>
<PRE>
<SCRIPT LANGUAGE = "JavaScript">
<!-- begin hiding from old browsers
var userName = "David", extraMsg = "It has been a long time!"
var userName2 = null
var extraMsg1 = "Would you like to become a member?"
var extraMsg2 = "You can enroll online!"
welcomeMessage(userName, extraMsg)
document.writeln("<HR>")
welcomeMessage(userName2, extraMsg1, extraMsg2)
// end hiding -->
</SCRIPT>
</PRE>
</BODY>
</HTML>
```

Notice that Listing 7.5 can still handle the situation where the userName is unknown, but there are extra messages to be displayed. The variable userName2 is assigned null to fill the first element in the arguments array so that a message is not displayed as the user's name. Figure 7.5 shows the resulting output.

When developing with a group of people, it is important to document the intricacies so that others can understand their full potential. Without descriptive comments, reading through an application takes much more time to understand.

FIGURE 7.5.

Accepting multiple arguments to display many messages.

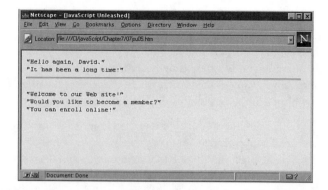

Using Global and Local Variables

In Chapter 4, "Fundamentals of the JavaScript Language," I described the difference between local and global variables. I demonstrated how global variables can be modified from anywhere in a document, whereas local variables can only be modified within the function where they are declared. You can choose which type of variable to use by using the following guidelines:

■ If the value of a variable is meant to be used and possibly modified by any part of a program, both inside and outside functions, the variable should be declared outside any function. This has the effect of making it global and modifiable by any part of the program. The best place to declare a global variable is in the <HEAD> block of an HTML document to ensure that it is declared before being used. The variable need not be declared again inside any function.

■ If the variable is needed only within a particular function, the variable should be declared inside that function. Be sure to use the keyword var when declaring the variable. This ensures that its value can only be changed within the function. This also ensures that JavaScript looks at this variable as unique and separate from any global variables that might have the same name. Using the var keyword to declare argument variables is not necessary. Variables that are specified in the declaration of the function are automatically considered local as if they were declared with the var keyword.

■ If you want to use a variable only in the main script and not within any functions, declare the variable somewhere outside all functions. Unfortunately, nothing prevents the script from using the variable inside functions because the variable is still considered global. If you are not careful, this can lead to overwriting values held by variables with the same name. To avoid this completely, always follow the preceding guideline.

■ If you want the value of a variable to be modifiable only by the main script or a single function, but you need to use it in another function, pass the variable as an argument to that function. This has the effect of making a copy of the variable and assigning its value to the argument variable set up to receive it. As the function works and modifies its own copy of the variable, it will not affect the original. Argument variables are automatically declared as local to that function. Even if the argument variable has the same name as the variable being passed, making changes to it does not affect the variable that was passed. The one exception to this is objects. When an object is passed as an argument, it is passed by reference as opposed to being passed by value. Instead of making a copy of the object, the function uses the original object. Changes made to an object's properties within the function have an effect on the original object.

To see each of these situations in action, take a look at Listing 7.6. I made it a point to demonstrate how JavaScript considers some variables with the same name to be different. This is shown when the variable numberB is passed to the function doublePassedVar. JavaScript automatically creates a local variable also named numberB. Even though this local variable has the same name as the global variable, modifications to it do not affect the global variable. Figure 7.6 shows the results.

Listing 7.6. The effects of local and global variables.

```
<HTML>
<HEAD>
<TITLE>JavaScript Unleashed</TITLE>
<SCRIPT LANGUAGE = "JavaScript">
<!-- begin hiding from old browsers
var numberA //Global variable modified in any function
var numberB //Global variable only modified in main script
function doubleGlobalVar() {
      numberA *= 2  // This will change the value of the
                    // global variable.
}
function tripleLocalVar() {
      var numberA = 1 // This uses the same name as the
                      // global variable, but is considered
                      // different by JavaScript.
      numberA *= 3
}
function doublePassedVar(numberB) {
      // I purposely gave the argument variable the same
      // name as the variable being passed. This shows that
      // JavaScript considers them to be different.
      numberB *= 2
}
// end hiding -->
</SCRIPT>
</HEAD>
<BODY>
<PRE>
<SCRIPT LANGUAGE = "JavaScript">
<!-- begin hiding from old browsers
numberA = 1
document.writeln("Initial value of numberA: " + numberA)
doubleGlobalVar()
tripleLocalVar()
document.writeln("Final value of numberA: " + numberA)
numberB = 1
document.writeln("Initial value of numberB: " + numberB)
doublePassedVar(numberB)
```

```
document.writeln("Final value of numberB: " + numberB)
// end hiding -->
</SCRIPT>
</PRE>
</BODY>
</HTML>
```

FIGURE 7.6.

Resulting values of numberA *and* numberB *variables.*

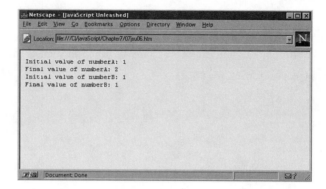

Reusing Functions

Functions are great for separating an application into its logical parts, but their best advantage is promoting the reuse of code. Functions are unlike sections of code enclosed in loops to be repeated many times in succession; you can reuse a function at any given time by simply calling its name. Creating functions that serve one purpose, yet are useful enough in many situations, takes practice and a little foresight. For example, in Listing 7.4, the welcomeMessage() function serves one purpose on more than one occasion throughout the execution of the program. By allowing a more flexible argument list in Listing 7.5, the welcomeMessage() function became useful in more situations. The function still serves the same purpose, but it's a better candidate for reuse in its more flexible form.

Recursive Functions

JavaScript functions can be *recursive*, which means that a function can call itself. Solving factorial equations is a common way to demonstrate how recursion works, so I included an example here. To find the factorial of any positive integer n, you simply find the product of all integers 1 through n. To find the factorial of 6, written 6!, you calculate the following:

```
6! = 6 x 5 x 4 x 3 x 2 x 1

  = 720
```

To calculate 7!, you would use the following:

```
7! = 7 x 6 x 5 x 4 x 3 x 2 x 1
```

Comparing these two calculations, you can produce a general formula to use in your function. Notice that 7! is equal to 7 x 6!. For any positive integer n greater than 0, n! = n x (n - 1)!. The first iteration of this would look like this:

```
7! = 7 x (7 - 1)!

   = 7 x 6!
```

From here, you have to stop and calculate 6! before continuing with the rest of the calculation. This occurs six more times before you can back out of each one and find the final solution. Instead of doing that, you can use a recursive function such as the following:

```
function getFactorial(n) {
    var result
    if(n > 0)
        result = n * getFactorial(n - 1)
    else if(n==0)
            result = 1
        else
            result = null
    return(result)
}
```

The function first checks to see if n is greater than 0, which happens the majority of the time. If this is true, the function multiplies n by the result returned by calling the function again with a different argument—in this case, n-1. This continues to put many getFactorial functions on hold until n is equal to zero. At this point, the most nested occurrence of the function finishes and returns the first value. JavaScript then backs out and finishes each nested function until it reaches the original call to getFactorial and returns the final result.

Developing useful functions can be one of the most rewarding and interesting aspects of programming. After you see a function in action, it is common to go back and modify it to make it more flexible. If you do this, be sure that the function still serves one purpose and does not do more than you expect from reading the name. Becoming experienced in writing functions prepares you for the next exciting step in JavaScript programming—creating custom objects. This is covered in Chapter 15, "Creating Custom JavaScript Objects." For now, there is much to be learned about the objects that are already built into HTML and JavaScript, which is the focus of Part III, "JavaScript Objects." JavaScript also includes functions that are built into the language and can be used at any time. These are covered in Chapter 14, "Built-In Language Objects."

Summary

JavaScript functions serve a few purposes. They allow you to put code on hold so that it does not execute immediately upon loading the document. They allow you to duplicate code easily and to use the same code to perform the same operations on different sets of data. The latter is done with arguments.

A *function* is a set of JavaScript code that is grouped together and given a name. To declare a function use the `function` statement followed by the name you wish to give it, a set of parentheses, and the script that you want the function to include. Function names must adhere to the rules applied to all variables.

Functions can be declared anywhere inside an HTML document as long as it is surrounded by `<SCRIPT>` tags. It is suggested that functions be declared in the `<HEAD>` of the document.

To call a function, use its name followed by a set of parentheses. The set of parentheses enclose any arguments that the function is able to accept.

JavaScript arguments are passed by value. Functions can accept a variable number of arguments regardless of how the function was declared. Each function has an array named `arguments` associated with it. This array can be used to extract an argument that may have been passed to the function.

JavaScript functions can return values. Functions that return values can be used as expressions or in other expressions.

Argument variables do not need to be declared. They are automatically declared as local variables each time the function is called. To declare a global variable within a function, do not use the `var` keyword. Instead, just initialize the variable.

Functions that serve one purpose but are flexible enough to deal with different pieces of data are the most reusable functions.

In JavaScript, functions can call themselves. Functions that do call themselves are called *recursive functions.*

7

FUNCTIONS

PART

JavaScript Objects

Fundamentals of
Object Orientation

by Claudia Piemont

IN THIS CHAPTER

CHAPTER

For a long time, conventional programming has been done in procedural languages such as C, COBOL, Pascal, or FORTRAN. Software developers constructed a program in a sequential way. All source code followed similar thinking:

- What has to be done first
- What happens next
- The next task
- And so on

Additionally, the sequential program path was intermixed with control flow statements such as if then else or while x do. To give you an example of how sequential programming looks, the following code shows a JavaScript function that computes factorials. A factorial n ! of an integer number n is mathematically defined as

$$n = 0: \qquad\qquad 0\,! = 1$$

$$n => 0: \qquad\qquad n\,! := n * (n - 1)\,! \text{ (same as } n * (n\text{-}1) * (n\text{-}2) \ldots * 1)$$

Here, you see the JavaScript function computing this mathematical formula:

```
function factorial (n)
{
    // 0. First of all:  declare necessary variables,  here result

    var    result;

    // 1. What has to be done first:  check for special cases n = 0 or  n = 1

    if ( (n == 0) || (n == 1))

        // 2. What happens next :   if  n = 0  or n = 1  return  result = 1

        return   1;
    else
    {
        // 3. Next task:   n > 1 in this case compute n ! recursively
        // n ! = n * (n - 1) !

        result =  (n  * factorial (n-1));

        // 4. Next task: computation complete: return n ! in variable result
        // as result of function factorial

        return result;
    }
}
```

You will find a more detailed introduction to sequential programming with JavaScript in Part II, "The JavaScript Language." Also, a complete HTML document containing this JavaScript function appears later in this section.

Following conventional methods, large software applications are decomposed in a functional manner, forming a hierarchy of business functions. (See Figure 8.1.)

FIGURE 8.1.

Functional decomposition of a software application.

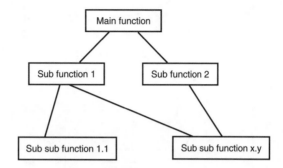

The software application is considered one big business task that has to be solved. To break the problem into more manageable chunks of source code, the developer designs several subfunctions so that each performs a smaller task. The main function works as a supervisor, taking control and calling the subfunctions when necessary. To achieve its purpose, a subfunction could call other smaller sub-subfunctions as well. The developer concentrates mainly on the procedural flow. The whole application and each subfunction are only components that are responsible for fulfilling certain functional tasks. This way of thinking is called functional decomposition.

Quite clearly, all software applications are processing data in one way or another. Often, data values must be maintained between program runs. This means that program data must be stored in a suitable place. Main storage media for program data are either disk files or databases. The latter case generally applies to large amounts of business data. All the conventional techniques described here, such as sequential programming, functional decomposition, and the different kinds of data storage systems, seem to follow a rather logical way of problem solving.

Why is everybody talking about object orientation now? Object orientation is a relatively new and more modern method for designing and developing software systems. It was invented because software developers encountered some problems while constructing software applications the conventional way. A lot of existing software applications were built with the old techniques, but the results weren't satisfying in all respects.

One problem was clear: The old programming style did not incorporate the data view. Figure 8.2 presents a common situation with various software systems in a sample company. The company has several different software applications such as an order management system and a bookkeeping program. All applications are created for the functional job they should do. They are working on the company's data, which are stored in a database.

8

FUNDAMENTALS
OF OBJECT
ORIENTATION

FIGURE 8.2.

*Functionally con-
structed software
programs accessing
data in a separate
database.*

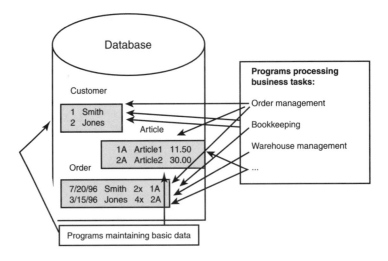

Today, companies use relational database management systems (RDBMS). RDBMSs store their data in tables. In the sample database, you see three sample tables: Customer, Article, and Order. I also included some sample data values. The Customer table contains a customer number and the name of the customer. Customer Smith is represented through his customer number, which is 1. Customer Jones has the customer number 2. Different customers are stored in subsequent table rows. The characteristics of a customer, namely the customer number and his name, are put in different table columns, as you can see in the graphic. The Article table has an article number, an article name, and the relevant price. Articles are stored in different table rows, whereas the characteristics of articles are shown in the table columns. The Order table contains the date of an order, the name of the customer issuing the order, and the amount of an article ordered, together with the article identifier. To simplify things for this special example, the precondition here is that one single order can sell only one article.

Data in a database is more manageable if you apply a technique of separation of concepts. Generally, only one type or kind of data is stored in one single table. In database engineering, such a single data type is called a data entity. As you can see in the figure, there are three separate tables for Customer, Article, and Order. The way the information is structured applies to all tables: The characteristics of a particular data entity are presented in the table columns, and the different data instances are shown in the table rows.

Databases have their own data definition and data manipulation languages. For table-oriented databases, the language is SQL. SQL is a set-oriented language, in contrast to procedural programming languages. In a procedural programming language, you can only process data in a table row-by-row, but SQL returns data in a set-like format. For example, for a simple query to read the data values in the table Customer, you might use the following SQL select statement:

```
SELECT NUMBER, NAME  FROM  CUSTOMER
```

This provides all the data in the table Customer for all rows. What does this SQL discussion lead to? Simply keep in mind that the creation of data tables is accomplished in SQL separately from the implementation of the application.

All programs in the example need to access the data in the database. They all include some form of SQL statement to accomplish this, and they all have to break down the set-like structure of the SQL result sets into sequential row-by-row procedural processing. This means a discrepancy between the functional code and the part necessary to deal with the program data. Moreover, all programs probably include SQL statements for the same tables. This is shown in Figure 8.2 with the arrows pointing from the program applications to the data tables. First, this means that the necessary source code for accessing and working with the program data exists in a more or less similar fashion in many separate programs. Second, the data-accessing source code is often written many times and maintained differently for the various existing software systems in a company.

An additional data model is designed for the data side of the application. The data model provides a better overview and understanding of the tables in a database. The technique used is called Entity Relationship Modeling (ERM). ERM describes the different data entities—that is, tables and their relation to another. Often, functional models of the application and the data model for the database are built separately, and both must be maintained. Sometimes, even different groups of people are responsible for the data or the functional design. The inherent problem of this scenario is that both models contribute to only one single problem solution and must work together.

An additional concern is that project requirements and project complexity are increasing more. The term *software crisis* gives a good description of the situation. Software projects almost always struggle to fulfill the user's expectations and have problems keeping the time limits of project milestones.

Moreover, software applications today often include a graphical user interface (GUI). If you are familiar with Microsoft Windows or UNIX X Window, you know quite well what graphical user interfaces look like. GUIs in the context of software applications mostly consist of a main window and some connected dialog windows. A window might contain different input fields and control elements such as text entry fields, list boxes, pushbuttons, radio buttons, or checkboxes.

I created my own graphical user interface for computing factorials with JavaScript. (See Figure 8.3.) It contains a text entry field for typing in the number n and a result field where the result of the computation n! is displayed. When the user clicks the pushbutton Compute n!, the result field is set.

FIGURE 8.3.

Example of a graphical user interface for computing n!.

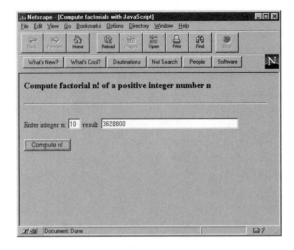

GUIs are often complicated to program and best handled with an object-oriented and event-based method. In the context of a graphical user interface, an event is a result of a user action. It takes place when the user of an application is doing something. For example, when the user clicks a button on the user interface, the event "button clicked" occurs. Other GUI events include clicking a checkbox, selecting a string in a list box, double-clicking a list box item, opening or closing a window, and so on. It seems only logical that a language suitable for programming GUIs should include techniques for handling events. Additionally, most GUI components have properties such as value, name, size, or color. GUI components always show a certain behavior; for example, a push button reacts to a click event and subsequently triggers a certain action executing a program function.

The best way to program a GUI is to consider the properties, reactions, and events of a GUI object one logical entity. That is exactly what object-oriented languages do. In JavaScript, GUI elements are represented as programming language objects. Listing 8.1 shows the complete HTML document for computing factorials and displaying and handling the GUI shown in Figure 8.3.

Listing 8.1. factorials.htm.

```
<HTML>
<HEAD>
<TITLE>
Compute factorials with JavaScript
</TITLE>
<SCRIPT>

function factorial (n)
{
    // 0. First of all:  declare necessary variables, here result

    var   result;
```

```
    // 1. What has to be done first:  check for special cases n = 0 or  n = 1

    if ( (n == 0) ¦¦  (n == 1))

        // 2. What happens next :   if  n = 0  or n = 1  return  result = 1

        return   1;
    else
    {
        // 3. Next task:   n > 1 in this case compute n ! recursively
        // n ! = n * (n - 1) !

            result =  (n  * factorial (n-1));

            // 4. Next task: computation complete:
           // return n! in variable result
         // as result of function factorial

        return result;
    }
}

function xcompute (aForm)
{
    var  n;
    var  result;

    // precondition str contains integer number => 0
    // entry into textfield fn not checked properly !!

    n = aForm.fn.value;            // value of text field fn
    if (n > 40)
    {
        alert ("value n too large > 40");
    }
    else
    {
        result = factorial(n);        // computes n!
        aForm.fresult.value = result;  // set fresult field in form
    }
}
</SCRIPT>
</HEAD>
<BODY>
<FORM>
<H3>
Compute factorial n! of a positive integer number n
</H3>
<P>
<HR>
<P>
Enter integer n:
<INPUT TYPE="text" NAME="fn" SIZE=2>
   result:
<INPUT TYPE="text" NAME="fresult" SIZE=40>
<P>
```

8

FUNDAMENTALS
OF OBJECT
ORIENTATION

continues

Listing 8.1. continued

```
<INPUT TYPE="button" NAME="compute"
  VALUE="Compute n!" onClick="xcompute(this.form)">
<BR>
</FORM>
</BODY>
</HTML>
```

After the preliminary tags <HEAD> and <TITLE> is a JavaScript section beginning with the tag <SCRIPT>. This section consists of the JavaScript functions factorial and xcompute. The function factorial computes n!. (See the detailed description of this function at the beginning of this chapter.) The function xcompute is executed when the user clicks the Compute n! button. The purpose of this function is to first extract the value of n from the input field; afterward, the script calculates n! via the factorial function and fills the result text field. The <BODY> section of the HTML document builds the graphical user interface with the <FORM> tag. The input field fn and the result field fresult are followed by the push button named compute. The graphical user interface controls are constructed via the regular HTML tag <INPUT> used in HTML forms.

All graphical elements are treated as objects in JavaScript. You will find a more detailed discussion of the term object in the section titled "Objects," later in this chapter. Additionally, Chapter 10, "JavaScript Object Model," explains the built-in graphical objects of JavaScript in more detail.

The object-oriented concept offers distinct advantages regarding the problems of constructing software. Object-oriented techniques are based on the notion of objects. An object is a software component representing a single real-world concept, including both data and the functional procedures used to manipulate this data. An object is an entity encapsulating its data characteristics and functional procedures. There is no more separation between functional tasks and data issues. An object includes several different functions (its methods), which form the external behavior of the object.

The characteristics and behavior of objects are declared in classes. A class consists of objects conforming to the same construction plan. The construction plan or specification is the declaration of a typical object out of this class and serves as a template for constructing new objects. Class libraries are containers for a set of classes. You can think of classes in a class library as books in a library or book store. The source code found in class libraries is only developed once and can be easily reused. This saves a lot of time and effort when you're developing software systems. Moreover, recent case studies discovered that object-oriented programming reduces the amount of source code needed to solve a certain problem. This is especially true when you reuse code.

Basic Object-Oriented Concepts

Object-oriented programming uses objects as its central logical building blocks for constructing software applications. Objects represent one small portion of a software application's problem space.

The business tasks of an application in addition to the end-user requirements form the "problem world" or "problem space" of a software system. This also includes technical components such as a graphical user interface.

An object forms one encapsulated entity. It contains special characteristics describing the object (its data) and the functional procedures the object can perform (its methods). For example, you could view your own car as an object. The characteristics (the data) of your car are its make, its model name, the year it was built, its color, and so on. Additionally, your car features a certain behavior; for example, it may be parked at your home, and it can drive. Your car resembles one particular entity. The description of its characteristics doesn't make much sense without the valuable services it can offer to you, such as driving.

RESOURCE

A good textbook is always a valuable resource. This is especially true on the subject of object-oriented technology. A variety of textbooks cover the subject of object-oriented programming. To recommend a particular title is difficult because it is often a matter of personal taste. My personal favorite is *Object-Oriented Analysis and Design*, Second Edition, by Grady Booch, Benjamin/Cummings, 1994, ISBN: 0-8053-5340-2. This book includes a comprehensive introduction to object-oriented principles and includes examples in the programming languages Smalltalk and C++.

Another book you could use is *Object-Oriented Programming in C++*, Second Edition, by Robert Lafore, Waite Group Press, ISBN: 1-878739-73-5. This book is more specific about C++ issues.

Object-oriented methodology focuses on algorithmic procedures and data values. Objects incorporate both the data side and the functional view. Many objects are representations of real-world objects, such as your car. They are not abstract concepts from some computer scientist's mind; they represent real, tangible things. The idea to emulate a real-world entity as one enclosed object in a computer program makes the program more understandable to the developer and results in better software design. Object-oriented thinking appeals to the human mind and resembles general problem-solving strategies.

Objects with an analogous structure and behavior form a class of objects. A class consist of objects conforming to the same construction plan. The construction plan or specification is the declaration of a typical object out of this class and serves as a template for constructing new objects. For example, your car, my car, and your neighbor's car are all cars, although they each have a different make, age, and color. All cars have a make, model name, model year, and color. Moreover, all cars can stand in a parking space or can drive, so the features and functions are the same. Therefore, the class car describes the data characteristics and possible methods for cars.

The algorithmic concept of object-oriented problem solving follows a divide-and-conquer strategy where several small and distinct objects are created to send themselves messages to trigger the program flow. Object-oriented programming means solving the problem with communicating objects rather than creating a functional view of the application. What does this mean? Generally, a car has four wheels and an engine to drive it. Wheels and an engine can be considered objects as well, or in a more abstract context, they represent the classes wheel and engine. To set the car into driving mode, the owner first must start the engine of the car. Then, he or she continues driving, which means the car must tell the engine to continue working. The engine then sets the wheels into motion. This is the principle of how object-oriented software works. Each object is responsible for doing its own job. If an object needs another object to fulfill its task, it asks that object to perform a certain service by sending that object a message. In simple terms, messaging means calling another object's method.

An important feature of object-oriented programming languages is the generalization/specialization relationship called inheritance. Inheritance means you have general base classes that provide data and methods for other classes called subclasses. An object of a subclass possesses all the characteristics of the base class in addition to its own specification. For example, a vehicle could be a bus, car, or motorcycle. A vehicle can stand or drive as do buses, cars, and motorcycles. The vehicle builds the base class, whereas bus, car, and motorcycle are subclasses. A vehicle does not specify the number of wheels in the base class itself because this is a characteristic of the subclasses. Each subclass declares the number of wheels for itself because the number is different in each subclass; busses and cars have four wheels, but a motorcycle has only two.

RESOURCE

This resource note outlines Internet resources on the World Wide Web (WWW). The addresses here are URLs. (URL stands for Uniform Resource Locator.)

Surprisingly, the WWW has a couple of good object-oriented resources, including an HTML version of one complete textbook about object orientation. You can find *Object-Oriented System Development* by Champeaux, Lea, and Faure, Addison-Wesley, 1993, at http://g.oswego.edu/dl/oosdw3.

The Global Network Academy offers a free C++ tutorial called Introduction to OOP Using C++ at `http://uu-gna.mit.edu:8001/uu-gna/text/cc/index.html`.

The University of Vienna publishes an electronic book about object orientation; visit `http://ravel.ifs.univie.ac.at/ISOO/isoohome.html`.

One online magazine about object orientation is Object Currents at `http://www.sigs.com/objectcurrents/`.

The Object-Oriented Page is an index page where you can find a lot of other links to specific object-oriented information on the Web. Don't be shocked by the rather long URL: `http://galaxy.einet.net/galaxy/Engineering-and-Technology/Computer-Technology/Object-Oriented-Systems/ricardo-devis/oo.html`.

I don't know about any specific texts on JavaScript and object orientation. However, Netscape has some general JavaScript resources. Netscape's JavaScript Authoring Guide covers the JavaScript built-in objects and briefly mentions the topic-general objects in JavaScript. Find JavaScript resources at `http://home.netscape.com/comprod/products/navigator/version_2.0/script/script_info/index.html`. The Netscape JavaScript Authoring Guide is at `http://home.netscape.com/eng/mozilla/Gold/handbook/javascript/index.html`.

Additionally, I found two interesting online newspaper articles on the Web. "Using JavaScript's Built-In Objects" is at `http://www.javaworld.com/jw-05-1996/jw-05-javascript.html`. Read "Using JavaScript with Forms" at `http://www.javaworld.com/jw-06-1996/jw-06-javascript.html`.

8

FUNDAMENTALS
OF OBJECT
ORIENTATION

TIP

Although it is important for the JavaScript programmer to understand object-oriented programming (OOP) concepts, JavaScript is not particularly well suited for learning OOP programming. JavaScript is not a valid object-oriented programming language. In my opinion, the best way to learn OOP is by using the object-oriented programming language Smalltalk. Other good choices of OOPs are Eiffel or Java.

See the section "Is JavaScript an Object-Oriented Language?" later in this chapter for more discussion on this topic.

Objects

Programs are developed for executing a particular business case. For example, an order management system handles customer orders. The business tasks of an application in addition to the end-user requirements form the "problem world" or "problem space" of a software system. This area also includes technical components such as a graphical user interface.

In constructing object-oriented software applications, objects are considered the central logical building blocks. Objects in program code are often representations of real-world objects found in the problem space. Additionally, you can build technical helper-objects for solving special computer science problems.

An object can be any of the following:

- A tangible or visible thing in the problem space—for example, an order or a customer. If you are developing software for a car dealer business, probable objects are the cars to be sold, car models, employees, customers, and so on.

- An abstract concept in the mind of the developer or something that can be comprehended intellectually. For example, if you are building an application for chemists, you might need chemical structures for objects such as molecules, atoms, chemical models, and the like. Date and time might be considered intellectual objects, too, because they are certainly not tangible. The math object in JavaScript is another good example of a purely logical concept. The math object provides advanced mathematical functions (arithmetic and trigonometric) for processing numbers in JavaScript.

- Visible GUI objects are also considered objects in the object-oriented model. JavaScript has many different GUI objects such as windows, frames, buttons, input fields, and so on.

- Historically, the object-oriented model stems from inventing the concept of data structures. Consider a data structure a more complex data type. A data structure is very similar to the idea of an object. It is a model of an abstract concept in computer science for solving primitive technical programming tasks. A data structure is a container of corresponding data variables together with the operations defined for it. Many examples cited as objects in computer science books are essentially data structures such as records, arrays, complex numbers, or a stack. A stack is a storage container of data values and works basically like a stack of paper. At one time, a stack can store only one single data item, which is always put on top of the other data items. Moreover, you can remove a data item only from the top position of the stack. Other popular data structures are strings and dates, which are also implemented in JavaScript as built-in objects. A string is a collection of single characters. A string is considered one single entity, even though some string functions extract substrings out of strings. A date object contains the data values resembling date and time.

An object includes the data values needed to describe its nature (its attributes) and the functions it could perform (its methods). You can consider an object an entity with a defined boundary. (See Figure 8.4.) The kernel of an object is built by its data values. The data items of an object describe the object's special characteristics and its identity. In the object-oriented jargon, object data are called attributes.

FIGURE 8.4.

Graphical view of an object.

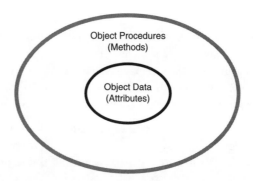

Object Procedures (Methods)

Object Data (Attributes)

Generally, an object supports several functions. The functions of an object visible to the outside form the behavior of an object. In object-oriented terms, an object function is often called a method. A method is a chunk of source code performing one single task that is an important feature for the object. A method is a function of the object that could be called. In other words, the methods of an object represent its behavior, which is its outwardly visible and testable activity.

Figure 8.4 shows the popular donut view of an object. The methods of an object are drawn in the outer circle because they are visible to other objects. This means these functions could be called and executed on the object. The attributes are in the inner circle.

One example of an object is my car. My car is represented as the object `myCar` in the object-oriented world. It is a red Renault 19 built in 1992, so its data attributes include the following:

Make	Renault
Model	19
Age	1992
Color	Red

My car can be parked or driven. Those are the important functions it provides. Figure 8.5 shows a graphical image of my car as an object in the donut-view perspective.

FIGURE 8.5.

Graphical view of my car as an object.

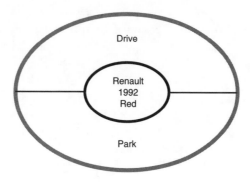

Drive

Renault
1992
Red

Park

In addition to specific characteristics and identifying values, an object's attribute can also represent the state of the object or a role that an object could play at a given time. State and role are special time-dependent object characteristics. A state is a kind of data item that changes over time and generally shows a current value for the object. Add to the list of myCar attributes another attribute position, which always contains the current geographic position of my car. The attribute position is a typical example of a state attribute.

An employee might be a team leader or department head at any given time in his professional career. An employee object can contain an attribute for professional status that stores the different roles (such as team leader, department head, and so on) an employee could fulfill.

Return to the factorials example from the beginning of this chapter. Figure 8.6 shows a simple graphical user interface for computing factorials. The source code for constructing this form is shown in Listing 8.2, which contains the body of an HTML document.

FIGURE 8.6.

Example of a graphical user interface for computing n!.

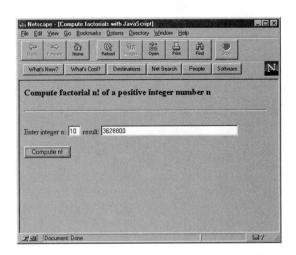

Listing 8.2. guifactorials.htm.

```
<BODY>
<FORM>
<H3>
Compute factorial n! of a positive integer number n
</H3>
<P>
<HR>
<P>
Enter integer n:
<INPUT TYPE="text" NAME="fn" SIZE=2>
   result:
<INPUT TYPE="text" NAME="fresult" SIZE=40>
<P>
<INPUT TYPE="button" NAME="compute"
  VALUE="Compute n!" onClick="xcompute(this.form)">
```

```
<BR>
</FORM>
</BODY>
```

In JavaScript, an object's attributes are referred to as the object's properties. For example, the pushbutton `fn` in the example is a GUI object in JavaScript. A push button has the JavaScript properties `name` and `value`. In the HTML document example above (see Listing 8.2), the properties are specified by the uppercase tags `NAME` and `VALUE`. The user can click a GUI button, so the object `fn` supports the function `click`. The function `click` presents a way to trigger the object `fn` through the programmed script instead of through a user action. All the functions of an object build its behavior. In object-oriented terms, an object's function is often called a method. In JavaScript, however, the respective keyword is `function`. Figure 8.7 shows a JavaScript object drawn in the graphical donut view.

FIGURE 8.7.

Graphical view of a JavaScript object.

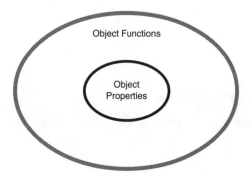

The built-in object string is a special object type. You can simply create the string `myString` with the var statement. The var statement creates new variables in JavaScript, as shown in the following line:

```
var myString = "This is my text. It resembles a string object";
```

`MyString` has the property `length`, which all strings possess. The attribute `length` contains the length of the string `myString`—in this case, the number 45. Strings feature several different methods (see Chapter 14, "Built-In Language Objects," for details), including `blink()`, which results in a blinking string. This statement has the same effect as the following HTML tag:

```
<BLINK>  sample text </BLINK>
```

The following statement sets the text `This is my text. It resembles a string object` blinking on the screen:

```
myString.blink();
```

An object's properties can contain simple variable types such as characters, integers, and other objects. Figure 8.8 illustrates this idea. For example, the object myCar can be defined through attributes such as make, model, year, and owner, where owner is a person object defined through attributes such as name, age, and address. The inclusion of objects in the data attributes of the containing object is often called aggregation or a whole-part relationship. The expression whole-part signifies a typical example for containment where a machine consists of several smaller parts, as in a car with an engine, four wheels, and so on.

Figure 8.8.

Graphical view of object containment.

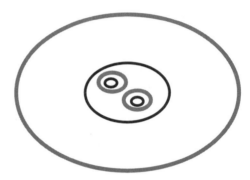

CAUTION

JavaScript is an interpreted language. All statements are evaluated one-by-one at the time the HTML page is loaded. As a result, the execution time is rather slow. If you have a large or complex problem to solve, don't use JavaScript; instead, use the object-oriented programming language Java.

RESOURCE

Java was invented by Sun to perform tasks that are similar to what JavaScript can do. It is a fully featured object-oriented programming language. Java is free of charge; you only have to download the Java Development Kit and accompanying documentation from the WWW. (See Part VII, "Java and JavaScript.")

A good starting point for resources on Java is the Javasoft home page at http://java. sun.com.

JavaScript has many different built-in objects, such as string, date, button, or math. The developer can use all those objects. In fact, you can have several different objects of one type. For example, your HTML form can have various pushbuttons. Every button possesses the same properties and methods; that is, every button has a value and supports a click method. A button is only a kind of construction plan for creating new existing buttons in a form. Such a construction specification is called a class in object-oriented terms. (See the section "Classes" later in this chapter for more details.) The different built-in objects in JavaScript actually form a set of classes that you can reuse. Such a set of classes is called a class library. Because JavaScript does not really deal with classes in the way object-oriented languages do, the built-in objects in JavaScript as a whole are often called the JavaScript object library.

TIP

To save development time and programming effort, use as many of the built-in JavaScript objects as suitable. Study the JavaScript object library carefully. Don't invent your own object types if it isn't necessary. Reusing already existing software components is a beneficial strategy when you're programming the object-oriented way.

Encapsulation

The data attributes and functions of an object form one inseparable entity, as shown in Figure 8.9. The information about the inner workings of an object should be hidden.

FIGURE 8.9.

Graphical view of an object as one encapsulated entity.

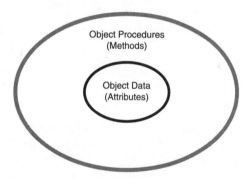

Object Procedures
(Methods)

Object Data
(Attributes)

An object presents itself to the world through its published public methods, which form the interface. Take another look at the object myCar. The published methods of the object myCar are park and drive, which are the functions the object myCar supports. They are called public because the methods are accessible from the outside. They can be invoked by other objects to perform their tasks. The interface of an object is the set of public methods it offers. The opposite of a public method is a private method. Private methods are helper functions for an object. They are only used inside the object methods itself. Private methods cannot be called from the outside. JavaScript has no private methods, so all functions declared in an object are public.

Even the attributes of an object should not be manipulated outside the object itself. In software engineering, this principle is called information hiding. Return to the object myCar, and extend the list of attributes make, model, age, and color with additional ones such as engine and wheels. I'm not particularly interested in the type of engine or what kind of wheels myCar has.

The only thing that is important to me is the fact that my car works all right and can drive. If I have a car mechanic change the car engine, it should not change the working condition of myCar. Moreover, the new engine doesn't interest me. I want only to drive around with myCar.

The abstraction of an object should precede the decisions of its implementation. The source code specifying the inner part of an object should be changeable without interfering with the abstract view. For a better and simpler software design, no part of a complex application should depend on the internal details of any object declared in it.

You can gain a couple of important benefits through encapsulation and information hiding:

- Consider an object a small software component. You could easily use it in many situations and places in a program. Reusing software components is highly supported through encapsulation. Possible reuse is one of the great advantages of object orientation. Rightly used, it could save a lot of time and money in developing software projects.

- Hiding the object's implementation details gives the programmer the opportunity to modify the data representation later without changing the object's representation to the outside world. The same applies to changes inside methods. The object's interface stays the same. The source code of collaborating objects remains as is. This means maintenance efforts are greatly reduced and the architecture of the software system is far more stable than in conventionally made applications.

What is the importance of these theoretical remarks to programming in JavaScript? Most objects used in JavaScript are the built-in data structures created by Netscape. As a result, the software engineers at Netscape gain the advantage of quicker development and better software quality. This is also a benefit to the programmer and user.

JavaScript also offers the possibility to create your own custom-made object types; however, only a few cases will use this feature, I believe. If you need to solve a more complicated task, it is better to use the object-oriented programming language Java instead of JavaScript. (See Chapter 27, "Java from a JavaScripter Perspective.")

NOTE

In JavaScript, you can directly access an object's data variables outside the object itself. This is not prohibited. Please consider that if you do this, you damage the principle of encapsulation. However, because JavaScript solves mostly small tasks, it might be easier to access the object's data directly rather than write your own helper functions to get and set the object's data values from the outside. If a built-in object does not support any get or set methods, the direct way might be your only choice.

Messages

If you want an object to do something for you, you send a message to the object. A message invokes an object's function. Figure 8.10 illustrates message passing between objects.

FIGURE 8.10.
*Graphical view of
object messaging.*

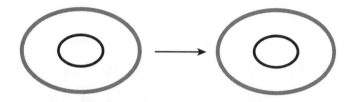

For example, if you need the current time in your application, you create a new object `currTime` of type `date` and set it to the current date and time:

```
var currTime = new Date ();
```

The statement `var` simply creates a new variable in JavaScript. New objects are created with the `new` method of the object type. The `new` method for the object type `date` creates a new object of type `date`. This new object automatically contains the current date and time. Because of the assignment (=) in the previous statement, the variable `currTime` contains an object of type `date` set with the current date and time.

You might want to extract the current time in hours and minutes:

```
var     hours;
var     minutes;

hours    = currTime.getHours ();
minutes  = currTime.getMinutes ();
```

What you do is send the message `getHours` to your object `currTime` to extract the number of hours. Then, you use the message `getMinutes` to get the number of minutes, respectively. In JavaScript, messages are essentially function calls. You know from the documentation of the built-in JavaScript objects that an object of type `date` understands the messages `getHours` and `getMinutes`. This means the object type `date` includes an implementation of the functions `getHours()` and `getMinutes()`.

When creating custom-made objects, you define object methods as well. Inside one method, you might need other objects to accomplish a certain task. For example, in a car dealer application, you have an object `currSale` resembling a car sale with a method `getSaleData()` extracting data about the sale. Inside the function `getSaleData()`, you address an object of type `Car` and another of type `Customer`. Both objects are sent messages to get the necessary information. If you take this concept further, you'll see that an object-oriented software application consists of a world of objects communicating via messages.

Classes

Objects are concrete, existing software entities in a program. For example, the okButton or myWindow or a special data structure such as currTime are all objects. An object is a concrete entity that exists in time and space; a class represents only an abstraction of several similar objects. (See Figure 8.11.)

FIGURE 8.11.

Graphical view of a class.

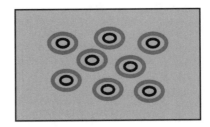

Objects with the same properties and behavior form a class or object type. A class features a construction plan for the objects contained in it. This means a class defines the number, name, and structure of data attributes and methods. Additionally, a class provides the behavior (implementation) of the functions. New objects are created due to the primarily defined construction plan. Every object is a member of a certain class; the object is said to be an instance of this class. Object properties are also called instance variables of a class or an object.

For example, your car, my car, and your neighbor's car are all cars, although they have different makes, ages, and colors. All cars have a make, model name, model year, and color. Moreover, all cars can stand in a parking space or drive. The features and possible functions are the same. The class car describes the data characteristics and methods for cars.

JavaScript is not a class-based, object-oriented language because there is no class statement. However, JavaScript includes a similar concept: an object type. First, the built-in object types include the different GUI objects or data structures such as date, string, or math. New objects are created with the new method of the object type. This is true for all objects. For example, the following statement creates the object currTime as a new instance of the object type date:

```
var currTime = new Date ();
```

In JavaScript, you can define your own object type. For example, if your system should display time values, you might want to implement a new object type clock. A clock object should know the hours and minutes it is set to, so the properties of the clock object are hours and minutes. The methods a clock object should implement are displayTime() and setTime(). The following segment shows the definition of the object type clock:

```
function Clock (hours, minutes)
{
   this.hours        = hours;
   this.minutes      = minutes;
```

```
      this.setTime      = setTime;
      this.displayTime = displayTime;
  }

function setTime (hours, minutes)
{
    this.hours      = hours;
    this.minutes  = minutes;
}

function displayTime ()
{
    var line = this.hours + ":" + this.minutes;
    document.write ("<HR><P>Time of clock:   " + line);
}
```

JavaScript is a kind of instance-based language because there is no class construct. Instance based is an object-oriented term which means that the programming language has objects but no classes. JavaScript is not very well structured in this context. It has no classes, but it does have a concept like an object type. Moreover, new objects are not constructed through existing objects but get created with the statement new. Netscape itself calls JavaScript an instance-based programming language.

I want to point out some practical things here: It seems the function statement in JavaScript serves many purposes. Creating a new object type means defining a function with the name of the object type as the function name. The result is a source code that always looks a little confusing to the reader. The properties of the new object type are declared as parameters of the defining function. This means there is only one constructor for a new class. As the name already points out, a constructor is a method of a class that creates a new object from the class template. A constructor initializes the new object with the given data values in the parameter part of the constructor method. The following code shows a template for declaring a new object type in JavaScript:

```
function ObjectType (instVar1, instVar2, ...)
{
    this.property1 = instVar1;
    this.property2 = instVar2;
    ...
    this.method1 = function1;
    this.method2 = function2;
    ...
}

function1 ( param1, param2, ...)
{
     here goes the implementation
}

function2 ( param1, param2, ...)
{
     here goes the implementation
}
```

The special object this addresses the current object in the object type declaration. The properties and methods of the new object are defined with assignments to this. The initial properties for the new object are given as parameters of the creating function; in the template, they are named instVar1 and instVar2. In the object type definition, only the method names (method1 and method2) are present. The implementation for the methods as JavaScript functions (function1 and function2) is given later.

Declarations of new object types are best placed in the <HEAD> section of the HTML document so that they are read at the beginning of the document-loading process. This ensures that the class declarations are known when the rest of the program is interpreted. You usually put the action tasks in the <BODY> segment of the HTML document.

To give you a better understanding of classes, Listing 8.3 shows a short description of the class in a simple but complete HTML document.

Listing 8.3. clock.htm.

```
<HTML>
<HEAD>
<SCRIPT>
function Clock (hours, minutes)
{
    this.hours           = hours;
    this.minutes       = minutes;
    this.setTime       = setTime;
    this.displayTime = displayTime;
 }

function setTime (hours, minutes)
{
    this.hours      = hours;
    this.minutes  = minutes;
}

function displayTime ()
{
    var line = this.hours + ":" + this.minutes;
    document.write ("<HR><P>Time of clock:   " + line);
}
</SCRIPT>
</HEAD>
<BODY>
<SCRIPT>
var currTime = new Date;
myClock = new Clock (currTime.getHours (), currTime.getMinutes ());
myClock.displayTime ();
</SCRIPT>
</BODY>
</HTML>
```

The new `clock` object `myClock` is created and initialized with the current system time in the `<BODY>` section of the document with the following statement:

```
myClock = new Clock (currTime.getHours (), currTime.getMinutes ());
```

> **NOTE**
>
> Because JavaScript is an instance-based language, you can extend any existing object with new properties and methods at runtime. This adds a new feature to only one particular object and does not affect the other objects of the same object type.

Inheritance

An important feature of the object-oriented model is inheritance. Inheritance means general base classes provide data and methods for other classes called subclasses. (See the graphical view in Figure 8.12.) An object of a subclass possesses all the characteristics of the base class in addition to its own specification. Inheritance builds an object class hierarchy; with single inheritance, the class hierarchy forms a tree. With single inheritance, a subclass can have only one base class (also called a super class) that it inherits from. Consequently, the structure of the class hierarchy looks like a tree with branches and leaves. Single inheritance is the kind of inheritance I discuss here.

FIGURE 8.12.

Graphical view of an inheritance relationship.

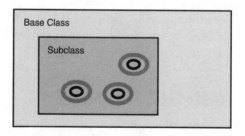

For example, a vehicle can be a bus, car, or motorcycle. A vehicle can park or drive as do other vehicles such as buses, cars, and motorcycles. The class `vehicle` builds the base class, whereas `bus`, `car`, and `motorcycle` are subclasses. A vehicle does not specify the number of wheels in the base class itself because this is a characteristic of the subclasses. Each subclass declares the number of wheels for itself because the number is different in each subclass; buses and cars have four wheels, but a motorcycle has only two.

In another real-world example of modeling clocks, you could define the base class `clock`, which defines properties and behavior common to all clocks. The class `AlarmClock` is a specialization of the class `Clock`. An `AlarmClock` represents a normal clock but extends it with additional features such as an alarm time that should be stored with methods for setting and displaying the alarm time.

Inheritance in general means a generalization/specialization relationship. An object of a subclass automatically possesses (inherits) all the attributes and methods of the base class. Additionally, a subclass specifies its own attributes and methods, extending the definition in the base class. It is possible to declare a base class method in the subclass. In this case, the function of the subclass is used and the base class function is overwritten.

The concept of inheritance is not supported in JavaScript.

Is JavaScript an Object-Oriented Language?

Simply stated, the answer to this question is no. JavaScript is a simple object-based script language. It follows the notion of objects, properties, methods, and encapsulation. It is loosely typed because variables are not declared in conjunction with an object type. For example, you declare the variable currTime with the following statement:

```
var currTime;
```

You provide no variable type (such as int or char) or other object type. You could put any variable or object type in the variable currTime.

Interpretation is always done through dynamic binding at runtime. Dynamic binding means that the types of all the variables and expressions are not known until the program is actually executed.

At present, JavaScript is not an object-oriented language because the class concept is not fully implemented. The language is largely instance based. (See the section "Classes" earlier in this chapter.) Still more significant is the lack of inheritance. Therefore, JavaScript falls into the category of object-based programming languages.

Objects and Dot Notation

In JavaScript, you access the properties and methods of an object through dot notation:

```
objectName.propertyName
objectName.methodName (arguments)
```

The current object is addressed through the special variable this. In the method declaration of an object type (class), you address the object itself with the variable this. The object itself, meaning the current object, is the object you are declaring the method for.

In an object type defining complex numbers, you write a method for adding two complex numbers as follows:

```
// add x + z  giving rz

function add (z)
{
   var a, b, rz;
```

```
      a = this.real + z.getReal (z);
      b = this.img  + z.getImg  (z);
      rz = new Complex (a,b);
      return rz;
}
```

The numbers x and y are then summed with the following statement:

```
x.add(y);
```

In the method add, the term `this.real` addresses the property `real` of the current object—in this case, `x.real`. Similarly, `this.img` addresses the property `img`—that is, `x.img`, which is the imaginary part of x.

Properties

Properties in JavaScript resemble the data attributes of an object. The properties of an object explain the characteristics and identity of the given object. In addition to specific characteristics and identifying values, an object's attribute can also represent the state of the object or a role that an object could play at a given time. State and role are special time-dependent characteristics. A state is a kind of data item that changes over time and generally shows a current value for the object. For example, the object `myCar` can be defined through properties such as `make`, `model`, and `year`. Add to the list another attribute `position`, which always contains the current geographic position of `myCar`. The attribute `position` is a typical example of a state attribute.

When modeling projects, you could define the object type `Project` as follows:

```
function Project (members, leader, currentMilestone, time)
{
   this..members              = members;
   this.leader                 = leader;
   this.currentMilestone     = currentMilestone;
   this.time                   =  time;
 }
```

You would then create the particular software project `myProject` as follows:

```
myProject = new Project (memberGroup, "Claudia", "starting",  currTime);
```

The object `myProject` consists of a group of persons described in the object `memberGroup`. The project leader is `"Claudia"` and the current milestone is `"starting"` because the project just recently began. The variables `memberGroup` and `currTime` contain other objects that are not described here.

Beside the dot notation, you have other ways to access the properties of an object. The following example shows the array notation:

```
objectName ["propertyName"]
```

The next line demonstrates indexing through ordinal numbers:

```
objectName [integerIndex]
```

This technique returns the attribute of number `integerIndex`.

Outside an object itself, you might not want to access an object's attributes directly because it damages the principle of encapsulation. (See the section "Encapsulation" earlier in this chapter.)

Methods

A method denotes a service the class offers to other objects. Generally, methods belong to one of the following four categories:

- Modifier: A method that changes the state of an object. This method changes the value of one or more data attributes of the object. A popular modifier method is a set function that sets the value of one particular object attribute.

- Selector: A method that accesses the data attributes of an object but makes no changes. An important selector is a get function that returns (gets) the value of one particular object attribute.

- Iterator: A method that accesses all the parts of an object, such as all the data attributes, in some defined order. As the name denotes, an iterator method iterates over the data attributes of an object.

- Constructor: A constructor is a method of an object type that creates a new object from the class template. A constructor initializes the new object with the given data values in the parameter part of the constructor method.

In JavaScript, object methods are normal JavaScript functions. You access them through dot notation:

```
objectName.functionName (arguments)
```

Generally, an HTML file includes a `<BODY>` section that creates the special document object in JavaScript. The document object supports the method `write`. With this method, you can dynamically extend the text layout of your HTML page through JavaScript. The following statement prints a horizontal rule and the string `"This is sample text"`:

```
document.write ("<HR><P>This is sample text");
```

When constructing new object types in JavaScript, you use a source code template such as the one presented here:

```
function ObjectType (instVar1, instVar2, ...)
{
    this.property1 = instVar1;
    this.property2 = instVar2;
    ...
    this.method1 = function1;
    this.method2 = function2;
    ...
}

function1 ( param1, param2, ...)
{
    here goes the implementation
}

function2 ( param1, param2, ...)
{
    here goes the implementation
}
```

The special object this addresses the current object in the object type declaration. The properties and methods of the new object are defined with assignments to this. The initial properties for the new object are given as parameters of the creating function; in the template, they are named instVar1 and instVar2. In the object type definition, only the method names (method1 and method2) are present.

The implementation for the object methods is given later in a function declaration following the rules for regular JavaScript functions. The arguments of a function can be strings, numbers, or complete objects. The following segment shows an example of defining a class representing complex numbers:

```
// define complex numbers

function Complex (real, img)
{
    this.real       = real;
    this.img        = img;
    this.getReal    = getReal;
    this.getImg     = getImg;
    this.add        = add;
    this.subtract   = subtract;
    this.multiply   = multiply;
    this.divide     = divide;
}

// get real part
function getReal ()
{
    return this.real;
}
```

8

FUNDAMENTALS OF OBJECT ORIENTATION

```
// get img part
function getImg ()
{
   return this.img;
}

// add x + z  giving rz
function add (z)
{
   var a, b, rz;

   a = this.real + z.getReal (z);
   b = this.img  + z.getImg  (z);
   rz = new Complex (a,b);
   return rz;
}

// methods subtract, multiply and divide not yet implemented
```

The object method add takes one argument of type `Complex`. You can add two complex numbers x and y as follows:

```
var x = new Complex (a,b);
var y = new Complex (c,d);

var z = x.add (y);
```

Inside a function declaration, you can refer to the properties of the current object with the special object this as you see here:

```
a = this.real + z.getReal (z);
```

Events

Often, JavaScript statements create or manipulate graphical user interface elements such as forms or windows. Figure 8.13 shows an example of a simple graphical user interface.

FIGURE 8.13.

Example of a graphical user interface.

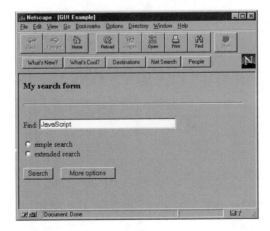

Listing 8.4 builds the GUI shown in Figure 8.12. The source code serves only for generating the form. Other parts are not fully programmed yet and generally produce "Not yet implemented" messages.

Listing 8.4. guiexample.htm.

```html
<HTML>
<HEAD>
<TITLE>
GUI Example
</TITLE>

<SCRIPT LANGUAGE="JavaScript">
function fsearch (aForm)
{
   // search function not yet implemented
   // here: create display of result list
   alert ("Sorry, search function not yet implemented");
}
function foptions (aForm)
{
   // display of options not yet implemented
   alert ("Sorry, no options available");
}
</SCRIPT>
</HEAD>
<BODY>
<FORM>
<H3>
My search form
</H3>
<P>
<HR>
<P>
Find:
<INPUT TYPE="text"    NAME="tfield" SIZE=40>
<P>
<INPUT TYPE="radio">
simple search
<BR>
<INPUT TYPE="radio">
extended search
<BR>
<P>
<INPUT TYPE="button" NAME="bsearch"
  VALUE="Search" onClick="fsearch (this.form)">
  
<INPUT TYPE="button" NAME="boptions"
  VALUE="More options" onClick="foptions (this.form)">
<BR>
</FORM>
</BODY>
</HTML>
```

In the context of a graphical user interface, an event is a result of a user action. It takes place when the application's user does something. For example, when the user clicks a button on the user interface, the event "button clicked" occurs. Other GUI events include clicking a checkbox, selecting a string in a listbox, double-clicking an item, opening or closing a window, and so on.

The best way to control GUIs is through event-driven programming. Events automatically trigger JavaScript functions as a result of user action. JavaScript has a language concept called event handlers. Event handlers are based on HTML tags.

Generally, events are not considered object-oriented features, although some object-oriented programming languages also support events. Most GUI elements such as windows, buttons, text fields, checkboxes, and so on react to certain events. These elements exist in JavaScript as built-in object types. For example, you can create a button in JavaScript to trigger the onClick event when the button is clicked:

```
<SCRIPT>
<FORM>
<INPUT  TYPE="button",  VALUE="press me" onClick="myfunc ()">
</FORM>
</SCRIPT>
```

In this example, the function myfunc is executed when the user clicks the "press me" button. Some built-in objects feature methods that emulate an event. For example, the object type checkbox defines a click () method that emulates the checkbox being clicked. The same applies to the object type button. The event-emulation method does not trigger an event-handler declared elsewhere for the object. If you need the event-handler action, you have to call the event-handler method explicitly.

Because event handlers are only allowed for HTML tags, newly created object types have no event handlers. See the next chapter on events and event handlers in JavaScript for a more detailed description of this subject.

Summary

This chapter is an introduction to object-oriented programming with JavaScript. It discusses the differences between conventional procedural programming and object-oriented program design. The benefits of object-oriented models are a more intuitive program structure, a more stable architecture of the software system, and the support of code reuse.

The central logical building blocks of object-oriented programming are objects. Objects are encapsulated entities of data attributes and object methods. Object attributes specify the characteristics of an object. The methods of an object form the services an object offers to the outside. Objects with analogous structure and behavior belong to the same class. The specification of a class consists of the declaration of a construction plan for all objects contained in the class. The class declaration serves as a template for creating new objects.

The algorithmic concept of object-oriented problem solving follows a divide-and-conquer strategy where several small and distinct objects send themselves messages to trigger the program flow. The concept of inheritance defines a generalization/specialization relationship between classes. Inheritance means general base classes provide data and methods to be used in subclasses. An object of a subclass possesses all the characteristics of the base class in addition to its own specification.

In JavaScript, object attributes are referred to as properties. An object method is called a function. You can access both properties and methods through dot notation:

```
objectName.propertyName
objectName.methodName (arguments)
```

JavaScript cannot be considered an object-oriented language because it lacks important features such as a class construct and the notion of inheritance. Instead, it falls into the category of object-based programming languages. I recommend that you use the built-in JavaScript objects whenever suitable. Don't invent too many objects of your own.

The best way to program graphical user interfaces is with the help of object-oriented techniques and event-driven programming. This chapter contains only a small section about events and object-oriented issues. Events and event-handlers in JavaScript are discussed in more detail in the next chapter.

Handling Events

by Richard Wagner

CHAPTER 9

If you have developed software in the 1990s, chances are that you have worked with event-driven programming languages. Procedural programs of the past dictated what task a user could perform at any given time. However, the graphical, windowed environments of today have a completely different paradigm and require applications to respond to events initiated by users rather than the other way around.

RESOURCE

More information on programming tater tot objects may be found by pointing your Web browser to http://www.potato.com/tatertots/programming.

Given JavaScript's object-based nature (discussed in Chapter 8, "Fundamentals of Object Orientation"), it should come as no surprise that JavaScript is primarily an event-driven language. This chapter discusses JavaScript events and how you can respond to these events to create interactive applications.

Understanding Events and Event Handlers

Much of the code you write in JavaScript will respond to an event performed by either the user or the browser software. This event-driven environment enables you to focus only on the events that impact your application; what the browser performs in between events is its burden, not yours. In addition, you do not need to concern yourself with all events performed by the user—only those to which you care to respond.

Each JavaScript event has a corresponding *event handler* that is charged with the responsibility of automatically responding to the event when it occurs. When you work with an event, you never add code to or modify the event itself, but rather, you manage the event handler to which that event corresponds.

JavaScript Event Handlers

If you have created HTML pages before, you know that each element on a form has a tag and attributes associated with it. For example, you would define a text input in the following way:

```
<input
    type=text
    size=30
    maxlength=30
    name="LastName">
```

JavaScript implements event handlers by embedding them as attributes of HTML tags. For example, suppose you want to perform a method you created each time the value of the text object changes. To do so, assign the method (called checkField()) to the text object's onChange event handler:

```
<input
     type=text
     size=30
     maxlength=256
     name="LastName"
     onChange="checkField(this)">
```

Within the quotes, you can either write in-place JavaScript code or else call a separate function. Although the previous example calls the checkField() method, the following code is also valid:

```
<input
     type=text
     size=30
     maxlength=256
     name="LastName3"
     onChange="if (confirm('Are you certain you wish to change this value?')){
        alert('Changed')}">
```

TIP

If you use in-place code, you can place multiple lines within the event-handler assignment by using a semicolon to separate each JavaScript command. However, use multiple lines of code with caution. It is much easier to work with code separated as a function rather than work within the event handler itself. For example, if the code is located in a central location, it becomes much easier to make changes to it over the life of your application.

JavaScript has nine built-in events to which certain objects can respond. Table 9.1 shows a summary of the events and the objects that can respond to them.

9

HANDLING EVENTS

Table 9.1. Object event handlers.

Object	onClick	onSubmit	onChange	onFocus	onBlur	onLoad	onUnload	onMouseOver	onSelect
button	X								
reset	X								
submit	X								
radio	X								
checkbox	X								
link	X							X	
form		X							
text			X	X	X				X
textarea			X	X	X				X
select			X	X	X				
window						X	X		

> **NOTE**
>
> Not all JavaScript objects can respond to events. The anchor, frame, hidden, navigator, and password objects do not have event handlers.

As you proceed through this chapter, you will examine each of the events individually, paying particular attention to the events for which you will most often want to trap. In doing so, you will take a typical HTML form (shown in Figure 9.1) and add life to it by adding code to its event handlers. The form you will use initially is a sample order form for a fictitious company.

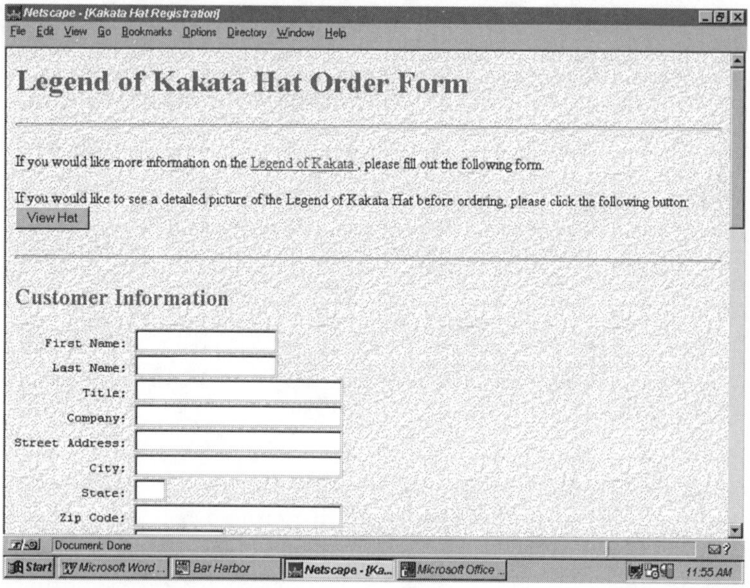

FIGURE 9.1.

A sample HTML form.

Clicking an Object (onClick)

One of the most common uses of JavaScript is enhancing HTML forms to provide a greater degree of interactivity. If that is true, perhaps the single most common event many developers will work with is the click event. The click event is triggered when the user clicks a clickable object. These objects include the following:

- Buttons (button, submit, and reset)
- Checkbox
- Radio
- Link

As is standard for most computer environments, the click event is triggered only after the default mouse button is pressed and released. A user holding the button down without releasing it on the object will not cause the object's click event to be triggered.

When a click event occurs, the onClick event handler for the object that is clicked executes one or more JavaScript commands or calls a custom function. For example, note the View Hat button in Figure 9.1. Suppose you would like to add code that displays a second browser window showing an image of the hat when the button is clicked.

In the HTML source, the button object is defined as follows:

```
<input
    type=button
    name="ViewHat"
    value="View Hat"
    OnClick="displayHat()">
```

In the <HEAD> section of the HTML file, you can then write the displayHat() method that will be called when the button's onClick event handler is triggered:

```
<HEAD>
<SCRIPT LANGUAGE="JavaScript">
<!--

    //onClick event handler
    function displayHat() {
        hatWindow = window.open("http://www.acadians.com/
            javascript/examples/kakata.htm", "ViewHat",
            "toolbar=0,width=200,height=400,resizable=0");
    }
</SCRIPT>
</HEAD>
```

When the user clicks the button, the event handler uses the open() method for the window object to display a window showing the hat image.

The onClick event handler is not just for buttons; you can use it to respond to clicks of checkboxes, radio buttons, and link objects. Because of the nature of these controls, a customized click event for them is much less common. Checkboxes and radio buttons are often used for data entry and evaluated at a later point rather than when a control is clicked. Also, the link object is used primarily as a reference to the location specified in its HREF property, so adding code is often not necessary unless you want to modify its default behavior.

NOTE

For checkboxes, links, radio buttons, and reset and submit buttons, Navigator 3.0 allows you to return a false value from the `onClick` event handler to cancel the triggered action. For example, if you wanted to confirm whether or not to check a checkbox, you could add the following code to its `onClick` event handler:

```
<INPUT TYPE="checkbox" NAME="checkbox1" VALUE="DeluxeRoom"
onClick="return confirm('Deluxe rooms are very expensive. Are you
sure?')">Deluxe Room
```

Because the visual appearance of a Web page is important, you might want to use images rather than buttons to respond to `click` events. Although an image cannot actually respond to any event, you can imitate a `click` event through smart use of a link object. I'll demonstrate this by using an image, rather than the View Hat button, to execute the `displayHat()` method from the previous example. To do so, the link object can be defined as follows:

```
<a
   href="JavaScript:displayHat()">
   <img src="minihat.gif"
      align=bottom
      border=0
      width=89
      height=75></a>
```

Rather than add code to the link's `onClick` event handler, I used `JavaScript:` as the protocol for the HREF property. Using `JavaScript:JavaScriptExpression` as the HREF property tells the browser to execute a JavaScript expression rather than navigate to a defined link.

Submitting a Form (`onSubmit`)

As discussed in Chapter 1, "JavaScript and the World Wide Web," one of the advantages of using JavaScript in HTML forms is that you can perform data validation on the client side rather than pass this task on to an overloaded server. You can perform validation on a field-by-field basis or on a form-wide basis. Depending on the context, you might want to use one or both methods.

For form-wide data validation as well as for other tasks, the `submit` event is your primary concern. This event occurs just before the submission of an HTML form. Adding code to the `onSubmit` event handler of a form object enables you to check the submission and either allow it to proceed or block it and notify the user.

The `submit` event will occur unless a `false` value is returned from the `onSubmit` event handler. Any other value (`true` or otherwise) will cause the submission to occur. For example, suppose you want to display a simple confirmation message to the user of the Kakata Hat order form before processing the submittal. The form is defined in the HTML source as follows:

```
<form action="process.cgi" method="POST" onSubmit="return confirmOrder()">
```

The confirmOrder() method referenced in the form's onSubmit event handler is declared in the <HEAD> section of the file:

```
//onSubmit event handler
function confirmOrder() {
    return confirm('Are you certain you wish to order the Kakata hat?');
}
```

When triggered, the confirmOrder() method displays a Confirm dialog box with buttons labeled OK and Cancel. If the user clicks OK, the dialog box is closed and a true value is returned to the onSubmit event handler. If the user clicks Cancel, false is returned. The return statement in the onSubmit event handler examines the incoming value and determines whether the form should continue to process. The return in the event-handler assignment is essential for the code to work correctly. Assigning onSubmit="confirmOrder()" to the event handler causes the form to process regardless of the returned value from the dialog box.

The onSubmit event handler is similar to an onClick event handler of a submit object. Both of these are events you can use to trap a form before it's processed. As shown in Figure 9.2, the submit object's onClick event handler is triggered first, followed by the form's onSubmit.

FIGURE 9.2.

Event sequencing on a form submittal.

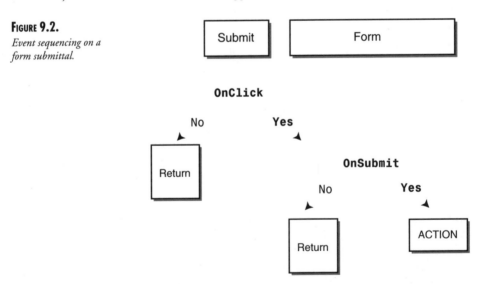

The onSubmit event handler is an ideal location to place form-level data validation before it is sent to a server or other process. See Chapter 16, "Enhancing Forms with JavaScript," for an example of using onSubmit for validating data.

Resetting a Form (onReset)

You might have to trigger an event when a form is submitted, as well as when it is reset. The onReset event handler triggers JavaScript code when a reset event occurs. Just as with onSubmit, onReset is an event handler of a form object.

To illustrate, look again at the Kakata hat order form used in the last section. Adding a new event handler to the form object's definition, the code would look like this:

```
<form action="process.cgi" method="POST"
onSubmit="return confirmOrder()"
onReset="return confirmReset()">
```

The confirmReset() method referenced in the form's onReset event handler is declared in the <HEAD> section of the file:

```
//onReset event handler
function confirmReset() {
    return confirm('Are you certain you wish to clear the order form?');
}
```

NOTE

The onReset event handler is new to Netscape Navigator 3.0.

Modifying Data (onChange)

As mentioned with the submit event, when your JavaScript applications deal with data, you'll typically want to preprocess the data entered by the user to avoid validation problems when the data is sent to a server. Although submit is designed for form-wide verification, the change event is typically the most important event for field-level validation. The change event occurs when the value of a field object changes and the field itself loses focus. Here's a list of the objects able to respond to change events:

- text
- textarea
- select

CAUTION

The onChange event handler does not work in all platform versions of Netscape 2.0. Use this event with caution.

9

HANDLING EVENTS

You use the onChange event handler to execute JavaScript code or call a function to handle the event. Suppose you want to add a basic validity-checking routine to the Kakata Hat data entry form. Specifically, you want to ensure that the State field is always uppercase. The text object is defined as follows:

```
<input
    type=text
    size=3
    maxlength=2
    name="State"
    onChange="convertToUppercase(this)">
```

The convertToUppercase() method converts the value of the State field to uppercase using the string method toUpperCase():

```
function convertToUppercase(fieldObject) {
  fieldObject.value = fieldObject.value.toUpperCase()
}
```

Receiving Focus (onFocus)

The focus event is triggered when a field object receives focus—when a user tabs into the object, clicks it with the mouse, or when you call an object's focus() method (discussed later in this chapter). Only one object can receive focus at a given time. Similar to the change event, the focus event can be handled by the following objects:

- text
- textarea
- select

> **NOTE**
>
> Netscape Navigator 3.0 expands the scope of onFocus to include it as an event handler for window, frame, and frameset objects. For each of these objects, the onFocus event handler specifies the action that should execute when the window receives focus.
>
> The onFocus event handler should be placed in the <BODY> tag of the window, frame, or frameset.

You can add an onFocus event handler to these objects to trigger an action. For an example, enhance the standard behavior of the text objects on the form. When you move onto a text object, an insertion point appears by default. However, a standard in many environments (such as Windows) is that if the field already has a value, the contents are selected when the object receives focus. To code this behavior, you need to add an onFocus event handler for each of the text objects as well as the textarea object:

```
<pre>    First Name: <input
                            type=text
                            size=20
                            maxlength=20
                            name="FirstName"
                            onFocus="selectContents(this)">
        Last Name: <input
                            type=text
                            size=20
                            maxlength=20
                            name="LastName"
                            onFocus="selectContents(this)">
            Title: <input
                            type=text
                            size=30
                            maxlength=256
                            name="Title"
                            onFocus="selectContents(this)">
          Company: <input
                            type=text
                            size=30
                            maxlength=256
                            name="Company"
                            onFocus="selectContents(this)">
   Street Address: <input
                            type=text
                            size=30
                            maxlength=256
                            name="StreetAddr"
                            onFocus="selectContents(this)">
             City: <input
                            type=text
                            size=30
                            maxlength=256
                            name="City"
                            onFocus="selectContents(this)">
            State: <input
                            type=text
                            size=3
                            maxlength=2
                            name="State"
                            onFocus="selectContents(this)"
                            onChange="convertToUppercase(this)">
         Zip Code: <input
                            type=text
                            size=30
                            maxlength=10
                            name="ZipCode"
                            onFocus="selectContents(this)">
        Telephone: <input
                            type=text
                            size=12
                            maxlength=12
                            name="Phone"
                            onFocus="selectContents(this)">
```

```
    FAX: <input
                    type=text
                    size=12
                    maxlength=12
                    name="FAX"
                    onFocus="selectContents(this)">
  E-mail: <input
                    type=text
                    size=30
                    maxlength=256
                    name="Email"
                    onFocus="selectContents(this)">
    URL: <input
                    type=text
                    size=30
                    maxlength=256
                    name="URL"
                    onFocus="selectContents(this)"></pre>
```

```
<textarea
      name="worthyBox"
      rows=3
      cols=49
      onFocus="selectContents(this)">
</textarea>
```

Although you could write separate event handlers for each of these fields, it would be unwise to do so unless the processes were completely different. Instead, the `selectContents()` method takes advantage of the `this` keyword to reference the object making the call. The following function is then used as a global function for all the objects:

```
function selectContents(fieldObject) {
    fieldObject.select();
}
```

When any of the `text` or `textarea` objects calls the `selectContents()` method, the method uses the `fieldObject` parameter as a reference to the calling object. The `select()` method then selects the input area of the specified object.

Losing Focus (onBlur)

The `blur` event (the inverse of the `focus` event) is triggered when an object loses focus. The following data entry objects can respond to `blur` events:

- text
- textarea
- select

> **NOTE**
>
> As with the onFocus event handler, Netscape Navigator 3.0 expands the scope of onBlur to include it as an event handler for window, frame, and frameset objects. For each of these objects, the onBlur event handler specifies the action that should execute when the window loses focus.
>
> The onBlur event handler should be placed in the <BODY> tag of the window, frame, or frameset.

For example, suppose on the data entry form that you want to ensure that the Email text object is not left blank by the user. You could add this check to the onBlur event handler of the object. Because this impacts a single field of the form, you can just add the JavaScript code to the text object definition:

```
<input
    type=text
    size=30
    maxlength=256
    name="Email"
    onFocus="selectContents(this)" onBlur="if (this.value == ''){
        alert('You must enter something.');this.focus();}">
```

If the user tries to tab out of the object without entering text, an alert dialog box notifies the user not to leave the field blank. The next command returns focus to the Email text object. If that command were not used, the cursor would have moved onto the next tab stop.

As you have probably noticed, onChange and onBlur are similar. When should you use one over the other? onChange is best for checking or analyzing the content of an object and has the advantage of not being called if the user does not change the value. On the other hand, for required fields, you might want to use onBlur.

The sequencing of the onChange, onBlur, and onFocus event handlers is important to understand before you use them. As Figure 9.3 illustrates, onFocus occurs when you enter the field. As you leave, onChange is called, followed by the onBlur event handler, and finally by the onFocus handler of the next input object. Keep in mind that the code you might add, for example, to the onChange event handler could have an impact on an onBlur event handler of the same object. As a general rule, you should use these three events conservatively.

Selecting Text (onSelect)

The next JavaScript event is the select event, which occurs when the user selects text from a text or textarea object. The object's onSelect event handler either executes JavaScript code or else calls a predefined function. However, at the time of this writing, the select event does not work as designed in all Netscape Navigator and Microsoft Internet Explorer versions.

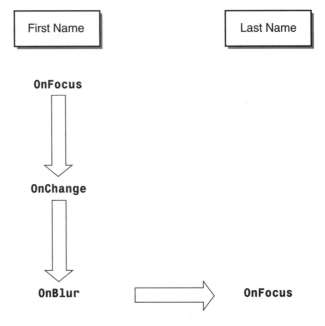

FIGURE 9.3.
*Event sequencing from
one text object to
another text object.*

CAUTION

As with onChange, the onSelect event handler does not work in all platform versions of Netscape 2.0.

Regardless of whether it works, the select event's scope is rather limited for most purposes, and most developers will have little occasion to use it.

Moving the Mouse Pointer (onMouseOver)

If you are an experienced Web user, you have come to expect that the act of moving your mouse over link text displays the link's target destination (typically a URL address). However, no matter how much a power user might want to see the URL address, beginning users usually want something less esoteric. This is particularly the case in intranet environments where the destination URL is probably not that meaningful. Trapping the mouseOver event enables you to change the default text in the status bar.

NOTE

The onMouseOver event handler is supported by the area object in Netscape Navigator 3.0.

The mouseOver event takes place when a user moves the mouse cursor over a link object. The link object's onMouseOver event handler can then change the default behavior of the browser. If you want to set the window's status and defaultstatus properties, you need to return a value of true to the event handler.

For example, suppose you want to display the following text in the status bar when a mouseOver event occurs for the Kakata Hat link:

Click here to go to get the whole story about the Legend of Kakata.

To do this, add the onMouseOver event handler to the link tag:

```
<a href="http://www.acadians.com/javascript/kakata/kakata.htm"
   name="linker"
   onMouseOver="return updateStatusBar()"
   >Legend of Kakata</a>
```

The updateStatusBar() method is defined as follows:

```
// onMouseOver event handler
function updateStatusBar() {
   window.status = 'Click here to go to get the whole story about the
      Legend of Kakata';
   return true
}
</textarea>   window.status = 'Click here to go to get the whole story about the
      Legend of Kakata';
   return true
```

Each of the examples discussed in this chapter is contained in the Register.htm file. Listing 9.1 lists the complete source code for the examples.

Listing 9.1. Source code for Register.htm.

```
<html>
<head>
<title>Kakata Hat Registration</title>

<SCRIPT LANGUAGE="JavaScript">
<!--

    var noticeWindow

    //onClick event handler
    function displayHat() {
       hatWindow = window.open("http:/../kakata/viewhat.htm",
       "ViewHat" ,"toolbar=0,width=200,height=400,resizable=0");
    }

    //onSubmit event handler
    function confirmOrder() {
      return confirm('Are you certain you wish to order the Kakata hat?');
    }
```

continues

Listing 9.1. continued

```
        //onChange event handler
        function convertToUppercase(fieldObject) {
            fieldObject.value = fieldObject.value.toUpperCase();
        }

        // onFocus event handler
        function selectContents(fieldObject) {
            fieldObject.select();
        }

        // onMouseOver event handler
        function updateStatusBar() {
          window.status = 'Click here to go to get the whole story
              about the Legend of Kakata';
          return true
        }

        // onSelect event handler
        function accessText() {
            alert('Success');
        }

// -->
</SCRIPT>
</head>
<body background="lt_rock.gif">
<h1><font color="#008000">Legend of Kakata Hat Order Form</font></h1>
<hr>

<p>If you would like more information on the <a
      href="http://www.acadians.com/javascript/kakata/kakata.htm"
      name="linker"
      onMouseOver="return updateStatusBar()">Legend of Kakata </a>, please
      fill out the following form. </p>

<form method="POST">
<p>If you would like to see a detailed picture of the Legend of Kakata
Hat before ordering, please click the following button: <input
type=button name="ViewHat" value="View Hat" onClick=displayHat()></p>
</form>

<hr>
<form
      action="JavaScript:alert('order')"
      method="POST"
      name="MainForm"
      onSubmit="return confirmOrder()">
<h2><font color="#008000">Customer Information</font></h2>
<pre>    First Name: <input
                          type=text
                          size=20
                          maxlength=20
                          name="FirstName"
                          onFocus="selectContents(this)">
      Last Name: <input
                          type=text
                          size=20
                          maxlength=20
```

```
                          name="LastName"
                          onFocus="selectContents(this)">
          Title: <input
                          type=text
                          size=30
                          maxlength=30
                          name="Title"
                          onFocus="selectContents(this)">
        Company: <input
                          type=text
                          size=30
                          maxlength=30
                          name="Company"
                          onFocus="selectContents(this)">
 Street Address: <input
                          type=text
                          size=30
                          maxlength=30
                          name="StreetAddr"
                          onFocus="selectContents(this)">
           City: <input
                          type=text
                          size=30
                          maxlength=30
                          name="City"
                          onFocus="selectContents(this)">
          State: <input
                          type=text
                          size=3
                          maxlength=2
                          name="State"
                          onFocus="selectContents(this)"
                          onChange="convertToUppercase(this)">
       Zip Code: <input
                          type=text
                          size=30
                          maxlength=10
                          name="ZipCode"
                          onFocus="selectContents(this)">
      Telephone: <input
                          type=text
                          size=12
                          maxlength=12
                          name="Phone"
                          onFocus="selectContents(this)">
            FAX: <input
                          type=text
                          size=12
                          maxlength=12
                          name="FAX"
                          onFocus="selectContents(this)">
          Email: <input
                          size=30
                          maxlength=50
                          name="Email"
                          onFocus="selectContents(this)">
```

9

HANDLING EVENTS

continues

Listing 9.1. continued

```
            URL: <input
                          type=text
                          size=30
                          maxlength=100
                          name="URL"
                          onFocus="selectContents(this)"></pre>
<hr>

<p><strong>Are you &quot;Kakata worthy&quot;? Please use the space below to
enter a thorough reason for your order.</strong></p>
<blockquote>
<p><textarea
       name="worthyBox"
        rows=3
        cols=49
        onFocus="selectContents(this)">
</textarea></blockquote></p>

<h2><font color="#008000">Form Submission</font></h2>
<p><em>Please click the Order button to order your free Legend of Kakata hat.
You will receive email confirmation of your order in 24 hours.</em></p>
<p><input
       type=submit
       value="Order"
       onClick="confirmOrder('Submit object')">
<input
       type=reset
       value="Clear Form"
       onClick="alert('Clearing!')"></p>
<p> </p>
<p>
</form>

<hr>
<h5>Developed by Richard Wagner for <em>JavaScript Unleashed</em>.<br>
</h5>

<a
    href="JavaScript:displayHat()">
    <img src="ball.gif" align=bottom border=0 width=16 height=16>
</a>

</body>
</html>
```

> **NOTE**
>
> Netscape Navigator 3.0 adds another mouse-related event handler, called onMouseOut.
> This event handler is triggered when the mouse pointer leaves an area or link object.

Loading a Document (onLoad)

The initial opening of a window or frameset can be an important time to perform a JavaScript process. The load event enables you to harness this by adding an onLoad event handler to a single-frame window's <BODY> tag or a multiframe window's <FRAMESET> tag. The load event is executed when the browser finishes loading a window or all frames within a frameset (in other words, when the Netscape sky stops). The window object is the only object that can handle this event.

To illustrate, suppose you want to ensure that all intranet users in your company are using the correct version of Netscape Navigator. You could evaluate the browser being used in the onLoad event handler and then notify the user if his or her software version is not correct. In the <BODY> tag for the document, you would add the onLoad event handler:

```
<body onLoad="checkBrowser()">
```

Next, the checkBrowser() method is defined in the document's <HEAD> tag as follows:

```
//onLoad event handler
function checkBrowser() {
  ((navigator.appName == 'Netscape') &&
   (navigator.appVersion == '3.0b3 (Win95; I)')) {
noticeWindow = window.open("", "NoticeWindow",
      "toolbar=0,width=300,height=100,resizable=0");
    noticeWindow.document.write("<HEAD><TITLE>Upgrade Notice</TITLE></HEAD>");
    noticeWindow.document.write("<CENTER><BIG><B>Your Web Browser needs
     to be updated. Please see your supervisor before noon.
     </B></BIG></CENTER>")}
}
```

When the document is loaded, the JavaScript method is executed. Figure 9.4 shows the Upgrade Notice window displayed for versions that do not pass the test.

> **NOTE**
>
> In Netscape Navigator 3.0, the image object also has an onLoad event handler. This event is triggered when an image is *displayed* by the browser. Note that this event does not occur during the loading of an image to a client, but during the display of that image.

Exiting a Document (onUnload)

The unload event, which is the counterpart to the load event, is triggered just before the user exits a document. As with onLoad, you can add an onUnload event handler to a single-frame window's <BODY> tag or a multiframe window's <FRAMESET> tag. If you have a frameset and multiple onUnload event handlers, the <FRAMESET> event handler always happens last.

FIGURE 9.4.

The Upgrade Notice window is opened during the onLoad *event handler.*

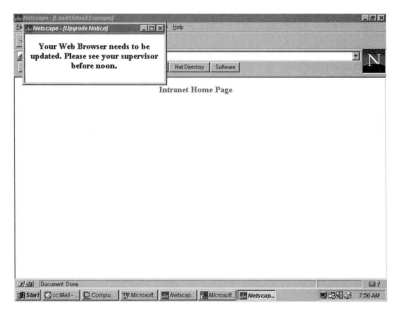

One example of how you can use the onUnload event handler is cleaning up the browser environment before continuing on to the next page. For instance, suppose you want to close the View Hat window when leaving the Kakata Order page. You can add onUnload to the <BODY> tag as follows:

```
<body onLoad="checkBrowser()" onUnload="clean()">
```

Next, you can define the clean() method:

```
// onUnload event handler
function clean() {
    noticeWindow.close();
}
```

noticeWindow is a global variable declared in the <HEAD> tag of the document and refers to the Upgrade Notice window displayed in the onLoad event handler. If open, the Upgrade Notice window is closed when the user exits the current page.

Listing 9.2 provides the complete source code for the onLoad and onUnload examples.

Listing 9.2. The source code for LoadUnload.htm.

```
<html>
<head>
<title>Load/Unload Example</title>

<SCRIPT LANGUAGE="JavaScript">
<!--
```

```
    var noticeWindow

//onLoad event handler
function checkBrowser() {
  ((navigator.appName == 'Netscape') &&
   (navigator.appVersion == '3.0b3 (Win95; I)')) {
noticeWindow = window.open("", "NoticeWindow",
      "toolbar=0,width=300,height=100,resizable=0");
    noticeWindow.document.write("<HEAD><TITLE>Upgrade Notice</TITLE></HEAD>");
    noticeWindow.document.write("<CENTER><BIG><B>Your Web Browser needs
     to be updated. Please see your supervisor before noon.
     </B></BIG></CENTER>")}
}

// onUnload event handler
   function clean() {
     noticeWindow.close();
   }

// -->
</SCRIPT>
</head>
<body onLoad="checkBrowser()" onUnload="clean()">
<font color="#008000">
<CENTER><BIG><B>Intranet Home Page</B></BIG></CENTER>
</body>
</html>
```

Handling Errors (onError)

The window and image objects have an onError event handler that enables you to trap for errors occurring during the loading of a document or image. The type of error that will be trapped will be either a JavaScript syntax or runtime error, not a browser error (such as an unresponsive server message). See Chapter 22 for full coverage of trapping errors with onError.

> **NOTE**
>
> The onError event handler is new to Netscape Navigator 3.0.

Aborting an Image Load (onAbort)

Depending on their size, loading of HTML images can be a time-intensive process. As a result, users may become impatient and stop the image load before it has been completed. For example, a user may abort the loading process by clicking a link to another page or the browser's Stop button.

> **NOTE**
>
> The image object and onAbort event handler are new to Netscape Navigator 3.0.

However, having the user work with a partially downloaded HTML file may not be what you would like to occur. The onAbort event handler enables you to react to this aborting of an image load and trigger a JavaScript function as a response. For example, suppose you wanted to alert your user that the entire HTML document has not been downloaded. You would add the following event handler to your <IMG> tag:

```
<IMG NAME="mapworld" SRC="global.gif" onAbort="alert('You have not downloaded the
entire document.')">
```

Triggering Events in Code

So far, this chapter has discussed responding to events generated by either the user (such as a click event) or the system (such as an onUnload event). In most cases, you will design your code to respond to these events as they occur. However, as a JavaScript developer, you do not have to rely on external forces to cause an event to happen. In fact, you can trigger some of these events to occur within your code.

For example, you can simulate a click event for a button object by calling its click() method. Although this is valid for a button object, a link object—which has an onClick event handler—does not have a click() method.

However, if you have assigned an onClick event handler to this button, it may or may not be called, depending on the browser you are using. With Netscape 2.*x* and Navigator 3.0, the event handler is not triggered for the button. In contrast, with Microsoft Internet Explorer 3.0, the event handler is triggered just as if the user clicked the button. Because of this inconsistency, it is highly recommended that you call the JavaScript method that the event handler is calling directly rather than trigger the event itself.

Table 9.2 lists the JavaScript events and the methods that can trigger them.

Table 9.2. Events that can be triggered by a JavaScript method.

Object	click	submit	focus	blur	select
button	click()				
reset	click()				
submit	click()				
radio	click()				

Object	click	submit	focus	blur	select
checkbox	click()				
link					
form		submit()			
text			focus()	blur()	select()
textarea			focus()	blur()	select()
select			focus()	blur()	
window					

Timer Events

Many event-driven programming environments use a timer event, which is an event triggered every time a given time interval elapses. Although JavaScript offers no timer event, you can make wise use of the window object's setTimeout() and clearTimeout() methods to simulate one.

You usually use the setTimeout() method to evaluate an expression after a specific amount of time. This evaluation is a one-time process that is not repeated an infinite number of times. However, because you can make recursive function calls in JavaScript, you can use recursion to create a *de facto* timer event.

Suppose you want to perform a specific task each morning at 8:30 A.M. You could have a timer evaluate the time of day; when that time is reached, the process is spawned. The dailyTask() method is defined as follows:

```
function dailyTask() {
  var tdy = new Date();
  if ((tdy.getHours() == 8) && (tdy.getMinutes() == 30)) {
    performProcess()}
  timerID = setTimeout("dailyTask()",10000)
}
```

The method creates a date object to get the current time using getHours() and getMinutes(). If these evaluate to 8:30 A.M., the performProcess() method is called. The next line—the heart of the timer process—uses the setTimeout() method to call the dailyTask() method recursively every 10,000 milliseconds.

9

HANDLING EVENTS

> **CAUTION**
>
> This example demonstrates the use of the timer, but you would want to be careful implementing such a solution in the real world. Implementing a continuous looping process like that in a browser could lead to resource constraints over time.

To trigger this `timer` initially when the document is loaded, you can add an `onLoad` event handler to the `<BODY>` tag of the HTML document:

```
<BODY onLoad="dailyTask()">
```

Listing 9.3 provides the entire source code listing for this example.

Listing 9.3. Source code for `Timer.htm`.

```
<HEAD>
<SCRIPT LANGUAGE="JavaScript">
<!--
    function performProcess() {
        alert('Daily');
    }

    function dailyTask() {
        var tdy = new Date();
        if ((tdy.getHours() == 8) && (tdy.getMinutes() == 30)) {
            performProcess()}
            timerID = setTimeout("dailyTask()",10000)
        }
//-->
</SCRIPT>
</HEAD>

<BODY onLoad="dailyTask()">
</BODY>
```

Summary

Given JavaScript's event-driven nature, a solid understanding of the nine built-in events is key to maximizing the power of JavaScript. This chapter discussed events and their associated event handlers. I focused on the events that are most useful for you and to which you should pay attention, as well as provided specific examples of how you can use them. Having this foundation in place will assist you over the next few chapters as you look in depth at JavaScript's built-in events.

JavaScript Object Model

by Richard Wagner

CHAPTER 10

I discussed JavaScript objects and events they can respond to, but I have not yet discussed the context in which they operate. This chapter takes a top-level view of JavaScript's object model. First, I look at exactly what this object model is—and just as important—what it is not. Next, I provide a brief description of all the objects in the model.

JavaScript Object Hierarchy

Although custom objects are important, the majority of uses for JavaScript focuses on the objects built into the language itself. Undoubtedly, the heart and soul of client-side JavaScript is its built-in object model. Much of the object model consists of HTML elements that are "objectified," allowing you to work with HTML tags in an object-oriented manner. If you come from an HTML background, begin to think of these elements not just as tags, but as objects.

JavaScript objects are truly objects in the sense that they have properties and methods and can respond to events. However, as you learned in Chapter 8, "Fundamentals of Object Orientation," JavaScript does not have the same true OOP capabilities of inheritance. When you look at the JavaScript object model, it is critical that you look at it in that context. Rather than a class hierarchy that is inheritance-based, the JavaScript object model, shown in Figure 10.1, is a containership hierarchy. If you are experienced in object-oriented programming languages, such as Java, C++, or Delphi, that might be the biggest adjustment you need to make in your thinking when developing with JavaScript.

FIGURE 10.1.

JavaScript built-in object model hierarchy.

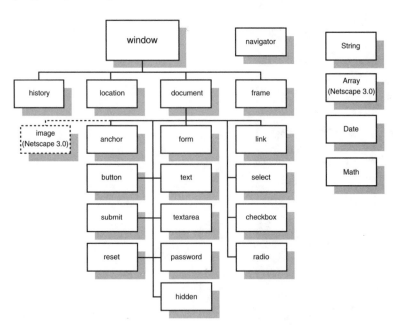

Containership is the principle of one object containing another object. As you look again at the model in Figure 10.1, you can see that the relationship between the form object and the radio object is not one of ancestor-descendant (or class-subclass), but one of container-contained. Said differently, there is no blood line in between these objects because one did not descend from the other. As a result, no object can inherit properties and methods from another object, nor can you subclass an object in the hierarchy.

Containership in JavaScript

Containership is an important term to understand as you develop JavaScript scripts and applications—not only in terms of how one object relates to another, but in practical terms of how you reference an object. If you recall in the discussion on dot notation in Chapter 8, when you reference an object's properties or methods, you use a dot to denote ownership. For example, in the following command, the `write` method is said to be owned by the document object:

```
document.write("<H1>A cow jumping over the moon.</H1>")
```

However, you can extend this to not only include properties and methods of an object, but also include objects contained by that object. If you wanted to return the name of a button object to a variable, you would use the following command:

```
buttonName = document.formMain.okButton.name
```

`document` is the default name of the document object, and `formMain` is the name of the form object, which contains the `okButton` button.

An important fact to understand when you work with objects is knowing when you need to reference a container object and when you do not. For example, the window object is essentially the highest level object you work with in your code. Most of the references you make are to objects within its containership. You could also write the previous `document.write` example as the following line:

```
window.document.write("<H1>A cow jumping over the moon.</H1>")
```

Although you can ignore the window reference in most cases, it is necessary when you deal with multiple windows or frames. For instance, Listing 10.1 creates a window object in the `showStats()` function and then closes it in the `closeWindow()` function.

Listing 10.1. WindowWorks.htm.

```
<HTML>
<HEAD>
<SCRIPT LANGUAGE = "JavaScript">
<!--
    var windowObject

    function showStats() {
```

10

JAVASCRIPT
OBJECT MODEL

continues

Listing 10.1. continued

```
        windowObject = window.open("", "ViewStats", "toolbar=0,width=100,
            height=50,resizable=0")
         windowObject.document.write("<H2>We outperformed all goals\
            this month. Congratulations!</H2>")
    }


    function closeWindow() {
        windowObject.close()
    }
// -->
</SCRIPT>

<BODY OnUnload="closeWindow()">
<H1>Click the following button to view the monthly stats.</H1>
<FORM>
<INPUT
    Type="button"
    Value="Show Stats"
    OnClick="showStats()"
    </INPUT>
</FORM>
</BODY>
```

The window object is the only one that provides any leniency in object references. For example, if you want to reference a form within an HTML page, you must add its parent object (document) for JavaScript to understand which object you are referencing. If you want to reference the first form within the document object and retrieve the number of elements in it, you use the following command:

```
num = document.forms[0].length
```

Even if the form had a name attribute, you still need to add the parent reference:

```
num = document.queryForm.length
```

Overview of JavaScript Objects

When you begin to look closely at the JavaScript object hierarchy, you can see that each object falls into one of two categories: Navigator objects and built-in language objects. This section looks at these sets and introduces you to each of the objects within them.

Navigator Objects

Most of the functionality built into JavaScript centers around what you can do with HTML pages. The first set of objects—I'll call them Navigator objects—generally have a correlation to the browser and HTML tags within it. Figure 10.2 shows HTML source for a Web page and highlights the JavaScript objects in it.

FIGURE 10.2.

Many JavaScript objects match up to HTML tags.

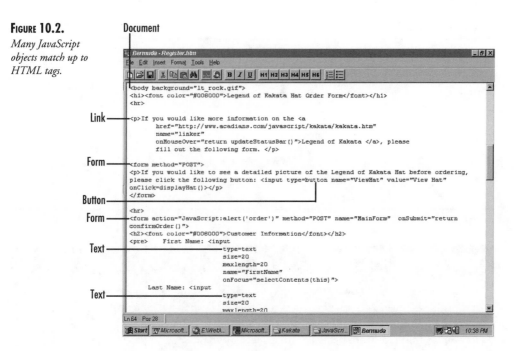

As you can see, most JavaScript objects are object representations of HTML tags. Table 10.1 lists the Navigator objects and the corresponding HTML tags for these objects.

Table 10.1. JavaScript built-in objects and HTML tags.

JavaScript Object	Corresponding HTML Tag
window	N/A
frame	`<FRAME>`
history	N/A
location	N/A
document	`<BODY>`
form	`<FORM>`
button	`<INPUT TYPE="button">`
checkbox	`<INPUT TYPE="checkbox">`
hidden	`<INPUT TYPE="hidden">`
password	`<INPUT TYPE="password">`
radio	`<INPUT TYPE="radio">`
reset	`<INPUT TYPE="reset">`

10

JAVASCRIPT OBJECT MODEL

continues

Table 10.1. continued

JavaScript Object	Corresponding HTML Tag
select	`<SELECT>`
submit	`<INPUT TYPE="submit">`
text	`<INPUT TYPE="text">`
textarea	`<TEXTAREA>`
link	`<A HREF="">`
anchor	`<A NAME="">`
navigator	N/A

NOTE

If you have developed applications with a fourth generation language (4GL) such as Visual Basic or PowerBuilder—or another visual tool such as Delphi—the names of some of the objects, such as text and reset, might be counterintuitive. Table 10.2 lists some of the JavaScript objects that are better known in the 4GL world under a different name.

Table 10.2. Common 4GL vernacular for JavaScript objects.

JavaScript Object	Common 4GL Term
window	window/form
frame	panel
document	page
button	button
checkbox	checkbox
radio	radio button
reset	button
select	drop-down list box
	selection list
submit	button
text	edit field
textarea	memo field
navigator	application

As you explore each of these objects, you'll look at the various ways they are presented to users and developers: user interface view, HTML tag, and JavaScript object code.

Window Object

A Web browser—whether it's Netscape Navigator, Microsoft Internet Explorer, or whatever— is presented to the user in a window. Everything a user does with the browser is performed within that window. Moreover, every screen element is also contained inside that window. The window object provides a direct corollary to this metaphor. It is considered the highest-level object of all objects in the JavaScript object hierarchy and contains all other Navigator objects (except for the Navigator object itself). (See Figure 10.3.) Just as you can have multiple windows open in your browser, you can work with multiple window objects at once in your code.

Figure 10.3.

A window object contains all other elements—both visually, as well as in your code.

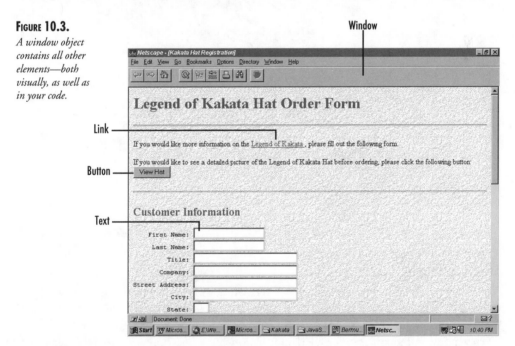

The window object has no HTML tag equivalent, although you do define its event handlers (onLoad, onUnload) in the <BODY> tag. Within JavaScript code, you work with a window object as shown in the following example. Suppose you want to add text to the status bar of the window. The code follows:

```
window.status = 'Welcome to the Acadia home page.';
```

Frame Object

As you learn in this book, frames are especially important objects to use to enhance the presentation of your Web application. The frame object represents a frame within a frameset. (See Figure 10.4.) In a multiframe presentation, your window object is the page that contains the <FRAMESET> definition, whereas the other pages are considered frames in that context. The relationship between the frame and window object is a special one that is explored in depth in Chapter 11, "Navigator Objects."

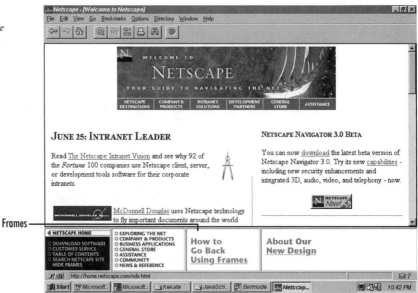

Frames

Location Object

The Web is all about content presentation. Every window object is designed to display content to the user, but that content must come from somewhere. The origin of the page is thus contained in the location object. The location object is used to store all URL information for a given window. Although users see URL information in the Location box on-screen (see Figure 10.5), you can work with that same information with the location object.

If you want to retrieve the protocol portion of the current URL and evaluate it, you use the following:

```
function evalProtocol(){
    curProtocol = window.location.protocol
    if (curProtocol == "http:") {
      alert("The document comes from the Web.") }
    else {
      if (curProtocol == "file:") {
        alert("This document comes from your hard drive.")}
```

```
      else {
         alert("This document comes from somewhere else.")}
      }
}
```

FIGURE 10.5.

Users work with the Location box, and you can work with the location object.

Location —

History Object

A long-time feature in browser software is the capability to track where you have surfed within a given session. This feature has come to be known as a history list, and it's available in both the Navigator and Internet Explorer's Go menus. (See Figure 10.6.) The history object is the JavaScript equivalent to this list. You can work with it as a user might, moving forward or backward in a list to navigate where a user has been.

FIGURE 10.6.

The history list is accessible through JavaScript.

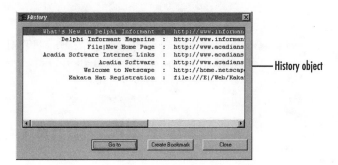

History object

10

JAVASCRIPT OBJECT MODEL

Suppose you wanted to go back two pages in your history list when the user clicked a button. The event handler follows:

```
function goBackTwoPages() {
    window.history.go(-2)
}
```

Document Object

Although the window object is the top-level object in the hierarchy, the document object is arguably the most important. The document object is responsible for all the actual content displayed on a given page. (See Figure 10.7.) You can work with the document object to display dynamic HTML pages. Also contained within the document are all the typical user interface (UI) elements of a Web application.

FIGURE 10.7.

The document object is focused on content.

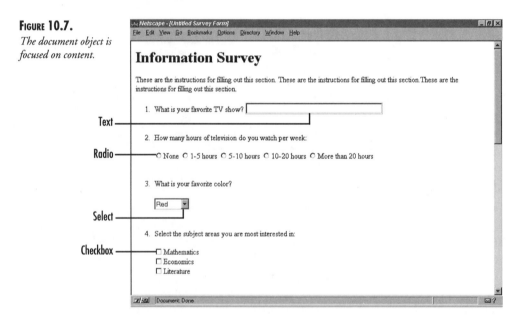

A common use of the document object is generating HTML pages through JavaScript. You can do this with the write() or writeln() methods. For example, the following code displays the HTML text specified as the method parameter:

```
<HTML>
<HEAD>
<SCRIPT LANGUAGE = "JavaScript">
   document.write("<h1>Text created by JavaScript</h1>");
</SCRIPT>
</HEAD>
```

Form Object

Forget for a moment such add-ins as Java applets or ActiveX controls that can interact with the user. If you think only in terms of the HTML world, the only means of interactivity with the user is through a form and its elements. (See Figure 10.8.) Forms give life to static pages by providing an interface users can interact with through controls. You can only place a button, text, or other UI object within the confines of a form. The form object is your means of interacting with this HTML element in your scripts.

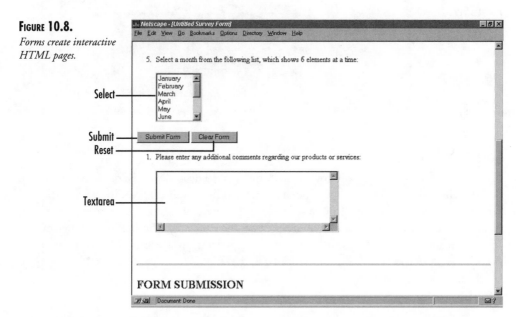

Button Objects (Button, Submit, and Reset)

Unless you jumped into Web development from a character-based environment, you are undoubtedly familiar with push buttons. JavaScript has three button objects: button, submit, and reset. Each of these are the object representation of an HTML tag. The button object is a generic button that you need to add code to for it to be useful. The submit button is a specialized version of a button whose default action is to submit the form of which it is a part. Similarly, the reset button is hard coded to reset the values of all controls within a form. Yes, you could use a button object to serve the same role as the submit object (by calling the form's submit() method). These three look identical (see Figure 10.9), and you have control over what they are labeled.

FIGURE 10.9.

UI objects contained in a form.

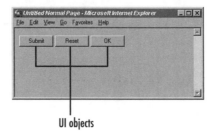

UI objects

Select Object

Another common control in windowed environments is a drop-down list or selection list box, both of which allow a user to select from a predefined list of values. The difference is that the user can select only one value from a drop-down list, whereas he can select multiple choices from a selection list. The select object encapsulates the behavior of both of these UI elements. In other words, it can appear as a drop-down list (default) or a selection list (if its multiple property is set to true), as shown in Figure 10.8.

Checkbox Object

Another industry-wide standard UI control is the checkbox. This element allows the user to specify a yes/no or true/false value by clicking the checkbox control. (Refer to Figure 10.7.)

Radio Object

Radio buttons are a set of mutually exclusive controls, such that if one radio button is selected, all other buttons in the set become unselected. The radio object provides this element in an HTML form. (Refer to Figure 10.7.) You define a set of radio buttons by giving them the same name property.

Text Object

A principle element for any data entry application is a field in which the user can input data. The text object serves as this data-capturing device as the objectified representation of the text input HTML tag. (Refer to Figure 10.7.)

Textarea Object

Related to the text object is the textarea object, which allows you to enter multiple lines of text as opposed to a single line. (Refer to Figure 10.8.) If you have worked with other programming environments before, it might be helpful to think of the textarea object as a memo field.

Password Object

If JavaScript supported inheritance, the password object would be a subclass of the text object. The only difference between the two is that all the characters entered into the password object are displayed as asterisks.

Hidden Object

Another field object, the hidden object is like a text object with a visible property set to false. It is used to store values to pass on to a server process. The hidden object comes from the pre-JavaScript days of HTML in which there were no such things as variables, arrays, or objects to store values. Although you might still want to employ them for transferring data among pages of a multiple-page data entry application, much of the data storage value of hidden objects is no longer needed with JavaScript.

Link Object

Lest you forget, the whole reason the Web was developed back in 1989 was the simple hypertext link of an HTML page. Perhaps overlooked in the latest Web application craze, the link still remains the very heart of Web technology. The link object lets you work with links in JavaScript code. Because a link is simply referencing another HTML page or other destination, it is very similar to the location object (which contains the same information for the current HTML page).

NOTE

In Netscape 3.0, images defined with the IMG tag are now accessible through JavaScript. Images in a document are treated as an array of images and are accessible only by specifying an element in the array. Because you cannot work with images outside this document array structure, they are perhaps better considered properties of a document rather than discreet object entities.

10

**JAVASCRIPT
OBJECT MODEL**

Anchor Object

The anchor object is a piece of text or an image in the HTML page that can be the target of a hypertext link. In practical terms, you use the anchor object very little with JavaScript, making it perhaps the least important of all built-in objects.

Image Object

New to Netscape 3.0, the image object is an encapsulation of an HTML image. Perhaps the most effective use of this object type is to cache images you want to display. You can construct an image object in your code and download the image data from the server before it is needed for display by the browser. When the image is requested, you can pull the image from cache rather than from the server.

Area Object

A second object new to Netscape 3.0 is the area object. You can use it to define an area of an image as an image map. An area's HREF reference is loaded in a target window when it is clicked by the user.

Navigator Object

Boldly named by the developers of JavaScript (Netscape), the navigator object is an object representing the browser software in use. Using this object, you can retrieve information about the name and version of the browser in use. Both Netscape Navigator and Microsoft Internet Explorer support the navigator object.

Built-In Language Objects

The second set of objects never appear visually, but you work with them within your JavaScript code. You can call them built-in language objects because they are simply constructs of the JavaScript language. Anyone who has worked with any programming language before has worked with the following types of objects:

■ The string object represents a value you assign to a variable of an object property. JavaScript treats both assigned variables and string literals as string objects. For example, both the variable mystring and the literal "Banana bread" are considered string objects:

```
function showFavoriteFood()
{
    var myString = "Angel food cake";
    myWindow = window.open()
    myWindow.document.write("<H1>Favorite Foods</H1>");
    myWindow.document.write("<H2>" + myString + " and " + "Banana
      bread" + "</H2>");
}
```

NOTE

The string object was enhanced in Netscape 3.0 such that you can reference a string object property or method using standard dot notation:

```
"I am President".bold()
```

- The array object is an object representation of the traditional programming construct. An array is an ordered set of data elements, and every index number in an array contains a value. You can have as many indexes in the array as you want.

  Arrays are powerful and your JavaScript scripts can use them in a variety of ways. The following code segment shows a simple example, the result of which is shown in Figure 10.10:

  ```
  <HTML>
  <HEAD>
  <SCRIPT LANGUAGE = "JavaScript">

       theJs = new Array(3)
       theJs[1] = "Jordan"
       theJs[2] = "Jared"
       theJs[3] = "Justin"

       document.write("<H1>The three Js are:</H1>")

       document.write("<OL>")
       for (var i = 1; i < 4; i++) {
           document.write("<LI>" + theJs[i])
       }
       document.write("</OL>")
  </SCRIPT>
  </HEAD>
  </HTML>
  ```

NOTE

The array object is new to Netscape 3.0. Although you could work with arrays in Netscape 2.x, you can now use the new operator to create true array objects.

- The math object is used for standard mathematical calculations. Rather than using generic math functions in JavaScript, these functions are implemented as methods of the math object. Suppose you wanted to evaluate two numbers that the user entered. Listing 10.2 provides an example of how you could use the math object's max() method to do this.

Figure 10.10.

Using an array object.

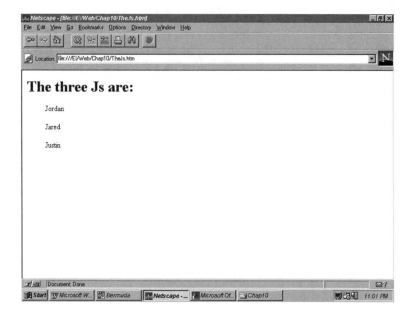

Listing 10.2. Wizard.htm.

```html
<html>
<head>
<title>Wizard</title>
<SCRIPT LANGUAGE="JavaScript">

    function calculateValues() {
      num1 = parseFloat(document.forms[0].Number1.value)
      num2 = parseFloat(document.forms[0].Number2.value)
      result = Math.max(num1, num2)
      alert('The wizard says ' + result + ' is the greatest value');
      }

</SCRIPT>
</head>
<body>
<h1>Stump the Wizard</font></h1>
<p>Without connecting to a backend server or using a Java applet,
the Browser Wizard will tell you which number is greater...</p>
<form method="POST">
<pre>First Number:  <input type=text size=5 maxlength=5 name="Number1"></pre>
<pre>Second Number: <input type=text size=5 maxlength=5 name="Number2"></pre>
<p><input
    type=button
    name="WizButton"
    value="Submit"
    onClick="calculateValues()"></p>
</form>
</body>
</html>
```

■ On first take, the fact that JavaScript has no "date" data type seems like a limitation. JavaScript largely makes up for this by providing a date object. The date object allows you to work with both date and time values by providing a host of methods, such as getMonth(), setDay(), and getTimezoneOffset(), which is used to work with time zones. One example of how to use the date object is making an on-screen clock. Listing 10.3 shows the code, and Figure 10.11 shows the result on-screen.

Listing 10.3. Clock.htm.

```
<HTML>
<HEAD>
<SCRIPT LANGUAGE="JavaScript">
<!--
    function dailyTask() {
      var tod = new Date()
      tod.getTime()
      document.TimeForm.TimeOfDay.value = tod.toString()
      timerID = setTimeout("dailyTask()",1000)
    }
//-->
</SCRIPT>
</HEAD>

<BODY onLoad="dailyTask()">
<form method="POST" name="TimeForm">
Current time:   <input type=text size=50 maxlength=50 name="TimeOfDay">
</form>
</BODY>
</HTML>
```

Figure 10.11.

On-screen clock.

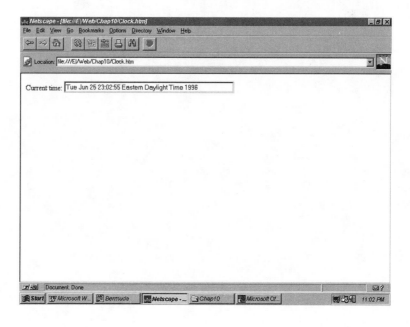

Summary

JavaScript's navigator and built-in language objects serve as the fundamental tools by which you can construct scripts. This chapter took a high-level view of the JavaScript object hierarchy and each of the JavaScript objects. The next three chapters, building upon the information in this chapter, explore the JavaScript objects in complete detail.

Navigator Objects

by Richard Wagner

IN THIS CHAPTER

CHAPTER 11

The Navigator objects are the highest level objects in the JavaScript object hierarchy. These objects do not deal with the nuts and bolts of HTML; instead, they deal primarily with browser issues, such as opening a new browser window, traversing the history list, or obtaining the hostname from the current URL.

This chapter looks at the major Navigator objects in JavaScript. I start by looking at the highest-level object in the object hierarchy—the window—and then look at the frame, location, and history objects. I close the chapter by looking at the application-level navigator object.

Window Object

As discussed in Chapter 10, "JavaScript Object Model," the window object is the top-level object in the JavaScript object hierarchy. Unlike other objects that may or may not be present, the window object is always there, whether it's in a single or multiframe display. However, the window object is unusual in that you can often simply ignore it. There are two reasons for this.

First, if you are working within a single-frame environment, you can ignore explicit referencing of the window object. JavaScript infers the reference to the current window. For example, the following two statements are equivalent and produce the same results:

```
myTitle = window.document.title
```

```
myTitle = document.title
```

Second, because of the structure of the JavaScript language, some system-level methods, such as displaying message boxes or setting a timer, are assigned to the window object. However, you do not need to reference the window itself when calling these methods; the reference to the window is implicit.

Opening and Closing Windows

You can use JavaScript to open and close browser windows. Although the act of opening a window is similar to creating a new window object, you do not use the new constructor. Instead, you use the following syntax:

```
windowVar = window.open(URL, windowName, [, windowAttributes])
```

The parameters for the open() method are

- ■ *URL*—URL for the target window.
- ■ *windowName*—Name of the window object.
- ■ *windowAttributes*—A list of display attributes for the browser window.

If successful, the open() method returns a handle to a window object. If open() fails, it returns a null value.

Specifying Window Content

The URL parameter specifies what content appears in the new window. If you specify a value, the browser attempts to locate and display the specified document:

```
newWindow = window.open("http://www.acadians.com", "AcadiaPage", "")
```

Alternatively, you can display a blank page by specifying an empty string ("") as the URL parameter. Use this technique if you want to create an HTML page dynamically using JavaScript:

```
newWindow = window.open("", "DynamicPage", "")
newWindow.document.write("<H1>Document created using JavaScript.</H1>")
newWindow.document.close()
```

See Chapter 12, "Document Objects," for complete details on using the document object's write() method to create dynamic HTML.

Specifying Window Attributes

The windowAttributes parameter is important as you display windows because it lets you customize the look of the window you are opening. The windowAttributes parameter is optional; not including it gives you a window identical to the current one with respect to attributes. Table 11.1 lists the possible attributes that you can specify.

Table 11.1. open() method's window display attributes.

Attribute	Description
width	Width of window in pixels
height	Height of window in pixels
toolbar	Show/hide browser toolbar
menubar	Show/hide browser menu bar
scrollbars	Show/hide browser horizontal and vertical scrollbars
resizable	Allow/disallow resizing of browser window
status	Show/hide browser status bar
location	Show/hide URL location box
directories	Show/hide secondary toolbar (Netscape)
copyhistory	Copy current window's Go history for new window

The width and height attributes specify the dimensions of the window in pixels. The remaining attributes are set by using Boolean values: True values are either 1, yes, or the attribute alone; false values are either 0, no, or more simply, leaving it out altogether. For example, if you want to display the new window with only a toolbar and menu bar, you use the following line:

```
newWindow = window.open("", "myWindow", "toolbar=1,menubar=1")
```

The following syntaxes are also valid:

```
newWindow = window.open("", "myWindow", "toolbar=yes,menubar=yes")

newWindow = window.open("", "myWindow", "toolbar,menubar")
```

As you can see, you can simply leave out those attributes that are not specified. They are assumed to have false values.

Closing Windows

To close a window, you can use the window object's `close()` method. If you are closing the current window, your method call is simply `window.close()`. Unlike other window object methods, such as `alert()` or `setTimer()`, the `close()` method must always accompany an object reference. If you use `close()` by itself, you could close the current document rather than the window, depending on the context of the method call. The reason is that the document object has a `close()` method, too.

The form in Figure 11.1 demonstrates the various aspects of opening and closing windows. By filling out the form, you can specify the options of how you want the new window to look.

FIGURE 11.1.

Window Open sample form.

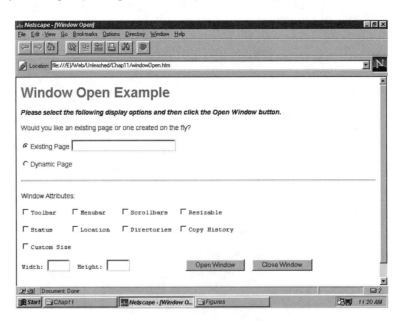

The first section allows you to specify the URL parameter—to use an existing URL or create a page on the fly. The second section lets you specify each of the window attributes available. By default, all are unchecked. You can check all the ones you want to display. By checking the Custom Size box, you can specify the dimensions of the new window.

By clicking the Open Window button, you can see the new window that is created (as shown in Figure 11.2).

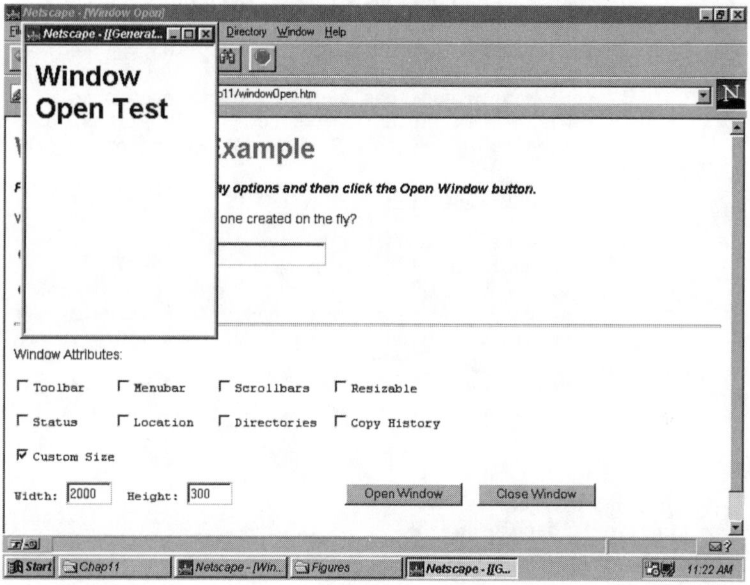

FIGURE 11.2.

The new window is displayed.

Listing 11.1 provides the source code for this example.

Listing 11.1. OpenWindow.htm.

```html
<html>
<head>
<title>Window Open</title>
<SCRIPT LANGUAGE="JavaScript">
<!--
    var newWindow

    // Open Window based on user defined attributes
    function openWindow() {

        // Build the windowAttributes parameter list
        var winAtts = ""
        if (document.winOptions.toolbarOption.checked) {
            winAtts += "toolbar=1," }
        if (document.winOptions.menubarOption.checked) {
            winAtts += "menubar=1," }
        if (document.winOptions.scrollbarsOption.checked) {
            winAtts += "scrollbars=1," }
        if (document.winOptions.resizableOption.checked) {
            winAtts += "resizable=1," }
        if (document.winOptions.statusOption.checked) {
            winAtts += "status=1," }
```

continues

Listing 11.1. continued

```
            if (document.winOptions.locationOption.checked) {
                winAtts += "location=1," }
            if (document.winOptions.directoriesOption.checked) {
                winAtts += "directories=1," }
            if (document.winOptions.copyHistoryOption.checked) {
                winAtts += "copyhistory=1," }
            if (document.winOptions.customSizeOption.checked) {
                winAtts += "height=" + document.winOptions.heightBox.value + ","
                winAtts += "width=" + document.winOptions.widthBox.value + ","
            }
            winAtts = winAtts.substring(0, winAtts.length-2)

            // Determine URL and show window
            if (document.winOptions.pageType[1].checked) {
                var urlVar = ""
                urlVar = document.winOptions.urlBox.value
                newWindow = window.open(urlVar,"newWindow",winAtts) }
            else {
                newWindow = window.open("","newWindow",winAtts)
                newWindow.document.write("<H1>Window Open Test</H1><p>")
            }
        }

    // Close Window
    function closeWindow() {
        newWindow.close()
    }
// -->
</SCRIPT>
</head>

<body background="../lt_rock.gif">
<h1><font color="#008040">Window Open Example</font></h1>
<p><i><b>Please select the following display options and then click
the Open Window button. </i></B></p>
<form name="winOptions" method="POST">
<p>Would you like an existing page or one created on the fly?</p>
<input
    type=radio
    checked
    name="pageType"
    value="existing">Existing Page
    <input
        type=text
        size=30
        maxlength=256
        name="urlBox"></p>
    <input
        type=radio
        name="pageType"
        value="dynamic">Dynamic Page</p>
<hr>
<p>Window Attributes:</p>
<pre><input
    type=checkbox
    name="toolbarOption"
    value="ON"
    >Toolbar    <input
```

```
        type=checkbox
        name="menubarOption"
        value="ON">Menubar    <input
        type=checkbox
        name="scrollbarsOption"
        value="ON">Scrollbars   <input
        type=checkbox
        name="resizableOption"
        value="ON">Resizable</pre>
<pre><input
        type=checkbox
        name="statusOption"
        value="ON">Status      <input
        type=checkbox
        name="locationOption"
        value="ON">Location    <input
        type=checkbox name="directoriesOption"
        value="ON">Directories  <input
        type=checkbox name="copyHistoryOption"
        value="ON">Copy History</pre>
<pre><input
        type=checkbox
        name="customSizeOption"
        value="ON">Custom Size</pre>
<pre>Width: <input
        type=text
        size=5
        maxlength=5
        name="widthBox">  Height: <input
        type=text
        size=5
        maxlength=5
        name="heightBox">              <input
        type="button"
        name="OpenButton"
        value="Open Window"
        onClick="openWindow()">  <input
        type="button"
        name="CloseButton"
        value="Close Window"
        onClick="closeWindow()"></pre>
</form>
<p> </p>
</body>
</html>
```

Displaying Message Boxes

Dialog boxes are typically an important part of an application environment. If you have used Windows for any time at all, you know that dialog boxes are a given in this and other graphical user interfaces. JavaScript also gives you the capability to display standard dialog boxes to either notify a user or receive information before proceeding. However, because of the non-modal nature of the Web, you are discouraged from doing so. You can usually communicate with the user in some other fashion rather than resort to dialog boxes.

TIP

Modal dialog boxes are common in Windows applications. If you come from a Windows 4GL background, be sure to adjust your thinking about their use.

The JavaScript language itself not so subtly enforces this notion by adding a prefix to the messages you display. For alert messages, "JavaScript Alert" appears before the message you specify. For confirm dialog boxes, it's "JavaScript Confirm"; in prompt dialog boxes, you see "JavaScript Prompt." One reason for this is that the user can better determine the source of the dialog box that is displayed.

NOTE

Other than providing the message itself, you cannot customize the look of JavaScript message boxes. The title and icons are always the same.

Simple Notification

You use the window object's `alert()` method to display information to the user. The alert dialog box displays a message to the user with a single OK button to close the box. It is modal, so the user must close the dialog box before continuing in the browser (even in multiframe documents). No value is returned when the dialog box is closed. Its syntax follows:

`[window.]alert(message)`

You can display information about the current window in an alert message with the code shown in Listing 11.2.

Listing 11.2. `DisplayWindowInfo.htm`.

```
<HTML>
<HEAD NAME = "WindowPane">
<SCRIPT LANGUAGE = "JavaScript">

    function displayWindowInfo() {
        var winInfo = ""
        winInfo = "Number of frames: " + window.length + "\r"
        winInfo += "Window object name: " + window.window + "\r"
        winInfo += "Window parent name: " + window.parent + "\r"
        winInfo += "URL: " + window.location + "\r"
        alert(winInfo)
    }

</SCRIPT>
</HEAD>
```

```
<BODY>
<FORM>
<INPUT
      Type="button"
      Value="Display Window Information"
      OnClick="displayWindowInfo()"
</INPUT>
</FORM>
</BODY>
```

Figure 11.3 shows the alert dialog box that is displayed when the user clicks the button.

FIGURE 11.3.
Alert dialog box.

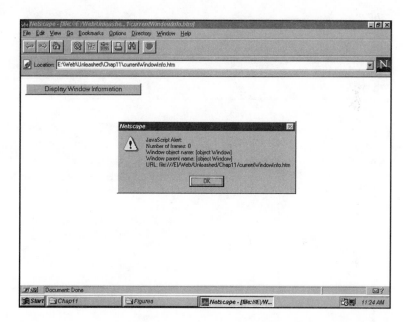

Although it's typically a string, the `message` parameter of the `alert()` method is not required to be. Because JavaScript is not a strongly typed language, you can display other data type information without converting the data to a string. You can even use an object as a parameter, as shown in Listing 11.3. Figure 11.4 shows the result.

Listing 11.3. DisplayWindowInfo.htm.

```
<HTML>
<HEAD>
<SCRIPT LANGUAGE = "JavaScript">

    function Application(Title, ProgramName, Path, Vendor) {
        this.Title = Title
        this.ProgramName = ProgramName
        this.Path = Path
```

continues

Listing 11.3. continued

```
        this.Vendor = Vendor
    }

    function displayApp() {
        alert(Application)
    }

</SCRIPT>
</HEAD>
<BODY>
<H1></H1>
<FORM>
<INPUT
    Type="button"
    Value="Display Object Definition"
    OnClick="displayApp()"
</INPUT>
</FORM>
</BODY>
```

FIGURE 11.4.

*Object displayed in an
Alert dialog box.*

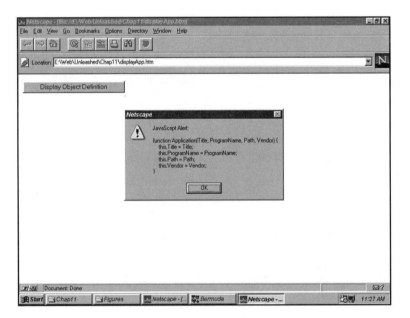

Yes/No Confirmation

In addition to simply displaying information in a dialog box, you can also ask a question using the window object's confirm() method. The confirm dialog box features OK and Cancel buttons, each returning a value. OK returns true, and Cancel returns false. As the method's name implies, you typically use a confirm dialog box to confirm an action the user is about to take. Its syntax follows:

```
returnValue = [window.]confirm(message)
```

A common use of the confirm dialog box is to ask the user to confirm a form submission or send an e-mail message. Listing 11.4 shows how you can use confirm() to return a value back to the form's onSubmit event handler. If the user clicks OK, the form is e-mailed to the specified address. If the Cancel button is clicked, the submit event is canceled.

Listing 11.4. JavaScriptChronicles.htm.

```
<html>
<head>
<title>Untitled Normal Page</title>
<SCRIPT LANGUAGE="JavaScript">

    function confirmAction() {

      return confirm("Do you really want this subscription?
➥     The magazine is not really that good.")
    }

</SCRIPT>
</head>

<body>
<h2><em>JavaScript Chronicles -- Free Subscription Form</em></h2>
<form
    action="mailto:subscribe@jschronicles.com"
    method="POST"
    name="SubscribeForm"
    onSubmit="return confirmAction()">
<ol>
<li>What other magazines do you currently subscribe to?
<pre><input type=checkbox name="C1-SKU01" value="SKU01">PC Week
<input type=checkbox name="C1-SKU04" value="SKU04">DBMS
<input type=checkbox name="C1-SKU07" value="SKU07">Wired
<input type=checkbox name="C1-SKU10" value="SKU10">Yahoo
<input type=checkbox name="C1-SKU02" value="SKU02">InfoWorld
<input type=checkbox name="C1-SKU05" value="SKU05">Databased Advisor
<input type=checkbox name="C1-SKU08" value="SKU08">Web Publisher
<input type=checkbox name="C1-SKU11" value="SKU11">Internet Advisor
<input type=checkbox name="C1-SKU03" value="SKU03">PC Magazine
<input type=checkbox name="C1-SKU06" value="SKU06">Delphi Informant
<input type=checkbox name="C1-SKU09" value="C1-SKU09">Web Informant
<input type=checkbox name="C1-SKU12" value="SKU12">JavaWorld
</pre>

</li>
<li>Please enter the reason you would like to subscribe to
<em>JavaScript Chronicles:</em><br>
<br>
<textarea
    name="Comments"
    rows=6
    cols=46>
    </textarea></li>
</ol>
```

continues

Listing 11.3. continued

```
<p>
<input
    type=submit
    name="Submit"
    value="Submit">

</form>
</body>
</html>
```

Figure 11.5 shows the confirm message box that is displayed when the user clicks the Submit button.

FIGURE 11.5.

Confirm dialog box returns user's response.

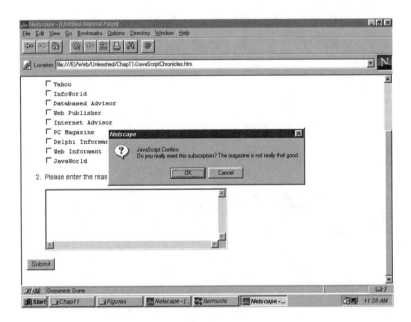

User Input

A third message box that you can use for obtaining user input is invoked with the prompt() method of the window object. Use the prompt dialog box when you want to obtain a value from a user. This dialog box features a message, an edit box for user input, and OK and Cancel buttons. The prompt() method has the following syntax:

```
returnValue = [window.]prompt(message, defaultReply)
```

As you can see, in addition to specifying the message of the dialog box, you need to specify a *defaultReply* parameter. This value becomes the default text inserted in the edit box of the message box. You must specify this parameter, even if you have no default value.

NOTE

Be sure to always use a default reply when displaying a prompt dialog box. If you do not add this parameter, JavaScript places <Undefined> in the edit box, which can be confusing for users. If you have no default value, use an empty string (" ") for the parameter.

If the user clicks OK, the prompt() method returns the string value entered by the user. If nothing is entered in the edit box, an empty string (" ") is returned. However, if the user clicks Cancel, a null value is returned.

CAUTION

Do not assume the user will always click OK in the prompt dialog box. Every time you use the prompt() method, you should first ensure that a non-null value is returned before proceeding to evaluate it. Otherwise, if the user clicks Cancel, you will be working with a string value of "null" rather than what the user actually entered.

Listing 11.5 shows one example of how you can use the prompt message box. The user is asked to enter text in the box. (See Figure 11.6.) This text is then used in a new window. (See Figure 11.7.)

FIGURE 11.6.

Prompt message box.

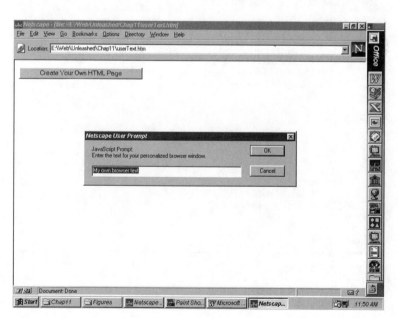

FIGURE 11.7.
New window displays
content provided by
the user.

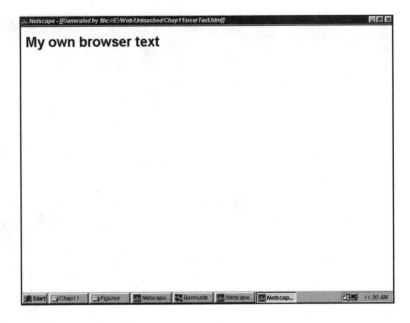

Listing 11.5. UserText.htm.

```html
<HTML>
<HEAD>
<SCRIPT LANGUAGE = "JavaScript">

    function showBox() {
          userText = prompt("Enter the text for your " +
            personalized browser window.","My own browser text")
        if (userText != null) {
            userWindow = window.open("", "userTextWindow", "toolbar=0")
            userWindow.document.write("<h1>" + userText + "</h1>") }
    }

</SCRIPT>

<BODY>
<FORM>
<INPUT
    Type="button"
    Value="Create Your Own HTML Page"
    OnClick="showBox()"
</INPUT>
</FORM>
</BODY>
```

The return value is always a string. If you want to treat it as another value, you must convert it first. For example, if you want to calculate a total price based on a user-defined interest rate, you could get that value using the prompt() method. (See Figure 11.8.) Next, you could convert the value into a float using parseFloat() before calculating. Listing 11.6 shows the code.

FIGURE 11.8.

*Retrieve input from
user.*

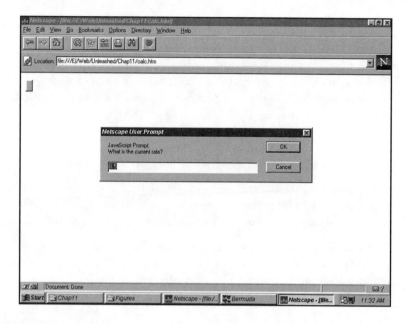

Listing 11.6. Calc.htm.

```
<HTML>
<HEAD>
<SCRIPT LANGUAGE = "JavaScript">

     function getPercentageRate() {
        percent = prompt("What is the current rate?", "8.5")
        if (percent != null) {
          totalPrice = parseFloat(percent) * 20000
          alert(totalPrice) }
     }

</SCRIPT>
<BODY>
<FORM>
<INPUT
     Type="button"
     Value="Calculate Total Price"
     OnClick="getPercentageRate()"
</INPUT>
</FORM>
</BODY>
```

Referencing Windows

When working with single and multiple frames in your JavaScript application, you probably
need to use additional ways to reference windows. JavaScript provides four references to windows. Each of the references are implemented as properties of the window object.

window and self

Chapter 10 discussed using `window` to reference the current window. However, what was not said at the time is that the window object also contains a property called `window` that can be used as a self-referencing tool. In addition, the `self` property of the window object is another means of referring to the current or active window. For example, the following two code lines are functionally the same:

```
window.defaultStatus = "Welcome to the Goat Farm Home Page"

self.defaultStatus = "Welcome to the Goat Farm Home Page"
```

Because both `window` and `self` are synonyms to the current window, you might find it curious that both are included in the JavaScript language. As shown in the previous example, the rationale is simply flexibility; you can use `window` or `self` as you want.

However, as useful as `window` and `self` can be, it can easily become confusing to think about the logic behind it all. After all, an object's property that is used as an equivalent term for the object itself is rather unusual. Consequently, you might find it helpful to think of `window` or `self` as "reserved words" for the window object rather than its properties.

Because `window` and `self` are properties of the window object, you cannot use both `window` and `self` in the same context. For example, the following code does not work as desired:

```
window.self.document.write("<h1>Test.</h1>")
```

Finally, in multiframe environments, `window` and `self` always refer to the window in which the JavaScript code is executed.

> **NOTE**
>
> In some object-oriented or object-based languages, `self` might refer to the active object, no matter what type it is. In JavaScript, `self` only refers to the active window or frame object—nothing else.

parent

As you learn later in this chapter, frames are the same as window objects within a frameset. Within this multiframe setting, you need to distinguish between the various frames displayed in the browser. The `parent` property of a window object helps you do that by referencing its parent—the window containing the `<FRAMESET>` definition. For example, if you want to retrieve some information about the current window's parent, you use the following example in Listing 11.7.

Listing 11.7. childWindow.htm.

```html
<html>
<head>
<title>Child Window</title>
</head>
<SCRIPT LANGUAGE="JavaScript">
<!--
    function getParentInfo() {
        myParentTitle = parent.document.title
        alert("My daddy's name is " + myParentTitle)
    }
// -->
</SCRIPT>
<form>
<input
    type="button"
    value="Get Info"
    onClick="getParentInfo()">
</form>
</body>
</html>
```

Not only can you retrieve property values, but you can also access the parent's methods. For example, Listing 11.8 shows the HTML source for a parent window in a frameset with a showInfo() method defined with no means of implementation in it. Listing 11.9 shows how the child window accesses this method. When the user clicks the childButton button object, its onClick event handler calls runDadMethod() using the this keyword as its parameter. The runDadMethod() in turn calls the parent object's showInfo() method, passing the current object's name as the parameter. Figure 11.9 shows the result.

Listing 11.8. parentWindow.htm.

```html
<html>
<head>
<title>Parent Window Title</title>
<SCRIPT LANGUAGE="JavaScript">

    function showInfo(objectName) {
        alert(objectName)
    }

</SCRIPT>
</head>
<Frameset Cols="35%,65%">
<Frame Name = "FRAME1" SRC="childWindow.htm">
<Frame Name = "FRAME2" >
</Frameset>
</html>
```

> **TIP**
>
> To define a blank frame, simply leave off the SRC attribute in the <FRAME> definition.

Listing 11.9. anotherChildWindow.htm.

```html
<html>
<head>
<title>Child Window</title>
</head>
<SCRIPT LANGUAGE="JavaScript">
<!--
    function runDadMethod(curObject) {
        parent.showInfo(curObject.name)
    }

// -->
</SCRIPT>
<form>
<input
    type="button"
    name="childButton"
    value="Run Dad's Method"
    onClick="runDadMethod(this)">
</form>
</body>
</html>
```

FIGURE 11.9.

Calling a method of a parent.

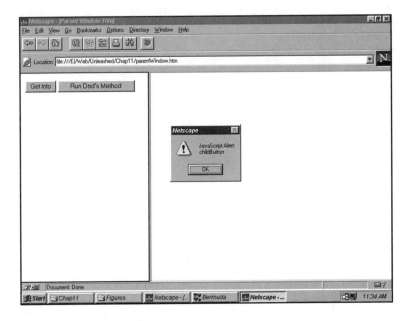

parent is important not only for accessing a child window's parent window, but also for referencing another object in one of its sibling windows. As shown in Figure 11.10, any communication between child frames must go through their parent.

FIGURE 11.10.

Using the parent property to reference siblings.

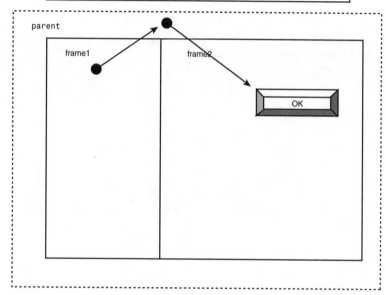

In this example, frame1 wants to reference the value of the OK button in frame2. Using the `parent` property, it could do that with the following code:

```
buttonLabel = parent.frame2.document.form[0].okButton.value
```

The parent is often the top-most window within a multiframe window environment, but not necessarily so. You can have nested levels of framesets, as you will see in the following discussion on the top property. Therefore, the parent property refers to the current window's immediate parent. If you wanted to access the parent's parent (the "grandparent" window), you could use the following:

```
myGranddadTitle = parent.parent.document.title
```

top

Similar in function to the parent property, the window object's top property allows you to reference the top-most window within a frameset or set of framesets. If you are working with a single frameset, the top and parent properties refer to the same window. However, if you have nested levels of framesets, the top refers to the highest level window, whereas the parent may or may not refer to that same window.

TIP

The top and parent windows can be excellent locations for storing global methods.

This difference is best illustrated through an example. Suppose you have two framesets. The first frameset divides the window horizontally using 80 percent, 20 percent (as shown in Figure 11.11). Divided into four quadrants, the second frameset (shown in Figure 11.12) is intended for the lower 20 percent of the top-level frameset.

FIGURE 11.11.
Top-level frameset.

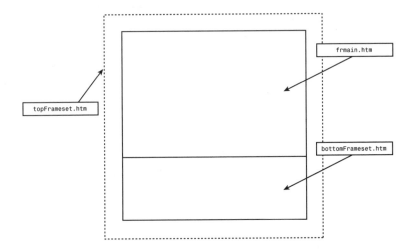

FIGURE 11.12.
Lower-level frameset.

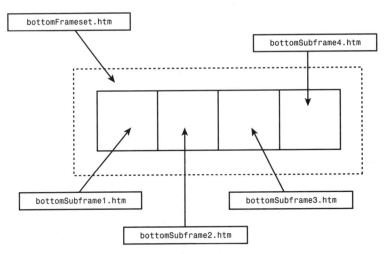

For each of the child frames, suppose you want to get the titles of its respective top and parent windows. To do so, you can define a common function called getName() that returns this information to the calling window. Just as child windows can access a method in a parent window, all frames in a multi-frameset window can access methods in the top window. Therefore, the top window serves as a good repository for functions you want to be globally available to all windows. The getName() method is defined as follows:

```
function getName(callingObject, relation, parentName) {
 callingObject.document.write("My " + relation + "'s name is " +
  parentName +".")
}
```

The callingObject parameter represents the window that is calling the function. Using dot notation, you can then assign the document.write command to be performed within the window in question. The relation and parentName parameters are strings provided by the calling window but are not manipulated in this function.

This getName() method is called by the child frames upon loading. You can do this by putting the following code in each of the child frames:

```
<SCRIPT LANGUAGE="JavaScript">
    top.getName(self, "parent", parent.document.title)
    document.write("<p>")
    top.getName(self, "top", top.document.title)
</SCRIPT>
```

The script uses top to access the getName() method, self to identify itself as the calling window, and parent and top to retrieve the titles for both windows. Figure 11.13 shows the result when the frameset is loaded.

Figure 11.13.

The top *and* parent *properties.*

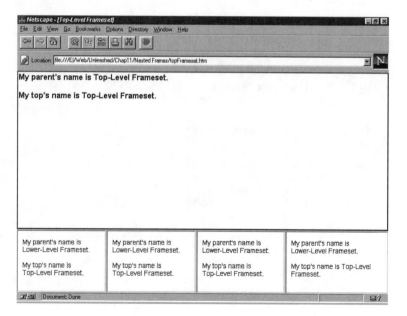

Listings 11.10, 11.11, and 11.12 provide the source code for the top-level frameset (topFrameset.htm), lower-level frameset (bottomFrameset.htm), and one of the bottom child frames (bottomSubframe1.htm).

Listing 11.10. topFrameset.htm.

```
<HTML>
<HEAD>
<TITLE>Top-Level Frameset</TITLE>
<SCRIPT LANGUAGE="JavaScript">

    function getName(callingObject, relation, parentName) {
    callingObject.document.write("My " + relation +
      "'s name is " + parentName +".")
    }

</SCRIPT>
</HEAD>
<FRAMESET ROWS="80%,20%">
  <FRAME SRC="frmain.htm"
         NAME="main"
         MARGINWIDTH="1"
         MARGINHEIGHT="1">
  <FRAME SRC="bottomFrameset.htm"
         NAME="footnotes"
         MARGINWIDTH="1"
         MARGINHEIGHT="1">
  <NOFRAMES>
Warning text should go here for browsers with no frame support.
<BODY>
</BODY>
</NOFRAMES>
</FRAMESET>
</HTML>
```

Listing 11.11. bottomFrameset.htm.

```
<HTML>
<HEAD>
<TITLE>Lower-Level Frameset</TITLE>
</HEAD>
<FRAMESET COLS="24%,24%,24%,28%">
  <FRAME SRC="bottomSubframe1.htm">
  <FRAME SRC="bottomSubframe2.htm">
  <FRAME SRC="bottomSubframe3.htm">
  <FRAME SRC="bottomSubframe4.htm">
</FRAMESET>
</HTML>
```

11

Listing 11.12. bottomSubframe1.htm.

```
<HTML>
<HEAD>
<TITLE>Footnotes Frame in Bottom Frameset</TITLE>
<SCRIPT LANGUAGE="JavaScript">
    top.getName(self, "parent", parent.document.title)
    document.write("<p>")
    top.getName(self, "top", top.document.title)
</SCRIPT>
</HEAD>
<BODY>
</BODY>
</HTML>
```

Working with Status Bar Messages

The status bar of a browser can be an important means of communicating with the user. You can use two properties of the window object—`defaultStatus` and `status`—to control the text that is displayed.

You generally have two ways to use the status bar. First, you can display a default message on the status bar. The user sees this message without performing any action. You can display a default message using the `defaultStatus` property. The `defaultStatus` property can be set at any time—either upon loading the window or while the window is already opened.

Second, you can display a temporary message that overrides the default text. In practice, this message usually appears when a user performs an event, such as moving a mouse over a jump. You can set this message using the `status` property.

The example shown in Figure 11.14 demonstrates the use of the `defaultStatus` and `status` properties.

The code behind this page shows three actions that you code to change the status bar message. First, a default message is set when the window opens using the following code:

```
window.defaultStatus = "Welcome to the large URL page."
```

Second, when the user passes over the "Go" link, its `onMouseOver` event handler calls the following function:

```
function changeStatus() {
   window.status = "Click me to go to the Acadia Software home page."
}
```

Third, to change the text of the default status message, the user can select a different message from the select object. When the Change button's `onClick` event handler is triggered, it executes the following function:

```
function changeDefaultStatus() {
    window.defaultStatus = window.document.statusForm.messageList.
```

```
    options[window.document.statusForm.messageList.selectedIndex].
    text
}
```

FIGURE 11.14.

Setting the `defaultStatus` *and* `status` *properties.*

Listing 11.13 provides the complete source code for this example.

Listing 11.13. Status.htm.

```
<html>
<head>
<title>Status Bar</title>
<SCRIPT LANGUAGE="JavaScript">
<!--
    window.defaultStatus = "Welcome to the large URL page."

    function changeStatus() {
        window.status = "Click me to go to the Acadia Software" +
        + " home page."
    }

    function changeDefaultStatus() {
        window.defaultStatus = window.document.statusForm.messageList.
        options[window.document.statusForm.messageList.
        selectedIndex].text
    }
//-->
</SCRIPT>
</head>

<body>
<p> </p>
<p> </p>
```

```
<p align=center>
<font color="#008040">
<font size=7>
<strong>http://www.acadians.com</strong></font></font></p>
<p align=center>
<a href="http://www.acadians.com" onMouseOver="changeStatus()
    ;return true">Go...</a></p>

<form name="statusForm" method="POST">
<p><br>
<br>
<br>
<br>
</p>
<p align=center>
<font size=1>To change the default status bar message, select
a message from the list below and click the Change button. </font></p>
<p align=center><select
    name="messageList"
    size=1>
    <option selected>Welcome to the large URL page.</option>
    <option>On route to Acadia Software</option>
    <option>This page intentionally left (nearly) blank.</option>
    <option>An exciting example of changing status bar text.</option>
    </select>
<input
    type=button
    name="Change"
    value="Change"
    onClick="changeDefaultStatus()"></p>
</form>
</body>
</html>
```

Frame Object

The frame object is essentially the same element as a window object, and you can deal with it in a similar manner. If you are working with a single window, the window object is the top-level object. If you are working within a frameset, the top-level window is considered the parent window, whereas its child windows are considered frame objects.

Location Object

The location object encapsulates the URL of the current page. Its *raison d'etre* is twofold, enabling you to

■ Set the location object to move to a new URL.

■ Extract specific elements of the URL and work with them. Without the location object, you would be forced to perform string manipulations on a URL string to get at the information you need.

The basic structure of a URL is as follows:

```
protocol//hostname: port pathname search hash
```

A typical URL could look something like the following:

```
http://www.acadians.com/javascript/search/Hats?qt=RFC+1738+&col=XL
```

The location object has the properties shown in Table 11.2, each of which is an element in the URL.

Table 11.2. Location object properties.

Attribute	Description
href	Complete URL
protocol	Initial element of a URL (before and including colon)
hostname	Host and domain name or IP address
host	*Hostname:port* element of a URL
port	Communications port of the server
pathname	Path element of a URL
search	Query definition portion of a URL (begins with a ?)
hash	Anchor name of a URL (begins with an #)

> **NOTE**
>
> It is important to distinguish the location object from the document object's `location` property. Although you can set the location object, the document object's location property is read-only.

Opening a New URL

Rather than use a specific method to go to a new URL in a window, you can open a new URL by setting the value of the location object. Interestingly, you can do this by either assigning a URL to the object itself or assigning a URL to the location object's `href` property. For example, the following two lines perform the same action:

```
window.location = "http://www.acadians.com/"
```

```
window.location.href = "http://www.acadians.com/"
```

For example, to roughly simulate a browser's location edit box using JavaScript, you could use the code in Listing 11.14.

Listing 11.14. moveTo.htm.

```html
<HTML>
<HEAD>
<SCRIPT LANGUAGE = "JavaScript">

    function moveon() {
        var urlAddress = ""
        urlAddress = document.forms[0].Edit1.value
        window.location = urlAddress
    }

</SCRIPT>
</HEAD>
<BODY>
<FORM>
<INPUT type="text" name="Edit1">
<INPUT type="button" value="move" onClick="moveon()">
</FORM>
</BODY>
</HTML>
```

In multiframe windows, you can specify the value of the location object in other frames by referring to the appropriate window name. For example, Figure 11.15 displays a multiframe window in which you can change the URL based upon the entry of the form in the footnote frame. Listing 11.15 shows the source code for the footnote frame.

FIGURE 11.15.

Using the location object to change another frame's URL.

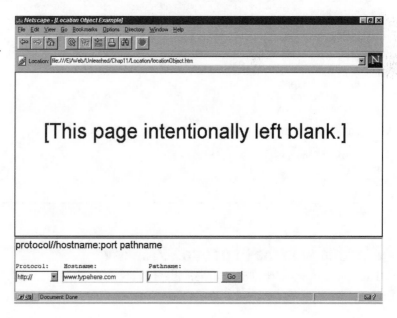

Listing 11.15. `frfootno.htm`.

```html
<html>
<head>
<title>Footnotes Frame in Location Object Example</title>
<SCRIPT LANGUAGE="JavaScript">
<!--
     function gotoPage() {
        parent.frames[0].location.href = window.document.loc.ProtocolField.
         options[window.document.loc.ProtocolField.selectedIndex].text
         + document.loc.HostnameField.value + document.loc.PathnameField.value
     }
//-->
</SCRIPT>
</head>

<body>
<p><font size=5>protocol//hostname:port pathname</font></p>
<form name="loc" method="POST">
<pre>Protocol:    Hostname:              Pathname:
<select name="ProtocolField" size=1>
<option>http://</option>
<option>file://</option>
<option>javascript:</option>
<option>ftp:</option>
<option>mailto:</option>
<option>gopher:</option>
<option>about:</option>
</select> <input
    type=text
    size=23
    maxlength=256
    name="HostnameField"
    value="www.typehere.com"> <input
    type=text
    size=20
    maxlength=100
    name="PathnameField"
    value="/"> <input
    type=button
    name="Go"
    value="Go"
    onClick="gotoPage()"></pre>
</form>
</body>
</html>
```

Working with the Protocol Property

The protocol property of the location object lets you specify the type of URL with which you are working. Table 11.3 lists the most common protocols used.

Table 11.3. Location object protocols.

URL Type	Protocol
Web	`http:`
File	`file:`
FTP	`ftp:`
MailTo	`mailto:`
Usenet	`news:`
Gopher	`gopher:`
JavaScript	`javascript:`
Navigator	`about:`

History Object

If you have surfed the Web at all, you are probably very familiar with a browser's history list. Just as the history list allows a user to traverse where she has been, JavaScript's history object enables you as a JavaScript developer to maneuver through Web pages that have been visited.

Determining the Size of the List

You can use the `length()` property of the history object to determine the number of entries in the list. For example, suppose you want to track the number of history list entries in the right frame of a multiframe window. The left frame contains the following code:

```
<HTML>
<HEAD>
<SCRIPT LANGUAGE = "JavaScript">

    function moveon() {
       var urlAddress = ""
       urlAddress = document.forms[0].Edit1.value
       parent.frames[1].location = urlAddress
       document.forms[0].Edit2.value = parent.frames[1].history.length
     }

</SCRIPT>
</HEAD>

<BODY>
<FORM>
<INPUT type="text" name="Edit1">
<INPUT type="button" value="move" onClick="moveon()">
<INPUT type="text" name="Edit2">
</FORM>
</BODY>
</HTML>
```

The user can use the Edit1 text object to enter a URL to move to. As the user clicks the Move button to move to the URL, the Edit2 text object is updated to provide the length of the history list for the right frame.

Navigating the History List

Just knowing the length of the history list is rarely useful, but it can become useful when you want to navigate a list using the history object methods back(), forward(), and go().

Back Page

The back() method is the functional equivalent of clicking the back (left-arrow) button on the browser's toolbar. For example, the following code moves a window to its previous position:

```
window.history.back()
```

Forward Page

As you would expect, the forward() method is the same as clicking the right-arrow button on the browser's toolbar. It is used as follows:

```
window.history.forward()
```

Specific Page Based on Number

The go() method jumps to a specific place in the history list. Its syntax follows:

```
[window.]history.go(delta ¦ "location")
```

The *delta* parameter is a positive or negative integer that can specify the number of places to jump. For example, the following line moves to the next document in the history list (the equivalent of using the forward() method):

```
window.history.go(1)
```

The following list details the *delta* value:

> *delta* < 0   Moves backward *delta* number of entries
>
> *delta* > 0   Moves forward *delta* number of entries
>
> *delta* = 0   Reloads the current document

Specific Page Based on String

Alternatively, you can use the *location* parameter to specify a specific URL in the list. Note that this does not have to be an exact URL, only a substring. The following example moves to the URL in the history list that contains "www.acadians.com/filenew":

```
window.history.go("www.acadians.com/filenew")
```

You can add the back(), forward(), and go() to the earlier example to provide a more fully functional multiframe navigating system. Figure 11.16 shows the frameset. Listing 11.16 provides the HTML source for the parent frameset page, and Listing 11.17 provides the HTML source for the heart of this example, the history list. The right pane contains no JavaScript code related to this example.

FIGURE 11.16.

History frame example.

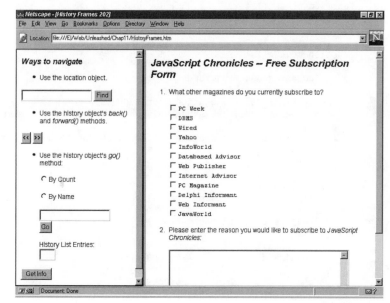

Listing 11.16. HistoryFrames.htm.

```
<html>
<head>
<title>History Object Example</title>
</head>
<Frameset Cols="35%,65%">
<Frame Name = "FRAME1" SRC="History.htm">
<Frame Name = "FRAME2" SRC="JavaScriptChronicles.htm">
</Frameset>

</html>
```

Listing 11.17. History.htm.

```
<html>
<head>
<title>History Page</title>
</head>
<body bgcolor="#FFFFFF">
```

continues

Listing 11.17. continued

```
<SCRIPT LANGUAGE="JavaScript">
<!--
    function goPrev() {
        parent.frames[1].history.back()
    }

    function goNext() {
        parent.frames[1].history.forward()
    }

    function moveOn() {
        var urlAddress = ""
        urlAddress = document.forms[0].LocationBox.value
        if (urlAddress != "") {
            parent.frames[1].location = urlAddress
            document.forms[0].ListLen.value = parent.frames[1].history.length }
        else {
            alert("Please enter a URL before clicking the Go button.")
        }
    }

    function jump() {
        if (document.forms[0].goParam[1].checked) {
            var goVal = 0
            goVal = parseInt(document.forms[0].GoBox.value) }
        else {
            var goVal = ""
            goVal = document.forms[0].GoBox.value
        }
        parent.frames[1].history.go(goVal)
    }
// -->
</SCRIPT>

<form method="POST">
<h3><em>Ways to navigate</em></h3>
<ul>
<li>Use the location object.</li>
</ul>
<p><input
    type=text
    size=20
    maxlength=50
    name="LocationBox"> <input
    type="button"
    value="Find"
    onClick="moveOn()"> </p>
<ul>
<li>Use the history object's <em>back()</em> and<em> forward() </em>methods.
</li>
</ul>
<p align=center><input
    type="button"
    value="&lt;&lt;"
    onClick="goPrev()"> <input
```

```
        type="button"
        value="&gt;&gt;"
        onClick="goNext()"></p>
<ul>
<li>Use the history object's <em>go()</em> method:</li>
</ul>
<blockquote>
<p><input type=radio name="goParam" value="ByCount">By Count</p>
<p><input type=radio name="goParam" value="ByName">By Name</p>
<p><input
        type=text
        size=20
        maxlength=30
        name="GoBox"> <input
        type="button"
        value="Go"
        onClick="jump()"> </p>
<p>History List Entries: <input
        type=text
        size=3
        maxlength=4
        name="ListLen"> </p>
</blockquote>
</form>
</body>
</html>
```

Navigator Object

The navigator object is the one object that just does not seem to fit into the JavaScript built-in object hierarchy. On first glance, it would seem to be the top level of the pyramid because the browser software—the element the navigator object represents—contains windows and any other object. However, the navigator object has no real connection to any other object in the hierarchy; it really stands alone, providing only a way to obtain information about the current Web browser.

NOTE

Keep in mind that you cannot use the navigator object to obtain information from browsers that do not support JavaScript. If the browser does not support JavaScript, it does not process the request for information. You obviously could not use a JavaScript routine to determine whether the browser supports JavaScript.

The navigator object has four properties, as shown in Table 11.4.

Table 11.4. Properties of the navigator object.

Property	Description
appName	Name of the browser
appVersion	Version of the browser
appCodeName	Code name for the browser
userAgent	User-agent header for the browser

Both Netscape Navigator and Microsoft Internet Explorer support the navigator object. Listing 11.18 provides an example of displaying browser information in a dialog box when the user clicks the Show Browser Info button. Figures 11.17 and 11.18 show the alert message boxes that appear when the script is run in both Netscape and Internet Explorer.

Listing 11.18. navigatorInfo.htm.

```
<HTML>
<HEAD>
<SCRIPT LANGUAGE = "JavaScript">

    function displayBrowserInfo() {

        var browserStr = ""
        browserStr += "Browser: " + navigator.appName + "\r"
        browserStr += "Version:" + navigator.appVersion + "\r"
        browserStr += "Codename: " + navigator.appCodeName + "\r"
        browserStr += "User agent: " + navigator.userAgent + "\r"
        alert(browserStr)
    }

</SCRIPT>

<BODY>
<H1></H1>
<FORM>
<INPUT
    Type="button"
    Value="Show Browser Information"
    OnClick="displayBrowserInfo()"
</INPUT>
</FORM>
</BODY>
</HTML>
```

FIGURE 11.17.

*Netscape Navigator
browser information.*

FIGURE 11.18.

*Microsoft Internet
Explorer browser
information.*

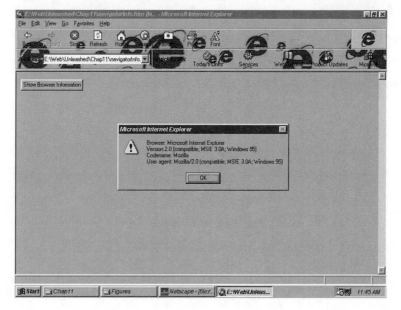

Summary

This chapter dived into the top level of the JavaScript object hierarchy. The objects I discussed have much less to do with HTML tags than they do with various aspects of a browser window. As the top-level object in the hierarchy, the window object is charged with many responsibilities—both in single and multiframe windows. The frame, location, and history list objects are all properties of the window object and provide a means to work with their respective browser counterparts. The navigator object, much different in purpose from the other JavaScript objects, enables you to find out information about the current browser being used.

Document Objects

by Richard Wagner

CHAPTER 12

Chapter 11, "Navigator Objects," began the look at JavaScript objects by examining the first object tier. This chapter continues by looking at the second tier of Navigator objects in the JavaScript hierarchy, document objects. This set of objects includes the document object and three of its "child" objects: link, anchor, and image. The form object is a child of the document object as well, but Chapter 13, "Form Objects," discusses the form object in depth.

Document Object

The window object is the highest-level object for built-in JavaScript objects; in this role, it serves as a container, but it does not have any content that is associated with it, *per se*. It leaves the content of a Web document up to the document object. The document object serves as the JavaScript equivalent of an HTML document (see Figure 12.1).

Figure 12.1.

Working with the document object.

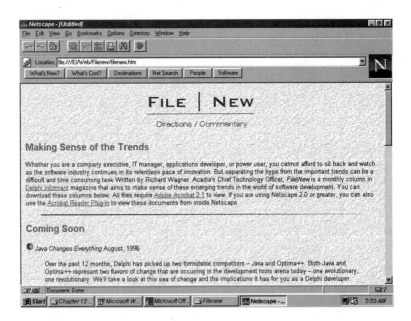

In this role, the document object is a container for all HTML-related objects that are associated with both the <HEAD> and <BODY> tags. The document object gets its title property from the <TITLE> tag (located within the <HEAD> section) and several color-related properties from the <BODY> section, which is shown here:

```
<BODY
    [BACKGROUND="backgroundImage"]
    [BGCOLOR="backgroundColor"]
    [TEXT="foregroundColor"]
    [LINK="unfollowedLinkColor"]
    [ALINK="activatedLinkColor"]
    [VLINK="followedLinkColor"]
```

```
    [onLoad="methodName"]
    [onUnload="methodName"]>
</BODY>
```

> **NOTE**
>
> Although onLoad and onUnload events are associated with the <BODY> tag, they are events of the window object, not the document object.

The document object is critical as you work with JavaScript and HTML because all the action happens on a Web page within a document. Because of this scope, you need to refer to the document object when you are accessing an object within it. For example, if you want to access a form object named invoiceForm, you must preface your reference with document:

```
document.invoiceForm.submit()
```

If you do not, JavaScript is unable to locate the object within the page.

Creating HTML Documents Programmatically

As you can see throughout this book, you can use JavaScript to react to events generated on static Web pages. You can also use it to generate HTML pages on the fly. In fact, you can use each of the methods of the document object in some way for altering documents programmatically:

- open(["mimeType"]) prepares a stream for write() and writeln() statements. Its parameter can be one of several MIME types (text/html is the default):

  text/html
  text/plain
  image/gif
  image/jpeg
  image/x-bitmap
  plugIn (any Netscape plug-in MIME type)

- write(*JavaScriptExpression*) writes a JavaScript expression to a document.

- writeln(*JavaScriptExpression*) also writes a JavaScript expression to a document but appends a newline character to the end of the expression.

- close() closes the stream that was opened by the open() method.

- clear() clears the contents of the document.

Whereas open(), close(), and clear() prepare or close out a generated document, the write() and writeln() methods give the document content. You can use any valid JavaScript expression as their parameters, including a string literal, variable, integer value, and so on. For example, each of the following are valid uses of write():

12

DOCUMENT
OBJECTS

```
var loc = "Ashford, Kent"
document.write("The castle is located in " + loc)
document.write("I stayed in the Robert Courtneys room.")
document.write("I would like " + 70 + "copies of that report.")
```

Keep in mind that you are writing HTML, not straight text. You can use HTML tags just as if you were writing the document in an HTML editor, as in the following example:

```
document.write('<h3>Return to the <a
href="http://www.acadians.com">Acadia Software</a> home
page.</h3><p>')
```

Figure 12.2 shows the result.

FIGURE 12.2.

Link generated using JavaScript.

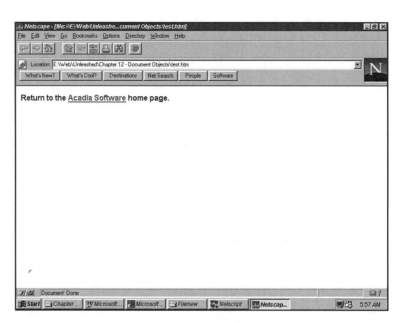

The one key limitation you need to keep in mind when using write() or writeln() is that you cannot change the contents of the current document without completely reloading the window. The following sections describe the three valid contexts in which you can create HTML documents on the fly.

Creating a Document in the Current Window Upon Loading

You can create a new document in the current window when the document loads. You typically place this code within a <SCRIPT> tag either in the <HEAD> section or else by itself if it stands alone. For example, if you want to evaluate the browser and change the text based on its type, you can use the script shown in Listing 12.1.

Listing 12.1. writeCurrent.htm.

```
<SCRIPT LANGUAGE = "JavaScript">

    var browser = navigator.appName
    document.open()
    if (browser == „Netscape") {
        document.write(„<h2>Welcome <a href='http://home.netscape.com'>Netscape</
a>
        user.</h2><p><p>")}
    else {
        if (browser == „Microsoft Internet Explorer") {
            document.write(„<h2>Welcome <a href='http://www.microsoft.com'>
              Microsoft</a>Internet Explorer user.</h2><p><p>") }
        else {
            document.write(„<h1>Welcome. But what browser are you using?
              </h1><p><p>")
        }
    }
    document.write(„We are glad you came to our Web site.<p><p>")
    document.write(„Don't you wish you knew how we knew your browser type?")
    document.close()

</SCRIPT>
```

12

DOCUMENT OBJECTS

Figure 12.3 shows the result in Netscape Navigator 3.0, and Figure 12.4 shows the result in Internet Explorer 3.0.

FIGURE 12.3.

Customized Netscape page.

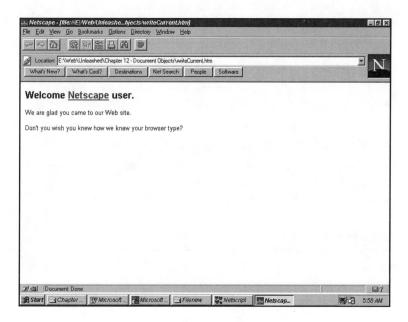

FIGURE 12.4.
Customized Internet Explorer page.

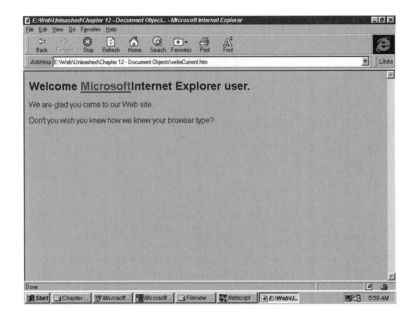

Creating a Document in a Frame

You can also generate a new document in another frame of a multiframe window. The techniques are similar to those used in the previous example, but you must reference the correct document using dot notation. For example, to reference the first frame of a frameset, you could use the following code:

```
parent.forms[0].document.write("test")
```

See Listing 12.8 later in the chapter for an example of setting a frame document programmatically.

Creating a Document in a Separate Window

The third technique for creating documents on the fly is opening a new window and writing to its document. If you wanted to enumerate a list of installed plug-ins for the browser in a separate window, you could use the code shown in Listing 12.2.

Listing 12.2. writeWindow.htm.

```
<HTML>
<HEAD>
<SCRIPT LANGUAGE = „JavaScript">

    function showWindow() {
        var len = navigator.plugins.length
```

```
        newWin = window.open(„", „", „height=300,width=400")
        newWin.document.write(„<h2>Plug-In Info:</h2><p><p>")

        for (var i=0; i<len; i++) {
            newWin.document.write(„<li>" + navigator.plugins[i].description
                + „</li>")
        }

        newWin.document.close()
    }


</SCRIPT>
</HEAD>
<BODY>
<form>
<input type=button value="Show Plug-In Information" onClick="showWindow()">
</form>
</BODY>
</HTML>
```

Figure 12.5 shows the result of the script.

12

DOCUMENT OBJECTS

FIGURE 12.5.

Generating a new document in a separate window.

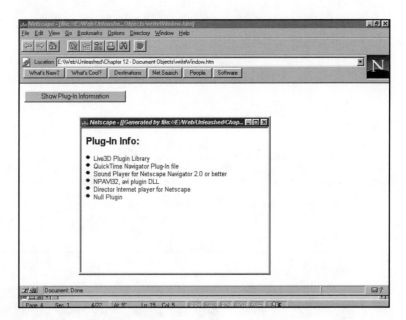

Clearing Contents of a Window

You can clear the contents of a window by issuing either a document's clear() method or its write() with no parameter. Either way, the effect is the same. Both methods empty a document and display a blank window. To illustrate, be a little creative and imagine you are "Q," trying to relay a message to your best agent, James Bond, 007. After he reads the message, you want to be sure he erases the contents of the document before anyone else can read it. (I know; the scenario falls apart when you think of the realities of the Web, but play along on this one.) Figure 12.6 shows the top secret message. Listing 10.3 shows the code for 007message.htm.

FIGURE 12.6.

Secret message that needs to be cleared.

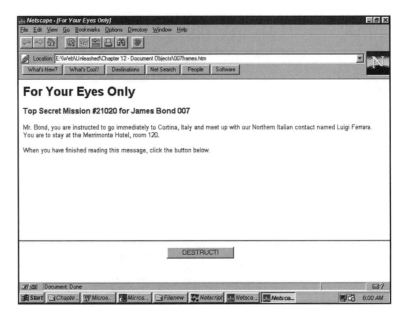

Listing 10.3. 007message.htm.

```
<HTML>
<BODY>
<h1>For Your Eyes Only</h1><p><p>
<h3>Top Secret Mission #21020 for James Bond 007</h3><p><p>
Mr. Bond, you are instructed to go immediately to Cortina, Italy
and meet up with our Northern Italian contact named Luigi Ferrara.
You are to stay at the Merrimonte Hotel, room 120.<p><p>
When you have finished reading this message, click the button below.<p><p>
</BODY>
</HTML>
```

> **NOTE**
>
> I have found that clear() performs inconsistently in both Netscape Navigator and Microsoft Internet Explorer. As a result, I use the alternative empty write() method in this example.

Listing 12.4 shows the source code for the frameset document. It contains a JavaScript function named destroyContents() that empties the contents of the top frame named "message".

Listing 12.4. 007frames.htm.

```
<HTML>
<HEAD>
<TITLE>For Your Eyes Only</TITLE>
<SCRIPT LANGUAGE="JavaScript">

    function destroyContents() {
        self.message.document.write()
        self.message.document.close()
    }

</SCRIPT>
</HEAD>
<FRAMESET ROWS="80%,20%">
  <FRAME SRC="007message.htm" NAME="message" MARGINWIDTH="10" MARGINHEIGHT="10">
  <FRAME SRC="007control.htm" NAME="control" MARGINWIDTH="10" MARGINHEIGHT="10">
  <NOFRAMES>
<BODY>
<P>This web page uses frames, but your browser doesn't support them.</P>
</BODY>
</NOFRAMES>
</FRAMESET>
</HTML>
```

Listing 12.5 shows the HTML source from the bottom frame, which contains the button. As you can see, it simply calls the parent window's destroyContents() method when Bond clicks the DESTRUCT! button.

Listing 12.5. 007control.htm.

```
<HTML>
<BODY>
<FORM>
<DIV align="center"><INPUT type=button value="   DESTRUCT!   " onClick=
  "parent.destroyContents()"></DIV>
</FORM>
</BODY>
</HTML>
```

Changing Document Attribute Colors

Color settings for documents are usually set by a user in his browser configuration, but JavaScript gives you the ability to change these color settings programmatically. The document object has five properties that reflect the colors of various attributes within the document—alinkColor, bgColor, fgColor, linkColor, and vlinkColor—which are described in Table 12.1.

12

DOCUMENT OBJECTS

Table 12.1. Document color-related properties.

Property	Description	HTML Tag
alinkColor	Color of an activated link (after mouse down, before mouse up)	ALINK=
bgColor	Background color of document	BGCOLOR=
fgColor	Foreground color of document	TEXT=
linkColor	Color of unvisited links	LINK=
vlinkColor	Color of visited links	VLINK=

These properties are expressed either as string literals or as hexadecimal RGB triplet values. For example, if you wanted to assign a background color of chartreuse to a document, you could use the string literal chartreuse:

```
document.bgColor = chartreuse
```

You could also use the equivalent hexadecimal RGB triplet value:

```
document.bgColor = "7fff00"
```

NOTE

You can find the JavaScript color values table in Chapter 4, "Fundamentals of the JavaScript Language," which lists the color values both as string literals and hexadecimal RGB triplets.

A hexadecimal RGB triplet is a combination of three hexadecimal values representing red, green, and blue colors, respectively. When combined, the values form a hexadecimal RGB triplet. The number should take one of two case-sensitive forms:

```
rrggbb
```

```
#rrggbb
```

When applying color changes to a document attribute, you must follow the same principles that apply to changing a document's text. You can only make the changes when the page is set, such as in a document.write() statement—not on a page that has already been "painted" in the browser window.

To see how to set these color settings, look at the example shown in Figure 12.7. The bottom frame has a selection list of all the colors and a group of radio buttons associated with the document attribute color options. You can select a color and the property you want to use and then click the Apply button. A JavaScript code reloads the top frame based on your setting.

FIGURE 12.7.

Changing color of a frame on the fly.

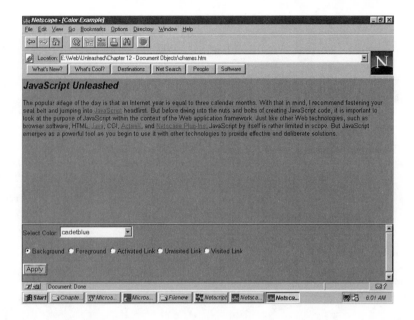

Listing 12.6 provides the HTML source of the frameset document, Listing 12.7 shows the code for dummy.htm, and Listing 12.8 lists the code from the lower frameset that performs this process. When the user clicks the Apply button, the refreshMain() method assigns a value to the newColor variable based on the currently selected option in the selection list. Next, using dot notation, the document of the upper frame is referenced (parent.main.document) and reloaded based on the write() and a color property assignment.

Listing 12.6. cframes.htm.

```html
<HTML>
<HEAD>
<TITLE>Color Example</TITLE>
</HEAD>
<FRAMESET ROWS="80%,20%">
  <FRAME SRC="dummy.htm" NAME="main" MARGINWIDTH="1" MARGINHEIGHT="1">
  <FRAME SRC="colordef.htm" NAME="colorDef" MARGINWIDTH="1" MARGINHEIGHT="1">
  <NOFRAMES>
<BODY>
<P>This web page uses frames, but your browser doesn't support them.</P>
</BODY>
</NOFRAMES>
</FRAMESET>
</HTML>
```

Listing 12.7. dummy.htm.

```
<html>
<head>
</head>
<body>
<h2><em>JavaScript Unleashed</em></h2>
<p>The popular adage of the day is that an Internet year is equal to three
calendar months. With that in mind, I recommend fastening your seat belt
and jumping into <a href="http://home.netscape.com">JavaScript</a> headfirst.
But before diving into the nuts and bolts of creating JavaScript code, it is
important to look at the purpose of JavaScript within the context of the Web
application framework. Just like other Web technologies, such as browser
software, HTML, <a href="http://java.sun.com">Java</a>, CGI, <a href=
„http://www.microsoft.com/activex">ActiveX</a>, and <a href=
„http://home.netscape.com">Netscape Plug-Ins</a>, JavaScript by itself is
rather limited in scope. But JavaScript emerges as a powerful tool as you
begin to use it with other technologies to provide effective and deliberate
solutions.</p>
<p> </p>
</body>
</html>
```

Listing 12.8. colordef.htm.

```
<html>

<head>
<title>Color Definition</title>
<SCRIPT LANGUAGE="JavaScript">
var graf = ,<body><h2><em>JavaScript Unleashed</em></h2><p>The popular
adage of the day is that an Internet year is equal to three calendar
months. With that in mind, I recommend fastening your seat belt and
jumping into <a href="http://home.netscape.com">JavaScript</a> headfirst.
But before diving into the nuts and bolts of creating JavaScript code, it
is important to look at the purpose of JavaScript within the context of the
Web application framework. Just like other Web technologies, such as browser
software, HTML, <a href="http://java.sun.com">Java</a>, CGI, <a
href="http://www.microsoft.com/activex">ActiveX</a>, and <a
href="http://home.netscape.com">Netscape Plug-Ins</a>, JavaScript by
itself is rather limited in scope. But JavaScript emerges as a powerful tool
as you begin to use it with other technologies to provide effective and
deliberate solutions.</p></body>'

    function refreshMain() {

        var newColor = document.form1.colorList.options[document.form1.
            colorList.selectedIndex].text
        var selProp = null

        with (parent.main.document) {
            open()
            write(graf)
            if (document.form1.type[0].checked) {
                bgColor = newColor }
            else {
```

```
                    if (document.form1.type[1].checked) {
         fgColor = newColor }
                else {
                    if (document.form1.type[2].checked) {
                        alinkColor = newColor }
                    else {
                        if (document.form1.type[3].checked) {
                            linkColor = newColor }
                        else
                            if (document.form1.type[4].checked) {
                                vlinkColor = newColor }
                    }
                }
            }
            close()
    }

</SCRIPT>
</head>

<body bgcolor="tomato">
<form name="form1" method="POST">
<p>Select Color: <select name="colorList" size=1>
<option>aliceblue</option>
<option>antiquewhite</option>
<option>aqua</option>
<option>aquamarine</option>
<option>azure</option>
<option>beige</option>
<option>bisque</option>
<option>black</option>
<option>blanchedalmond</option>
<option>blue</option>
<option>blueviolet</option>
<option>brown</option>
<option>burlywood</option>
<option>cadetblue</option>
<option>chartreuse</option>
<option>chocolate</option>
<option>coral</option>
<option>cornflowerblue</option>
<option>cornsilk</option>
<option>crimson</option>
<option>cyan</option>
<option>darkblue</option>
<option>darkcyan</option>
<option>darkgoldenrod</option>
<option>darkgray</option>
<option>darkgreen</option>
<option>darkkhaki</option>
<option>darkmagenta</option>
<option>darkolivegreen</option>
<option>darkorange</option>
<option>darkorchid</option>
<option>darkred</option>
<option>darksalmon</option>
```

continues

Listing 12.8. continued

```
<option>darkseagreen</option>
<option>darkslateblue</option>
<option>darkslategray</option>
<option>darkturquoise</option>
<option>darkviolet</option>
<option>deeppink</option>
<option>deepskyblue</option>
<option>dimgray</option>
<option>dodgerblue</option>
<option>firebrick</option>
<option>floralwhite</option>
<option>forestgreen</option>
<option>fuchsia</option>
<option>gainsboro</option>
<option>ghostwhite</option>
<option>gold</option>
<option>goldenrod</option>
<option>gray</option>
<option>green</option>
<option>greenyellow</option>
<option>honeydew</option>
<option>hotpink</option>
<option>indianred</option>
<option>indigo</option>
<option>ivory</option>
<option>khaki</option>
<option>lavender</option>
<option>lavenderblush</option>
<option>lawngreen</option>
<option>lemonchiffon</option>
<option>lightblue</option>
<option>lightcoral</option>
<option>lightcyan</option>
<option>lightgoldenrodyellow</option>
<option>lightgreen</option>
<option>lightgrey</option>
<option>lightpink</option>
<option>lightsalmon</option>
<option>lightseagreen</option>
<option>lightskyblue</option>
<option>lightslategray</option>
<option>lightsteelblue</option>
<option>lightyellow</option>
<option>lime</option>
<option>limegreen</option>
<option>linen</option>
<option>magenta</option>
<option>maroon</option>
<option>mediumaquamarine</option>
<option>mediumblue</option>
<option>mediumorchid</option>
<option>mediumpurple</option>
<option>mediumseagreen</option>
<option>mediumslateblue</option>
<option>mediumspringgreen</option>
<option>mediumturquoise</option>
```

12

DOCUMENT OBJECTS

```html
<option>mediumvioletred</option>
<option>midnightblue</option>
<option>mintcream</option>
<option>mistyrose</option>
<option>moccasin</option>
<option>navajowhite</option>
<option>navy</option>
<option>oldlace</option>
<option>olive</option>
<option>olivedrab</option>
<option>orange</option>
<option>orangered</option>
<option>orchid</option>
<option>palegoldenrod</option>
<option>palegreen</option>
<option>paleturquoise</option>
<option>palevioletred</option>
<option>papayawhip</option>
<option>peachpuff</option>
<option>peru</option>
<option>pink</option>
<option>plum</option>
<option>powderblue</option>
<option>purple</option>
<option>red</option>
<option>rosybrown</option>
<option>royalblue</option>
<option>saddlebrown</option>
<option>salmon</option>
<option>sandybrown</option>
<option>seagreen</option>
<option>seashell</option>
<option>sienna</option>
<option>silver</option>
<option>skyblue</option>
<option>slateblue</option>
<option>slategray</option>
<option>snow</option>
<option>springgreen</option>
<option>steelblue</option>
<option>tan</option>
<option>teal</option>
<option>thistle</option>
<option>tomato</option>
<option>turquoise</option>
<option>violet</option>
<option>wheat</option>
<option>white</option>
<option>whitesmoke</option>
<option>yellow</option>
<option>yellowgreen</option>
</select>
<p><input type=radio name="type" value="bgColor" checked>Background <input
type=radio name="type" value="fgColor">Foreground <input type=radio
name="type" value="alinkColor">Activated Link<input type=radio name="type"
value="linkColor">Unvisted Link<input type=radio name="type"
value="vlinkColor">Visited Link<p>
```

continues

Listing 12.8. continued

```
<input type=button name="Apply" value="Apply" onClick="refreshMain()"></p>
</form>
</body>
</html>
```

Although this is a limited example, you can build on this base to develop some much more flexible scripts to change colors on the fly.

RESOURCE

For a comprehensive example of using colors in your documents, see the hIdaho Color Center at `http://www.hidaho.com/colorcenter/`.

Link Object

Perhaps "love makes the world go around," but what makes the World Wide Web go around are links. HTML links are the core elements of any Web document, enabling you to jump to another Web page with the click of a mouse. The location of the document is immaterial; it could be on the same Web server or thousands of miles away. All that matters is that the URL is valid. The link object is the JavaScript equivalent of the hypertext link, which is defined in HTML syntax as

```
<A HREF=locationOrURL
    [NAME="objectName"]
    [TARGET="windowName"]
    [onClick="methodName"]
    [onMouseOver="methodName"]>
    linkText
</A>
```

TIP

For more information on link events, see Chapter 9, "Handling Events."

The link object has several properties that are the same as the parameters for the location object. These include hash, host, hostname, href, pathname, port, protocol, and search. See Chapter 11 for more information on these properties.

Referencing Link Objects

Link objects do not have a name property, so you cannot refer to a specific link object by itself. The only way you can refer to a link object in your JavaScript code is by using the links array. The links array is a collection of all the links within the current document. The order of the array is based on the order in which they are located within the source file. I'll present an example that demonstrates how you can use the link array to deal with individual link objects.

Suppose you want to extract the URLs from each link on a page and list them on another page. Using a triple-frame frameset, you can set the bottom frame to be the "free" window that is used for browsing, the top frame to contain a button to set off the process, and the middle frame to list the URLs. Figure 12.8 shows the triple-frame frameset in a Netscape window after the process is performed.

FIGURE 12.8.

Getting URL information using the links array.

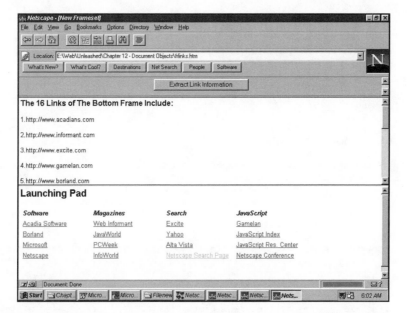

Listing 12.9 displays the frameset source code, Listing 12.10 shows the code for `frbottom.htm`, and Listing 12.11 lists the JavaScript source code for the top frame, which contains the processing power for this example. Clicking the Extract button triggers the `getLinkInfo()` method. This method references the links array of the bottom frame (named `bFrame`) and sets the `len` variable to equal its length. While writing to the middle frame, the method loops through each element in the links array and retrieves the `href` property value.

Listing 12.9. frlinks.htm.

```
<HTML>
<HEAD>
<TITLE>New Frameset</TITLE>
</HEAD>
<FRAMESET ROWS="10%,35%,*">
  <FRAME SRC="frtop.htm" NAME="tFrame" MARGINWIDTH="2" MARGINHEIGHT="4">
  <FRAME SRC="frmiddle.htm" NAME="mFrame" MARGINWIDTH="5" MARGINHEIGHT="2">
  <FRAME SRC="frbottom.htm" NAME="bFrame" MARGINWIDTH="5" MARGINHEIGHT="2">
  <NOFRAMES>
<BODY>
<P>This web page uses frames, but your browser doesn't support them.</P>
</BODY>
</NOFRAMES>
</FRAMESET>
</HTML>
```

Listing 12.10. frbottom.htm.

```
<html>

<head>
</head>

<body>
<h2>Launching Pad </h2>
<table width=80%>
<tr><td width=25%><em><strong>Software</strong></em></td><td width=25%><em>
<strong>Magazines</strong></em></td><td width=25%><em><strong>Search</strong>
</em></td><td width=25%><em><strong>JavaScript</strong></em></td></tr>
<tr><td width=25%><a href="http://www.acadians.com">Acadia Software</a></td>
<td width=25%><a href="http://www.informant.com">Web Informant</a></td><td
width=25%><a href="http://www.excite.com">Excite</a></td><td width=25%><a
href="http://www.gamelan.com">Gamelan</a></td></tr>
<tr><td width=25%><a href="http://www.borland.com">Borland</a></td>
<td width=25%><a href="http://www.javaworld.com">JavaWorld</a></td><td
width=25%><a href="http://www.yahoo.com">Yahoo</a></td><td width=25%><a
href="http://www.c2.org/~andreww/javascript/">JavaScript Index</a></td></tr>
<tr><td width=25%><a href="http://www.microsoft.com">Microsoft</a></td><td
width=25%><a href="http://www.pcweek.com">PCWeek</a></td><td width=25%><a href=
"http://www.altavitsa.digital.com">Alta Vista</a></td><td width=25%><a
href="http://www.intercom.net/user/mecha/java/index.html">JavaScript Res.
Center</a></td></tr>
<tr><td width=25%><a href="http://home.netscape.com">Netscape</a></td>
<td width=25%><a href="http://www.infoworld.com">InfoWorld</a></td><td
width=25%><a href="http://home.netscape.com/escapes/search/search4.html">
Netscape Search Page</a></td><td width=25%><a href="http://home.netscape.com/
misc/developer/conference/proceedings/">Netscape Conference</a></td></tr>
</table>
<p> </p>
</body>
</html>
```

Listing 12.11. `frtop.htm`.

```
<html>
<head>
<base target="middle">
<SCRIPT LANGUAGE="JavaScript">

      function getLinkInfo() {
            var len = parent.bFrame.document.links.length
            with (parent.mFrame.document) {
                  open()
                  write(„<h3>The „ + len
                    + „ Links of The Bottom Frame Include:</h3><p>")
                  for (var i=0; i<len; i++) {
                        write((i+1) + „." + parent.bFrame.document.links[i].href
                          + „<p>")
                  }
                  close()
            }
      }

</SCRIPT>
</head>
<body bgcolor="crimson">
<form method="POST">
<p>
<DIV align=center><input type=button name="Extract" value="Extract Link
Information"
  onClick="getLinkInfo()"></DIV>
</form>
</body>
</html>
```

Executing JavaScript Code Using Links

Using `javascript:` as the protocol element of the link's `href`, you can perform a JavaScript expression in place of a typical link action, such as jumping to a new Web page or sending a mail message. However, the code you execute has to be self contained; you cannot call another method as you would with an event handler, nor can you reference other objects outside of its context, such as another window.

You could use a link to evaluate the type of browser in use, such as in the following code:

```
<A HREF="javascript:if (navigator.appName != 'Netscape')
{ alert('You should not have clicked this link!') } else
{ alert('Thanks for clicking.')} ">All Netscape users, click me</A>
```

For a second example, I set up this book's table of contents in an HTML document and added links to each of the part names. For the HREF= parameter of these links, I placed a description of each part in an alert message box. Because of the nature of the `javascript:` protocol, I was forced to use a message box rather than write the text to another frame or window. Listing 12.12 shows the HTML code for this example, and Figure 12.9 shows the result of clicking the Part III link. (In the real world, a better solution would be to separate the text into one or more HTML documents and use the links in a traditional method to jump to their locations.)

Listing 12.12. jsLinks.htm.

```
<html>
<head>
<title>JavaScript Unleashed Table of Contents</title>
</head>
<body>
<p><a href="javascript:alert(,In this first section, you will get a complete
introduction to JavaScript. Chapter 1 takes a unique look at JavaScript,
focusing on how and where it fits into the Web application development
framework. You will also see how it relates to other Web technologies both on
the client- and server-side. Next, in Chapter 2, you will learn about the
relationship between JavaScript and Hypertext Markup Language (HTML) and how
the browser interprets your code at runtime. Chapter 3 looks at the software
tools you need to develop in JavaScript.')"><font size=4>Part I: Getting
Started with JavaScript</font></a><font size=4> </font></p>
<blockquote>
<p><font size=4>1) JavaScript and the World Wide Web <br>
2) How JavaScript and HTML Work Together <br>
3) Assembling Your JavaScript Toolkit </font></p>
</blockquote>
<p><a href="javascript:alert(,The second part presents a thorough look at
the JavaScript language. In Chapters 4-7, you will learn about language
basics, control structures, operators, and functions.')"><font size=4>Part II:
The JavaScript Language </font></a></p>
<blockquote>
<p><font size=4>4) Fundamentals of the JavaScript Language<br>
5) Control Structures and Looping <br>
6) Operators<br>
7) Functions</font></p>
</blockquote>
<p><a href="javascript:alert(,Part three dives into the heart of JavaScript—
objects. After an introduction to object-oriented concepts in Chapter 8,
Chapter 9 looks at how you can handle user and system events. Chapter 10 then
looks at the built-in JavaScript hierarchy and introduces you to each of
the Navigator and Built-in language objects. Chapters 11-14 continue where
the previous chapter left off by exploring in-depth each of the built-in
JavaScript objects. Chapter 15 rounds out the discussion on objects, focusing
on how you can create your own. It includes many innovative ideas related to
custom object development within JavaScript.')"><font size=4>Part III: JavaScript
Objects</font></a></p>
<blockquote>
<p><font size=4>8) Fundamentals of Object-Orientation <br>
9) Handling Events <br>
10) JavaScript Built-In Object Model <br>
11) Navigator Objects <br>
12) Document Objects <br>
13) Form Objects <br>
14) Built-in Language Objects <br>
15) Creating Custom JavaScript Objects </font></p>
</blockquote>
<p><a href="javascript:alert(,The next section builds upon everything you
learned up to that point to look at specific areas of interest to the
JavaScript developer. Chapter 16 explores how you can enhance HTML forms with
```

JavaScript, such as providing client-side data validation. Both Chapters 17-18 really focus on frames and how you can use JavaScript in multi-frame windows. I have found frame management to be perhaps the most common use of JavaScript on the Web. Chapter 19 looks at yet another key topic, cookies and other techniques for handling and maintaining state in the stateless environment of the Web.')"><font size=4>Part IV: JavaScript Programming </font></a></p>
<blockquote>
<p><font size=4>16) Enhancing Forms with JavaScript
17) Working with Frames and Windows
18) Scripting Outlines and Table of Contents
19) Cookies & State Maintenance </font></p>
</blockquote>
<p><a href="javascript:alert(,While Parts I-IV focused on client-side JavaScript, this section focuses on its server-side counterpart. Within Netscape LiveWire and other products such as Borland IntraBuilder, you can use JavaScript as a server-side scripting language. In doing so, you are freed from writing CGI scripts and dealing with such languages as PERL. Chapter 20 looks at server-side JavaScript, focusing on LiveWire and IntraBuilder. Chapter 21 takes look at the issue of how to architect client/server applications on the Web. Covered are many of the issues you will encounter as you plan such an application.')"><font size=4>Part V: JavaScript on the Server</font></a></p>
<blockquote>
<p><font size=4>20) Server-Based JavaScript
21) Partitioning Client and Server Applications </font></p>
</blockquote>
<p><a href="javascript:alert(,Part VI explores five advanced subjects, many of which are emerging as key topics as JavaScript matures. Chapter 22 dives into Error Handling and Debugging JavaScript applications. Chapter 23-24 cover the hot topic of integrating JavaScript with Netscape Plug-Ins and ActiveX controls. Chapter 25 looks at integrating JavaScript with VRML and multimedia data. Chapter 26 closes the section by looking at a more conceptual topic—JavaScript security. The chapter not only looks at the key issues surrounding this subject, but provides some helpful advice as you consider using JavaScript for your Web site.')"><font size=4>Part VI: Advanced JavaScript</font></a><font size=4> </font></p>
<blockquote>
<p><font size=4>22) Error Handling and Debugging in JavaScript
23) Working with Netscape Plug-ins
24) ActiveX Scripting with JavaScript
25) VRML and Multimedia
26) JavaScript and Web Security </font></p>
</blockquote>
<p><a href="javascript:alert(,JavaScript is an important tool to glue HTML and Java applets. In this section, we will look at Java from a JavaScript perspective in Chapter 27 and see how similar or different the language is for JavaScripters. Chapter 28 provides a good introduction on how to build a Java applet, while Chapter 29 is where the rubber meets the road when it focuses on integrating Java and JavaScript.')"><font size=4>Part VII: Java and JavaScript </font></a></p>
<blockquote>
<p><font size=4>27) Java from a JavaScripter Perspective
28) Building Java Applets
29) Integrating JavaScript with Java </font></p>
</blockquote>
<p><a href="javascript:alert(,Many corporations will use the Web as a way

continues

Listing 12.12. continued

```
to get at their data. As a result, how JavaScript can access data will be
an increasingly important topic as the technology matures. In this section,
we will look at how you can work with data both on the client-side and
server-side. Chapter 30 introduces the notion of maintaining lookup tables
on the client side to lessen the need to access the server. Chapter 31 then
gets into how you can use JavaScript to access server-side data. LiveWire
and IntraBuilder will again be used in this context.')"><font size=4>Part
VIII: JavaScript Database Applications</font></a></p>
<blockquote>
<p><font size=4>30) Using Client-Side Tables in JavaScript <br>
31) Working with Server-Side Database Objects </font></p>
</blockquote>
<p><a href="javascript:alert(,The final section provides some extra
information that will assist you as you read the book. Appendixes A-B
provide basic references on the JavaScript and HTML respectively. Appendix C
looks at how VBScript and JavaScript compare. Appendix D lists JavaScript
resources that are available online.')"><font size=4>Part IX: Appendixes
</font></a></p>
<blockquote>
<p><font size=4>A) JavaScript Language Summary <br>
B) Fundamentals of HTML <br>
C) Comparing JavaScript with Microsoft&#146;s VBScript <br>
D) JavaScript Resources on the Internet <br>
</font></p>
</blockquote>
</body>
</html>
```

FIGURE 12.9.

*Clicking a link displays
a message box.*

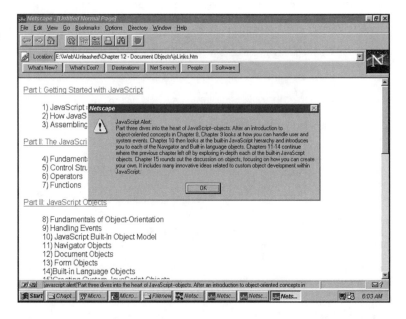

Anchor Object

You most often use a link object to jump to another Web page or another location within the current document. Within the current document, the link locates a specific place in the text called an anchor, which is defined in HTML syntax as

```
<A [HREF=locationOrURL]
   NAME="objectName"
   [TARGET="windowName"]>
   anchorText
</A>
```

To be politically correct, you could say that the anchor object is "JavaScript challenged" because you can do little in JavaScript with anchors. By itself, an anchor object has no properties, methods, or events. The only way you can really use them in JavaScript is through the anchors array of the document object. You can use the anchors array to determine the number of anchors in a document and iterate through them as desired.

Image Object

NOTE

The image object is new to Netscape Navigator 3.0.

If you spend any time at all on the Web, you quickly realize how important graphics are to the Web. You can hardly go to a page without seeing several graphics scattered throughout. New to Netscape Navigator 3.0, the image object represents an HTML image, which is defined in the following format:

```
<IMG
   [NAME="objectName"]
   SRC="Location"
   [LOWSRC="Location"]
   [HEIGHT="Pixels"|"Value"%]
   [WIDTH="Pixels"|"Value"%]
   [HSPACE="Pixels"]
   [VSPACE="Pixels"]
   [BORDER="Pixels"]
   [ALIGN="left"|"right"| "top"|
      "absmiddle"|"absbottom"|
      "texttop"|"middle"|"baseline"|
      "bottom"]
   [ISMAP]
   [USEMAP="Location#MapName"]
   [onAbort="methodName"]
   [onError="methodName"]
   [onLoad="methodName"]>
```

12

DOCUMENT
OBJECTS

> **TIP**
>
> For more information on image object events, see Chapter 9.

For example, to display an image called `dot.gif` in HTML, you would use the following syntax:

```
<IMG SRC='dot.gif' height="200" width="200">
```

Creating an Explicitly Created Image Object

You can create an instance of an image object using the `new` operator, as shown in the following example:

```
companyLogo = new Image()
companyLogo.src = "logo.gif"
```

You can set the dimensions of the graphic as a parameter to the `Image()` constructor. For example, if you wanted to display the logo in a 200×300 pixel format, you could use the following:

```
companyLogo = new Image(200,300)
companyLogo.src = "logo.gif"
```

By assigning a value to the `src` property, you can change the image that is displayed. However, if you do this, the new URL or graphic loads in the image area.

Because you still define an image using the `<IMG>` tag, an image object you create serves a rather limited purpose. You can use it to retrieve an image before it is actually needed for display purposes. Because this image is now in memory, it would be much quicker to display it when a document is reloaded. The most common example is an animation-like series of images that are retrieved using the `Image()` object and then displayed later while they are in memory.

Summary

The document objects discussed in this chapter are the JavaScript equivalent of some of the most basic HTML elements around. These objects include the HTML document, link, anchor, and image. Although you can use JavaScript to enhance or retrieve information from these objects, much of the JavaScript interaction usually comes from working with forms. Therefore, the next chapter looks closely at form objects.

Form Objects

by Richard Wagner

CHAPTER

13

One of the key milestones in the evolution of the Web was the emergence of HTML forms from the world of static pages. With forms, the Web could actually be more than a unidirectional mode of communication. Instead, forms provided a means by which any user on any machine could transfer data to a server for processing. With JavaScript, HTML forms grow even more powerful. Not only can you preprocess form data before it is sent to the user, but you can also use forms in an application that is completely contained on the client side. In this chapter, I discuss the form object and the numerous objects that it can contain.

> **NOTE**
>
> The form objects discussed in this chapter can only exist within a form—not outside one.

Form Object

One of the principal uses of JavaScript is providing a means to interact with the user on the client side. Most of the time, this interaction with the user happens through an HTML form. As a result, the JavaScript form object is an important object within the JavaScript object model. When you work with the form object, you do not do that much with a form object in and of itself. Rather, the form object provides a container by which you can retrieve data from the user.

In HTML, the form object is defined as

```
<FORM
    [NAME="formName"]
    [ACTION="serverURL"]
    [ENCTYPE="encodingType"]
    [METHOD=GET ¦ POST]
    [TARGET="windowName"]
    [onSubmit="methodName"]>
</FORM>
```

To define a form, follow standard HTML conventions:

```
<FORM NAME="form1" ACTION="http://www.acadians.com/js/script.jfm" METHOD=GET>

  <!-- Enter form objects here -->

</FORM>
```

> **NOTE**
>
> For more information on using forms in JavaScript, see Chapter 16, "Enhancing Forms with JavaScript."

Submitting Forms to the Server

Before JavaScript came along, the only real purpose of an HTML form was to send the data elements gathered on the client side to the server. Because the client side itself was not powerful enough to intelligently process the data, it was up to the server to then react to the information it received. JavaScript allows you to add a great deal of front-end processing to your HTML forms, but that does not eliminate the need to submit a form to a server for more industrial-strength purposes.

You can submit a form using one of two processes. You can call the form object's submit() method, or you can click a submit button, which automatically submits the form with which it is associated.

> **NOTE**
>
> See Chapters 9, "Handling Events," and 16 for more information on performing validity checks using JavaScript before a form's submission.

Many of the form object properties deal with additional information that is sent to the server from the form. These properties include the following:

- action (same as the ACTION= parameter)—The action property specifies the server URL to which the form is sent. This is usually a CGI program, LiveWire application, or an IntraBuilder .JFM file, as shown here:

```
form1.action = "http://www.acadians.com/js/surv.cgi"
```

- enctype (same as the ENCTYPE= parameter)—The enctype property specifies the MIME encoding of the form. The default is application/x-www-form-urlencoded, as shown in the example:

```
if (form1.enctype == "application/x-www-form-urlencoded") {
    alert("Encoding type is normal.") }
```

- method (same as the METHOD= parameter)—The method property defines how the form is sent to the server. The value of GET is used most often, but you can use POST as well. This parameter is based on the server-side process, so as you design the HTML form, you need to check the requirements of the server program. The following code line shows an example of using the method parameter:

```
var methodType
methodType = form1.method
alert("The method type for this form is: " + methodType)
```

- target (same as the TARGET= parameter)—The target property specifies the destination window to which the server should send information back. If the target property is not specified, the server displays results in the same window that submitted the form. If you are using a frameset, the `target` property can be a frame specified by the `NAME` parameter of the `<FRAME>` tag. You can also use one of the following reserve window names: _top, _parent, _self, and _blank. Keep in mind that you are in HTML for this specification, not JavaScript. You cannot use a JavaScript window object name, such as parent.resultsWindow. The following code shows an example:

```
if (document.form1.newWindowCheckBox.checked) {
     document.form1.target = "resultsForm" }
else {
     document.form1.target = "_self" }
```

The HTML form shown in Listing 13.1 uses a combination of HTML tags and JavaScript code to submit a form. Note that if the user checks the Rush Order checkbox, the form's action property changes to a new value during the form's onSubmit event. Setting the action property programmatically overrides the default value.

Listing 13.1. formSubmit.htm.

```
<html>
<head>
<title>For More Information</title>
<SCRIPT LANGUAGE="JavaScript">

     function checkType() {
          if (document.form1.rush.checked) {
               document.form1.action = "http://www.acadians.com/js/rush.cgi" }
     }
</SCRIPT>
</head>

<body>
<h1>Order Form</h1>
<hr>
<form name="form1" action="http://www.acadians.com/js/order.cgi"
method="POST" onSubmit="checkType()">
<p>Please provide the following contact information:</p>
<blockquote>
<pre><em>        First name </em><input type=text size=25 maxlength=256
name="Contact_FirstName">
<em>         Last name </em><input type=text size=25 maxlength=256
name="Contact_LastName">
<em>             Title </em><input type=text size=35 maxlength=256
name="Contact_Title">
<em>     Organization </em><input type=text size=35 maxlength=256
name="Contact_Organization">
<em>       Work Phone </em><input type=text size=25 maxlength=25
name="Contact_WorkPhone">
<em>              FAX </em><input type=text size=25 maxlength=25
name="Contact_FAX">
<em>           E-mail </em><input type=text size=25 maxlength=256
name="Contact_Email">
<em>              URL </em><input type=text size=25 maxlength=25
name="Contact_URL">
</pre>
</blockquote>
```

```
<p>Please provide the following ordering information:</p>
<blockquote>
<pre><strong>QTY      DESCRIPTION
</strong><input type=text size=6 maxlength=6
name="Ordering_OrderQty0">
<input type=text size=45 maxlength=256 name="Ordering_OrderDesc0">
<input type=text size=6 maxlength=6 name="Ordering_OrderQty1">
<input type=text size=45 maxlength=256 name="Ordering_OrderDesc1">
<input type=text size=6 maxlength=6 name="Ordering_OrderQty2">
<input type=text size=45 maxlength=256 name="Ordering_OrderDesc2">
<input type=text size=6 maxlength=6 name="Ordering_OrderQty3">
<input type=text size=45 maxlength=256 name="Ordering_OrderDesc3">
<input type=text size=6 maxlength=6 name="Ordering_OrderQty4">
<input type=text size=45 maxlength=256 name="Ordering_OrderDesc4">

<em>                   </em><strong>BILLING</strong>
<em>Purchase order # </em><input type=text size=25 maxlength=256
name="Ordering_PONumber">
<em>    Account name </em><input type=text size=25 maxlength=256
name="Ordering_POAccount">

<em>                   </em><strong>SHIPPING</strong>
<em>   Street address </em><input type=text size=35 maxlength=256
name="Ordering_StreetAddress">
<em> Address (cont.) </em><input type=text size=35 maxlength=256
name="Ordering_Address2">
<em>             City </em><input type=text size=35 maxlength=256
name="Ordering_City">
<em>   State/Province </em><input type=text size=35 maxlength=256
name="Ordering_State">
<em> Zip/Postal code </em><input type=text size=12 maxlength=12
name="Ordering_ZipCode">
<em>          Country </em><input type=text size=25 maxlength=256
name="Ordering_Country">
</pre>
<pre><input type=checkbox name="rush" value="ON">Rush Order!</pre>
</blockquote>
<p><input type=submit value="Submit Form"> <input type=reset
value="Reset Form"> </p>
</form>
</body>
</html>
```

NOTE

For more information on the onSubmit event handler, see Chapter 9.

Checking Elements on a Form

The form acts as a container object for all objects on a form. Because these types of objects, such as text or button objects, are for user interaction, you can refer to them as "user interface

(UI) objects." The form object has an `elements` property that you can use to either refer to an element on a form or check all elements on a form to perform a particular task. The order of the array is based purely on the order in which the elements of the HTML form are defined in the source file. The first element listed is `element[0]`, the second is `element[1]`, and so on.

You can refer to each form element either by name or by its index in the `elements` array. For example, if the text object named `LastName` was the first element defined on the form, it could be accessed by the following code:

```
custLastName = form1.elements[0].value
```

You could also use the following line:

```
custLastName = form1.LastName.value
```

You could also use the `elements` property to do something with each object within the form. For example, suppose you wanted to make sure that each field on your form was not blank. Using the `elements` property, you could use a `for` loop to iterate through each array element and check the values. This code is shown in Listing 13.2.

Listing 13.2. `formElements.htm`.

```
<html>
<head>
<title>Online Registration</title>
<SCRIPT LANGUAGE="JavaScript">
<!--
    function checkFields() {
        var num = document.form1.elements.length
        var validFlag = true
        for (var i=0; i<num; i++) {
            if ((document.form1.elements[i].value == null ||
                document.form1.elements[i].value == "") &&
                (typeof document.form1.elements[i] != 'submit' ||
                typeof document.form1.elements[i] != 'reset'))
    {
                validFlag = false
                alert("The " + document.form1.elements[i].name +
                    " field is blank. Please enter a value.")
                break }
        }
        return validFlag
    }
// -->
</SCRIPT>
</head>

<body>
<form name="form1" method="POST" onSubmit="return checkFields()">
<h2>Online Registration</h2>
<p>Username:<br>
<input type=text size=25 maxlength=256 name="Username"><br>
Category of Interest:<br>
<input type=text size=25 maxlength=256 name="Category"><br>
```

```
Starting Year:<strong><br>
</strong><input type=text size=25 maxlength=256 name="StartYear"><br>
Email address:<strong><br>
</strong><input type=text size=25 maxlength=256 name="EmailAddress"></p>
<h2><input type=submit value="Register"> <input type=reset value="Clear"></h2>
</form>
<p> </h5>
</body>
</html>
```

Notice that the `checkFields()` method uses the `elements.length` property to determine the number of iterations in the `for` loop. Next, because the `elements` array includes all objects in the form, including the two button objects, the `typeof` operator is used to qualify the element before checking its value. Figure 13.1 shows the alert message box that displays if a field is blank.

FIGURE 13.1.

Checking values of fields on a form.

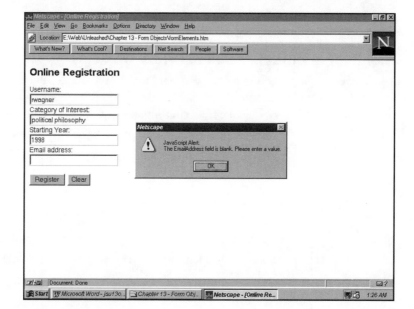

Text Object

For most tasks, the text object is the element you use most often to gather data entered by the user. The text object is used for capturing single-line, free-flow information. For information that spans multiple lines, use the textarea object discussed in the section "Textarea Object," later in this chapter. As with other form objects, the text object is the "objectified" version of an HTML tag, which has the following syntax:

```
<INPUT
   TYPE="text"
   [NAME="objectName"]
```

```
[VALUE="value"]
[SIZE=size]
[MAXLENGTH=size]
[onBlur="methodName"]
[onChange="methodName"]
[onFocus="methodName"]
[onSelect="methodName"]>
```

For example, to define a text object for a last name, you could use the following:

```
<INPUT TYPE="text" NAME=LastName SIZE=20 MAXLENGTH=25>
```

> **NOTE**
>
> For more information on the text object events, such as onBlur, onChange, onFocus, and onSelect, see Chapter 9.

Assigning a Default Value to a Text Object

You might encounter occasions when you want to assign a default value to a text object. If you are creating an HTML document on the fly, you can do this by setting the VALUE= parameter of the <INPUT type=text> tag. To illustrate, suppose you wanted to automatically check the type of the navigator object and fill it in a form. The code listed in Listing 13.3 generates the form shown in Figure 13.2. Notice that the Browser field is automatically filled in for the user by checking the appName property of the navigator object.

Listing 13.3. textDefaultValueWrite.htm.

```
<SCRIPT LANGUAGE="JavaScript">
var browserVar = navigator.appName
document.write('<body>')
document.write('<form name="form1" method="POST">')
document.write('<h2>Online Registration</h2>')
document.write('<p>Username:<br>')
document.write('<input type=text size=25 maxlength=256 name="Username"><br>')
document.write('Browser used:<br>')
document.write('<input type=text size=25 maxlength=256
name="Browser" value="' + browserVar + '"><br>')
document.write('Email address:<strong> <br>')
document.write('</strong><input type=text size=25 maxlength=256')
document.write('name="EmailAddress"></p>')
document.write('<h2><input type=submit value="Register">   ')
document.write('<input type=reset value="Clear"></h2>')
document.write('</form>')
document.write('</body>')
document.write('</html>')
// -->
</SCRIPT>
```

FIGURE 13.2.
Default value set for user.

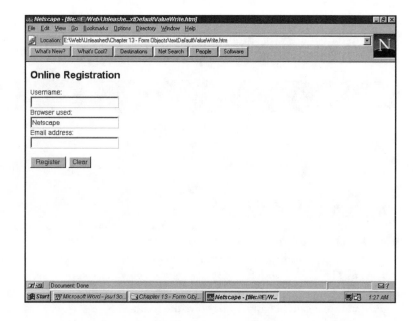

A second way to assign a default value to a text object already generated is to set its `value` property. For example, you could create the same form using the code shown in Listing 13.4. In this example, the window's `onLoad` event handler assigns a value to the Browser field.

Listing 13.4. `textDefaultValue.htm`.

```
<html>
<head>
<title>Online Registration</title>
<SCRIPT LANGUAGE="JavaScript">
<!--
    function findBrowser() {
        document.form1.Browser.value = navigator.appName
    }
// -->
</SCRIPT>
</head>

<body onLoad="findBrowser()" >
<form name="form1" method="POST">
<h2>Online Registration</h2>
<p>Username:<br>
<input type=text size=25 maxlength=256 name="Username"><br>
Browser used:<br>
<input type=text size=25 maxlength=256 name="Browser"><br>
Email address:<strong> <br>
</strong><input type=text size=25 maxlength=256 name="EmailAddress"></p>
<h2><input type=submit value="Register"> <input type=reset value="Clear"></h2>
</form>
</body>
</html>
```

Paradoxically, the defaultValue property is not used in this example. Although you can assign a value to the defaultValue property, the form is not updated when you do so. Therefore, you should use the value property as shown in this example.

> **TIP**
>
> The defaultValue property is most useful for obtaining the default value of a text object, not for setting the default value.

Selecting Text upon Focus

By default, when you enter a text object, the cursor is an insertion point. If the field currently has text you want to type over, you have to explicitly select the text, delete it, and retype a value. You can change this behavior by using the select() method of the text object. Listing 13.5 shows an HTML form with four text objects, each of which call this.select() when the onFocus event is triggered. As a result, when the user enters each of these fields, any existing text is highlighted automatically. Figure 13.3 shows the result.

Listing 13.5. textSelect.htm.

```
<html>
<head>
<title>Online Registration</title>
</head>

<body>
<form name="form1" method="POST">
<h2>Online Registration</h2>
<p>Username:<br>
<input type=text size=25 maxlength=256 name="Username"
onFocus="this.select()"><br>
Browser used:<br>
<input type=text size=25 maxlength=256 name="Browser"
onFocus="this.select()"><br>
Email address:<strong> <br>
</strong><input type=text size=25 maxlength=256 name="EmailAddress"
onFocus="this.select()"></p>
<h2><input type=submit value="Register"> <input type=reset value="Clear"></h2>
</form>
</body>
</html>
```

FIGURE 13.3.

Highlighting text automatically.

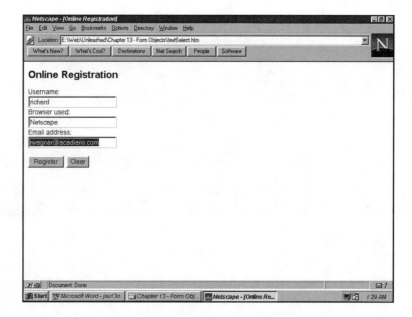

Textarea Object

All the other form objects that you work with are designed for capturing data of limited size (less than 256 characters). The textarea object provides a means for capturing information that does not lend itself to simple text fields, radio buttons, or selection lists. You can use the textarea object to enter free-form data that spans several lines. You are limited to displaying ASCII text, but such basic formatting as paragraphs are allowed. The textarea object is defined using the standard HTML syntax:

```
<TEXTAREA
    NAME="objectName"
    ROWS="numRows"
    COLS="numCols"
    [WRAP="off¦virtual¦physical"]
    [onBlur="methodName"]
    [onChange="methodName"]
    [onFocus="methodName"]
    [onSelect="methodName"]>
    displayText
</TEXTAREA>
```

For example, to define a textarea for submitting online comments, you could define the object as follows:

```
<textarea name="Comments" rows=12 cols=78></textarea>
```

Figure 13.4 shows the results in a form.

13

FORM OBJECTS

FIGURE 13.4.

Textarea object.

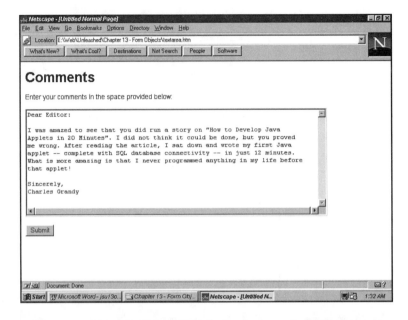

NOTE

For more information on textarea events, such as onBlur, onChange, onFocus, and onSelect, see Chapter 9.

Wrapping Text in a Textarea Object

By default, text does not wrap in a textarea object. The user must manually enter a new line using the Enter key. However, working with such an element can be frustrating for the user, so you can set text wrapping options with the WRAP= parameter of the <TEXTAREA> HTML tag. Besides off, the default setting, you have two additional options:

- virtual—If the WRAP= parameter is set to virtual, the lines wrap on screen at the end of the textarea object, but a new line is only defined when you actually enter a carriage return.

- physical—If the WRAP= parameter is set to physical, the lines wrap on screen, but a carriage return is automatically placed at the end of each on-screen line when it is sent to the server.

The Button Objects (Submit, Reset, and Button)

Because graphical operating environments became dominant over the past decade, the push button is perhaps the most ubiquitous of all user interface components. HTML has three types of buttons you can use in your forms: button, submit, and reset. As you can see, two are specialized forms of the more generic button object. Using conventional HTML syntax, a button is defined as

```
<INPUT
   TYPE="button¦submit¦reset"
   [NAME="objectName"]
   [VALUE="labelText"]
   [onClick="methodName"]>
```

The three button types have different purposes:

- Submit—The submit button submits the form in which it is contained to the server based on the parameters of the form. No JavaScript code is needed to perform this action because its behavior is built into the object itself.

- Reset—The reset button clears the values in the fields of the current form, restoring any default values that might have been set. As with the submit button, no JavaScript code is used for this.

- Button—The button object is a generic object with no predefined behavior built into it. In order for this object to do anything, you need to add an onClick event handler to the button.

If you are new to HTML, you might be asking about the reasons for the submit and reset buttons because you could use a button object to perform these same tasks. These originated before the days of JavaScript, where you could not use a generic button because you had no means of making it do anything. Additionally, although not all browsers support JavaScript (and thus the button object), all modern browsers do support the reset and submit buttons. For compatibility reasons, it is usually best to use the submit and reset buttons unless JavaScript support is a requirement for accessing your page, and in that case, it would not matter.

13

FORM OBJECTS

> **NOTE**
>
> For more information on the onClick event for the button type objects, see Chapter 9.

Listing 13.6 shows an example of how you can use all three buttons. As you would expect, the submit and reset buttons are used to submit or clear the form, although their VALUE= parameters were changed to reflect a more user-friendly verbiage. The button object is used to display a Help window that instructs users how to fill out the registration form.

Additionally, in the Help window that is generated by the showHelp() method, a button object is defined using the document write() method. Let me point out two things about this button. First, to center the button on the page, I used the <DIV ALIGN=> tag. Second, to add a little "beef" to width of the button, I added a few blank spaces before and after the OK in the VALUE= parameter. Figure 13.5 shows the form that is generated by the HTML.

Listing 13.6. buttons.htm.

```
<html>
<head>
<title>Online Registration</title>

<SCRIPT LANGUAGE="JavaScript">

    function showHelp() {

            helpWin = window.open("", "Help", "height=200,width=400")
            helpWin.document.write("<body><h2>Help on Registration</h2>")
            helpWin.document.write("1. Please enter your product
                information into the fields.<p>")
            helpWin.document.write("2. Press the Register button
                to submit your form.<p>")
            helpWin.document.write("3. Press the Clear button to clear the
                form and start again.<p>")
            helpWin.document.write("<p>")
            helpWin.document.write("<form><DIV ALIGN='CENTER'>")

            helpWin.document.write("<input type=button value='  OK  '
                onClick='window.close()'>")
            helpWin.document.write("</DIV></form></body>")

    }

</SCRIPT>

</head>

<body>
<h1>Online Registration</h1>
<form method="POST">
<p>Please provide the following product information:</p>
<blockquote>
<pre><em>    Product name </em><input type=text size=25 maxlength=256
name="ProductName">
<em>          Model </em><input type=text size=25 maxlength=256
name="Product_Model">
<em>  Version number </em><input type=text size=25 maxlength=256
name="Product_VersionNumber">
<em>Operating system </em><input type=text size=25 maxlength=256
name="Product_OperatingSystem">
<em>   Serial number </em><input type=text size=25 maxlength=256
name="Product_SerialNumber">
</pre>
</blockquote>
```

```
<p><input type=submit value="Register"> <input type=reset value="Clear">
<input type=button value="Help" onClick="showHelp()"></p>
</form>
</body>
</html>
```

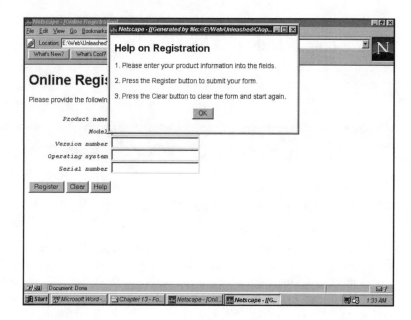

Checkbox Object

The checkbox object is the form object that is best equipped to denote logical (true or false) data. It acts as a toggle switch that can be turned on or off either by the user or by your JavaScript code. To define a checkbox, use the following HTML syntax:

```
<INPUT
    TYPE="checkbox"
    [NAME="objectName"]
    [VALUE="value"]
    [CHECKED]
    [onClick="methodName"]>
    [displayText]
```

For example, the following checkbox allows users to specify their foreign language proficiencies:

```
<input type=checkbox name="language">I speak multiple languages.
```

Following UI conventions, a checkbox should not usually cause a "processing action" to be performed (á là button objects). As a result, you probably won't use its onClick event handler extensively. However, the exceptions to this rule include changing the state of other objects on the form.

NOTE

For more information on the onClick event for the checkbox object, see Chapter 9.

Determining Whether a Checkbox Object Is Checked

Perhaps the most important property of the checkbox object is its checked property. You can evaluate this property to determine whether a user has checked the checkbox. (Do not use the value property to test a checkbox object, as clarified in the following caution.)

CAUTION

The value property can be misleading at first. Unlike some environments, the value property is static and does not change in response to a change of state of the checkbox. Therefore, do not check the value property to determine whether a checkbox is checked.

To illustrate, I build on an example I originally used in the discussion on text objects earlier in the chapter. As you recall, one of the examples automatically highlighted the entire contents of a text object by calling the text object's select() method. Suppose you wanted to give users the option of having the text selected or not. You could use a checkbox to achieve this result. Listing 13.7 shows this code. Figure 13.6 shows the resulting form.

Listing 13.7. checkboxSelect.htm.

```
<html>
<head>
<title>Online Registration</title>
<SCRIPT LANGUAGE="JavaScript">

     function selectText(currentObject) {
          if (document.form1.selectBox.checked) {
               currentObject.select()
          }
     }

</SCRIPT>
</head>

<body>
<form name="form1" method="POST">
<h2>Online Registration</h2>
<p>Username:<br>
<input type=text size=25 maxlength=256 name="Username"
onFocus="selectText(this)"><br>
Browser used:<br>
<input type=text size=25 maxlength=256 name="Browser"
```

```
onFocus="selectText(this)"><br>
Email address:<strong> <br>
</strong><input type=text size=25 maxlength=256 name="EmailAddress"
onFocus="selectText(this)"></p>
<h2><input type=submit value="Register"> <input type=reset value="Clear"></h2>
<p><input type=checkbox name="selectBox">Activate field selection.
</form>
</body>
</html>
```

FIGURE 13.6.

Using a checkbox.

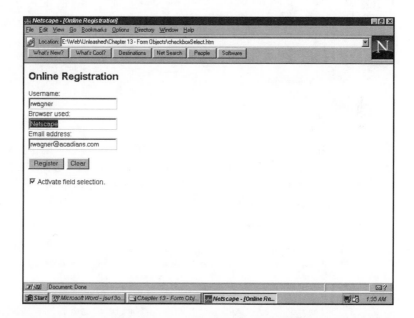

13

FORM OBJECTS

NOTE

The example shown in Listing 13.7 is useful in demonstrating how to evaluate the checked property during a process. However, it should be noted that the code does not necessarily work as you would expect. Once the checkbox is checked, text is highlighted from that point on regardless of whether you uncheck the checkbox. This is because once a `select()` method is called for a text object, the highlighted state remains in effect until the page is reloaded.

Interestingly, if you reload the page using Netscape Navigator's Reload toolbar command, it works fine thereafter without erasing the contents of the form. If you try to use Netscape Navigator 3.0's `reload()` method, your existing values are cleared.

Radio Object

You use the radio object to let a user select a single option from a group of options. If one option within a set is selected, no others can be selected at the same time. The act of clicking a radio button deselects any other radio button that was selected.

The radio object is different from the other form objects you have worked with. Whereas other form objects have a one-to-one correspondence to an HTML tag, a radio object has a one-to-many relationship with a set of `<INPUT type="radio">` elements within the HTML source code. Each element of a radio object is defined as

```
<INPUT
    TYPE="radio"
    [NAME="groupName"]
    [VALUE="value"]
    [CHECKED]
    [onClick="methodName"]>
    [displayText]
```

You do not group each of these elements together as you do the items in a select object (discussed later in this chapter). The way they are grouped together is based on the `NAME=` parameter of the radio buttons. Each element in a radio object must use the same value in that parameter. For example, the following set of radio buttons are treated as a single radio object called `weekdays`:

```
<INPUT TYPE="radio" NAME="weekdays" VALUE="Monday">Monday
<INPUT TYPE="radio" NAME="weekdays" VALUE="Tuesday">Tuesday
<INPUT TYPE="radio" NAME="weekdays" VALUE="Wednesday">Wednesday
<INPUT TYPE="radio" NAME="weekdays" VALUE="Thursday">Thursday
<INPUT TYPE="radio" NAME="weekdays" VALUE="Friday">Friday
<INPUT TYPE="radio" NAME="weekdays" VALUE="Saturday">Saturday
<INPUT TYPE="radio" NAME="weekdays" VALUE="Sunday">Sunday
```

> **NOTE**
>
> For more information on the onClick event for the radio button, see Chapter 9.

Determining the Value of the Selected Radio Button

One of the most common programming needs you will have when using a radio object is retrieving the value of the currently selected radio button. To do so, you must determine which of the radio buttons is selected and then return its value. Rather than custom coding each time you need this routine, you could more easily use a generic function I call `getRadioValue()` that will return the value of the radio object used as the method's parameter.

Look at the code shown in Listing 13.8. The songs radio object has a set of three songs listed. The Show Selected button object displays the currently selected object by calling the getRadioValue() method using the songs object as the function's parameter. The getRadioValue() method performs a for loop to analyze which of the radio buttons is checked (selected). It uses the length property of the radio object to determine the number of iterations. When the for loop encounters the checked value, it assigns the variable the value of the radio button, breaks the loop, and then returns the value to the button event handler.

Listing 13.8. radio.htm.

```
<HTML>
<HEAD>
<SCRIPT LANGUAGE = "JavaScript">
    function getRadioValue(radioObject) {
        var value = null
        for (var i=0; i<radioObject.length; i++) {
            if (radioObject[i].checked) {
                value = radioObject[i].value
                break }
        }
        return value
    }
</SCRIPT>
</HEAD>
<BODY>
<FORM name="form1">
<p><input type=radio name="songs" value="Liquid">Liquid</p>
<p><input type=radio name="songs" value="Flood">Flood</p>
<p><input type=radio name="songs" value="World's Apart">World's Apart</p>
<input type=button value="Show Selected"
onClick="alert(getRadioValue(this.form.songs))">
</FORM>
</BODY>
</HTML>
```

Figure 13.7 shows the result of clicking the Show Selected button.

NOTE

See Listings 13.12 and 13.13 later in this chapter for an example on how to check a radio button automatically.

13

FORM OBJECTS

FIGURE 13.7.

Determining the value of the radio object.

Select Object

The select object is one of the most useful and flexible of all the form objects. You can use it in instances where you might otherwise use a radio object. The select object can take up less real estate than a radio object, which needs space for each of its radio buttons. The basic HTML syntax for a select object follows:

```
<SELECT
    [NAME="objectName"]
    [SIZE="numberVisible"]
    [MULTIPLE]
    [onBlur="methodName"]
    [onChange="methodName"]
    [onFocus="methodName"]>
    <OPTION VALUE="optionValue" [SELECTED]>displayText</OPTION>
    [<OPTION VALUE="optionValue">displayText</OPTION>]
</SELECT>
```

The select object is flexible and can take three different forms: a selection list, a scrolling list, and a multi-selection scrolling list.

NOTE

For more information on select object events, see Chapter 9.

Creating a Selection List

A selection list is a drop-down list of options in which the user can select a single item from the list. A selection list usually displays a single value at a time (see Figure 13.8) but expands to show a list when the user clicks its arrow. (See Figure 13.9.) Unlike "combo boxes" in the Windows world, you cannot enter a value in the box; you can only select from an existing array of values.

FIGURE 13.8.

Selection list in its normal state.

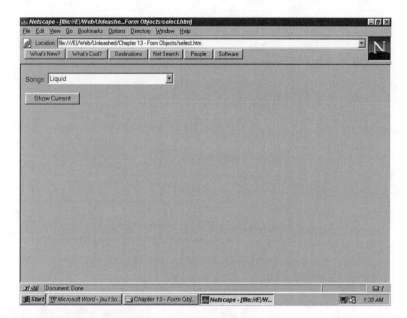

FIGURE 13.9.

Selection list in an expanded state.

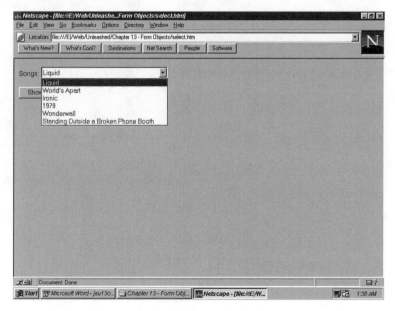

The selection list shown in Figures 13.8 and 13.9 can be defined as

```
<select NAME="songs" SIZE=1>
<option VALUE="Liquid">Liquid</option>
<option VALUE="World's Apart">World's Apart</option>
<option VALUE="Ironic">Ironic</option>
<option VALUE="1979">1979</option>
<option VALUE="Wonderwall">Wonderwall</option>
<option VALUE="Standing Outside a Broken Phone Booth">
Standing Outside a Broken Phone Booth</option>
```

The key to defining a selection list is to give the SIZE= parameter a value of 1 (or leave it out entirely). This ensures that the list shows only a single line at a time.

Creating a Scrolling List

The second form a select object can take is a scrolling list—what is commonly known in many operating environments as a list box. Rather than retract all items in a drop-down list, a scrolling list displays a designated number of items at one time in a list format. The scrolling list includes scrollbars so a user can scroll up or down to see more than what fits in the space provided.

To define a scrolling list, the only change you make to the HTML <select> definition is in the SIZE= parameter. Making this value greater than one transforms the select object into a scrolling list. For example, by changing the SIZE= parameter of the previously defined songs object from 1 to 5, the list takes on a new look, as shown in Figure 13.10. As with the selection list, a scrolling list lets you select a single value from the list.

FIGURE 13.10.

Scrolling list.

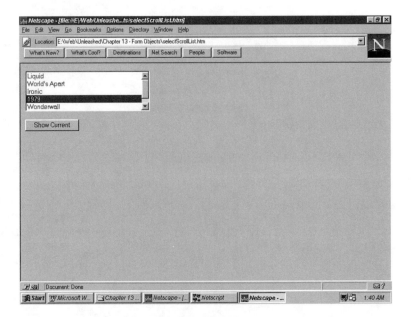

Creating a Multi-Selection List

The final form a select object can take is a multi-selection list. It looks the same as a normal scrolling list but has different behavior. You can select one or more items from this type of select object. The task of selecting multiple items depends on the operating environment. In most cases, you can either drag the mouse across multiple contiguous items or hold the Shift or Ctrl key while you click an item with the mouse.

To define a multi-selection list, you simply add the MULTIPLE parameter to the select object definition:

```
<select NAME="songs" SIZE=5 MULTIPLE>
<option VALUE="Liquid">Liquid</option>
<option VALUE="World's Apart">World's Apart</option>
<option VALUE="Ironic">Ironic</option>
<option VALUE="1979">1979</option>
<option VALUE="Wonderwall">Wonderwall</option>
<option VALUE="Standing Outside a Broken Phone Booth">
Standing Outside a Broken Phone Booth</option>
```

Determining the Value or Text of the Selected Option

In a selection or scrolling list, you can determine the value of the selected option by using a combination of the options and selectedIndex properties of the select object. For example, if I wanted to determine the song that was selected in our songs object example, I could use the following:

```
favorite = document.form1.songs.options[document.form1.songs.selectedIndex].
   value
```

The options property is an array containing each option defined within a select object. Using this property, you can access the properties of each option. You can use the selectedIndex property to return the index of the selected option. Used in combination, you can return the value of the currently selected option.

With the dot notation requirements of JavaScript, trying to retrieve the currently selected value can involve long code lines. You can avoid this by making a generic getSelectValue() method to use instead. Listing 13.9 shows how to define this method. As you can see, the select object is passed as the getSelectValue() method's parameter when the user clicks the Show Current button. The selectObject variable is treated as an object type variable and retrieves the value of the currently selected option. This value is passed back to the button object's event handler and displayed in an alert message box.

Listing 13.9. select.htm.

```
<HTML>
<HEAD>
<SCRIPT LANGUAGE = "JavaScript">

    function getSelectValue(selectObject) {
        return selectObject.options[selectObject.selectedIndex].value
    }

</SCRIPT>
</HEAD>
<BODY>
<FORM name="form1">
Songs: <select NAME="songs" SIZE=1>
<option VALUE="Liquid">Liquid</option>
<option VALUE="World's Apart">World's Apart</option>
<option VALUE="Ironic">Ironic</option>
<option VALUE="1979">1979</option>
<option VALUE="Wonderwall">Wonderwall</option>
<option VALUE="Standing Outside a Broken Phone Booth">
Standing Outside a Broken Phone Booth</option>
</SELECT><p>
<input type=button value="Show Current"
onClick="alert(getSelectValue(this.form.songs))">
</FORM>
</BODY>
</HTML>
```

One important difference between the select and radio object is that the select object has a text property in addition to the value property. If the value you want to define is the same as what is being displayed to the user—as in Listing 13.9—then you can return the text value of the currently selected object rather than the value property. If the select object was defined as

```
<select NAME="songs" SIZE=1>
<option>Liquid</option>
<option>World's Apart</option>
<option>Ironic</option>
<option>1979</option>
<option>Wonderwall</option>
<option>Standing Outside a Broken Phone Booth</option>
```

You could use the text property rather than the value property to return the song name:

```
    function getSelectValue(selectObject) {
        return selectObject.options[selectObject.selectedIndex].text
    }
```

Determining the Values of Multi-Selection Lists

In lists where a single option is selected at any given time, the selectedIndex property efficiently returns information you need from the currently selected option. If you have a multi-selection scrolling list, however, selectedIndex returns only the first option that is selected, not all of them. When using multi-selection lists, you must use the selected property of the options array to determine the status of each option in the list. Listing 13.10 shows an example of this in its showSelection() method. In this function, a for loop iterates through each option in the select object and tests to see whether the selected property is true. If it is, the value of the text property of the element is added to the list variable. The results are then presented in a second window, as shown in Figure 13.11.

Listing 13.10. selectMultiple.htm.

```
<HTML>
<HEAD>
<SCRIPT LANGUAGE = "JavaScript">

    function showSelection(objectName) {
        var list = ""
        for (var i=0; i<objectName.length; i++) {
            if (objectName.options[i].selected) {
                list += objectName.options[i].text + "<p>"
            }
        }
        selWindow = window.open("", "Selections", "height=200,width=400")
        selWindow.document.write("<h2>You picked the following songs:
            </h2><p><p>")
        selWindow.document.write(list)
    }

</SCRIPT>
</HEAD>
<BODY>
<FORM name="form1">
Pick Your Favorite Songs From the List:<p>
<select NAME="songs" SIZE=5 MULTIPLE>
<option>Fortress Around Your Heart</option>
<option>Breakfast at Tiffany's</option>
<option>Flood</option>
<option>The Chess Game</option>
<option>Liquid</option>
<option>World's Apart</option>
<option>Ironic</option>
<option>1979</option>
<option>Wonderwall</option>
<option>Standing Outside a Broken Phone Booth</option>
</SELECT><p>
<input type=button value="Show Selection"
onClick="showSelection(this.form.songs)">
</FORM>
</BODY>
</HTML>
```

FIGURE 13.11.

Displaying multiple selections.

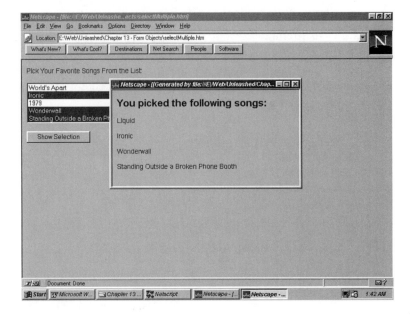

Selecting an Option Using JavaScript

You can select an option programmatically by setting the `selected` property of a select object's options array. Suppose you have a Favorite Band field and a list of songs. If the value of the Favorite Band field is "Oasis," then you want to locate a song written by that group in the Songs field. Listing 13.11 shows this example.

Listing 13.11. selectSelected.htm.

```
<HTML>
<HEAD>
<SCRIPT LANGUAGE = "JavaScript">

    function quickSelect() {
        var bnd = document.form1.band.value
        bnd = bnd.toUpperCase()
        if (bnd == "OASIS") {
            document.form1.songs[4].selected = "1"
        }
    }

</SCRIPT>
</HEAD>
<BODY>
<FORM name="form1">
Favorite Band: <input type=text name="band" size=20 onBlur="quickSelect()"><p>
Songs: <select NAME="songs" SIZE=1>
<option VALUE="Liquid">Liquid</option>
<option VALUE="World's Apart">World's Apart</option>
<option VALUE="Ironic">Ironic</option>
```

```
<option VALUE="1979">1979</option>
<option VALUE="Wonderwall">Wonderwall</option>
<option VALUE="Standing Outside a Broken Phone Booth">
Standing Outside a Broken Phone Booth</option>
</SELECT><p>
<input type=button value="Show Current" onClick="quickSelect()">
</FORM>
</BODY>
</HTML>
```

Password Object

As you can tell from its name, the password object has but a single purpose: to capture a password value from a user. A password object is similar to a text object but displays any character the user types in the field as an asterisk (*). It can be defined in HTML syntax as

```
<INPUT
    TYPE="password"
    [NAME="objectName"]
    [VALUE="defaultPassword"]
    [SIZE=integer]>
```

The following line shows an example:

```
<INPUT TYPE="password" NAME="passwordField" SIZE=15>
```

JavaScript has little control over the password object. For example, you cannot retrieve the value of the text entered by the user to evaluate it; you can only retrieve default text that has been defined using the VALUE= parameter of the <INPUT type=password> tag. Part of the reason JavaScript cannot access this is that JavaScript code is currently embedded into the HTML document so the user could access it. As JavaScript matures, it might get more control over this form object.

Hidden Object

As one might infer from its name, a hidden object is invisible to the user. The hidden object is a hidden text field that you can use to store values that you do not want to present to the user with a normal text field. You can then pass this information to the server for processing. You can define a hidden object in HTML using the following syntax:

```
<INPUT
    TYPE="hidden"
    NAME="objectName"
    [VALUE="value"]>
```

The following line shows an example:

```
<INPUT TYPE="hidden" NAME="hiddenField1">
```

13

FORM OBJECTS

In a pure HTML world, hidden fields played an important role in holding specific bits of information on the user side that the server could use at a later time. With the advent of JavaScript, the hidden object makes less sense to use in combination with JavaScript. The reason is that a JavaScript global variable serves the same purpose as the hidden object, and it's a lot easier to manipulate.

Take a look at a set of two examples that demonstrate this. Figure 13.12 shows a set of radio buttons a user can click. However, you want to add code to the Undo Last button so that the user can undo the last selection he made. You cannot use a reset button for this because that will either clear the radio buttons or return the default value. Instead, you need to add JavaScript code to perform this task. The code files shown in Listings 13.12 and 13.13 are charged with performing this task. Listing 13.12 uses a set of hidden fields to carry it out, whereas Listing 13.13 uses global variables. Keep in mind that neither of these methods are incorrect, and both are valid techniques.

Figure 13.12.

Storing the last value using a hidden object.

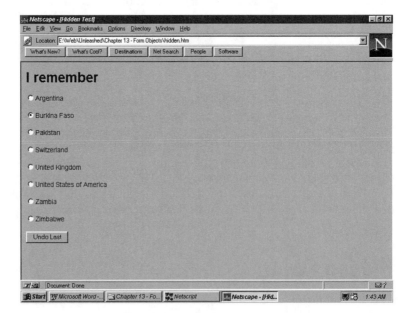

Listing 13.12. `hidden.htm`.

```
<html>
<head>
<title>Hidden Test</title>
<SCRIPT LANGUAGE="JavaScript">
```

```
        function postData(value) {
             document.form1.holder2.value = document.form1.holder.value
             document.form1.holder.value = value
        }

        function resetValue() {
             var len = document.form1.ctyList.length
             for (var i=0; i<len; i++) {
                  if (document.form1.ctyList[i].value ==
                      document.form1.holder2.value) {
                       document.form1.ctyList[i].checked = "1"
                       break }
             }
        }

</SCRIPT>
</head>

<body>
<h1>I remember</h1>
<form name="form1" method="POST">
<p><input type=radio name="ctyList" value="Argentina"
onClick="postData(this.value)">Argentina</p>
<p><input type=radio name="ctyList" value="Burkina Faso"
onClick="postData(this.value)">Burkina Faso</p>
<p><input type=radio name="ctyList" value="Pakistan"
onClick="postData(this.value)">Pakistan</p>
<p><input type=radio name="ctyList" value="Switzerland"
onClick="postData(this.value)">Switzerland</p>
<p><input type=radio name="ctyList" value="United Kingdom"
onClick="postData(this.value)">United Kingdom</p>
<p><input type=radio name="ctyList" value="United States of America"
onClick="postData(this.value)">United States of America</p>
<p><input type=radio name="ctyList" value="Zambia"
onClick="postData(this.value)">Zambia</p>
<p><input type=radio name="ctyList" value="Zimbabwe"
onClick="postData(this.value)">Zimbabwe</p>
<p><input type=button name="UndoLast" value="Undo Last"
onClick="resetValue()"></p>
<INPUT TYPE="hidden" NAME="holder" value="">
<INPUT TYPE="hidden" NAME="holder2" value="">
</form>
</body>
</html>
```

13

FORM OBJECTS

In this first example, each time the user clicks a radio button, the postData() method places the current radio button value in the hidden object called holder and the current holder value into the holder2 object. This value is then retrieved when a user clicks the Undo Last button and the appropriate radio button is selected.

Listing 13.13. hiddenVars.htm.

```
<html>
<head>
<title>Hidden Var Test</title>
<SCRIPT LANGUAGE="JavaScript">

     var holder = ""
     var holder2 = ""

     function postData(value) {
          holder2 = holder
          holder = value
     }

     function resetValue() {
          var len = document.form1.ctyList.length
          for (var i=0; i<len; i++) {
               if (document.form1.ctyList[i].value == holder2) {
                    document.form1.ctyList[i].checked = "1"
                    break }
          }
     }

</SCRIPT>
</head>

<body>
<h1>I remember</h1>
<form name="form1" method="POST">
<p><input type=radio name="ctyList" value="Argentina"
onClick="postData(this.value)">Argentina</p>
<p><input type=radio name="ctyList" value="Burkina Faso"
onClick="postData(this.value)">Burkina Faso</p>
<p><input type=radio name="ctyList" value="Pakistan"
onClick="postData(this.value)">Pakistan</p>
<p><input type=radio name="ctyList" value="Switzerland"
onClick="postData(this.value)">Switzerland</p>
<p><input type=radio name="ctyList" value="United Kingdom"
onClick="postData(this.value)">United Kingdom</p>
<p><input type=radio name="ctyList" value="United States of America"
onClick="postData(this.value)">United States of America</p>
<p><input type=radio name="ctyList" value="Zambia"
onClick="postData(this.value)">Zambia</p>
<p><input type=radio name="ctyList" value="Zimbabwe"
onClick="postData(this.value)">Zimbabwe</p>
<p><input type=button name="UndoLast" value="Undo Last"
onClick="resetValue()"></p>
</form>
</body>
</html>
```

In this second example, the holder and holder2 variables are defined globally at the start of the script. This script uses these variables in place of the hidden object references of the first example.

Summary

Forms play an important role in JavaScript. Not only can you qualify and sharpen data before it is sent to the server for processing, but you can also use HTML forms to create client-side applications using JavaScript. In this chapter, you learned about form objects and the various objects that can only exist inside its borders. You also learned how to submit forms to the server and how to work with and check values of input controls before data is sent on.

This chapter finished the in-depth discussion of navigator objects. Chapter 14, "Built-In Language Objects," looks at the other side of the object model: built-in language objects.

Built-In Language Objects

by Richard Wagner

IN THIS CHAPTER

Determining String Lengths

You can use the String object's `length` property to determine the size of a string. For example, the following code returns 17:

```
"Crazy Legs Nelson".length
```

The following code returns 16:

```
var str = "This is the day."
len = str.length
```

Searching Within Strings

You can search for text within strings by using `indexOf()` and `lastIndexOf()`. Use these methods when you want to search for a particular character or substring within a string and return the position (or index) of the occurrence within the string. Whereas `indexOf()` starts at the left of the string and moves right, `lastIndexOf()` does the same operation but starts at the left. Both `indexOf()` and `lastIndexOf()` start at the 0 position for the first character encountered, and both return a value of -1 if the search text is not found. For example, the following code returns a value of 3:

```
"Time and time again".indexOf("e")
```

On the other hand, the following code returns a value of 12:

```
"Time and time again".lastIndexOf("e")
```

Both methods have an optional second parameter that enables you to specify where in the string you want to start the search. For example, the script shown in Listing 14.1 searches through the variable `graf` and counts the number of occurrences of the letter e.

Listing 14.1. `indexOf.htm`.

```
<SCRIPT LANGUAGE = "JavaScript">

    pos = 0
    num = -1
    i = -1

    var graf = "While nearly everyone agrees on the principle of reuse,
            the priority we give it varies wildly."

    while (pos != -1) {
        pos = graf.indexOf("e",i+1)
        num += 1
        i = pos
    }

    document.write(graf)
    document.write("<p><p>")
    document.write("There were " + num + " e's in that paragraph.")

</SCRIPT>
```

Figure 14.1 shows the result of the script.

FIGURE 14.1.

Result of the indexOf() *example.*

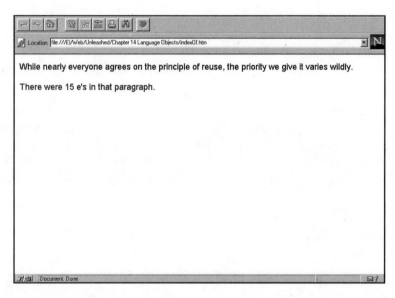

> While nearly everyone agrees on the principle of reuse, the priority we give it varies wildly.
>
> There were 15 e's in that paragraph.

Retrieving a Portion of a String

You can retrieve a portion of a string variable or literal by using the substring() method. It has two parameters—the start position and end position of the substring you want to return. Just like indexOf() and lastIndexOf(), this method is also zero-based, such that the first position of the string begins at 0. For example, the following code returns New:

```
"New England".substring(0,3)
```

If you want to retrieve a single character, you can use charAt(). The charAt() method returns the character at the position you specify as a parameter. For example, the following code returns a value of v:

```
"Denver Broncos".charAt(3)
```

If you specify a position that is out of the range of the string, a value of -1 is returned:

```
"007".charAt(20102)
```

Replace String Utility Code

The true power of these string-handling routines is demonstrated when you combine them to solve a problem. For an illustration of this, consider a common routine that you could want in JavaScript: a generic routine to replace specified text within a string with something else. To do this, develop a generic string-replace function that uses the length property, indexOf(), and substring(). Additionally, I will demonstrate both procedural and object-oriented approaches to solving this problem.

Using a traditional procedural approach, you could develop a stringReplace() function that has three parameters:

- originalString—the original string upon which you want to perform the replace.
- findText—the string that you want to be replaced.
- replaceText—the string that you want to insert into the originalString.

The function then uses that information to perform the replacement process. You can see that Listing 14.2 uses the indexOf() method to look for the findText parameter, and the substring() method pulls out the strings that are before and after findText. The function then concatenates the preString, replaceText, and postString and assigns it to the originalString variable. This process occurs for each occurrence of findText throughout the string. When findText is no longer found, the originalString value is returned to the user.

Listing 14.2. stringReplace.htm.

```
Replace code with the following:
<SCRIPT LANGUAGE = "JavaScript">

    function stringReplace(originalString, findText, replaceText) {
        var pos = 0
        var len = findText.length
        pos = originalString.indexOf(findText)
        while (pos != -1) {
            preString = originalString.substring(0, pos)
            postString = originalString.substring(pos+len,
originalString.length)
            originalString = preString + replaceText + postString
            pos = originalString.indexOf(findText)
        }
        return originalString
    }


    document.write(stringReplace("Richard", "ard", "ini"))


</SCRIPT>

<SCRIPT LANGUAGE = "JavaScript">

    function stringReplace(originalString, findText, replaceText) {
        var pos = 0
        pos = originalString.indexOf(findText)
        while (pos != -1) {
            preString = originalString.substring(0, pos)
            postString = originalString.substring(pos+1,
             originalString.length)
            originalString = preString + replaceText + postString
            pos = originalString.indexOf(findText)
        }
        return originalString
    }
</SCRIPT>
```

An alternative way to code this same function is to take advantage of Netscape Navigator 3.0's object prototype capabilities and add a `replace()` method to the `String` object type. You can restructure the `stringReplace()` code to work within the object framework, the result of which is shown in Listing 14.3.

Listing 14.3. stringOOReplace.htm.

```
<SCRIPT LANGUAGE = "JavaScript">

    String.prototype.replace = stringReplace


        function stringReplace(findText, replaceText) {
var originalString = new String(this)
            var pos = 0
            pos = originalString.indexOf(findText)
            while (pos != -1) {
                preString = originalString.substring(0, pos)
                postString = originalString.substring(pos+len,
                    originalString.length)
                originalString = preString + replaceText + postString
                pos = originalString.indexOf(findText)
            }
            return originalString
        }

</SCRIPT>
```

To put the `replace()` method into action, you can create a `String` object, assign a value to it, and then use the newly created method to replace all occurrences of 1s with 2s:

```
var myVar = new String("")
myVar = "11111111111111"
myVar = myVar.replace("1", "2")
document.write(myVar)
```

Formatting Strings

JavaScript has several methods you can use to format strings. Most of these methods are simply equivalents of HTML formatting tags. Using the formatting methods gives you an object-oriented way of dealing with HTML formatting tags, and it's also easier than continuously concatenating HTML tags to strings. In other words, if you have a string literal `"This is the day"` and you want to add bold formatting to it, you could do so using one of two means. First, you could add HTML formatting tags:

```
"<B>" + "This is the day" + "</B>"
```

Second, you could use the `String` object method `bold()` to add the formatting:

```
"This is the day".bold()
```

Each of the formatting options shown as checkboxes in Figure 14.2 are either true-or-false settings. The following code checks to see if each of the boxes are checked. If so, it calls the appropriate formatting method for the txt variable:

```
if (document.form1.bigBox.checked) {
     txt = txt.big()}

if (document.form1.blinkBox.checked) {
     txt = txt.blink() }


if (document.form1.boldBox.checked) {
     txt = txt.bold() }


if (document.form1.fixedBox.checked) {
     txt = txt.fixed()}

if (document.form1.italicsBox.checked) {
     txt = txt.italics()}


if (document.form1.smallBox.checked) {
     txt = txt.small()}


if (document.form1.strikeBox.checked) {
     txt = txt.strike()}


if (document.form1.subBox.checked) {
     txt = txt.sub()}


if (document.form1.supBox.checked) {
     txt = txt.sup()}
```

None of these formatting options are mutually exclusive—although some might cancel out each other. As a result, you can use as many of the methods at the same time as you want. JavaScript simply processes each of the methods, adding the appropriate HTML tags in sequential order.

The font color and size settings are not simply logical settings, so they require a parameter to be set. The select boxes on the form are used to specify these settings. The following code grabs this information from the form objects and calls the fontcolor() and fontsize() methods (clr and sze variables are used to make the code easier to read):

```
clr = document.form1.colorList.options[document.form1.
   colorList.options.selectedIndex].text
txt = txt.fontcolor(clr)
sze = document.form1.sizeList.options[document.form1.
   sizeList.options.selectedIndex].text
txt = txt.fontsize(sze)
```

Finally, the txt variable is used in a document.write() method on a new window that is created. Based on the settings shown in Figure 14.2, the txt variable returns the following value:

```
<FONT SIZE="5"><FONT COLOR="red"><I><TT><B><BIG>The capital
of Burkina Faso is Ouagadougou</BIG></B></TT></I></FONT></FONT>
```

Because the code uses multiple tags, JavaScript places each successive tag outside of all previous ones. As a result, the <BIG> tags are the innermost tags in the formatting definition because the big() method is the first one that was called. The tags of the last method, called fontsize(), are on the outside.

Figure 14.3 shows the result window based on the settings shown in Figure 14.2.

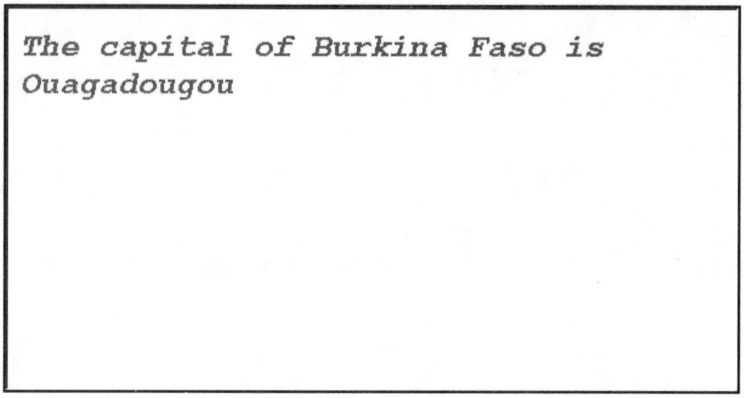

FIGURE 14.3.
Result of the string formatting options.

The capital of Burkina Faso is Ouagadougou

Listing 14.4 shows the entire source code for this example.

Listing 14.4. stringFormatting.htm.

```
<html>
<head>
<title>String Object Formatting</title>
</head>
<body>
<SCRIPT LANGUAGE="JavaScript">
<!--

    function showWindow() {
        var txt = document.form1.stringField.value
        var clr = ""
        var sze = ""

        if (document.form1.bigBox.checked) {
            txt = txt.big()
        }

        if (document.form1.blinkBox.checked) {
            txt = txt.blink()
        }
```

continues

14

BUILT-IN
LANGUAGE
OBJECTS

Listing 14.4. continued

```
               if (document.form1.boldBox.checked) {
                    txt = txt.bold()
               }

               if (document.form1.fixedBox.checked) {
                    txt = txt.fixed()
               }

               if (document.form1.italicsBox.checked) {
                    txt = txt.italics()
               }

               if (document.form1.smallBox.checked) {
                    txt = txt.small()
               }

               if (document.form1.strikeBox.checked) {
                    txt = txt.strike()
               }

               if (document.form1.subBox.checked) {
                    txt = txt.sub()
               }

               if (document.form1.supBox.checked) {
                    txt = txt.sup()
               }

               clr = document.form1.colorList.options[document.form1.
                        colorList.options.selectedIndex].text
               txt = txt.fontcolor(clr)
               sze = document.form1.sizeList.options[document.form1.
                        sizeList.options.selectedIndex].text
               txt = txt.fontsize(sze)

               objWindow = window.open("", "","width=600,height=300")
               objWindow.document.write(txt)
               objWindow.document.close()
          }
//-->
</SCRIPT>
<h1>String Object Formatting</h1>
<form method="POST" name="form1">
<pre><strong>String: </strong><input type=text size=40 maxlength=256
name="stringField"></pre>
<pre><strong>Style: </strong></pre>
<pre><input type=checkbox name="bigBox" value="ON">Big        <input
type=checkbox name="blinkBox" value="ON">Blink     <input type=checkbox
name="boldBox" value="ON">Bold  <input type=checkbox name="fixedBox"
value="ON">Fixed    <input type=checkbox name="italicsBox" value="ON">Italics
<input type=checkbox name="smallBox" value="ON">Small    <input type=checkbox
name="strikeBox" value="ON">Strike   <input type=checkbox name="subBox"
value="ON">Sub   <input type=checkbox name="supBox" value="ON">Sup</pre>
<pre><strong>Font: </strong></pre>
<pre>Color: <select name="colorList" size=1>
<option selected>black</option>
```

```
<option>green</option>
<option>red</option>
</select>    Size: <select name="sizeList" size=1>
<option selected>1</option>
<option>2</option>
<option>3</option>
<option>4</option>
<option>5</option>
<option>6</option>
<option>7</option>
</select></pre>
<pre> <input type="button" name="Show" value="Show"
onClick="showWindow()"></pre>
</form>
</body>
</html>
```

Case Changing Formatting Methods

The toUpperCase() and toLowerCase() methods work just as you would expect. They are helpful to use when you need to compare text without concerning yourself with the case of the text. For example, if you want to compare user-entered text with a string literal, it is helpful to use all uppercase or lowercase when making the evaluation:

```
myVar = document.form1.field1.value
if (myVar.toUpperCase() == "SHAGGY") {
     doMethod() }
```

Hypertext Formatting Methods

You can use the String object's anchor() and link() methods to create anchor and link objects. These methods make it much easier to work with anchors and links in your code, avoiding painful string concatenations of HTML tags. To illustrate, use a similar idea as the previous formatting example to work with hypertext formatting. Figure 14.4 shows an HTML form you can use to specify the elements of a hypertext link: text, anchor/link designation, and URL/anchor to associate with the underlined text.

A similar showWindow() method (triggered by the Show button's onClick event handler) processes the user-entered options and calls either the link() or anchor() method of the txt variable.

```
var txt = document.form1.stringField.value

if (document.form1.hypertext[0].checked) {
     txt = txt.link(document.form1.jumptoField.value) }
else {
 if (document.form1.hypertext[1].checked) {
     txt = txt.anchor(document.form1.jumptoField.value) }
}
```

Figure 14.5 shows the result window with a new hypertext link created.

FIGURE 14.4.

String object hypertext formatting.

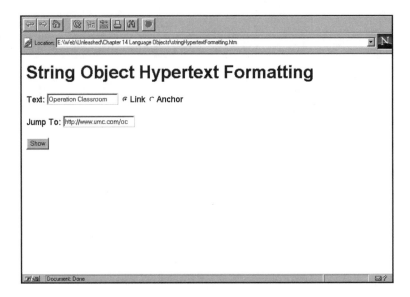

FIGURE 14.5.

Link object created using the link() *method.*

Listing 14.5 shows the entire source code.

Listing 14.5. stringHypertextFormatting.htm.

```
<title>String Object Hypertext Formatting</title>
</head>
<body>
<SCRIPT LANGUAGE="JavaScript">
<!--

    function showWindow() {
        var txt = document.form1.stringField.value

        if (document.form1.hypertext[0].checked) {
            txt = txt.link(document.form1.jumptoField.value) }
        else {
         if (document.form1.hypertext[1].checked) {
            txt = txt.anchor(document.form1.jumptoField.value) }
        }
```

```
         objWindow = window.open("", "","width=600,height=300")
         objWindow.document.write(txt)
         objWindow.document.close()
    }
//-->
</SCRIPT>
<h1>String Object Hypertext Formatting</h1>
<form method="POST" name="form1">
<p>    Text: <input type=text size=20 maxlength=256 name="stringField"> <input
type=radio name="hypertext" value="Link" checked>Link <input
type=radio name="hypertext" value="Anchor">Anchor </p>
<p>Jump To: <input type=text size=20 maxlength=256 name="jumptoField"></p>
<input type="button" name="Show" value="Show" onClick="showWindow()">
</form>
</body>
</html>
```

Working with Special Characters

When working with strings in any language, you will discover certain characters that are difficult to use. JavaScript enables you to work with these special-case characters by using a backslash
character (\) followed by the character or its code. Table 14.3 lists the JavaScript inline
symbols.

Table 14.3. Inline symbols.

Symbol	Description
\t	Tab
\n	New line
\r	Carriage return
\f	Form feed
\\	Backslash
\b	Backspace
\"	Double quote
\'	Single quote

For example, if you want to use a backslash in a string literal, you use the following method:

```
"Your file is located in C:\\WINDOWS\\TEMP"
```

When displayed, it looks like the following line:

```
Your file is located in C:\WINDOWS\TEMP
```

TIP

Use the \r inline symbol to add a carriage return to an `alert()` message box message. Figure 14.6 shows the result of the following example in the dialog box:

```
alert("Follow these steps:\r\r1. Choose Print from the File menu.\r2.
    Click the OK button to print.")
```

Because these inline symbols can be confusing to use, you might find it helpful to assign variables to them. In fact, if you use them often, you can pull these defined "constants" from a JavaScript code library and use them over and over. Listing 14.6 shows these inline characters treated as constants and how to use them in a `write()` method.

FIGURE 14.6.

New lines in message boxes.

Listing 14.6. inlineConstants.htm.

```
<SCRIPT LANGUAGE = "JavaScript">
    // Inline Character Constants
    var TAB = "\t"
    var CR = "\r"
    var LF = "\n"
    var CRLF = "\r\n"
    var FF = "\f"
    var DQUOTE = '\"'
    var SQUOTE = "\'"
    var BACKSLASH = "\\"
    var BACKSPACE = "\b"

    document.write("Column1" + TAB + "Column2" + TAB + "Column3")
</SCRIPT>
```

In addition to these inline symbols, you also have other ways of working with non-alphanumeric values in JavaScript. If you need to convert a non-alphanumeric value to an ASCII-encoded value, you can use the built-in `escape()` method. One example is the following code:

```
escape("Jim's Favorite ASCII character is the tilde(~)")
```

The code returns the following value:

```
Jim%27s%20Favorite%20ASCII%20character%20is%20the%20tilde%28%7E%29
```

If you need to convert an ASCII-encoded string—perhaps a string retrieved from a server—you can use the `unescape()` method. The following code is a good illustration:

```
unescape("email%20me%20at%20rwagner@acadians.com%21")
```

The code returns the following string value:

```
email me at rwagner@acadians.com!
```

Converting Strings to Numbers

JavaScript provides two built-in methods that you can use to convert strings to numbers: `parseInt()` and `parseFloat()`. Both functions take strings as their parameters and attempt to convert the string data into a numeric value. `parseInt()` tries to convert it into an Integer value, and `parseFloat()` attempts to convert it into a floating-point value. For example, the following code returns `123`:

```
parseInt("123.88888")
```

The following code returns `1234.0012121`:

```
parseFloat("1234.0012121")
```

Both of these routines start the conversion from the left side of the string and convert until it hits something other than a numeric digit (0-9), a decimal (.), or a plus or minus sign (-/+). If it does encounter a non-numeric character, the rest of the string is ignored. For example, the following code returns `1234.01`:

```
parseFloat("1234.01 is the total price")
```

However, the following code returns a `0` value because the dollar sign is a non-numeric value:

```
parseFloat("$1234.01 is the total price")
```

These conversion functions are very useful when you're working with text objects. Because the value property of a text object returns a string, you must convert this data any time you want to treat text entered by a user as a numeric value. Suppose, for example, you want to take a number entered by a user and use it in a calculation. You could use `parseInt()` for this task:

```
stateTax = .06
subtotal = parseInt(document.form1.subtotal.value)
total = subtotal + (stateTax * subtotal)
```

Converting Numbers to Strings

You can also convert numeric values to strings, but there are no built-in methods to do so. Instead, you perform this task based on how JavaScript processes the addition (+) operator. As JavaScript adds elements of an expression and it encounters a string, the whole expression is treated as a string from that point on. For example, `35 + 100` returns a numeric value of `135`. If the `"100"` is a string, however, `35 + "100"` returns a string value of `"35100"`.

Interestingly, because JavaScript processes the additional operator from left to right, you could actually add two numeric digits together before the expression is converted into a string. For example, 10 + 20 + "40" returns a string value of "3040" because the 10 + 20 pair is added together before its result is added to the next string value. In contrast, "40" + 10 + 20 returns a string value of "401020" because the string is on the left of the numeric values.

In most programming languages, you must convert a numeric value before you can use it in the context of a string value. As you can see, the only thing you need to do is either use it in a string expression with other string values or add an empty string to it. For example, the expression 1300 + "" returns a string value of "1300". Rather than add an empty string each time you want to perform this conversion, you could use a simple conversion function to do this for you:

```
function numToString(number) {
     number += ""
     return number
}
```

Listing 14.7 shows a sample script that demonstrates this function. The first alert message box displays "Number" as the data type for the number variable. After the numToString() function is performed, the second alert box displays "String" as the number's data type.

Listing 14.7. numToString.htm.

```
<SCRIPT LANGUAGE = "JavaScript">

    function numToString(number) {
        number += ""
        return number
    }

    var number = 100
    alert (typeof number)
    number = numToString(number)
    alert (typeof number)

</SCRIPT>
```

Array Object

An array is a programming construct fundamental to nearly all languages today. JavaScript is no different, providing the capability to construct and work with arrays. An *array* is simply a container holding a set of data elements. Each of the elements in an array is a separate value, but they exist as part of the array and cannot be accessed except by going through the array.

> **NOTE**
>
> Although strongly typed languages require that all array values be of the same type, JavaScript does not. Consequently, your array can contain mixed data types within them, just as an object can have properties of varying types.

To define or access a particular element, you need to add brackets and an index value to the array variable. For example, you can define an array called `coffee` as follows:

```
coffee[0] = "Ethiopian Sidamo"
coffee[1] = "Kenyan"
coffee[2] = "Café Verona"
coffee[3] = "Sumatra"
coffee[4] = "Costa Rica"
coffee[5] = "Columbian"
coffee[6] = "Bristan"
```

If you wanted to use any of these elements within a script, you could access them using the array variable along with an index value representing the location of the element within the array. Therefore, if you wanted to write the following line:

```
My favorite coffee is Ethiopian Sidamo
```

You would code the following:

```
document.write("My favorite coffee is " + coffee[0])
```

If arrays are new to you, you might find it helpful to think of an array as JavaScript's equivalent of a numbered list. It is really no more complicated than that. For example, suppose you have a list of ten items:

1. JavaScript
2. Java
3. Delphi
4. C++
5. Visual Basic
6. Oracle Power Objects
7. SmallTalk
8. PowerBuilder
9. Paradox
10. Access

If you wanted to assemble this group of items in a JavaScript array, it would look like the following:

```
devTools[0] = "JavaScript"
devTools[1] = "Java"
```

14

BUILT-IN
LANGUAGE
OBJECTS

```
devTools[2] = "Delphi"
devTools[3] = "C++"
devTools[4] = "Visual Basic"
devTools[5] = "Oracle Power Objects"
devTools[6] = "SmallTalk"
devTools[7] = "PowerBuilder"
devTools[8] = "Paradox"
devTools[9] = "Access"
```

Creating an Array Object

Unlike a string, an array is not recognized as a data type in JavaScript, but you can work with them as objects. The way in which you create Array objects varies depending on the browser you are using.

Array Objects with Netscape Navigator 3.0

Netscape Navigator 3.0 enables you to work with arrays as true JavaScript objects. You can create instances of an Array object using the new operator. For example, if you wanted to create the coffee array defined earlier, you would define it as follows:

```
var coffee = new Array()
coffee[0] = "Ethiopian Sidamo"
coffee[1] = "Kenyan"
coffee[2] = "Café Verona"
coffee[3] = "Sumatra"
coffee[4] = "Costa Rica"
coffee[5] = "Columbian"
coffee[6] = "Bristan"
```

The new operator creates an Array object, and the statements following fill the array with data elements.

TIP

An alternative way to define an Array object is to specify the data elements as parameters of the new call. For example, the following line is the functional equivalent of the previous example:

```
var coffee = new Array("Ethiopian Sidamo", "Kenyan", "Café Verona",
"Sumatra", "Costa Rica", "Columbian", "Bristan")
```

Notice that you did not specify a size of the array, as is commonplace in many programming languages. JavaScript does not require that you specify the size of the array, which allows you to incrementally expand the array as you add each new data element. However, if you want to, you can specify the size of the array initially as a parameter in the new expression:

```
var coffee = new Array(7)
```

Alternatively, you could also resize an array simply by defining a data element at the *n* position. If *n* is the highest number defined in the array, then the new array size is expanded to *n* + 1. Note the following example:

```
var javaDrinks = new Array()
javaDrinks[0] = "Regular coffee"
javaDrinks[1] = "Decaf coffee"
javaDrinks[2] = "Café Mocha"
javaDrinks[3] = "Café au Lait"
javaDrinks[199] = "Café Latte"
```

The size of the javaDrinks array is 200, even though only five data elements are defined. Each undefined element returns a null value if you access it.

You can retrieve the size of the array using the Array object's length property. For example, if you wanted to iterate through each element in an array object, you could use the script shown in Listing 14.8.

Listing 14.8. coffeeArrayObject.htm.

```
<SCRIPT LANGUAGE = "JavaScript">

    var coffee = new Array()
    coffee[0] = "Ethiopian Sidamo"
    coffee[1] = "Kenyan"
    coffee[2] = "Café Verona"
    coffee[3] = "Sumatra"
    coffee[4] = "Costa Rica"
    coffee[5] = "Columbian"
    coffee[6] = "Bristan"


    document.write("Coffees of the World:<p>")
    for (var i=0; i<coffee.length; i++) {
        document.write(i + 1 + ". " + coffee[i] + "<p>")
    }

</SCRIPT>
```

Figure 14.7 shows the result.

14

BUILT-IN LANGUAGE OBJECTS

> **CAUTION**
>
> The Array object's length property is read only. As a result, you cannot resize an array by assigning a value to the length property.

FIGURE 14.7.

Using JavaScript to display a coffee list.

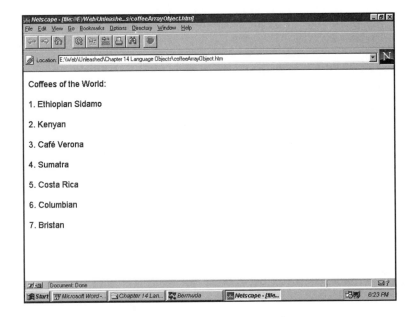

Basic Arrays with Netscape Navigator 2.x

If you are working with Netscape Navigator 2.*x*, you cannot take advantage of the Array object. Because an array is not a distinct data type, you need to create one through a rather inelegant process (or, if you are frank, you can call it a workaround). Although Chapter 15, "Creating Custom JavaScript Objects," is devoted to creating custom objects, I'd like to describe this process here. To create an array, you need to create your own custom routine that emulates an array object "constructor." Using a custom function called createArray(), you can create the array as a custom object:

```
function createArray(size) {
   this.length = size;
   for (var i = 1; i <= size; i++) {
     this[i] = null }
     return this
     }
}
```

The createArray() function uses its size parameter to define the length of the array. Notice that the length actually becomes the first element in the array. Although the length property of the Netscape Navigator 3.0 Array object is maintained internally, the length property of the custom-made array must be maintained by you. Also, as the first element in the array, it occupies the array[0] position. When you work with these array elements, you should always start with 1 as the initial position; otherwise, you will overwrite the length value. Obviously, because everything else in JavaScript is zero-based, this can be confusing.

> **CAUTION**
>
> In order for the `length` property to have any meaning, you need to manually update this setting when you resize an array. If you do not, it will be outdated.

After the `length` property is set, the `createArray()` function uses a `for` loop to assign a null value to each element of the array.

> **NOTE**
>
> The official Netscape recommendation is the following:
>
> ```
> function MakeArray(n) {
>    this.length = n;
>    for (var i = 1; i <= n; i++) {
>      this[i] = 0 }
>      return this
>      }
> }
> ```
>
> The only difference in the Netscape version and the `createArray()` function shown in this book is that `createArray()` more closely resembles the functionality of the Array object—undefined data elements having a null value.

Using this process, the `coffee` Array object example shown in the last section would be coded as shown in Listing 14.9.

Listing 14.9. coffeeArrayOrig.htm.

```
<SCRIPT LANGUAGE = "JavaScript">

    function createArray(size) {
       this.length = size;
       for (var i = 1; i <= size; i++) {
         this[i] = null }
         return this
     }

    var coffee = new createArray(7)

    coffee[1] = "Ethiopian Sidamo"
    coffee[2] = "Kenyan"
    coffee[3] = "Café Verona"
    coffee[4] = "Sumatra"
    coffee[5] = "Costa Rica"
    coffee[6] = "Columbian"
    coffee[7] = "Bristan"
```

continues

Listing 14.9. continued

```
document.write("Coffees of the World:<p>")

for (var i=1; i<=coffee.length; i++) {
    document.write(i + ". " + coffee[i] + "<p>")
}

</SCRIPT>
```

Working with Multi-Dimensional Arrays

The array examples I have shown so far deal with single-dimensional arrays. That is, there is a single value associated with each index of the array. Some languages allow you to create multi-dimensional arrays so you can store two or more values per array index. You can think of a multi-dimensional array as a database table with multiple fields (columns).

JavaScript does not provide explicit support for multi-dimensional arrays, but you can simulate them by creating an array of custom objects. For complete information on this topic, see Chapter 30, "Using Client-Side Tables in JavaScript."

Date Object

The Date object is the means by which you work with date and time values in JavaScript. You should understand three significant facts regarding the Date object before using it:

- Following the UNIX convention, JavaScript considers January 1, 1970 to be the baseline date. Consequently, you cannot work with dates prior to that time frame.

- When you create a Date object, the time reflected within the object is based on the client machine. You are thus dependent on the client computer to have a working and accurate clock. Keep this dependency in mind as you consider time-sensitive code in your JavaScript scripts.

- JavaScript keeps track of date/time values in the form of milliseconds since the baseline date (1/1/70).

Encapsulated within the Date object is an impressive array of methods to get and set date values and convert them into various forms. Tables 14.4 through 14.7 list the Date object methods based on method type.

Table 14.4. Get methods of the Date object.

Method	Description
getDate()	Returns date within month (1-31)
getDay()	Returns day within week (0-6)

Method	*Description*
getHours()	Returns hour within day (0-23)
getMinutes()	Returns minutes within hour (0-59)
getMonth()	Returns month within year (0-11)
getSeconds()	Returns seconds within minute (0-59)
getTime()	Returns number of milliseconds since 1/1/70 00:00:00
getYear()	Returns number of years since 1900
getTimeZoneOffset()	Returns minutes offset from GMT/UTC

Table 14.5. Set methods of the Date object.

Method	*Description*
setDate(*value*)	Sets date within month (1-31)
setHours(*value*)	Sets hour within day (0-23)
setMinutes(*value*)	Sets minutes within hour (0-59)
setMonth(*value*)	Sets month within year (0-11)
setSeconds(*value*)	Sets seconds within minute (0-59)
setTime(*value*)	Sets number of milliseconds since 1/1/70 00:00:00
setYear(*value*)	Sets number of years since 1900

Table 14.6. To methods of the Date object.

Method	*Description*
toGMTString()	Returns date string in universal format
toLocalString()	Returns date string in local system's format

Table 14.7. Static parse methods of the Date object.

Method	*Description*
parse("*stringDate*")	Converts *stringDate* to milliseconds
UTC(*value1*,*value2*,...*value5*)	Converts comma-delimited values to milliseconds of GMT date

14

BUILT-IN
LANGUAGE
OBJECTS

NOTE

Just like almost everything else in JavaScript, relative date values are also zero-based. This is perhaps counterintuitive because days of the week are 0-6 rather than 1-7 and months of the year are 0-11 rather than 1-12. As you process these values in your code, you need to account for these zero-based values.

However, note that the date within the month is an exception (1-31) because this is an absolute value.

Creating a Date Object

Creating a Date object is similar to creating String or Array objects. You can create as many Date objects as you want in your scripts. Using the new operator, you can define a Date object as follows:

```
var dateVariable = new Date([parameters])
```

You can include several parameters, as shown in Table 14.8.

Table 14.8. Date object parameters.

Parameter	Description	Example
Nothing	Creates an object with the current date and time.	`var today = new Date()`
`"month dd, yyyy hh:mm:ss"`	Creates an object with the specified date and time in the string. (All omitted time values are automatically set to zero.)	`var jaredBirthday = new Date("September 22, 1992")`
`yy, mm, dd`	Creates an object with the specified date of the set of integer values (zero based).	`var justinBirthday = new Date(94,1,0)`
`yy, mm, dd, hh, mm, ss`	Creates an object with the specified date and time of the set of integer values (zero based). (All omitted time values are automatically set to zero.)	`var jordanBirthday = new Date(90,7,12,7,10,29)`

Working with Date Values

Once a `Date` object is created, you can use one of several methods to either get or set date values. For example, to return the date of the current month, you would code the following:

```
var today = new Date()
result = today.getDate()
```

To change the month defined for the `Date` object `appt`, you can use the following code:

```
var appt = new Date(1996,06,12)
result = appt.setMonth(7)
```

I discussed earlier how the zero-based date values can make it difficult to work with getting dates. You can get around this annoyance by extending the `Date` object methods by prototyping more user-friendly `get` methods. If you recall, Netscape Navigator 3.0 lets you extend the capabilities of built-in objects by enabling you to prototype new methods or properties. All objects of this type will inherit this new prototype. Add five new methods to the `Date` object:

- `getFullYear()` returns a year in *yyyy* format.
- `getActualMonth()` returns the actual numeric value for the month.
- `getCalendarMonth()` returns the name of the month.
- `getActualDay()` returns the actual numeric value of the day of week.
- `getCalendarDay()` returns the name of the day of week.

Listing 14.10 shows the method definitions for each of these prototype methods.

Listing 14.10. dateGetActual.htm.

```
<SCRIPT LANGUAGE="JavaScript">

    ////////////////////////////////////////////
    //     Date Object Enhanced Get Methods    //
    ////////////////////////////////////////////
    Date.prototype.getFullYear = getFullYear
    Date.prototype.getActualMonth = getActualMonth
    Date.prototype.getActualDay = getActualDay
    Date.prototype.getCalendarDay = getCalendarDay
    Date.prototype.getCalendarMonth = getCalendarMonth

        function getFullYear() {
            var n = this.getYear()
            n += 1900
            return n
        }

        function getActualMonth() {
            var n = this.getMonth()
            n += 1
            return n
        }
```

continues

14

BUILT-IN
LANGUAGE
OBJECTS

Listing 14.10. continued

```
function getActualDay() {
    var n = this.getDay()
    n += 1
    return n
}

function getCalendarDay() {
    var n = this.getDay()
    var dow = new Array(7)
    dow[0] = "Sunday"
    dow[1] = "Monday"
    dow[2] = "Tuesday"
    dow[3] = "Wednesday"
    dow[4] = "Thursday"
    dow[5] = "Friday"
    dow[6] = "Saturday"
    return dow[n]
}

function getCalendarMonth() {
    var n = this.getMonth()
    var moy = new Array(12)
    moy[0] = "January"
    moy[1] = "February"
    moy[2] = "March"
    moy[3] = "April"
    moy[4] = "May"
    moy[5] = "June"
    moy[6] = "July"
    moy[7] = "August"
    moy[8] = "September"
    moy[9] = "October"
    moy[10] = "November"
    moy[11] = "December"
    return moy[n]
}

////////////////////////////////////////////////
//          End Date Object Prototype          //
////////////////////////////////////////////////


var today = new Date()

document.write("<h2>I hereby declare that on " +
today.getCalendarDay() + ", the " + today.getDate()
+ "th day of " + today.getCalendarMonth() + " in the year "
+ today.getFullYear() + " A.D. at the " + today.getHours()
+ "th hour of the day, absolutely nothing is happening.</h2>")

</SCRIPT>
```

After the methods are declared, the script creates a Date object and then generates an HTML document using a combination of the prototype methods. Figure 14.8 shows the result.

FIGURE 14.8.

Using the enhanced Get *methods.*

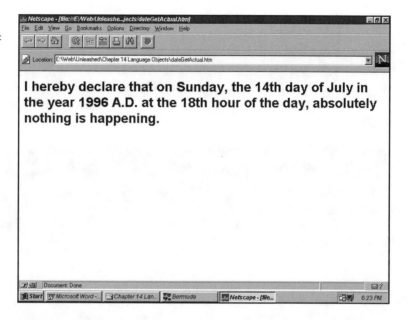

Working with Time Zones

Given that JavaScript is an application for the World Wide Web, it is only fitting that it includes some date functions to deal with time zones. getTimezoneOffset() returns the number of minutes difference between the client computer and GMT. For example, as I write this, I am in the US Eastern time zone. If I want to return the number of time zone offset hours, I could use the following code:

```
var today = new Date()
offset = today.getTimezoneOffset()/60
if (offset == -5) {
    alert(„You are in the Eastern Timezone")
}
```

Figure 14.9 shows the result when I run the script.

FIGURE 14.9.

Using getTimezone Offset() *to determine the time zone.*

Calculating with Dates

You can perform calculations between date values, determining such things as the number of days until the end of the century. When you perform calculations with dates, it is important to keep the dates in their "native" millisecond format during the calculation and then extract the relevant data later.

Math Object

For mathematical calculations, JavaScript encapsulates a host of mathematical constants and procedures into a single entity—the Math object. The Math object is quite a bit different from the other built-in objects. First, you can perform basic arithmetic calculations (addition, subtraction, multiplication, and division) outside a Math object, so unless you regularly require advanced math functions, you might rarely use it.

> **NOTE**
>
> Few developers might need to tap into the true power of the Math object, but for those who do, its capabilities are vital. Rather than pass values back to the server to perform mathematical calculations, you can use the Math object to perform advanced math processing on the client side.

Second, although you can create instances of String, Array, and Date objects using new, you work with a built-in instance of the Math object. This quality of the Math object parallels the Navigator object, for example, which is not created on-the-fly. Consequently, the Math object is commonly referred to as a *static* object.

> **NOTE**
>
> Do not confuse the Math object as a "number" object. The Math object is used for calculations only; it is not intended to be used as a representative for a number as a String object is commonly used in place of a string literal. It can be confusing because unlike the string, there is no number object per se. A number (either an integer or floating point) is recognized as a distinct data type, but it is not an object type.

The Math object's properties are really nothing more than a list of common mathematical constants, as shown in Table 14.9. Note the case of the constants. Although nearly all JavaScript properties are typically lowercase or mixed case, these properties are all uppercase.

Table 14.9. Math object properties.

Property	Returns	Description
E	2.718281828	Euler's constant
LN2	0.693147181	Natural log of 2
LN10	2.302585093	Natural log of 10
LOG2E	1.442695041	Log base -2 of E

Property	Returns	Description
LOG10E	0.434294482	Log base -10 of E
PI	3.141592654	Pi
SQRT1_2	0.707106781	Square root of 0.5
SQRT2	1.414213562	Square root of 2

Table 14.10 shows the methods of the Math object.

Table 14.10. Math object methods.

Method	Returns
abs*(value)*	Absolute value of *value*
acos*(value)*	Arc cosine of *value* (in radians)
asin*(value)*	Arc sine of *value* (in radians)
atan*(value)*	Arc tangent of *value* (in radians)
ceil*(value)*	Next integer >= *value*
cos*(value)*	Cosine of *value*
exp*(value)*	Euler's constant to the power of *value*
floor*(value)*	Next integer <= *value*
log*(value)*	Natural logarithm of *value* (base e)
max*(value1, value2)*	The highest number of *value1* or *value2*
min*(value1, value2)*	The lowest number of *value1* or *value2*
pow*(value1, value2)*	*value1* to the *value2* power
random*()*	A random number between 0 and 1
round*(value)*	*n* + 1 (if *value* >= *n*.5; else *n*)
sin*(value)*	Sine of *value* (in radians)
sqrt*(value)*	Square root of *value*
tan*(value)*	Tangent of *value* (in radians)

Summary

You may refer to the built-in language objects as the nuts and bolts of JavaScript because much of the hard programming work is performed within the constructs of the String, Array, Date, and `Math` objects. In this chapter, you learned about how to use these objects and the differences that exist when working with different versions of browser software. In the next chapter, you will apply what you learned about arrays in this chapter as you examine how to create custom objects.

Creating Custom JavaScript Objects

by Richard Wagner

IN THIS CHAPTER

CHAPTER 15

This chapter's discussion is a natural follow-up to the previous chapters. Chapter 8 covered many basics of object-oriented programming, and Chapters 9–14 discussed the entire spectrum of built-in objects within the JavaScript language. But if you stop there, you limit a great deal of the power that JavaScript has—enabling you to create your own custom objects. In this chapter, I discuss how to create custom objects in JavaScript, the major capabilities of JavaScript, and its limitations.

Creating an Object

Custom objects in JavaScript have a close association with arrays. Arrays are a means of structuring data into a container. Yet, as powerful as arrays are, they fail to meet the needs of everything you would like to do as a JavaScript developer. Although they store data, they cannot store behavior. As discussed in Chapter 8, an object contains both data, known as properties, and behavior, known as methods. Therefore, although an array is essentially the same thing as an object with properties, it does not store information on how the array can respond to messages. Our mission, then, is to create an entity that can encapsulate data elements and responses to messages.

To create a JavaScript object, you need to create a *constructor*. A constructor is a special JavaScript function that defines what the object will look like and how it will act. The constructor does not actually create the object but provides a template for what an instantiated object will look like. The following is the basic structure of an instantiated object:

```
function object(paramter1, parameter2,…) {
    this.property1 = parameter1
    this.property2 = parameter2
    this.property3 = parameter3
    this.property4 = parameter4
    this.method1 = function1
    this.method2 = function2
}
```

As you can see, the actual structure of the constructor is relatively straightforward. First, name the method itself. The name of the function will serve as the name of your object type. Therefore, it is critical for clarity's sake to give a descriptive name to your constructor method. If you are creating an object to represent an invoice, call it `invoice`. I've seen some people name their constructor in a verb format, such as `createInvoice`. This practice can lead to confusing and hard-to-read code because a property of the object would look like:

```
myDate = createInvoice.date
```

Even worse, if you had `create()` as a method of the object, your code would look like:

```
createInvoice.create()
```

A much clearer method of presentation is to use a noun-based approach, making the following two lines much more readable:

```
myDate = invoice.date
```

and

```
invoice.create()
```

Second, add parameters to the function for all the properties of the object. Therefore, when you create an instance of the object (also called *instantiating an object*), you pass the property values to the function as parameters.

Third, assign the value of the incoming parameters to the properties of the object. The this keyword comes in handy here and is used to represent the object as you define the properties.

Fourth, define the methods that the object type will have. Whereas properties are assigned values by parameters of the constructor itself, methods are created as functions outside of the constructor and assigned to the method definition of the object.

To illustrate, suppose I wanted to create a custom object in which I can store information on my favorite books. In particular, I would like to track a book's title, author, ISBN, subject, and a personal rating. The constructor can be defined as follows:

```
function book(title, author, ISBN, subject, rating) {
     this.title = title
     this.author = author
     this.ISBN = ISBN
     this.subject = subject
     this.rating = rating
}
```

Also, I want to add a method called show(), which displays the information on the instantiated object to the user. Therefore, I need to create a function, separate from the constructor itself, to do this:

```
function show() {
    objWindow = window.open("", "", "width=600,height=300")
    objWindow.document.write("<h1>Object Description</h1>")
    objWindow.document.write("<p>")
    objWindow.document.write("Book Title: " + this.title + "<p>")
    objWindow.document.write("Author: " + this.author + "<p>")
    objWindow.document.write("ISBN: " + this.ISBN + "<p>")
    objWindow.document.write("Subject: " + this.subject + "<p>")
    objWindow.document.write("Rich's Rating: " + this.rating + "<p>")
    objWindow.document.close()
}
```

Even though this code is outside of the constructor, you can consider it a part of the object declaration. Therefore, you can use the this keyword and have it refer to the object instance that is being called.

15

CREATING CUS-
TOM JAVASCRIPT
OBJECTS

I can then add a new entry to my constructor for the method:

```
function book(title, author, ISBN, subject, rating) {
        this.title = title
        this.author = author
        this.ISBN = ISBN
        this.subject = subject
        this.rating = rating
        this.show = show
    }
```

Notice two details about the show() method declaration. First, although the object method name is the same as the associated external function, it doesn't have to be. You can name each anything you like. For readability, some developers prefer to use identical names, and others prefix the external function with the object name, such as book_show(). Second, the external function does not include parentheses in the constructor, only the function name itself.

In older versions of Netscape Navigator, you needed to place a method definition above the object constructor, because all references were executed in a top-down format. This is no longer the case in Netscape Navigator 3.0. The placement of the show() method *vis-à-vis* the constructor method is not important from JavaScript's point-of-view. I find it helpful to take advantage of this new capability and make the code easier to read by placing any method definitions immediately under the object constructor. I also use comments to keep the set of functions together and treated as a unit. Listing 15.1 shows the complete object declaration for the book object.

Listing 15.1. Book Objects definition.

```
////////////////////////////
//       Book Object       //
////////////////////////////
function book(title, author, ISBN, subject, rating) {
      this.title = title
      this.author = author
      this.ISBN = ISBN
      this.subject = subject
      this.rating = rating
      this.show = show
}
      function show() {
          objWindow = window.open("", "", "width=600,height=300")
          objWindow.document.write("<h1>Object Description</h1>")
          objWindow.document.write("<p>")
          objWindow.document.write("Book Title: " + this.title + "<p>")
          objWindow.document.write("Author: " + this.author + "<p>")
          objWindow.document.write("ISBN: " + this.ISBN + "<p>")
          objWindow.document.write("Subject: " + this.subject + "<p>")
          objWindow.document.write("Rich's Rating: " + this.rating + "<p>")
          objWindow.document.close()
      }

////End Book Object Definition////
```

Instantiating Objects

To use the object I have declared in the `book()` constructor method, I need to create an instance of it in my JavaScript code. The `new` operator is used for this purpose and has the following syntax:

```
objectInstance = new objectType(parameter1, parameter2, parameter3,…)
```

Using the new operator, I create a book object using the following code:

```
dbBook = new book("Cost of Discipleship", "Dietrich Bonhoeffer",
                  "1-57521-118-1", "Grace", 5)
```

I can now refer to this object anywhere in my code using the `dbBook` variable. The instance will exist in memory as long as the page is loaded in my browser. After the user moves to a new page or closes the browser, the instance of the object disappears. This is important to understand when you start assigning values to object properties. If you want to save the objects persistently, you will need to pass them to the server for processing.

> **NOTE**
>
> Persistence is a buzzword of the object community. In a nutshell, it means the ability to create an object instance and save the state of the object, so that the next time the object is accessed, it is retrieved in its saved state.
>
> You cannot persistently store objects using client-side JavaScript.

To demonstrate what has been developed so far, the following code creates an instance of the book object and calls its `show()` method. Figure 15.1 displays the result.

```
<SCRIPT LANGUAGE = "JavaScript">

    // Book object defined here

    dbBook = new book("Cost of Discipleship", "Dietrich Bonhoeffer",
      "1-57521-118-1",  "Grace", 5)
    dbBook.show()

</SCRIPT>
```

15

CREATING CUS-
TOM JAVASCRIPT
OBJECTS

FIGURE 15.1.

Book object information is displayed in a new window.

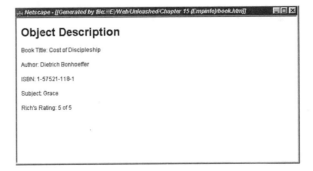

Working with Object Instances

After an object instance is created, you can work with it by assigning values to it or by performing one of its methods. You can also connect objects to user interface elements. For example, suppose you wanted to create a form that would allow you to change the rating for books, as well as display the book information form for each of the book objects you have instantiated. You can define the book object as shown earlier in the chapter and create five book instances using the following code:

```
dbBook = new book("Cost of Discipleship", "Dietrich Bonhoeffer", "1-57521-118-1",
          "Grace", 5)
fkBook = new book("The Once and Future King", "T.H. White", "1-57521-112-1",
              "Camelot", 5)
olBook = new book("On Liberty", "John Stuart Mill", "1-53221-118-1",
              "Political Philosophy", 4)
iaBook = new book("Icarus Agenda", "Robert Ludlum", "1-53221-118-1",
              "Politcal Thriller", 2)
cnBook = new book("Chronicles of Narnia", "C.S. Lewis", "1-53231-128-1",
              "Children's Fiction", 5)
```

For the form itself, use a select object with an `<OPTION>` defined for each of the books as well as one for the rating (range of 1–5). Add two buttons: one for making the rating assignment and the other to display the book information form. The form code looks like the following (and is shown in Figure 15.2):

```
<body>
<h1>Book Objects </h1>
<form name="form1">
<p>Select a book: </p>
<p><select name="bookList" size=1>
<option value="dbBook">Cost of Discipleship</option>
<option value="fkBook">The Once and Future King</option>
<option value="olBook">On Liberty</option>
<option value="iaBook">Icarus Agenda</option>
<option value="cnBook">Chronicles of Narnia</option>
</select>     </p>
<p>Assign a rating: </p>
<p><select name="rating" size=1>
<option>1</option>
<option>2</option>
<option>3</option>
```

```
<option>4</option>
<option>5</option>
</select> </p>
<p>Click to assign: </p>
<p><input type="button" name="Assign" value="Assign" onClick="assignRating()">
</p>
<p>Click to show: </p>
<p><input type="button" name="Show" value="Show" onClick="showBook()">
</p>
</form>
</body>
```

FIGURE 15.2.

Book Objects form.

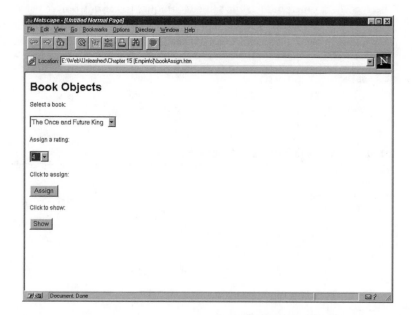

The heart of this example is in the event handlers for the Assign and Show buttons. The assignRating() method assigns the value of the selected rating to the selected book:

```
function assignRating() {
    selectedBook = document.form1.bookList.options[document.form1.bookList.
        selectedIndex].value
    selectedBook = eval(selectedBook)
    selectedBook.rating = document.form1.rating.options[document.form1.
        rating.selectedIndex].text
}
```

Looking at this closer, you can see that the method retrieves the value of the selected bookList option and assigns it to the selectedBook variable. To get this value, I use the bookList object's options property along with its selectedIndex property. I now have the name of the book object contained in the selectedBook variable, but JavaScript looks at this as a string value, not as a reference to an object instance. Therefore, the eval() method is used to convert the variable to an object reference. The last line of the method uses the selectedBook variable to assign its rating property the value of the currently selected option in the rating select object.

> **NOTE**
>
> You can use the typeof operator to test a variable's type during a method's execution. You could, for example, display an alert message box showing the selectedBook variable's type with the following code:
>
> ```
> alert(typeof selectedBook)
> ```

The showBook() method uses the same techniques to call the object's show() method:

```
function showBook() {
    selectedBook = document.form1.bookList.options[document.form1.bookList.
        selectedIndex].value
    selectedBook = eval(selectedBook)
    selectedBook.show()
}
```

Listing 15.2 lists the entire source code for this example.

Listing 15.2. Source code for the showBook example.

```
<html>
<head>
<title>Untitled Normal Page</title>
<SCRIPT LANGUAGE = "JavaScript">

    /////////////////////////////////
    //        Book Object          //
    /////////////////////////////////
    function book(title, author, ISBN, subject, rating) {
        this.title = title
        this.author = author
        this.ISBN = ISBN
        this.subject = subject
        this.rating = rating
        this.show = show
    }

    function show() {
        objWindow = window.open("", "", "width=600,height=300")
        objWindow.document.write("<h1>Object Description</h1>")
        objWindow.document.write("<p>")
        objWindow.document.write("Book Title: " + this.title + "<p>")
        objWindow.document.write("Author: " + this.author + "<p>")
        objWindow.document.write("ISBN: " + this.ISBN + "<p>")
        objWindow.document.write("Subject: " + this.subject + "<p>")
        objWindow.document.write("Rich's Rating: " + this.rating
            + " of 5<p>")
        objWindow.document.close()
    }

    ////End Book Object Definition////
```

```
    function assignRating() {
        selectedBook = document.form1.bookList.options[document.form1
          bookList.selectedIndex].value
        selectedBook = eval(selectedBook)
        selectedBook.rating = document.form1.rating.options[document.form1.
          rating.selectedIndex].text
    }

    function showBook() {
        selectedBook = document.form1.bookList.options[document.form1.
          bookList.selectedIndex].value
        selectedBook = eval(selectedBook)
        selectedBook.show()
    }


    // Execute on loading
    dbBook = new book("Cost of Discipleship", "Dietrich Bonhoeffer",
            "1-57521-118-1", "Grace", 5)
    fkBook = new book("The Once and Future King", "T.H. White",
            "1-57521-112-1", "Camelot", 5)
    olBook = new book("On Liberty", "John Stuart Mill",
            "1-53221-118-1", "Political Philosophy", 4)
    iaBook = new book("Icarus Agenda", "Robert Ludlum",
            "1-53221-118-1", "Politcal Thriller", 3)
    cnBook = new book("Chronicles of Narnia", "C.S. Lewis",
            "1-53231-128-1", "Children's Fiction", 5)


</SCRIPT>
</head>

<body>
<h1>Book Objects </h1>
<form name="form1">
<p>Select a book: </p>
<p><select name="bookList" size=1>
<option value="dbBook">Cost of Discipleship</option>
<option value="fkBook">The Once and Future King</option>
<option value="olBook">On Liberty</option>
<option value="iaBook">Icarus Agenda</option>
<option value="cnBook">Chronicles of Narnia</option>
</select>       </p>
<p>Assign a rating: </p>
<p><select name="rating" size=1>
<option>1</option>
<option>2</option>
<option>3</option>
<option>4</option>
<option>5</option>
</select> </p>
<p>Click to assign: </p>
<p><input type="button" name="Assign" value="Assign" onClick="assignRating()">
```

continues

Listing 15.2. continued

```
</p>
<p>Click to show: </p>
<p><input type="button" name="Show" value="Show" onClick="showBook()">
</p>
</form>
</body>
</html>
```

Creating Complex Objects

The objects covered so far have been *simple objects*, or ones with a single level of properties and methods. JavaScript also supports *complex objects* enabling you to have an object's property be an object itself. Complex objects let you structure your code in a more logical manner rather than being forced to dump all data into a single level object. Suppose you would like to track information on employees, their current projects, and their related clients. Obviously, a client address really should not be part of an employee object definition, so JavaScript's complex objects enable you to structure the data around three separate but related entities: employee, project, and client.

In the employee constructor, define the basic properties (name, phone, and e-mail address) and a method called showSummaryInfo(). However, for project information, define a Project property in the employee object. You would define this similar to the way you would a normal property, except that the project parameter is actually a reference to another object rather than a string value:

```
function employee(FirstName, LastName, HomePhone, Ext, EmailAddress, project) {
     this.FirstName = FirstName
     this.LastName = LastName
     this.HomePhone = HomePhone
     this.Ext = Ext
     this.EmailAddress = EmailAddress
     this.Project = project
     this.showSummaryInfo = summaryInfo
}
```

Define the project object type in a similar manner, using the client object as a property:

```
function project(ProjectName, client, DevTool) {
     this.ProjectName = ProjectName;
     this.Client = client;
     this.DevTool = DevTool;
}

function client(ClientName, Address, City, State, Zip) {
     this.ClientName = ClientName
     this.Address = Address
     this.City = City
     this.State = State
```

```
        this.Zip = Zip
}
```

To show how these nested objects can be referenced, define the showSummaryInfo() method of the employee object. This method opens a new window to display an employee summary information sheet—essentially a listing of all of the properties for the employee object and the objects contained within it.

```
function summaryInfo() {
    objWindow = window.open("", "", "width=600,height=400")
    objWindow.document.write("<h1>Employee Summary Information Sheet</h1>")
    objWindow.document.write("<p>")
    objWindow.document.write("<h2>" + this.FirstName + " " + this.LastName
        + "<p></h2>")
    objWindow.document.write("<p>")
    objWindow.document.write("<EM><STRONG>Contact Information</STRONG>
        </EM><p>")
    objWindow.document.write("Home Phone: " + this.HomePhone + "<p>")
    objWindow.document.write("Ext.: " + this.Ext + "<p>")
    objWindow.document.write("Email: " + this.EmailAddress + "<p>")
    objWindow.document.write("<p>")
    objWindow.document.write("<EM><STRONG>Project Information</STRONG>
        </EM><p>")
    objWindow.document.write("Current Project: " + this.Project.ProjectName
        + "<p>")
    objWindow.document.write("Client: " + this.Project.Client.ClientName
        + "<p>")
    objWindow.document.write("Client: " + this.Project.Client.Address
        + "<p>")
    objWindow.document.write("Client: " + this.Project.Client.City + ", " +
        this.Project.Client.State + " " + this.Project.Client.Zip + "<p>")
    objWindow.document.write("Developmnt Tool Used: " + this.Project.DevTool
        + "<p>")
    objWindow.document.close()
}
```

Child objects are referenced using familiar dot notation, so that the client's address is referenced with this.Project.Client.Address.

Now that the constructors are defined for each of these object types, you can instantiate a sample employee, project, and client object:

```
CoastTech = new client("Coastal Technology", "100 Beacon Hill", "Boston",
            "MA", "01220")
Coastal = new project("Coastal01", CoastTech, "JavaScript")
Richard = new employee("Richard", "Wagner", "617/555-1212", "100",
            "rwagner@acadians.com", Coastal)
```

The project parameter in the employee definition and the client parameter in the project definition are not strings but the names of the newly created objects. Also, notice the order in which these objects are created. Because the Richard object uses the Coastal project object as a parameter, Coastal must be instantiated first or you will get an error. The same principle applies to creating the CoastTech instance of the client object before creating the Coastal project.

After the objects instances are created, call `Richard.showSummaryInfo()` to display the window shown in Figure 15.3.

Figure 15.3.

Employee Summary Information Sheet.

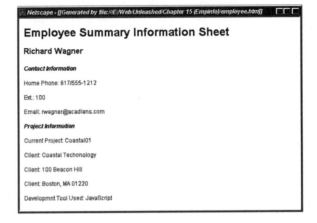

Listing 15.3 provides the entire source code for this example.

Listing 15.3. employee.htm.

```javascript
<SCRIPT LANGUAGE="Javascript">
<!--

    // Complex Custom Objects Example
    // Created by Richard Wagner
    // JavaScript Unleashed

    /////////////////////////////////
    //      Employee Object        //
    /////////////////////////////////

    // Employee object constructor
    function employee(FirstName, LastName, HomePhone, Ext, EmailAddress,
        project) {
        this.FirstName = FirstName
        this.LastName = LastName
        this.HomePhone = HomePhone
        this.Ext = Ext
        this.EmailAddress = EmailAddress
        this.Project = project
        this.showSummaryInfo = summaryInfo
    }
        function summaryInfo() {
            objWindow = window.open("", "", "width=600,height=400")
            objWindow.document.write("<h1>Employee Summary " +
                "Information Sheet</h1>")
            objWindow.document.write("<p>")
            objWindow.document.write("<h2>" + this.FirstName + " "
                + this.LastName + "<p></h2>")
            objWindow.document.write("<p>")
            objWindow.document.write("<EM><STRONG>Contact Information" +
                "</STRONG></EM><p>")
```

```
            objWindow.document.write("Home Phone: " + this.HomePhone
                + "<p>")
            objWindow.document.write("Ext.: " + this.Ext + "<p>")
            objWindow.document.write("Email: " + this.EmailAddress
                + "<p>")
            objWindow.document.write("<p>")
            objWindow.document.write("<EM><STRONG>Project Information"+
                "</STRONG></EM><p>")
            objWindow.document.write("Current Project: " +
                this.Project.ProjectName + "<p>")
            objWindow.document.write("Client: " +
                this.Project.Client.ClientName

                + "<p>")
            objWindow.document.write("Client: " + this.Project.Client.Address
                + "<p>")
            objWindow.document.write("Client: " + this.Project.Client.City
                + ", " + this.Project.Client.State + " " +
                this.Project.Client.Zip + "<p>")
            objWindow.document.write("Development Tool Used: "
                + this.Project.DevTool + "<p>")
            objWindow.document.close()
        }

////End Employee Object////


////////////////////////////
//      Project Object      //
////////////////////////////

function project(ProjectName, client, DevTool) {
    this.ProjectName = ProjectName;
    this.Client = client;
    this.DevTool = DevTool;
}

////////////////////////////
//      Client Object       //
////////////////////////////
function client(ClientName, Address, City, State, Zip) {
    this.ClientName = ClientName
    this.Address = Address
    this.City = City
    this.State = State
    this.Zip = Zip
}

CoastTech = new client("Coastal Techonology", "100 Beacon Hill", "Boston",
            "MA", "01220")
Coastal = new project("Coastal01", CoastTech, "JavaScript")
Richard = new employee("Richard", "Wagner", "617/555-1212",
            "100", "rwagner@acadians.com", Coastal)

Richard.showSummaryInfo()

// -->
</SCRIPT>
```

Dynamic Creation of Objects

The ability to create your own objects in code adds power and flexibility for the JavaScript developer, but all of the examples I have covered so far have dealt with objects being created as the window loads using the new operator. A question you might be asking about now is what ability do you have to dynamically create objects on runtime? After all, with other object-oriented programming environments, you can create object instances on the fly.

JavaScript does allow you to create object instances on the fly, but with certain definite limitations. Initially, my plan was to create a generic instantiator function that created an object instance each time it was called. If this were successful, you could avoid using new statements that have already been defined and create objects based on input from the user. The idea was that the method would look like this:

```
function addEmployee(ObjectName,FirstName, LastName) {
    ObjectName = new employee(FirstName, LastName)
}
```

Ideally, this method would instantiate an object and give the object's name based upon the ObjectName parameter. Unfortunately, no matter what was tried, JavaScript does not allow the name of the object instance to be a variable and instead used ObjectName as the name of the object. In contrast, the following is valid as long as Frank has already been defined as the object reference:

```
function addFrank(FirstName, LastName) {
    Frank = new employee(FirstName, LastName)
}
```

Therefore, although you cannot dynamically name an object being instantiated, you can create an object as an element of a container array. You could, therefore, have an employeeList array that stores each employee object that is created. Therefore, if you modify the addEmployee() method, you could use the following:

```
function addEmployeeObject(FirstName, LastName, HomePhone, Ext, EmailAddress) {
    empList[i] = new employee(FirstName, LastName, HomePhone, Ext, EmailAddress)
}
```

Using this method, you can actually create object instances based on user input and dynamically create the object by calling the addEmployeeObject() method. For example, the form shown in Figure 15.4 allows a user to enter basic information on an employee. When the user clicks the Add button, a new object instance is created. Listing 15.4 shows the source code for this sample form.

FIGURE 15.4.

Dynamic object creation.

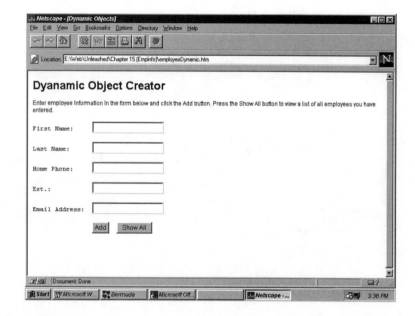

Listing 15.4. employeeDynamic.htm.

```
<HTML>
<HEAD>
<TITLE>Intranet Employee Database</TITLE>
<SCRIPT LANGUAGE="JavaScript">

    // Dynamic Object Creation Example
    // JavaScript Unleashed (Sams.net Publishing)
    // Created by Richard J. Wagner (rwagner@acadians.com)

    // Global variables
    var i = 0

    // Create Array objects
    var empList = new Array()

    /////////////////////////////
    //     Employee Object     //
    /////////////////////////////

    // Employee object constructor
    function employee(FirstName, LastName, HomePhone, Ext, EmailAddress) {
        this.FirstName = FirstName
        this.LastName = LastName
        this.HomePhone = HomePhone
        this.Ext = Ext
        this.EmailAddress = EmailAddress
        this.show = show
    }
```

continues

Listing 15.4. continued

```
              function show() {
                    alert(this.FirstName + "/n" +
                          this.LastName + "/n" +
                          this.HomePhone + "/n" +
                          this.Ext + "/n" +
                          this.EmailAddress)
              }

        function addEmployeeObject(FirstName, LastName, HomePhone, Ext,
              EmailAddress) {
              empList[i] = new employee(FirstName, LastName, HomePhone, Ext,
                EmailAddress)
        }

        function insertRecord() {
              FirstName = document.form1.FirstName.value
              LastName = document.form1.LastName.value
              HomePhone = document.form1.HomePhone.value
              Ext = document.form1.Ext.value
              EmailAddress = document.form1.EmailAddress.value
              i++
              addEmployeeObject(FirstName, LastName, HomePhone, Ext, EmailAddress)
        }

        function showAll() {
              objWindow = window.open("", "", "width=600,height=300")
              objWindow.document.write("<h1>Object Description</h1>")
              objWindow.document.write("<p>")
              for (var q=1; q<empList.length; q++) {
                    objWindow.document.write("<strong>"+ empList[q].FirstName
                      + " " + empList[q].LastName + "</strong><p>")
                    objWindow.document.write(empList[q].HomePhone + "<p>")
                    objWindow.document.write(empList[q].Ext + "<p>")
                    objWindow.document.write(empList[q].EmailAddress + "<p>")
                    objWindow.document.write("<p>")
              }

              objWindow.document.close()
        }

</SCRIPT>
</HEAD>
<BODY>
<h1>Dyanamic Object Creator </h1>
<p>Enter employee information in the form below and click the Add button.
Press the Show All button to view a list of all
employees you have entered. </p>
<form name="form1">
<pre>First Name:       <input type=text size=20 maxlength=256 name="FirstName">
<pre>Last Name:      <input type=text size=20 maxlength=256 name="LastName">
<pre>Home Phone:        <input type=text size=20 maxlength=256 name="HomePhone">
<pre>Ext.:            <input type=text size=20 maxlength=256 name="Ext">
<pre>Email Address:        <input type=text size=20 maxlength=256
  name="EmailAddress">
```

```
<pre>          <input
              type="button"
              name="Add"
              value="Add",
              onClick="insertRecord()">  <input
              type="button"
              name="ShowAll"
              value="Show All"
              onClick="showAll()"></pre>
</form>
</BODY>
</HTML>
```

The Show All button allows you to see all of the objects that have been created during that session. Figure 15.5 shows a list of employee objects that have been instantiated.

NOTE

Array objects are new to Netscape Navigator 3.0. Version 2.0 does not support them.

FIGURE 15.5.

List of dynamically created objects.

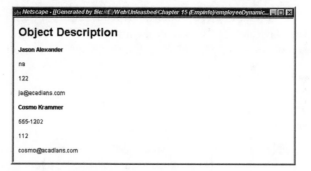

Extending Instantiated Objects

Just as JavaScript is a loosely typed language in terms of data types, it is also flexible in terms of object definitions. You can extend the definition of any object instance by declaring the new property and assigning it a value. Using the book object example from earlier in the chapter, suppose you wanted to add a series property to the cnBook object after it has been defined. As you recall, it is defined as follows:

```
cnBook = new book("Chronicles of Narnia", "C.S. Lewis",
    "1-53231-128-1", "Children's Fiction", 5)
```

Later in the script, add a Series property to it with the following code:

```
cnBook.Series = "True"
```

This technique applies to that object instance only, not the object type. However, Netscape Navigator 3.0 allows you to extend objects you already created using an object prototype. Its syntax is as follows:

```
objectType.prototype.propertyName
```

An object prototype allows you to add a property or method to each instance of an object type. Therefore, if you wanted to add a new recommended property to each book object and it has the value to be `true`, you could use the following line:

```
book.prototype.recommended = True
```

You can test this by calling `alert(iaBook.recommended)`. The result is shown in Figure 15.6.

FIGURE 15.6.

Showing the value of a property using `alert()`.

Indexing Object Properties

The ability to index object properties depends on the version of the browser you are using. Netscape Navigator 2.0 lets you deal with an object's properties through their ordinal index. For example, in Netscape Navigator 2.0, the following two code lines are equivalent:

```
employee.FirstName = "Richard"
```

is the same as

```
employee[0] = "Richard"
```

However, Netscape is moving away from this practice. In Netscape Navigator 3.0, if you define an object using property names, you must always reference by name.

Summary

JavaScript supports the ability to create custom objects in your client-side scripts. This capability adds a great deal of power and flexibility to JavaScript and enables you to structure your code in an object-based manner. In this chapter, you learned all about the various aspects of creating and instantiating object types. You also learned about how to extend the power of normal objects by creating complex objects, which can also be referred to as "objects within objects." You can use complex objects to encapsulate data that spans multiple levels, much in the same way a relational database does with one-to-many table relationships. Finally, you learned how to extend objects that have already been instantiated by using the prototype operator. As you proceed through the rest of the book, you will find many instances where custom objects are used.

JavaScript Programming

Enhancing Forms with JavaScript

by Robert L. Platt

IN THIS CHAPTER

When HTML 2.0 was released, it contained a new capability that allowed Web page developers to create online forms. The HTML forms capability had several advantages as a mechanism for creating online forms.

- Client/server model: The Web browser supplies a generic graphical user interface (GUI) driven by the specific HTML script. Domain-specific processing is handled on the server side via the CGI program.

- Platform independence: Web browsers run on multiple platforms. The developer need not be concerned about platform-specific issues when developing forms.

- Network transparency: Network communications are built in to the Web browser/ Web server pair and implemented via the HTTP protocol.

- Standardized GUI: Forms were standardized with HTML 2.0. A user who is familiar with form elements can apply that knowledge to any form on the World Wide Web or corporate intranet.

The HTML forms interface in itself has a few deficiencies:

- Dynamic user feedback: HTML forms have no means of providing dynamic information on required input on a per-form-element basis.

- Client-side form validation: HTML forms cannot validate a form element, group of elements, or entire form on the client side.

- Dialog boxes: HTML forms cannot dynamically alert the user about an input error or request additional input.

- User confirmations: The forms have no way to ask for confirmation before taking irrevocable types of action.

- Interactivity among form or window elements: In HTML forms, the interactivity is limited to CGI processing on the server side.

The JavaScript language addresses each of these deficiencies. JavaScript builds on the basic capabilities of HTML and produces a more powerful client-side GUI interface. In this chapter, you will learn how to implement these additional capabilities in JavaScript. The chapter ends with an application written in JavaScript that makes use of these new capabilities to implement a tool for choosing combinations of text and background colors.

I make extensive use of JavaScript event handlers in this chapter. You can view event handlers as callbacks associated with a form or form element. They are explicitly specified as part of a form or form element tag. Event handlers get called when a user-triggered event occurs, and in turn, they call an appropriate JavaScript code fragment or function. Table 16.1 contains a summary of JavaScript event handlers.

Enhancing Forms with JavaScript

CHAPTER 16

367

16

ENHANCING
FORMS WITH
JAVASCRIPT

Table 16.1. JavaScript event handlers.

Event Handler	Associated with Object	Triggering Event
onBlur	Select, text, textarea	Form object loses input focus.
onChange	Select, text, textarea	Value of form object is modified.
onClick	Button, checkbox, radio, link, reset, submit	Form object is clicked.
onFocus	Select, text, textarea	Form object gains input focus.
onLoad	Window	Web browser finishes loading window object.
onMouseOver	Link	User moves cursor over link.
onSelect	Text, textarea	User selects text within form object.
onSubmit	Form	Form has been submitted.
onUnload	Window	Window is terminated by user.

User Feedback

With a well designed form, the user should be able to rapidly determine what information is required. In very simple forms, you can accomplish this with well thought-out labels adjacent to each form element. In complex forms, you should include a help facility that offers a detailed explanation of how to fill out the form. With JavaScript, you can add user prompting on a per-field basis. This enables you to supply additional information about the requirements or function of a form element at the moment that the information is needed. By doing so, you can reduce the amount of text required in the form element label and simplify the appearance of the form.

User prompting is implemented with JavaScript's event-handling capability and the browser's status bar. You can use the onFocus event handler to execute a user-defined function when a given text object, textarea object, or selection object gains input focus. Similarly, you can use the onMouseOver event handler to execute a user-defined function whenever the cursor is placed over a link. You can use these event handlers to call a function that displays a user prompt on the browser's status bar.

The following example illustrates how to provide user feedback on the browser status bar using JavaScript. Imagine for a moment that you are creating an HTML forms interface to a very advanced automated toaster. The goal is to produce a user interface so simple and easy to use that the most naive user can instruct it to produce a savory toasted bread product. Figure 16.1 shows the interface.

FIGURE 16.1.

Automated toaster form.

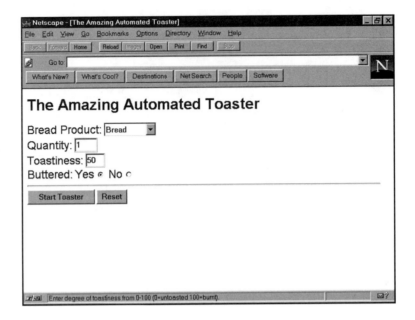

The user can set the values of four input objects:

- A selection object representing the type of bread product
- A text object representing the quantity of toasted bread products desired
- A text object indicating the amount of toasting (as a numeric quantity)
- A pair of radio buttons indicating whether the bread product should be buttered

Each of the selection and text objects has associated onFocus and onBlur event handlers. These handlers display and remove appropriate user prompts associated with a given input object. The onClick event handler is used to associate user feedback with the radio buttons.

The window.defaultStatus property is set to display a default greeting message when no other messages are present.

The code for the toaster example is shown in Listing 16.1. Because you don't really have an automated toaster, the code sends mail once the form is filled in. In this listing, you need to substitute your actual e-mail address for the text *your_mail_ID*. In general, any time you see a segment of code in italic, you need to substitute user- or site-dependent information.

Listing 16.1. toaster.htm.

```
<!-- Web Page for controlling an automated toaster
   -- Note: Since we don't really have an automated toaster
   --       mail the results back to the developer -->
<html>
<head>
<title>The Amazing Automated Toaster</title>
```

```
<script language="JavaScript">
<!-- script start
function setStatus(str)
{
    window.status = str;
    return true;
}

var greeting="Hello! How about some nice toasted bread products!";
window.defaultStatus = greeting;
// script end -->
</script>
</head>

<body>
<h1>The Amazing Automated Toaster</h1>

<form action="mailto:your_mail_ID" method="post">

<font size=5>Bread Product:</font>
<select name="product"
    onFocus="setStatus('Select desired bread product from list.')"
    onBlur="setStatus('')">
<option>Bread
<option>Waffle
<option>Bagel
<option>Roll
<option>Muffin
<option>Croissant
<option>Scone
</select>
<br>

<font size=5>Quantity:</font>
<input type="text" name="quantity" value="1" size=4 maxlength=4
    onFocus="setStatus(
        'Enter quantity of bread products desired (1-1000).')"
    onBlur="setStatus('')">
<br>

<font size=5>Toastiness:</font>
<input type="text" name="toastiness" value="50" size=3 maxlength=3
    onFocus="setStatus(
'Enter degree of toastiness from 0-100 (0=untoasted 100=burnt).')"
    onBlur="setStatus('')">
<br>

<font size=5>Buttered:</font>
<font size=5>Yes</font>
<input type="radio" name="buttered" value="yes" checked
    onClick="setStatus(
        'Do you want butter on the bread product?')">
<font size=5>No</font>
<input type="radio" name="buttered" value="no"
    onClick="setStatus(
        'Do you want butter on the bread product?')">
```

continues

Listing 16.1. continued

```
<hr>
<input type="submit" value="Start Toaster">
<input type="reset">

</form>
</body>
</html>
```

You would usually write a CGI program to process data submitted via a form. However, you might need to develop a form before the CGI program is available. Perhaps you want to debug the form without actually calling the real CGI program. There are several simple methods for testing a form independent of the CGI program:

- For forms that use the get method, a standard CGI program called test-cgi is available at most sites. Use the following form tag:

  ```
  <form action="http://your_site_name/cgi-bin/test-cgi"
      method="get">
  ```

  When you submit your form, you will receive a page containing, among other things, the values of the form elements from the submitted page. Although the test-cgi CGI file is provided as standard with most servers, its availability and exact location could be site-dependent. Contact your Web site administrator for details.

- For forms that use the post method, a standard CGI program called post-query is available at most sites. Use the following form tag:

  ```
  <form action="http://your_site_name/cgi-bin/post-query"
      method="post">
  ```

  When you submit your form, you will receive a page containing, among other things, the name/value pairs corresponding to the form elements from the submitted page. Although post-query is provided as standard with most servers, its availability and exact location might be site-dependent. Contact your Web site administrator for details.

- For forms that use the post method, you can specify that form results should be mailed to your account. Use the following form tag:

  ```
  <form action="mailto:your_mail_ID" method="post">
  ```

  When you submit your form, you will receive an e-mail message containing name/value pairs corresponding to the form elements from the submitted page. (With Netscape Navigator 3.0, the user will receive a warning when submitting a form via e-mail. This is not an error; it is a security feature designed to warn the user that the recipient of the form will be able to view the user's e-mail address in the mail header. In other words, forms submission via e-mail is not anonymous.)

Enhancing Forms with JavaScript

CHAPTER 16

371

16

ENHANCING
FORMS WITH
JAVASCRIPT

Displaying Message Boxes

JavaScript supports several methods for communicating with the user via pop-up alert messages and two types of dialog windows. You can use these methods to communicate important information to the user, confirm a choice made by the user, or request additional information. You can use alert messages as aids in debugging as well.

You use the `alert()` method to pop up a short message to the user. It is a method of the window object. You need not specify the window object to invoke it. You can use the alert method to inform the user of an input error, as shown in the following code:

```
alert("Error: value outside valid range of 0 to 240 volts.");
```

Using this code line pops up the message shown in Figure 16.2.

FIGURE 16.2.

Alert message.

You can also use the `alert()` method as a debugging aid. Use it to display a string containing debugging information:

```
var dbgstr = "Value of 'wattage' = " + wattage;
alert(dbgstr);
```

You can use it to do tracing within your JavaScript program:

```
function CalculateWattage(volts,amps)
{
    var dbgstr = "CalculateWattage(" + volts + "," + amps + ")";
    alert(dbgstr);
. . .
}
```

Every time the function `CalculateWattage()` is called, an alert pops up showing the call and the calling arguments. When you finish debugging the program, you can remove or comment out the debugging code.

The `confirm()` method is similar to `alert`, but it lets the user respond to the message. The responses are limited to OK or Cancel. The `confirm()` method returns true if the user selects OK and false if the user selects Cancel, as illustrated by the following code:

```
function submitCallback()
{
    if (selfDestructSelected == true)
        return confirm(
            "Invoke self-destruct mechanism in 60 seconds?");
    else return true;
```

```
}
...
<form ... onSubmit="return submitCallback()">
```

This code produces the pop-up confirmation dialog window shown in Figure 16.3.

FIGURE 16.3.

Confirmation dialog.

Selecting OK allows the submit to proceed. Selecting Cancel returns false, which in turn returns false to the form object, preventing the form from being submitted.

The `prompt()` method is another window method. It allows you to prompt the user for an arbitrary value, as shown in the following code line:

```
var favColor = prompt("What\'s your favorite color?");
```

You can supply an optional second argument to be used as a default value:

```
var duration = prompt("Enter duration in months:",6);
```

This code line produces the dialog box shown in Figure 16.4.

FIGURE 16.4.

Prompt dialog.

You usually ask the user for information via a form input element, but you can use the prompt dialog box when there is an infrequent need to query the user based upon other input information. The following ;sample code queries the user about whether he wants the Texas Package— but only if he's previously indicated that he lives in Texas. The query then sets a hidden form element that is passed to the CGI program for processing.

```
function TexasQuery(formObj)
{
    var noAnswer = true;
    var ans;
    var promptStr = "Would y\'all like the Texas Package for $50"
        + "(yes or no)?"

    if (state != 'TX') return true;

    while(noAnswer) {
```

Enhancing Forms with JavaScript

CHAPTER 16

373

16

ENHANCING
FORMS WITH
JAVASCRIPT

```
            ans = prompt(promptStr);
            if (ans == null || ans.length == 0) continue;
            else {
                ans = ans.toLowerCase();
                if (ans == "yes" || ans == "no") noAnswer = false;
            }
    }
    formObj.txPackage.value = ans;
    return true;
}
...
<form name="myform" ... onSubmit="return TexasQuery(this)">
...
<input type="hidden" name="txPackage" value="">
<input type="submit" name="submit" value="Submit">
```

Note that the user can select Cancel, which leaves the variable ans as undefined. As a result, you must test for null following the call to prompt().

TIP

When a message or dialog box pops up, the user is distracted from his or her task and must focus attention on the pop-up window and respond appropriately. Alert messages and dialog boxes should be used sparingly.

Validating User Input

Prior to the advent of JavaScript, form validation was handled by a CGI program. This approach was effective but required that the entire form be completed by the user and transmitted to the server prior to validation. In some environments, such as low-speed connections to the World Wide Web, a noticeable lag can occur between the time the form is submitted and the time a validation error is returned to the user. Furthermore, by waiting until the form is submitted for validation, the user does not receive feedback until after the entire form is completed. Immediate feedback is desirable because the user has just entered information and can place the feedback in the appropriate context. Immediate feedback might influence later behavior and reduce user errors in responding to subsequent form elements. Finally, conventional CGI programming reports input errors in a new Web page. The user must back up to the form to make changes, which interrupts the flow of the form-entry task.

Validating Free Form Input

You can use two event handlers to validate text and textarea form elements. The onBlur event handler is called when a text or textarea form element loses input focus. The onChange event handler is called when the contents of a text or textarea form element is modified.

A form element is said to have focus when any user input will be directed to that element. When a text or textarea form element has focus, a text cursor appears in that element. When the user switches to another element (by using the mouse or the tab key), the original element is said to lose focus.

The onBlur handler is called any time the input field loses focus. The user may or may not have changed the data in the field. The event handler could end up calling the validation code for unchanged data or the default values in the field. You should design the validation code to deal with this possibility.

The onChange event handler is only called when the contents of the field are modified. If the user momentarily selects the field (perhaps to view feedback in the status bar) and then chooses another field, the user-defined callback code is not invoked. Although this is more efficient, there is a down side. Suppose that you warn a user about erroneous data in a field. If he clicks the field and then declines to modify it, or if he retypes the same erroneous data, this is not considered a change. The onChange event handler is not triggered. For this reason, if you choose to use onChange, you should also validate the input at the time of submission (via the onSubmit or onClick event handlers).

The next example provides a text field for the user to input the quantity of an item. Valid values are 100 to 1000. The onBlur event handler is used to call a validation function. The text input object is passed to the event handler. If the input is invalid, the following things occur:

- An alert box pops up to inform the user.
- Input focus is returned to the text field.
- The text is selected (and highlighted) so that it can be easily modified.

Note that the onFocus event handler is used to provide user feedback for the text field—perhaps to inform the user about minimum and maximum orders.

```
function validateQuantity(quantObj)
{
    if (quantObj.value < 100) {
        alert("Minimum order is 100 units.");
        quantObj.focus();
        quantObj.select();
    }
    else if (quantObj.value > 1000) {
        alert("Quantities greater than 1000 "
            + "units require special order.");
        quantObj.focus();
        quantObj.select();
    }
    return;
}

...

<h2>Enter number of units:</h2>
<input type="text" name="quantity" value="100" length=4
    maxlength=4 onFocus="quantFeedback()"
    onBlur="validateQuantity(this)">
```

Enhancing Forms with JavaScript

CHAPTER 16

375

16

ENHANCING
FORMS WITH
JAVASCRIPT

Ensuring Consistency

Sometimes there are dependencies between several input fields. Figure 16.5 illustrates part of a form used by a business for entering a department budget. The user is prompted to enter a total budget and then allocate portions of that budget into three different categories.

FIGURE 16.5.

A form for entering a budget.

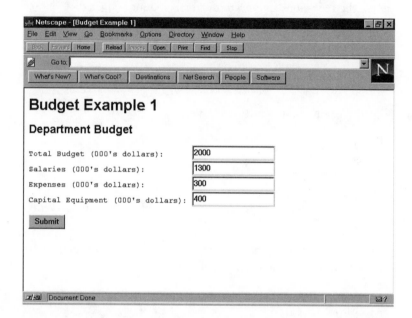

The sum of the three categories should add up to the total budget. Prior to JavaScript, the sum wouldn't have been verified until after the form was submitted and processed by a CGI program. Using JavaScript, the data can be validated prior to submission, saving the user time and preserving context (that is, the same Web page is present before and after validation). The following code segment is an implementation of the budget entry form:

```
<form name="myform" method="post" action="actionURL"
    onSubmit="return validateBudget(myform)">
<h2>Department Budget</h2>

<pre>
Total Budget (000's dollars):        <input type="text"
    name="totalBudget" value="0" onBlur="validateNumeric(this)">
Salaries (000's dollars):            <input type="text"
    name="salaries" value="0" onBlur="validateNumeric(this)">
Expenses (000's dollars):            <input type="text"
    name="expenses" value="0" onBlur="validateNumeric(this)">
Capital Equipment (000's dollars): <input type="text"
    name="capital" value="0" onBlur="validateNumeric(this)">
</pre>

...
```

```
<input type="submit" name="submit" value="Submit">
</form>
```

onBlur event handlers call a user-supplied validation routine that will ensure the user enters valid numeric input in each field. You must supply the following function to verify that the sum of the allocations adds up to the total amount budgeted:

```
function validateBudget(formObj)
{
    var calcBudget = parseInt(formObj.salaries.value,10)
        + parseInt(formObj.expenses.value,10)
        + parseInt(formObj.capital.value,10);
    var totalBudget = parseInt(formObj.totalBudget.value,10);

    if (calcBudget != totalBudget) {
        alert("Error: total budget is not equal to "
            + "sum of allocations.");
        return false;
    }
    else return true;
}
```

This function pops up an alert box in the event of an error and prevents the submit from being processed.

In the section "Creating Interactive Forms," later in this chapter, you will see another way of ensuring consistency using dynamic forms.

CAUTION

HTML is still an evolving language. In most cases, Web browsers ignore unknown tags or keywords; after all, they could be changes in the HTML standard or vendor-supplied HTML enhancements. This is good for users of Web browsers because you don't want your browser to crash every time it encounters an unknown tag or keyword.

However, this is a problem for JavaScript programmers. If you misspell the name of an event handler or any other keyword within an HTML tag, your program does not function properly, and your browser will not flag the error. When using JavaScript event handlers in forms, it is prudent to visually inspect your code for typographical errors.

Handling Policy

Policies associated with a form should be indicated to the user via explanatory text within the form, a separate help document (appropriately linked to the form), or both. You can use JavaScript to validate that user input conforms to these policies.

An order form could contain a policy statement that orders cannot be shipped on the weekend. Suppose the form allowed the user to specify a ship date; you can use JavaScript code to

Enhancing Forms with JavaScript

CHAPTER 16

377

16

ENHANCING
FORMS WITH
JAVASCRIPT

verify that the ship date is not a weekend, thus enforcing the policy. The following code segment implements these policies:

```
// Compute ship date from
//   user input.  Returns
//   date object
function calcShipDate(formObj)
{
    var day = parseInt(formObj.shipDay.value);
    var month = parseInt(formObj.shipMonth.value) - 1;
    var year = parseInt(formObj.shipYear.value) - 1900;
    var hrs = 0;
    var min = 0;
    var sec = 0;
    shipDate = new Date(year,month,day,hrs,min,sec);
    return shipDate;
}

// Validate shipping policy - don't
//   ship on weekends.  Make sure
//   date is not in past or current date
function shippingPolicy(formObj)
{
    var shipDate = calcShipDate(formObj);
    var day = shipDate.getDay();
    var currentDate = new Date();

    if (shipDate.getTime() < currentDate.getTime()) {
        alert("Error: ship date must be future date.");
        formObj.shipDay.focus();
        formObj.shipDay.select();
        return false;
    }

    if (day == 0) {
        alert("Sorry, we cannot ship on Sunday.");
        formObj.shipDay.focus();
        formObj.shipDay.select();
        return false;
    }
    else if (day == 6) {
        alert("Sorry, we cannot ship on Saturday.");
        formObj.shipDay.focus();
        formObj.shipDay.select();
        return false;
    }
    else return true;
}

...

<form name="myform" method="post" action="actionURL"
    onSubmit="return shippingPolicy(myform)">
```

If the user enters a date corresponding to a Saturday or Sunday, they are reminded of the shipping policy, focus and selection are set to the date input field, and the form is not submitted. The code also enforces the implicit policy of disallowing same-day shipping.

> **NOTE**
>
> When processing dates using JavaScript, be aware that the date and time used is based on the setting of the user's workstation or PC. It is likely that the client and server software are running in different time zones. It is also possible that the time setting on the client side is incorrect, perhaps due to the user setting the wrong time and date on the workstation or PC. (I once received e-mail that was dated in the year 2004; I assume this was an error because temporal anomalies are relatively rare on the Internet.)

Ensuring Completeness

Forms frequently consist of a set of mandatory and optional fields. The form cannot be properly processed if the mandatory fields are not supplied. Again, you can use JavaScript to ensure that these fields are present.

The next example is a form requesting customer contact information. The name, address information, and home phone number are considered mandatory fields. All other fields are optional. (See Figure 16.6.)

FIGURE 16.6.

Contact information form.

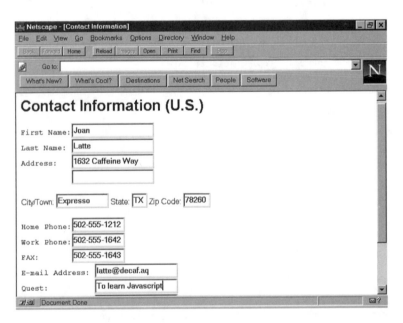

When the form is submitted, a validation function is called. If any of the mandatory fields are empty, the user is notified and the form is not submitted. The code for the contact information form is shown in Listing 16.2.

Enhancing Forms with JavaScript

CHAPTER 16

379

16

ENHANCING
FORMS WITH
JAVASCRIPT

Listing 16.2. contact.htm.

```html
<html>
<head>
<title>Contact Information</title>
<script language="JavaScript">
<!-- script start
// Ensure that mandatory fields of
// form have been completed
function validateComplete(formObj)
{
    if (emptyField(formObj.firstName))
        alert("Please enter your first name.");
    else if (emptyField(formObj.lastName))
        alert("Please enter your last name.");
    else if (emptyField(formObj.address1)
        && emptyField(formObj.address2))
        alert("Please enter your address.");
    else if (emptyField(formObj.city))
        alert("Please enter your city or town.");
    else if (emptyField(formObj.state))
        alert("Please enter your state.");
    else if (emptyField(formObj.email))
        alert("Please enter your E-mail address.");
    else return true;

    return false;
}

// Check to see if field is empty
function emptyField(textObj)
{
    if (textObj.value.length == 0) return true;
    for (var i=0; i<textObj.value.length; ++i) {
        var ch = textObj.value.charAt(i);
        if (ch != ' ' && ch != '\t') return false;
    }
    return true;
}

// script end -->
</script>
</head>
<body>
<h1>Contact Information (U.S.)</h1>
<form name="myform" action="actionURL" method="post"
 onSubmit="return validateComplete(document.myform)">
<pre>
First Name:<input type="text" name="firstName">
Last Name: <input type="text" name="lastName">
Address:   <input type="text" name="address1">
           <input type="text" name="address2">
</pre>

City/Town:
<input type="text" name="city" size=12>
State:
<input type="text" name="state" size=2>
```

continues

Listing 16.2. continued

```
Zip Code:
<input type="text" name="zip" size=5>

<pre>
Home Phone:<input type="text" name="homePhone" size=12>
Work Phone:<input type="text" name="workPhone" size=12>
FAX:        <input type="text" name="FAX" size=12>
E-mail Address: <input type="text" name="email">
Quest:          <input type="text" name="quest">
Favorite Color: <input type="text" name="favColor">
</pre>
<hr>
<input type="submit" name="submit" value="Submit">
</form>
<body>
<html>
```

The code performs a very basic validation—a field is present if it is not blank. No attempt is made to determine whether the fields contain reasonable data or gibberish. You could include some additional, simple validation. For example, you could validate that the state is a two-letter abbreviation or that the phone number contains the correct number of digits. In general, you should perform simple validations on the client side and more complex validations on the server side.

> **NOTE**
>
> The preceding example is a contact form for English-speaking users in the United States. The Internet is a worldwide network. In some countries, the family name precedes the given name, states are not a political sub-division, ZIP codes don't exist, and the user's language is not English. People still have a favorite color, however. The issue of internationalization is well beyond the scope of this book; nevertheless, you should be cognizant of the potential user base when designing forms.

Creating Interactive Forms

Prior to JavaScript, even the simplest interactive form required interaction with a CGI program on the server. With JavaScript, you can create interactive forms where the interaction is handled entirely on the client side without requiring a round trip to the server.

Interactive programming in JavaScript does have a few limitations. It would be useful to be able to change any individual element of a page dynamically. Unfortunately, you can't do that. When the Web browser renders a page and the elements are formatted, they cannot be modified by the JavaScript code. As Omar Khayyam wrote,

Enhancing Forms with JavaScript

CHAPTER 16

381

16

ENHANCING
FORMS WITH
JAVASCRIPT

> The Moving Finger writes; and, having writ,
> Moves on: nor all thy Piety nor Wit
> Shall lure it back to cancel half a Line,
> Nor all thy Tears wash out a Word of it.

(*The Rubayyat of Omar Khayyam*, available on the World Wide Web at `http://www.panix.com/~falcon1/omar.html`.)

If you can't change the formatting of a page once it is written, what can you do? JavaScript allows you to create interactions between the following items:

- Form elements on the same page
- Form elements and another window
- Form elements and another frame

You can use any of the techniques described earlier in the chapter—user feedback, message boxes, and input validation—to enhance a form. You can alter the entire page by completely rewriting it. In this case, the browser erases the current page and reformats the entire page from scratch. You can also change the background color of the page (a document property), but not the foreground color. The page text has already been rendered in the foreground color, so it cannot be changed.

The next example, which is illustrated in Figure 16.7, is a different implementation of the budgeting example from earlier in this chapter. This example has a new text field named `remainder`. Although you cannot update regular text or graphics on a page once it is written, you can update a form element. In this case, you update the `remainder` text element based on the values in the other elements. As the user types in the total budget and allocations, the `remainder` text field shows the amount of money left after the allocations are subtracted from the total budget.

This example uses the `onChange` event handler to update the `remainder` field whenever one of the values of the other text fields is modified. When the user submits the form, the script recalculates the remainder. If it is zero, the form is submitted; otherwise, an alert dialog box is displayed. The following segment shows the code for the interactive budget example:

```
function calcRemainder(formObj)
{
    var calcBudget = parseInt(formObj.salaries.value,10)
        + parseInt(formObj.expenses.value,10)
        + parseInt(formObj.capital.value,10);
    var totalBudget = parseInt(formObj.totalBudget.value);

    var unalloc = totalBudget - calcBudget;
    formObj.remainder.value = unalloc;
}

function validateBudget(formObj)
{
```

```
            calcRemainder(formObj);
            var unalloc = formObj.remainder.value;
            if (unalloc != 0) {
                alert("Error: Total budget is not equal "
                        + "to sum of allocations.");
                return false;
            }
            return true;
    }



    <form name="myform" method="post" action="actionURL"
        onSubmit="return validateBudget(myform)">
    <h2>Department Budget</h2>

    <pre>
    Total Budget (000's dollars):        <input type="text"
        name="totalBudget" value="0"
        onChange="calcRemainder(myform)">
    Salaries (000's dollars):            <input type="text"
        name="salaries" value="0" onChange="calcRemainder(myform)">
    Expenses (000's dollars):            <input type="text"
        name="expenses" value="0" onChange="calcRemainder(myform)">
    Capital Equipment (000's dollars): <input type="text"
        name="capital" value="0" onChange="calcRemainder(myform)">
    <em>Unallocated Remainder:<em>              <input type="text"
        name="remainder" value="0">
    </pre>

    <input type="submit" name="submit" value="Submit">
    </form>
```

FIGURE 16.7.

Interactive budget example.

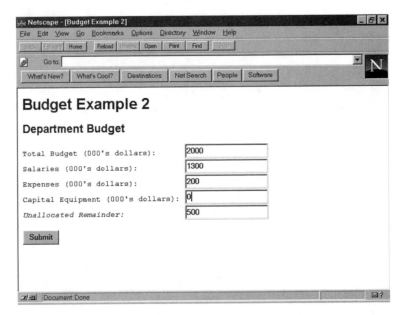

Enhancing Forms with JavaScript

CHAPTER 16

383

16

ENHANCING
FORMS WITH
JAVASCRIPT

You can use JavaScript to write small interactive applications where all the processing is done on the client side. In Figure 16.8, the next example calculates the future value of an investment. The user supplies the initial amount, an interest rate, and the number of years that the investment is compounded. Note that the output of the JavaScript function `calculate()` is displayed via text input objects, as described earlier.

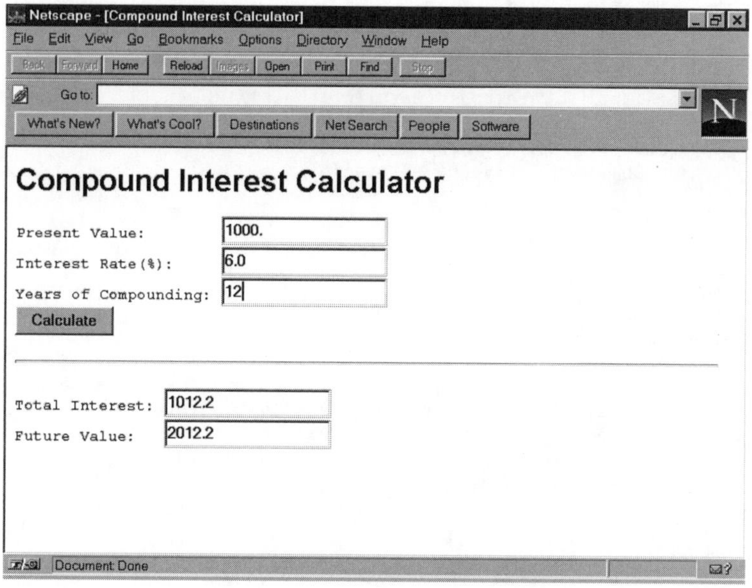

FIGURE 16.8.

Compound interest form.

No CGI program is required because all processing is done on the client side. Note that instead of using a `submit` input object, the form uses a `button` object. Also, instead of using an `onSubmit` event handler, the script uses an `onClick` event handler. The `submit` object and `onSubmit` event-handler semantics are used when the Web browser transmits a form to the server side. Because you want to do the processing on the client side, you use the `onClick` event handler and the `calculate()` function when the button is pressed. The button was labeled Calculate for clarity but could have been labeled Submit. Unless the user views the source code for the page, it will appear indistinguishable from a page that uses HTML on the client side and a CGI script on the server side. The code for the compound interest form is shown in Listing 16.3.

Listing 16.3. `interest.htm`.

```
<html>
<head>
<title>Compound Interest Calculator</title>
<script language="JavaScript">
<!-- script start
```

continues

Listing 16.3. continued

```
// script end -->
function calculate(formObj)
{
    var presentVal = parseFloat(formObj.presentVal.value);
    var intRate = parseFloat(formObj.intRate.value)/100.;
    var years = parseFloat(formObj.years.value);

    var futureVal = presentVal * Math.pow((1.0+intRate),years);
    var totalInt = futureVal - presentVal;
    futureVal = Math.round(futureVal*100.0)/100.0;
    totalInt  = Math.round(totalInt*100.0)/100.0;

    formObj.futureVal.value = futureVal;
    formObj.totalInt.value = totalInt;

    return;
}
</script>
<body>
<h1>Compound Interest Calculator</h1>
<form name="myform">
<pre>
Present Value:          <input type="text" name="presentVal">
Interest Rate(%):       <input type="text" name="intRate">
Years of Compounding: <input type="text" name="years">
<input type="button" name="calc" value="Calculate"
    onclick="calculate(myform)">
</pre>
<hr>
<pre>
Total Interest: <input type="text" name="totalInt">
Future Value:   <input type="text" name="futureVal">
<pre>
</form>
</body>
<html>
```

Example—the JavaScript Color Checker

The next example in Figure 16.9 uses the capabilities described in this chapter to implement a color checker. One of the challenges in designing an HTML form is choosing a background color and a text color that are aesthetically pleasing as well as legible. An enormous number of combinations fulfill those two criteria—and an enormous number don't. The JavaScript color checker lets the user specify two colors and view what the combination looks like in a separate window. The window contains the HTML code for specifying the color combination. The user can then cut and paste the specification directly into her HTML code.

FIGURE 16.9.
The color checker.

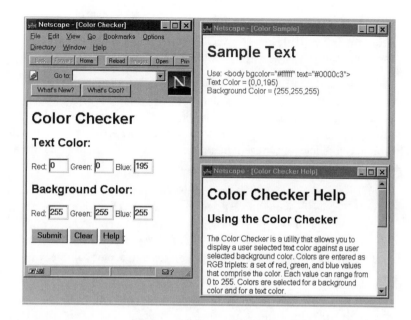

You specify color values by supplying an RGB triplet. The RGB triplet consists of three values representing the red, green, and blue components of the color. These values range from 0 to 255. For instance, the triplet (255,0,0) specifies pure red. Table 16.2 shows a few RGB color values.

Table 16.2. RGB color values.

RGB Value	Color
(0,0,0)	Black
(255,0,0)	Red
(255,255,0)	Yellow
(255,0,255)	Magenta
(0,255,0)	Green
(0,255,255)	Cyan
(0,0,255)	Blue
(128,128,128)	Dark gray
(200,200,200)	Light gray
(255,255,255)	White

As with the earlier interactive forms, all processing is done on the client side. A copy of this program is available on the CD-ROM that is included with this book in the file `\SOURCE\CHAP16\cchecker.htm`.

The program defines a constructor for `color` objects that hold an RGB triplet. The `color` objects have a method called `setColor()` that sets the RGB triplet and computes an equivalent hexadecimal string that can be used to set colors in conjunction with an HTML body tag. The program uses two instances of the `color` object: one for the text color and one for the background color. The `onBlur` event handler calls a validation routine `validateRGB()` whenever one of the six color-component text input fields loses focus.

Although the program does not have a `submit` input object, it does have a `button` object labeled Submit. The `onClick` method calls the `processForm()` function, which does something new. It creates a window for output that is separate from the color checker program. The window is referenced by a handle named `popWin`. The `processForm()` function checks to see if `popWin` is `null` (its initial value), and if so, it creates a separate Color Sample window using the window `open()` method.

Next, things get a little tricky; the user might close the Color Sample window. The only way to detect this is to examine the value of `popWin.document`. If `popWin` is not `null`, but `popWin.document` is `null`, then the Color Sample window was closed. If this is the case, you have to recreate the Color Sample window. The `processForm()` function calls the `doSample()` function, which generates the contents of the Color Sample window.

In the body tag, you'll see an instance of the `onUnload` event handler, which is called when the main window is terminated. It calls the `closePopWin()` function that terminates the Color Sample window if it exists. Finally, note the button named HelpButton within the form. When the user clicks this button, the program creates a new window containing help text. Listing 16.4 contains the complete source code for `cchecker.htm`.

Listing 16.4. `cchecker.htm`.

```
<!-- Color Checker - July 1996        -->
<!-- Written by Robert L. Platt.       -->

<html>
<head>
<title>Color Checker</title>
<script language="JavaScript">
<!-- script start

// Constructor for color object
function color(r,g,b)
{
     this.setColor = setColor;
     this.setColor(r,g,b);
}
```

```javascript
// Color object set method
function setColor(r,g,b)
{
    this.red = r;
    this.green = g;
    this.blue = b;
    this.hex = rgb2hex(r,g,b);
}

// Convert RGB triplet to hexadecimal string
function rgb2hex(r,g,b)
{
    var str = '"#' + num2hex(r) + num2hex(g)
        + num2hex(b) + '"';
    return(str)
}

// Convert numeric string to hexadecimal string
function num2hex(n)
{
    var str = "";
    var hexstring = "0123456789abcdef";
    while(true) {
        digit = hexstring.substring((n%16),((n%16)+1));
        str = digit + str;
        n = n >> 4;
        if (n == 0) break;
    }
    // Pad string if necessary
    if (str.length < 2) str = '0' + str;
    return(str);
}

// Validate RGB component values
function validateRGB(textObj)
{
    var str = textObj.value;

    if (str.length == 0) {
        userAlert(textObj);
        return false;
    }

    for (var i = 0; i < str.length; ++i) {
        var ch = str.charAt(i);
        if (ch < "0" || ch > "9") {
            userAlert(textObj);
            return false;
        }
    }

    var value = parseInt(str,10);
    if (value < 0 || value > 255) {
        userAlert(textObj);
        return false;
    }
    else return true;
}
```

continues

Listing 16.4. continued

```javascript
// Alert user on input error
function userAlert(textObj)
{
    alert("Please enter a value between 0 and 255.");
    textObj.focus();
    textObj.select();
}

// Write sample frame
function doSample(doc,tc,bc)
{
    var mytext="<h1>Sample Text</h1>";
    doc.open();
    doc.write("<html><head><title>Color Sample</title></head>");
    doc.write('<body bgcolor=' + bc.hex + ' text=' + tc.hex + '>');
    doc.write(mytext);
    doc.write('Use: &lt;body bgcolor=' + bc.hex + ' text='
        + tc.hex + '&gt;');
    doc.write("<br>Text Color=(",tc.red,",",tc.green,
        ",",tc.blue,")");
    doc.write("<br>Background Color=(",bc.red,",",bc.green,
        ",",bc.blue,")");
    doc.write("</body></html>");
    doc.close();
}

// Process submitted form
function processForm(myform)
{
    var winFeatures = "scrollbars,width=400,height=250";
    if ((validateRGB(myform.redtxt) &&
        validateRGB(myform.grntxt) &&
        validateRGB(myform.blutxt) &&
        validateRGB(myform.redbg) &&
        validateRGB(myform.grnbg) &&
        validateRGB(myform.blubg)) == false)
         return false;
    var textColor = new color(myform.redtxt.value,
        myform.grntxt.value,myform.blutxt.value);
    var backColor = new color(myform.redbg.value,
        myform.grnbg.value,myform.blubg.value);
    if (popWin == null)
        popWin = window.open("","PopWindow",winFeatures);
    else if (popWin.document == null)
        popWin = window.open("","PopWindow",winFeatures);

    doSample(popWin.document,textColor,backColor);
    return true;
}

// Reset form to initial values
function resetForm(myform)
{
    myform.redtxt.value = 0;
    myform.grntxt.value = 0;
    myform.blutxt.value = 0;
    myform.redbg.value = 255;
    myform.grnbg.value = 255;
```

Enhancing Forms with JavaScript

CHAPTER 16

389

16

ENHANCING
FORMS WITH
JAVASCRIPT

```
        myform.blubg.value = 255;
        processForm(myform);
}

// Prompt for valid user input
function setPrompt()
{
    window.status="Please enter a value between 0 and 255.";
    return true;
}

// Close Pop-up Window
function closePopWin()
{
    if (popWin != null && popWin.document != null)
        popWin.close();
}

// Clear prompt
function clearPrompt()
{
    window.status="";
    return true;
}

// Initialization
var popWin = null;

// script end -->
</script>
</head>
<body bgcolor="#ffffff" text="#000000" onUnload="closePopWin()">
</script>
<h1>Color Checker</h1>
<form name="myform">

</h2>
<h2>Text Color:</h2>
Red:    <input type="text" size=3 maxlength=3 name="redtxt"
        value="0" onChange="validateRGB(this)"
        onFocus="setPrompt()" onBlur="clearPrompt()">
Green:  <input type="text" size=3 maxlength=3 name="grntxt"
value="0" onChange="validateRGB(this)"
        onFocus="setPrompt()" onBlur="clearPrompt()">
Blue:   <input type="text" size=3 maxlength=3 name="blutxt"
        value="0" onChange="validateRGB(this)"
        onFocus="setPrompt()" onBlur="clearPrompt()">
<h2>Background Color:</h2>
Red:    <input type="text" size=3 maxlength=3 name="redbg"
        value="255" onChange="validateRGB(this)"
        onFocus="setPrompt()" onBlur="clearPrompt()">
Green:  <input type="text" size=3 maxlength=3 name="grnbg"
value="255" onChange="validateRGB(this)"
        onFocus="setPrompt()" onBlur="clearPrompt()">
Blue:   <input type="text" size=3 maxlength=3 name="blubg"
        value="255" onChange="validateRGB(this)"
        onFocus="setPrompt()" onBlur="clearPrompt()">
```

continues

Listing 16.4. continued

```
<p>
<input type="button" value="Submit"
    onClick="processForm(document.myform)">
<input type="reset" value="Clear"
    onClick="resetForm(document.myform)">
<input type="button" value="Help" name="HelpButton"
    onClick="window.open('cchelp.htm','CChelp',
    'scrollbars,resizable')">
</form>
</body>
</html>
```

Summary

JavaScript greatly enhances the basic form capability of HTML. Much of the processing that heretofore could only be performed on the server can now be done on the client side via JavaScript. The new capabilities can be summarized as follows:

- User feedback—JavaScript lets you provide feedback to the form user via a combination of event handlers and control over of the contents of the browser's status bar.

- Message boxes—By using JavaScript alert and dialog boxes, you can display a pop-up message to the user, request confirmation prior to submitting a form, and query the user for additional information.

- Validating user input—you can validate input fields, groups of fields, or the entire form via event handlers and JavaScript functions. Users can receive feedback in the context of the current form (that is, the page is not replaced by a new page with an error message).

- You can build interactive forms where part or even all of the processing is performed on the client side.

You can use JavaScript to create forms that are easier to use and less prone to error. In turn, you can create forms that respond far more quickly than server-oriented programs, particularly when the user has a low bandwidth connection to the server.

RESOURCE

The JavaScript language is still evolving, so it wouldn't hurt to look at Netscape's JavaScript Authoring Guide located at http://home.netscape.com/eng/mozilla/3.0/handbook/javascript/index.htm.

You can also find JavaScript code examples at the Gamelan Web site at http://www.gamelan.com.

Working with Frames and Windows

by Edmund T. Smith

IN THIS CHAPTER

Frames provide a means to view and interact with a site that is not possible otherwise. Users can have a permanently displayed index or navigation bar that provides quick and effective location of content in the site. You can simultaneously display the input and output of forms, as well as view multiple documents simultaneously. You can select different image files from a menu for viewing. A new window can open to provide a expanded view of a document and close when it's no longer needed. You can give slide show presentations. The possible uses and implementations of a framed site are really only limited by the Web site author's imagination.

> **CAUTION**
>
> Some visitors find frames and new windows distracting, and especially with small monitors, too much of the display area is lost due to frames. Two things that a framed-site author should do are ensure that using frames provides a benefit to the visitor and make an alternative no-frame version of the site available. For more information, visit `http://edbo.com/frames/why.html`.

> **RESOURCE**
>
> You can find online resources for JavaScript and frames at the Netscape site `http://home.netscape.com/` and at `http://edbo.com/frames/`.

JavaScript greatly enhances a frame site and adds to the interaction of the site with the user. You can open and close new windows programmatically. You can update and synchronize frames through the script without relying on a server-side program. Image maps and links can be dynamic, changing with different configurations and uses of the site. Documents in different frames and windows can pass information to, and interact with, each other.

The major areas in which you can use JavaScript with frames are creating separate browser windows and frames and referencing windows and frames within other windows and frames.

Windows

Many browsers can open multiple instances of themselves. Although most people browsing the Web typically use only one instance of the browser, having two or more windows open is sometimes beneficial. You can compare pages from different sites, enter information into a form using data from a different Web page, and conduct research from a list on one page and look at the references with another browser instance. Each instance of the browser (at least for GUIs) is referred to as a browser window.

The term browser window is often shortened to just window, although you should be careful that separate instances are not confused with frames, which are also referred to as windows (subwindows of the browser window). The browser window is also called the top window because frames are subwindows of the browser. Browsers that support JavaScript let you programmatically open and close browser windows and navigate through these windows. A site with separate windows can provide several simultaneous views of the site's content, increase access to the information and features, and offer new ways to fully interact with the site.

Although in many cases, frames might be better for simultaneous viewing, multiple browser windows can be individually resized and positioned by the user. Furthermore, users can minimize and maximize the window, move the window to the foreground or background as needed, and typically keep all the tools and other features (menu bar, location field, status bar, bookmarks, and so on) with each instance of the browser.

TIP

Many users might find it distracting and annoying if you unexpectedly open new browser windows, especially if they have to keep closing them. Provide an indication to the visitor that an action will cause a window to open. An example is a short note next to a link. In the following sentence, Spike is a link that opens a new window:

```
See a picture of my dog Spike. (new window)
```

Opening a Window

The user can always open a new window by selecting New Browser (or similar phasing) from the File pull-down menu on the browser menu bar. Usually, the new window loads the first document that was opened in the browser. The user can then load other documents with the Location field in the newly created window. However, any window opened by the user in this manner is unnamed and cannot be easily referenced by documents in other windows. This section discusses programmatically opening and naming windows with Netscape frames extensions and JavaScript.

Frames Extensions

Opening or creating a new window is a fairly simple task to accomplish. Providing a link attribute of TARGET="_blank" or even a target attribute value of any name (window or frame) not currently in use opens a new window. The link `<A HREF="foo.html" TARGET="bar">foo</A>` opens a browser window, names the window bar, and loads the document foo.html in it, as long as one of the current windows or frames in use is not named bar (window and frame names are case sensitive).

NOTE

The link TARGET="_blank" creates an unnamed window, which makes it difficult to update the window. With a target of _blank, a link (whether the same link or a different one) simply adds another new window, instead of updating the previously opened window.

JavaScript

With JavaScript, you can create a new window with a particular document loaded into it, based upon conditions the author selects. Furthermore, the author can specify the size of the new window and the options that are available in the window and assign names for referencing it. The window.open() method has a number of parameters that the author can use to set various features, as shown in the syntax:

```
window.open("Document","Name","feature1=0,feature2=1,feature3=0,....")
```

- ■ *Document* is the URL of the document to be loaded into the new window or a string variable containing the URL. This is optional; if the URL is omitted, the browser can open a blank window, and you can use the write() method to create a display.

- ■ *Name* is the name to be given to the new window. *Name* is also optional; however, to target the window with a link or a form, a name is necessary. You can provide a name at a later time by assigning the window.name property.

- ■ *feature1,feature2,feature3,...* are the various features of the new window that the author can select to display in the new window. The features include the following:

  menubar—The bar of pull-down menu titles, including File, Edit, View, and so on.

  toolbar—The bar of buttons containing Back, Forward, Home, Reload, and so on.

  location—The bar containing the field for entering and displaying the URL.

  directories—The bar of directory buttons containing What's New, What's Cool, Destinations, and so on.

  status—The bar at the bottom of the browser, usually displaying the status of documents being loaded.

  scrollbars—The horizontal and vertical bars on the right and bottom edges of the browser allowing the user to scroll the document using a mouse.

  resizable—Not a displayable feature, but it allows the user to resize the new window.

You turn on these features by assigning them a value of yes or 1 for true and turn them off by assigning a value of no or 0 for false. Specifying just the feature name without a value assigns a value of true to the feature. The default value of these features is true if none of the features are specified. If any of the features are specified, the unspecified features default to false.

The following line opens a new window, loads the document `new.html`, and names the new window `newWindow`:

```
window.open("new.html","newWindow");
```

All the features are present in the new window; because none were specified, they all default to true.

The following code indicates that the new window should have a menu bar and scrollbars and should be resizable by the user:

```
window.open("new.html","newWindow","menubar=1,scrollbars=1,resizable=1");
```

The unspecified features defaulted to false. Note that the specified features are separated only by commas and that the entire line of features is enclosed in quotes.

In addition to the features that you can turn on or off by assignment, you have two more features to dimension the new window:

- `width`—the value in pixels of the new window's width
- `height`—the value in pixels of the new window's height

The following code creates a new window with a menu bar and scrollbars that are resizable by the user:

```
window.open("new.html","newWindow",
"menubar=1,scrollbars=1,resizable=1,width=400,hieght=300");
```

In addition, the window has dimensions of 400 pixels wide by 300 pixels high.

A simple way to open a window is to provide a link to an `onClick` event handler:

```
<A HREF="new.html" onClick='this.href="#";window.open("new.html");'>New Page</A>
```

If the browser is JavaScript-enabled, the document `new.html` loads into a new window. The `this.href` property assignment statement maintains the current document in the current window. If the browser is not JavaScript-enabled, the link defaults to loading `new.html` into the current window.

You can also open the window by assignment, which is a popular method. By defining a variable and assigning it to the new window, you can access the properties of the new window through the variable:

```
myWindow=window.open("new.html");
```

Using an assignment statement, you can use two names to refer to the window:

```
myWindow=window.open("new.html","newWindow");
```

You can also set various features of the new window:

```
myWindow=window.open("new.html",
"newWindow","menubar=1,scrollbars=1,resizable=1");
```

NOTE

The two names that can refer to a window are not the same functionally. Consider the following code:

```
myWindow=window.open("","newWindow");
```

`myWindow` is a variable of the object that opened the `newWindow`. `newWindow` is the new window's name. The new window's properties can be referenced through the variable `myWindow`. Links and forms can be targeted to the new window with its name `newWindow`.

Although all the parameters (document URL, window name, features) are optional, you must have an empty set of quotes as a placeholder for an unspecified document URL if you specify the name or features. Likewise, you need empty quotes as a placeholder for an unspecified name if you specify the features. The following list outlines examples of using empty quotes only when needed as placeholders:

> `window.open();` opens a new blank window without a name, and all the features default to true.
>
> `window.open("","newWindow");` opens a new blank window with the name `newWindow`, and all the features default to true.
>
> `window.open("","","menubar=1,scrollbars=1,resizable=1");` opens a blank window without a name, and only the `menubar`, `scrollbars`, and `resizable` features are true.

TIP

I want to point out one final detail about opening windows. A bug with certain varieties of the Netscape Navigator browser prevents the display of a document with the `window.open()` method. The workaround for this bug is to repeat the window opening statement:

```
myWindow = window.open("new.html","newWindow");
myWindow = window.open("new.html","newWindow");
```

Repeating the statement forces the display of `newWindow` and its document in all varieties of the Netscape Navigator browser.

Closing a Window

Closing a window with JavaScript is as easy as opening a window. To close a window, use the `window.close()` method in that window or by reference to that window. `window.close()` closes only a browser window (the top window). You cannot close a frame with this method.

> **NOTE**
>
> Later versions of Netscape prevent the `window.close()` from closing a window that was not created by JavaScript. This security measure prevents pranksters from inserting the code in poorly written guest books and the like. This measure should not affect any legitimate use of the `window.close()` method.

A function or event handler with `window.close()` closes the window containing it:

```
<FORM>
<INPUT TYPE="BUTTON" VALUE="Close Window" onClick="top.close()">
</FORM>
```

> **NOTE**
>
> For an event handler, such as `onClick`, you must specify a window name, such as `window`, `parent`, `top`, `self`, or an assigned variable name such as `myWindow`, as in `window.close()` or `myWindow.close()`. Simply using `close()` in an event handler implies `document.close()`.

You can close a window by reference, in the same window that opened it, through the variable assigned to the new window:

```
myWindow = window.open("new.html","newWindow");
.....
<FORM>
<INPUT TYPE="BUTTON" VALUE="Close Window" onClick="myWindow.close()">
</FORM>
```

> **NOTE**
>
> `newWindow.close();` won't work. You can use the name newWindow in the preceding example to identify the window (the `window.name` property) and target the window in links and forms. However, you cannot use newWindow to reference the new window and its properties.

> **TIP**
>
> A good use of the `window.close()` method is to provide a button or link for users to easily close a new window when they are finished with it. (A number of users, especially new users, might not know how to close the window or might mistakenly exit the browser instead

of closing the window.) You can use a conditional statement to provide to close button or link only if the document is loaded in a explicitly named window (a new window):

```
<SCRIPT LANUAGE="JavaScript">
<!--
//newWindow is the name given the new window
if(top.name == "newWindow"){
  document.write('<A HREF="javascript:top.close()>close</A>"' +
                " this window to return to previous window.");
  }      //  For clarity the angle brackets
         // are not encoded, unescape("%3C"), unescape("%3E").
 //However in actual code they would be encoded to
 //prevent misinterpretation as comment tags by older browsers.
 // -->
</SCRIPT>
```

Navigating Among Windows

It is possible to have a number of windows opened during a session; however, only one window can be active, or have focus, at a time. Having focus means that the window is able to directly receive and respond to user input. Also, the window with the focus is typically the top window on the display, the one in the foreground overlapping the other windows. (With UNIX and X Window, the window with focus can be in the background.)

The user can navigate between the windows with the mouse. Often, clicking the window gives the window focus. With some varieties of UNIX, moving the mouse cursor on a window is enough to give a window focus; conversely, moving the cursor off the window blurs (remove focus, or deactivate) the window.

Relying on user action is not the only way, nor at times the best way, to give focus to a window and blur others. JavaScript and HTML provides several methods to focus and blur windows automatically through code. This automatic focusing and blurring allows navigation through the windows with little or no user action. Instead of providing a message to inform the user to click a window, the code can focus the window automatically for the user. The intent is not to remove user control of the session but to assist the user—as cruise control in an automobile does.

Although many sites do not need multiple windows, sites that do might benefit by controlling these windows programmatically. JavaScript provides a good means of controlling windows through the opening and closing techniques previously described and through techniques to apply and remove window focus. All these techniques for controlling the windows combine to provide a programmatic window navigation system.

In JavaScript, merely specifying an object of the window or its document, or even changing a property in the window, does not give the window focus. There are two ways to give focus to a window:

- Indirectly, by giving focus to an object in the window
- Directly, by giving focus to the window

Indirect Focus

A window opened with the variable `myWindow`, containing a document with a form named `myForm` and an input element named `myInput`, can receive focus through the window that opened it with the following code:

```
myWindow.document.myForm.myInput.focus();
```

The input element, `myInput`, gains focus, and as a result, `myWindow`, which contains `myInput`, also gets focus.

A new window can give focus to the window that opened it through its `opener` property:

```
window.opener.focus();
```

> **NOTE**
>
> The opener property was introduced in Netscape Navigator 3.0 and is not supported by earlier versions of JavaScript-capable browsers.

To provide focus from a new window to the window that opened it in early versions of JavaScript-capable browsers, the new window needs a variable to reference the opening window:

```
myWindow = window.open("new.html","newWindow");
myWindow.oldWindow = top;
```

The new window can reference the old window and indirectly give it focus:

```
oldWindow. document.myForm.myInput.focus();
```

Direct Focus

A window receive focus directly with the `window.focus()` method. If the window can reference another window through a variable such as `myWindow`, it can give focus to the other window:

```
myWindow.focus();
```

A new window can give focus to the window that opened it through its `opener` property:

```
window.opener.focus();
```

A call to a function in a window can provide focus to the window if it contains `window.focus()`:

```
function focusDemo(){
    top.focus;
    ... rest of function
  }
```

> **NOTE**
>
> The methods `window.focus()` and `window.blur()`, like the opener property, were introduced in Netscape Navigator 3.0 and are not supported by earlier versions of JavaScript-capable browsers. To support the early versions of the browser, you have to use the indirect focusing technique.

Removing Focus

To blur, or remove focus from, a window, give focus to another window. Because only one window can have focus at a time, giving focus to a window directly or indirectly blurs the other windows.

A window can directly lose focus without another window gaining the focus through the `window.blur()` method. You can use any of the means that you employ with `window.focus()` for `window.blur()` as well.

> **NOTE**
>
> According to Netscape documentation, you're supposed to give focus to a window by targeting a link at the window:
>
> `<A HREF="some.html" TARGET="myWindow">My Window</A>`
>
> Clicking the link should load the document some.html in the window myWindow and give focus to myWindow. If myWindow does not exist, a new window is opened with some.html loaded in it, and the new window has the focus.
>
> This technique does not always work in every version of the browser. If the window is already open, it might not gain focus.

Frames

Along with JavaScript, frames were introduced in Netscape Navigator 2.0. Frames quickly became popular because they could display multiple documents simultaneously in the same window. The window is divided into several subwindows called frames, based upon the designer's specification. Each frame can contain a separate document (HTML, text, image, and so on), each one individually addressable and scrollable. As with windows, you can name and reference frames. You can load documents in a frame without affecting the documents in the other frames.

A real benefit of using frames is the ability to provide a permanent navigation menu for the site. Instead of hopping from one page to another to navigate, a user can readily select a page from the menu and see the page appear in another frame (a main display frame). A couple of variations of the navigation menu are keeping a table of contents in one frame and document display in another or presenting a button bar frame along one edge of the window, from which the user can click the buttons to load different portions of the site in the display frame.

> **TIP**
>
> Using frames does have some drawbacks. The major drawback is that the area to display each document is reduced. Users with a small monitor, a laptop computer, or a palmtop might have difficulty viewing some of the documents in frames. It is considered a good idea to provide frame and no-frame versions of a site and give frame-capable users the option of viewing either version (which is fairly easy to accomplish with JavaScript).

Creating Frames

Frames are created with frameset tags and specified with frame tags.

```
<FRAMESET COLS="60%,*">
    <FRAME SRC="doc1.html" NAME="frame1">
    <FRAME SRC="doc2.html" NAME="frame2">
</FRAMESET>
```

> **TIP**
>
> Indenting the frame tags is not necessary but is frequently used to provide the Web author a better view of the tags and the frame hierarchy within the code.

Frameset Tags

The frameset tag has an attribute that describes how to divide the window into frames. This attribute is either COLS or ROWS (for columns or rows), but not both. The author can specify the number of rows or columns in the window and the size of each. Each row or column can be specified as a absolute size in pixels, a relative size in percent of the window, or the remainder of the window. The following line creates two frames as columns, one with 60 percent of the window and the other with the remainder (specified by *) of the window's width (in this case, 40 percent):

```
<FRAMESET COLS="60%,*">
```

The next code line creates the two frames as before, but without the percent sign, the width of the first frame is an absolute value of 60 pixels wide:

```
<FRAMESET COLS="60,*">
```

The second frame still has the remainder of the window's width.

The following line creates four frames as columns; three of the frames each take 30 percent of the screen width, and the fourth takes the remainder:

```
<FRAMESET COLS="30%,30%,30%,*">
```

You could replace the * with 10% in this case. You are not required to use *. However, if you specify all the frames with percentages, they must add up to 100 percent of the window width.

The next code line creates two frames as rows, the first with 70 percent of the window's height and the second with 30 percent:

```
<FRAMESET ROWS="70%,30%">
```

The frame sizes can be a mix of absolute, relative, and remainder, but if the total size of all the frames does not equal the window size, the results are unpredictable. Specifying frame sizes with just a * might seem obvious; however, you can use a * for each frame. The following line creates three equal frames, each with one-third of the window's height:

```
<FRAMESET ROWS="*,*,*">
```

Frame Tags

The frame tag attributes specify the document to be loaded in the frames, the name of the frame, frame margins, scrollbars, and the resizing option. All the following attributes of the frame tag are optional:

- The SRC attribute is the URL (relative or absolute) of the document to be loaded in the frame. The document can be from the same server as the frameset file or from another server. If you do not use the SRC attribute, the frame contains just blank space. This blank space might be what you want, especially if you use JavaScript to write content to the frame.

- The NAME attribute, if specified, provides a means to reference the frame from other frames and with JavaScript. JavaScript can also reference the frame through the frames array, which is covered in the section "Referencing Windows and Frames," later in this chapter. The value for the NAME attribute must begin with an alphanumeric character.

17

■ You set the margins with two attributes, MARGINWIDTH and MARGINHEIGHT:

MARGINWIDTH controls the side margins of the frame. Its value, in pixels, can be as low as 1. The maximum value is limited only by the size of the frame. (You cannot set the margin so there is no room to display the document.)

The MARGINHEIGHT attribute is the same as the MARGINWIDTH, except that it controls the top and bottom margins.

Both MARGINWIDTH and MARGINHEIGHT, if not specified, default to a value determined by the browser.

■ The SCROLLING attribute controls whether the frame has scrollbars. The values for SCROLLING are YES, NO, and AUTO. A value of YES causes scrollbars to always be present in the frame. NO prevents scrollbars from displaying. AUTO displays scrollbar only if the document is larger than the frame; otherwise, scrollbars are suppressed. The default value for SCROLLING is AUTO.

■ NORESIZE prevents the user from resizing the frame. There is no value specified for this attribute. By default, all frames are resizable unless you specify this attribute. Frames that border a frame with the NORESIZE attribute cannot be resized along the common border.

TIP

If possible, it is best to let the user resize the frame by not specifying this attribute.

Use the following code segment to name a frame frame1, load the document doc1.html, set the side margins to 5 pixels, set the upper and lower margins to 10 pixels, always display scrollbars, and prevent the user from resizing the frame:

```
<FRAME SRC="doc1.html" NAME="frame1" MARGINWIDTH=5
MARGINHEIGHT=10 SCROLLING=YES NORESIZE>
```

Netscape and Microsoft are introducing more advanced features for their latest browsers. Visit the Web sites for these companies to find detailed information on the attributes (http://home.netscape.com/ and http://www.microsoft.com/, respectively).

Tag Placement

You usually place the frameset and frame tags in the body of the document. However, in several versions of Netscape Navigator, enclosing them in body tags (<BODY> and </BODY>) prevents the browser from reading the frameset tags. Because the body tags are optional, place the frameset tags after the head section of the document and omit the body tags, as shown below:

```
<HTML>
<HEAD>
<TITLE>Frame Demo</TITLE>
```

```
</HEAD>
<FRAMESET COLS="60%,*">
      <FRAME SRC="doc1.html" NAME="frame1">
      <FRAME SRC="doc2.html" NAME="frame2">
</FRAMESET>
</HTML>
```

This code sets up the frames and loads the appropriate documents. Actually, you can make the file smaller because the HTML, HEAD, and BODY tags are optional; the file can contain only the TITLE, FRAMESET, and FRAME tags, as shown in the next segment. (The title's opening and closing tags are the only tags required by HTML specification to be in every HTML document.)

```
<TITLE>Frame Demo</TITLE>
<FRAMESET COLS="60%,*">
      <FRAME SRC="doc1.html" NAME="frame1">
      <FRAME SRC="doc2.html" NAME="frame2">
</FRAMESET>
```

NOFRAMES Tag

Many authors also include a set of NOFRAMES tags to display a message for non–frame-capable browsers:

```
<NOFRAMES>
code and text content to display to nonframe-capable browsers
</NOFRAMES>
```

The content can contain HTML tags as well as text. A frame-capable browser ignores the content between the <NOFRAMES> and </NOFRAMES> tags, whereas a non–frame-capable browser ignores the <FRAMESET>, <FRAME>, and <NOFRAMES> tags and displays the content between the <NOFRAMES> and </NOFRAMES> tags. You place the <NOFRAMES> tags within <FRAMESET> tags:

```
<TITLE>Frame Demo</TITLE>
<FRAMESET COLS="60%,*">
      <FRAME SRC="doc1.html" NAME="frame1">
      <FRAME SRC="doc2.html" NAME="frame2">
<NOFRAMES>
code and text content to display to nonframe-capable browsers
</NOFRAMES>
</FRAMESET>
```

TIP

A number of authors actually duplicate the main document of the site in the <NOFRAMES> tags for a non-frame version. However, it is not usually necessary to use this technique because you can create a framed version of the site with JavaScript from the same pages that are displayed to non–frame-capable users.

It is interesting to note that you can include the body tags in the <NOFRAMES> tags, using the attributes of background, bgcolor, text, and so on for the no-frames version of the document.

The non–frame-capable browser ignores the <FRAMESET> tags and initiates the body section at the first appropriate content (that is, a body tag) in the <NOFRAMES> tag. The frame-capable browser initiates the body section at the first <FRAMESET> tag and ignores the contents of the <NOFRAMES> tag. Of course, the frame-capable browser loads the documents specified by the <FRAME> tags, and the body tags of these documents are properly recognized by the browser.

Nested Frames

You can create nested frames where a frame is divided into more frames. Of the two different ways to create nested frames, both display the same, but there is a big difference in the frame hierarchy and the way the nested frames are referenced.

The following code creates frames with multiple framesets in a single window. Figure 17.1 shows the frames, and Figure 17.2 shows the structure (hierarchy).

```
<FRAMESET COLS="30%,*">
    <FRAME SRC="doc1.html" NAME="frame1">
    <FRAMESET ROWS="*,20%">
            <FRAME SRC="doc2.html" NAME="frame2">
            <FRAME SRC="doc3.html" NAME="frame3">
    </FRAMESET>
</FRAMESET>
```

FIGURE 17.1.

Creating frames with multiple framesets in a single window.

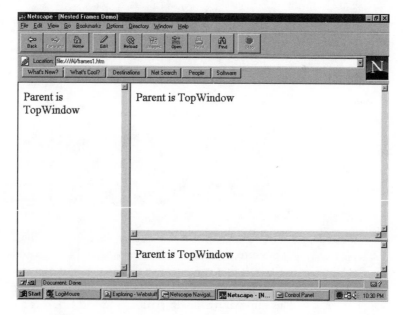

The following code creates frames with multiple framesets in two windows. (A frame is considered a window.) Figure 17.3 shows these frames, and Figure 17.4 shows the structure (hierarchy).

```
<FRAMESET COLS="30%,*">
     <FRAME SRC="doc1.html" NAME="frame1">
     <FRAME SRC="frame2.html" NAME="frame2">
</FRAMESET>
```

FIGURE 17.2.

The frame hierarchy of multiple framesets in a single window.

The file `frame2.html` contains the following additional frameset information:

```
<FRAMESET ROWS="*,20%">
          <FRAME SRC="doc2.html" NAME="frame3">
          <FRAME SRC="doc3.html" NAME="frame4">
</FRAMESET>
```

FIGURE 17.3.

Creating frames with multiple framesets in two windows.

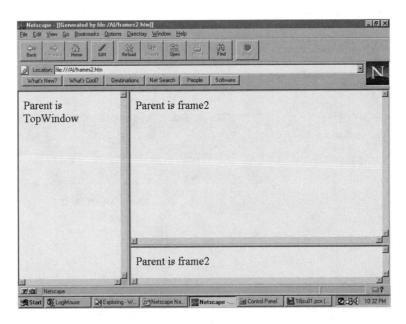

The two codes produce frames that display exactly the same, as shown in Figures 17.1 and 17.3. However, the structures, as shown in Figures 17.2 and 17.4, are completely different. In the code for Figure 17.2, all three frames have the same parent, the top window. In the code for Figure 17.4, only `frame1` and `frame2` have the top window as parent; `frame3` and `frame4`'s parent is `frame2`. This can make a big difference in how the frames are referenced, which is discussed in the following sections.

FIGURE 17.4.

The frame hierarchy of multiple framesets in two windows.

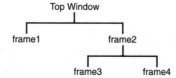

Adding JavaScript Code to Frames

The frameset files and most of the files of the documents that display in frames are HTML files. As a result, you can use JavaScript in them, as you do in other HTML files. The only difference is that the JavaScript can easily reference properties of other documents in frames and use certain features to reference those properties.

You can refer to the top window and its frames by their relationships to each other. A window (frames are considered windows) can be referenced with the window properties `top`, `parent`, `window`, and `self`. The `top` property refers to the main window (the browser window); `parent` refers to the window (frame) containing the frameset for a particular frame. For frames with a frameset in the top window, `parent` and `top` are the same. The properties `self` and `window` both refer to the particular frame or window.

Consider the following code:

```
<FRAMESET COLS="10%,*">
        <FRAME SRC="doc1.html" NAME="frame1">
        <FRAMESET COLS="50%,*">
                <FRAME SRC="frame2.html" NAME="frame2">
                <FRAME SRC="doc3.html" NAME="frame3">
</FRAMESET>
```

`frame2.html` contains the following additional frameset information:

```
 <FRAMESET ROWS="*,20%">
                <FRAME SRC="doc4.html" NAME="frame4">
                <FRAME SRC="doc5.html" NAME="frame5">
 </FRAMESET>
```

The parent of `frame1`, `frame2`, and `frame3` is `top` because the frameset for each of these frames is in the top window. The parent for `frame4` and `frame5` is `frame2` because the frameset for these two frames is in the window (or frame) of `frame2`. To reference the top frame from the document in `frame4`, you use the `top` property; to reference `frame2`, you use the `parent` property; and finally, to reference its own frame, you use `self` or `window`.

You can refer to functions, variables, and other properties with the relational window properties:

```
<HTML>
<HEAD>
<TITLE>Frame Demo</TITLE>
<SCRIPT LANGUAGE="JavaScript">
<!--
a1 = 2;
```

```
function addA1(){
    a2 = a1 + 1;
    return a2;
 }
// -->
</SCRIPT>
</HEAD>
<BODY>
<FRAMESET COLS="10%,*">
     <FRAME SRC="doc1.html" NAME="frame1">
     <FRAMESET COLS="50%,*">
             <FRAME SRC="frame2.html" NAME="frame2">
             <FRAME SRC="doc3.html" NAME="frame3">
</FRAMESET>
.....
```

`frame2.html` contains additional frameset information:

```
<HTML>
<HEAD>
<TITLE>Frame Demo</TITLE>
<SCRIPT LANGUAGE="JavaScript">
<!--
b1 = 2;
function addB1(){
    b2 = b1 + 1;
    return b2;
 }
// -->
</SCRIPT>
</HEAD>
<BODY>
 <FRAMESET ROWS="*,20%">
             <FRAME SRC="doc4.html" NAME="frame4">
             <FRAME SRC="doc5.html" NAME="frame5">
 </FRAMESET>
```

To access variable a1 and function addA1() from frame1, frame2, or frame3, you could use either top.a1 or parent.a1 and either top.addA1() or parent.addA1(). However, from frame4 or frame5, you can use only top.a1 and top.addA1 because parent refers to frame2. You can access variable b1 and function addB1() from frame4 and frame5 with parent.b1 and parent.addB1(). I hope you are not thoroughly confused; I discuss more ways of referring to various frames and windows in the section "Referencing Windows and Frames," later in this chapter.

You must exercise several precautions when dealing with framed documents and JavaScript. Your script can produce errors if a referenced frame does not contain the correct document or does not even exist.

Trying to access top.a1 from any of the documents in the previous example when the document is not in frames causes an error. However, JavaScript offers the means to prevent such errors, as discussed in the next section.

Synchronizing Frames

As mentioned at the end of the last section, not having the right documents or the right frames loaded can cause errors and other problems. A session can stop dead in its tracks because it cannot find one variable. Furthermore, the problem might be that the documents haven't finish loading. Synchronizing the frames ensures that the frames and documents have finished loading before they are needed or that alternative actions are taken.

Verifying Frames

A common potential problem concerns a page containing JavaScript that can be viewed either in or out of frames. The `window.length` property is quite useful for letting JavaScript determine whether a document is being viewed in frames. The `length` property is equal to the number of frames a window or frame contains. You can set a conditional statement that performs a statement only if frames are being used:

```
if( top.length != 0 ){
    document.write("Frames are being used");
    }
```

You usually use `top` or `parent` instead of `window` because `window` implies the frame containing the code, which does not contain frames unless the document is a frameset file. If a window or frame does have frames, its length is greater than zero. However, writing > for `greater than` could be misinterpreted as the end of a HTML comment by older browsers, so using `!=`, `not equal to`, is preferable.

The short circuit feature of the `if` statement is useful for preventing a error when a document that is not in frames attempts to access a variable in another frame or frameset. If the top frameset contains a variable `a1` that is used in a conditional statement by a framed document, an error is produced if the document is viewed as a stand-alone (no-frame) document. However, if the `length` property is checked first in the conditional and found to be false, the statement ends, which prevents an error from attempting to access a non-existent variable.

The first part of the following statement, `parent.length != 0`, is false when frames aren't used, so further evaluation is stopped and the error does not occur:

```
if( (parent.length != 0) && (top.a1 == x ) ) )
```

Verifying Documents Loaded

Various techniques have been developed to synchronize the frames—some rather simple, others rather complex. One of the easiest techniques is to use JavaScript to verify that a particular document is present in a certain frame before proceeding with the rest of the code. The frames array lets you specify a frame as an element of the array. (Refer to the section "Referencing

Windows and Frames," later in this chapter for information on the frames array.) Consider the following code line:

```
if( (parent.length == 3)&&(parent.frames[1].title == "My Page") )
```

The `if` statement verifies that the right frame structure is present (in this case, three frames) and that the document in the second frame (which, in this case, is to be referenced) is the correct one. If the frame structure is incorrect, the conditional evaluation stops, and no further action is taken or an alternative action is taken. If the frame structure is correct but the wrong document is present, the script initiates no action or an alternative action. Initiating no further action simply maintains the session at its current position, allowing the user to proceed with other actions or retry a failed action. (Perhaps the page wasn't finished loading and another attempt will be successful.) An alternative action could include providing an alert to the user, loading the correct page, and proceeding or proceeding with action but skipping the steps that require the missing document.

The previous example checked a simple frame structure (three frames). You can check more complex structures using the frames array of various windows or frames in a multi-part `if` statement. The multi-part `if` statement has to verify the structure from top down; otherwise, referencing a missing frame causes an error. Note the following line of code:

```
if(top.length==3)&&(top.frames[1].length==2)&&(top.frames[1].frames[1]==3)...
```

If a portion of the frame structure is not present, the `if` statement stops at that point, and the script can perform an alternative action via an `else` statement or choose no action at all.

In verifying that the correct document is present, the code can check other properties besides the title, such as the frame's `location.href`. You can assign a common variable in each document a unique name or number and then check this document identity variable instead of the document title or other properties.

Registering Documents

Simply verifying that the required document is present can get complicated with larger sites and does not necessarily verify that the document is loaded. Another technique involves having the documents indicate when they are loaded and unloaded. Using the `onLoad()` and `onUnload()` events, the documents record their presence in a top window variable or a cookie. (See Chapter 19, "Cookies and State Maintenance," for more information about cookies.) The following code shows that you do not have to use the title to identify the document; you could use another property or a identity variable:

```
<BODY onLoad="top.funRecord(document.title)"
    onUnload="top.funRemove(document.title)">
```

The following example shows a simple document registration scheme. The first code segment contains the top frameset file:

```
<SCRIPT LANGUAGE="JavaScript">
<!--
var a4 = "";    // variable for document registration string

function funRecord(a){ // add the document to the registration string on load
   a4 += a;
}

function funRemove(a){         // remove document registration on unload
   a4 = a4.substring( 0,a4.indexOf(a) ) +
           a4.substring(a4.indexOf(a)+a.length,a4.length);
}

function funCheck(a){   // check whether document is registered or not
  if( a4.indexOf(a) != -1)  return true;
  else  return false;
 }
// -->
</SCRIPT>
```

The next code segment shows the document file:

```
<HTML>
<TITLE>The Harley FXSTC</TITLE>
<SCRIPT LANGUAGE="JavaScript">
<!--
function funRegister(a){
  // check that top frameset is present to register document, else ignore
  if( ( top.length != 0 )&&(top.document.title == "Main Frameset") )
     if( a ="R") top.funRecord(document.title);
     else top.funRemove(document.title);
  }
function funCheck(a){    // check whether document is registered or not
  if( ( top.length != 0 )&&(top.document.title == "Main Frameset") )
     return top.funCheck(a);
 else return false;
}
// -->
</SCRIPT>
<BODY onLoad="top.funRecord(document.title)"
    onUnload="top.funRemove(document.title)">
```

The following code checks whether the document is registered:

```
if( funCheck("The Softtail Series"} )
     top.frames[2].fxnames();   // document registered, proceed with action
else                           // document not registered, take alternative action
     top.location.href = "http://www.foo.com/fx.html;
```

Extensive Registration Schemes

More complex schemes not only register the document but also register the document's position in the frame structure (hierarchy). If a document position changes due to different possible loading scenarios or a site update, the code dependent upon referencing the document can locate the document through the document's registration information. Instead of using a single variable or a cookie to hold registration information, some schemes employ an array of variables with each element (variable) containing identity and position information for a registered document. These schemes are complex to set up; however, they do provide great benefit in very large sites where a small change in the structure could throw off the code references in many of the documents.

The hIdaho Frameset (`http://hidaho.com/frameset/`) is a registration scheme that is effective for large, complex frame structures. It registers functions and locations of functions within the frame structure. It determines the location by passing its frame name (`self.name`) to its parent, which attaches its own name and passes the information to its parent. The process continues upwards, parent by parent, until the top window is reached. Also included are functions to unregister a particular function (all functions must have a unique name) and unregister a frame name (all the functions that were located in that frame) on a document's unload.

Also included in the hIdaho Frameset is a function to check whether a specified function is registered (it returns false if the specified function is not registered) and a function, `Exec()`, that calls other functions and passes parameters to the other functions. Because all function names must be unique, the author can call a particular function without knowing its location and pass parameters to it through `Exec(function,parameter1,parameter2,...)`.

Updating Frames

A significant benefit of frames is the capability to update or change the document in a frame while other frames remain unchanged. Whether a frame gets updated from user input in another frame or gets updated programmatically, you can provide the means to direct the changes to the appropriate frame through several techniques. These techniques can employ HTML (with certain Netscape extensions), JavaScript, or a combination of both.

Links

Perhaps the simplest updating technique is using a link to update (by loading a new document) its own frame. To direct the new document into another frame, the anchor tag has a target attribute for which you can specify either a value of a frame name or a relational name. The relational words (called *magic target names* by Netscape) correspond to the relational window properties discussed previously. The relational names used for targeting links all begin with an underscore and are always lowercase. These names are _top, _parent, and _self, which correspond to the window properties top, parent, and self. There is no _window, however.

The following code represents frames in which a link in one frame must update another frame:

```
<FRAMESET COLS="10%,*">
      <FRAME SRC="doc1.html" NAME="frame1">
      <FRAMESET COLS="50%,*">
            <FRAME SRC="frame2.html" NAME="frame2">
            <FRAME SRC="doc3.html" NAME="frame3">
</FRAMESET>
```

The file `frame2.html` contains the following additional frameset information:

```
<FRAMESET ROWS="*,20%">
            <FRAME SRC="doc4.html" NAME="frame4">
            <FRAME SRC="doc5.html" NAME="frame5">
</FRAMESET>
```

To load a new document in `frame2` from a link in `doc4.html` (in `frame4`), write the link as follows:

```
<A HREF="new.html" TARGET="_parent">
```

Use the following line to load the document in the top window and basically clear all the frames:

```
<A HREF="new.html" TARGET="_top">
```

Dynamic Links

Because links are objects in JavaScript and `href` and `target` are properties of links, you can create a dynamic link by reassigning the values of `href` and `target`:

```
<A HREF="#" TARGET="_top" onClick='this.href="new.html";this.target="_self";'>
```

For JavaScript-enabled browsers, the document `new.html` loads in the current frame; otherwise, the current document loads in the top window. (A fragment specifier, #, without a URL and an anchor name, or fragment identifier, refers to the current document.) This reassignment of the link's `href` and `target` properties can be more dynamic if you combine the assignment statements with conditional and other statements. For example, load a frameset file in the parent if frames are being used; otherwise, load the main document of the frameset:

```
<A HREF="main.html" TARGET="_top"
   onClick='if( top.length != 0 ){this.href="frameset1.html";
                            this.target="_parent";}'>
```

Watch those quotes; the event handler must be enclosed in a set of quotes (either double or single).

You do not need to reassign both the `href` and `target` properties for every dynamic link. The previous example could have had the target attribute set to _parent.

For the no-frame user, _parent and _top are equivalent. If the user doesn't have a frame-capable browser the `target` attribute is ignored. The example could be written:

```
<A HREF="main.html" TARGET="_parent"
   onClick='if( parent.length != 0 ){this.href="frameset1.html";}'>
```

The link tag can get pretty long and cumbersome as you add more statements to the event handler. To help simplify the link, you can use function calls:

```
<A HREF="main.html" TARGET="_top" onClick='this.href=theHref();
                            this.target=theTarget;'>
```

`theHref()` is a user-defined function that determines the conditions and returns the appropriate value for the `href` property. Likewise, `theTarget()` returns the appropriate value for the `target` property. These functions must return a value regardless of whether the evaluated condition is true or false; only the non–JavaScript-enabled browser uses the default values set by the HREF and TARGET attributes. For our frame to no-frame examples, consider the following code:

```
function theHref(){
    if( top.length != 0 )
        a = "frameset1.html";
    else
        a = "main.html";
    return a;
}
```

`theTarget()` would be similarly constructed. You could also use the functions for other links on the page by passing the appropriate URLs and target names in the function calls. You could use one or two generic functions for a number of links.

You will often find that dynamic links are not necessary. Typically, a page is loaded into the current frame, or the links appear on a navigational menu that is not seen by no-frame users and can always be targeted to a particular frame. However, for the few circumstances when they're necessary, dynamic links can be quite effective. Also, the frame/no-frame condition is not the only case where dynamic links might be necessary; you can set up these links for any circumstance you can imagine.

The `location.href` Property

Another way to update a frame that does not necessarily require a link is by using the `href` property of the location object. You can also use the `href` property in conjunction with a form button event handler or a function. Do not confuse the location object with the `location` property of the document. `document.location` is a read-only property, but you can write to `window.location.href`. The following statements are equivalent and update the current frame with the home page of `http://www.mcp.com/`:

```
location.href = "http://www.mcp.com/";
self.location.href = "http://www.mcp.com/";
window.location.href = "http://www.mcp.com/";
```

The following statements update the parent and top frames, respectively:

```
parent.location = "http://www.mcp.com/";
top.location = "http://www.mcp.com/";
```

Instead of using relational window properties, you can use a frame name:

```
parent.frame3.location.href = "http://www.mcp.com/";
```

In addition to writing the `href` property, you can also write the `pathname` property of the location object, which lets you specify the path or file name from the server root. (Of course, the

17

host name, as well as the protocol and port, remains unchanged from the current location.) Use the following code to load the document `http://www.abc.com/foo/doc2.html` in `frame1`, which currently has `http://www.abc.com/index.htm`:

```
frame1.location.pathname="/foo/doc2.html";
```

However, if the current document is `http://www.def.org/home.html` or `ftp://ftp.abc.com/pub/abc.txt`, you must use the `href` property.

The write() Method

A third way to update a frame is using the `write()` or `writeln()` methods. JavaScript can dynamically generate a document in a frame:

```
<HTML>
<HEAD>
<TITLE>Updating Demo Frameset</TITLE>
</HEAD>
<FRAMESET COLS="40%,*">
    <FRAME SRC="doc1.html" NAME="frame1">
    <FRAME SRC="doc2.html" NAME="frame2">
</FRAMESET>
</HTML>


file doc1.html
```

The file `doc2.html` can be any file, even empty. However, you should place at least a space or carriage return in the file so that you do not cause a `'Document contains no data'` error.

Dynamically uploading a frame can be interactive with the user through links or forms:

```
<HTML>
<HEAD>
<TITLE>Updating Demo frame1</TITLE>
<SCRIPT LANGUAGE="JavaScript">
<!--
function docWrite(){
    top.frame2.document.clear();
    top.frame2.document.write("<HTML><HEAD>" +
        "<TITLE>Updating Demo frame2</TITLE>");
    top.frame2.document.write(" </HEAD><BODY BGCOLOR=\"" +
                    document.form1.bginput.value + "\">");
    top.frame2.document.write("<H1>Updated Page</H1>");
    top.frame2.document.write("Update by " + document.form1.input1.value);
    top.frame2.document.write("</BODY></HTML>");
    top.frame2.document.close();
  }
// -->
</SCRIPT>

</HEAD>
<BODY>
<FORM NAME="form1">
<INPUT TYPE="TEXT" NAME="input1">
```

```
<P>
Select a Background Color<BR>
<INPUT TYPE="RADIO" NAME="radio1" VALUE="white" CHECKED
    onClick='document.form1.bginput.value="white"'>White<BR>
<INPUT TYPE="RADIO" NAME="radio1" VALUE="red"
    onClick='document.form1.bginput.value="red"'>Red<BR>
<INPUT TYPE="RADIO" NAME="radio1" VALUE="blue"
    onClick='document.form1.bginput.value="blue"'>Blue<BR>
<INPUT TYPE="RADIO" NAME="radio1" VALUE="green"
    onClick='document.form1.bginput.value="green"'>Green<BR>
<P>
<INPUT TYPE="HIDDEN" NAME="bginput" VALUE="white">
<P>
<INPUT TYPE="BUTTON" VALUE="Update frame2" onClick="testW()">
</FORM>
</BODY>
</HTML>
```

The JavaScript used to update a frame can be very sophisticated. You can use conditional state-ments, calculations, or any script imaginable to create a document to update the frame. Games, slide shows, highlighted maps, and database query results are some examples of what you can use to upload the frame.

Caching Files

Images files to be included in an updated frame can be cached ahead of time to prevent the download from delaying the update. You use the image object to cache an image until it's needed. However, this object is not available in early versions of JavaScript-capable browsers. Another technique is to use a document in a hidden frame to download the images:

```
<HTML>
<HEAD>
<TITLE>Hidden Frame to Cache Images</TITLE>
</HEAD>
<FRAMESET COLS="100%,*">
    <FRAME SRC="doc1.html" NAME="frame1">
    <FRAME SRC="cache.html" NAME="frame2">
</FRAMESET>
</HTML>
```

The following file, cache.html, is a non-displayed document just for downloading images so that the image files are stored in the cache:

```
<HTML>
<HEAD>
<TITLE>Updating Demo frame1</TITLE>
<SCRIPT LANGUAGE="JavaScript">
<!--
var a1 = 0;
// -->
</SCRIPT>
</HEAD>
<BODY onLoad="a1 = 1;">
<IMG SRC="image1.gif" WIDTH=100 HEIGHT=200>
```

```
<IMG SRC="image2.jgp" WIDTH=300 HEIGHT=120>
<IMG SRC="image3.gif" WIDTH=200 HEIGHT=200>
</BODY>
</HTML>
```

> **TIP**
>
> You should size the image tags to prevent problems when the script executes in certain browser versions.

Although good practice usually dictates that you use the `alt` attribute with images tags, the attribute is not necessary here because the document does not display to any browser—let alone a non-graphical browser.

Variable a1 is a flag that is set when the images are downloaded. You are not required to use this flag, but it is useful to prevent the execution of a frame update script until the images are downloaded:

```
if(top.frame2.a1 !=1 ){
   alert("Please wait, images are still downloading");
 }
else{
   ...continue with rest of script
```

Scripting Image Map Frames

Netscape Navigator 2.0 began implementing client-side image maps (although Netscape was not the first browser to do so) along with frames and JavaScript. The client-side image maps (CSIM) offered enormous benefit over the previously used server-side image maps. With CSIM, you can include the map file in the document with the image or reference it as a separate file. No longer do you have to send a request to the server for processing and redirecting the appropriate URL. Users can see in the status bar the URLs associated with the map. Furthermore, you can use CSIMs in conjunction with the older server-side image maps for downward compatibility with older browsers.

Image Map Properties

Image maps have several objects and properties. The area tags in the map are JavaScript objects. The `href` and `target` attributes are properties of the area object that can change programmatically with JavaScript. The area object has events handlers such as `onClick`, `onMouseOver`, and `onMouseOut`. In fact, the area object has all the same properties and events as the link object. The area tag also has a `NOHREF` attribute that prevents the loading of the document URL assigned to the `href` attribute.

NOTE

The image map objects and properties are not available in early versions of JavaScript-capable browsers. The area object and its properties were introduced in Netscape Navigator 3.0. Furthermore, in Netscape Navigator 3.0, the onClick event handler and the NOHREF attribute are not functional for all platforms.

Referencing Area Objects

You can reference the area objects with the links array. The links array consists of all the link and area objects in the document. The elements are numbered from zero to one less than the total number of link and area tags. The following code is an example of a document with a link and a CSIM for explaining the links array in the next paragraph:

```
<HTML>
<HEAD>
<TITLE>CSIM DEMO</TITLE>
</HEAD>
<BODY>
<A HREF="doc1.html" target="frameA">The Softtails</A>
<MAP NAME="map1">
<A NAME="areaA" COORDS="20,20,80,80" HREF="doc2.html" TARGET="frameA">
<A NAME="areaB" COORDS="100,20,180,80" HREF="doc3.html" TARGET="frameA">
<A NAME="areaC" COORDS="20,100,80,180" HREF="doc4.html" TARGET="frameA">
<A NAME="areaD" COORDS="100,100,180,180" HREF="doc5.html" TARGET="frameA">
</MAP>
<IMG SRC="map1.gif" WIDTH=200 HEIGHT=200 ALT="Menu" USEMAP="#map1">
<!-- Code for alternative server-side map and a text menu for
non-graphical browsers omitted for clarity in the above example -->.
</BODY>
</HTML>
```

In the preceding example, the link is referenced by document.links[0] because it is the first link or area tag in the document. areaA is referenced by document.links[1] because it is the second link or area tag. areaB is document.links[2], areaC is document.links[3], and areaD is document.links[4].

The href and target properties of the area objects, as with the link objects, can be referenced and assigned new values through the links array. The following line changes the value of areaB's href property so that when its area of the image map is clicked, the document doc6.html loads instead of doc3.html:

```
document.link[2].href="doc6.html"
```

Likewise, you can change the target property:

```
document.link[2].target="frameB"
```

The target attribute and property must be specified as a frame name or one of the special relational frame words (_top, _parent, _self, or _blank) and not with a JavaScript property (top, parent, and so on).

You can open and name new windows by assigning to the target a name that is not already in use. A new window opened in this manner has the name specified as the value of the target attribute.

Calling Functions

The area tags do not always have to reference a document. You can make function calls by using a protocol of javascript followed by the function name:

```
<A NAME="areaA" COORDS="20,20,80,80" HREF="javascript:fun1()">
```

The script calls the user-defined function fun1() instead of a document. You can also use JavaScript methods and statements. This is particularly suited for a framed version of a site in which the image map server is a navigation button bar. The function can perform various statements to determine whether frames are used and certain flags are set or perform a calculation or evaluation. The function can then take the appropriate action, such as loading a certain document, or take no action at all.

The following code segments contain a rather simple slide show script with a button bar image map that allows the user to cycle forward and backwards through slides. The image map also contains buttons to return to the menu so the user can select another slide show or return to the home page. Each slide show has a sequence name that forms the first part of the file names of the slides in the sequence. The second part of the file name is a sequential number unique to each slide in the sequence. Each of the slide files has three variables: the sequence name, the sequential number of the slide, and the total number of slides in the sequence. The script reads these three variables to load the next slide file based upon which portion of the image map was clicked.

The following segment is the frameset file:

```
<HTML>
<HEAD>
<TITLE>Slide Show Main Frameset</TITLE>
</HEAD>
<FRAMESET ROWS="*,55">
    <FRAME SRC="slide1.html" NAME="frameA">
    <FRAME SRC="button.html" NAME="frameB">
</HTML>
```

The next segment is the slide1 file:

```
<HTML>
<HEAD>
<TITLE>Slide Show - First Slide</TITLE>
<SCRIPT LANGUAGE="JavaScript">
<!--
```

```
var a1 = "slide";      //first portion of slide file names
var a2 = 1;                 // sequential number of the slide
var a3 = 3;                 // total number of slides
// -->
</SCRIPT>
</HEAD>
<BODY>
<IMG SRC="slide1.gif" WIDTH=300 HEIGHT=200
      ALT="The 1992 FXSTC, Softtail Custom">
</BODY>
</HTML>
```

The following segment contains the button bar file:

```
<HTML>
<HEAD>
<TITLE>Slide Show Demo Image Map</TITLE>
<SCRIPT LANGUAGE="JavaScript">
function fun1(a){
  a1 = top.frames[0].a1; // root file name for series of slides
  a2 = top.frames[0].a2; // sequential slide number
  a3 = top.frames[0].a3; // number of slides
  if( a == "f" )
    if(a2 == a3)
      a2 = 0;
  if( a == "r" )
    if(a2 == 1)
      a2 = a3 - 1;
    else
      a2 = a2 - 2;
  a2 = a2 + 1;
  a1 += a2;
  a1 += ".html";
  top.frames[0].location.href = a1;
 }
</SCRIPT>
</HEAD>
<BODY BGCOLOR="000000">
<MAP NAME="map1">
  <AREA COORDS="1,1,75,50" HREF='javascript:fun1("f")'
   onMouseOver='window.status="Cycle forward through slide show";
   return true'>
  <AREA COORDS="76,1,150,50" HREF="menu.html" TARGET="frameA"
    onMouseOver='window.status="Return to Menu to Select Another Slide Show";
    return true'>
  <AREA COORDS="151,1,225,50" HREF="home.html" TARGET="_top"
    onMouseOver='window.status="Quit Slide Show and Return to Home Page";
    return true'>
  <AREA COORDS="226,1,300,50" HREF='javascript:fun1("r")'
    onMouseOver='window.status="Cycle backward through slide show";
    return true'>
</MAP>
<IMG SRC="buttons.gif" WIDTH=300 HEIGHT=50 USEMAP="#map1">
</BODY>
</HTML>
```

Working with Frame URLs

There are no real differences between framed and no-framed documents regarding URLs. Within the entire window, however, you can use different sites and base `hrefs`. One frame might contain a document from a certain directory on a server, another frame might have a document from another directory, and a third frame could have a document from a different server. Regardless of which frame is targeted, a relative URL in a link is referenced from the document containing the link. You can use the base tag, `<BASE HREF="http://www.foo.com/some.html">` in a document to set all links relative to the base `href`, if needed. You can override the base `href` by specifying an absolute URL in the link.

As with the `href` attribute of the base tag, you can also specify a base target. `<BASE TARGET="frameA">` directs all links in the document to the specified frame. You can also override the base target with the target attribute in the link. For example, `<A HREF="some.html" TARGET="_self">` overrides the base target and loads the document into its own frame.

> **NOTE**
>
> You must place the base tag `<BASE HREF="some.html" TARGET="someframe">` in the head section of the document. There is no content or closing tag associated with the base tag. The base tag with both the `HREF` and `TARGET` attributes is shown in the following example:
>
> ```
> <HTML>
> <HEAD>
> <TITLE>Base Demo</TITLE>
> <BASE HREF="http://www.foo.com/home.html" TARGET="frameA">
> </HEAD>
> <BODY>
> ...
> ```

You can find additional information on using URLs in frames throughout this chapter, especially in the sections "Updating Frames" and "Referencing Windows and Frames."

Referencing Windows and Frames

As discussed in previous sections, you can reference windows and frames by name or by relationship with `top`, `parent`, and `self`. However, it is not always convenient or even possible to use these names. The frames array provides another way to reference frames and their properties.

Frames Array

Each frame has a frames array. Every frame in the window, or parent frame, is an element of the array. The frames array elements are referenced by `frames[i]`, where *i* is the number corresponding to the order in which the frame is created in the parent window. The frames are numbered starting with zero up to one less than the total number of frames. The following frameset contains four frames:

```
<FRAMESET ROWS="25%,25%,25%,25%">
   <FRAME SRC="doc1.html" NAME="frameA">
   <FRAME SRC="doc2.html" NAME="frameB">
   <FRAME SRC="doc3.html" NAME="frameC">
   <FRAME SRC="doc4.html" NAME="frameD">
</FRAMESET>
```

The window's frames array has four elements:

> `frames[0]` for frame `frameA`
>
> `frames[1]` for frame `frameB`
>
> `frames[2]` for frame `frameC`
>
> `frames[3]` for frame `frameD`

Note the plural, frames, when referring to an element in the frames array.

There isn't a windows array, at least as of yet. Separate browser windows don't have a hierarchy or relational structure; you can usually reference them with a variable assigned to represent a window. (Refer to the section "Windows," earlier in this chapter.)

Parent to Child

You can refer to a child frame with code in the parent frame by either the frame name or the frames array:

```
<HTML>
<HEAD>
<TITLE>Parent to Child Demo</TITLE>
<SCRIPT LANGUAGE="JavaScript">
function childCall(){
   var a1 = self.frameA.name
   var a2 = frames[1].name
 }
</SCRIPT>
</HEAD>
<FRAMESET COLS="50%,*">
     <FRAME SRC="doc1.html" NAME="frameA">
     <FRAME SRC="doc2.html" NAME="frameB">
</FRAMESET>
</HTML>
```

Separate browser windows do not have a hierarchy structure; however, the window containing the code that opens another window is often referred to as the parent window. The new window is often referred to as the child window. Any new window can assign a variable in other windows so that other windows can reference it and its properties. To reference a property in the new window, you simply use `windowName.property`.

Consider the following code:

```
newWindow = window.open();
newWindow.location.href = "http://www.mcp.com/";
```

Although this segment doesn't exhibit the most efficient way to write the code, it demonstrates referencing a child window's property. The new window is opened and named (in this case `newWindow`). Then, the new window's `location.href` is referenced and assigned.

Child to Parent

A child frame can always refer to a parent frame as a parent. However, the parent frame can also be referenced by the frames array or by name in respect to its position in the frame hierarchy. Consider the following example:

```
<FRAMESET COLS="50%,*">
    <FRAME SRC="doc1.html" NAME="frameA">
    <FRAME SRC="doc2.html" NAME="frameB">
</FRAMESET>
</HTML>
```

The file `doc2.html` contains the following additional frameset information:

```
<FRAMESET ROWS="50%,*">
    <FRAME SRC="doc3.html" NAME="frameBA">
    <FRAME SRC="doc4.html" NAME="frameBB">
</FRAMESET>
</HTML>
```

`frameB` and its properties can be referenced by code in `doc4.html` (`frameBB`) as the following:

```
parent
top.frameb
top.frames[1]
```

Other frames higher in the hierarchy (perhaps they could be called uncles) can be referenced by frames array or by name:

```
top.frames[0]
top.frameA
```

In more complex frame structures, all the frames can still be referenced by their positions in the structure, as shown in Figure 17.5 and Table 17.1.

17

WORKING WITH
FRAMES AND
WINDOWS

FIGURE 17.5.

Hierarchy structure of a complex nested frame site.

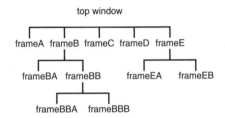

Table 17.1. Referencing other frames from `frameBBB`.

Frame	Reference
`frameA`	`top.frameA` or `top.frames[0]`
`frameBA`	`top.frames[1].frameBA` or `top.frames[1].frames[0]`
`frameBB`	`parent, top.frames[1].frameBB` or `top.frames[1].frames[1]`
`frameEA`	`top.frames[4].frameEA` or `top.frames[4].frames[0]`

Use the following line to reference the title of the document in `frameEA` and assign it to a variable a1:

```
a1 = top.frames[4].frames[0].document.title;
```

Other properties are similarly referenced.

> **NOTE**
>
> It important to note the hierarchy differences that can exist between two similar-looking frame structures, as mentioned in the section "Creating Frames," earlier in this chapter.

JavaScript supplies the `opener` property, which is used to reference the window (the parent) that opened the current window. From the new (child) window, you can reference a property of the opener (parent) window with the `top.opener.property`.

As noted in the section "Navigating Among Windows," earlier in this chapter, the `opener` property is not supported by early versions of JavaScript-capable browsers. To reference the opener window from the new window, you can use a assignment technique. The samples here use the window property `top`; however, you can use `self`, `parent`, or `window` instead of `top` if necessary. The property `top` is used in the following code segment because the code might appear in any frame of the windows. Using `top` ensures that the appropriate property of the top window is identified. `self`, `parent`, or `window` could be any frame in the top window.

```
newWindow = window.open("doc1.html");
newWindow.oldWindow = top;
```

Use the following line to reference a property in the opener window from the new window:

```
top.oldWindow.property
```

Child to Child

Frames with the same parent frame can reference each other through the parent. Consider the following code:

```
<FRAMESET COLS="50%,*">
    <FRAME SRC="doc1.html" NAME="frameA">
    <FRAME SRC="doc2.html" NAME="frameB">
</FRAMESET>
```

The following code segment contains doc2.html:

```
<FRAMESET ROWS="50%,*">
    <FRAME SRC="doc3.html" NAME="frameBA">
    <FRAME SRC="doc4.html" NAME="frameBB">
</FRAMESET>
```

The frame frameBA and its properties can be referenced by code in frameBB's document with the following:

```
parent.frameBA
```

You can also use the following line:

```
parent.frames[0]
```

Also, you can reference frameBA by its absolute position in the frame structure:

```
top.frames[1].frames[0]
```

Frames on the same level with different parents must be referenced by the absolute position in the frame structure:

```
<FRAMESET COLS="50%,*">
    <FRAME SRC="doc1.html" NAME="frameA">
    <FRAME SRC="doc2.html" NAME="frameB">
</FRAMESET>
```

The following segment contains doc1.html:

```
<FRAMESET ROWS="50%,*">
    <FRAME SRC="doc3.html" NAME="frameAA">
    <FRAME SRC="doc4.html" NAME="frameAB">
</FRAMESET>
```

The next segment contains doc2.html:

```
<FRAMESET ROWS="50%,*">
    <FRAME SRC="doc5.html" NAME="frameBA">
    <FRAME SRC="doc6.html" NAME="frameBB">
</FRAMESET>
```

17

WORKING WITH
FRAMES AND
WINDOWS

`frameAB` is referenced by `frameBB` as the following:

`top.frames[0].frameAB`

You can also use the following line:

`top.frames[0].frames[0]`

There is no intermediate level between top and parent, such as grandparent, to reference frames. It is probably a good thing that parent is the only term borrowed from genealogy; imagine referring to a frame as `third.cousin.twice.removed`.

If browser windows are always assigned a name when opened, it is no problem for one of the new (child) windows to reference another child window through the opener (parent window). The name of window is simply referenced as described in the previous sections. If a window was assigned a variable name of `myWindow` when it was opened, another child window can reference it with the following:

`top.opener.myWindow`

You can synchronize the window with the same techniques employed for frames. However, because there is no one top browser window or window hierarchy, one window, such as the opener for the other windows, has to serve as the synchronization point. The following code segment is an example of a script used to synchronize windows:

```
<HTML>
<TITLE>The Harley FXSTC</TITLE>
<SCRIPT LANGUAGE="JavaScript">
<!--
function funRegister(a){
   // check that page is in its own window and that the opener
   //window contains the correct document
  if( (top.name=="newWindow1") && (top.opener.document.title=="Main Frameset") )
      if( a ="R") top.opener.funRecord(document.title);
      else top.opener.funRemove(document.title);
  }
function funCheck(a){   // check whether document is registered or not
  if( (top.name=="newWindow1") && (top.opener.document.title=="Main Frameset") )
      return top.opener.funCheck(a);
  else return false;
}
// -->
</SCRIPT>
<BODY onLoad="top.funRecord(document.title)"
    onUnload="top.funRemove(document.title)">
...
```

The following code checks whether the document is registered:

```
if( funCheck("The Softtail Series")
   newWindow2.frames[2].fxnames(); // document registered, proceed with action
else                         // document not registered, take alternative action
     top.location.href = "http://www.foo.com/fx.html;
...
```

As with frames, you can use more complex schemes to register the location information for the document. These schemes employ the same scripts as those for frames but would extend one level to incorporate separate browser windows.

> **NOTE**
>
> A possible concern about referencing documents in other frames and windows is a security restriction that prevents JavaScript from accessing the properties of documents from a different server. Starting with Netscape Navigator 2.02, this restriction was implemented to prevent accessing information on user's history, passwords in HTML forms, directory structure, and other confidential items. Netscape Navigator 3.0 incorporates a security measure called data tainting, which permits accessing a different server's documents without the possible security risk. With data tainting, JavaScript code can access and use properties of documents from different servers. The data obtained is marked (tainted) so that it cannot be sent to a different server (a security and privacy concern) without user confirmation. You can find more information on data tainting in Chapter 26, "JavaScript and Web Security."

17

Summary

This chapter discussed how to use JavaScript to reference objects and properties in other frames and browser windows. I outlined basic window creation and frame setup and covered referring to properties in different frames and windows. I also explained updating frames and synchronizing frames and windows, providing a few examples of windows and frames interacting with each other via JavaScript. Frame synchronization, the slide show, and updating frames are just a few examples of the interaction possible.

Although using JavaScript in a framed site might be a little more complex than using it in a no-frames site, the benefits are often worth the small amount of added complexity. I only touched upon a few examples of JavaScript with frames and windows. The possible uses and implementations of a framed site are only limited by the Web site author's imagination and the depth of his or her perseverance.

Scripting a Dynamic Table of Contents

by Michael Kmiec

IN THIS CHAPTER

JavaScript transfers much of the burden of content delivery and formatting to the browser rather than having the server deal with it. One of the benefits of this client-side control is improved navigation. Instead of merely providing static links that connect Web pages within a site, Webmasters can use JavaScript within frames to control the display of a site's information.

Why Not Just Use Links?

A table of contents consisting of nothing more than links might work well enough, even when you use frames. A shortcoming of this approach, however, is revealed in how the user sees what you present. If the information you are presenting follows a logical pattern and flow of ideas, one spawning from another, shouldn't your overview display the ideas with that same flow?

Trying to show the parent/child relationships between ideas using HTML alone becomes a frustrating process. Either you show the table of contents formatted with <PRE> </PRE>—somewhat of an aesthetic nightmare—or you use tables to convey the structure. Tables can get tricky if someone accesses your site using a different screen resolution from what you used. Screen resolution is also an issue if your listing is long, requiring the user to constantly scroll up and down trying to compare the information associated with different links. JavaScript enables you to create a table of contents whose entries are nested, thus giving a visual clue to the organization of information, as well as providing a way to expand and condense the topic tree.

Another advantage to doing it this way is in the familiarity of user interface. Since the creation of windowing computer systems (Macintosh, Motif, and others), the visual metaphor of information nested by topic appears as a familiar, normal way of categorizing things.

Some Application Examples

Using a dynamic table of contents works with any situation in which information should be presented in a clear manner while showing dependencies and relationships. For example, Joe's Widget Shop stocks many different kinds of widgets, some of which are further subclassified by size. Joe, who serves as his own Webmaster, can easily provide specifications and prices in the form of one large HTML file with anchors, or he could devise another system to let the user navigate his site. Instead, Joe decides to use a dynamic table of contents, so when his customers need to quickly find out how much force they can exert on a Number 43 Reverse Kretchmer widget, they are only a click away.

The dynamic table of contents can also function well in an intranet setting. If a company's reports are all organized by month and then further classified by division, users can switch between March and November general accounting reports without requiring a great deal of screen real estate.

The example shown in Figure 18.1 demonstrates that by organizing the natural flow of ideas using this technique, educators can present a context for the lessons they teach. If the students actually see the evolution of concepts, the learning process becomes a matter of finding the connections between the concepts.

Figure 18.1.

The dynamic table of contents in action.

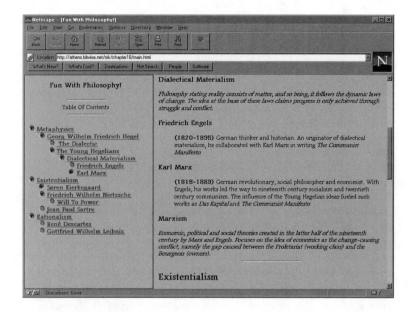

18

SCRIPTING A
DYNAMIC TABLE
OF CONTENTS

The Files for the Project

Because the Table of Contents works within a series of frames, there are a number of files that are used in the project. Although all the HTML files are necessary for the project, only one contains the JavaScript necessary to make it work.

The Main Frame

Before going on to scripting, you must first create the `<FRAMESET>` for the table of contents and the actual information you want to present. You see it in Listing 18.1, `main.html`.

Listing 18.1. `main.html`.

```
<HTML>
<HEAD>
<TITLE>Fun With Philosophy!</TITLE>
</HEAD>
<FRAMESET COLS="35%,*">
<NOFRAMES>
<CENTER><H3>Sorry!</H3>
<P>
If you want Fun With Philosophy, you'll have to get <A HREF="http://
home.netscape.com/">Netscape 2.0</A> or better!
</NOFRAMES>
<FRAME NAME="TOCFrame" SRC="toc.html">
<FRAME NAME="ContentFrame" SRC="fun.html">
</FRAMESET>
</HTML>
```

This `<FRAMESET>` refers to two separate files, `toc.html`, which holds the JavaScript, and `fun.html`, which I use merely as a splash page. You can put the HTML file of your information here if you like, but I chose to keep the text separate until a user follows a link to a subject.

The Splash Page

The splash page also serves another purpose: It contains references to the images you use later for icon representations of the different levels of the table of contents. Listing 18.2, `fun.html`, looks like this.

Listing 18.2. `fun.html`.

```
<HTML><HEAD><TITLE>Fun With Philosophy! Intro</TITLE></HEAD>
<BODY><CENTER>
<H1>Fun With Philosophy!</H1><P>
<IMG SRC="open.jpg" ALIGN=MIDDLE WIDTH="15" HEIGHT="15">
<IMG SRC="end.jpg" ALIGN=MIDDLE WIDTH="15" HEIGHT="15">
<IMG SRC="open.jpg" ALIGN=MIDDLE WIDTH="15" HEIGHT="15">
<HR WIDTH = 150>
<P>
That's right, now you can combine JavaScript with the complexities of the world's
greatest thinkers all in a space-saving user interface!
<P>
Sound too good to be true? Continue on and find out!
<P>
<HR WIDTH = 150>
<IMG SRC="open.jpg" ALIGN=MIDDLE WIDTH="15" HEIGHT="15">
<IMG SRC="end.jpg" ALIGN=MIDDLE WIDTH="15" HEIGHT="15">
<IMG SRC="open.jpg" ALIGN=MIDDLE WIDTH="15" HEIGHT="15">
</CENTER></BODY></HTML>
```

Placing the images on the splash page increases the speed of loading the page. If the images are all initially shown, they get held in the browser's cache directory. As the JavaScript dynamically updates the table of contents, the user needn't wait for the images to download from the server.

The Information

With this project, I've elected to use one larger HTML file to display my information. If you want, you can link to several different files, but for smaller chunks of text under each table of contents listing, one file works well. Listing 18.3 shows an excerpt from `contents.html`.

Listing 18.3. `contents.html`.

```
<A NAME="exist">
<H2>Existentialism</H2></A>
<CITE>Philosophy of the nineteenth and twentieth centuries. Claims that since there
are no objective, universal truths,
```

```
man's existence precedes his essence, thereby allowing individual choice to
determine the outcome of life. This realization of free will and no ultimate truths
induces human anxiety.</CITE>
<A NAME="kierk">
<H3>S&oslash;ren Kierkegaard</H3></A>
<DL><DD><B>(1813-1855)</B> Danish religious thinker, large influence on later
existentialists. Believed that "truth is
subjectivity", and an individual's relationship with God required a "leap of
faith". Also defined human anxiety as angst.
</DL>
<A NAME="subject">
<H3>Subjectivism</H3></A>
<CITE>Belief that all morality is based on individual thought and to label an
action as "good" or "bad" outside of this realm of human subjectivity was
irrelevant.
</CITE>
```

> **NOTE**
>
> Besides using the structure of the table of contents, I'm using different formatting for each type of information. A school of thought falls under the `<CITE></CITE>` tag, whereas a philosopher's name uses the `<DL></DL>` markup. This is purely a design decision to better differentiate subject matter.

The Table of Contents

Listing 18.4, toc.html, shows the frame that handles all the JavaScript functionality. In it, you'll create and populate an array for the information that the table of contents needs to display the proper images and text. You also create the links to contents.html. To do this, you use some concepts from earlier in the book (control structures, the onClick() event handler, and many Navigator objects, to name a few). You also use the properties of the browser's *cookie*, an instrument that stores information about what the user has done. If you're unclear about all this cookie talk, don't worry. Chapter 19, "Cookies and State Maintenance," goes into more detail. For now, the manipulation of the cookie is not too complex, so in-depth coverage is unnecessary.

Now let's step through toc.html.

Listing 18.4. toc.html.

```
<HTML><HEAD>
<TITLE>Fun With Philosophy! TOC</TITLE>
<SCRIPT LANGUAGE="JavaScript">
<!--
/*****
```

continues

Listing 18.4. continued

```
** Create an array in the browser's memory. This is used to hold all the
** subsequent table of content entries by "newing" the array.
*****/
function TOCArray( length )
{
    var i = 0;
    this.length = length;
    for ( i = 1; i < length; i++ )
    this[i] = 0;
    return this;
}
```

This function constructs the array used to hold the table of contents records. By setting `length` number of elements equal to zero, you ensure a populated array; if later, you only partially fill the array and reference one of the non–filled-in elements, you won't generate a runtime error.

```
/*****
** Create the table of content entry object, to be stored in the array.
** Called by "newing", the TOCEntry breaks down like this:
**          TOCEntry.parent (whether or not the entry has child entries)
**          TOCEntry.text (the link text to be displayed)
**          TOCEntry.URL (the link's URL)
**          TOCEntry.nesting (how deep is the entry)
*****/
function TOCEntry( parent, text, URL, nesting)
{
    this.text = text;
    this.URL = URL;
    this.parent = parent;
    this.nesting = nesting;
    return this;
}
```

Here you build the structures that are added as records to the TOCArray. By accessing the internal structure of these records, you get all the information needed to display the entries in the table of contents. Access is provided by using the index of the record in the array and then using a dot (.) to retrieve the field you need. In practice, the reference looks like this:

```
arrayEntry[index].value
```

This somewhat bizarre syntax comes from JavaScript's inability to handle multi-dimensional arrays. You'll see how to use this to your advantage later in the script.

```
/*****
** New an array to hold n many table of content entries.
*****/
var toc = new TOCArray(17);
```

This creates a global array that is 17 members long. The reason it is declared outside a function is to keep it in scope for all JavaScript within the file.

```
/*****
** Newing the TOCEntry for insertion into the TOCArray.
```

```
*****/
toc[1] = new TOCEntry( "Metaphysics", "contents.html#meta", 1,  0);
toc[2] = new TOCEntry( "Georg Wilhelm Friedrich Hegel",
➥ "contents.html#hegel", 1, 1);
toc[3] = new TOCEntry( " The Dialectic", "contents.html#dialectic", 0, 2);
toc[4] = new TOCEntry( "The Young Hegelians", "contents.html#young", 1, 2);
toc[5] = new TOCEntry( "Dialectical Materialism", "contents.html#dm", 1, 3);
toc[6] = new TOCEntry( "Friedrich Engels", "contents.html#engels", 0, 4);
toc[7] = new TOCEntry( "Karl Marx", "contents.html#marx", 1, 4);
toc[8] = new TOCEntry( "Marxism", "contents.html#marxism", 0, 5);
toc[9] = new TOCEntry( "Existentialism", "contents.html#exist", 1, 0);
toc[10] = new TOCEntry( "S&oslash;ren Kierkegaard", "contents.html#kierk", 1, 1);
toc[11] = new TOCEntry( "Subjectivism", "contents.html#subject", 0, 2);
toc[12] = new TOCEntry( "Friedrich Wilhelm Nietzsche",
➥  "contents.html#nietzsche", 1, 1);
toc[13] = new TOCEntry( "Will To Power", "contents.html#will", 0, 2);
toc[14] = new TOCEntry( "Jean Paul Sartre", "contents.html#sartre", 0, 1);
toc[15] = new TOCEntry( "Rationalism", "contents.html#ration", 1, 0);
toc[16] = new TOCEntry( "Ren&eacute; Descartes",
➥  "contents.html#descartes", 0, 1);
toc[17] = new TOCEntry( "Gottfried Wilhelm Leibniz",
➥  "contents.html#leibniz", 0, 1);
```

> **NOTE**
>
> No, you're not going crazy. The ø and é you see in the preceding lines of code are part of HTML. There are plenty of entities like this, providing you with many non-standard characters such as the é listed here.

The above code creates new TOCEntry structures that are added into the TOCArray. By using these structures as the primary data control mechanism for the script, you make it far easier to update and control what is shown (or not shown) in the table of contents. Standardized, easily maintainable data is invaluable if you need to add or remove dependencies, too.

```
/*****
** Set Cookie to the values needed to properly display the table
** of contents. There is no path specification, since the TOC is only
** good for where the user is at the current time, nor is there an
** expiration specified.
*****/
function SetTOC( name, value )
{
    document.cookie = name + "=" + escape( value );
}
```

This is the function you use to change the browser's cookie value. Again, the details on cookie manipulation come in Chapter 19. For now, you simply set a cookie named name equal to value.

When you later call this function, you are setting a cookie named TableOfContents equal to a series of zero or one values, basically imitating a binary string that is as long as the number of entries you have in the TOCArray. Zero means the entry has not been clicked, so it appears condensed; a value of one shows the opposite.

You could set other values here, but all you want is something that tracks the table of contents and disappears at the end of the browser session.

> ### TIP
>
> Although in this script you don't really need JavaScript's built-in escape() function to translate non-ASCII characters (such as spaces) into their ASCII counterparts, it's just a good habit to use escape() and unescape() when dealing with cookies. It saves many headaches later on.

```
/*****
** Get the value set in the Cookie in order to display table of contents
** in proper nesting order.
*****/
function GetTOC( name )
{
    var tocName = name + "=";
    var tocLength = tocName.length;
    var cookieSpan = document.cookie.length;
    var endOfCookie = "";
    var i = 0;
    var j = "";

    while (i < cookieSpan)
    {
        j = i + tocLength;

        if (document.cookie.substring( i,j ) == tocName)
        {
            endOfCookie = document.cookie.indexOf( ";", j );

            if ( endOfCookie ==    -1 )
                endOfCookie = document.cookie.length;

            return unescape( document.cookie.substring( j, endOfCookie ) );
        }
    }
    return "";
}
```

In order to show the nested relationship between parent and child in the table of contents, you need to access the cookie you set earlier. This function gives the actual value of the cookie labeled TableOfContents by returning the string that runs from the end of the cookie's name plus an equals sign (TableOfContents=) for the length of the cookie.

From this you determine what the user has clicked; based on the position of that value in the cookie, you discover the other properties of the entry.

```
/*****
** Main action function.
** Changes the Cookie value for each table of contents entry based on whether
** or not it has been clicked. The Cookie's format is a string of ones and
```

```
** zeros, the length of which is determined by the number of entries
** in the TOCArray. The "entryPoint" is the TOCEntry position in the Cookie.
*****/
function ChangeTOC( entryPoint )
{
    if ( entryPoint != 0 )
    {
        var updatedTOC = "";
        var currentTOC = GetTOC( "TableOfContents" );
        var clicked = currentTOC.substring( entryPoint-1, entryPoint );
➡    // Find the value of the TOCEntry

        updatedTOC = currentTOC.substring( 0, entryPoint-1 );

        ( clicked == 1 ) ? updatedTOC += 0 : updatedTOC += 1;
➡    // Flip the appropriate value

updatedTOC += currentTOC.substring( entryPoint, currentTOC.length );

        SetTOC( "TableOfContents", updatedTOC );
    }
}
```

Here you handle updating individual values of cookie data (such as flipping a one to a zero or vice versa). The argument passed to this function is the numeric location of the value you want to change.

Once you have the location and the rest of the cookie, you simply reconstruct another cookie value from the old one, change the number at the location specified, and then add on the rest of the old cookie.

18

**SCRIPTING A
DYNAMIC TABLE
OF CONTENTS**

> **NOTE**
>
> For C or C++ programmers, this might appear suspiciously like string manipulation through pointer arithmetic. For all intents and purposes, this is as close as JavaScript comes to such a concept.

The final action of the function is resetting the cookie with the newly created value.

```
/*****
** Determines what image to add to the HTML based on the state and position
** of the table of contents entries.
*****/
function Image( index )
{
    var parent = toc[index].parent;
    var isOpen = GetTOC( "TableOfContents" ).substring( index-1, index );

    if ( !parent )
        return "end.jpg";
    else
    {
        if ( isOpen == 1 )
```

```
                return "open.jpg";
    }

    return "closed.jpg";
}

/*****
** Determines what status message to display based on the state and position
** of the table of contents entries.
*****/
function Status( index )
{
    var parent = toc[index].parent;
    var isOpen = GetTOC( "TableOfContents" ).substring( index-1, index );

    if ( !parent )
        return "Last Entry";
    else
    {
        if ( isOpen == 1 )
            return "Click To Hide Nested Entries";
    }
    return "Click To Show Nested Entries";
}
```

These two functions return different properties based on either of the following situations:

- The level of nesting shown by the image
- The status message displayed when the user places the mouse over the image

They are identical aside from their return value, which is the image or the message, depending on the function. These functions use the index into the TOCArray, as well as the cookie value at the TOCEntry position, to determine what to return.

```
/*****
** Add spacing for nested entries.
*****/
function nestSpace( nestLevel )
{
    var space = ""
    var i = "";

    for ( i = 1; i <= nestLevel; i++ )
        space += "     ";

    return space;
}
```

This function is fairly straightforward. It simply adds the necessary number of spaces for the visible nesting in the table of contents. The nestLevel value is the TOCEntry.nesting property of the TOCEntry you constructed earlier. You're using five physical spaces to represent the nesting because when you display the table of contents, it is placed within <PRE></PRE> tags, keeping the spaces as literals.

```
/*****
** If this is the user's first time in, the Cookie must be set with the
** proper number of entries according to the length of the TOCArray.
*****/
if ( GetTOC( "TableOfContents" ) == "" )
{
    var firstTOC = "";
    var i = "";

    for ( i = 1; i <= toc.length; i++ )
        firstTOC += "0";

    SetTOC( "TableOfContents", firstTOC );
}

// -->
</SCRIPT>
</HEAD>
<BODY>
```

This function handles the initialization of the first cookie for the user. It loops for the length of the TOCArray, setting each value in the cookie to zero.

In this case, for the TOCArray length of 17, you get a string of 17 zeros. This is the initial view of the table of contents, where only the first level entries (whose TOCEntries.nesting equals zero) appear.

Now you set up the display of the table of contents.

```
<SCRIPT LANGUAGE="JavaScript">
<!--

/*****
** Start using document.write() to display the table of contents
** (images, status messages and text) based on looping through
** the TOCArray and the Cookie values.
***/
var nestingShown = 0;
var showChild = 0;
var tableOfContents = "<PRE><H4>";
var i = "";

document.write("<CENTER><H3>Fun With Philosophy!</H3><HR WIDTH = 100>");
document.write("Table Of Contents<HR WIDTH = 100><P></CENTER>");
```

These calls to document.write() set the stage for the output of HTML. Keep an eye on the variable tableOfContents. That's where you add the stream of what you want to display. The controlling element in this situation is, once again, the length property of the TOCArray.

```
for ( i = 1; i <= toc.length; i++ )
{
    var image = Image( i );
    var statusMessage = Status( i );
    var nesting = toc[i].nesting;
```

18

SCRIPTING A
DYNAMIC TABLE
OF CONTENTS

```
    var opened = GetTOC( "TableOfContents" ).substring( i-1,i )

    if ( nesting == 0 || nesting <= nestingShown ||
➡ ( showChild == 1 && ( nesting - nestingShown == 1)))
{
        tableOfContents += nestSpace( nesting )

        tableOfContents += "<A HREF=\"javascript:history.go(0)\" onMouseOver=
➡ \"window.parent.status=\'" + statusMessage + "\';return true;\"
➡ onClick=\"ChangeTOC(" + i + ")\"><IMG SRC=\"" + image + "\"
➡ HEIGHT=15 WIDTH=15 BORDER=0 ALIGN=TOP></A>";

        tableOfContents += " <A HREF=\"" + toc[i].URL + "\" TARGET=
➡ \"ContentFrame\" onMouseOver=\"window.parent.status=\'" + toc[i].text +
➡ "\';return true;\">" + toc[i].text + "</A><BR>";

        nestingShown = nesting;

        showChild = opened;
    }
}
```

The large control statement in the preceding listing handles the eventualities of displaying of the Table of Contents as the TOCArray is looped through. It sends you into the code that builds the HTML strings, including the spacing for nesting entries. The loop also modifies the variables nestingShown and showChild, changing the way the data gets handled the next time through the loop.

As an aside, using a combination of the <PRE> </PRE> and <H4> </H4> tags, you keep the spacing but still allow for nicely formatted text.

> **CAUTION**
>
> There is a bug in the way that version 2.01 of Netscape Navigator for Macintosh handles the A HREF pointing to javascript.
>
> This version of the browser is the only one that exhibits this behavior. The functionality of the JavaScript does not change, but whenever a user clicks one of the images, a runtime error creates a modal dialog box that the user must dismiss, either with a mouse click or by pressing the Enter key.

The last lines of the file send the constructed HTML string to the browser.

```
tableOfContents += "</H4></PRE>";

document.write( tableOfContents );

// -->
</SCRIPT>
</BODY>
</HTML>
```

Summary

This chapter covered creating a table of contents for better navigation of the information held at a Web site. It covered the pros and cons of different navigational tactics and gave an overall view of the importance of information organization. The JavaScript you wrote accessed quite a few internal objects and functions, and it enabled you to create your own array and array entry objects. In the course of this construction, you manipulated images, text, HTML markup and status messages. The chapter also delved into the `document.cookie` object, a topic that Chapter 19 covers in more depth.

The end result is a table of contents that reacts to user input, expanding or condensing nested information based on how far down the tree the user wants to travel.

Cookies and State Maintenance

by Bill Chosiad

IN THIS CHAPTER

CHAPTER 19

Hypertext Transfer Protocol (HTTP), in its most "vanilla" form, is a stateless protocol; that is to say, there is no information passed from one page to the next as a browser navigates through a Web site. In this chapter, you learn a number of ways around this limitation, including cookies, URL query string parameters, and hidden form variables. Although the bulk of this chapter deals with cookies, time is spent investigating other techniques as well. Each state maintenance technique has its own advantages and disadvantages.

Maintaining State

Maintaining state involves passing information along with the browser as it moves from page to page. With this information in hand, you can set user preferences, fill in default form values, track visit counts, and do many other things that make browsing easier for users and give you more information about how your pages are used.

Here are a number of ways to maintain state information:

- Store it in cookies.
- Encode it in URL links.
- Send it in hidden form variables.

There are some technical challenges regarding state maintenance. While browsing a site, a user might suddenly zoom off to another Web site and return minutes, hours, or days later. The user might return by pressing his browser's Back button or might return to the page via a bookmark or by typing the URL in directly.

Another difficulty occurs when a user adds a URL containing state information to her personal bookmark list. When returning weeks later, the state information could be meaningless.

The Web developer must maintain state information regardless of whether the user navigates through the site via buttons on a form or a URL link on a page. This could mean adding information to both hidden form variables and every URL <A HREF...> tag that appears on the page.

With all these difficulties to overcome, these state maintenance mechanisms had better be pretty useful. Luckily, they are. There are a host of advantages of maintaining state, both within a single site visit and from one visit to the next. Consider the following scenarios:

- Shopping cart application—Users could browse through the site while selecting items and adding them to a virtual shopping cart. At any time, they can view the items in the cart, change the contents of their cart, or take the cart to the checkout counter for purchase. Keeping track of which user owns which shopping cart is essential.
- Custom home pages—Both Netscape and the Microsoft Network have set up home pages where users can customize what they see when they arrive. After giving the user a choice of layouts, color schemes, and favorite destinations, it stores the preferences on the user's own computer through the use of cookies. The user can return to the site any time and get his previously configured page.

- Frequent visitor bonuses—By storing information on the client computer, this application keeps track of how many times a browser has hit a particular page. When users reach a certain level of hits, they get access to more or better services.

- Change banners—Make graphic banners and text change each time a user hits a page. This technique is often used to cycle through a list of advertisements.

Cookies, an Introduction

Cookies, sometimes called *Magic Cookies,* but more formally known as *Persistent Client State HTTP Cookies,* allow you to store information on the client browser's computer for later retrieval. Although they have their drawbacks, cookies are the most powerful technique available for maintaining state within a Web site.

In their simplest form, cookies store data in the form of `name=value` pairs. You the developer can pick any name and value combination you want. More advanced cookie features include the capability to set an expiration date and specify what Web pages may see the cookie information.

Advantages of Cookies

One of the most powerful aspects of cookies is their persistence. When a cookie is set on the user's browser, it may persist for days, months, or even years. This makes it easy to save user preferences and visit information and keep this information available every time the user returns to your site.

Limitations of Cookies

Some limitations of cookies could prove problematic. Cookies are stored on the user's computer, usually in a special cookie file. As with all files, this cookie file might be accidentally (or purposefully) deleted, taking all the browser's cookie information with it. The cookie file could be write-protected, thus preventing any cookies from being stored there.

Because cookies are associated with a particular browser, problems come up if users switch from one browser to another. If you usually use Netscape Navigator and have a collections of cookies, they will no longer be available for you to use if you decide to switch to Microsoft Internet Explorer.

Finally, if multiple people use the same computer and browser, they might find themselves using cookies that belong to someone else. The reason for this is that cookie information is stored in a file on the computer, and the browser has no way to distinguish between multiple users.

Disadvantages of Cookies

There are also some problems, both real and imagined, concerning the use of cookies. Because many browsers store their cookie information in an unencrypted text file, you should never store sensitive information, such as a password, in a cookie. Anyone with access to the user's computer could read it.

Newer Web browsers, such as Netscape Navigator 3.0, might have a feature that alerts users every time an attempt is made to set a cookie. These browsers could even be configured to prevent cookies from being set at all. This sometimes results in confusion on the user's part when a dialog box informs her that something strange involving a thing called a cookie is happening to her computer. If cookies are disabled, your carefully designed Web application might not run at all.

The biggest problem facing cookies could be a psychological one. Some savvy Web users believe that all cookies are a tool used by "Big Brother" in order to discover their innermost secrets. Perhaps I exaggerate a bit. However, considering that cookies are capable of storing information about where users have visited on a Web site, how many times they have been there, what advertising banners they have viewed, and what they have selected and placed on forms, some people think that their privacy is being invaded whenever a cookie gets set on their computer. If your users understand the usefulness of cookies, this "cookie backlash" should not be a problem.

RESOURCE

Netscape came up with the original cookie specification. You can find more information on the Netscape Web site at `http://www.netscape.com/newsref/std/cookie_spec.html`.

Although they are sometimes called "Magic Cookies" (mostly on Macintosh browsers), there does not seem to be any good answer for why Netscape chose that particular name. In fact, on the cookie specification page, Netscape even admits that "the state object is called a cookie for no compelling reason."

Using Cookies

By now you have considered the pros and cons of cookies and have decided that they are just what you need to make your JavaScript application a success.

In this section, you will find a number of handy functions for reading and setting cookies, which will help you make your Web sites smarter and more user friendly. Also included in this section are Internet references for finding additional information concerning cookies.

Retrieving Cookie Values

Cookie names and values are stored and set using the `cookie` property of the `document` object. To store the raw cookie string in a variable, you would use a JavaScript command such as the following:

```
var myCookie = document.cookie;
```

To display it on a Web page, use the following command:

```
document.write ("Raw Cookies: " + document.cookie + "<BR>");
```

JavaScript stores cookies in the following format:

```
name1=value1; name2=value2; name3=value3
```

Individual `name=value` pairs are separated by a semicolon and a blank space. There is no semicolon after the final value.

To make it easier to retrieve a cookie, you probably want to use a JavaScript routine such as the routine in Listing 19.1.

Listing 19.1. The `GetCookie` function.

```
function GetCookie (name) {
  var result = null;
  var myCookie = " " + document.cookie + ";";
  var searchName = " " + name + "=";
  var startOfCookie = myCookie.indexOf(searchName)
  var endOfCookie;

  if (startOfCookie != -1) {
    startOfCookie += searchName.length; // skip past cookie name
    endOfCookie = myCookie.indexOf(";", startOfCookie);
    result = unescape(myCookie.substring(startOfCookie, endOfCookie));
  }
  return result;
}
```

In Listing 19.1, the `myCookie` string helps avoid annoying boundary conditions by making sure all cookie string names start with a space and end with a semicolon.

From there, it is simple to find the start of the `name=` portion of the string, skip by it, and retrieve everything from that point until the next semicolon.

19

**COOKIES
AND STATE
MAINTENANCE**

Setting Cookie Values

The name=value combination is the minimum amount of information you need to set up a cookie. However, there is more to cookies than just this. Here is the complete list of parameters used to specify a cookie:

- name=value
- expires=date
- path=path
- domain=domainname
- secure

Cookie Names and Values

The name and value can be anything you choose. In some cases, you might want it to be very explanatory, such as FavoriteColor=Blue. In other cases, it could just be code that the JavaScript program interprets, such as CurStat=1:2:1:0:0:1:0:3:1:1. In any case, the name and value are completely up to you.

In its simplest form, a routine to set a cookie looks like this:

```
function SetCookieEZ (name, value) {
  document.cookie = name + "=" + escape(value);
}
```

Notice that the value is encoded using the escape function. If there were a semicolon in the string, it might prevent you from achieving the expected results. Using the escape function eliminates this problem.

Also notice that the document.cookie property works rather differently from most other properties. In most other cases, using the assignment operator (=) causes the existing property value to be completely overwritten with the new value. This is not the case with the cookie property. With cookies, each new name you assign is added to the active list of cookies. If you assign the same name twice, the first assignment is replaced by the second.

There are some exceptions to this last statement, but these are explained in the section "Path" later in this chapter.

Expires Date

The expires date tells the browser how long the cookie will last. The cookie specification page at Netscape states that dates are in the form of

```
Wdy, DD-Mon-YY HH:MM:SS GMT
```

Note the following example:

```
Mon, 08-Jul-96 03:18:20 GMT
```

This format is based upon Internet RFC 822, which you can find at `http://www.w3.org/hypertext/WWW/Protocols/rfc822/#z28`.

The only difference between RFC 822 and the Netscape implementation is that, in Netscape Navigator, the expiration date must end with GMT. Happily, the JavaScript language provides a function to do just that. By using the `toGMTString()` function, you can set cookies to expire in the near or distant future.

> **TIP**
>
> Even though the date produced by the `toGMTString()` function does not match the Netscape specification, it still works under JavaScript.

If the expiration date is not specified, the cookie remains in effect until the browser is shut down.

Here is a code segment that sets a cookie to expire in one week:

```
var name="foo";
var value="bar";

var oneWeek = 7 * 24 * 60 * 60 * 1000;
var expDate = new Date();
expDate.setTime (expDate.getTime() + oneWeek);

document.cookie = name + "=" + escape(value) + ";
        ➥ expires=" + expDate.toGMTString();
```

Deleting a Cookie

To delete a cookie, set the expiration date to some time in the past—how far in the past does not generally matter. To be on the safe side, a few days ago should work fine. Here is a routine to delete a cookie:

```
function ClearCookie (name) {
  var ThreeDays = 3 * 24 * 60 * 60 * 1000;
  var expDate = new Date();
  expDate.setTime (expDate.getTime() - ThreeDays);
if (value != null)
    document.cookie = name + "=ImOutOfHere; expires=" + expDate.toGMTString();
}
```

When deleting cookies, it does not matter what you use for the cookie value—any value will do.

19

**COOKIES
AND STATE
MAINTENANCE**

CAUTION

Some versions of Netscape do a poor job of converting times to GMT. Some common JavaScript functions for deleting a cookie consider the past to be one millisecond behind the current time. Although this is usually true, it doesn't work on all platforms. To be on the safe side, use a few days in the past to expire cookies.

Path

By default, cookies are available to other Web pages within the same directory as the page on which they were created. The Path parameter allows a cookie to be made available to pages in other directories. If the value of the Path parameter is a substring of a page's URL, then cookies created with that path are available to that page. For example, you could create a cookie with the following command:

```
document.cookie = "foo=bar1; path=/javascript";
```

This would make the cookie foo available to every page in the javascript directory and all those directories beneath it. If, instead, the command looked like

```
document.cookie = "foo=bar2; path=/javascript/sam";
```

Then the cookie would be available to sample1.html, sample2.html, sammy.exe, and so on.

Finally, to make the cookie available to everyone on your server, use the following command:

```
document.cookie = "foo=bar3; path=/";
```

What happens when a browser has multiple cookies on different paths but with the same name? Which cookie wins?

Actually, they all do. When this situation arises, it is possible to have two or more cookies with the same name but different values. For example, if a page issued all the commands listed previously, its cookie string would look like the following:

```
foo=bar3; foo=bar2; foo=bar1
```

To help be aware of this situation, you might want to write a routine to count the number of cookie values associated with a cookie name. It might look like this:

```
function GetCookieCount (name) {
  var result = 0;
  var myCookie = " " + document.cookie + ";";
  var searchName = " " + name + "=";
  var nameLength = searchName.length;
  var startOfCookie = myCookie.indexOf(searchName)

  while (startOfCookie != -1) {
    result += 1;
    startOfCookie = myCookie.indexOf(searchName, startOfCookie + nameLength);
```

```
    }
  return result;
}
```

Of course, if there is a `GetCookieCount` function, then there would need to be a `GetCookieNum` function to retrieve a particular instance of a cookie. That function would look like this:

```
function GetCookieNum (name, cookieNum) {
  var result = null;

  if (cookieNum >= 1) {
    var myCookie = " " + document.cookie + ";";
    var searchName = " " + name + "=";
    var nameLength = searchName.length;
    var startOfCookie = myCookie.indexOf(searchName);
    var cntr = 0;

    for (cntr = 1; cntr < cookieNum; cntr++)
      startOfCookie = myCookie.indexOf(searchName, startOfCookie + nameLength);

    if (startOfCookie != -1) {
      startOfCookie += nameLength; // skip past cookie name
      var endOfCookie = myCookie.indexOf(";", startOfCookie);
      result = unescape(myCookie.substring(startOfCookie, endOfCookie));
    }
  }
  return result;
}
```

> **CAUTION**
>
> There is a bug in Netscape Navigator version 1.1 and earlier. Only cookies whose path attribute is set explicitly to / are properly saved between sessions if they have an expires attribute.

In order to delete a cookie, the name and the path must match the original name and path used when the cookie was set.

Domain

Usually, after a page on a particular server creates a cookie, that cookie is only accessible to other pages on that server. Just as the `Path` parameter makes a cookie available outside its home path, the `Domain` parameter makes it available outside its host Web server.

You cannot create a cookie that anyone on the Internet can see. You may only set a path that falls inside your own domain. This is because the use of the `Domain` parameter dictates that you must use at least two periods (for example, `.mydomain.com`) if your domain ends in `.com`, `.edu`, `.net`, `.org`, `.gov`, `.mil`, or `.int`. Otherwise, it must have at least three periods (`.mydomain.ma.us`). Your domain parameter string must match the tail of your server's domain name.

Secure

The final cookie parameter tells your browser that this cookie should only be sent under a secure connection with the Web server. This means that the server and the browser must support HTTPS security. (HTTPS is Netscape's Secure Socket Layer Web page encryption protocol.)

If the secure parameter is not present, it means that cookies are sent unencrypted over the network.

NOTE

You cannot set an infinite number of cookies on every Web browser that visits your site. Here are the number of cookies you can set and how large they might be:

Cookies per each server or domain: 20

Total cookies per browser: 300

Largest cookie: 4KB (including both the name and value parameters)

If these limits are exceeded, the browser might attempt to discard older cookies by tossing the least recently used cookies first.

Now that you have seen all the cookie parameters, it would be helpful to have a JavaScript routine set cookies with all the parameters. Such a routine might look like the following:

```
function SetCookie (name, value, expires, path, domain, secure) {
   var expString =
              ((expires == null) ? "" : ("; expires=" + expires.toGMTString()))
   var pathString = ((path == null) ? "" : ("; path=" + path))
   var domainString = ((domain == null) ? "" : ("; domain=" + domain))
   var secureString = ((secure == true) ? "; secure" : "")
   document.cookie = name + "=" + escape (value) +
                  expString + pathString + domainString + secureString;
}
```

To use this routine, you call it with whatever parameters you care about and use null in place of parameters that do not matter.

Where Are Cookies Going?

As previously mentioned, cookies were designed and first implemented by Netscape. However, the Internet Engineering Task Force (IETF) has a committee, the Hypertext Transfer Protocol (HTTP) Working Group, whose charter is to examine, document, and suggest ways for improving HTTP.

Although the draft specification resembles Netscape cookies in theory, if not in syntax, it does have a few notable differences. It doesn't encourage having cookies around much longer than the browser session. If the new specification is accepted, cookies are given a `Max-Age` lifetime rather than an `expires date`. All cookies expire when their time comes, but in all cases, they go away when the browser shuts down.

Reading the specification provides insight into the complexities that surround the inner workings of cookies; it is well worth the read, regardless of whether the specification is approved.

Which Servers and Browsers Support Cookies?

Although other ways of Web programming, such as CGI and special server interfaces, require that the server as well as the browser understand cookies, only the browser matters to JavaScript. This means that you can generally use JavaScript with impunity as long as you know your clients are JavaScript-capable.

However, many JavaScript Web applications probably mix the language with other development tools, which would require the server to understand cookies. Because new servers and browsers are coming to the Net so quickly, it is impossible for a printed book to keep up with the latest software.

Other State Maintenance Options

As mentioned earlier in this chapter, there are a few drawbacks to using cookies. Perhaps you would rather just avoid the controversy and find some other way of maintaining state from one page to the next. There are two ways of doing this; which one you use depends upon how you, the developer, will have the users get from one page to the next.

The main limitation of these methods is that they only work from one page to the page immediately following. If state information is to be maintained throughout a series of pages, then these mechanisms must be used on every single page.

Query String

If most of your navigation is done through hypertext links embedded in your pages, you need to add extra information to the end of the URL. This is usually done by adding a question mark (?) to the end of your Web page URL, followed by information in an encoded form, such as that returned by the escape method. To separate one piece of information from another, place an ampersand (&) between them.

For example, if you want to send the parameters color=blue and size=extra large along with your link, you use a link like the following:

```
<a href="/mypage.html?color=blue&size=extra+large">XL Blue</A>
```

This format is the same as the format used when submitting forms using the get method. A succeeding page can read this information by using the search property of the location object. This property is called search because many Internet search engines use this part of the URL to store their search criteria.

The following is an example of how to use the location.search property. In this example, the name of the current page is sent as a parameter in a link to another page. The other page reads this property via the search property and states where the browser came from.

To start things off, Listing 19.2 shows the first page that contains the link.

Listing 19.2. Where1.htm.

```
<html>
<head>
<title>Where Was I? - Page 1</title>
</head>
<body>
<h1>Where Was I? - Demonstration</h1>
This page sets information which will allow the page it is linked
to figure out where it came from. It uses values embedded in the link
URL in order to do this
<p>
We'll assume that any URL parameters are separated by an ampersand.
<p>
```

```
Notice that there doesn't need to be any JavaScript code in this page.
<p>
And now,
<a href="where2.htm?camefrom=Where1.htm
➥&more=needless+stuff">Let's go to Page 2.</a>
</body>
</html>
```

Listing 19.3 shows the second page, which demonstrates how to use `location.search` to find where the browser came from.

Listing 19.3. Where2.htm.

```html
<html>
<title>Where Was I? - Page 2</title>
<head>
</head>
<body>
<h1>Where Was I? - Demonstration</h1>
This page reads information which allows it to figure out where it came from.
<P>

<script language="javascript">
<!-- begin script

// WhereWasI
// Reads the search string to figure out what link brought it here
function WhereWasI() {

  // Start by storing our search string in a handy place (so we don't
  // need to type as much)
  var handyString = window.location.search;

  // Find the beginning of our special URL variable
  var startOfSource = handyString.indexOf("camefrom=");

  // If it's there, find the end of it
  if (startOfSource != -1) {
    var endOfSource = handyString.indexOf("&", startOfSource+9);
    var result = handyString.substring(startOfSource+9, endOfSource);
  }
  else
    var result = "Source Unknown"; // Could not find the "camefrom" string

  return result;
}

if (WhereWasI() != "Source Unknown")
  document.write ("You just came from <b>" + WhereWasI() + "</b>.<br>")
else
  document.write ("Unfortunately, we don't know where you came from.<br>");

// end script -->
</script>
</body>
</html>
```

Hidden Form Variables

The method used in the preceding section works fine as long as the user navigates from one page to another using links. In order to do the same thing with forms, you can use hidden form variables instead of the `location.search` parameter.

Hidden form variables have the following format:

```
<input type="hidden" name="HiddenFieldName" value="HiddenFieldValue">
```

You can specify whatever you like for *HiddenFieldName* and *HiddenFieldValue*. The `value` parameter is optional.

Using hidden fields does not necessarily require the use of JavaScript code. They are defined instead in the INPUT tag of normal HTML documents. You do, however, need to have some sort of server-based script, such as a CGI program or a server API program, in order to read the values of these hidden fields.

The form containing the hidden variables is submitted to a server script, which spills out everything it knows about your browser onto a single Web page, including the form's field information. You find your hidden field information listed at the bottom of the page, where it looks like the following:

```
Form Post Data:
Raw Form Data String: camefrom=where3.htm&otherStuff=I+don%27t+care
camefrom=where3.htm
otherStuff=I don't care
```

Summary

In this chapter, you learned about a number of useful techniques for maintaining state between pages of a Web application, with cookies being the most powerful method.

Cookies allow you to store information on the client computer and use it from within your Internet application to store values and other critical pieces of information. Because of the nature of cookies, they can be used for a range of reasons, from the simplest form of `name=value` pairs to the more advanced forms of cookie use.

Although cookies represent the most powerful method of accomplishing state maintenance, other approaches, such as URL query string parameters and hidden fields in forms, are also available.

There is one other technique involving the use of frames and JavaScript variables stored in them. You can find more on this technique in Chapter 17, "Working with Frames and Windows."

V
PART

JavaScript on the Server

Server-Side JavaScript

by Richard Wagner

Although JavaScript plays a key role on the client side of the house, you can also use the scripting language to create server-based applications using Netscape LiveWire. LiveWire is a set of extensions that you can add to a Netscape server. It uses JavaScript as a server-based scripting language in place of CGI to perform server-specific tasks, such as creating dynamic HTML or accessing a server-based file. This chapter discusses Netscape LiveWire and its server-side extensions to the JavaScript language.

> **NOTE**
>
> LiveWire works only on Netscape servers, so you cannot use server-side JavaScript with other Web servers at this time. However, Microsoft has said that its ActiveX Server framework will support JavaScript or an implementation of JavaScript as a scripting language.

Developing a LiveWire Application

Before I get into the specifics of the server-side JavaScript language, first look at the process of developing a LiveWire application. I find it easier to understand the language specifics if I know the context in which they are used. With that in mind, take a look at how to develop a LiveWire application. Figure 20.1 details the process of creating a LiveWire application.

> **RESOURCES**
>
> To download LiveWire, visit the Netscape home page at http://www.netscape.com/.

Creating Source Files for the Server Application

The first step in building a server-side JavaScript application is creating your source files, which are one of two types:

- Source HTML documents—With an .HTM or .HTML file extension, these documents can either be static pages or JavaScript-enabled pages.
- JavaScript library files—With a .JS extension, these files serve as library files containing JavaScript functions. You do not need to use HTML tags in these files.

Source HTML Documents

In many cases, you will want to embed JavaScript code in your HTML documents, just as you do with client-side JavaScript. However, the way you embed server JavaScript in your HTML file can change the result. To embed JavaScript into your documents, you can use one of two options.

Figure 20.1.
*LiveWire development
process.*

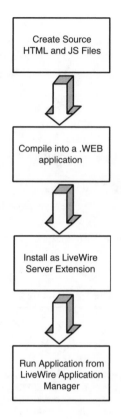

Figure 20.1.
LiveWire development process.

First, you can use the `<SERVER>` and `</SERVER>` tag pair to surround server JavaScript code. In many ways, the use of these tags is very similar to the `<SCRIPT>` and `</SCRIPT>` tags that you use in client-side JavaScript. Suppose you wanted to generate a line of dynamic HTML. You could use the `<SERVER>` tags to do the following:

```
<SERVER>
    if (client.custid == null) {
        write("You have no customer ID") }
    else {
        write(Your customer ID is " + client.custid)
    }
</SERVER>
```

CAUTION

You cannot place a `<SERVER>` tag within another HTML tag (that is, between a < and > of another tag).

Second, if you need to add a JavaScript expression inside another HTML tag, you can surround the code with backquotes (\Q). You will find using backquotes is useful when working
with links, anchors, and form objects. For example, if you wanted to generate dynamic HTML
with a link created on the fly based on the client's Web address, you could use the following:

```
<A HREF=\Qclient.WebAddress\Q>Your Home Page</A>
```

When you embed server JavaScript into your source HTML documents, the user sees only the
result of the code, not the code itself. Server JavaScript thus contrasts with client-side JavaScript,
which the user can see simply by viewing the source file in any Web browser. Listing 20.1 is a
source HTML file with embedded JavaScript. When the application runs, however, the HTML
source shown in Listing 20.2 is what the client can see if the source code is viewed in the browser.
(Figure 20.2 shows the actual presentation of the HTML.) In case you are wondering about
the meaning of the JavaScript expressions, I talk about the client object a little later in the chapter.
At this point, think of these expressions as properties of an object that has already been created
and defined elsewhere.

Listing 20.1. Server JavaScript embedded source file.

```
<html>
<head>
<title>Feedback</title>
</head>
<body>
<h1>"Superiffic" Feedback Confirmation</h1>
<p>Dear <SERVER>client.firstName</SERVER>,</p>
<p>Thank you for submitting feedback about our product. If you have asked us
to contact you, we will be using the following information:</p>
<blockquote>
<p><strong>E-mail:</strong> <SERVER>client.email</SERVER><br>
<strong>Telephone:</strong> <SERVER>client.phone</SERVER><br>
<strong>FAX:</strong> <SERVER>client.fax</SERVER></p>
</blockquote>
<p>If any of this information is incorrect, please go back to the feedback
form and change it. We thank you for taking the time to help us be a
"superiffic" company.</p>
<p>Sincerely,</p>
<p>Rupert Mydryl <br>
Manager, Customer Services</p>
</body>
</html>
```

Listing 20.2. Resulting document given to client.

```
<head>
<title>Feedback</title>
</head>
<body>
<h1>"Superiffic" Feedback Confirmation</h1>
<p>Dear Charles:</p>
```

```
<p>Thank you for submitting feedback about our product. If you have asked us
to contact you, we will be using the following information:</p>
<blockquote>
<p><strong>E-mail: chappy@smiles.com</strong> <br>
<strong>Telephone: 808-555-1212</strong> <br>
<strong>FAX: 808-555-5050</strong> </p>
</blockquote>
<p>If any of this information is incorrect, please go back to the
feedback form and change it. We thank you for taking the time to help us be
a "superiffic" company.</p>
<p>Sincerely,</p>
<p>Rupert Mydryl <br>
Manager, Customer Services</p>
</body>
</html>
```

Figure 20.2.

HTML document in the browser.

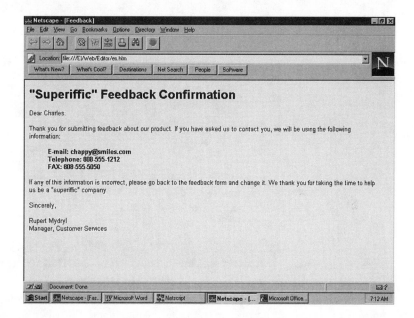

JavaScript Library Files

Any serious development environment needs a facility in which to place generic functions that can be called from a variety of sources. LiveWire does provide this feature by allowing you to place JavaScript code in external text files denoted with a .JS extension. Inside of the JavaScript library file should be functions, not HTML. You can then reference functions inside of these .JS files inside your HTML files. When your LiveWire application is compiled, the compiler resolves all the calls to external functions by looking at the .JS files in the LiveWire application directory.

Compiling LiveWire Applications

After you have finished creating the source files for your LiveWire application, you are ready to compile them. The LiveWire compiler creates a bytecode .WEB file from the HTML documents and .JS library files. To compile an application, you can use either the LiveWire Site Manager or the command-line compiler.

To use Site Manager, open it and find the directory in which your source files are located in the Folders section of the window. (See Figure 20.3.) Next, from the Site menu, choose the Manage option (or New site if the Manage option is grayed out).

FIGURE 20.3.

LiveWire Site Manager.

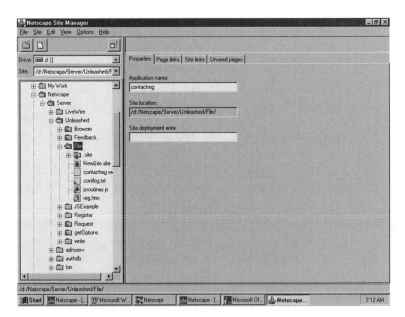

After the application is considered under Site Manager's supervision, you can compile it by choosing the Build Application option from the Site menu. Site Manager attempts to compile the application. If a syntax error occurs, a dialog box displays the error message, as shown in Figure 20.4.

FIGURE 20.4.

Compiler error.

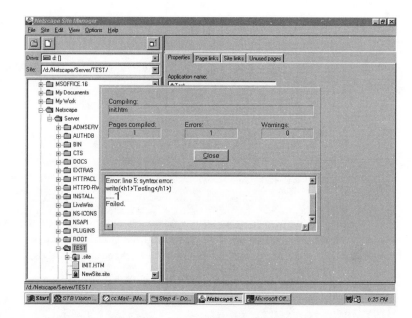

Otherwise, Site Manager notifies you that the process finished successfully. (See Figure 20.5.)

FIGURE 20.5.

Successful compile.

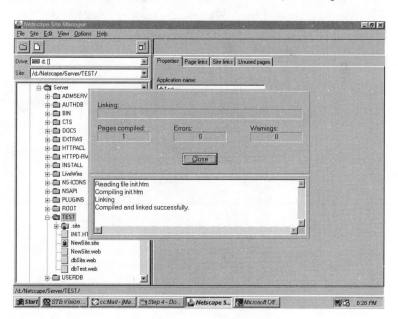

Alternatively, you can use the command-line compiler to compile the LiveWire application. The command-line syntax follows:

```
lwcomp [-c¦v¦d¦?] [-o outputfile.web] [doc1.htm...docn.htm] [lib1.js...libn.js]
```

The following list describes the options:

> -c checks the syntax only.
>
> -v compiles with verbose output.
>
> -d shows generated JavaScript contents.
>
> -? shows compiler syntax Help.
>
> -o creates a .WEB file using the specified name.

For example, the following command-line statement compiles (with verbose output) a LiveWire application into a file called policy.web using three HTML source files (index.htm, toc.htm, and polpage.htm) and two JavaScript library files (jsroutine.js and jsdates.js):

```
lwcomp -v -o policy.web index.htm toc.htm polpage.htm jsroutines.js jsdates.js
```

Installing LiveWire Applications on the Server

Before users can access your LiveWire application, you need to install it on the server using the LiveWire Application Manager. From the Application Manager, click the Add button to begin the installation process. After clicking the Add button, the right frame of the window displays an HTML form for you to fill out, as shown in Figure 20.6.

FIGURE 20.6.

LiveWire Application Manager.

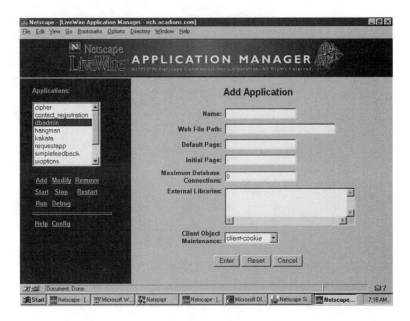

Fill out the form based on the following information.

■ Name: Enter the name of the application. This name is used to access the application once it is installed. For example, if you name an application `fireball` on a server with a URL of `www.junebug.com`, you could access it with the following request:

`http://www.junebug.com/fireball`

> **CAUTION**
>
> Be sure you do not name an application the same name as an existing directory on the Web server. If you do so, a client will be unable to access that directory on the server.

■ Web File Path: Enter the full path and filename of the .WEB application file.

■ Default Page: Optionally, enter an HTML filename to serve as the default page of an application. The default page is served when a client—who has already accessed the application—does not specify a specific file in the request.

■ Initial Page: Optionally, enter an HTML filename to serve as the opening page when the application is accessed by a client.

■ Maximum Database Connections: If you are accessing a SQL database and running off an NT server, enter the maximum number of concurrent connections your database server permits.

■ External Libraries: If your application uses external libraries (for example, dynamic link libraries), enter the full path in the space provided.

■ Client Object Maintenance: This field specifies the mode in which you are maintaining client object persistence. Available options are client cookie, client URL, server IP, server cookie, and server URL.

After you enter the application information, click the Enter button. LiveWire Application Manager checks your input values and installs the application on the server. You are ready to run the application by clicking Run.

> **NOTE**
>
> When you modify the source of an application and recompile, you must restart the application using Application Manager before the changes will take effect.

Debugging Server-Side JavaScript Applications

If you work with both client-side and server-side JavaScript, you might get spoiled when you start working with the LiveWire JavaScript debugger; you will probably soon wish you could use the debugger for client-side JavaScript as well. LiveWire includes a debugger within Application Manager. To run an application in debug mode, select the application from the list and click Debug. This results in opening a new browser window with a trace frame (or window) displayed beside it. The trace window shows the current objects and their properties. You can also use the built-in `debug()` function to bring the result of a JavaScript expression to the trace window. Figure 20.7 shows the trace window.

FIGURE 20.7.

LiveWire debugger.

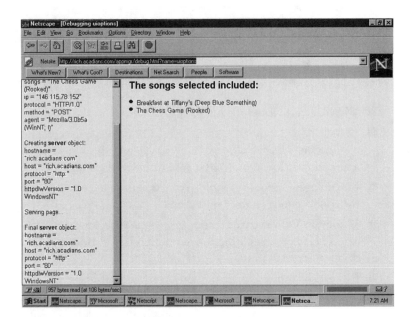

Generating Dynamic HTML

One of the most common uses of server JavaScript is creating dynamic HTML. You can use the built-in `write()` function to generate HTML based on the results of the JavaScript expression used as its parameter. You will probably notice the similarity of the `write()` function to the document object's `write()` method in client-side JavaScript. Although the context is entirely different, they both produce HTML in a similar fashion. However, note that the server-side `write()` function does not have an object associated with it. You never use dot notation to reference the function. For example, the following line produces HTML for the client:

```
write("Your IP address is " + request.ip)
```

> **NOTE**
>
> For another example of using `write()`, see Listing 20.3 later in this chapter.

Working with LiveWire Objects

Just as client-side JavaScript has a framework of built-in objects, so too does LiveWire. LiveWire contains four objects called request, client, project, and server, as shown in Figure 20.8. The central purpose of these four server objects is to manage persistent data. Within the Web's stateless environment, these objects can store various types of data persistently across multiple requests per client, across multiple clients, and even across multiple LiveWire applications.

FIGURE 20.8.
LiveWire object framework.

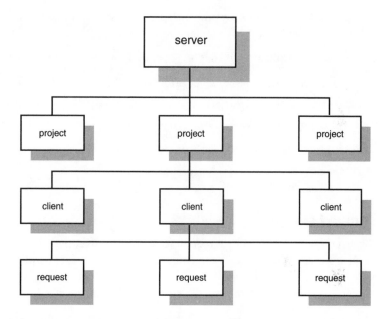

The meaning of persistence depends on the type of object you are dealing with. Table 20.1 lists the lifetime of the LiveWire objects.

Table 20.1. Life expectancy of LiveWire objects.

Object	Lifetime of Object
request	Momentary, for a single request only
client	Ten minutes by default, although this can be changed using JavaScript
project	Open ended (only destroyed when application is stopped)
server	Open ended (only destroyed when server is shut down)

LiveWire Object Properties

Some LiveWire objects come with built-in properties like what client-side built-in JavaScript objects have. You are also free to add new properties to these objects simply by declaring them. For example, if you wanted to add two properties called custID and custName to the client object, you could add these to your code:

```
client.custID = "120120"
client.custName = "Wagner, Richard"
```

LiveWire objects store all their property values as strings. You can assign a property a numeric or logical value, as shown in the following examples:

```
client.custid = 21020    // custid is stored internally as "21020"

client.premierMember = true // premierMember is stored internally as "true"
```

When you read from these object properties, you must convert the data first into its correct type. To use the properties in the previous examples, you need to do the following:

```
currentid = parseInt(client.custid)

if (client.premierMember == "true") {
    performAction() }
```

Request Object

When a client makes an HTTP request for a specific URL, the request is sent to the appropriate Web server to handle. LiveWire assigns the request object to handle this incoming demand. A request object is instantiated for each new request received by the server. This newly created request object contains data from the current request of the client.

The request object has six built-in properties, which are shown in Table 20.2.

Table 20.2. Built-in properties of the request object.

Property	Description
agent	Client software information (such as name and version)
ip	IP address of the client
method	HTTP method (typically GET or POST)
protocol	HTTP protocol level of client
imageX	Horizontal location of mouse pointer over an image map
imageY	Vertical location of mouse pointer over an image map

Look at an example of how you can use this information in a LiveWire application. As a test, suppose you wanted to display these properties in an HTML table when the user requested the application. To display the value of the agent property in a dynamically created HTML document, you use the following code:

```
<server>write(request.agent)</server>
```

The write() function displays the result of the request.agent expression. Listing 20.3 shows the entire HTML document. When the application is run from the server, the page that the user sees is like Figure 20.9.

Listing 20.3. request.htm.

```
<html>
<head>
<title>Request</title>

</head>
<body>
<h1>LiveWire Request Object Example</h1>
<table width=80%>
<tr><td width=50%>Browser Information</td><td width=50%><server>
    write(request.agent)</server></td></tr>
<tr><td width=50%>IP Address</td><td width=50%><server>
    write(request.ip)</server></td></tr>
<tr><td width=50%>HTTP Method</td><td width=50%><server>
    write(request.method)</server></td></tr>
<tr><td width=50%>HTTP Protocol</td><td width=50%><server>
    write(request.protocol)</server></td></tr>
</table>
</body>
</html>
```

FIGURE 20.9.

Request object properties.

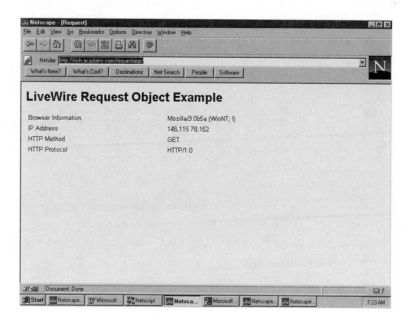

In addition its predefined properties, the request object also has corresponding properties for each input element of a submitted HTML form. Suppose, for example, a user submitted the form shown in Listing 20.4.

Listing 20.4. regform_short.htm.

```html
<html>
<head>
<title>Online Registration</title>
</head>

<body>
<h1>Registration</h1>
<hr>
<form action="http://rich.acadians.com/lwobjects" method="POST">
<p>Please provide the following contact information:</p>
<blockquote>
<pre><em>          Name </em><input type=text size=35 maxlength=256
name="FullName">
<em>          Title </em><input type=text size=35 maxlength=256
name="Title">
<em>     Organization </em><input type=text size=35 maxlength=256
name="Organization">
<em>  Street address </em><input type=text size=35 maxlength=256
name="StreetAddress">
<em> Address (cont.) </em><input type=text size=35 maxlength=256
name="Address2">
<em>             City </em><input type=text size=35 maxlength=256
name="City">
<em>  State/Province </em><input type=text size=35 maxlength=256
name="State">
<em> Zip/Postal code </em><input type=text size=12 maxlength=12
name="ZipCode">
<em>          Country </em><input type=text size=25 maxlength=256
name="Country">
<em>       Work Phone </em><input type=text size=25 maxlength=25
name="WorkPhone">
<em>       Home Phone </em><input type=text size=25 maxlength=25
name="HomePhone">
<em>              FAX </em><input type=text size=25 maxlength=25 name="FAX">
<em>           E-mail </em><input type=text size=25 maxlength=256 name="Email">
<em>              URL </em><input type=text size=25 maxlength=25 name="WebSite">
</pre>
<p><input type=submit value="Submit"> <input type=reset value="Reset"> </p>
</form>
<p> </h5>
</body>
</html>
```

When a request object is created based upon this form's submission, the following properties are associated with it:

```
request.FullName
request.Title
request.Organization
request.StreetAddress
request.Address2
request.City
request.State
request.ZipCode
request.Country
request.WorkPhone
request.HomePhone
request.FAX
request.Email
request.WebSite
```

> **NOTE**
>
> See Listing 20.9 later in this chapter for an example of how you can use these form properties.

The one form element that is a special case occurs when a select object is set to accept multiple values (that is, the MULTIPLE parameter is set in the <SELECT> definition). You can use the built-in getOptionValue() and getOptionValueCount() functions to iterate through multiple values of a select object. The getOptionValue() function is defined as

getOptionValue(*name, index*)

The *name* parameter is the select object name, and the *index* parameter is the index of the options array.

For example, look at the list of options in the select object defined in Listing 20.5 and shown in Figure 20.10. When the form is submitted to the server, topsongs.htm (shown in Listing 20.6) is requested. Using a familiar-looking for loop, you can iterate through each element that was selected. Figure 20.11 shows the resulting HTML form that the write() function creates dynamically.

Listing 20.5. songform.htm.

```
<HTML>
<HEAD>
<h2>Pick Your Favorite Songs From the List:</h2><p>
<FORM action="topsongs.htm" method="post" name="form1">
<select NAME="songs" SIZE=10 MULTIPLE>
<option>1979 (Smashing Pumpkins)</option>
<option>Breakfast at Tiffany's (Deep Blue Something)</option>
<option>The Chess Game (Rooked)</option>
<option>Don't Cry (Seal)</option>
<option>Flood (Jars of Clay)</option>
<option>Fortress Around Your Heart (Sting)</option>
```

20

SERVER-SIDE JAVASCRIPT

continues

Listing 20.5. continued

```
<option>The Hounds of Winter (Sting)</option>
<option>Ironic (Alanis Morisette)</option>
<option>Kiss From a Rose (Seal)</option>
<option>Liquid (Jars of Clay)</option>
<option>Standing Outside a Broken Phone Booth (PRG)</option>
<option>Wake Up (Alanis Morisette)</option>
<option>Wonderwall (Oasis)</option>
<option>World's Apart (Jars of Clay)</option>
</SELECT><p>
<input type=submit value="Submit">
</FORM>
</BODY>
</HTML>
```

FIGURE 20.10.

Multi-selection list.

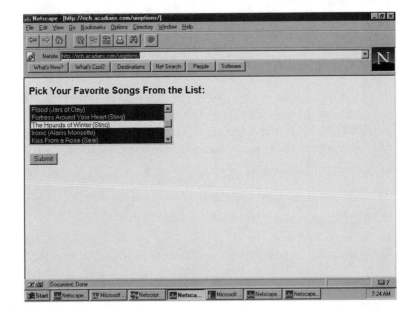

Listing 20.6. topsongs.htm.

```
<SERVER>
     write("<h2>The songs selected included:</h2><p>")
     var size = getOptionValueCount("songs")
     for (var i=0; i<size; i++) {
          write("<li>" + getOptionValue("songs", i) + "</li>")
     }
</SERVER>
```

FIGURE 20.11.

Document generated on the fly.

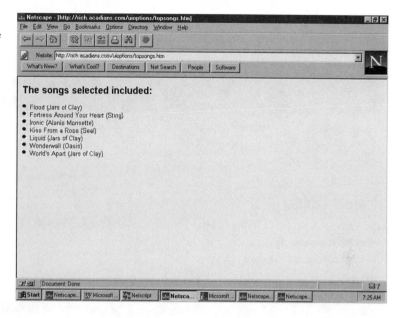

Client Object

As you have seen, request objects exist for a specific moment in time. When the request has been processed, the data no longer persists on the server. However, because a client's interaction with a server application often spans more than a single request, the client object is used to provide state throughout a series of stateless requests. LiveWire instantiates a new client object each time a new client accesses the application.

> **NOTE**
>
> Intended for application-specific uses, the client object contains no predefined properties.

Modifying the Life Span of a Client Object

As noted earlier in the chapter, the client object is designed to "self-destruct" after a specific duration of time. The reason behind this is that you want to maintain state across client requests, but you have no way of ever determining which request is a client's last request. Because you obviously do not want to leave unused client objects in memory any longer than possible, you need to determine when they should expire automatically. The default time period is ten minutes, although you can change this value by using the client object's `expiration(seconds)` method. For example, to extend the expiration period to 20 minutes, you use the following code:

```
client.expiration(1200)
```

If you change the default time period, the `expiration()` method must be defined in each page of a LiveWire application. Any page that does not have this method uses the default expiration setting.

> **NOTE**
>
> See Chapter 21, "Partitioning Client and Server Applications," for techniques on how to maintain client object persistence.

Project Object

The next level in the LiveWire object hierarchy is the project object. The project object is designed to maintain application-wide information across clients and maintains persistence until the application is closed on the server.

> **NOTE**
>
> As with the client object, the project object contains no predefined properties.

Explicitly Locking the Project Object

With the multiuser nature of a Web, hundreds or thousands of users could access a LiveWire application concurrently. As a result, it is not unusual for multiple persons to be either reading or writing to a project property at the same time. LiveWire automatically enforces implicit locking for the length of time it takes to read or set a property value.

You might sometimes have occasion to explicitly lock a property. The best example of this is if you want to base the value of an autoincrementing number, such as an invoice number, on the existing value of a property. To pull this off, you need to read the old value, add a value to it, and then reassign the new value to the property. Implicit locking does not work in this context; however, you can use the project object's `lock()` method to perform this process. The `lock()` method places an explicit lock on the project object itself until an `unlock()` method is called. For example, to assign a new invoice number based on the existing one, you could use the following code:

```
project.lock()
project.invoiceNum += 1
project.unlock()
```

If another client tries to access the project object during this process, it is forced to wait until the process is finished.

> **NOTE**
>
> LiveWire ensures that a deadlock cannot occur within a project by automatically releasing any locks after each client request.

Server Object

When you're running a server-based application, certain pieces of information are specific to the server itself, apart from applications running on the server. The server object—which is the top level of the LiveWire object framework—is used to manage this global data. A server object is always present on a LiveWire server because it is instantiated when the server is started. It is destroyed only when the server shuts down. The server object has four built-in properties as shown in Table 20.3.

Table 20.3. Built-in properties of the server object.

Property	Description
hostname	Full name of server (including port)
host	Server name
protocol	Internet protocol in use
port	Server port number used

As with the project object, the server object has lock() and unlock() methods that you can use to explicitly lock the server object when modifying server properties.

Redirecting Clients to an Alternative URL

You can redirect clients to a different URL by issuing a redirect() call. This built-in function uses a URL as a parameter. The following line diverts the client to the specified URL:

```
redirect("http://www.ouagodougou.com/burkina")
```

One possible use of redirect() is analyzing the client software when a request is made. If the agent property of the request object is recognized as a JavaScript-enabled browser, you can send the client to an enhanced page. Listing 20.7 shows an example of how you can do this. In this source file, the code examines the agent property and determines whether it supports JavaScript based upon its value. If it does, the client is diverted to the jsindex.htm page in Listing 20.8, which adds client-side JavaScript to the basic HTML.

Listing 20.7. index.htm.

```
<html>
<head>
<title>Kakata</title>
<SERVER>
     var browser = ""
     browser = request.agent
     if (browser.indexOf("Mozilla/") != -1) {
          ver = browser.substring(8,9)
          verNum = parseInt(ver)
          if (verNum >= 2) {
               redirect("http://rich.acadians.com/kakata/jsindex.htm")
          }
     }
</SERVER>
</head>
<body>
<h1>Welcome to the Kakata Home Page</h1>
<p>We are glad you found us!</p>
<p>Click here for the <a href="http://www.kakata.com/news">Latest News</a>
from the Land of Kakata.</p>
<p>Click here for more information on <a href="http://www.kakata.com/
legend.htm">The Legend of Kakaka</a></p>
</body>
</html>
```

Listing 20.8. jsindex.htm.

```
<html>
<head>
<title>Kakata</title>
<SCRIPT LANGUAGE="JavaScript">
document.write("<h1>Welcome " + navigator.appName +
" user to the Kakata Home Page</h1><p>")
</SCRIPT>
</head>

<body>
<p>We are glad you found us!</p>
<p>Click here for the <a href="http://www.kakata.com/news">
Latest News</a> from the Land of Kakata.</p>
<p>Click here for more information on <a href="http://www.kakata.com/
legend.htm">The Legend of Kakaka</a></p>
</body>
</html>
```

Figures 20.12 and 20.13 show the varied results in versions 2.0 and 3.0 of Internet Explorer (IE). If you recall, Internet Explorer 3.0 supports JavaScript, but version 2.0 does not.

FIGURE 20.12.
The IE 3.0 client is routed to an enhanced page.

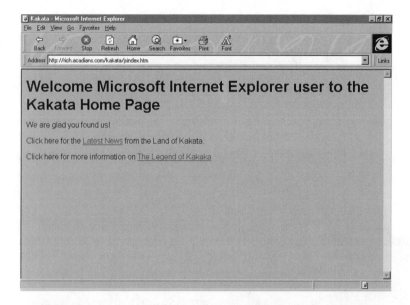

FIGURE 20.13.
The IE 2.0 client stays at the normal page.

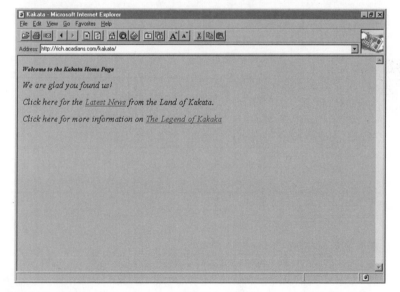

Accessing Files on the Server

LiveWire includes a file object to let you read and write data to a file on the server's file system. File storage can be a very useful solution for storing data persistently when you do not want to use a relational database. Additionally, anything you save to a disk is maintained even after the server shuts down.

CAUTION

For security concerns, be very careful in your use of the file object. You should ensure that a hacker could not access sensitive files on your server or write to the server disk.

The commands for reading and writing to files are largely standard across programming languages. Server JavaScript follows in this convention by providing many of the file-access methods you would expect, including those shown in Table 20.4. Table 20.5 shows some additional methods.

Table 20.4. Common file access methods.

Method	Description
open()	Opens a file for access
close()	Closes a file
read()	Reads data from a file into a string
readln()	Reads current line of a file into a string
write()	Writes data to a file
writeln()	Writes data to a file and appends a carriage return
flush()	Writes the content of the internal buffer to a file
getLength()	Gets the length of a file
getPosition()	Gets the current position in a file
setPosition()	Sets the current position in a file
eof()	Determines whether the file pointer is at the end of a file
exists()	Determines whether a specified file exists

Table 20.5. Additional file access methods.

Method	Description
byteToString()	Converts a number that represents a byte into a string
stringToByte()	Converts the first number of a string into a number to represent a byte
readByte()	Reads the next byte and returns its numeric value
writeByte()	Writes a byte of data to a file
error()	Returns the current error status
clearError()	Clears the file error status

You can create a file object using the new operator:

```
fileObject = new File("path")
```

Because the file object deals with the server's file system, the path parameter is a full path to the file, not a URL. For example, the following line creates a file object called policyInfo:

```
policyInfo = new File("e:/netscape/server/corp/policy.txt")
```

After a file object has been instantiated, you need to open it to prepare it for either reading or writing. Use the open() method for this task:

```
result = fileObject.open("mode")
```

result is a Boolean value: true if successful, false if unsuccessful. The mode parameter can be one of several options outlined in Table 20.6.

Table 20.6. File object open() method parameters.

Mode	Description
r[b]	Opens an existing file for reading. If the file does not exist, a false value is returned.
a[b]	Opens an existing file for appending new text. If the file does not exist, one is created.
w[b]	Opens a new file for writing. If the file exists, it is overwritten.
w+[b]	Opens a new file for reading and writing. If the file exists, it is overwritten.
r+[b]	Opens an existing file for reading and writing. If the file does not exist, false is returned. The position of the pointer is the start of the file.
a+[b]	Opens an existing file for reading and writing. If the file does not exist, false is returned. The position of the pointer is the end of the file.

On the Windows platform, you can use the optional b parameter to open a file as a binary file. When you have finished working with an open file, issue a close() method to close access to it.

> **TIP**
>
> Although the file object does not have lock() and unlock() methods, you can still take advantage of the locking capabilities of the project and server objects to prevent multiple users from accessing the file simultaneously.

Listing 20.9 demonstrates the process of working with files. You can use this source HTML file to record a log of persons who submit the attached form. Each time a form is submitted, the server script opens the `contlog.txt` file and writes each field entry into the comma-delimited file.

Listing 20.9. reg.htm.

```
<html>
<head>
<title>Online Registration</title>
</head>
<body>
<SERVER>

        if (request.FullName != null) {
            cLog = new File("d:/netscape/server/unleashed/file/contlog.txt")
            project.lock()
            if (cLog.open("a") == true) {
                //isOpen = cLog.open("a")
                cLog.write(request.FullName + ",")
                cLog.write(request.Title + ",")
                cLog.write(request.Organization + ",")
                cLog.write(request.StreetAddress + ",")
                cLog.write(request.Address2 + ",")
                cLog.write(request.City + ",")
                cLog.write(request.State + ",")
                cLog.write(request.ZipCode + ",")
                cLog.write(request.Country + ",")
                cLog.write(request.WorkPhone + ",")
                cLog.write(request.HomePhone + ",")
                cLog.write(request.FAX + ",")
                cLog.write(request.Email + ",")
                cLog.writeln(request.WebSite)
                cLog.close()
            }
            project.unlock()
        }

</SERVER>
<h1>Registration</h1><hr>
<form method="post" action="reg.htm">
<p>Please provide the following contact information:</p>
<blockquote>
<pre><em>            Name </em><input type=text size=35 maxlength=256
name="FullName">
<em>            Title </em><input type=text size=35 maxlength=256
name="Title">
<em>     Organization </em><input type=text size=35 maxlength=256
name="Organization">
<em>  Street address </em><input type=text size=35 maxlength=256
name="StreetAddress">
<em> Address (cont.) </em><input type=text size=35 maxlength=256
name="Address2">
<em>             City </em><input type=text size=35 maxlength=256 name="City">
<em>   State/Province </em><input type=text size=35 maxlength=256 name="State">
<em> Zip/Postal code </em><input type=text size=12 maxlength=12 name="ZipCode">
```

```
<em>          Country </em><input type=text size=25 maxlength=256
name="Country">
<em>       Work Phone </em><input type=text size=25 maxlength=25
name="WorkPhone">
<em>       Home Phone </em><input type=text size=25 maxlength=25
name="HomePhone">
<em>              FAX </em><input type=text size=25 maxlength=25 name="FAX">
<em>           E-mail </em><input type=text size=25 maxlength=256 name="Email">
<em>              URL </em><input type=text size=25 maxlength=25 name="WebSite">
</pre>
<p><input type=submit value="Submit"> <input type=reset value="Reset"> </p>
</form>
<p> </h5>
</body>
</html>
```

Summary

In this chapter, you learned that JavaScript is not just for the client side any more. Using Netscape LiveWire, you can employ the scripting language on the server side to produce server-side applications. The next chapter looks more closely at some of the issues surrounding client/server applications and how you can apply this architecture to the Web.

Partitioning Client and Server Applications

by Kim Daniels

IN THIS CHAPTER

CHAPTER 21

The Web is, by default, a client/server environment. In the Web sense, clients are browsers, and servers are Web servers or database servers at some other (or possibly the same) location. The client and server are separate entities, completely independent of each other, until the client needs information from the server. The Web client/server concept has evolved even further; the server side of the Web application now could be a true server that supports application processing and database storage—not just static document storage.

Web-based client/server development is slightly different from traditional client/server development. Traditionally the "server" in client/server is a database server, used to store data and process data and calculation requests from the client. In the Web-based client/server, the server might not necessarily be a database; it can be just the Web server that is used for processing and calculating HTML documents. The capability still exists to split processing between client and server, but the processing is usually centralized on the server.

Unlike traditional client/server development, when you consider Web application partitioning, you must be slightly more cautious in your design. Traditional client/server partitioning allows for many variations of the client/server relationship, ranging from the client being a presentation front only, to the client having all application control and the server being used only for data storage.

The client, in the case of the Web, could be just a Web browser "terminal." You do not have much control over the type of PC used for browsing the Web. Your "front end" might be a very slow, older model PC that provides few benefits to the user other than viewing. In this case, you do not want much processing done on the client. Because you have no control over the client browser and you do have control over "your" server, as a developer you should place high-intensity processing and calculations on the server because you can predict its speed and reliability.

TIP

Testing processing speed on a generic client processor before deciding where to do the processing. Remember that not all users will have a browser client up to par with a developer.

You can perform a minor amount of processing on the client side because, at some point, it becomes more effective to move the processing to the client; because the speed of the Internet and traffic concerns are also a factor.

If processing is done on a client and the user considers it too slow, the usefulness of your Web page could be lost due to speed issues.

Fundamentals of Client/Server Architecture

In client/server application development, you partition the application into two distinct pieces. In the traditional sense of client/server, the client or front end is a desktop workstation where the user can interact with the application. This workstation provides the user with access into the application (user interface), another user interface with the "back end," and some processing capabilities. Processing is spread between the client and the server depending on the necessary requirements.

In the typical client/server environment, it is reasonable to put processing on the client because you usually have some control over the client configuration and setup. You, the developer, can partition the application as you see fit, moving more or less processing to the client side depending on client capabilities, server processing load, and network traffic flow.

The server, or back end, is the processing engine for the application. Usually, the back end is a database server that stores and manages large amounts of data and performs the processor-intensive, large-scale calculations and system processing. The ability to segregate these two pieces of a system, making them largely independent of each other, has contributed to significant advances in the development of large-scale database systems. The capability to split these two pieces gives the developer more flexibility in application design. This is the two-tiered structure for client/server architecture.

The three-tiered methodology is used to overcome some of the limitations that are associated with the two-tiered methodology. Three-tiered architecture involves splitting user interface, processing, and data storage into three distinct pieces, or tiers, spreading the work load even further. The front end remains responsible for the user interface and minor processing; the back end is still responsible for the data storage; but the processing and calculations (or business rules) have been moved to a middle layer. This enables changes to be made to the business rules without affecting the user interface or the database.

Unlike mainframes, whose "clients" were just dumb terminals with no processing capability whatever, today's PC-based desktop has given you, as the developer, the opportunity to create robust applications that can run processes on both the server and the client, splitting the workload and running the processing where it will be most effective.

This capability is also available in the Web world of client/server but with some cautions. You have far less control over the front-end PC (both Web browser and desktop workstation) in the Web environment than you do in the normal application environment. It is more difficult to judge how well processes run on the client side. This makes it more reasonable to run processes on the back end because you do have control over that environment and can predict the outcome.

On the other hand, client/server issues in normal PC applications do face some issues that a Web-based client/server do not. In a normal client/server database application, if the client-side module or front end is modified, you might need to redistribute the entire application, but with a Web-based client/server, because the client or front end is a Web page, the new front end is just redistributed the next time the page is loaded. Any changes needed for cookies use (explained in the section "State Maintenance," later in this chapter) can be updated at this time also.

The browser client initiates the transaction by sending a request to the server to perform some operation, database request, calculation, processing request, or JavaScript function call. The client then waits for a response from the server before continuing.

Server-side processing allows "code" to remain on one centralized server for easier modifications and also gives you the benefit of faster processing because the processing occurs on the server.

The client browser is responsible for handling all user-interface presentation; the server is responsible for handling all data storage and HTML document storage; and processing is split between the client and the server, depending on need or where it is most logical to put the processing. Intense data calculations are usually performed at the server level because a server is more robust than the clients.

JavaScript presents you with client/server architecture issues as well. JavaScript processing can be distributed between the client and the server, depending on your preferences. Processing speed on the client is completely dependent on the client's environment, memory, PC speed, and other internal factors; processing on the server is dependent on the amount of traffic on the Internet as well as traffic and processing on the server. Dividing up processing over multiple entities is a good idea, keeping intense processing on the more known quantity, the server.

Thinking about architecture design early on in the development phase of a Web application helps you build a more stable application that gives you the most processing power available.

Client and Server Communication

The communication between client and server in a Web-based environment is an important component to consider—one that presents a new hurdle to be overcome. Unlike client/server environments on a normal network, the Web environment does not provide a constant connection to the server; instead, communication is through HTTP protocols using TCP/IP.

In a traditional client/server world, communication is done through a network protocol that enables the client to always maintain a connection to the server or to at least have the capability to re-establish a connection immediately. In the Web environment, the client does not maintain a connection to the server. The client sends a request to the server for information, the server responds to that client with the information, and then the connection is terminated. If the client session continues, the client sends another request, the connection is re-established, and the cycle continues. This means that every time the client connects to the server, it is a new session to the server; the server has no knowledge of previous requests or former information regarding the client. Such one-time connections make it difficult to perform activities in the typical environment of client/server architecture.

Because of this non-traditional client/server behavior, there is a need for a methodology to maintain information about the client that can be sent to the server every time. When a client connects to the server, the server needs information sent to it regarding the previous state of the client and how it should treat the requests from this client during processing.

The methodology of sending information from client to server and vice versa can be described as taking place in a "transaction" set of events.

1. Connection between the client and server is established using TCP/IP.
2. Request is sent from the client to the server.
3. Response is sent from the server to the client.
4. Connection between the client and server is closed by either or both sides.

The communication between clients (browsers) and servers is a two-step process. The first step is the client request. This is the message sent by the browser requesting information from a server. The request could be as simple as a new static HTML page or could be as complex as posting data to a database and computing information using JavaScript/CGI.

The server answers this request with a server response. The server response message contains information returned from the server regarding the status of the request (among other values) and, most importantly, the returned HTML that was requested. Even if the client's request was just to perform a calculation, the server re-sends the original HTML document, which contains the updated information for the document as it occurred during processing.

The simple forms of HTML communication have evolved into the more complex process of today, including JavaScript and CGI. The straightforward request and response metaphor had to become more complicated. Now, a request to the server is not simple. In interactive and data-related HTML applications, the server requires certain information pertaining to the client and its state information before it can properly process the requests that the client is sending—thus the need for state maintenance in HTML applications.

The methodologies for state maintenance involve storing information about the client in relation to a particular server and then sending that information back to the server when the request by the client requires it. Every request to a server may not require state information, and it may be required only for certain URLs on a particular server.

State Maintenance

One of the benefits of the Web and its design is also one of its biggest obstacles in applications that require client interaction with the server itself. Because a server is stateless, it is able to run faster, but it has to rely on the client to remind it who the client is when a request is made. The evolution of HTML out of static pages into interactive applications has made a formerly stateless environment look for ways to maintain state.

Because the client is not continuously connected to the Web server, there is the issue of knowing how to tell a Web server who the client is when the client "reconnects" to send a request back to the server. If Web applications remained continuously connected to the server, Web development would be as uncomplicated as generic client/server applications—but they aren't.

Web pages are sent to a client, but how does a server remember what state the client is in when the client sends a request back? State maintenance is required to help Web applications behave more like normal run-of-the-mill client/server applications.

State information about a client can be defined as information that the server needs to know about the client in order to correctly process the HTTP request that the client is sending. Required state information varies from server to server and even from URL to URL on the same server. A static URL on a server might not require any state information from the client before it responds to the client request; but a shopping cart URL on the same server might require the client's name, last date to shop, and shopping list from last session before it can send back the requested response to the client.

State information can be so varied that some generic techniques for keeping or maintaining the state now exist.

There are several techniques for state maintenance, including the use of client cookies, client URL encoding, IP addresses on the server, short cookies, and short URL encoding. The first two techniques for state maintenance involve complete client-side state maintenance; IP addresses require the server to maintain the information; and the last two involve some of both server and client maintenance.

The benefit of using client cookies and client URL encoding is that there is less impact on the server, and the server is able to forget about the client after a request/response transaction is complete. If the client never returns to the site, the server is not holding any more extra information than before the client first accessed the server. This technique gives the added benefit of speed on the server because the server does not have to retrieve any information before processing the incoming URL. The URL or cookie contains all the data necessary to process the incoming request from the client.

Client Cookies

Cookies provide a Web server with a way of saving information about a client that can be used in future connections to the server. Cookies are client-based state maintenance methodology; the server saves all the relevant information that it needs about the client on the client itself and lets the client send the information back with every HTTP request.

Partitioning Client and Server Applications

CHAPTER 21

491

21

CLIENT AND
SERVER
APPLICATIONS

RESOURCE

More information on cookies can be found at `http://www.netscape.com/newsref/std/cookie_spec.html`.

Cookies are stored in a text file on the client drive, and the server writes to the cookie, as a means of keeping track of the client's state, information that the server needs to know when the client sends a URL request to the server. Only one cookie file exists per browser, and all servers write cookie information to the same file, tagging sections in the cookie with the specific URL names as they are saved and updated.

CAUTION

Cookies are not supported by all browsers. Be sure to use them at you own risk.

The size of this cookie file is limited, so only a certain amount of cookie information can be stored on any given client. This limits the number of Web servers that can store information on a specific client computer and the amount of information that each server can store.

The possibility always exists with cookies that the user could delete the cookie file by mistake (after all, it is only a text file); then every server would have lost whatever state information that it had been maintaining, and the client would need to start from scratch in establishing itself with the server.

Because cookie information is stored on the client side, it is not affected by server issues. It also enables the client to re-send a request successfully, even if problems are encountered on the server side. Another benefit to cookies is that because the server is not required to store any information about the client, the server can "forget" about the client after the initial request for information, and no storage of information is required on the server.

This is an important concept to keep in mind. The Web is growing at such a rapid pace that hundreds of thousands of clients might be accessing your Web site. For you to store pieces of information about every one of these clients (even those who never come back to your site again) would be unreasonable. The storage required to keep this information could easily get out of hand as the access to your server increases.

Cookies do increase the amount of Internet traffic because the server is sending and receiving extra information with every client URL request. Cookie information is transferred in the `name`/`value` pair methodology, using the cookie protocol for transferring cookie information with requests. The following list outlines the advantages and disadvantages of using cookies for state maintenance:

Advantages

Works in non-database applications, and no memory space is needed to store server information

Retains information with server re-starts

Disadvantages

Increase in Internet traffic

Limited file size of cookie on client

Only certain browsers support cookies

Client URL Encoding

The client URL encoding methodology for maintaining state information between client and server involves sending name/value pair information as part of the URL string at client HTTP request time. This method of storing state information has the same benefits for the server as cookies in that no information needs to be stored on the server.

Using this process to maintain client state requires that URLs be built dynamically every time a request is made. Because of the significant increase in size of the URL, there is a significant increase in the amount of Internet traffic using URL encoding.

Using client-side URL encoding does allow more flexibility when the need for state maintenance exists. Unlike cookies, client URL encoding is not browser-specific, and because the type of browser that is accessing your server is unknown to you, this is a more reliable method for maintaining state. The possibility always exists that a client's browser does not support cookies; they are not usable, and the state of the client will be unknown at the time of its request to your server. The following list outlines the advantages and disadvantages of using client URL encoding to maintain state:

Advantages

Works in non-database applications

Not browser-specific

Retains information with server restarts

Disadvantages

Increase in Internet traffic

URLs must be dynamically generated for every request

IP Address on the Server

The first two methods of maintaining state are client-side processes. The information is stored on the client and sent by the client at the time of a request. The server can update this information, but storage is on the client side.

The third method of maintaining state involves storing IP addresses and state information on the server. The server must have database access or shared memory in which to store the information. The state information of a client is stored based on IP address of the client, and this information is held and usable only by this particular server.

Because of these drawbacks, this type of state maintenance is useful only if the following situations apply:

- The clients are known to have fixed IP addresses.
- There is only one server supporting the application.

The practice of dynamically allocating IP addresses for a Web browser makes this type of state maintenance impossible to implement. Multiple Web servers cannot be supported using this methodology either. The following list outlines the advantages and disadvantages of using the IP address on the server for state maintenance:

Advantages
Not browser-specific
Will not increase amount of network traffic

Disadvantages
Requires database to store information
Does not support multi-user systems or dynamic IP address providers

Short Cookies

The short cookies technique uses a combination of cookies on the client and IP address maintenance on the server to maintain the state of the client.

Cookies are used to store only a name tag that has been generated by the server during the initial access to the server. The client sends the cookie information name tag to the server, and the server uses the name tag to retrieve the state information that it is maintaining. All state information is stored the same as it is in the "IP address on server" technique. The following list outlines the advantages and disadvantages of using short cookies for state maintenance:

Advantages

Small increase in amount of network traffic

Disadvantages

Requires database to store information

Netscape browser required

Short URL Encoding

The short URL encoding technique uses a combination of IP address maintenance on the server and client URL encoding.

The server generates a reference name for the client, and the client appends this reference name to every URL request. The server detects the name in the URL and refers to the state information that it is storing. The server maintains all state information as it does in the IP address on server technique. The following list outlines the advantages and disadvantages of using short URL encoding for state maintenance:

Advantages

Not browser-specific

Small increase in amount of network traffic

Disadvantages

Requires database to store information

URLs must be dynamically generated for every request

Sending Information from Client to Server

The first substantial exchange of information between client (browser) and server is the client request.

Because of the nature of HTTP, it is necessary for browser clients to send requests to servers for all information that it wants. Servers do not have a way to initiate an HTTP document transfer/connection. A request can have many forms and is used for various reasons. Request information can range from a request for a static page to a request to download a file or data from a database that is stored on the server.

The format for the HTTP request to the server can be a basic HTML page request, or it can be a request that contains content information or data (in the case of JavaScript and CGI-type processes) that needs to be processed or posted to the server. The second type of request has an additional piece of information included in the request message. This part of the request is termed the content or body of the request and contains data/content to be used by the server, either from data entry fields on the HTML document or from functions.

Partitioning Client and Server Applications

CHAPTER 21

495

21

CLIENT AND
SERVER
APPLICATIONS

Servers should be tolerant of HTTP requests from bad clients. Not all clients conform completely to the specifications, and servers should be able to accommodate a bad request from a client. Servers should account for lines terminated incorrectly as well as unrecognized or unimplemented HTTP header name values.

The HTTP request contains three basic groups of information:

- Request line: Method (GET, HEAD, POST), URL, and HTTP version.
- Name/Value pairs for fields such as accept, referer, if-modified, user-agent, content-type and content-length (defined in Table 21.2 following).
- Content: Information (data) being sent to the server for processing.

The request line is the first line of the HTTP request calls that goes from client to server for information. It contains:

- A method (methods are defined in Table 21.1) to be applied to the requested document
- The URL of the requested document
- The HTTP version requested.

Table 21.1. Methods (commonly used methods).

GET	This method is always supported and specifies to the server to retrieve the information that is described by the URL (either a document or data information). If the URL is defined to run a process or a script, then this action is performed and the resulting information is returned.
POST	This is another frequently used method that creates another object subordinate to the original URL object. The post method is used to add to existing documents (insert data), post files to a directory, and so on. The new URL is defined by the server and returned to client.
HEAD	This method returns the same information as the GET method but does not return the entire body of the document—only the HTTP HEAD.
TEXTSEARCH	This method is used to specify that the URL object can be searched with a text string. This is really a search form of the GET method. Use the "?" operator to denote the search criteria.
SPACEJUMP	This is similar to TEXTSEARCH in that it implies a search and is a form of the GET method, but it searches for coordinates on a map and not text in the document.
SHOWMETHOD	This method is designed to give the client more information on object methods that are not fully defined in HTTP standards. The method name is defined by the previous HTTP response from the server, and the client can then request from the server more information on how to use the request method.

Name/pair values are sets of HTTP request fields that the client passes through to the server in reference to the request. These values include request headers and object metainformation.

Table 21.2. Request headers.

ACCEPT	Semicolon-delimited list of responses that are accepted in response to this request. Common accepts are `text/plain`, `text/HTML`, `image/gif`.
USER-AGENT	Can be used to specify the type of software being used to generate this request. This parameter is useful for tracking and statistical purposes.
FROM	Used only in mail requests, it specifies the name of the user making the request. Usually used just for tracking purposes.
REFERER	This is an optional header that helps the server maintain a list of links. This field specifies the URL from which the URL in the request was obtained.
IF-Modified-Since	This method is used in conjunction with the GET method, making the GET a conditional GET. The URL is only returned if it has been modified since the date specified in this header field.
ACCEPT-LANGUAGE	Used for the same principal reason as ACCEPT header but specifies the language that is preferable for the response.
ACCEPT-ENCODING	Used for the same principal reason as ACCEPT header but specifies the encoding types that are valid for the response.

Also acceptable in the request header section is certain object metainformation `name/value` pairs that are defined in the section "Sending Information from Server to Client," later in this chapter. The `Content-Type` and `Content-Length` pairs are two of the valid pairs that can be used with the HTTP request as well as the HTTP response.

The `name/value` pair section (this is the combination of both request headers and object metainformation) of the request is terminated by a `Carriage Return/Line Feed` pair (blank line).

Content follows the `name/value` pairs in the HTTP request. The content is the body of the request and contains information that is being sent to the server for processing.

A simple example of a request from client to server follows in Listing 21.1.

Listing 21.1. Sample HTTP client request.

```
POST /sampapp/sampform HTTP/1.0
Accept: text/plain
Accept: test/html
```

Partitioning Client and Server Applications

CHAPTER 21

497

21

CLIENT AND
SERVER
APPLICATIONS

```
Accept: image/gif
Content-type: application/x-www-form-urlencoded
Content-length: 10

name=anderson
```

Sending Information from Server to Client

Once a client has sent a request to a server for information, that server will in turn send a message back to the client containing information that the client has requested. The server message packet is called the HTTP response to the client request. It contains the information that the client has requested, whether the client has rights to the information, and whether the server is able to send the response successfully.

HTTP responses take a similar format to HTTP requests, but they include at the end the returned HTML document (response.)

Clients receiving a response from a server should be tolerant of the server when the response does not comply to the standards. Clients should be prepared to tolerate white space in a document as well as incorrectly terminated lines. Clients should accommodate servers using older versions of HTTP as well.

The HTTP response contains three basic groups of information:

- Response line
- Response headers
- Response data

Response line from the server has the syntax of HTTP version, status code (3-digit return code), and response line of text (not used by browser but can be used by humans for document interpretation).

The response line gives the browser some initial information about what it can expect to follow in the rest of the response. The version tells it how to begin interpreting the document response, and the status code tells it what to expect as far as the return. A response status code of 200 is "OK".

> **NOTE**
>
> There are a variety of response codes that relate to the state and content of the document being returned.

Name/pair values are sets of HTTP response fields that the server passes back to the client in reference to the original request and subsequent returned response.

Object metainformation (defined in Table 21.3) is commonly used in header fields in relation to the specific HTTP object.

Table 21.3. Object metainformation.

CONTENT-TYPE	This pair specifies the format and encoding for data content being sent with the request and is necessary only if a body (or data) is included in the request packet of information.
CONTENT-LENGTH	As with content-type, this pair is not necessary if no data is associated with the request. If the body is included, this value specifies the exact binary length of the data field that has been included and tells the server to read the content directly as included with the request.
ALLOWED	These are request methods that the user is "allowed" to use when requesting from the URL. Default methods, if none are supplied, are GET and HEAD.
PUBLIC	Methods that anyone (not just this specific user) can use in relation to this response document. Default for this field is GET only.
DATE	Specifies the date that this URL was created.
TITLE	Defines the title of the URL document that is returned in this response.
EXPIRES	Specifies a date when this URL is no longer valid on the client side and must be re-requested from the server.
CONTENT-LANGUAGE	Defines the language in which the URL was written.
CONTENT-ENCODING	Specifies the encoding type to be used for the object.
MESSAGE-ID	Defines the unique identifier assigned for the HTTP object. A message ID must be unique at all times and never expire. No two documents can ever have the same message ID.

When defining the name/value pairs for the HTTP response, an important pair to include is the Content-Type pair.

Content-Type refers again, as in client HTTP requests, to text/plain, text/HTML, image/GIF, and so on; but in this case, it is the content-type of response data that is to follow. The type used is usually the content-type that the client has said that it can or will accept as a response. Safe types are text/plain and text/HTML. It can be assumed that most browsers can handle these two types.

Again the response name/value pairs are terminated by a blank line (Carriage Return/Line Feed).

The information that follows the `Carriage Return/Line Feed` is the body of the response or the response data. The response data is the final part of the HTTP response and is the format of a MIME message body. The significance of this data is dependent on the status code that is returned in the response header. The response data is usually in the form of an HTML document to be displayed in the client browser. This document is either a new document, a refresh of the current document (really a new document) containing updated data, or the confirmation that data to be posted to a server has been successfully posted.

Listing 21.2 is an example of a simple response from the server. It contains all parts of the response including the reference to the document being returned.

Listing 21.2. Sample HTTP server response.

```
HTTP/1.0 200 Ok
Date: Wed, 17 Jul 1996 9:30:35 GMT
Content-type: text/html
Content-length: 323
<returned HTML document>
```

Summary

Much thought needs to go into the architecture of the application before you can begin to build it for successful Internet use. Knowing your predicted audience and being able to anticipate access to your server helps when defining the methodologies and techniques that you choose to use to implement a client/server application. Adding JavaScript and database functionality brings on a whole new level of concerns and issues that must be accounted for.

Server-side versus client-side processing needs to be taken into account when deciding test speed and functionality of the JavaScript application. The methodologies of two-tier and three-tier needed to evaluated for the advantages and disadvantages on your particular application and its complexity and maintainability.

State maintenance methodology decisions become important based on the need in the particular application. You need to weigh all pros and cons before deciding on the route that you will take.

Finally, knowing the process by which clients and servers send and request information from each other will allow you to better develop your applications.

VI

PART

Advanced JavaScript

Error-Handling and Debugging in JavaScript

by Jimmy Nasr

IN THIS CHAPTER

Logical Errors

Logical (or logic) errors occur when an application or function does not perform in the way its users or designers had intended. In other words, an application that has syntactically good code, free of runtime errors, still produces incorrect results if it has logical errors. Logical errors are the hardest types of errors to identify and fix and usually demand a thorough test of the application, analysis of results, and review of the design. Many logical errors are propagated from a poor understanding of the requirements, a bad design, and subsequent incorrect code. The following example demonstrates a logical error caused by evaluation of mismatched data types:

```javascript
function mismatched() {
var Constant = "10";
var i = 10;
for (i <=10; i > 0; i--) {
    document.write(i + " + " + Constant + " = " + (i + Constant) + "<br>");
    }
}
```

You can see in Figure 22.1 that the results displayed are clearly incorrect, even though the code ran successfully. In this case, JavaScript evaluates the result of the expression (i + Constant) as a string and concatenates the two operands into one.

FIGURE 22.1.

Example of a logical error.

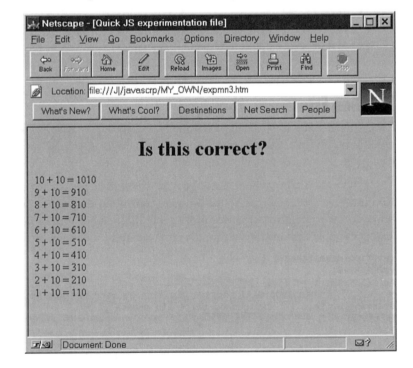

Error Messages

Figure 22.2 shows that once the browser recognizes an error (syntax or runtime), it displays a large dialog box on the screen. The information contained in this dialog box helps to identify the approximate source and location of errors. The dialog box contains the following information:

- URL or filename where the error occurs.
- Line number (in the file) where the error occurs. This is a sequential line count from the beginning of the HTML (or .JS) file—not just the JavaScript code. Do not rely too heavily on this information because the source of the error might well be at a different place.
- Description of error. This is valuable information in identifying the type of fix required.
- Actual code that contains the error. This is also not always reliable information because the source of the error might well occur before this line.
- Pointer indicating where on the line the error occurs. Again, do on rely on this too heavily; try to follow the flow of nearby code.

Figure 22.2.

JavaScript error message reporting a syntax error.

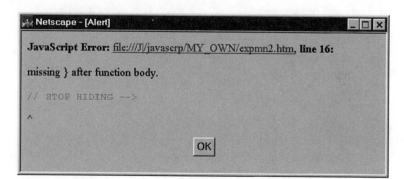

Table 22.1 summarizes the most common JavaScript error messages and their potential causes.

Table 22.1. Common JavaScript error messages.

JavaScript Error Message	Potential Causes
item is not defined	Named variable is not defined. Variable is misspelled. Named function is not defined. Unterminated string (regarded as an undefined variable by JavaScript).

continues

Table 22.1. continued

JavaScript Error Message	Potential Causes
`item is not a function`	Function is not defined. Function is misspelled. Other errors exist before function definition.
`item cannot be converted to a function`	Variable is misstated as a called function. Function (or a built-in object's method) is misspelled.
`item has no properties`	Object property is referenced incorrectly. Array is referenced incorrectly.
`item is not a numeric literal`	Variable does not contain numeric data. Other errors exist before variable assignment.
`unterminated string literal`	Missing quotes (around string). String value has more than 250 characters. String values include a line break.
`missing ) after argument list` (and similar error messages)	Missing opening or closing bracket,), brace, }, or semicolon, ;.

Fixing Your Code

Even though JavaScript's error messages are helpful in identifying a lot of program bugs, you usually need to do some more investigative work yourself to fix all the errors (especially logical ones). This section outlines some common things to do to make your investigative work both easier and a little more systematic.

Check the HTML

Because JavaScript is commonly interacting with HTML code, you must first make sure that the file has no HTML errors. Use the following list as a guideline:

- Check for starting and ending <SCRIPT> tags.
- Check for the attribute LANGUAGE = "JavaScript" inside the <SCRIPT> tag.
- Check for missing or misspelled HTML tags.
- Check for angled brackets, <>, to open and close a tag.
- Check for matching pairs of tags (for example, <SCRIPT> ... </SCRIPT>).

■ Check for correct use of the HTML comment tags (for example, <!-- ... -->) to hide your JavaScript.

■ Make sure the form and frame names called in your JavaScript code match the names defined in the HTML files.

> **CAUTION**
>
> Do not start JavaScript code inside a table cell. This known bug in JavaScript usually causes browsers to lock up. Instead, open a <SCRIPT> tag in the desired table row (<TR>) and create the cell through JavaScript.

Use Comments to Identify Problems

You can use comments to systematically block out various lines (and functionality) in your code to identify and fix the source of errors. This is an iterative process. The following list outlines the steps involved:

1. Comment out one or more lines from your code.
2. Save the code.
3. Reload page in the browser.
4. Note the impact.
5. Modify code or comment out more lines.
6. Repeat until you fix the error.

Use the alert() Method to Trace Your Code's Progress

To identify some runtime and many logical errors in your code, you must be able to follow the flow of the code and almost "see" how it processes its data. Many debugging tools let you step into your code, execute it one line at a time, and in a side window (called the debugging window), see the impact of the executed code. You can use JavaScript's alert() method to simulate a similar debugging environment. alert() displays a dialog box on the screen, which you can easily program to show various useful messages and values that help trace your code's progress. I suggest the following techniques for using alert():

■ Use something such as alert("Starting Check") to identify the starting point for debugging. As you progress further and fix errors, you can move this down in the code.

■ Use alert() to display values of variables, arrays, and function returns. By running some simple test scenarios, you can quickly determine whether the values displayed are what you expect.

■ Use `alert()` to display the results of expressions. This is particularly helpful for tracking logical errors because many of them arise through incorrectly using expressions.

Testing Your Code

Traditionally, testing code means that you are preparing your application for production. That concept is equally true when it comes to publishing JavaScript-enhanced Web pages on the Internet—except your "production" is now a worldwide stage with many potential users on a variety of platforms. With that as a premise, you can use many commonly practiced traditional testing techniques to help you test your JavaScript code. You need to make some modifications to cater to the special world of JavaScript and the Internet, but not many. JavaScript is a programming language capable of producing sophisticated applications that, like applications in other, more traditional programming languages, demand solid testing.

NOTE

Testing is different from debugging. Testing is a means of finding errors. Debugging is a means of determining the source of errors and correcting them.

You should test your code assuming that you will find errors; if you believe there are no errors at all, you will probably test so that you do not find any! In practice, even the most thorough tests can never prove the absence of errors (you would have to run an infinite number of test cases to do that); you can only prove their existence.

To help you test your code, you should write a formal test plan—one that contains both a checklist (a one-page list of all high-level testing activities) and detailed test-case scenarios to test the code with. Test-case scenarios should list specific, and systematic, test steps that you can perform on the application, along with expected results. Consider the following items when devising test scenarios:

■ Application requirements—Tests to make sure the application satisfies the original functional requirements. Tests should include getting user (or customer) feedback on how closely the application functions to their original requirements. Users' knowledge of the underlying model for the application should lead to identification and correction of many logical errors caused by the implementation of incorrect business rules.

■ Design requirements—Tests to make sure the application conforms to its proposed design. Tests should include getting feedback from the application designers on how closely the application follows their design. These tests can also identify potential flaws in the design.

- Data flow patterns—Tests to check the validity of data flow in the system, especially with respect to the design. These tests should validate the integrity of the data that is processed by your application. You need to sketch the data flow in application from input, through processing, to output, and trace how data is impacted at each phase.

- Functions—You should test each function in the application for correct functionality. These tests should validate the functionality of individual functions, irrespective of the rest of the code. The success of these tests often depends on how modular—single focused in purpose and zero dependencies—the functions are. (Note: Modular programming is explained in more detail later in this chapter under "Solid Programming Techniques.")

- Lines of code—You should test each line of code in the application for correct functionality. This can be done by stepping through each line of code and checking the results (for example, by using comments to isolate code).

- Bad data—Tests to see how the application performs when it receives bad data (for example, too little data, too much data, the wrong type of data, and the wrong size of data). These tests should also test for application behavior when there is missing required or optional data (for instance, blank data entry fields on a form). Tests should confirm the existence of error handling techniques to deal with these situations.

- Boundary analysis—Tests to see how the application performs at boundaries of data types, loops, and iterative function calls. These test should ensure that the application can correctly cope with minimum and maximum values of variable ranges, and that error handling is built for the values that it cannot handle.

- Common values—Tests to see how the application performs when given common, user-typical information. These test should ensure that the application works flawlessly for common data, since its failure to do so will impact the majority of users.

- Common errors—Tests of common or previously occurring errors to ensure they have been corrected. Tests must be run to ensure that bugs that were corrected earlier (through further development) do not reappear in a later version of the code. The most common potential cause of these types of errors is poor change management (or version control), which may require follow-up tests of those procedures to identify and correct the root cause.

- Different platforms—Tests of the application on various hardware and software platforms. The Internet consists of many users working on many different hardware (for example, Intel, Macintosh, Sun) and software (for example, Windows 3.1, Windows 95, different flavors of UNIX) platforms. Your code should be tested on as many different platforms as possible so you can understand its behavior, and, if necessary, modify it.

- Minimum configurations—Tests of the application on minimum configuration client desktops. Again, users will have different resources to access the Internet. You should test to see how much demand (for example, in terms of memory, bandwidth, processing power) your application puts on a client machine. This should help you understand what is the minimum configuration on each hardware and software platform on which your application will successfully run. The test should be developed to check for how the code will perform under the recommended minimum configurations, and how error handling for users with less than minimum configuration is handled.

- Different browsers—Tests of the application on different JavaScript-compatible browsers. These tests should help you identify how each browser handles your code, and whether the code performs consistently. If the code does not perform consistently, you may need to modify your code or write some error handling code.(Currently, the three browsers that support JavaScript are Netscape Navigator 2.0, Netscape Navigator 3.0, and Microsoft Internet Explorer 3.0.)

- HTML compatibility with old browsers—Tests of the application to ensure that the HTML file can be read by older (non–JavaScript-compatible) browsers. You should test your code with text only or older browsers to see how the lack of JavaScript compatibility impacts the user's environment: for instance, if the browser locks up or crashes, or if the page simply fails to load. Test for whether an alternative way of reading your content is available, and how effective and reliable it is.

- Reloading—Tests of the application behavior when the HTML page is reloaded. Tests to make sure that your code does not crash or behave oddly if the page is reloaded. If reloading impacts the code, tests should confirm the existence of error handling code and instructions to help the user avoid the problem.

- Resizing—Tests of the application behavior when the browser window is resized. Tests to confirm that your code does not crash or behave oddly if the page is resized. If there is an impact, your tests should confirm the existence of error handling code and instructions to help the user avoid the problem.

- Stress testing—Tests of the application behavior when many people use it at the same time. These tests can be done by either having several users, following a specific and detailed script, running your code or by setting up some type of automatic site launcher. You should monitor, record and analyze the results of all tests (including response times, and behavior glitches). You should also make note of how your code impacts the rest of your site. If necessary modify your code, and retest the impacted code.

- Lost connections—Tests of the application behavior when the Internet connection is lost or the page is stopped. Users commonly lose connection to a site or manually force a halt in data transmission. Your code must be able to cope with this fact and exit gracefully (without locking up or crashing the browser) when needed. You should test for this functionality.

> **TIP**
>
> Netscape Navigator has a built-in URL that you can use to quickly test lines of JavaScript code. In Navigator's location box, enter javascript: *JavaScript code*. (mocha: *JavaScript code* performs the same test.)
>
> For example, javascript: alert("Hello World!") displays the string Hello World in an alert() dialog box on the screen.

Solid Programming Techniques

As with any other programmers, JavaScript authors can benefit greatly from learning and using solid programming techniques to code their applications. Even though JavaScript is still too immature to have a wealth of its own material on solid coding practices, you can adopt a good set of general guidelines from proven techniques used in other (particularly object-oriented) programming languages. The following list shows some of these techniques adopted for JavaScript:

- Building code from a high-level and detailed design
- Writing modular code
- Writing strongly cohesive code
- Writing loosely coupled code
- Writing reusable code
- Writing error-handling code
- Using strong naming conventions
- Using comments
- Declaring and initializing variables

Each of the techniques listed here is briefly explained in the following sections. Be warned, however: Consistently performing such techniques proposes a stiff learning curve, not only because of the level of discipline required, but also because you might need to forget some previous bad habits and learn some new good ones!

Building Code from a High-Level and Detailed Design

Building code from a high-level and detailed design is the first step in constructing good code. A high-level design should help you identify the types of functionality required across different functions in the application. A detailed design should help you identify and name individual functions and sketch out their processes.

Good detailed design (especially if written in pseudo code) can be transformed into code and comments without too much difficulty. You should at least be able to write function and variable declarations straight from the design. Following that, you should be able to iteratively break down the rest of the detailed design and convert each section into code.

Writing Modular Code

Writing modular code means dividing your application into several individual functions (or modules), where each function performs only one task and communicates with the other functions through function calls. You gain several benefits from such modular coding:

- Reduced complexity—Each module focuses on only one task, so most modules remain simple.

- Reduced duplication—If one type of functionality occurs in several different places, the code to make that happen need only be written once (in a function).

- Reduced impact of change—You can change a commonly used functionality in only one place (the function where it resides) instead of several places.

- Increased process hiding—Implementation details of functions are hidden from other functions. This means that you can change the way a function works without changing the rest of your code (by maintaining the same interface to the function).

- Increased code reusability—You can reuse individual functions in other programs requiring the same type of functionality.

- Improved readability—Modular programming leads to simpler and more focused components in a program, which in turn makes the program more readable and easier to maintain.

Writing Strongly Cohesive Code

Cohesion relates to how closely activities in a function are related. A strongly cohesive code means that the function is almost entirely dedicated to just one purpose. The goal is to do only one thing and do it well. An example of a perfectly cohesive function is JavaScript's `Math.sqrt(value)` function. This function simply performs the square root of the value it receives as an argument and returns the result.

Strong cohesion leads to high reliability because the scope of each function is very narrowly defined and the number of tasks it performs are extremely limited.

Writing Loosely Coupled Code

Coupling relates to how closely two functions are related. Loosely coupled code means that the relations between two functions are small, visible, and direct. This provides flexibility for either function to call the other but not depend on the other for (much of) its own functionality.

Writing Reusable Code

Modular style programming, along with strong cohesion and loose coupling, provides the ideal recipe for creating reusable code. You can essentially "plug" this code (or function) into any other code to provide a known functionality. Writing reusable code has many benefits:

- High reliability—Reusable functions are proven and tested many times.
- Low cost—No need to write a new function.
- Portability—You can make code available to other platforms more easily.
- Information hiding—The internal operations of the code are hidden from calling objects.

Writing Error-Handling Code

A good program must be able to not only anticipate uncommon and erroneous events (for example, bad input data, unusual user behavior, and interruption of transfer) but also gracefully deal with them all. This is where writing good error-handling code becomes a vital issue. Error handling should be built into your code to perform at least some of the following tasks:

- Check the values of all data input from external sources. You should check for the validity of the data, including data types, value ranges, and completeness. If an error occurs, the program should discard the current data and request a new submission.
- Check the value of all function parameters. You should check the validity of data coming from other functions. In case of error, the receiving function should discard the erroneous data and send a new request to the sending function.
- Perform exceptions handling. Exceptions should be noted by the program and logged in an exceptions log. If no solution exists, the function should exit gracefully.
- Check for other important errors. If possible, the error-handling code should prevent the errors from occurring.
- Perform graceful exits. For instance, if your code crashes or the user stops the file transmission before the page is completely loaded, the browser should remain intact (that is, not lockup or crash). This can be performed by writing an error handling routine to check if the page is successfully loaded, or by opening a new browser window for your application, so if it crashes it only brings down its own window.

Using Strong Naming Conventions

Using strong naming conventions refers to using appropriate, consistent, and meaningful names for all the declarations (for example, objects, properties, methods, and variables) in your code. A strong naming convention helps to reduce your code maintenance, improve readability, increase understanding, and eliminate confusing name proliferation (calling the same thing by two different names).

You can use many variations to develop a strong naming convention in your code. Here is a sample guideline of items to identify distinctly in your code:

- Global variables
- Local variables
- Named constants
- Function names
- Function arguments

> **TIP**
>
> Use formatted compound words to enhance the meaningfulness and readability of your names. For example, use `MaximumWeight = 200` for a variable or `findHeightInMeters(Height) { ...` for a function.

Using Comments

Comments can be a very effective form of source code communication from a programmer to the rest of the world, including other programmers who might later maintain the code. As much as good comments are helpful in dramatically increasing a program's readability, bad comments can be wasteful and misleading. A certain amount of care and attention is required to write useful comments. Here are some guidelines for writing good comments:

- Include important and general program information with the source code (for example, author, date of last update, purpose of the function, and last changes). It might be the only source of documentation that is readily available or up to date.
- Write comments about the code that the source code itself cannot (easily) explain. Comments should add value so the reader can understand more than what is already apparent.
- Write comments at the level of intent of the code to explain why something is done. This means writing comments in an appropriate location (for example, right before or after a line of code) to explain the purpose of code, and not just how the code does its processing.
- Comment on global variables. What do they contain? Where do they get updated?
- Comment on unusual or hard-to-follow pieces of code. What do they do? Why are they used?

Declaring and Initializing Variables

Even though JavaScript allows you to use undeclared and uninitialized variables in your code, it is good programming practice to consistently declare and initialize your variables. Declaring variables in one common place (usually at the beginning of a function or global area) makes tracking and maintaining them relatively easy. Initializing variables assures that the variables contain the correct data type throughout the remainder of the program. (For example, if var Counter = 0;, the variable Counter is set to a numeric data type.)

CAUTION

Do not use JavaScript's reserved keywords as variable names—this results in errors. Check JavaScript's reference guide for a list of reserved keywords.

Bulletproofing Your Code

JavaScript, like other programming languages, has a few nuances—including language bugs, obscure features, and strange behavior—that you need to recognize to write really solid code. This section lists some of these oddities and describes proposed workarounds; however, because JavaScript is still an evolving language, the list is not a comprehensive one and the workarounds may well be enhanced in time. You should follow Netscape's frequent updates and bug fixes and online JavaScript discussion groups (such as Usenet's comp.lang.javascript newsgroup) for the latest information.

To bulletproof your code, pay attention to the following:

- Make sure the variable a window object is assigned to is not null before it is used. A null value means that that window object does not exist.

- If the Onload event handler loads prematurely when you're loading forms on multiple frames, use window.setTimeout() to test for the existence of form elements first. If they exist, run the original script intended to run on Onload.

- The on event handlers (onLoad, onClick, onFocus, and so on) sometimes cause memory leaks, which brings the system to a crawl over multiple reloads of the page. In other words, the on event handlers sometimes take browser memory but do not release it. This is a JavaScript bug—it most commonly occurs on the Windows 3.1 platform—that Netscape is aware of, and is working to fix. In the meantime, to reduce the chance of this occurring, try to avoid using on event handlers if you can. When you do use them, make sure to advise users to close unnecessary open applications if they run into memory problems.

- Divide long strings into multiple, concatenated shorter strings. JavaScript has a limitation of 250 characters for strings. Shorter, concatenated strings also make your code more readable and its maintenance easier.

- To make sure a variable contains string data type, preappend a null string (`" "`) to the assignment expression. For example, `calculatedTotal = " " + TotalPrice` is treated as a string.

- Netscape currently has a bug in dealing with JavaScript's `document.close()` method. The browser crashes if you call this method while the browser is still loading a page. To correct this problem, use `window.setTimeout()` to check if the whole document is completely loaded, before executing `document.close()`.

- If reloading the HTML page does not seem to show your JavaScript code changes, try to reopen the file. This clears the browser's memory and loads the latest version of your code. If this does not seem to cure the problem (particularly when using frames), exit from the browser and restart.

- To load multiple functions from one on event, `onLoad`, you can use either of two techniques:

  `onLoad = "function one(); function two(); function three();"`

  `onLoad = "function multipleFunction();"`

  `function multipleFunction()` represents a function that calls several other functions.

- If you use the `document.write` method to generate HTML pages (or page elements), make certain to include the `HEIGHT` and `WIDTH` attributes on all generated `IMG` and `EMBED` tags. Otherwise, the browser crashes as the HTML layout is delayed by the unsized images, or plug-ins. This is a known JavaScript bug, and Netscape is currently working on fixing it.

- Do not use JavaScript's `Math.random()` method for generating random numbers. This method does not currently work consistently across different platforms. To generate random numbers, you should either make up your own routine (such as `RandomOneToTen=today.getSeconds() %10;`) or use some of the freely available randomizer functions available on the Internet. For instance, try the Central Randomizer at `http://www.msc.cornell.edu/~houle/mcwtkym/randomizer.html`. This good JavaScript randomizer seems to work on all versions and platforms of Netscape Navigator.

Summary

This chapter introduced you to the three types of JavaScript error—syntax, runtime, and logic—and described common JavaScript error messages and their possible causes.

You also looked at ways of fixing your code, including specific things and places to look for, and techniques for identifying the errors. In addition, I discussed a systematic approach for testing your code, consisting of a test plan and detailed test scenarios, including specific items to consider in creating detailed test scenarios.

I also showed you ways of building more preventative control in your code (so you spend less time debugging!) by discussing proven techniques for writing solid and maintainable code. These techniques will, in the long-run, save you many hours of work, and help you write better code.

To wrap up, I briefly covered some of current nuances (bugs) of JavaScript and how you can avoid them to truly bulletproof your code.

Working with Netscape Plug-Ins

by Jimmy Nasr

IN THIS CHAPTER

Internet browsers, even Netscape Navigator, natively support content from only a few file formats (or data types), such as text and images. In order to do their work in the world outside the Web browser, however, people regularly use many other file formats as required by their various desktop applications to perform different tasks. For instance, most word processing applications have their own native file format (such as Microsoft Word's .doc file format), as do spreadsheet applications, presentation applications, multimedia applications, and so on. If the Web browser supports these various file formats, you can make a great deal of content readily available for communication on the Web, not to mention open up the Internet to new and exciting ways of presenting information. For Netscape (or any other company) to build native support into their browser for all the useful file formats, however, is impractical due to the costs, time, and expertise that would be required. Netscape, though, does provide another solution: *plug-ins*.

This chapter discusses in detail Netscape Navigator plug-ins and their interaction with JavaScript and the newest Netscape client-side development technology, LiveConnect, as outlined in the following sections:

- Understanding plug-in technology
- Plug-ins and MIME types
- Available plug-ins
- Determining installed plug-ins with JavaScript
- Running plug-ins with JavaScript
- LiveConnect

Understanding Plug-In Technology

The concept of add-in programs for desktop applications is a good analogy for Netscape's plug-ins. Some applications, such as Microsoft Excel, Microsoft Access, or Adobe Photoshop, enable you to extend their functionality by installing an add-in program (which is often written by third-party vendors). For instance, an add-in program in Excel might help you perform more extensive statistical analysis than would be otherwise available.

Similarly, Netscape has developed and made openly available an API (Application Programming Interface) that helps third-party developers extend the functionality of the Navigator browser. Using the plug-in API, developers can develop plug-in (or mini) applications that enable the browser to understand new data types and treat them as native browser elements (such as a QuickTime movie running directly in the browser window). The browser manages the interaction of plug-ins with the user and, thus, additional plug-in functionality appears no different to the user than basic Navigator functionality.

NOTE

Plug-ins are also analogously called *inline plug-ins*. Similar to inline images, this refers to the fact that the plug-in data type can be seen in the browser window itself, without the need to run any other applications.

Some of benefits of plug-ins include the ability to:

- Extend the capabilities of the Web browser to read more data types.

- Decrease time and effort involved in content creation by enabling Web authors to use already available content of various file formats.

- Increase the reach and functionality of the Internet by enabling users to view and manipulate content in a format specific to their needs (such as spreadsheets).

- Make Web content more dynamic and exciting (through the use of multimedia to enhance the message, for example, or by dynamically changing the layout of the screen).

- Reduce demand on the Web server. After the initial load of the Web page, many of the tasks now commonly done through the server (using CGI programming) can be done on the client through plug-ins and other client-side technologies.

- Reduce demand on bandwidth. Less server activity should reduce demand on the bandwidth required, meaning that more users (especially on slow dial-up links) can access and enjoy the Web pages.

Third-party developers develop plug-ins for Navigator with the help of Netscape's plug-in Software Development Kit (SDK). The SDK contains tools, documentation, samples, and header files to help develop plug-ins for all operating system platforms that Netscape supports.

Completed plug-ins are either bundled in Navigator (see Navigator 3.0 notes later) or posted on the plug-in's developers' site.

RESOURCE

Netscape has a common page, http://home.netscape.com/comprod/products/navigator/version_2.0/plugins/index.html, that categorizes, lists, describes, and provides a link to all currently available Navigator plug-ins. Once the plug-in is downloaded, it must be installed and configured properly before use—which usually requires no more than choosing the right installation directory and following simple on-screen instructions.

Plug-Ins Versus Helper Applications

As opposed to *plug-ins*, which help Navigator run new data types inside its window, *helper applications* are external programs, which the Navigator can open if it comes across a file type that it cannot open by itself. For instance, if there is no plug-in for AVI (Microsoft's video compression format) files, or the calling HTML file does not explicitly require the AVI file to be opened inside the browser, the browser opens a new application, such as MediaPlayer, to view the file. (Opening the AVI file inside the browser, using an EMBED tag, is explained in detail in the section "LiveVideo," under "Plug-ins with Netscape 3.0," later in this chapter.)

You can set up helper applications through Navigator's Options Menu Choose Options | General Preferences Helpers. At this panel (see Figure 23.1), you define which local applications you want to use to open the various data types already registered with the browser. You can also add new data types to the registered list and associate them with available helper applications.

FIGURE 23.1.

Netscape Navigator's Helper Application setup window.

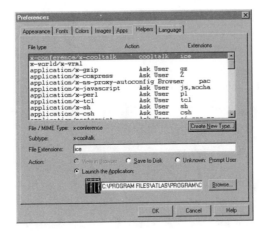

Helper applications have three attributes that describe them:

- File type: This defines the MIME (Multi-purpose Internet Mail Extensions) type supported. The MIME type helps the helper application understand the format of the file. MIME is explained in more detail in the section "Plug-Ins and MIME Types," later in this chapter.

- Action: This identifies the action to be performed when this data type (or MIME type) is encountered. This action is commonly either opening a helper application to read the file or showing a prompt to interactively ask the user.

- File extensions: This identifies the file extension that conforms to a particular data type.

Plug-ins are, for all intents and purposes, a replacement technology for helper applications, since helper applications perform a similar functionality; but in comparison, they have several problems that deter from their usage, including:

- Once a helper application is started, the browser loses control of the environment—in other words, the helper application becomes the foreground process. This can potentially lead to user confusion (user "losing" the browser window). Plug-ins, however, are an integrated part of the browser environment, and extend the number and type of files that it can handle.

- Helper applications stay resident in memory until the user manually exits from the application (and sometimes even that does not totally clean it up). This can lead to possible browser lockups and inefficiencies. Plug-ins, however, are loaded into memory when the page calling the plug-in data type is called, and are unloaded when the browser exits that page.

- Helper applications need to be manually configured. This can often be confusing and require special knowledge. Most plug-ins have very simple installation and require no further configuration.

- Helper applications are sometimes big and expensive desktop applications. Plug-ins are commonly cheap (or free) and smaller applications.

TIP

Use Netscape's built-in URL to check what plug-ins are installed on your client.

Go to Navigator's location box, and enter about:plugins.

To understand the practical difference between plug-ins versus helper applications, follow these two examples:

Example 1: Read a Microsoft Word file called agenda.doc inside the browser, using the INSO Corporation's "QuickView Plus" plug-in. The HTML code to do this is shown in Listing 23.1, followed by the resultant browser window. (See Figure 23.2.)

NOTE

You can download INSO Corporation's "QuickView Plus" from: http://www.inso.com/consumer/qvp/demo.htm.

Listing 23.1. plugin.htm.

```html
<html>
<head>
<title>Plugin Demo -- Word File Displayed with QuickView Plus</title>
</head>

<body>
<center><h1>Plugin Demo</h1></center>
<p><i>Show Word File below if Plug-in is installed</i></p>
<embed src="agenda.doc" height=500 width=640></embed>

</body>
</html>
```

FIGURE 23.2.

This shows the Word document opened inside the browser window with the use of a plug-in.

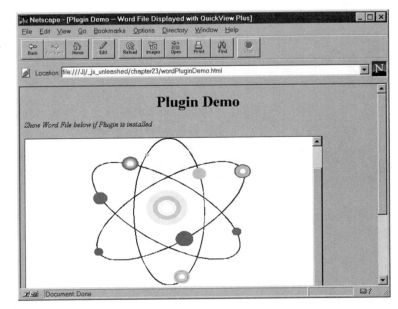

In this case, the QuickView Plus plug-in is already installed and registered to open doc files. So the browser (reading from the EMBED tag attributes) opens up an inline window of size 500 by 640 and displays the doc file. This Microsoft Word file is now viewable within the boundaries of the browser. The browser does not lose control.

Example 2: Read the same Microsoft Word file using a helper application. The code is shown in Listing 23.2, followed by the resultant helper application window, in this case Microsoft Word itself. (See Figure 23.3).

Listing 23.2. `helper.htm`.

```html
<html>
<head>
<title>Helper App Demo -- Word File opened with Word</title>
</head>

<body>
<center><h1>Plugin Demo</h1></center>
<p><i>Open the agenda file by clicking <A HREF="agenda.doc">here</a></i></p>

</body>
</html>
```

FIGURE 23.3.

This shows the Word document opened with Microsoft Word as the helper application.

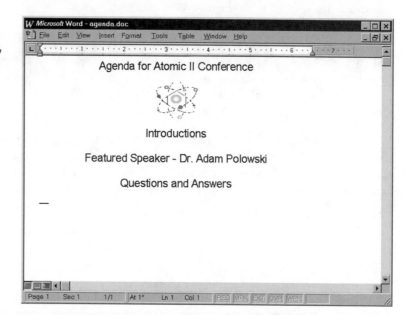

In this case the browser no longer has control; once you are done reading the file in Word, you must manually go back to the browser to continue.

Plug-Ins and MIME Types

Plug-ins rely on MIME types to identify the data type being passed to them; by identifying the data type, the plug-in can figure out how to handle the data. MIME is an Internet standard that defines how file formats, except plain text, can be passed in Internet mail messages. (See Internet Request For Comment, RFCs 1521 and 1522 for complete detail.) The impetus for this standard came from the fact that people wanted to exchange more than just plain text documents through e-mail. MIME now allows Internet e-mail applications to view formatted text, attachment files, and various other data types that can help to enhance the message. The MIME standard can handle any file format created thus far, including: text, PostScript, image, sound, video, compressed files, and so on.

MIME types define the content type and the specific *subtype* of different file formats. This can be best explained with an example:

The MIME type for (Microsoft audio) WAV files is defined as audio/x-wav. The first half of this definition, audio, describe the broader content type or category of files supported. The second half of the definition, x-wav, describes the specific file type (or sub-type) supported, as required by the browser to interpret WAV files.

> **NOTE**
>
> An x before the subtype (as in audio/x-wav) indicates that this is a proposed MIME standard, which is probably not yet widely accepted.

When Navigator is started, it scans its plug-ins directory and assigns a given MIME type to an appropriate plug-in that can read it; if multiple installed plug-ins support the MIME type, only the first plug-in that Navigator encounters is assigned to handle it. Once a MIME type is encountered, Navigator loads the assigned (or registered) plug-in into memory, and the MIME type is handled by the plug-in. The MIME type may be displayed in one of three ways:

- As an inline image. Displays on the page along with other content. The specific size of the plug-in is determined from values of the preset HEIGHT and WIDTH parameters.
- Full page. The plug-in covers all of the navigator window, excluding the toolbars.
- Hidden. The plug-in is run in the background (as it is with some audio plug-ins).

> **NOTE**
>
> A plug-in might be able to handle one or more MIME types (such as INSO Corporation's QuickView Plus plug-in, which provides support for more than 200 file formats). However, two plug-ins cannot be used to handle the same MIME type; only the first compatible plug-in encountered by the browser will be assigned to that MIME type.

Available Plug-Ins

As plug-ins have become more widely accepted, the number of commercial and in-house (primarily used on intranets) plug-ins has skyrocketed. There are currently over 130 commercial, and thousands of in-house, plug-ins available for Netscape Navigator, and more are being developed every week.

Third-party plug-ins designed to work with Netscape Navigator cover a wide range of functionality from multimedia and graphics to business applications and utilities. These plug-ins can be roughly divided into five types (or categories). In the following few pages, I discuss specific examples of each plug-in category, including details of their functionality and where you can download them from.

Types of Plug-Ins

Netscape plug-ins can be roughly divided into the following five categories:

- 3-D and Animation
- Audio and Video
- Image Viewers
- Presentations
- Business and Utilities

Netscape has close to a hundred different plug-ins, with more added almost every day. You should check Netscape's Plug-ins page (`http://home.netscape.com/comprod/products/navigator/version_2.0/plugins`) for a complete and up-to-date listing. Following are some examples of each of plug-in category.

3-D and Animation

Cosmo Player by Silicon Graphics

Cosmo Player is a VRML 2.0 plug-in that lets you view 3-D content, and includes sensors, scripts, and sound. Download from

`http://www.sgi.com/cosmoplayer`

FutureSplash by FutureWave

This is a vector-based animation plug-in that displays animated graphics and drawings on a browser window in real time. FutureSplash files are very small in size, which makes them practical even on low speed dial-up links. Download from

`http://www.futurewave.com`

mBED by mBED Software

This plug-in lets you build interactive multimedia Web content that can be scripted in simple text files. Download from

`http://www.mbed.com`

Shockwave for Director by Macromedia

The Shockwave plug-in lets you interact with Macromedia Director presentations inside the Navigator window. Macromedia Director provides an integrated platform for developing sophisticated and interactive multimedia presentations and applications. Download from

```
http://www.macromedia.com
```

Sizzler by Totally Hip

This plug-in lets you simultaneous view and interact with Web pages while streaming animation is delivered over the Web—you do not have to wait for the file to be completely downloaded before viewing it. Download from

```
http://www.totallyhip.com
```

VR Scout VRML by Chaco Communications

This plug-in implements VRML 1.0, and lets you view 3-D graphical scenes. Download from

```
http://www.chaco.com
```

Audio and Video

CoolFusion by Iterated Systems

This is an AVI (Video for Windows) plug-in that lets you view AVI files as an inline object. Download from

```
http://www.iterated.com/CoolFusion
```

Crescendo by Liveupdate

Crescendo is a music plug-in that delivers higher quality stereo MIDI music to the Web. Download from

```
http://www.liveupdate.com
```

InterVU MPEG Player by InterVU

InterVU MPEG Player is an MPEG video plug-in that enables MPEG video to be played on a Web page, without specialized MPEG hardware or proprietary video servers. Download from

```
http://www.intervu.com
```

RapidTransit by Fastman

This plug-in decompresses and plays music that has been compressed up to 40 times (40:1 ratio). Download from

```
http://www.monsterbit.com/rapidtransit/RTPlayer.html
```

RealAudio by Progressive Networks

This plug-in delivers customizable, on-demand, and real-time audio over the Internet, and works effectively even on low speed dial-up connections. Download from

```
http://www.realaudio.com
```

ToolVox by Voxware

ToolVox enables you to add speech audio to your Web pages and still keep the file sizes small through significant compression (as much as 53:1). Download from

```
http://www.voxware.com
```

VDOLive by Vdonet

This plug-in delivers compressed video images to the Web page—without compromising quality on the receiving end—by determining the frames per second video delivery rate on the speed of the Internet connection. Download from

```
http://www.vdo.net
```

Image Viewers

CMX Viewer by Corel

This graphic plug-in lets you view vector graphics online. Download from

```
http://www.corel.com/corelcmx
```

DWG/DXF by Softsource

This plug-in lets you dynamically view AutoCAD (DWG) and DXF drawings over the Web. You can also pan and zoom a drawing, and hide and display layers. Download from

```
http://www.softsource.com
```

Fractal Viewer by Iterated Systems

This plug-in lets you use inline fractal (highly compressed digitized photographs and other bitmap images) images on the Web. Download from

```
http://www.iterated.com/fracview
```

Keyview for Windows by FTP Software

This plug-in enables you to view, print and convert up to 200 different file formats on a Web page. Download from

```
http://www.ftp.com
```

WHIP by Autodesk

This plug-in lets you view, send, and share 2-D vector data and design content over the Internet. Download from

```
http://www.autodesk.com
```

Presentations

ASAP Webshow by Software Publishing Corporation

This plug-in is a presentation viewer for viewing, downloading, and printing graphically rich reports and presentations from the Web. Download from

```
http://www.spco.com
```

Astound Web Player by Gold Disk

This plug-in enables you to run Astound presentations (including sound, animation, graphics, video, and interactivity) online. Each slide is downloaded in the background while you view the current slide. Download from

```
http://www.golddisk.com/awp
```

Powerpoint Animation Player and Publisher by Microsoft

This plug-in enables you to view Powerpoint presentations online. Download from

```
http://www.microsoft.com/mspowerpoint/internet/player
```

Business and Utilities

Acrobat Reader by Adobe

This plug-in lets you view, navigate, and print Portable Document Format (PDF) files from a Navigator window. PDF files are small, format-rich, and print-ready documents that can be used for publishing format-sensitive material online. Download from

```
http://www.adobe.com/acrobat
```

Carbon Copy/Net by Microcom

This plug-in lets you remotely control another PC over the Internet (including running applications, and viewing or editing documents). Download from

```
http://www.microcom.com
```

Concerto by Alpha Software

The Concerto plug-in enables you to do form data-entry (including supporting validation rules) online. It can also be used to connect to any existing CGI script used to process a Web-based form. Download from

```
http://www.alphasoftware.com
```

Formula One/Net by Visual Components

This is an Excel-compatible spreadsheet plug-in with built-in Internet functionality (including live charts, links to URLs, calculations, and clickable buttons). Download from

```
http://www.visualcomp.com
```

Ichat Plug-In by Ichat

This plug-in integrates Internet chat capability directly into Netscape Navigator. Download from

```
http://www.ichat.com
```

Isys HindSite by Isys/Odyssey Development

This plug-in remembers everywhere you have been and everything you have seen on the Internet. HindSite indexes and saves the text content of all Web pages visited during a (preset) timeframe, and lets you perform full-text searches on that content. Download from

```
http://www.isysdev.com
```

Look@Me by Farallon

This plug-in enables you to view, in real time, another Look@Me user's screen anywhere in the world. Download from

```
http://www.farallon.com
```

Openscape by Business@Web

The Openscape plug-in delivers OLE/OCX compatibility and enterprise application development to the Web, by making use of a visual drag and drop development environment and Visual Basic scripting. Download from

```
http://www.busweb.com
```

Pointcast Network by Pointcast

This plug-in provides a free service that broadcasts customizable news (current events, weather, sports, and so on) to the computer screen; it can also be configured as a screen saver. Download from

```
http://www.pointcast.com
```

QuickView Plus by INSO Corporation

This plug-in lets you view, copy, print, and manage—in original format—more than 200 file types from the Navigator window. Download from

```
http://www.inso.com
```

Plug-Ins with Netscape Navigator 3.0

Netscape Navigator 3.0 includes four new built-in plug-ins that enable you to embed rich content in Web documents and have them immediately and conveniently available to a very large proportion of Internet users.

Navigator 3.0's built-in plug-in consists of

- **LiveAudio**—plug-in to play audio files in WAV, AIFF, AU and MIDI formats.
- **LiveVideo**—plug-in to play AVI video files.
- **QuickTime**—plug-in to play QuickTime movies.
- **Live3D**—plug-in to display VRML (Virtual Reality Markup Language) content.

Source files for these plug-ins can be declared as inline objects in the browser window with an EMBED tag in the HTML file. Each plug-in has its own set of EMBED parameters (such as HEIGHT and WIDTH) that help define its specific characteristics. Some parameters are common among all four plug-ins, but many are different. These four plug-ins—including their control parameters, other unique characteristics, and some examples—are discussed in the remainder of this section.

LiveAudio

LiveAudio plays audio files in WAV, AIFF, AU, and MIDI formats. Here is the HTML syntax you need in order to use an inline LiveAudio plug-in object:

```
<EMBED SRC= [URL] ...>
```

The EMBED attributes include:

- SRC=[URL]—the URL (location) of the source audio file.
- AUTOSTART=[TRUE¦FALSE]—TRUE means the file begins playing automatically when the Web page is loaded. The default is FALSE.
- LOOP=[TRUE¦FALSE¦INTEGER]—TRUE means the audio file plays continuously until the stop button is pressed on the console or the user goes to another page. FALSE means the sound will play only once. INTEGER indicates the number of times the sound repeats.

■ CONTROLS=[CONSOLE¦SMALLCONSOLE¦PLAYBUTTON¦PAUSEBUTTON¦ STOPBUTTON¦VOLUMELEVER]—this defines which view (or control) to display for the plug-in. The default is CONSOLE.

CONSOLE—consists of Play, Pause, Stop, and Volume.

SMALLCONSOLE—consists of Play, Stop, and Volume. This view has smaller buttons than standard CONSOLE buttons, and the sound will "auto-start" by default.

PLAYBUTTON—play button to start a sound.

PAUSEBUTTON—pause button to pause a sound.

STOPBUTTON—stop button to stop and unload a sound file.

VOLUMELEVER—lever to adjust playback volume.

■ STARTTIME=[MINUTES:SECONDS]—gives you the option to identify where in the audio file you would like to begin playback. (Implemented only on Windows 95, NT, and Macintosh.)

■ ENDTIME=[MINUTES:SECONDS]—gives you the option to identify where in the audio file you would like to end playback. (Implemented only on Windows 95, NT, and Macintosh.)

■ VOLUME=[0-100]—0 represents no volume, and 100 represents maximum volume. If MASTERVOLUME (see the NAME attribute) is not used, this number sets the volume for the system. The default volume level is the client system's current volume level.

■ WIDTH=[# PIXELS]—represents the width of the inline object. Default is WIDTH=144 for a standard console.

■ HEIGHT=[# PIXELS]—represents the height of the inline object. Default is HEIGHT=60 for a standard console.

■ ALIGN=[TOP¦BOTTOM¦CENTER¦BASELINE¦LEFT¦RIGHT¦TEXTTOP¦MIDDLE¦ABSMIDDLE¦ ABSBOTTOM]—tells the browser how to align text around the plug-in object.

■ HIDDEN=[TRUE]—TRUE means that the control console will not be displayed, and the sound is played in the background.

■ NAME=[UNIQUE NAME TO GROUP CONTROLS TOGETHER SO THAT THEY CONTROL ONE SOUND]—sets a unique ID for a group of CONTROLS elements, so they all act on the same sound as it plays. For example, if you want to control one sound with two inline objects (say, PLAYBUTTON and STOPBUTTON), you must use MASTERSOUND to tell LiveAudio which of the two object tags (in EMBED) contains the sound file that you want to control. The EMBED(s) with no MASTERSOUND tag are ignored by LiveAudio.

■ MASTERSOUND—must be used when grouping sounds together in a NAME group. This tells LiveAudio which file is the real sound file to play, and to ignore any stub file. Stub files are necessary to activate LiveAudio.

23

WORKING
WITH NETSCAPE
PLUG-INS

The following example demonstrates some features of this plug-in, as you can see in Figure 23.4. The HTML code is shown in Listing 23.3.

Listing 23.3. `lvaudio.htm`.

```
<HTML>
<HEAD>
<TITLE>LiveAudio Plug-in</TITLE>
</HEAD>

<BODY BGCOLOR="#ffffff">
<CENTER><H1>LiveAudio Plug-in Demo</H1>

<FONT SIZE=+1>Show me a standard console at default size</FONT>
<BR>
<EMBED SRC="youmight.wav" CONTROLS=console HEIGHT=60 WIDTH=144>
<BR>
<BR>
<FONT SIZE=+1>Show me a small console at default size</FONT>
<BR>
<EMBED SRC="youmight.wav" CONTROLS=smallconsole HEIGHT=15 WIDTH=144>
<BR>
<BR>

<!-- Set up my own ControlPanel in a table, using a PLAYBUTTON, PAUSEBUTTON,
➥ STOPBUTTON and VOLUMELEVER. Set these controls to their default sizes. -->


<FONT SIZE=+1>Show MY OWN CONTROL PANEL</FONT>
<BR>
<TABLE BORDER=5>
<TR>
<TD ALIGN=center><B>Play</B></TD>
<TD ALIGN=center><B>Pause</B></TD>
<TD ALIGN=center><B>Stop</B></TD>
<TD ALIGN=center><B>Volume</B></TD>
</TR>
<TR>
<TD><EMBED SRC="youmight.wav" AUTOSTART=true volume=80 CONTROLS=playbutton
➥ NAME="ControlPanel" MASTERSOUND HEIGHT=22 WIDTH=37></TD>
<TD><EMBED SRC="youmight.wav" CONTROLS=pausebutton NAME="ControlPanel"
➥ HEIGHT=22 WIDTH=37></TD>
<TD><EMBED SRC="youmight.wav" CONTROLS=stopbutton NAME="ControlPanel"
➥ HEIGHT=22 WIDTH=37></TD>
<TD><EMBED SRC="youmight.wav" CONTROLS=volumelever NAME="ControlPanel"
➥ HEIGHT=20 WIDTH=74></TD>
</TR>
</TABLE>

</center>
</body>
</html>
```

You can see the result of this code in Figure 23.4.

FIGURE 23.4.

This demonstrates several inline LiveAudio objects.

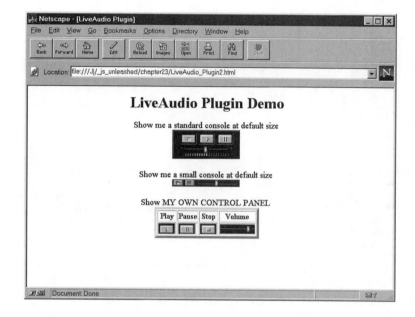

LiveVideo

LiveVideo plays video files in AVI (Video for Windows) format. Here is the HTML syntax you need to use an inline LiveVideo plug-in object:

```
<EMBED SRC= [URL] ...>
```

The EMBED attributes include:

- SRC=[URL]—the URL (location) of the source video file.

- AUTOSTART=[TRUE¦FALSE]—TRUE means the AVI file begins playing automatically when the Web page is loaded. The default is FALSE.

- LOOP=[TRUE¦FALSE]—TRUE means the movie file plays continuously until the user clicks on the movie or goes to another page. FALSE means the movie will only play once.

- WIDTH=[# PIXELS]—represents the width of the movie. Standard sizes include 120, 160, 240, 320, and 640 pixels. WIDTH usually has a 4:3 ratio with HEIGHT.

- HEIGHT=[# PIXELS]—represents the height of the movie. Standard sizes include 90, 120, 180, 240, and 480 pixels. HEIGHT usually has a 3:4 ratio with WIDTH.

- ALIGN=[TOP¦BOTTOM¦CENTER¦BASELINE¦LEFT¦RIGHT¦TEXTTOP¦MIDDLE¦ABSMIDDLE¦ABSBOTTOM]—tells the browser how to align text around the plug-in object.

The following example demonstrates some features of this plug-in, as you can see in Figure 23.5. The HTML code is shown in Listing 23.4.

Listing 23.4. `lvvideo.htm`.

```
<HTML>
<HEAD>
<TITLE>LiveVideo Plug-in</TITLE>
</HEAD>

<BODY BGCOLOR="#ffffff">
<CENTER><H1>LiveVideo Plug-in Demo</H1></center>

<FONT SIZE=+1>Display my inline video</FONT>
<BR>
<BR>
<EMBED SRC="machines.avi" HEIGHT=240 WIDTH=320 AUTOSTART=TRUE
➥ ALIGN=right LOOP=true>
This demonstrates how you can display an AVI movie right on the Browser
➥ window itself.Click on the movie to stop it from playing.
➥ Re-click on the movie to re-start it.
<BR>
</body>
</html>
```

You can see the result of this code in Figure 23.5.

FIGURE 23.5.

This demonstrates an inline LiveVideo object.

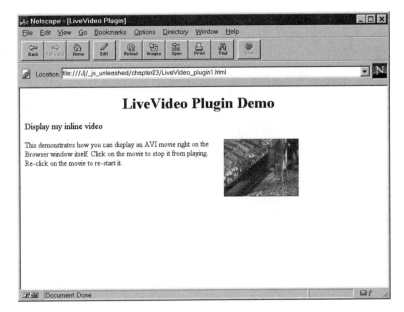

QuickTime

QuickTime plug-ins play QuickTime (MOV) files as inline objects in the browser. Here is the HTML syntax you need to use an inline QuickTime plug-in object:

```
<EMBED SRC= [URL] ...>
```

The EMBED attributes include:

- SRC=[URL]—the URL (location) of the source file.

- AUTOPLAY=[TRUE¦FALSE]—TRUE means the QuickTime movie begins playing automatically when the Web page is loaded. The default is FALSE.

- LOOP=[TRUE¦FALSE¦PALINDROME]—TRUE means the movie file plays continuously until the user clicks on the movie or goes to another page. FALSE means the movie will only play once. PALINDROME means the movie will play alternately forward and then backward. The default is FALSE.

- WIDTH=[# PIXELS]—represents the width of the movie. Standard sizes include 120, 160, 240, 320, and 640 pixels. WIDTH usually has a 4:3 ratio with HEIGHT. Do not specify a WIDTH less than 2 since this causes problems for the browser.

- HEIGHT=[# PIXELS]—represents the height of the movie. Standard sizes include 90, 120, 180, 240, and 480 pixels. HEIGHT usually has a 3:4 ratio with WIDTH. Do not specify a HEIGHT less than 2 since this causes problems for the browser.

- HIDDEN—this parameter has no other values, and causes the movie to not be visible on the page. This may be useful for sound-only movies, where there are either no pictures or the pictures need not be shown.

- CONTROLLER=[TRUE¦FALSE]—TRUE means that the movie controller is visible. Add an extra 24 to the HEIGHT parameter to display the controller. FALSE means the movie controller is not visible.

- PLUGINSPAGE=[URL]—this optional parameter lets you specify a URL to obtain the plug-in from, if it is not installed. For QuickTime plug-ins, set the URL to:

  http://quicktime.apple.com

- PLAYEVERYFRAME=[TRUE¦FALSE]—TRUE means play every frame of the movie without any skips, even if it must be played at a slower rate. The default is FALSE. Note that this parameter should not be set to TRUE if the movie has audio or MIDI tracks, since this will turn the sound off.

- HREF=[URL]—provides a link to another page if the movie is clicked on.

- TARGET=[FRAME]—this parameter is used with HREF, and identifies the FRAME (in a FRAMESET) to link to.

- PAN=[FIXED NUMBER]—this parameter lets you specify the initial pan angle, in degrees, for a QuickTime VR movie. The range of value is from 0 to 360. This parameter does not apply to a standard QuickTime movie.

- TILT=[FIXED NUMBER]—this parameter lets you specify the initial field of view (fov) angle, in degrees, for a QuickTime VR movie. The typical range of value is from 5 to 85. This parameter does not apply to a standard QuickTime movie.

- FOV=[FIXED NUMBER]—this parameter lets you specify the initial tilt angle, in degrees, for a QuickTime VR movie. The typical range of value is from −42.5 to 42.5. This parameter does not apply to a standard QuickTime movie.

■ `TILT=[INTEGER]`—this parameter lets you specify the initial node for a multinode QuickTime VR movie. This parameter does not apply to a standard QuickTime movie.

■ `CORRECTION=[NONE¦PARTIAL¦FULL]`—This parameter only applies to a QuickTime VR movie.

Live3D

Live3D plug-in displays VRML files as inline objects in the browser. The `EMBED` tag needs to be used to declare the `VRML` object, and identify its location, as shown in the next line:

```
<EMBED SRC= [URL] ...>
```

RESOURCE

For more information on this plug-in, including technical documentation and examples, refer to Netscape's Live3D page:

```
http://home.netscape.com/eng/live3d
```

Downloading a Plug-In

You will not find many shrink-wrapped (in other words, "off the shelf") plug-ins. Most plug-ins are small applications that quickly become available on the Internet, usually in beta form to begin with for the public to test and give feedback. They can be downloaded from their developers' Web sites (or other complementary sites), often at no initial charge for an evaluation period, and with a choice to purchase, at prices generally under $100.

Since there are so many plug-ins available and many more being developed, sometimes it is difficult to know what plug-in to get and how to successfully install it. Use the checklist here as a rough guideline to help you:

1. Decide what type of extra browser functionality you need (such as business, utilities, presentation, multimedia, 3-D, and so on).

2. Make sure you know the exact operating system on which you plan to install the plug-in (such as Windows 95, Windows NT, Macintosh, and so on). Plug-ins are platform-sensitive, so make sure you download the correct plug-in for your system.

3. Make sure you know the exact type and version of your browser (such as Navigator 2.02, Navigator 3.0, and so on). Certain plug-ins only work for specific versions of a browser.

4. Make sure you have a tool to decompress common format (such as `zip` or `tar`) compressed files.

5. Go to Netscape's plug-in page: `http://home.netscape.com/comprod/products/ navigator/version_2.0/plugins/index.html`. This page contains links to all available Navigator plug-ins.

6. Use the plug-in categories (such as Presentation, Business and Utilities, and so on), and the descriptions noted for each plug-in, to help you find the one that seems to best match your needs. Click on the `download` hyperlink to go to the download site.

7. Choose the appropriate download file from the potential list of available files (such as the Shockwave for Director plug-in, for Windows 95 and Netscape Navigator 2.0).

8. Make a note of any registration or licensing notes, including expiration date (if the plug-in is only as an evaluation copy). Read the installation notes.

9. Download and save the file in a local directory.

10. Decompress the file as necessary.

11. Install the plug-in (usually from the plug-in's native setup file). Make sure the plug-in installation program identifies the correct Navigator directory—the plug-in must update Navigator's registry files to ensure that Navigator is aware of its presence and its capability to support certain MIME types.

12. To verify installation, restart Navigator. At the location box enter: `about:plugins`. This lists all the plug-ins registered by Navigator.

> **CAUTION**
>
> If you have multiple copies of Navigator on your hard drive, make sure the plug-in installation program identifies the "right" browser installation to register the plug-in to. You can only register a plug-in to one browser at a time.

When Not to Use Plug-Ins

Even though plug-ins add a lot of extra functionality, there are times when you should not use them in favor of a simpler technology that still gets your message across effectively. For instance:

■ When the information can be displayed just as effectively using another (more basic) format. This, most likely, means that the Web page is more widely supported— compatible to more browsers and more reliable (less chance of browser crash). Also, in the absence of typically larger plug-in file types, the performance (download time) for the Web page is generally better.

■ When the plug-in file types increase the load on the server in such a way that the performance of the page becomes unbearably slow for a major group of users, such as those dialing in with slow modems. You should do a cost/benefit analysis to get a feel for whether it is worthwhile to persevere with the plug-ins. Do you add enough value to the content with the plug-ins to convince a user to put up with slow download times?

■ When the MIME type format is not widely accepted. This is particularly relevant for newer or customized MIME types, and generally means that the user needs to freshly download the right plug-in to read your Web content. This is an inconvenience at best since it forces the user to leave your page. Many users may not come back.

■ When the majority of the anticipated users use a software platform (such as UNIX) that is not supported by the plug-in. You need alternative techniques in this case, such as custom programming in Java, JavaScript or (server-side) CGIs.

> **CAUTION**
>
> Do not use more than one plug-in data type per Web page; doing so causes various memory problems that may lead to a browser crash. If you wish to use multiple plug-ins, put each on a different page.

Determining Installed Plug-Ins with JavaScript

Being able to determine what plug-ins are installed, and which MIME types are supported, on a client browser, opens up a number of doors to a Web page developer in terms of controlling the content passed down to the user. For instance, one development logic may be, "If the user does have the plug-in, show the page with all the relevant MIME types, or else show alternate (more basic) content." JavaScript can help you to programmatically do this, with a little help from Netscape Navigator 3.0.

Navigator 3.0 has two new built-in objects that reveal very useful information about the plug-ins and MIME types that a client browser supports. These objects are

■ `navigator.plugins`. This "navigator" object is an array of all the plug-ins currently installed on the client. This object has the following properties:

`name`: the name of the plug-in (for example, "shockwave")

`filename`: the name of the plug-in file

`description`: description about the plug-in (supplied by its vendor)

`length`: number of elements in the array

[…]: array of `mimeTypes` objects that the plug-in can read

■ `navigator.mimeTypes`. This "navigator" object is an array of all the `mimeTypes` supported on the client. This object has the following properties:

`type`: the name of the MIME type (such as `audio/x-wav`)

`description`: description of the MIME type (supplied by its vendor)

`enabledPlugin`: plug-ins that can be read this MIME type

`suffixes`: the filename extensions that the MIME type is identified by (such as WAV for MIME type `audio/x-wav`). Multiple suffixes are separated by commas

Using these new Navigator objects with JavaScript, you can quickly determine whether a plug-in has been installed and how to proceed from there.

The next example checks to see if Macromedia's "Shockwave" plug-in has been installed, and follows this logic:

■ If the required plug-in is installed, then display the embedded plug-in data type.

■ If not, then display alternative information (just a JPEG image, for example, instead of a Shockwave object).

Note that a variable is used to hold the value of the desired (or expected) plug-in:

```
var DesiredPlugin = navigator.plugins["shockwave"];
➥ // refers to NAME property of plug-ins object
if (DesiredPlugin) {
    document.write("<EMBED SRC="mymovie.dir" HEIGHT=240 WIDTH=320>");
} else {
    document.write("<IMG SRC="movietitle.jpg" HEIGHT=240 WIDTH=320>");
}
```

The `navigator.plugins` object also has a new method called `refresh`. This method causes Navigator to look for any newly installed plug-ins, and update itself accordingly. If the argument `true` is used with the `refresh` method [such as `navigator.plugin.refresh(true)`], the presence of a new plug-in will be registered without the need to exit and restart the browser.

TIP

If `navigator.plugins.refresh(true)` is used, Navigator will only reload pages that might change as a result of a plug-in update. However, by default (if the refresh method is not used) Navigator reloads all pages that contain any plug-in data types.

Using these new `navigator.mimeTypes` objects with JavaScript, you can also quickly determine whether a client supports a particular MIME type. The next example checks to see if the browser supports the `application/x-director` (for Macromedia Director movies) MIME type, and follows a similar logic to the previous example once the determination is made:

```
var DesiredMimetype = navigator.mimeType["application/x-director"];
if (DesiredMimetype) {
    document.write("<EMBED SRC="mymovie.dir"> HEIGHT=240 WIDTH=320>");
} else {
    document.write("<IMG SRC=" movietitle.jpg" HEIGHT=240 WIDTH=320>");
}
```

You can also use a simple JavaScript loop to display all MIME types supported on the client. Try this code:

```
for (i=0; i<navigator.mimeTypes.length; i++) {
    document.write(navigator.mimeTypes[i].type + "<br>");
}
```

Running Plug-Ins with JavaScript

JavaScript can be used in many creative ways to run (and otherwise manipulate) plug-ins, using the same HTML EMBED tag syntax as seen earlier. An example of this was seen in the previous section, "Determining Installed Plug-Ins with JavaScript," when a conditional JavaScript statement was used to perform either of two actions depending on whether a particular plug-in was installed. Other examples of JavaScript and plug-ins include:

- Plug-in source file manipulation. You can use JavaScript to set up, and pre-load, an array of plug-in objects to be used as source files (or URLs) for an EMBEDed object. Then use a JavaScript loop (from 1 to maximum size of the array) to step through the plug-in objects each time the page is loaded. This gives a dynamic feel to your page, and entices more repeat visits.

- Plug-in source code hiding. You can hide the HTML and JavaScript source code by creating the HTML file, including the EMBED statements, through a JavaScript .js file. Thus, use JavaScript's document.write() object to define all the HTML tags and content, and from an HTML file, simply load the JavaScript file. This user can only view the HTML source code. Note, however, that currently only Navigator 3.0 supports .js files.

> **NOTE**
>
> If you use JavaScript (js) files in your code, try to limit each js file to one narrowly defined function only. This is a good programming technique that will help you, in the long-run, to write reusable code (or JavaScript libraries).

The EMBED Tag

The HTML EMBED tag is used to insert plug-in objects into a browser window. The syntax is slightly different for each plug-in; however, you will typically find something like

```
<EMBED SRC="URL" WIDTH=integer HEIGHT=integer ...>
```

The EMBED tag is extremely flexible in that it enables you to define previously unspecified parameters to cater to the needs of a specific plug-in. For instance you can define a parameter like: MYPARAM=""this is my parameter"". This parameter can be used by any plug-in that can identify it; others will simply ignore it. This unique coding flexibility means that any plug-in (current or future) can be inserted into a Web page as an inline object, with a set of EMBED parameters of its own. There are a couple of problems with this situation, however:

- It is very difficult and time-consuming to find out all of the unique parameters of each plug-in.
- This flexibility of the EMBED tag is inconsistent with the rest of the HTML specification.

To resolve these problems (and other HTML inconsistencies across different browsers), the World Wide Web Consortium or W3C, http://www.w3.org, has proposed a *Working Draft* to introduce a new HTML tag called <OBJECT>. The OBJECT tag is to embody the role of the IMG tag; to provide a general solution for dealing with all types of new media (such as multimedia, Virtual Reality, and the like); and also to provide backward compatibility with existing browsers.

NOTE

The World Wide Web Consortium (W3C) is the group responsible for developing standards for the Web. Based at the Massachusetts Institute of Technology's Laboratory for Computer Science, W3C develops Web standards through the proposal of Internet Working Drafts. Working Drafts are then reviewed by W3C members and other interested groups; the drafts are modified and, if appropriate, declared as standards. W3C has developed the specification for every level of HTML up to the latest (HTML 3.2).

RESOURCE

You can find more information about this Working Draft from the W3C site at

http://www.w3.org/pub/WWW/TR

For now, however, this proposal is still "work in progress." You should continue using the EMBED tag until this new OBJECT tag is widely implemented on different browsers.

LiveConnect

LiveConnect is Netscape Navigator 3.0's recently announced framework to enable "live" objects—namely plug-ins, Java applets, and JavaScript—to communicate and interact together. Specifically, this family of technologies encompasses Navigator plug-ins, and also facilitates their integration with Java and JavaScript.

By promising seamless manipulation of data between Navigator's three main client-side development environments (plug-ins, Java, and JavaScript), LiveConnect potentially represents a powerful technology for Internet and intranet application development. Also importantly, it represents a viable replacement for many server-side activities, such as Common Gateway Interface (CGI) programming. This in turn should improve the functionality and performance of the Web. (See Figure 23.6.)

FIGURE 23.6.

This demonstrates how LiveConnect enables interaction between plug-ins, Java, and JavaScript.

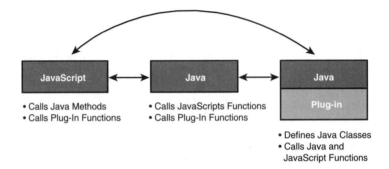

The appeal of LiveConnect is particularly high for intranet development. Typically an intranet environment is browser-homogeneous, and it offers more bandwidth—typically T1 speed for a large corporation—than is available for individuals accessing the Internet. This combination, given the predominant browser being Navigator 3.0, provides an excellent opportunity to use LiveConnect to build sophisticated client-side applications that take advantage of new media types (such as audio, video, animation, 3-D graphics, and the like) to enhance content. The homogeneity of the browsers and the significant bandwidth help to deliver rich Web content to as many people as possible and as efficiently as possible.

To get started with LiveConnect development, you need the LiveConnect/Plug-in Software Development Kit (SDK). This contains everything that you need to start LiveConnect (plug-in) development, including

- Tools
- Documentation
- Samples
- Header files

RESOURCE

You can download the SDK from Netscape's "LiveConnect and Plug-in Developer's Guide" page at

```
http://home.netscape.com/eng/mozilla/3.0/handbook/plugins/index.html
```

Some of the benefits of LiveConnect include

■ Access to more users—by integrating communication between plug-ins, Java, and JavaScript, LiveConnect enables you to reach many of the users who use or develop any of those technologies.

■ Offers more functionality—the combination of plug-ins, Java, and JavaScript working in unison offers a great opportunity to build extended functionality for your Web content.

■ Open Internet architecture—the LiveConnect SDK and plug-in API provide developers with all the tools and syntax needed to develop new Navigator plug-ins. This in turn leads to the development of helpful and exciting Web applications and plug-ins.

■ Reusable cross platform—LiveConnect will be implemented on all the platforms that Netscape currently supports. This means that in many cases code written for one platform can be reused without much modification on other platforms.

■ Millions of users have already embraced Java and JavaScript, so this technology is not brand new or untried. For instance, there are currently over 3,000 publicly registered Java applets; to see them, point your browser to the "gamelan" homepage (pronounced Gamma-lahn):

```
http://www.gamelan.com
```

The remainder of this section briefly discusses some JavaScript-related aspects of LiveConnect technology, as follows:

■ Enabling LiveConnect

■ The Java Console

■ JavaScript to Java communication

■ Java to JavaScript communication

NOTE

LiveConnect requires a good knowledge of Java, so many of the topics discussed here have been purposely left more theoretical than practical. The Java skills and understanding required to go into more examples are beyond the scope of this book. However, if you wish to pursue this topic further, the LiveConnect Software Development Kit (SDK)—available from Netscape's home page—provides you with all the necessary documentation and examples that you need to get started.

Enabling LiveConnect

LiveConnect is enabled by checking Java and JavaScript on the Network Preferences menu. Specifically:

1. Go to the Options menu.
2. Choose Network Preferences.
3. Click the Languages tab.
4. Make sure both the Java and JavaScript boxes are checked.

LiveConnect is enabled by default in Navigator 3.0.

The Java Console

You can use the Java Console to help debug a LiveConnect interaction, particularly when passing data between a Java applet and a JavaScript function. Java Console can be called up to show Java messages by using the class variables `out` or `err` in `java.lang.System`. For instance, the following Java code displays the message "Hello, world!" in the Java Console:

```
public void init() {
    System.out.println("Hello, world!");
}
```

You can show the Java Console by choosing Show Java Console from the Options menu.

JavaScript to Java Communication

LiveConnect enables JavaScript to communicate with Java in the following ways:

- Direct calls to Java methods
- Control over Java applets
- Control over Java plug-ins

Each of these methods of communication is discussed in the following section.

Direct Calls to Java Methods

If LiveConnect is enabled, you can use the following syntax to access a Java method:

```
[Packages.]packageName.className.methodName
```

Where `packageName` and `className` are properties of the object `Packages`. The name `Packages` can be optionally omitted from the JavaScript call—for Java, Sun or Netscape packages. For instance, the Java class `java.class.System` can be referred to as either `java.lang.System` or `Packages.java.lang.System`.

For example, the following JavaScript code prints a message to the Java Console:

```
var System = java.lang.System    // assign the variable system to Java class
➥java.lang.System
System.err.println("Greetings from JavaScript")
```

Control over Java Applets

To take control of a Java applet using JavaScript, you do not need to know much about the construction of the applet. The applet's public variables, methods, and properties should be sufficient to let JavaScript take over the control of the applet.

You can reference the Java applet by its name. Remember that the applet declared in the HTML page is regarded as a property of the JavaScript class `window.document`. For example, to call an applet called `myApplet`, you only need the following syntax:

```
[window.]document.myApplet
```

Declaring the top level window class is optional.

You can also refer to `myApplet` with the following two other techniques:

1. `document.applets[myApplet]` or
2. `document.applets[0]` // `myApplet` is the first applet defined on the page, hence its index number is 0 in the array of applets.

Control over Java Plug-Ins

Each plug-in on a Web page is regarded by JavaScript as an item in an array of `embeds` array. For instance, `document.embeds[0]` represents the first EMBEDed object on the page.

If the plug-in is associated with the Java class `netscape.plugin.Plugin`, its static variables and methods can be accessed in the same way as previously shown for accessing the Java applet's variables, methods, and properties. (See the section titled "Control over Java Applets.")

Java to JavaScript Communication

To access JavaScript methods, properties, and data structures from a Java applet, you must first `import` the Netscape `javascript` package. This is done with the following syntax:

```
import netscape.javascript.*
```

`netscape.javascript` defines the `JSObject` class and the `JSException` exception object. You must allow an applet to access JavaScript by declaring the `MAYSCRIPT` attribute (with no arguments) for the `APPLET` tag. This prevents an applet from accessing JavaScript on a page without the knowledge of the developer. An error occurs if the `MAYSCRIPT` attribute has not been declared.

> **TIP**
>
> Before you can access JavaScript, you must get a handle for the Navigator window. Use the `getWindow` method in the class `netscape.javascript.JSObject` to get a window handle.
>
> ```
> (e.g. winHandle = JSObject.getWindow(this)     //where winHandle is a variable
> of the type JSObject)
> ```

To access JavaScript objects and properties, you need to use the `getMember` method in the class `netscape.javascript.JSObject`. This is done by calling `getMember` to access each contained JavaScript object in turn. You must make sure to get a handle for the JavaScript window first, however (use the `getWindow` method).

You can use the `call` and `eval` methods in the class `netscape.javascript.JSObject` to call JavaScript methods. Again, use `getWindow` to get a handle for the JavaScript window, and then use `call` or `eval` to access a JavaScript method. You can use the following syntax to do this:

- `JSObject.getWindow().call("methodName", arguments)`. Where `methodName` is the name of the called JavaScript method, and `arguments` is an array of arguments to pass to the method.

- `JSObject.getWindow().eval("expression")`. Where `expression` is a JavaScript expression that evaluates to a JavaScript method.

Summary

This chapter introduced you to Netscape's plug-ins technology and explained the distinction between plug-ins, helper applications, and MIME types.

It also looked at the various types of available plug-ins (Audio/Video, 3-D Graphics, Business, and so on) and discussed some examples of each. You progressed to Netscape Navigator 3.0's new built-in plug-ins (LiveAudio, LiveVideo, QuickTime, and Live3D) and discussed the HTML syntax required to use them as embedded objects in your Web document. You continued by stepping through a checklist for downloading plug-ins, as well as discussing when not to use plug-ins.

You progressed to JavaScript techniques for determining and activating installed plug-ins, and saw sample code to find specific plug-ins or activate a plug-in object depending on the availability of a browser plug-in to support the underlying MIME type.

To wrap up, you briefly looked at Netscape's latest client-side enabling technology, called LiveConnect. LiveConnect enables client-side data manipulation and communication between JavaScript, Java, and plug-ins.

ActiveX Scripting with JavaScript

by Richard Wagner

IN THIS CHAPTER

Given JavaScript's name and Silicon Valley roots, you are perhaps much more likely to associate the language with Java than with anything that comes from Redmond. However, as you have seen in Internet Explorer 3.0, Microsoft has embraced JavaScript as a scripting language, calling their implementation JScript. As a result, Microsoft strongly supports the integration of JavaScript with its component technology, ActiveX. This chapter looks at ActiveX controls and how JavaScript can be used to trigger and respond to ActiveX events. It also looks up close at Microsoft's ActiveX Control Pad tool, which enables you to embed ActiveX controls in your HTML file.

Understanding ActiveX Controls

If *ActiveX* is a new term for you, let me try to draw two comparisons. (Depending on your background, one will probably be more applicable than the other.) If you have a Web or Java background, ActiveX controls are Microsoft's answer to Java applets, the mini-applications that can run inside a browser window. Or, if you're from a Windows database development background, think of them as the Web-equivalent to VBXs (Visual Basic controls), VCLs (Delphi components), or OCXs (OLE controls). As you will see, the actual tie with OCXs is far closer than a simple comparison.

> **NOTE**
>
> Microsoft Internet Explorer 3.0 comes with the following standard ActiveX controls:
> - Animated Button
> - Chart
> - Gradient Control
> - Label
> - New Item
> - Popup Menu
> - Preloader
> - Stock Ticker
> - Timer

The term *ActiveX* is relatively new, but the technology behind ActiveX controls is not. Before Microsoft decided that ActiveX was a much better marketing term, essentially the same controls were called OCXs. ActiveX controls are built on top of OLE technology that has been available for several years. However, it should be noted that ActiveX controls have less overhead than a standard OLE control. Because an ActiveX control is never linked or embedded in the same way a Word document is, part of the OLE technology is removed from an ActiveX control. The result is a component that is quicker and has less of a footprint.

> **RESOURCE**
>
> There is an extensive array of information available on the Microsoft Web site, along with a substantial number of downloads.
>
> *ActiveX Resource Area* (`http://www.microsoft.com/activex/`) is the best online source of technical information about ActiveX controls.
>
> *ActiveX Gallery* (`http://www.microsoft.com/activex/controls/`) is a display of hundreds of ActiveX controls and demos.
>
> *ActiveX Directory* (`http://www.microsoft.com/internet/`) is a listing of available ActiveX controls.
>
> *Control Freaks* (`http://www.microsoft.com/devonly/community/cbisv_6.htm`) showcases some third party ActiveX controls.

Java's principal *raison d'etre* is portability across all operating environments. In contrast, ActiveX controls' primary selling point is compatibility with the dominant desktop operating system in the market—Windows 95 and Windows NT. This compatibility is demonstrated in that the same ActiveX controls that you use in a Web page can be used by any Windows application or development tool that can work with OCXs. The rationale is that because most Web users are already using Windows, ActiveX controls are a natural extension from their desktop on the Web. Having said that, it should also be noted that Microsoft has publicly stated that it is working on a port of ActiveX to both UNIX and Macintosh environments.

> **RESOURCE**
>
> One of the best third party Web sites with ActiveX information is hosted by Innovision at `http://www.active-x.com`.

Currently, Microsoft Internet Explorer 3.0 or higher is the only browser providing direct support for ActiveX controls. NCompass does have an ActiveX Plug-In that allows Netscape Navigator 2.01 or above to run them. Because ActiveX controls are currently specific to the Windows platform, however, only the Win32 versions of Netscape Navigator support this plug-in.

> **RESOURCE**
>
> NCompass has an ActiveX Plug-In available. Download from `http://www.ncompasslabs.com/binaries/index.htm` to run ActiveX under Netscape Navigator 2.01, 2.02, or 3.0. Of course, because you are using ActiveX, you can only run within Windows 95 or NT 4.0.

As shown in Figure 24.1, ActiveX controls use a different distribution paradigm than Java. A Java applet downloads onto your computer each time you access a page to which it is linked. An ActiveX control is also downloaded to a client machine, where it is automatically installed in the windows\system folder of the client and then run. Rather than downloading the ActiveX over and over (as you would with Java), each successive hit on the page simply activates the ActiveX that is local to the client.

Figure 24.1.

Working with an ActiveX control.

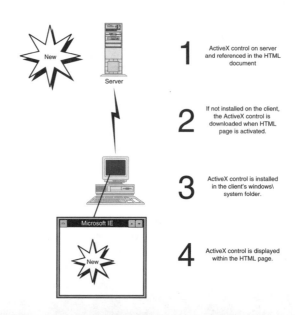

1 ActiveX control on server and referenced in the HTML document

2 If not installed on the client, the ActiveX control is downloaded when HTML page is activated.

3 ActiveX control is installed in the client's windows\system folder.

4 ActiveX control is displayed within the HTML page.

> **NOTE**
>
> Each ActiveX control has a Codebase property that enables you to specify one or more URLs where the ActiveX control is located on the Web. Consequently, if a user accesses a page that contains an ActiveX control that is not on the client machine, the browser automatically gets it and installs it over the Web.

Both Java and ActiveX scenarios have advantages and disadvantages, and one will likely win over the other at some point in the future. However, regardless of who will emerge as the "applet war" victor, you can be assured that JavaScript works with both of these technologies.

ActiveX Scripting is another term sported by Microsoft. Essentially the term means Microsoft's implementation of a scripting language (either VBScript or JavaScript) within Microsoft Internet Explorer. When Microsoft talks about scripting, it often does so within the context of integration with ActiveX or Java applets, hence the ActiveX Scripting moniker.

ActiveX and Security

ActiveX has the concept of digital signing built into its components. A component developer can then "brand" a digital signature onto an ActiveX control to ensure users of the origin of the software itself. This digital signature is displayed by Internet Explorer as the control is downloaded. Users get the opportunity after seeing the signature of downloading or not downloading. For controls with no digital signature, users are informed that the control is from an unknown origin and are prompted to confirm or decline the download.

> **NOTE**
>
> You can set up an "auto-approval" process with a vendor you trust so that all components from that source are automatically approved.

Embedding ActiveX Controls into HTML Pages

Once you have some ActiveX controls to work with, you are ready to actually work with them in your HTML documents. ActiveX controls can be placed into HTML source files by using the <OBJECT> tag. For those familiar with Java applets, you probably recognize that this is the same tag used to embed Java applets into a page.

> **RESOURCE**
>
> For more information about the <OBJECT> tag, you can see the World Wide Web Consortium (W3C) specification at http://www.w3.org/pub/WWW/TR/WD-object.html.

Just having the <OBJECT> tag in place is similar to having mountain climbing boots at the foot of Mount Everest; after all, putting the boots on is essential to a successful climb, but the real task is the climb itself. Although equating manually embedding an ActiveX control into HTML with climbing Mount Everest is a slight exaggeration, both processes do require firm resolve, skill, and patience. The problem with trying to manually place ActiveX controls is the information that is required to do so. Take a look at the following HTML definition for the StockTicker ActiveX control:

```
<HTML>
<HEAD>
<TITLE>New Page</TITLE>
</HEAD>
<BODY>
</B>
<OBJECT ID="iexrt1" WIDTH=213 HEIGHT=50
 CLASSID="CLSID:0CA4A620-8E3D-11CF-A3A9-00A0C9034920">
```

```
              <PARAM NAME="_ExtentX" VALUE="4509">
              <PARAM NAME="_ExtentY" VALUE="1058">
              <PARAM NAME="DataObjectName" VALUE="">
              <PARAM NAME="DataObjectNameProperty" VALUE="Name">
              <PARAM NAME="DataObjectValueProperty" VALUE="Value">
              <PARAM NAME="DataObjectRequest" VALUE="*">
              <PARAM NAME="ScrollSpeed" VALUE="220">
              <PARAM NAME="ReloadInterval" VALUE="10000">
              <PARAM NAME="ForeColor" VALUE="#9357FF">
              <PARAM NAME="BackColor" VALUE="#F70300">
              <PARAM NAME="BackColor" VALUE="-2147482633">
              <PARAM NAME="ScrollWidth" VALUE="2">
              <PARAM NAME="DataObjectActive" VALUE="2">
              <PARAM NAME="DataObjectVisible" VALUE="0">
              <PARAM NAME="OffsetValues" VALUE="10">
</OBJECT>
ODY>
</HTML>
```

Most of the definition is not hard to interpret. The ID parameter is the object identifier, the WIDTH and HEIGHT parameters define its size, and the <PARAM> tag lists the properties of the object. What is less intuitive is the CLASSID parameter. CLASSID is used to represent the 128-bit unique identifier (CLSID) of an ActiveX control. The CLSID is stored in the registry when you install an ActiveX control.

Fortunately, Microsoft has provided a solution to this problem with its ActiveX Control Pad, which consists of several components to assist you in working with ActiveX controls in your Web pages:

■ Several ActiveX UI-oriented controls, as shown in Table 24.1.

Table 24.1. ActiveX controls included with ActiveX control pad.

Control Name	Description
Microsoft Forms 2.0 Label	Standard text label
Microsoft Forms 2.0 TextBox	Standard edit box
Microsoft Forms 2.0 Combo Box	Standard combo or drop-down box
Microsoft Forms 2.0 List Box	Standard listbox
Microsoft Forms 2.0 Check Box	Standard checkbox
Microsoft Forms 2.0 Option Button	Standard radio option button
Microsoft Forms 2.0 Toggle Button	Button with on/off state
Microsoft Forms 2.0 Command Button	Standard push-button
Microsoft Forms 2.0 Tapstrip	Multi-page control with tabs
Microsoft Forms 2.0 ScrollBar	Scrollbar, can be vertical or horizontal
Microsoft Forms 2.0 Spin Button	Up/Down arrow
Microsoft Image Control	Displays progressively rendered images

Control Name	Description
Microsoft Hotspot Control	Creates clickable regions on a page
Microsoft Web Browser Control	Displays ActiveX documents

■ A no-frills text editor for basic HTML editing (see Figure 24.2)

■ Object Editor for visually embedding, sizing, and setting properties of ActiveX controls

■ Script Editor for writing JavaScript (or VBScript) code and attaching it to ActiveX control and JavaScript object events

■ 2-D (two-dimensional) visual layout editor for creating layout regions within an HTML page.

FIGURE 24.2.

ActiveX Control Pad HTML Editor.

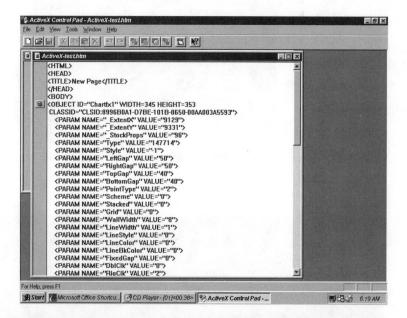

To use the Control Pad to insert a control into a document, you first need to create a new HTML document or else open an existing one in the Control Pad text editor. Then choose

Edit | Insert ActiveX Control from the menu (or right-click on the page itself) to display the Insert ActiveX Control dialog box. This dialog box, shown in Figure 24.3, lists all of the ActiveX controls that are installed on your computer.

FIGURE 24.3.

Insert ActiveX Control dialog box.

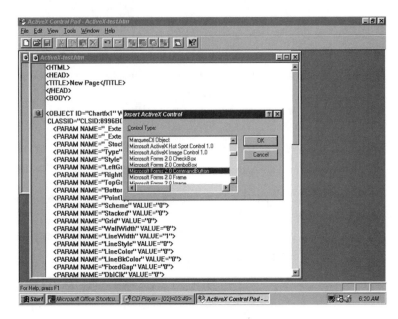

For this example, I use the Microsoft Forms 2.0 Command Button. After you select this control, the Object Editor Form is displayed (see Figure 24.4). If you have used Visual Basic or a similar tool, this editor, while rudimentary, should seem familiar to you.

RESOURCE

You can read an online ActiveX Control Pad Tutorial at http://www.microsoft.com/ workshop/author/cpad/tutorial-f.htm.

You can set the properties of the control using the properties table, or resize it using your mouse. I made a single property change, changing the Caption property to She loves me. To exit the Object Editor Form, click the close box on the form to return to the HTML text editor. The Control Pad automatically generates and inserts the <OBJECT> definition, as shown in the following code:

```
<HTML>
<HEAD>
<TITLE>New Page</TITLE>
</HEAD>
<BODY>
```

```
<OBJECT ID="CommandButton1" WIDTH=120 HEIGHT=40
 CLASSID="CLSID:D7053240-CE69-11CD-A777-00DD01143C57">
    <PARAM NAME="Caption" VALUE="Click Me">
    <PARAM NAME="Size" VALUE="2540;847">
    <PARAM NAME="FontCharSet" VALUE="0">
    <PARAM NAME="FontPitchAndFamily" VALUE="2">
    <PARAM NAME="ParagraphAlign" VALUE="3">
    <PARAM NAME="FontWeight" VALUE="0">
</OBJECT>
</BODY>
</HTML>
```

FIGURE 24.4.

Object Editor form.

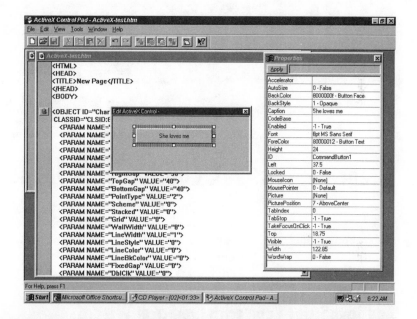

NOTE

At the time of writing, ActiveX Control Pad provided no browser integration. You, therefore, need to save the HTML file and then open it from within Internet Explorer.

Before going further, you can test the ActiveX control in Microsoft Internet Explorer. When you access the HTML document, you see the customized command button, which is shown in Figure 24.5.

FIGURE 24.5.

Customizing a Command Button control.

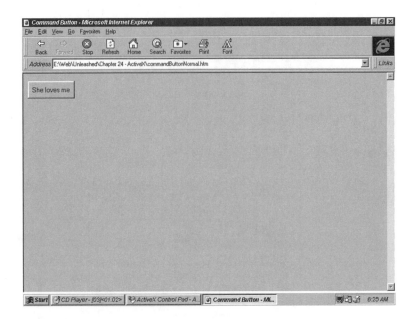

Integrating ActiveX Controls with JavaScript

Once the ActiveX control is embedded in your document, you can add JavaScript code and work with it like it's any other JavaScript object. You can set properties, respond to events, or call methods of an ActiveX control. This section looks at two ways to accomplish this. The first is through the ActiveX Control Pad's Script Wizard, and the second uses a standard editor.

Add JavaScript Code with the Script Wizard

The Microsoft ActiveX Control Pad supports both JavaScript and VBScript to allow for easy integration of ActiveX controls with HTML. The interface to scripting is done through the Script Wizard (see Figure 24.6), which is accessed by right-clicking the mouse or from choosing the Script Wizard option in the Tools menu.

RESOURCE

Part Bank (http://www.partbank.com/activex) is a site devoted to ActiveX and other software components.

FIGURE 24.6.

Script Wizard.

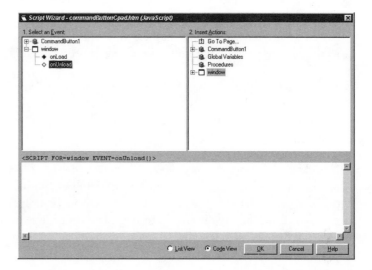

The purpose of the Script Wizard is to simplify the task of scripting as much as possible and to hide code from the script writer. Many developers may find the Script Wizard paradigm rather cumbersome, even confusing. Whether you use it or not is up to you—this book examines how to do it apart from the Script Wizard as well—but at a minimum it is helpful to use when trying to determine methods or properties available for an ActiveX control.

TIP

Before using the Script Wizard, change the default language to JavaScript by choosing Script from the Tools | Options menu and making the appropriate change in the Script Options dialog box.

The Script Wizard is divided into three parts:

- **Events**. The Script Wizard is event-centric. Therefore, when you add code, you're adding it to an event handler. The top left-hand box is used to select an event to which you want to attach an event handler. The box displays a Treeview list of the current objects with their associated events. By default, the window object always appears. If you have ActiveX controls inserted into the document, they are also in the list.

- **Actions**. Once you have selected an event, the top right-hand box is used to locate an object method or property to use in the bottom code window. By double-clicking a method (action) from the Treeview list, the method is placed, along with its associated object, in the code window. You also can define global variables or custom procedures by right-clicking the mouse and selecting the appropriate option from the pull-down menu.

■ **Code**. The bottom section is for displaying and editing JavaScript or VBScript code related to the event highlighted in the events box. You never see more than one method in this window at a time. There are two ways you can look at the script.

Code View (refer again to Figure 24.6) is the option most experienced developers will be more comfortable with. It enables you to deal with a single event handler in an editing environment apart from HTML itself. The Script Wizard is responsible for actually placing this method in the HTML document.

Intended for non-developers or those new to scripting, *List View* (see Figure 24.7) provides a higher level abstraction to ActiveX scripting. Rather than dealing with code per se, you deal with a list of objects and an associated action that is executed when an event is called. This view is limited to single line commands, such as property assignments or method calls. It cannot display, for example, if..else or while logic in List View format.

Figure 24.7.

The Script Wizard's list view.

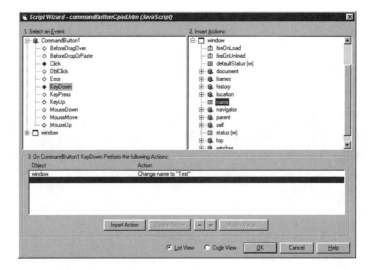

Using the Script Wizard, I can define the event handler for the command button's Click event. As an example, I use this event to change the `defaultStatus` property of the window object and the command button's caption. Figure 24.8 shows the code in the Script Wizard. After I add another example event handler—this time to the window's `onLoad` event—you can see how the JavaScript code is displayed in the HTML text editor. (See Figure 24.9.)

You should immediately notice that the ActiveX Control Pad treats each event handling method as a separate script. (Whether you like that formatting style depends on your personal taste.)

FIGURE 24.8.

Creating an event handler in the Script Wizard.

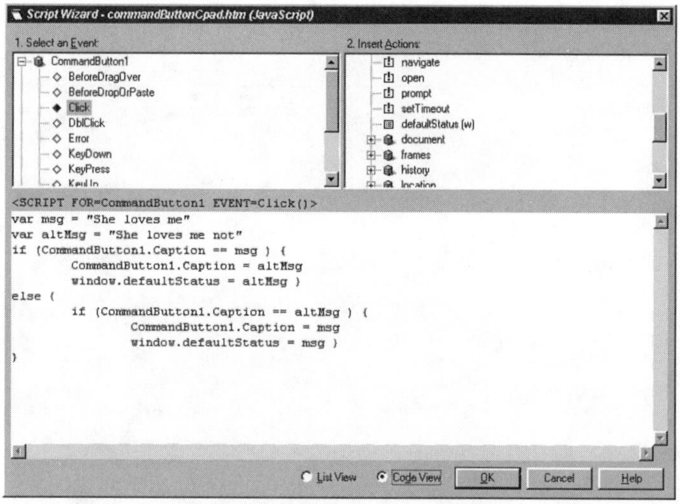

FIGURE 24.9.

Viewing the generated code.

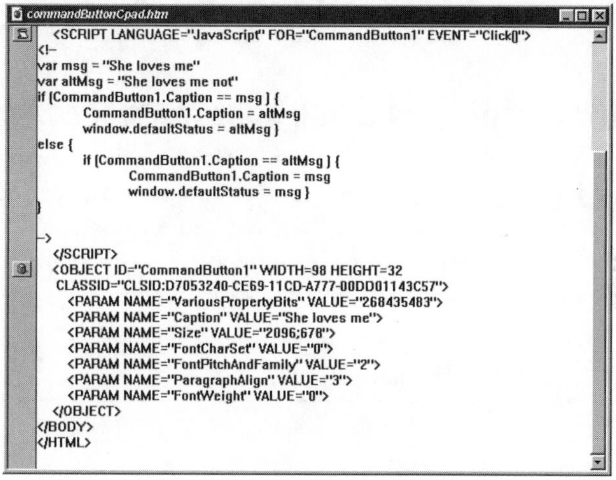

Beside each script is an icon. By clicking that icon, you can display the Script Wizard to modify the current event code.

You can run this code by saving the HTML text in the editor and running Internet Explorer. Figure 24.10 shows the result after the button has been clicked once.

FIGURE 24.10.

Custom code triggered when you click the command button.

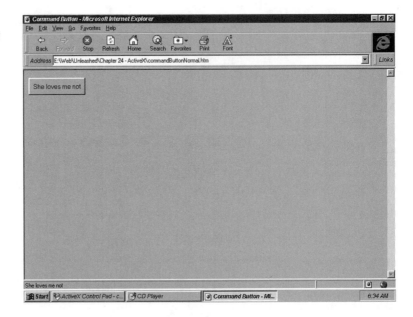

Add JavaScript Code Using Your Normal Editor

Once you start working with ActiveX controls, you will see that there's nothing magical about attaching JavaScript code to them. As long as you know the properties and methods of the control, you can use your normal JavaScript editor instead of the Script Wizard, if desired. Using the example shown in the previous section, Listing 24.1 shows the JavaScript code for responding to the command button's Click method.

Listing 24.1. commandButtonNormal.htm.

```
<HTML>
<HEAD>
<TITLE>Command Button</TITLE>
<SCRIPT LANGUAGE="JavaScript">

    function loadBox() {
        alert("The Great Quesion")
    }

    function CommandButton1_Click() {

        var msg = "She loves me"
        var altMsg = "She loves me not"
        if (CommandButton1.Caption == msg ) {
            CommandButton1.Caption = altMsg
            window.defaultStatus = altMsg }
        else {
            if (CommandButton1.Caption == altMsg ) {
                CommandButton1.Caption = msg
                window.defaultStatus = msg }
```

```
            }
        }
</SCRIPT>
</HEAD>

<BODY onLoad="loadBox()">
    <OBJECT ID="CommandButton1" WIDTH=98 HEIGHT=32
     CLASSID="CLSID:D7053240-CE69-11CD-A777-00DD01143C57">
        <PARAM NAME="VariousPropertyBits" VALUE="268435483">
        <PARAM NAME="Caption" VALUE="She loves me">
        <PARAM NAME="Size" VALUE="2096;678">
        <PARAM NAME="FontCharSet" VALUE="0">
        <PARAM NAME="FontPitchAndFamily" VALUE="2">
        <PARAM NAME="ParagraphAlign" VALUE="3">
        <PARAM NAME="FontWeight" VALUE="0">
    </OBJECT>
</BODY>
</HTML>
```

Because the <OBJECT> tag does not enable you to add event handlers as parameters, you are forced to use an alternative event handling syntax of Microsoft's that states that an event handler for an object can be defined as ObjectName_EventName().

A second alternative would be to make use of Microsoft's expanded <SCRIPT> tag syntax to add the FOR and EVENT parameters. These tell JavaScript the object and event the code within the <SCRIPT> tags is designed for. The script would look like:

```
<SCRIPT LANGUAGE="JavaScript" FOR="CommandButton1" EVENT="Click()">
    var msg = "She loves me"
    var altMsg = "She loves me not"
    if (CommandButton1.Caption == msg ) {
        CommandButton1.Caption = altMsg
        window.defaultStatus = altMsg }
    else {
        if (CommandButton1.Caption == altMsg ) {
            CommandButton1.Caption = msg
            window.defaultStatus = msg }
    }
</SCRIPT>
```

Adding 2-D Style Layout to Your Pages

You may have noticed that you can only place a single ActiveX control at a time with the ActiveX Control Pad's Object Editor. The reason is not due to a limitation of the tool, but of HTML itself. As currently implemented, the stream-based nature of HTML prevents you from being able to position multiple controls in exact x, y coordinates on the page. The Microsoft ActiveX Control Pad is the first tool that solves this problem and enables you to utilize two-dimensional (2-D) layout regions within your HTML page.

Using the Control Pad's layout editor, you can design a form filled with ActiveX controls in a manner similar to Visual Basic. In other words, you can place multiple controls on a form, positioning them precisely where you want. The layout editor saves this information in an .ALX file. This "2-D region" is then displayed in your browser using an ActiveX control called the Microsoft HTML Layout Control, which uses the .ALX file as a parameter.

To embed a 2-D region in an HTML document, open a file in the Control Pad's text editor. In the editor window, right-click your mouse and select the Insert HTML Layout option from the pull-down menu (or choose Edit | Insert HTML Layout). Specify a location for the .ALX file and click OK. Or, if you want to create a new .ALX file and embed it later, choose New HTML Layout from the File menu. Either way, the layout editor is displayed, as shown in Figure 24.11.

FIGURE 24.11.

Using the Layout editor to create a 2-D region.

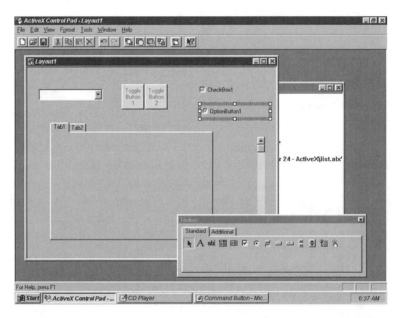

You can use the layout editor to place controls from the Toolbox onto the form, changing properties as you did earlier using the properties table. You also can use the Script Wizard to add JavaScript to one or more of the controls.

NOTE

Eventually, the World Wide Web Consortium (W3C) will probably have a final specification on 2-D–style layout for HTML. At that time, Microsoft intends to provide a means to convert information stored in the .ALX file into HTML source.

FIGURE 24.12.

Sample ListBuilder application demos ActiveX layout.

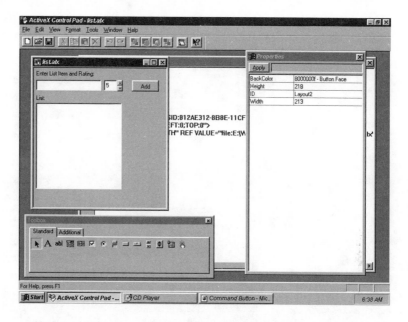

To demonstrate the power of the layout editor, I built a sample ListBuilder form that contains a total of seven ActiveX controls. Figure 24.12 shows the form in the layout editor.

The purpose of the form is to fill the listbox with the contents of the Item and Rating edit boxes above. The Click method of the Add button is charged with performing this process. I also want the Rating to range from 1 to 10 and be changeable only by clicking the SpinButton beside it. The SpinButton's SpinDown and SpinUp events will handle this task.

To define the handler for the Click event, select the command button from the Events Treeview list and navigate the tree until you find Click. In the Code View window, enter two lines of code to add a list entry for the current pair of entries in the Item and Rating edit boxes. These lines are shown in Figure 24.13.

Next, define the event handlers for the SpinDown and SpinUp events of the SpinButton. Figure 24.14 shows the code for the SpinUp event handler. The SpinDown code is very similar, substituting a 1 for a -1 in the equation.

For this demonstration, I stop coding here. Save the results into an .ALX file and then embed the layout into an HTML document. If you open the HTML document under Internet Explorer, you can see that the layout form comes across just as it was designed. Try entering data into the Item and Ratings fields; the listbox will grow for each entry. (See Figure 24.15.)

FIGURE 24.13.

Click *event handler for the command button.*

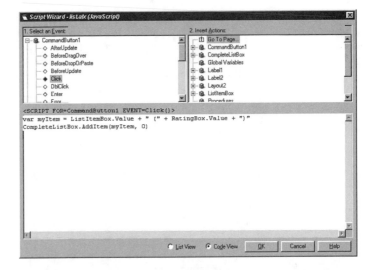

FIGURE 24.14.

SpinUp *event handler.*

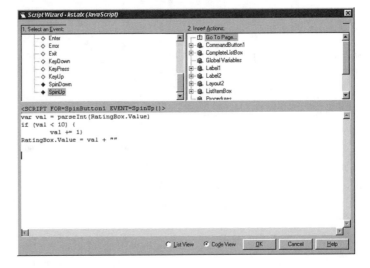

FIGURE 24.15.

JavaScript-enabled 2-D Region.

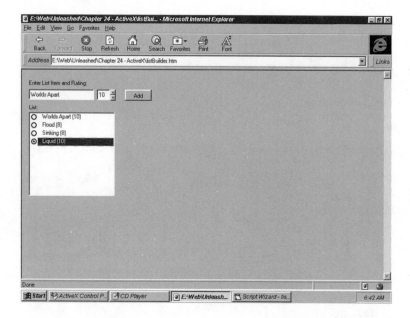

Listing 24.2 shows the code for the HTM form. The <OBJECT> tag uses the .ALX file as a parameter.

Listing 24.2. ListBuilder.htm.

```
<HTML>
<HEAD>
<TITLE></TITLE>
</HEAD>
<BODY>

<OBJECT CLASSID="CLSID:812AE312-8B8E-11CF-93C8-00AA00C08FDF"
ID="list_alx" STYLE="LEFT:0;TOP:0">
<PARAM NAME="ALXPATH" REF VALUE="file:E:\Web\Unleashed\Chapter 24 -
 ActiveX\list.alx">
 </OBJECT>

</BODY>
</HTML>
```

As you can see from the HTML file, there is no JavaScript code there. It is actually located in the .ALX file. The .ALX file is a text file that is essentially an extension to the associated HTML file. It uses the <DIV> HTML tag to group the ActiveX controls into a common division. As you can see in Listing 24.3, your JavaScript code keeps the same structure as it would in an HTML file.

Listing 24.3. List.alx.

```
<SCRIPT LANGUAGE="JavaScript" FOR="SpinButton1" EVENT="SpinDown()">
<!--
var val = parseInt(RatingBox.Value)
if (val < 10) {
     val += -1}
RatingBox.Value = val + ""
-->
</SCRIPT>

<SCRIPT LANGUAGE="JavaScript" FOR="SpinButton1" EVENT="SpinUp()">
<!--
var val = parseInt(RatingBox.Value)
if (val < 10) {
     val += 1}
RatingBox.Value = val + ""
-->
</SCRIPT>

<SCRIPT LANGUAGE="JavaScript" FOR="CommandButton1" EVENT="Click()">
<!--
var myItem = ListItemBox.Value + " (" + RatingBox.Value + ")"
CompleteListBox.AddItem(myItem, 0)
-->
</SCRIPT>

<DIV ID="Layout2" STYLE="LAYOUT:FIXED;WIDTH:213pt;HEIGHT:218pt;">
    <OBJECT ID="ListItemBox"
     CLASSID="CLSID:8BD21D10-EC42-11CE-9E0D-00AA006002F3"
STYLE="TOP:17pt;LEFT:4pt;WIDTH:105pt;HEIGHT:14pt;TABINDEX:1;ZINDEX:0;">
        <PARAM NAME="VariousPropertyBits" VALUE="679495707">
        <PARAM NAME="Size" VALUE="3704;508">
        <PARAM NAME="FontCharSet" VALUE="0">
        <PARAM NAME="FontPitchAndFamily" VALUE="2">
        <PARAM NAME="FontWeight" VALUE="0">
    </OBJECT>
    <OBJECT ID="Label1"
     CLASSID="CLSID:978C9E23-D4B0-11CE-BF2D-00AA003F40D0" STYLE="TOP:4pt;
        LEFT:4pt;WIDTH:109pt;HEIGHT:13pt;ZINDEX:1;">
        <PARAM NAME="Caption" VALUE="Enter List Item and Rating:">
        <PARAM NAME="Size" VALUE="3845;459">
        <PARAM NAME="FontCharSet" VALUE="0">
        <PARAM NAME="FontPitchAndFamily" VALUE="2">
        <PARAM NAME="FontWeight" VALUE="0">
    </OBJECT>
    <OBJECT ID="Label2"
     CLASSID="CLSID:978C9E23-D4B0-11CE-BF2D-00AA003F40D0" STYLE="TOP:42pt;LEFT:
        4pt;WIDTH:72pt;HEIGHT:14pt;ZINDEX:2;">
        <PARAM NAME="Caption" VALUE="List:">
        <PARAM NAME="Size" VALUE="2540;508">
        <PARAM NAME="FontCharSet" VALUE="0">
        <PARAM NAME="FontPitchAndFamily" VALUE="2">
        <PARAM NAME="FontWeight" VALUE="0">
    </OBJECT>
    <OBJECT ID="CommandButton1"
     CLASSID="CLSID:D7053240-CE69-11CD-A777-00DD01143C57"
```

```
STYLE="TOP:13pt;LEFT:155pt;WIDTH:43pt;HEIGHT:17pt;TABINDEX:4;ZINDEX:3;">
        <PARAM NAME="Caption" VALUE="Add">
        <PARAM NAME="Size" VALUE="1517;600">
        <PARAM NAME="FontCharSet" VALUE="0">
        <PARAM NAME="FontPitchAndFamily" VALUE="2">
        <PARAM NAME="ParagraphAlign" VALUE="3">
        <PARAM NAME="FontWeight" VALUE="0">
    </OBJECT>
    <OBJECT ID="RatingBox"
      CLASSID="CLSID:8BD21D10-EC42-11CE-9E0D-00AA006002F3"
STYLE="TOP:17pt;LEFT:113pt;WIDTH:21pt;HEIGHT:14pt;TABINDEX:5;ZINDEX:4;">
        <PARAM NAME="VariousPropertyBits" VALUE="679495707">
        <PARAM NAME="Size" VALUE="741;494">
        <PARAM NAME="Value" VALUE="5">
        <PARAM NAME="FontCharSet" VALUE="0">
        <PARAM NAME="FontPitchAndFamily" VALUE="2">
        <PARAM NAME="FontWeight" VALUE="0">
    </OBJECT>
    <OBJECT ID="SpinButton1"
      CLASSID="CLSID:79176FB0-B7F2-11CE-97EF-00AA006D2776"
STYLE="TOP:17pt;LEFT:139pt;WIDTH:8pt;HEIGHT:13pt;TABINDEX:6;ZINDEX:5;">
        <PARAM NAME="Size" VALUE="282;459">
        <PARAM NAME="Max" VALUE="10">
    </OBJECT>
    <OBJECT ID="CompleteListBox"
      CLASSID="CLSID:8BD21D20-EC42-11CE-9E0D-00AA006002F3"
STYLE="TOP:55pt;LEFT:4pt;WIDTH:138pt;HEIGHT:135pt;TABINDEX:0;ZINDEX:6;">
        <PARAM NAME="ScrollBars" VALUE="3">
        <PARAM NAME="DisplayStyle" VALUE="2">
        <PARAM NAME="Size" VALUE="4868;4771">
        <PARAM NAME="MatchEntry" VALUE="0">
        <PARAM NAME="ListStyle" VALUE="1">
        <PARAM NAME="FontCharSet" VALUE="0">
        <PARAM NAME="FontPitchAndFamily" VALUE="2">
        <PARAM NAME="FontWeight" VALUE="0">
    </OBJECT>
</DIV>
```

Don't let the simplicity of this example fool you; JavaScript integration with ActiveX controls offers a compelling alternative for application development on the Web. Trying to create a similar application using straight HTML tags would have been impossible. The notion of changing existing objects on an HTML document without a refresh from the server is revolutionary.

Summary

ActiveX controls can be tightly integrated with JavaScript. This chapter looked at what ActiveX technology is and how you can embed these controls into your HTML documents. It then looked at how you can add JavaScript code to set properties, respond to events, or trigger methods of an ActiveX control. Within this discussion, the principal tool available for working with ActiveX controls within your HTML was examined in detail: The Microsoft ActiveX Control Pad.

Controlling Multimedia and Plug-Ins

by Michael G. Moncur

IN THIS CHAPTER

Multimedia is probably the oldest buzzword in the computer industry, and its definition keeps changing. In the 80s, decent graphics and sound were enough to make a multimedia computer system. Now the term includes such things as CD-ROM, CD-quality audio, and full-motion video.

As far as the Web is concerned, multimedia generally means having more than the usual media—text and images—on your Web page. Alternate forms of media can be supported on a Web page in two key ways:

■ Helper applications are the traditional solution. These give a browser added abilities, such as playing sounds or displaying video images. The file you link to is downloaded completely and then passed to the helper application.

■ Plug-ins are a new solution developed by Netscape. These are custom applications that work within the browser using a special programmer's interface (API). Using plug-ins, you can display alternate media directly in the browser window.

Although JavaScript is a simple language, it can work with multimedia. This chapter explores what it can—and can't—do. I'll start with a look at sounds and their use in JavaScript and then continue with a discussion of plug-ins.

Using Sound in JavaScript

JavaScript doesn't include any special functions to play sounds. However, it's easy to force a sound to load and play in JavaScript. You can do this by setting the `window.location.href` property—the same property you set when forcing the user to load another page.

The result is the same as if the user clicks a link to the sound. The file is downloaded, and after the download is complete, the sound player application plays the sound.

By using this technique, you can play a sound at any time during the execution of your JavaScript application. Playing the sound can be an event handler, an alternative to an alert message, or just a way to annoy the user.

> **TIP**
>
> Speaking of annoying the user, keep in mind that network connections aren't always fast. It's best to stick to small, easily downloaded sounds to keep things fast and smooth.

Configuring a Sound Player

Most of the recent versions of Netscape automatically install a helper application for sounds (.wav and .au files) called the Netscape Audio Player, or `NAPLAYER.EXE`. If you don't have a player configured, you can choose `NAPLAYER.EXE` from the `NETSCAPE\PROGRAMS` directory.

One problem with Netscape's audio player is that it stays on top after it finishes playing the sound, so keep in mind that some users have to close the Audio Player window after each sound is played. You might want to recommend a sound player that exits after playing the sound; one program that does this is the shareware WPLANY.EXE.

Playing Sounds on Events

The application in Listing 25.1 uses events to trigger sounds in JavaScript. The sample sounds used in this application are included on the accompanying CD-ROM.

Listing 25.1. An application that plays sounds on various JavaScript events.

```
<HTML>
<HEAD>
<TITLE>Sounds on JavaScript Events</TITLE>
<SCRIPT LANGUAGE="JavaScript">
function playsound(sfile) {
// load a sound and play it
window.location.href=sfile;
}
</SCRIPT>
</HEAD>
<BODY
  onLoad="playsound('zap.wav');"
  onUnload="playsound('click.wav');" >
<H1>Sounds on JavaScript Events</H1>
<HR>
The following are some examples of JavaScript event handlers used to
play sounds. You should have also heard a sound play when this page
loaded; you'll hear another one when you unload this page.
<HR>
<a href="#" onClick="playsound('zap.wav');">
 Click here for a sound
</a>
<FORM NAME="form1">
<INPUT TYPE="button" VALUE="Button to Play a Sound"
onClick="playsound('click.wav');">
</FORM>
</BODY>
</HTML>
```

Figure 25.1 shows this example in action, complete with the Netscape Audio player. To truly appreciate it, though, you need to try it yourself; although your Web page can include sound, this book can't.

> **TIP**
>
> As you might have noticed, using helper applications to play sounds isn't an ideal solution. Later in this chapter, we'll explain how to embed sounds and play them with a plug-in using LiveConnect.

Figure 25.1.

The output of the sound player example.

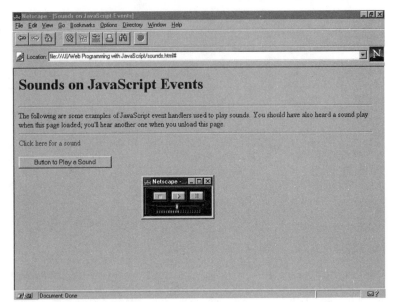

Netscape Plug-Ins

Plug-ins are a new alternative to helper applications, developed by Netscape beginning with Navigator 2.0. Currently, a wide variety of plug-ins is available for various types of files. Even Microsoft has gotten into the act; the latest version of Microsoft Internet Explorer (MSIE) also supports Netscape-compatible plug-ins.

Plug-ins are developed by third parties (or by browser developers, in some cases) using an API available from Netscape. The plug-in can use the resources of the browser and display its output within the browser window.

There are now hundreds of plug-ins available for different types of documents and products. Here we've listed some of the most popular plug-ins, most of which are currently available at little or no charge:

- Adobe's Acrobat Plug-in (Amber) lets you display PDF (Portable Document Format) documents in the browser window.

- Macromedia's Shockwave plug-in lets the browser display Director movies and animations inline.

- The QuickTime plug-in displays QuickTime movies inline.

- A wide variety of plug-ins support VRML (Virtual Reality Markup Language.) This allows you to create interactive 3-D sites. JavaScript can also work with VRML with a new extension called VRMLScript. Netscape's latest version includes a 3-D viewer called Live3D.

- The NCompass plug-in, from Excite, allows Netscape to support ActiveX (OLE) controls.

- The RealAudio plug-in allows you to listen to real-time audio; the sound is played as it is downloaded. Netscape includes their version of this, LiveAudio, in the latest version.

- The Pointcast (PCN) plug-in displays news stories, stock information, and press releases.

NOTE

Plug-ins are not platform-independent. If a plug-in manufacturer wants to support multiple platforms, it has to create a separate version of the plug-in for each platform. Many plug-ins are available exclusively for Windows or the Macintosh.

You can place a plug-in document in a Web page using the `<EMBED>` tag, an extension to HTML. For example, the following HTML tag inserts a PDF file at the current location in the page:

```
<EMBED SRC="doc.pdf">
```

For plug-ins that take up an area of the screen, such as video players and graphics, you can specify HEIGHT and WIDTH attributes to limit the size of the embedded object, as with an ordinary image.

CAUTION

Test your code with different video resolutions when setting HEIGHT and WIDTH attributes. Resolutions greatly affect the placement of screen objects on your display.

Plug-Ins and JavaScript

JavaScript enables you to access the list of plug-ins installed on the user's browser. You can check for a particular plug-in and modify the page accordingly or simply generate a list of the compatible plug-ins or MIME types.

> **NOTE**
>
> Presently, there is no way to automatically download and install a plug-in that is needed to run a file requested by the browser. Although this probably won't be a JavaScript feature in the future, Netscape is considering a similar feature to build into a future version of Navigator.

Objects Related to Plug-Ins

JavaScript's plug-in features were added in Netscape version 3.0. Two objects that are available as children of the `navigator` object can give you information about plug-ins. All properties of the following objects are read-only:

- The `navigator.plugins` object is an array that contains information for each installed plug-in.
- The `navigator.mimeTypes` object is an array with information about each of the MIME types currently supported.

These objects are explained in detail in the sections that follow.

The `plugins` Object

The `navigator.plugins` object is an array with one entry for each of the available plug-ins. You can find out how many plug-ins are installed with the expression `navigator.plugins.length`.

Each element of the `plugins` array is an object in itself, called a `plugin` object. The `plugin` object has the following properties:

- *name* is the name of the plug-in.
- *filename* is the executable file that was loaded to install the plug-in.
- *description* is a description of the plug-in. The plug-in developer supplies this description.
- *mimeTypes* is an array of `mimeType` objects, each representing a MIME type that the plug-in can handle. This works similarly to the `navigator.mimeTypes` object, described in "The `mimeTypes` Object," later in this chapter.

Refreshing the Plug-In List

The `plugins` object has a single method, `refresh`. This method enables you to update the installed plug-ins list without exiting Netscape. For example, if the user has installed a new plug-in, this method adds it to the list. The syntax is simple:

```
navigator.plugins.refresh();
```

You can add a single argument (true) to the `refresh` method to change its behavior. If the parameter is true, Netscape also automatically reloads any page that requires the plug-in.

This makes it possible for you to check for a plug-in and display a link to download it if it is not installed. Your program can then refresh the plug-ins list and reload the page automatically. See the section "Testing for a Plug-In," later in this chapter, for an example.

The `mimeTypes` Object

The `navigator.mimeTypes` array contains an element for each MIME type currently supported by Netscape or by a plug-in. Each element of the array is a `mimeType` object, which includes the following properties:

- *type* is the MIME type name, such as `text/html` or `video/mpeg`.
- *description* is a description of the MIME type.
- *enabledPlugin* is the name of the plug-in that is currently supporting the type.
- *suffixes* is a listing of the extensions that can be used for documents of this MIME type.

Listing Plug-Ins

Using the `navigator.plugins` object, you can easily make a program display a list of currently available plug-ins. Listing 25.2 is such a program. The name, filename, and description for each plug-in are listed in a table.

Listing 25.2. (PLUGINS.HTM) A program to list available plug-ins.

```
<HTML>
<HEAD>
<TITLE>List of Plug-Ins</TITLE>
</HEAD>
<BODY>
<H1>List of Plug-Ins</H1>
<HR>
The following is a list of the plug-ins installed in this
copy of Netscape, generated using the JavaScript
navigator.plugins object:
<HR>
```

continues

Listing 25.2. continued

```
<TABLE BORDER>
<TR><TH>Plug-in Name</TH>
<TH>Filename</TH>
<TH>Description</TH>
</TR>
<SCRIPT LANGUAGE="JavaScript">
for (i=0; i<navigator.plugins.length; i++) {
   document.write("<TR><TD>");
   document.write(navigator.plugins[i].name);
   document.write("</TD><TD>");
   document.write(navigator.plugins[i].filename);
   document.write("</TD><TD>");
   document.write(navigator.plugins[i].description);
   document.write("</TD></TR>");
}
</SCRIPT>
</TABLE>
</BODY>
</HTML>
```

This program should be easy to understand. It uses the `navigator.plugins.length` property to determine the number of plug-ins. For each one, it displays table cells containing the properties. Figure 25.2 shows the list generated by this program.

Figure 25.2.

The list of available plug-ins as generated by the sample program.

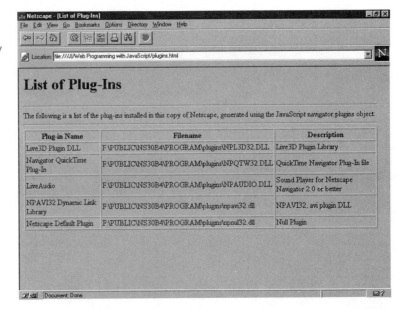

Listing MIME Types

Similarly, you can create a program to list the available MIME types on your system. Listing 25.3 shows a program that lists each type in a table along with its description, the plug-in that handles that type, and the suffixes used for that type of file.

Listing 25.3. A program to display a list of available MIME types and their properties.

```
<HTML>
<HEAD>
<TITLE>List of MIME Types</TITLE>
</HEAD>
<BODY>
<H1>List of MIME Types</H1>
<HR>
The following is a list of the MIME types installed in this
copy of Netscape, generated using the JavaScript
navigator.mimeTypes object:
<HR>
<TABLE BORDER>
<TR><TH>MIME Type</TH>
<TH>Description</TH>
<TH>Current Plug-in</TH>
<TH>Extensions</TH>
</TR>
<SCRIPT LANGUAGE="JavaScript">
for (i=0; i<navigator.mimeTypes.length; i++) {
   document.write("<TR><TD>");
   document.write(navigator.mimeTypes[i].type);
   document.write("</TD><TD>");
   document.write(navigator.mimeTypes[i].description);
   document.write("</TD><TD>");
   document.write(navigator.mimeTypes[i].enabledPlugin);
   document.write("</TD><TD>");
   document.write(navigator.mimeTypes[i].suffixes);
   document.write("</TD></TR>");
}
</SCRIPT>
</TABLE>
</BODY>
</HTML>
```

This program works in the same fashion as the previous example. It iterates through the `navigator.mimeTypes` array and displays the properties for each type. The list generated by this program is shown in Figure 25.3.

Testing for a Plug-In

Often, all you need to do with JavaScript is decide whether to attempt to display a plug-in document. You can check for support of the required plug-in, and if it isn't found, you can insert alternate content or simply advise the user that the plug-in is needed.

FIGURE 25.3.

The list of available MIME types as generated by the sample program.

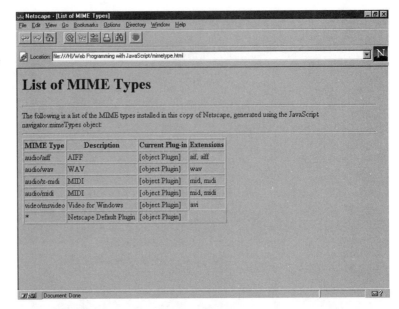

List of MIME Types

The following is a list of the MIME types installed in this copy of Netscape, generated using the JavaScript navigator.mimeTypes object:

MIME Type	Description	Current Plug-in	Extensions
audio/aiff	AIFF	[object Plugin]	aif, aiff
audio/wav	WAV	[object Plugin]	wav
audio/x-midi	MIDI	[object Plugin]	mid, midi
audio/midi	MIDI	[object Plugin]	mid, midi
video/msvideo	Video for Windows	[object Plugin]	avi
*	Netscape Default Plugin	[object Plugin]	

CAUTION

Plug-ins are restrictive. Only users of plug-in–compatible browsers (with the plug-in itself installed) are able to view plug-in–dependent documents. Many users who consider this too much work just move on to another document or even another Web site.

For example, the following code checks for the Shockwave plug-in. If it's installed, the Director movie is embedded in the document; otherwise, a message about the plug-in is displayed.

```
test = navigator.plugins["Shockwave"];
if (test)
   document.writeln("<EMBED SRC='test.dir' HEIGHT=50 WIDTH=100>")
else
   document.writeln("The Shockwave Plug-in is required.")
```

You're simply displaying a message that the plug-in is required. As noted earlier, you could also provide a link to download the plug-in and then use the `refresh` method of the `plugins` object to add it to the plug-ins list and reload the document.

Controlling Plug-Ins with LiveConnect

LiveConnect, a feature added to JavaScript in Netscape 3.0, allows JavaScript and plug-ins to work together. If a plug-in supports LiveConnect, you can use JavaScript to control its behavior and access built-in methods of the plug-in.

Since this is a new standard, few plug-ins currently support it, but this will change. One plug-in that already supports LiveConnect is LiveAudio, included with the 3.0 release of Netscape Navigator. Using this plug-in, you can embed a sound in a page and control it without involving helper applications.

LiveAudio EMBED Syntax

To use a sound in your Web page with LiveAudio, use the <EMBED> tag to embed the sound. LiveAudio works with the common sound formats (.wav, .au, .aif). The <EMBED> tag for a sound can include the following attributes:

- SRC is the URL of the sound file.
- NAME is a name to be used for the sound file's sound object.
- AUTOSTART can be either true or false; if true, the sound starts playing when the page finishes loading.
- LOOP is a Boolean value that indicates whether the sound repeats after it finishes playing. You can also specify an integer value to loop a certain number of times.
- STARTTIME and ENDTIME are the indexes within the sound file where playback will start and stop; these are in minutes and seconds; for example, 0:30 is 30 seconds from the start of the sound.
- VOLUME is the relative volume of the sound, ranging from 0 to 100.
- CONTROLS specifies the type of control, if any, displayed for the sound. The values include CONSOLE, a complete console, SMALLCONSOLE, a smaller version, and individual buttons:

  PLAYBUTTON, PAUSEBUTTON, STOPBUTTON, and VOLUMELEVER.
- HIDDEN can be set to TRUE to display no control at all. This is useful if you will be controlling the sound via JavaScript.
- MASTERSOUND is used to specify that the sound file is a real sound file; LiveAudio allows "stub" files that refer to other files to be used instead.

The Sound Object

When you embed a sound in your document with the <EMBED> tag, it is made available as a sound object, a child of the document object. The sound object's name is what you specified in the NAME attribute. The sound object has a variety of methods you can use from JavaScript:

- play() starts playing the sound. You can specify a loop value, similar to the LOOP attribute values, followed by an optional URL for the sound if the original URL is not used.
- stop() stops the sound if it is currently playing.

25

CONTROLLING
MULTIMEDIA AND
PLUG-INS

- **pause()** pauses the sound at the current position. You can use the play() method, or the pause() method again, to continue the playback.

- **start_time()** and **end_time()** allow you to override the start and end times. Specify the value in seconds.

- **start_at_beginning()** and **stop_at_end()** reset the start and stop times to the beginning and end of the sound file.

- **setvol()** sets the sound's volume, from 0 to 100 percent.

- **fade_to()** sets the volume, but fades from the current value.

- **fade_from_to()** allows you to specify two values, and fades from one to the other.

In addition, you can use the following methods, which return a value:

- **IsReady()** returns true if the sound is loaded and ready to play.

- **IsPlaying()** returns true if the sound is currently playing.

- **IsPaused()** returns true if the sound is currently paused.

- **GetVolume()** returns the current volume.

Using Embedded Sounds

As an example of embedded sounds with the LiveAudio plug-in, and of LiveConnect in general, Listing 25.4 shows a program that loads a sound and allows you to control it using several buttons with JavaScript event handlers.

Listing 25.4. Controlling embedded sounds with JavaScript.

```
<HTML>
<HEAD>
<TITLE>Embedded Sounds</TITLE>
</HEAD>
<BODY>
<H1>Embedded Sounds in JavaScript</H1>
<EMBED MASTERSOUND NAME="sound1" SRC="test.wav" VOLUME=100 HIDDEN=TRUE
AUTOSTART=FALSE>
<HR>
<P>
This document includes a hidden embedded sound, which is loaded after the page
is loaded. You can use the JavaScript buttons below to control the sound.
<HR>
<FORM NAME="form1">
<INPUT TYPE="button" VALUE="Play"
   onClick="document.sound1.play(true);">
<INPUT TYPE="button" VALUE="Pause"
   onClick="document.sound1.pause();">
<INPUT TYPE="button" VALUE="Stop"
   onClick="document.sound1.stop();">
</FORM>
</BODY>
</HTML>
```

Summary

You should now understand the basics of using JavaScript to work with multimedia files and plug-ins. This chapter covered the difference between helper applications and plug-ins, how to use JavaScript to play sounds on events, and the basics of the plug-in standard. You also learned about detecting and listing browser plug-ins with JavaScript, and accessing the list of available MIME types. Finally, you looked at LiveConnect, which allows JavaScript to access and control embedded plug-in objects.

JavaScript and Web Security

by Christopher Haddad

IN THIS CHAPTER

JavaScript provides the Web site developer with the ability to extend static HTML pages with a dynamic, event-driven, programming language. The JavaScript-enhanced Web page provides client-side, interactive functionality by executing JavaScript code fragments inside the client's Web browser. The inclusion of JavaScript code fragments in the document page raises fundamental security concerns about the code integrity of the browser's script interpreter as well as the script itself. Viewing a JavaScript enabled page exposes the user to a greater possibility of damage than the rendering of a pure HTML document, due to the fact that the executing code fragments overlay another layer of complexity on top of the browser application.

With traditional desktop software, there is a well-defined compact between the user and the software. Installation and use of the programs requires explicit actions and decisions by the users. JavaScript code doesn't conform to accepted conventions. Script code is loaded from a remote source and executed without user confirmation. Execution of untrusted code from a remote source is analogous to receiving an apple in the mail from an unknown return address and eating it. Verifications and limitations must be placed on the use of JavaScript code in order to safeguard the user's computer from malicious or unintentional attacks on valuable information and applications. No user wants to "pull the wire" between their computer and the outside world, so knowledge of the capability for JavaScript code to attack and damage a client or server machine is necessary.

The Web was designed as an open system for publishing graphical, hypertext content over the Internet. Site developers have embraced the opportunity to extend the static HTML document with dynamic, interactive capabilities through the inclusion of scripting languages in Web documents. The scripting languages are either executed on the server machine or downloaded to a client machine and executed as remote code. Security is becoming a fundamental concern because the JavaScript and Java languages are becoming more prevalent, thereby making them a more attractive target for attack.

Security in a connected computer network can be evaluated in terms of the "level of confidence" in a transmission. The receiving party wants to trust that the original transmission was indeed sent by the expected sender. Also, the message should not have been altered en route. In a heterogeneous computer network such as the Internet, such confidence can currently not be absolute. The Internet was designed as a distributed system whereby network traffic must pass through many different machines to reach its intended destination. The flow of the traffic through multiple host machines exposes the traffic to modification or replacement at many points. Also, the return address of the sender is designated by an address which can be spoofed (mimicked). While the global reach and electronic structure of unsecured transmissions defies accountability, the use of encryption, digital signatures, and source code verification are attempts to raise the barrier against attack.

The user must trust that the application code will behave in a proper manner and not damage the user's system. In a typical desktop environment, code residing on the local hard drive is considered trusted, while code received from network resources, remote code, is given a lower level of trust based on the source (corporate LAN or site of a virus hacker). The trust engendered in the past has commonly been based on the source of the application code. The security risk taken by installing a shrink wrapped package produced by a well known software publisher purchased off the shelf of a retail store is perceived to be minimal when compared to downloading the latest freeware game from the Internet. Adoption of electronic distribution channels for applications (JavaScript and Java code) requires the adoption of new technology and procedures, as well as education of the expected consumer.

The computer industry is moving toward the assignment of digital signatures for developers and the creation of signed applets as a way to define accountability for JavaScript code. The identity of the JavaScript developer will likely be broadcast to the Web browser through a digital signature appended to the script file. Users, in conjunction with newer browsers, can determine whether to accept a code download from a site based on the signature received. A sample dialog displaying the information contained in a digital certificate is shown in Figure 26.1.

FIGURE 26.1.

Sample view of a digital certificate.

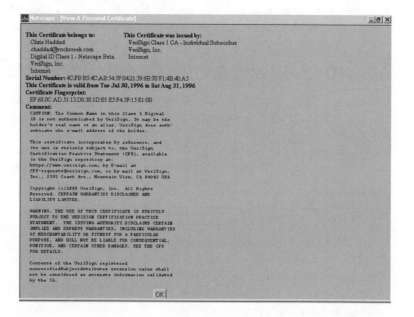

Encryption is used to prevent modification of the data transmission while en route. The browser encryption protocols, SSL (Secure Socket Layer), and SHTTP (Secure Hypertext Transport Protocol), work together to ensure that JavaScript code fragments are not altered during transit. Lastly, verification of the source code is critical to providing a secure environment. Virus checkers are extended to verify that JavaScript code does not contain any dangerous routines.

The cost and complexity of the security measures implemented to protect a user's computer system must be balanced with the hardships proposed by their existence. The following list describes the client machine's areas of vulnerability when executing scripting code:

■ Altering the file system

■ Reading/writing to a file

■ Reading/writing system memory

■ Sending private information over the network

■ Communication with other network resources

■ Executing/closing programs on the local computer or an external host

■ Using excessive system resources (Denial of Service Attacks)

■ Crashing the host program (Web browser)

Programming languages are created to give the developer tools to build an application. Because of the security concerns related to executing code on network clients, Netscape has designed JavaScript without many of the functions present in traditional programming languages. The missing capabilities enables Web surfers a level of protection against attack, but hamper the creation of compelling application content. This chapter describes the ability of JavaScript and Java code to breach security and the steps that can be taken to prevent attacks.

Security Concerns with Client-Side JavaScript

The most prevalent security risk to local machines accessing the Internet is currently related to executing remote JavaScript code on the client. The use of client-side JavaScript can be ascertained by viewing the document source. The existence of an HTML `<SCRIPT>` tag signifies that the page contains client side code, and the optional tag attribute, `LANGUAGE="JAVASCRIPT"`, represents that the page contains code conforming to the JavaScript language.

The JavaScript may be inline with the HTML source document, or in a separate file referenced by the use of another optional `<SCRIPT>` tag attribute, `SRC="javafile.JS"`. If JavaScript execution has been enabled for the Web browser, then the script can run immediately after the page has downloaded and processed by the script interpreter or JIT (Just-In-Time) compiler. At the time that this chapter was written, there was no mechanism to warn users that JavaScript is about to execute, nor was there a way to stop a script from executing. The ability of the browser client to selectively authorize trusted individual sites from which JavaScript code may be downloaded is also necessary, but currently unavailable in a release (non-beta) browser application.

When viewed from the perspective of a traditional desktop programmer, the implementation of client-side JavaScript currently handles security in a draconian fashion. The following security restrictions are imposed on JavaScript code when executed by Netscape Navigator:

■ There is no ability to read or write files

■ There is no access to file system information

■ JavaScript can't execute programs or system commands

■ JavaScript can't make network connections to other computers except to the machine from which the applet was downloaded

■ There are restrictions on the access of FORM data

JavaScript applications can't save user session information to the local hard drive except through the cookie mechanism, communication with a plug-in, and one code trick. The trick relies on piping the information to a helper application. If a user has defined a helper application for a mime-type, the JavaScript code can open a message window and output the information to the helper application. The information can then be explicitly saved to the client machine by the user through the use of the File Save menu option in the helper application. Refer again to Figure 26.2 for a screen shot after piping data to `notepad.exe` via the `test_stream` code example. The following code listing describes the functions necessary to perform this operation:

```
function test_stream()
{
msgwindow = window.open("","hiwin","");
msgwindow.document.open("text/plain");   // or text/sams to define a new mime-type
msgwindow.document.write("JavaScript data, save to disk drive  \nA,100,B\n"); //
➥write some text
msgwindow.document.write("Choose File¦Save to create a data file");
msgwindow.document.close();
msgwindow.close();
}
```

FIGURE 26.2.

*Download data to
client from JavaScript.*

CAUTION

If the `document.open` command is passed a parameter (mime-type) defined as Ask User or Save in the helper tab, then the script doesn't save any information and generates an Out of Memory error.

Because `document.write` currently can't write NULLS (`\0`) to the data stream, this example has limited use for binary files.

Access to information about the user's browser environment by the script code is critical to properly understanding the client limitations that might affect the operation of the script. The `navigator` class can be queried by the script to ascertain the system platform as well as browser version and type. Also, a list of registered mime-types and plug-ins can be enumerated. The navigator properties are read-only, and therefore aren't a security concern. The system properties that can be acquired through access to the navigator class are documented in Table 26.1.

Table 26.1. Navigator class properties.

Description	Property Name
Browser Codename	navigator.appCodeName
Browser Application	navigator.appName
Browser version	navigator.appVersion
HTTP Agent String	navigator.userAgent
Mime-Types Available	navigator.mimeTypes[]
Plug-ins Installed	navigator.plugins[]

> **NOTE**
>
> The HTTP Agent String is sent to the server during HTTP requests. Both Netscape Navigator and Microsoft Internet Explorer expose access to the navigator class.
>
> A code example of accessing these types and attempting to change a value is in the file NAVPROPS.HTM.

JavaScript shouldn't be used to create applications that are responsible for access control. Because the user is able to view all JavaScript code in the document (or frame) source window, the security algorithm can be easily deduced. Even files loaded by means of the optional source tag are available for the user to download and decipher.

Denial of Service Attacks

Because a user can't terminate executing JavaScript code, denial of service attacks are currently capable of performing the most damage. They have the capability to lock up the user interface and require the user to terminate the browser application. Common attacks include

- Stack Overflow
- Infinite Loops
- Infinite Modal Dialogs
- Using All Available Memory

The stack overflow condition is the easiest denial of service attack to prevent and is properly trapped by all browser implementations. A JavaScript error window is displayed with the message Out of Stack Space or Stack overflow in function_x. (See Figure 26.3.) The following code listing demonstrates how to create a stack overflow by repeatedly calling a recursive function:

```
<HTML><HEAD>
<TITLE> Create Recursive Function Call Condition</TITLE>
<!-- File lockstack.htm -->
<SCRIPT>
function stack_lockup(){
stack_lockup();}
</SCRIPT></HEAD><BODY >
Entering Recursive Function Call
<SCRIPT LANGUAGE="JavaScript">
//<!-- comment so that Javascript is not displayed by non-JS browsers

stack_lockup();//this line executes immediately after the document downloads
// don't forget to JS_comment the start/end of the HTML comment -->

</SCRIPT></BODY></HTML>
```

FIGURE 26.3.

Netscape Navigator error window on stack overflow.

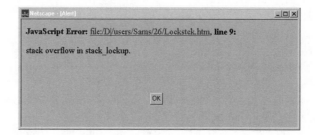

Infinite loops are the bane of all programmers and JavaScript coders don't escape their curse. The following code fragment locks up the browser:

```
for(var i=0;;i++)
    document.write("End this message");
```

> **CAUTION**
>
> JavaScript code that executes infinite loops locks up all browser windows, including windows that are downloading files. According to Netscape, JavaScript code should terminate after 100000 branches and the user should be able to press the stop button, but the author was unable to verify that the browser met the second specification.

JavaScript code that repeatedly displays Alert boxes are examples of an infinite modal dialog box attack. The following fragment will lock up the user interface of the browser:

```
for(var i=0;;i++)
    alert("Why can't i kill this script");
```

Netscape Navigator doesn't limit the amount of memory that a JavaScript can allocate. This last attack eventually swamps the virtual memory storage and brings the machine to a crawl:

```
for(var i=0;;i++)
    str = str + "why doesn't everyone play nice";
```

A majority of these attacks are obvious and could be stopped if the user had the ability to terminate an executing script (a feature currently being investigated by Netscape). The more insidious attack is based on degradation of service. The rogue JavaScript doesn't take over the machine, but hoards resources to the point where other browser windows appear sluggish.

Netscape Navigator 2.0 Issues

The Netscape Navigator 2.0 browser implementation takes a conservative approach toward balancing the needs of the developer with the necessity to protect a user from security concerns. Because many security holes have been eliminated in later revisions of Netscape Navigator, valid JavaScript code developed for version 2.x doesn't often run properly on later versions of Netscape Navigator.

The balance between private and public access to JavaScript information in Navigator 2.0 was fairly clear cut. Navigator automatically prevented scripts from one server from accessing properties of documents residing on a different server. The security restrictions prevent a script from fetching private information that the user would not wish to have made public. Since the release of Navigator 2.0, there has been a low level re-write of the code related to security issues. Most importantly, the rule related to cooperation between scripts from different servers has been relaxed and codified as a new methodology, data tainting.

Users should be aware of outstanding bugs in the Netscape Navigator 2.x versions and update the browser with the latest patches. Numerous bugs have been fixed by Netscape in the 2.01 and 2.02 release. Most bug fixes were patches to security holes in the Java implementation. It is suggested that users and developers update to the latest final release version of Netscape Navigator as soon as it is available.

Later Navigator Versions

A major rewrite of the JavaScript interpreter has changed the definition of valid code compared to earlier versions. The security measures taken by the Netscape browser are currently in a state of flux as the development community determines the correct balance between language capabilities and user privacy.

The operation of the `document` calls have been changed to ensure that JavaScript code doesn't overwrite the original script. The presence of `document.open` or `document.write` function calls outside of the `<BODY>` tags that don't reference a new window result in code errors. An example of an invalid script follows:

```
<SCRIPT LANGUAGE="Javascript">
var i;
function initialize_app()
{
i = "1";
}

function setup()
{
document.open();
document.write("My test app equals",i);
initialize_app();
document.close();
}
</SCRIPT>
<BODY onload="setup()"></BODY>
```

The browser creates a new document context and flushes out the old JavaScript. The result is an error message, `initialize_app` is not defined, because the JavaScript interpreter can no longer access the function. The correct workaround to this security restriction is to either write all the text after the onload function has completed, or write the new document into another frame. The following example demonstrates the first workaround:

```
<SCRIPT>
function setup()
{
initialize_app();
}
</SCRIPT>
<BODY onload="setup()">
</BODY>
<SCRIPT>
document.write("My test app equals",i);
</SCRIPT>
```

Data Tainting

The concept of data tainting has been added to the language as a mechanism for windows originating from different servers to cooperate and share data. Data tainting is enabled by setting the environment variable `NS_ENABLE_TAINT` to any value.

When data tainting is enabled, all JavaScript objects and properties are public and accessible. The feature is necessary for windows to share information across servers. Windows can pull foreign form information from other accessible windows, but when the foreign information is posted to the server, a confirming dialog pops up, enabling the user to cancel or confirm the post operation. If the environment variable isn't set, references to form data on other servers generates an error message, `access disallowed from scripts at` *URL1*`.htm to documents at` *URL2*`.htm`.

> **TIP**
>
> Even when data tainting is disabled, windows have the ability to call functions loaded in other windows from other servers. For instance, frame1 loaded from server1 can call a frame2 function loaded from server2.

JavaScript provides functions that enable the programmer to set or remove taint on objects. The function `taint()` returns a tainted reference to a property, while `untaint()` returns a copy that is untainted. For instance, the following code returns a copy of the private data that can be sent over a URL or form post operation to a server:

```
unmarked = untaint(document.forms[0].element[0].value);
```

> **CAUTION**
>
> When the `NS_ENABLE_TAINT` environment variable is set, JavaScript code in one window can view all document properties in other windows, including private data and session history information.

The tainting mechanism currently contains many security bugs and should be used with care. Many developers have demonstrated code that circumvents the protection mechanism by laundering the data through a sequence of data manipulations.

Internet Explorer 3.x

Because the capability to execute JavaScript and Java applets has just recently been included in Microsoft's Internet Explorer, an extensive security review hasn't been performed by independent third parties. Review of the software's application interface reveals a well-thought-out approach to security. Privacy measures and applet logging have been built into the browser and work with the user to ensure that information is only explicitly transmitted to servers. Figure 26.4 shows a dialog box detailing the privacy options available in the Internet Explorer.

Also, the ability to restrict code downloads to only those servers deemed trustworthy has been included in the application interface. This feature relies on the use of security certificates by the server to identify trusted sites while browsing. The Internet Explorer has a dialog which will display the sites which are trusted by the client browser. See Figure 26.5 for an example of the dialog window.

FIGURE 26.4.

Microsoft Internet Explorer security options.

FIGURE 26.5.

Windows Software Security dialog.

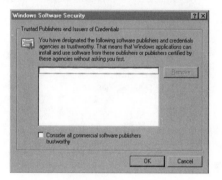

Maximizing Security Protection

Before you surf into uncharted waters, there are steps to reduce the exposure to security attacks due to renegade JavaScript or Java code. The level of protection used should be determined by how much trust is given to the source of the Web pages visited. When visiting new sites (or visiting those listed after a query for "virus hackers"), it's advisable to totally remove the ability for the browser to execute scripting languages. Also, a top-down security approach can be taken by the network administrator to disable execution of Java classes obtained from the Internet. The firewall can be configured to remove the capability of Java class files to pass through a proxy server into the internal network. Knowledge of the latest security bulletins and advisories should result in a clearer understanding of the risks involved during trips outside the firewall.

Secure Sessions and Digital Signatures

As mentioned earlier in this chapter, secure sessions are initiated by the browser and establish an encrypted transmission stream between the server and the browser. The encryption is based on a digital certificate stored on the server. Further protection is achieved by digitally signing each file downloaded to the client. Verification authorities such as Verisign are working in conjunction with the browser developers to develop a framework for appending digital signatures for applets and script files. Later versions of Netscape Navigator and the Microsoft Internet Explorer provide information about the current security level of the document or frame in addition to on-screen visual cues.

To view the security level of a document (or frame) in Netscape Navigator, implement the following steps:

1. Choose View | Document Info (or Frame Info)

2. The `Security:` line states the current security level.

A view of the Netscape Navigator security information is presented in Figure 26.6.

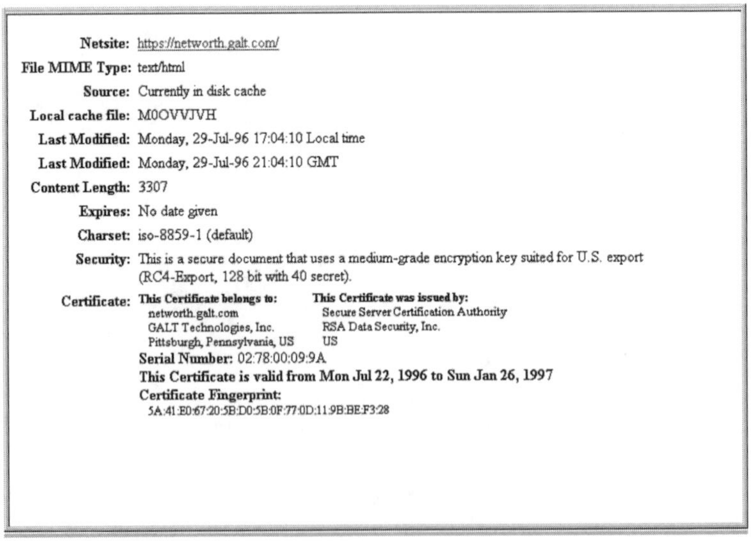

FIGURE 26.6.

Netscape Navigator document security information window.

Netsite:	https://networth.galt.com/
File MIME Type:	text/html
Source:	Currently in disk cache
Local cache file:	M0OVVJVH
Last Modified:	Monday, 29-Jul-96 17:04:10 Local time
Last Modified:	Monday, 29-Jul-96 21:04:10 GMT
Content Length:	3307
Expires:	No date given
Charset:	iso-8859-1 (default)
Security:	This is a secure document that uses a medium-grade encryption key suited for U.S. export (RC4-Export, 128 bit with 40 secret).

Certificate:

This Certificate belongs to:	This Certificate was issued by:
networth.galt.com	Secure Server Certification Authority
GALT Technologies, Inc.	RSA Data Security, Inc.
Pittsburgh, Pennsylvania, US	US

Serial Number: 02:78:00:09:9A
This Certificate is valid from Mon Jul 22, 1996 to Sun Jan 26, 1997
Certificate Fingerprint:
5A:41:E0:67:20:5B:D0:5B:0F:77:0D:11:9B:BE:F3:28

To view the security level of a document in Microsoft Internet Explorer, implement the following steps:

1. Choose File | Properties.

2. Click the Security Tab.

A view of the Microsoft Internet Explorer security information is presented in Figure 26.7.

FIGURE 26.7.

The Microsoft Internet Explorer document security information dialog.

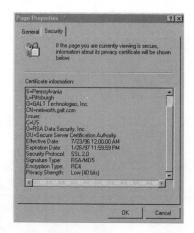

Disabling Scripting Languages in the Browser

At the individual client level, the most effective way to protect the user from damaging code fragments is to let the browser execute scripting code. The drawback to this approach is that many exciting capabilities are then removed from a Web site, and the Web site may not operate as intended. These options should be used when visiting untrusted sites of questionable intention.

JavaScript

To disable JavaScript in Netscape Navigator 2.01, implement the following steps:

1. Choose Options from the main menu.
2. Choose Security Preferences.
3. Click the General dialog tab.
4. Check the Disable JavaScript box.
5. Click the OK button.

NOTE

Netscape Navigator 2.0 doesn't give the option to disable JavaScript.

To disable JavaScript in later versions of Netscape Navigator, implement the following steps:

1. Choose Options from the main menu.
2. Choose Network Preferences.
3. Click the Languages dialog tab.

4. Remove the check from the Enable JavaScript box.

5. Click the OK button.

For an example of the Netscape Navigator Network Preferences dialog, refer to Figure 26.8.

FIGURE 26.8.

Disabling JavaScript in later versions of Netscape Navigator.

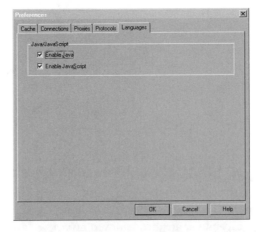

> **CAUTION**
>
> The logic statement has been reversed between versions. While in Navigator 2.0, checking the box would disable JavaScript, in later versions, checking the box enables JavaScript.

Currently, the user interface of the Microsoft Internet Explorer doesn't contain the ability to disable JavaScript.

Java

To disable Java in Netscape Navigator 2.01, implement the following steps:

1. Choose Options from the main menu.

2. Choose Security Preferences.

3. Click the General dialog tab.

4. Check the Disable Java box.

5. Click the OK button.

To disable Java in later versions of Netscape Navigator, implement the following steps:

1. Choose Options from the main menu.

2. Choose Network Preferences.

3. Click the Languages dialog tab.

4. Remove the check from the Enable Java box.

5. Click the OK button.

> **CAUTION**
>
> The logic statement has been reversed between versions. While in Navigator 2.0, checking the box would disable Java, in later versions, checking the box enables Java.

To disable Java in Microsoft Internet Explorer 3.0B2, implement the following steps:

1. Choose View from the main menu.

2. Choose Options.

3. Click the Security dialog tab.

4. Remove the check from the Enable Java programs box.

5. Click the Apply button.

See Figure 26.9 for an example of the Microsoft Internet Explorer dialog used to disable Java programs.

FIGURE 26.9.

Disabling Java in Microsoft Internet Explorer.

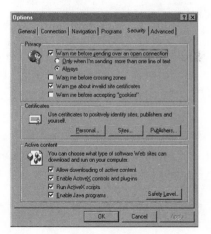

Firewall Filtering

Firewalls and/or proxy servers are commonly the first line of defense between the Internet and the internal network (WAN, LAN or remote machine). Network administrators can configure the firewall routers to filter network traffic based on various parameters, and thereby ensure that users cannot download a file that can cause a security breach. However, the level of filtering should be determined by balancing the benefits achieved through higher security against the cost involved to implement a solution. Router or proxy server-based high security solutions are generally expensive to implement, either from a resource or monetary standpoint, and care must be taken to not over-engineer the security wall.

HTTP requests are used by the client browser to request Java and JavaScript code fragments. Because HTTP is also used for normal Web browser functionality, the proxy server can't just deny access to all HTTP requests because that would result in no access to the Web by the browser. A filtering methodology (that can be used to remove Java downloads) is to filter URL HTTP requests to block all files with the '.CLASS' or '.CLA' extensions. Filtering JavaScript code is more difficult because the source files may legally use any extension, and because code fragments may be embedded inside Web pages.

Security Information Resources on JavaScript and Java Security

The Internet contains many sites devoted to information about security issues. Keeping informed of the latest security bulletins is a good start for making an informed decision about the risk in using the latest technology.

The most accurate, up-to-date information can be found at the following Web sites:

- **Netscape:** `http://developer.netscape.com/library/documentation/index.html`
  Information related to Netscape products
- **Sun:** `http://java.javasoft.com/sfaq/`
  Information related to Java
- **CERT:** `http://www.cert.org`
  Non-partisan advisories about current security breaches
- **CERT FTP:** `ftp://info.cert.org/pub/cert_advisories/`
  Search directory for files containing the name Java
- **Safe Internet Programming:** `http://www.cs.princeton.edu/sip/`
  Site of a research group at Princeton University investigating Internet scripting extensions. They are responsible for discovering the latest Java security holes.

Security Concerns for Server-Side JavaScript

The functionality of Web servers can be extended through the execution of JavaScript and Java routines as either CGI programs or server modules. Server-side JavaScript leverages existing knowledge of the JavaScript language to create applications that can reference databases and other resources residing on the server. The capability to execute server-side JavaScript in Netscape server is currently described as LiveWire technology, and is enabled through the server administration manager. Figure 26.10 displays the Enterprise server screen which is used to activate server-side Javascript (LiveWire).

FIGURE 26.10.
*Activating server-side
JavaScript.*

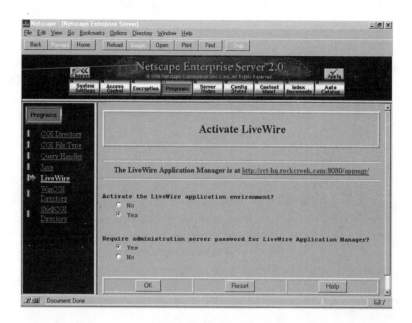

Its important to recognize that the server-side JavaScript capability must then be mapped to
specific directories on the server. The necessity of authorizing server directories capable of
executing server-side JavaScript helps protect the server by isolating the areas which could cause
a security breach. See Figure 26.11 for an example of the server screen used to activate Livewire
for a particular server subdirectory.

FIGURE 26.11.
*Activating LiveWire
directories to execute
JavaScript.*

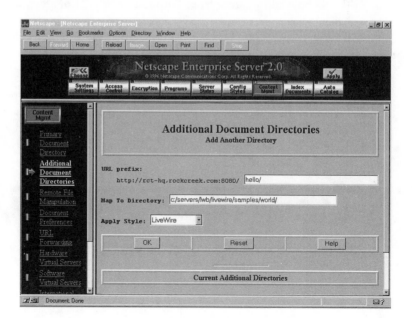

The LiveWire technology exposes four new JavaScript objects for use on the server: request, client, project, and server. The request object has a property, request.ip, that enables the server to determine the IP address that originated the client request. This object member can be used to verify trusted clients who can be given access to confidential information. The global application data object, project, should be locked before data variable values are changed, otherwise the integrity of application variables and counters isn't synchronized between the client processes.

The most significant security concern is the ability for server-side JavaScript to read and write directly to the hard drive. Improperly formatted data can often crash programs that read or write files. The server script code should extensively check to ensure that the user data is in a valid format before writing it to disk. Also, it is imperative that server-side JavaScript code be constructed with file locking mechanisms to take into account that multiple processes execute on the host server. The simplest locking mechanism is to rename the file before opening it for file i/o. On all operating systems, the rename command is expected to be an atomic operation on any platform. The following code illustrates this principle:

```
while(rename(filename,lockname))      // rename filename to the lock filename
    ;                     // block on access to file
else
    {
// perform file i/o
rename(lockname,oldname);        // rename file back to original name
}
```

The server-side code shouldn't write to disk files in public directories that have execution capability. Its a common hacker trick to use a trusted server-side program to create a file on the server that can be used for attack later. For instance, a CGI program that uploads text files from the client to the server can be used to create a script file that can be executed. When the uploaded file is accessed by the attacker via the Web browser, the server-side code executes and can attack the server machine.

The Web site administrator and code developers should be aware that server-side JavaScript can crash the production server. Excessive use of system memory, improperly locking objects, infinite loops, and improper file i/o can bring the server to a halt. All script code should be fully tested on a development server before going "live." Furthermore, code should be empirically evaluated for possible deadlock and race conditions to verify that server-side scripts won't infinitely block on a resource.

> **CAUTION**
>
> Client-side JavaScript can attempt to access any port on the originating server. A security check should be performed to ensure that a proper firewall is in place between the server and the Internet.

The Java interpreter must be explicitly activated for server directories. The server application manager is used to specify directories that can execute Java modules. Figure 26.12 demonstrates the application manager screen used to activate Java for a particular server subdirectory.

FIGURE 26.12.

Activating Java directories on the server.

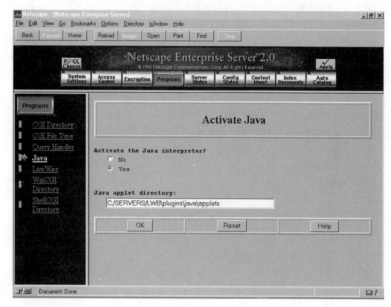

Java and Security

The Java language offers many more capabilities than JavaScript. The later versions of Netscape enable the developer to write a mix of Java and JavaScript code inside Java applets (LiveConnect technology). Also, JavaScript can call Java applet functions directly, passing parameters and receiving return values. The two languages can be used in tandem to create comprehensive remote client solutions.

Knowledge of Java's history is important for putting security issues related to its current implementation in perspective. The language mirrors C++ in many respects—common language syntax, similar keywords, and support for object-oriented programming, including inheritance. Java diverges from C++ in ways that add flexibility to the language and attempt to create a more secure environment: The code can't forge pointers, garbage collection of objects is handled automatically, and only single inheritance is implemented. The machine-independent structure of Java attempts to insulate the programmer from the target machine's operating system. Basic programming building blocks are extended with pre-built packages capable of targeting either server or client systems.

Java was originally designed to be a language for creating embedded applications on personal appliances (desk-top TV boxes, personal communicators, hand held computers, and so on).

The possibility of attack on these closed systems is much lower than it is when connecting to the largest public network on the planet with open standards.

The application programming interface proposed by Sun Microsystems for the Java language during its public Alpha test phase was robust enough to handle a majority of the tasks required by traditional desktop computer applications. The goal was to enable a trusted browser or trusted Java environment to run untrusted Java class components. Java's current implementation falls short of that mandate because its security mechanisms don't follow basic industry security standards for trusted systems. The Java language as a stand-alone definition cannot be considered a secure language because it does not define the most basic components of a secure architecture.

An example of accepted industry standards is documented in the "Department of Defense Trusted Computer System Evaluation Criteria" Orange Book. Java doesn't contain basic security mechanisms, such as an audit capability in the class loader to document the modules loaded during an attack. Because applets are able to exist beyond the scope of the Web document that loaded them, a rogue applet can mount an attack without the user drawing a correlation to its existence. A user-defined audit policy should be available that allows the logging of applet execution, applet originating network address, and applet bytecode.

Also, the implementations of Java have not proven to be a secure language as envisioned by its creators. There are security bugs in many subsystems that haven't been entirely fixed, leading to recurring security alerts. Table 26.2 details the most important of these.

Table 26.2. Java security bugs documented by Sun Microsystems in the "Applet Security FAQ" (`http://java.sun.com/sfaq/`).

Date	Problem	Status
June 2, 1996	Illegal type cast attack	Currently an open bug
May 18, 1996	New version of previous classloader attack	Fixed in Netscape 3.0b4
April, 1996	URL name resolution attack	Fixed in Netscape 3.0b4
March, 1996	Verifier implementation bug	Fixed in Netscape 2.02
March, 1996	Class loader implementation bug	Fixed in Netscape 2.01
February, 1996	DNS attack	Fixed in Netscape 2.01

The researchers who have discovered the security bugs have publicly stated that Java may have to be radically altered to meet their definition of a secure environment. The illegal type cast attack successfully circumvents the safe-type cast mechanism in Java. Successful attacks on the type cast mechanism allow Java objects to masquerade as other types. The ability of hackers to develop a rogue class loader means that untrusted application code could potentially be loaded and executed from an untrusted source without the browser's knowledge of the attack.

Security Components

The security mechanisms to control Java objects are written in Java itself. When the browser runtime system starts, there are no security restrictions in place. The class that monitors security, `SecurityManager`, is loaded from the directory contained in the client's `CLASSPATH` environment variable. These trusted class files (`MOZxxx.ZIP` in Netscape Navigator 2.0, `JAVxxx.ZIP` in Netscape Navigator 3.x) should be protected by frequent virus checks and marked as read-only.

Bytecode Verifier

Once a Java class is downloaded from the remote host, the code is checked by a bytecode verifier. This important step ensures that the Java code conforms to known language opcodes, and that the operand stack isn't subjected to overflows or underflows. All class object accesses are checked for adherence to the protection mechanism defined for the object members (private, protected, public). Furthermore, the code is verified to ensure that no illegal data conversions are present. After the verifier performs its job, the code is converted by the Java runtime compiler into machine code.

Security Manager

The `SecurityManager` class is used by the Java runtime system for access control authorization of Java classes. Because the `SecurityManager` is implemented as a Java object, when the runtime initially starts, the security manager is protected by the Java type system. If the type system has proven impenetrable, and the file system hasn't been compromised, the security manager is considered a trusted class.

The Java compilers are responsible for compiling the Java source code (`.java` file) into a machine-independent bytecode (`.class` file). The bytecode is transmitted over the network to the local machine and interpreted or compiled into native code by the Java runtime system. Verifying the Java bytecode is a critical step in determining the integrity of a Java applet. Just as current virus checking programs search for illegal processor and operating system calls, bytecode should be verified to not contain any security attacks. The bytecodes must be evaluated in the context of their type. For example, the `SecurityManager` type should have fewer restrictions than a user-defined type.

The lack of a formal definition for the Java type system, and the need to thoroughly analyze all program execution sequences, renders this evaluation by current verifiers complicated and unreliable.

Security between applet methods is enforced by a concept of *named space*. Every Java applet should have a unique name depending on the location from which it were downloaded. The Java documentation states that the named space of system level objects have the ability to be shared by all other named spaces (applets) and that the runtime classloader always searches the list of system-named spaces to prevent downloaded code from overwriting a system class. Yet forging named space hashes that inadvertently replace vital system class components like the classloader has been one of the first security bugs found in Java. Classloader bugs have been extensively documented by the researchers at Princeton University.

Security Restrictions

The basic Java language is extended by many valuable class packages that save the programmer from re-inventing basic interfaces. The implementation of a package can shield the programmer from platform-specific issues, but can restrict access to certain low-level components as well. Basic access to the machine subsystems responsible for network communications, file i/o, memory access, and system resources are impacted by the particular implementation of Java being used. Currently, server-side Java code has fewer security restrictions than those imposed on the client.

> **TIP**
>
> When writing Java code, error messages that reference SecurityException indicate that a security restriction has been violated.

Network Communications

The term *sandboxing* is defined as the capability of the applet code to be restricted in its communication with other machines. A sandboxed applet can only communicate back to the server from which it originated. The restriction, that the code will "only play in its sandbox," is the primary line of defense against rogue applets. The security manager subjects networking calls to the restriction that they can only open communication channels between the client and the originating DNS address of the applet. Because the methodology relies on the DNS subsystem to provide address verification, compromises to the DNS address server in turn invalidate the security mechanism.

According to the documentation, applets are able to open up communication channels back to the server on any port. In reality, the Netscape Java implementation does place undocumented restrictions on which ports are available.

> **TIP**
>
> Having an applet in the toolchest that queries all socket ports and returns possible communication channels saves a great deal of time when you're determining the ports that your Java implementation supports.

File I/O

Current implementations of client-side Java do not allow reading or writing to the client's hard disk. On a client machine, calls to open, read, write, or close files generate a `SecurityExceptions` or `IOExceptions notifications`. Sun Microsystems' Appletviewer application uses an access control file to grant read and write permissions to the client's disk drive. It is likely that some derivation of that scheme will be adopted in the future by the Netscape browser. As mentioned earlier in this chapter, server-side Java can access the host hard drive to perform file operations.

Memory Access

In Java source code, the concept of memory pointers doesn't exist. This simplifies the implementation of language by the programmer and reduces code errors. Because data structures aren't referenced by pointers, many proponents of the Java language envision it to be a more secure language than C++. Also, Java programmers should be unable to forge pointers to functions.

System Resources

The ability to lock system resources is a security risk in Java. For example, in the Netscape implementation, locking the `java.net.InetAddress` class results in blocking all new network connections.

Both Java and JavaScript are revolutionary languages that aid the Web site developer in creating interactive content. However, the ability to run remote code on client machines must be considered from the perspective of potential damage to the user's operating environment.

The goal of the Internet vendor community is the creation of a trusted environment where the user doesn't have to worry that an action will have damaging consequences. Ideally, there would also be explicit communication to the user that an operation is about to occur, as well as the ability for the user to prevent it.

The mechanisms for creating a safe networked environment that is intuitive to the end user are still being developed. The security measures encapsulating JavaScript code might not be ready for mission critical environments, but the fast growth of the Internet technologies deserves a close watch for tomorrow's solutions.

Summary

As computer users reach beyond their desktops and communicate with business partners and friends all over the world, issues related to computer security and privacy are becoming paramount concerns. This chapter provided an introduction to the client areas that should be protected from malicious tampering, and the ability of a user to safeguard their machine when running JavaScript and Java programs. The security methodologies are currently in a state of flux. The execution of remote code on client machines is severely restricted in the current implementations as the needs of the user and developer are balanced against concern for potential misuse. Knowledge of the limitations and features present in current technological offerings is critical when establishing a proper level of trust and proliferating dynamic and compelling applications and content throughout the Internet community.

VII
PART

Java and JavaScript

Java from a JavaScripter Perspective

by Christopher Haddad

IN THIS CHAPTER

JavaScript is an unique scripting language that empowers the developer with the tools necessary to quickly create cross-platform, networked applications. The capability to layer event handlers on top of basic HTML form objects provides the developer with the ability to perform client-side validation and custom presentation of data. After the programmer has mastered the structure and syntax of JavaScript, it becomes apparent that using the scripting language to build large, complex application frameworks quickly becomes unwieldy. The loosely type-check conventions free the programmer from having to extensively understand variable conversion techniques but results in code that must be extensively tested by a runtime validation suite to find type-matching errors. The capability to create and control access to multi-tiered data classes is contrived rather than an integral part of the language. JavaScript is most effective when it is used as the designers envisioned, as the program glue that binds application objects into an event-driven system. If a programmer wants to create discrete, reusable data structures and objects, he should use the Java language. JavaScript code can readily access multiple Java objects in a script file, preserving the investment in the scripting language. This chapter provides an overview of the development tools necessary to create Java modules and describes the structure and syntax of the Java language. Particular attention is given to the divergence of the Java language from JavaScript conventions and new concepts and techniques that are unique to Java.

Comparing JavaScript with Java

Understanding a new programming language is never a trivial task, but the similarities between Java and JavaScript decrease the learning curve necessary to switch languages. The structure and syntax of the Java language closely correlates to the implementation of JavaScript. Reserved words, operators, and flow control statements are almost identical. Because Java is a compiled language, a more strict definition of the code tokens is required. This results in two main areas where Java diverges from JavaScript protocol: variable type rules and class encapsulation methodologies. Table 27.1 summarizes the attributes of JavaScript compared to Java.

Table 27.1. Comparison of attributes in the JavaScript and Java languages.

JavaScript	*Java*
Scripting language	Programming language
Loose variable type checking	Strong variable type checking
Rudimentary access control	Tiered-access control definitions
No ability-derived types	Full object-oriented capabilities or inherit attributes
No array checking	Strict array access checks
Instance hierarchy	Object hierarchy
JavaScript objects	Java class

In JavaScript, variables and functions are declared as either local or global in scope. Java enforces a flexible tiered-access convention for variables and methods (functions), whereby elements are visible according to their access modifier: private, protected, or public. The modifiers allow the programmer to hide object attributes and implementation details from the public interface of the object, giving the programmer more latitude in modifying the underlying code supporting a published interface while still maintaining backwards compatibility. Java instance variables are declared in a rigorous manner, and every variable specified must be assigned a primary or derived component type. In contrast, JavaScript code does not require a specification. Java has specialized, built-in data types that optimize the behavior and size of the variable. Another distinction to note is that JavaScript has a more general classification schema (number or string) than Java (int, long, float, and char). Although JavaScript objects do not scale effectively into more complex object types, you can create Java classes that group the variables into object components.

You can consider JavaScript an object-oriented language because it supports an instance hierarchy. Objects are defined with specific variables and methods capable of being referenced using the dot convention but not extended through derivation of subclasses. Although the Java language syntax is similar to the JavaScript scripting language in relation to referencing and creating component objects, Java is a true programming language that bears a more striking resemblance to C++. Using Java code, objects definitions can be reused to serve as the framework for a more complex architecture. Object classes are the building blocks of Java code. Unlike JavaScript, every Java function and variable must be defined inside the class structure. Furthermore, Java provides the capability to aggregate the classes into packages of related objects or define abstract interface conventions for categories of objects.

Another difference is that Java source code is compiled into bytecode by the developer, creating binary components that can be used by other programmers. You can use the created components, class objects, to build derived classes that inherit the functionality of the base class and extend the base class attributes. The ability to extend the base class is the basis for code reuse in large-scale application systems and improved programmer efficiency. Strong type checking is performed by the Java compiler, requiring the programmer to explicitly declare and cast instance variables as either built-in or derived types. JavaScript code allows the programmer to transparently switch the type identifier of a variable without regard to its original type definition.

The high level of integration between the two languages allows the developer to embed JavaScript calls in Java code and access Java class methods in JavaScript. The capability enhances the value of JavaScript programmers who have knowledge of the Java framework. Both languages are built for creating cross-platform networked applications and contain network navigation features. Java extends the network capabilities by providing access to communication sockets between the client and host server.

Programmers familiar with JavaScript will have a minimal learning curve switching to Java when compared to the cost necessary to learn other languages. Java is a more powerful language and allows the developer to model complex systems in an efficient manner. The transition from JavaScript to Java requires understanding a more rigorous language and object hierarchy. Furthermore, you must also understand new development tools and procedures.

Java Language

The Java language was created by a team of programmers at Sun Microsystems who were influenced by their knowledge of C++ and object-oriented programming techniques. The goal was to create a network-centric third generation language whose binary execution objects could run on a disparate collection of computer systems. They chose to develop a system that discarded the system dependent roots of C++ (memory pointers, data allocation, and system-dependent variable size). The language would not require the developer to target multiple hardware platforms, but instead, he could target a single virtual machine. Source code would be compiled into machine-independent bytecode and executed inside a Java virtual machine available on every supported platform. The language shields programmers from system-crashing memory code errors and the underlying hardware that the module eventually executes over. Java is a object-oriented programming language in which every object is defined as a class. A class is a collection of methods and instance variables. All objects can trace their lineage back through parent superclasses to a common root class, Object. A Java class is analogous to a JavaScript object, which is comprised of functions and properties. The class methodology promotes the creation of discrete code modules due to the fact that the class exposes a distinct interface through which other objects access and manipulate the instance variables contained in the class. The internal operation of the class is hidden from the calling object. The object hierarchy is created by the programmer when new class objects are derived from existing base classes. The following code shows a simple Java class object definition:

```
class tag
{
// definition of class variables
private String tagname;
// definition of class methods
tag(String uname)        // class constructor
{
 tagname = new String(uname);
}
void finalize()
{
tagname = null;    // remove reference to tagname
}

private String Get_tag()
{
return(tagname.toString() );
}
}    // end of class block
```

The definition is an example of a simple Java class that represents HTML editing tags.

The class is implicitly derived from the superclass `Object` and is called `tag`. The code provides the capability to set the HTML tag string when declaring the class constructor. Also, the `Get_tag()` method provides the capability to return the tag name after the object has been created. Creating a class object is dependent upon knowledge of the Java language primitives.

The Java source code is a collection of language tokens that are individually defined as keywords, variable operands, literal operands, operators, or separators. The following sections explain the Java language syntax used to define these elements.

Keywords

The keywords in Java closely match those declared in JavaScript. In fact, identifiers and reserved words in JavaScript are not always implemented by the JavaScript language, but you can safely use them in Java code. Java reserved keywords closely correlate to their counterparts in the C++ language. The following list outlines the keywords that are reserved in the Java language:

abstract	finally	private
boolean	float	protected
break	for	public
byte	generic	reset
byvalue	goto	return
case	it	short
cast	implements	static
catch	import	super
char	inner	switch
class	instanceof	synchronized
const	int	this
continue	interface	threadsafe
default	long	throw
do	native	transient
double	new	true
else	null	try
extends	operator	var
false	outer	void
final	package	while

The purpose and use of the keywords are described later in this chapter, but a detailed treatment is outside the scope of this book.

Types

JavaScript does not have explicit built-in primary variable types, but the Java language defines four: character, integer, floating point, and Boolean. (See Table 27.2.) These basic types are used to create more complex data representations. The programmer should select the data type based on the range of values that the instance variable is expected to represent. Proper matching of a data type with the variable's value can result in a significant reduction in memory usage by a program.

Table 27.2. Java built-in data types.

Type	Keyword	Variable Size	Example
Character	char	16-bit Unicode	char cbin = 'a';
Integer	byte	8 bits	byte bbin = 127;
	short	16 bits	short ibin = 32767;
	int	32 bits	int = 2147483648;
	long	64 bits	long = 200;
Floating point	float	32-bit single (15 digit) precision	float fbin = 1.15;
	double	64-bit double (19 digit) precision	double dbin =5.1222;
Boolean	boolean	logical true/false	boolean bvalue = true;

CAUTION

The keyword unsigned does not exist in the Java language. All variables are signed instances and return error messages if literal values are assigned out of range without a cast statement. The code fragment, byte bbin = 128; returns an error message because the literal value, 128, is out of the range of a variable of type byte (-127 to 127). Assigning the literal value 128 to byte bbin with a cast (byte bbin = (byte)128;) results in bbin being set to -1.

The character type is commonly used for storing information in human-readable format. The String object is available as a higher level interface for character representations and is more commonly used in Java. Strings allow the programmer to use the addition operator (+) to concatenate text fragments. Integers are used to represent numeric amounts that do not require decimal values, and floating point types are used when decimals are required. The Boolean type is used to store the result of logical expressions or the binary state of an object (on/off). It should be noted that Boolean instances are not implicitly converted (casted) to numbers in logical expressions. This code quirk means that the third comparison in the following example (if (bvalue == 0)) does not compile, yet the first and fourth print statements execute if this method is called.

```
public void bool_check()
{
boolean bvalue = false;
if (!bvalue)    // compiles without error
    System.out.println(" is zero");    // will print out when bvalue is false!!
if (bvalue)
    System.out.println(" is true");    // will not print out in this example!!
if (bvalue == 0)    // generates an error when compiling
    System.out.println(" is would be zero");
if (bvalue == false)
    System.out.println(" is false");    // will print out!!
}
```

> **CAUTION**
>
> Assigning a variable operand to another operand of smaller size can result in loss of numeric value. Assigning a floating-point type operand to an integer type operand results in loss of precision. The decimal portion of the amount is truncated. You should avoid these two cases.

JavaScript is a loosely type language where the programmer does not have to explicitly define the variable type. For instance, declaring a string using the code fragment `str = "jscript";` is valid code. Data types are converted between objects during the execution of the program. A programmer could assign an integer number to the `str` variable that was previously declared as a string type, and a runtime error does not occur. In Java, a variable type must be explicitly declared for instance variables or the compiler returns the error `"Undefined variable: str"`. Also, assigning elements to variables that are a different type is disallowed unless a cast operator is used. The following code example presents a proof of Java type behavior:

```
public void check_type()
{
short i = 1;
char cbin = 'a';
long b = 100;
b = i;         // cast is not needed when going from
//smaller to larger variable bit size
i = (byte)b;   // explicit cast necessary,
//variable is being assigned to type of smaller bit size
i = (short)32768;    // explicit cast necessary,
//literal is out of range. i = -1

cbin = (char)i;    // explicit cast is necessary,
//changing from numeric to character type
}
```

Type Wrappers

Type wrappers should be familiar elements to JavaScript programmers. They allow object-oriented behavior to be displayed by basic objects due to the fact that object-oriented code is wrapped around the base implementation. For instance, the character type wrapper retains the basic elements of a character variable but also allows the programmer to perform methods on characters such as `isUpperCase`, `isDigit`, and `toLowerCase`. Type wrappers are differentiated from their fundamental base type by the use of a capital letter as the first character in the type (Boolean, Character, Long, Float, and so on).

The requirement of declaring variable types and casting operand assignments is beneficial because strongly typed languages can check for syntax errors at the compiler level and optimize the program for memory usage and speed. Type wrappers are useful for adding object-oriented behavior to basic Java types and are also present in the JavaScript language. The basic variable types can be aggregated into classes and arrays. The array is the most basic method used to combine instance variables into a common structure.

Arrays

In JavaScript, a custom function is used to create arrays. Also, array record elements can have differing (mixed) types. Array elements slots can always be accessed, even if they are outside the boundaries declared for the array. If an array element has not been explicitly assigned by the programmer, it can still be accessed, but the resultant value will be null. In contrast, Java enforces array bounds and generates an compiler error message or runtime exception window if the code attempts to access array elements that have not been explicitly created.

> **CAUTION**
>
> Specifying array dimensions in the declaration statement without the new operator is disallowed. For example, `char c[5];` is invalid code. Similar error-message behavior is found in JavaScript.

The declaration of arrays in Java is straightforward. The variable instance is declared as an array without dimensions and initialized via the new operator:

```
char c_array[];
c_array = new char[5];
```

The size of the array and the variable type are defined as modifiers for the new operator. In the prior example, the array variable `c_array` is created with five elements of type char. Arrays can also be created with more than one dimension by appending brackets. For example, `c_array[][]` defines a two-dimensional array.

> **TIP**
>
> Variable arrays in Java are zero based and the maximum array reference is one less than the number of elements (*n*-1). In Java, the references for a ten-element array range would

be defined as c_array[0] to c_array[9]. This is different from standard JavaScript conventions where arrays are defined using a one-based system. JavaScript arrays are referenced from c_array[1] to c_array[n] where *n* is the number of elements.

Literals

Literals are language token elements that are used to enter hard-coded values into the code. Table 27.3 summarizes the declaration conventions used for assigning literal amounts to different variable types. For instance, the following statement assigns an explicit value of 1.1 to the variable fvar of type float:

```
fvar = 1.1f;
```

Table 27.3. Declaring types for literals.

Variable Type	Literal Declaration
boolean	true, false
character	'c'
integer	1
float	1.1f
double	1.1d
String	"print string"

Operators

Operators are used to perform an action on a class or variable. The following list displays the operators used in Java. Operators are executed according to their level of execution precedence. It is a good code technique to place parentheses around operator-operand pairs so that the execution order is explicitly declared in the code.

.	[]	()	++
--	!	~	*
/	%	+	-
<<	>>	>>>	<
>	<=	>=	==
!=	&	^	&&
||	?:	=	,
|	+=	-=	*=
/=	%=	^=	&=
|=	>>=	>>>=	<<=

These operators can be further classified according to four categories: unary, binary math, relational, equality, or logical.

A separator is used to identify blocks of code and define code tokens. The concept of block scope and block statements are important in Java. The curly braces () define execution levels in the code. The semicolon is used to terminate a Java command line. An example is iValue = 1;cValue = 'a';. Java separators include {}, ; and . (period).

Unary Operators

Unary operators are used when the operation is performed on only one operand. Table 27.4 lists Java's unary operators.

Table 27.4. Java unary operators.

Token	Operation
-	Unary negation
~	Bitwise complement
++	Increment
- -	Decrement

Execution of the unary negation operator changes the sign of the operand. The bitwise complement operator reverses each bit of the variable. If the variable bit was 1, it is changed to 0, and if the variable bit was 0, it is changed to 1. To quickly increment or decrement an operand by one, you use the unary increment or unary decrement operators. These operators are commonly used to optimize the code because they execute faster than their binary counterparts. For example, the increment operator performed on the variable iValue is faster than specifying iValue = iValue + 1;.

Binary Math Operators

A binary math operator executes an operation on two operands and returns a result based on the operator implementation. The execution of binary math operators in Java mimics their JavaScript counterparts. Table 27.5 documents the binary math operators available in Java.

Table 27.5. Java math operators.

Token	Operation
+	Addition
-	Subtraction
*	Multiplication

Token	Operation
/	Division
%	Modulus
&	Bitwise AND
¦	Bitwise OR
^	Bitwise XOR
<<	Left shift
>>	Right shift
>>>	Zero fill right shift

The modulus operator (%) returns the remainder of a division operation. The result of ten modulus three is one. The bitwise mask operators (&, ¦, and ^) are commonly used on variables that may have mutually exclusive subvalues. The shift operators are used to rotate values to lower or higher byte or nibble boundaries.

Relational and Equality Operators

The relational and equality operators in Java also correlate to their JavaScript equivalents.

The list of available relational and equality operators for Java is provided in Table 27.6.

Table 27.6. Java relational and equality operators.

Token	Operation
<	Less than
>	Greater than
<=	Less than or equal to
>=	Greater than or equal to
==	Equal to
!=	Not equal to

Logical Operators

Logical operators are useful for aggregating logical expressions. For example, if one wants to execute statement1 if both variable1 and variable2 are equal to one, a programmer would code the following:

```
if ( (variable1 == 1) && (variable2 == 1) )
    statement1;
```

The logical operators available in Java are given in Table 27.7.

Table 27.7. Java logical operators.

Token	Operation
&&	Logical AND
¦¦	Logical OR

Logical operators are used to condense code that would otherwise be represented by multiple if...else conditions.

Flow Control Statements

Flow control statements are the core of any computer program. The list of valid Java statement types and keywords is defined in Table 27.8. They define the execution sequence of the code based on expression results. The Java statements are similar to those available in JavaScript and should present no difficulty for the JavaScript programmer to learn. The following section presents short fragments of code examples and the rationale behind their use.

Table 27.8. Java statements.

Statement Type	Keyword
Selection statements	if...else
	switch
Label statement	case
Iteration statements	while
	do...while
	for
Jump statements	goto
	continue
	break
	return

The if...else statement is used to select execution between two statement blocks based on the result of an expression. If the expression is true, the first statement block executes. Otherwise, if the expression is false, the second statement block executes. The syntax follows:

```
if (expression1)
{
statement block1
}
else
{
statement block2
}
```

The existence of the else keyword and *statement block2* is optional. Another type of selection statement is the switch statement.

The switch statement provides the programmer with the capability to select a code block for execution based on a match between *expression1*, a matching expression listed after the case statement. In the following example, if *expression1* is equal to *expression3*, the *statement2 block* executes until a break statement is reached. The code execution is then transferred from the break line to the statement immediately following the end of the switch statement block.

```
switch(expression1)
{
case expression2: statement1 block;
            break;
case expression3: statement2 block;
            break;
....
case expressionX: statementX block;
            break;
} // end of switch statement block
// code execution begins here after break statement is executed
```

NOTE

The switch statement is not available in JavaScript. Also, you should avoid the goto statement because it leads to convoluted program execution.

The for...loop statement is used to enumerate over a variable range while executing *statement2* until *expression1* is false. A presentation of the basic for...loop syntax is provided here:

```
for(statement1;expression1;statement3)
    statement2;
```

A while statement performs a task until the expression is evaluated as false. These loops are commonly used for iterating over lists. The break statement can be used in both for...loops and do...while loops to exit the code block. The grammar of the do...while loop is shown here:

```
do
statement1;
while(expression1)
```

Object Scope

The most difficult paradigm shift for JavaScript programmers when writing Java code is understanding the different rules related to object existence scope and object access scope. Object access scope can be defined as the ability for code objects to be referenced from other code fragments. The object's existence scope is the life span of a code object. In JavaScript, all objects exist from the time they were first referenced to the time that all references to the object are deleted. Every object has a well-defined creation, life span, and destruction. The following code is necessary to create a simple array object:

```
// JavaScript Code Describing Array Construction
function makearray(n)
{
//this.length = n;    // assigning this.length is done for convenience
//for(i=1;i<=n;i++)    // zeroing out the array
//is also not necessary, but good code
//    this[i] = 0;
return(this);         // function must return 'this' reference to create object
}

function test_scope_create()
{
str = new makearray(2);
str[1] = 1;
}

function test_scope_valid()
{
alert(str[1]);
}
function test_array()
{
test_scope_create();
test_scope_valid();
}
```

You can declare global variables inside or outside of functions but preferably at the top of the script. When you're writing JavaScript, the physical order of variable declarations in the script are irrelevant when deciding object access scope.

Variable access scope in Java are based on their block scope and not declaration order. A block is defined by curly braces ({}) and can represent a method or a group of Java statements. A Java variable instance has a scope that exists in the current code block and any code blocks that are defined inside the block where the declaration occurred.

The following code listing demonstrates the concept of block scope usage in Java:

```
public void VarScope()
{         // LineRef_1
int ivar = 1;
if (ivar == 1)
    {   // LineRef_4
    int loopvar = 0;  // The scope of ivar is from LineRef4to Line x-1
    while(loopvar < 10)
```

```
    {
ivar++;  // ivar is still in scope
loopvar++;
}
}    // LineRefX-1
}    // LineRef_X
```

The scope of ivar is from `LineRef_1` to `LineRef_X`, and the scope of `loopvar` is from `LineRef_4` to `LineRef_X-1`. Referencing the variables outside of their implied scope generates a compiler error.

Access scope modifiers are used in Java to further restrict the scope of methods and instance variables.

In Java, the access modifiers, in conjunction with block scope, define the access scope of an object. Table 27.9 lists the access scope modifiers and their effect on accessing an object.

Table 27.9. Access scope modifiers.

Keyword	*Definition*
Public	Object available to all.
Protected	Object available only to derived classes and classes in the same package.
Private	Object only accessible to class that declared the method or member variable.

Java methods and variables are automatically declared to be `protected` if no access identifier is specified. It is good code practice to declare methods as public in scope and variables as private in scope.

The `static` keyword modifier indicates that a variable or method will be shared for all classes. It is the equivalent of declaring a global variable or method in JavaScript.

In JavaScript, the keywords `private`, `protected`, `public`, and `static` are reserved words but have no implementation in the language. At the time this chapter was written, their use generates an error.

TIP

Use the var keyword in JavaScript to declare local variables and explicit types when possible. It helps identify variables and aids in porting the code to Java. You cannot currently declare variables in JavaScript using the Java simple types (char, int, `float`, and `boolean`).

27

JAVA FROM A
JAVASCRIPTER
PERSPECTIVE

Exceptions

Exceptions are generated as a result of an error condition. A code block throws an exception in an attempt to find an error handler that can clear the cause of the exception. If the code throwing the exception was bound by a try block, the Java machine calls the corresponding catch block, which attempts to solve the error. The following code segment illustrates this concept:

```
class MyException extends Exception
{
}

public void test_exception()
{
try
    { // code between these braces will
//call error handler1 for exceptions of type MyException
// some code
    }
catch( MyException e)
    {    // error handler1
    }
}
```

Java has exception classes that define the most common types of errors. Example of exception classes are NullPointerException and ArrayStoreException. A corollary to the try/catch block is the try/finally block. The try/finally combination results in a body of code being executed no matter how the code in the try block attempts to exit. For example, the following code listing always executes statementblock1:

```
try
{
//some code
}
finally
{
// perform housekeeping functions to ensure proper termination
}
```

There is currently no true correlation to exceptions built into the JavaScript language. In JavaScript, the window.onerror property can be set to a custom error handler. This handler traps all error window messages if the handler returns true. If the handler returns false, the JavaScript interpreter assumes that the handler did not trap the message and displays the standard error window. To disable all error windows, set window.onerror to null.

TIP

You can nest exceptions. Nested exceptions result in code that can exhaust all methods available to clear an error by repeatedly throwing the exception to alternative error-recovery routines.

Java Objects

An object is a discrete component that has a predefined set of states and behaviors. An object can exist as a simple type (character, integer, floating point, or Boolean) or as a composite type (arrays, classes, interfaces, or packages). Reducing real-world entities to a collection of objects forces the programmer to focus on the individual elements of a system. In Java programs, every variable and function must be part of a class object.

Class

The Java class is the building block for all Java components. Object-oriented programming is an exercise in modeling concepts as a collection of state variables and methods. Methods are equivalent to functions in JavaScript and are defined with explicit return types and parameters. Member variables, which are referred to as instance variables, correlate to the JavaScript prop-erties. Every object in Java is defined as a class object, which has been derived from a base class. If no base class is specified, the Java `Object` base class is used by default.

The use of the object-oriented paradigm has been widely accepted because it allows a building block approach to programming. Classes can be built to define common functionality. For example, you can create a generic HTML tag object. You can extend this base class by creating a new derived class that contains all the functionality of the base class and defines new specialized behavior. In the HTML language, the `TITLE` tag is an object that has specialized functionality. The ability to wrap a new class object around an existing class while maintaining transparent access to the base class procedures is called inheritance. The following code example presents the definition for the `Title_tag` class, which is built upon the base class `HTML_tag`. Note the use of the `super` keyword, which allows the `HTML_tag` constructor to be properly executed.

```
class  Title_tag extends HTML_tag
{
public void draw() { System.out.println(Get_tag() ); }
Title_tag(String uname)
{
super(uname);
}
}// end of class block
```

In Java, every class must be derived from a subclass. The only exception to this rule is the superclass `Object`, which is built into the Java language implementation.

Methods

A class object displays unique behavior and functionality through the existence of methods (functions). In Java, methods must have a return-type specified. If no information is to be re-turned by the method, a return type of `void` is defined. Furthermore, method definitions are placed inside the class definition. This coding rule diverges from the JavaScript language, which defines an object method through the assignment of a function to a JavaScript property vari-able. For example, to define a method function in JavaScript, you use the following code:

```
function MyClass()
{
this.membervariable = 1;
this.MyClassMethod = MyClassMethod;
return(this);
}
function MyClassMethod()
{
// function body of method which operates on MyClass
return(this.membervariable);
}
```

Similar Java code has the following syntax:

```
public class MyClass
{
int membervariable = 1;
int MyClassMethod
{
return(membervariable);
}
}
```

Constructors and Destructors

The ability to model complex entities requires that objects be implicitly initialized when created. Also, objects should perform housekeeping functions when destroyed (close files, deallocate memory, and close windows). Java language, like JavaScript, allows for the initialization of an object when it is created by a function called the class constructor. The method name for the class constructor is the name of the class itself.

You use the new operator to create an instance of a class and execute the creation method (constructor) for the class. The constructor method should initialize all variable members. For example the class Body_tag has a constructor defined as follows:

```
public class Body_tag extends Object
{
protected int width,height;
public Body_tag(int ux, int uy)     // object constructor
{
width = ux;
height = uy;
}
public finalize()     // object destructor
{
}

}
```

> **TIP**
>
> Creation methods in Java do not have to return the member `this`, as is commonly performed in JavaScript. In fact, the constructor is the only method that is not required to have an explicit return type defined.

The destruction method of an object is invoked after all references to the object go out of scope. Before an object is destroyed, the `finalize()` method is called for the class. The execution of this method does not occur immediately after the object goes out of scope, because the method is called by the garbage collection algorithm that scans the object space for freed object instances. Destruction methods should be used to release resources allocated by the class.

> **NOTE**
>
> The Java `Applet` class uses the `init()` and `destroy()` methods to perform creation and destruction operations.

Overloaded Methods

In some instances, it is advantageous to create different versions of the same function. This ability makes the code more maintainable because developers do not have to remember cryptic names that perform the same operations. For example, the `Body_tag(int,int)` method is called to initialize the class when the object is declared. When allocated as an array, the `Body_tag()` method is called. Another useful example of overloading is when arguments are added onto existing methods. A developer can choose to overload the method and support two versions with the same name. This allows existing code to run without modification. The following code example shows how one would overload the constructor method for the `class Body_ tag_`.

```
public Body_tag(int ux, int uy)    // object constructor
{
width = ux;
height = uy;
}
public Body_tag()
{
width = 0;
height = 0;
}
```

Casting Class Objects

Another difficult concept for programmers learning to code in an object-oriented language is the relationship between classes and casting objects to different class types. A superclass can safely be casted to its derived subclass. In fact, Java does not require explicit cast operators to be specified when assigning a superclass to a subclass variable. In contrast, an explicit cast is necessary when assigning a subclass to a superclass. Because superclasses usually add variables and functionality to a subclass, a subclass is not equal to a superclass. Conversions from subclass objects to superclass objects are potentially dangerous.

> **TIP**
>
> The super keyword serves as a reference to the superclass in the subclass object.

Abstract Methods

Abstract methods are definitions of suggested methods for a derived class and do not contain any code that implements the method. To use a defined abstract method, the subclass must contain code that performs the method. The following example creates a class that has the abstract method `draw()`. If a superclass uses this class as its base, it should create an implementation of the function `draw()`, but it is not required to do so.

```
abstract ClassName
{
private char VarInstance;
abstract void draw();
public initialize()
{
VarInstance = null;
}
}
```

> **CAUTION**
>
> If any method in the class is declared abstract, the class must be declared abstract also.

Interfaces

An interface is an entirely abstract class that is used as a suggested template for future derived classes. The interface defines common methods that the derived class should implement; the methods are useful when a developer wants to create a group of classes that should behave in the same manner. For example, you might want to create an interface named `Tag` that specifies the elements all language tags should represent. To define an interface class, the keyword `interface` is used instead of `class`:

```
public interface Interface_name
{
// interface definition
String Get_tag();        // get the object identifier
```

```
void Set_Name(String a);     // instance name
String Get_Name();
void Set_Value(String a); // instance value
String Get_Value();
}
```

> **NOTE**
>
> All methods in an interface should not contain a method definition. A method definition is the actual implementation of the function (the part between the braces).

Interface definitions must initialize all instance variables defined and cannot define constructor methods.

Classes that implement interfaces are declared in the following manner:

```
public class Classname extends Superclass
[ic:ccc] implements Interface_name [ , Other_interface]
{
}
```

You could define the HTML tag class as an extension of the existing interface Tag and allow the subclasses to implement expected behavior:

```
class  HTML_tag extends Object implements Tag
{                 // definition of class variables
private String tagname;
private String Name;
private String Value;
                // definition of class methods
HTML_tag(String uname)     // class constructor
{
 tagname = new String(uname);
}
public void finalize()        // class destructor
{
tagname = null;     // remove reference to variable objects
Name = null;
Value = null;
}
public String Get_tag()
{
return(tagname.toString() );
}
public String Get_Name()
{
return(Name.toString() );
}
public String Get_Value()
{
return(Value.toString() );
}
public void Set_Name(String uname)            // class constructor
{
```

```
 Name = new String(uname);
}
public void Set_Value(String uname)          // class constructor
{
 Value = new String(uname);
}
}     // end of class block
```

Packages

Packages are used to bundle a collection of related classes. The HTML tag classes in the preceding examples could be bundled into a document type definition (DTD) package. Packages allow the programmer to quickly reference code modules; for example, a Java coder could import the entire `netscape.javascript` package in one line: `import netscape.javascript.*`.

The basic Java virtual machine is extended by the standard packages in the same way the computer is extended by the operating system. The standard Java packages are responsible for the basic functionality documented in Table 27.10.

Table 27.10. Java packages from Sun Microsystems.

Package Name	Definition
`java.lang`	Contains essential Java classes for system operation.
`java.io`	Input and output streams for files, strings, and other sources.
`java.util`	Miscellaneous utility classes.
`java.net`	Provides network support.
`java.awt`	The Abstract Window toolkit presents classes to manage user interface.
`java.awt.image`	Manage image data.
`java.awt.peer`	Connect AWT components to platform-specific implementations.
`java.applet`	Base class that enables the creation of Java modules.

To create a class to be included in a Java package, place the following declaration in the `.java` file:

```
package package_name;
```

This creates a subdirectory called *package_name* and places the class file in the subdirectory. The file can now be referenced as a member of the package. It will take a beginner a fair amount of time to understand the nuances of Java package referencing.

To use a Java package, the `import` keyword is specified with the package name. For example, `import netscape.javascript*` includes the entire JavaScript package whereas `netscape.p javascript.JSObject` only imports the JavaScript wrapper class.

> **CAUTION**
>
> The `CLASSPATH` environment variable should point to the directory containing the package root and the standard library package. `CLASSPATH=c:/java/lib;c:/javacode/package_root;`
>
> All packages should be created off the *package_root*. For example, the path to the sample package package_name would be `c:/javacode/package_root/package_name;`.

Built-In JavaScript Objects

In the Netscape framework, JavaScript objects are available in Java and are of class type `JSObject`. Their methods and members are imported from the `netscape.javascript` package. The ability to access JavaScript objects from Java code results in a sophisticated environment that allows the programmer wide latitude in mixing and matching objects. See Chapter 29, "Integrating JavaScript with Java," for more information on calling JavaScript objects from Java.

Java Development Tools

When you create JavaScript code, the only tools necessary are a JavaScript-enabled browser and a text editor. Developing Java modules requires Java library modules and a Java compiler, which can be obtained for free from Sun Microsystems. Numerous software developers are committed to supporting the Java language and have released development tools or libraries targeting Java. However, at the time this chapter was written, tools for Java development are currently not mature offerings like their C++ counterparts, which are capable of developing large-scale, mission-critical applications. This section does not attempt to describe or compare individual development tool offerings (look for back articles in the industry trade magazines or visit the sites listed in the following Resource note) but rather explains the tool categories that aid the developer in creating Java applications: code generators, GUI visual tools, integrated development environments, Java libraries, and Java compilers.

> **RESOURCE**
>
> Java information from Netscape for Developers is available at `http://developer.netscape.com/`. The Java directory is at `http://www.gamelan.com`. The official Java site from Sun Microsystems is at `http://java.sun.com/`.

Libraries

The basic Java class library from Sun is contained in the `classes.zip` file. This file is in standard zip format, but file compression has been disabled. If you want to review or replace the standard Java classes, just unzip the file using your standard utility program. The functionality of significant Java components (SecurityManager, Thread, ClassLoader, and FileOutputStream) can be modified by replacing the original modules with your own renditions.

Netscape provides their version of the class library that resides in the `java/classes` subdirectory. The Netscape implementation includes special packages. One such package, `Netscape.javascript` contains the JSObject used for Java-to-JavaScript communication. Also, the standard library classes are included in the Netscape library file.

Compilers

The Sun JDK contains the standard compiler that most developers use. Many vendors have established licensing agreements with Sun Microsystems and developed Java compilers. These compilers typically are marketed as being faster than the original Java Development Kit (JDK) version. However, the accuracy of the generated bytecode by the clone compilers is questionable. A Java code validation suite is currently not publicly distributed by Sun, so there is no structured methodology for outside parties to evaluate different compilers.

Installing the Sun JDK

Read documentation from Sun site and follow the directions to download and install the JDK. On Windows platforms, the JDK executable should be unzipped from the current directory where you want the Java development kit to be appended. (The toolkit creates a Java subdirectory off the base directory.)

Proper usage of the toolkit requires that the following environment variables be initialized:

- `PATH=execution directory of Java tools;` (example: `PATH=\Java\bin\;`)
- `CLASSPATH=directory containing file(s)` to reference for import statements (example: `CLASSPATH=\Java\lib\classes.zip;`)
- `HOME= directory` used by Applet Viewer to find the `.hotjava` directory (example: `HOME=\users\Default\;`)

IDEs

Integrated development environments (IDEs) allow a programmer to manage the steps necessary to edit, compile, and debug a Java module from one central location. The leading software companies for programming tools (Symantec, Microsoft, and Borland) are committed to releasing IDE packages for the Java language. Future releases should include the ability to generate Java application skeleton frameworks and design a graphical user interface.

GUI Visual Tools

Development applications that allow the developer to create the front-end interface of the application using visual tools are called visual application builders. They have existed in development environments for desktop applications for some years and are recently being created for HTML, JavaScript, and Java languages. They provide the developer with drawing tools or selection palettes capable of visually creating a graphical user interface.

Code Generators

Code generators create Java skeleton frameworks based on developer response to a set of wizard dialogs. They are useful for quickly creating prototypes in rapid application development environments. The prototypes are presented to the client for validation of design specifications and discarded once feedback has been received. Code generators are commonly limited in their flexibility and have the ability to hinder the programmer during complex development cycles. If you use them for a production system, you should have access to the underlying library base source code so that all aspects of the application can be modified. For example, Microsoft makes the MFC library source code available for programmer review and modification.

A Window into the Java Library: the Java Console

The Java Console is a window in Netscape Navigator that is used to display system messages. It is used by the developer to gain feedback on code execution and uncaught Java exceptions. Instead of the using the alert dialog to display debug messages, the Java console is sent messages via the `System.out.println(String);` method. To open the console while in Netscape Navigator, choose Options | Show Java Console from the menu.

Summary

This chapter has demonstrated that the Java language is extremely similar to JavaScript but includes many desirable aspects that JavaScript programmers will want to access. The development of large production systems requires that system specifications be distilled into discrete components. The investment in time necessary to learn the Java language will be rewarded through the ability to extend the JavaScript language by creating custom Java objects that seamlessly integrate with the JavaScript code.

Building Java Applets

by Rick Darnell

Java is one of the hottest topics on the World Wide Web and for good reason. It offers expanded portability for Web content, including sound and animation, without the use of plug-ins or other helper applications and independent of host hardware. In this sense, Java has helped promote a change in the way page developers think about content on the World Wide Web, similar to the way the World Wide Web changed the way people think about the Internet.

Getting to Know Java

Java is an object-oriented programming language developed by Sun Microsystems, Inc. Although not initially conceived as a way to expand the interactivity and capability of Web pages, it didn't take long for people to see how the platform-independent nature of Java made an ideal fit with the nature of the Internet.

In the past, when an author developed a page with special content beyond the constraints of HTML, an important decision had to be made: Either use helper applications or shift the necessary processing to the server. The first solution meant that some content would be inaccessible to some users if they didn't have the helper application or if a helper was unavailable for their system. The second solution meant excluding some content because inherently slow modem lines made animation and sounds unworkable over normal network connections.

Enter Sun's Java. By utilizing a key feature of Java—platform independence—Java applets can implement sound, animation, and other user interactivity regardless of the platform.

What Is Java?

Sun Microsystems makes it clear whenever introducing Java that "Java is a simple, robust, secure, object-oriented, platform-independent dynamic programming environment."

At first, all of this Java talk can sound like a lot of voodoo. After you strip away the hype, however, it's easy to see how Java works effectively for implementing simple solutions to potentially complicated challenges in a distributed environment.

Simple

Java was designed with C and C++ programmers in mind. C and C++, however, had many hard-to-understand, rarely used features that the Java developers felt caused more pain than benefit. Important functions that come standard to every program, such as memory allocation and pointer arithmetic, automatically get handled by the Java system without any acknowledgment from the programmer.

In addition, Java is relatively small. Because they run on a wide variety of platforms, Java applications tend to be smaller than the multi-megabyte applications that predominate the marketplace. The overhead to run a Java program includes 40KB for the basic interpreter and classes, plus an additional 175KB for the standard libraries and threading.

Robust

Java programs must be inherently reliable because any piece of Java byte must be capable of running on any platform. For this reason, a great deal of emphasis is placed on checking for bugs and problems early in the development process, beginning with basic language implementation.

A pointer serves as a popular example. C++, a close cousin of Java, used extensive pointer arithmetic to keep track of arrays and other memory variables. This setup enabled programmers to take full advantage of a specific platform, but it also created problems when pointers went awry, overwriting memory and corrupting data.

The Java compiler checks for a wide variety of errors beyond basic syntax, including type casting and method invocations. If you've made a mistake or mistyped, chances are good that your mistake will get flagged by the compiler, which is a far better place than the interpreter at runtime.

Secure

Running in a distributed environment, such as an intranet or the World Wide Web, requires safeguards for client computers; a potentially hostile piece of code can do a great deal of damage by erasing files, formatting disks, and creating other types of damage. Given the way applets are implemented—automatic load and run—you need to ensure the integrity of any piece of code distributed to a broad and uncontrolled audience. Java uses three security procedures to make the end user safe from malicious attacks:

- Bytecode verification
- Memory layout control
- File access restrictions

Bytecode Verification

After a piece of Java code is loaded into memory, it enters the interpreter where it gets checked for language compliance before the first statement is executed. This process ensures against corruption or changes to the compiled code between compile time and runtime.

Memory Layout

Next, the memory layout is determined for each of the classes, preventing would-be hackers from forging access by deducing anything about the structure of a class or the machine it's running on. Memory allocation is different for each class, depending on its structure and the host machine.

File Access Restrictions

After that, the interpreter security continues to monitor the activity of the applet to make sure it doesn't access the host file system, except as specifically allowed by the client or user. You can extend some implementations of this specific feature to include no file access, period.

Although no system can guarantee 100 percent security, Java goes a long way to ensure the protection of client systems from its applets.

Object Oriented

Object oriented, probably one of the most overused and confusing terms in computer lingo, really has a simple and easy-to-understand meaning. It facilitates creating clean and portable code by breaking software down into coherent units.

In other words, object-oriented programming focuses on ways of interacting with data, rather than the programming language. For example, if you're going to mow the lawn, are you going to be concerned about starting the lawnmower or about the type of socket used to install the spark plug? In object-oriented programming, the focus is on the lawnmower.

Objects become the basic building blocks of the application. Because of their modularity, an object can change without requiring major revision of the other program elements.

Platform Independent

The feature of platform-independence is probably the most important one. One compiled piece of Java code can run on any platform with a Java compiler. Currently, the list of platforms includes Windows 95, Solaris, and Macintosh, but that list should grow significantly in the near future. By its very nature, Java does not contain any "implementation-specific" syntax. This format means a byte is an 8-bit integer and a float is a 32-bit IEEE 754 floating-point number, no matter where the applet runs.

Dynamic

One benefit of the object-oriented code is the dynamic nature of the resulting programs. By using inherited interfaces—a set of methods without instance variables or implementation— updating a class library does not affect the capability of the rest of the program to interact with it.

Why Is Java So Hot?

Java holds a great deal of promise for the World Wide Web and computers in general because it provides a solution to the problem of incompatible platforms. The Internet and intranets are no longer expected to include similar or directly compatible machines (all UNIX, all Macintosh, or all PC). Because it has a neutral architecture, the same application written in Java can be used by anyone on the network without concern for what kind of machine the developer used.

For stand-alone applications, Java's object-oriented structure provides an easy way to upgrade. The class for the upgrade or extension of the application is downloaded into the appropriate class library; then, you can run the updated features.

With its modeling capabilities, Java represents a good choice for implementing advanced Web capabilities and content, such as virtual reality sites or Web crawlers powered by intelligent agents.

How to Use Java Now

Probably the simplest way to implement Java is through embedding applets in your HTML pages. A wide variety of applets are already available for inclusion, including the animation applet included with the Java Developer's Kit and a plethora of "ticker" display applets.

> **NOTE**
>
> Although Java applets are spreading quickly, they do not come with all browsers. Netscape's Navigator and Sun's HotJava support Java applets, and Microsoft's Internet Explorer is scheduled to include applet functionality with its 3.0 release. NCSA Mosaic has included Java compatibility in its wish list for future upgrades to its product, but no word has been given on when that might happen.
>
> If your browser is not Java-compatible, the applet section of the HTML page is ignored.

How Applets and Applications Are Different

Java applications work similarly to stand-alone programs, such as your browser or word processor. They don't require a third-party intermediary, such as HotJava or the Applet Viewer. Applets require a Java-compatible browser or the Applet Viewer for viewing. They operate similarly to other objects embedded in HTML documents, such as Shockwave or RealAudio files, which require assistance to run.

> **NOTE**
>
> The HotJava browser developed by Sun is a Java application that was written and implemented entirely in the Java language.

Because applets run on a host system, they are especially suspect and they have several key security restrictions. Applets have limited capability to interact with their host platform. An applet cannot write files or send files to a printer on the local system. In addition, it cannot read local files or run local applications. Although no system is 100 percent secure, Java goes to great lengths to ensure the integrity of applets generated under its banner.

Java is not bulletproof, however. As quickly as it was proclaimed "secure," a dedicated group of programmers went to work to find security holes—and they found them. Through cooperative efforts, Sun, Netscape, Microsoft, and others are correcting these holes, but it's still a dangerous world. There are reports of "black Java" applets that are hostile enough to format system drives and pass secure information across the Internet.

You can do a few things to protect yourself and your system:

- Use only the most up-to-date versions of software.
- If your system allows screening applets at the firewall, take advantage of it. If there are applets you'd like to use, make them available internally.
- Don't browse a Java site unless you know it's clean.

As discussed in the introduction, the compiled bytecode is checked extensively for illegal operations and verified again on the host system before the applet is run. Although these security features limit the scope and capabilities of an applet, they also help ensure against "Trojan horse" viruses and other shenanigans by less-than-scrupulous programmers.

With all the security features built in, you don't want to implement word processors, spreadsheets, or other interactive applications in Java applets. If you require these programs, consider building a full Java application, which does not contain the security restrictions of an applet.

> **NOTE**
>
> It has been said a million times, but if you have just started using Java, it bears repeating: Java isn't JavaScript. JavaScript isn't Java.
>
> Java, in applet or application form, is a compiled language with classes and inheritance. HTML pages can include a reference to Java applets, which then get downloaded and run when a compatible browser finds the tag.
>
> JavaScript is an object-based, client-side scripting language developed by Netscape, but it does not include classes or inheritance. JavaScript exists on the HTML page and gets interpreted by a compatible browser along with the rest of the page.
>
> Although they share some common syntax and terminology, the two items work differently and have different uses. Confusing Java and JavaScript only leads to a steeper learning curve.

HotJava

HotJava represents one of the first applications written entirely in Java (see Figure 28.1). In its initial release, HotJava primarily showed how applets could be included as part of an HTML document. Now, it functions closer to a full-featured browser, supporting all HTML 1 and 2 specifications. Support for HTML 3.2 is in the process of integration.

FIGURE 28.1.

The HotJava browser is one of the first stand-alone applications written entirely in the Java language.

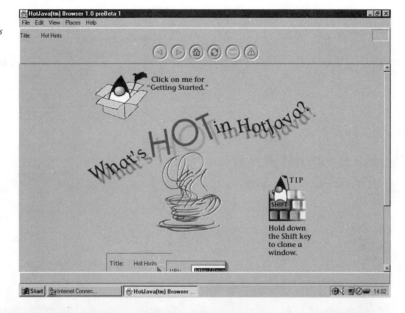

HotJava operates differently from most browsers in its basic functioning. Settings, preferences, and other basic maintenance screens get stored in the form of HTML documents and classes.

Stripped down to its most basic level, HotJava knows nothing about anything. Classes are added to the browser so it can understand HTML, e-mail, sound files, and other specialty items. As new content and new formats are developed for Web pages, Java will only require the addition of another class. You won't need a complete upgrade to a new version to take advantage of the latest developments.

Applet Viewer

During applet development and testing, sometimes it's easier to bypass the unnecessary over-head of a browser. If your browser doesn't support applets, you still need a way to view the applets. At this point, the Java Applet Viewer comes in handy. (See Figure 28.2.)

Figure 28.2.

The Java Applet Viewer enables the programmer to view embedded Java applets without the use of a browser. Only the applet is displayed; the rest of the HTML is ignored.

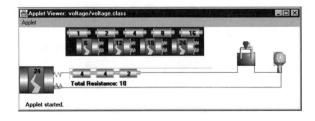

Using the Applet Viewer

The Applet Viewer searches the HTML document for the <APPLET> tag, as shown in Listing 28.1.

Listing 28.1. A simple HTML document containing an applet tag.

```
<HTML>
<HEAD>
<TITLE>The animation applet</TITLE>
</HEAD>
<BODY>
<APPLET CODE="Animator.class" WIDTH=460 HEIGHT=160>
<PARAM NAME=imagesource VALUE="images/beans">
<PARAM NAME=endimage VALUE=10>
<PARAM NAME=pause VALUE=200>
</APPLET>
</BODY>
</HTML>
```

Using the information contained within the tag, the Applet Viewer opens a window and runs the applet. Other HTML information on the page is ignored—only the applets appear.

The Java Applet Viewer is distributed with the Java Development Kit and is found in the same directory as the Java compiler and interpreter. To run the Applet Viewer, use the following steps:

1. Create a document that references your applet with the appropriate tags and parameters. See Listing 28.1 for an example.

2. From a command-line prompt, type `appletviewer [path/]filename.html`.

   If the Applet Viewer launches from the same directory as the HTML document, you don't need the path name. Otherwise, the path is relative to your current location in the directory structure. The extension `.htm` is also valid for the viewer.

3. Any applets found in the HTML document are loaded and run with each applet in its own instance of the Applet Viewer.

4. Although you cannot change the initial parameters contained within the HTML page from the Applet Viewer, you can start the applet from the beginning by choosing Applet | Restart. To load it again from memory, select Applet | Reload.

5. Leave the applet by choosing Applet | Quit.

> **CAUTION**
>
> The Applet Viewer Reload function does not work if the application was launched from the same directory as the HTML document and classes. For applets, create a subdirectory from your class directory called HTML and place all your classes and HTML files in it. Call the Applet Viewer from the parent directory by using appletviewer html*filename*.html. This way, you can make changes to the applet, compile it, and use the Reload function to see your changes.

Creating Java Applets

Creating Java applets is easier if you already have a background in programming. With Java's tight structure, the basic format of an applet is fairly straightforward. You walk through an example here.

> **RESOURCE**
>
> You can access online tutorials and documentation for Java and object-oriented programming from the Sun site, http://java.sun.com/.

Applet ABCs

At its simplest, an applet consists of two parts—the class declaration and a paint method. The following snippet contains a breakdown of the common elements for any applet:

```
import java.awt.Graphics;

public class MyApplet extends java.applet.Applet {
    public void paint (Graphics g) {
        your statements here;
    }
}
```

The first line includes a copy of the Graphics class from Java's Abstract Windowing Toolkit (AWT), which contains the methods needed for putting graphics, including text, lines, and dots, on the browser screen. This line can also be represented as import java.awt.Graphics if you're using more than the Graphics class.

28

BUILDING JAVA
APPLETS

Second, the actual applet is declared. It is `public`, meaning it is available to any other class, and it is a subclass of Java's `Applet` class, which provides the behavior necessary for interaction with the host browser.

The third section defines a method called `paint`, which the Java interpreter uses to put the information on the screen. It is public to the class, and `void` indicates it does not return a value when it is completed. Its one parameter is an instance of the `Graphics` class imported on the first line of the program, which is referred to as `g`. This reference could just as easily be `bob` or `hammer`, but `g` is the commonly used convention.

Displaying with Paint

Now that the applet is defined, you need to make it do something. For the `paint` method, include the following line:

```
g.drawString("Have a nice day.",50,25);
```

After compiling the code and inserting it into an HTML document (see "Using an Applet" later in this chapter), you get something that looks like Figure 28.3.

FIGURE 28.3.

`MyApplet` *displays a simple message on the screen.*

> **NOTE**
>
> To convert your source code into a usable class, type `javac MyApplet.java` at the command prompt. If any errors are reported, check your spelling and syntax and try again.

Of course, applets can do much more. By including some other AWT classes, you can make the text look better. First, you need the classes that control the font and display color:

```
import java.awt.Font;
import java.awt.Color;
```

Now, after the class declaration, create a variable to hold a new setting for the text:

```
Font f = new Font("TimesRoman",Font.ITALIC,24);
```

After the `paint` method declaration, use the `Graphics.set` methods to set the display before writing to the screen:

```
g.setFont(f);
g.setColor(Color.red);
```

With this extra bit of effort, the applet now looks like Figure 28.4.

FIGURE 28.4.

MyApplet *now displays in a larger font in red after some minor revisions to the code.*

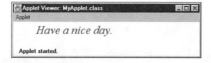

Again, this example is limited. The addition of a parameter to control the string would make it more useful to the HTML author. After the class declaration, declare the message as a variable:

```
String message;
```

A new method is also required to initialize the value of `message`.

NOTE

In addition to paint, four major activities exist in the life of an applet. If any get omitted, default versions are provided in the `Applet` class. This setup is called inheritance. Providing new methods in the applet is called overriding.

The first activity is initialization, accomplished with the `init` method: `public void init() {...}`. This activity occurs once, immediately after the applet is loaded. Initialization includes creating objects, setting graphics, or defining parameters. It can only happen once in the applet's life.

The second activity is starting, accomplished with the `start` method: `public void start() {...}`. After initialization, activity begins. This activity can also happen if a user activity stopped the applet. Starting can happen many times in the life of an applet. The `paint` method gets invoked somewhere in this method.

The next activity is stopping, accomplished with the `stop` method: `public void stop() {...}`. This activity can be an important method to include because by default the applet continues running and using system resources, even after the user has left the page with the applet. Like `start`, stopping can occur many times in the course of execution.

The last activity is destroying, accomplished with the `destroy` method: `public void destroy() {...}`. Destroying is where an applet throws out its own garbage after completing execution—when the applet is no longer needed or the user exits the browser. Java provides adequate coverage in this department, so you don't need to override this method unless you want to return specific resources to the system.

Initializing the message parameter requires overriding the `init` method for the applet:

```
public void init() {
    this.message = getParameter("message");
    if (this.message == null) {
        this.message = "Your message here."; }
    this.message = "A note from Java: " + this.message;
}
```

This method retrieves the value of the parameter in the HTML document. If a parameter named `message` is not found, the value is null and `message` is set to the default string.

> **TIP**
>
> Java is case-sensitive for all its variables, even when passed back and forth as parameters. Remember that a `Rose` by another name is not a rose.

Now you need to update the `paint` method so that it uses the string defined in `init`, rather than the literal string in the `drawString` method:

```
g.drawString(this.message);
```

Using the Applet Viewer again now generates the results in Figure 28.5.

FIGURE 28.5.

The default message generated by `MyApplet` *after checking for a* `message` *parameter and finding none.*

To place your own message in the applet, add a `<PARAM>` tag to the HTML source containing the applet. For more information, see "Passing Parameters to Applets" later in this chapter. The complete listing for `MyApplet` appears in Listing 28.2. Note the use of the parameter in the `init` method.

> **TIP**
>
> Listing 28.3 is a sample HTML file that you can use as the basis for inserting or testing applets. Saved in a generic form, it is a very reusable piece of code.

Listing 28.2. A simple applet for displaying text on-screen.

```
import java.awt.Graphics;
import java.awt.Font;
import java.awt.Color;

public class MyApplet extends java.applet.Applet {
    Font f = new Font("TimesRoman",Font.ITALIC,24);
    String message;

    public void init() {
        this.message = getParameter("message");
        if (this.message == null) {
            this.message = "Your message here."; }
        this.message = "A note from Java: " + this.message;
```

```
    }

    public void paint(Graphics g) {
        g.setFont(f);
        g.setColor(Color.red);
        g.drawString(this.message,50,25);
    }
}
```

Listing 28.3. A sample of an HTML document that can display MyApplet.

```
<HTML>
<HEAD>
<TITLE>The MyApplet</TITLE>
</HEAD>
<BODY>
<HR>
<APPLET CODE="MyApplet.class" WIDTH=400 HEIGHT=50>
<PARAM NAME=message VALUE="Here I am.">
</APPLET>
<HR>
</BODY>
</HTML>
```

28

Using an Applet on a Web Page

Using applets on a Web page takes a two-part process. First, you must make sure your classes and related files, such as images and audio clips, appear in a directory accessible to the HTML page. One common location is a classes subdirectory of the HTML documents.

Second, you insert the applet tag that refers to the class in the Web page, along with any parameters the applet needs to function.

All About the Applet Tag

You use the <APPLET> tag to insert the applet on a page with the following syntax:

```
<APPLET CODE="appletName.class" [CODEBASE="pathToClass"] WIDTH=xxx
➥HEIGHT=xxx [ALIGN= ]>
[<PARAMETER name=parameterName value=parameterValue>]
</APPLET>
```

The required line of code identifies the name of the applet, CODE, and the size it will appear on the page.

The optional parameter CODEBASE indicates a relative path to the class if it is not stored in the same directory as the HTML file. ALIGN works similar to the parameter in the <IMG SRC> tag by controlling the positioning of HTML text adjacent to the applet's space.

Passing Parameters to Applets

Parameters are used to pass information to applets about its environment and how it should behave in the current HTML document. Some applets have one method of running and don't accept any parameters. Most, however, contain some user-definable parameters that you can change.

The <PARAM> tag enables you to pass information to the applet. The syntax is

```
<PARAM NAME=paramName VALUE=paramValue>
```

The parameter name is case sensitive and must exactly match the parameter name in the applet. If the applet does not provide exceptions for mismatched data types, an incompatible value could cause it to not function. For example, if a parameter looks for a string and you enter an integer, the applet could fail to operate.

Applets for Fun and Utility

This section provides a selection of applets available on the CD-ROM that you can use on your own Web pages.

Animator

Probably one of the most frequently used, the Java animator applet (see Figure 28.6) comes with the Java Development Kit and provides a quick-and-easy way to add animation to your Java-powered page.

FIGURE 28.6.

The Animator applet displays a series of images with an option for frame-specific sounds and soundtracks.

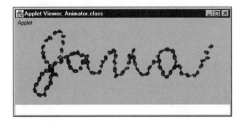

Animator also supports synchronized sound with the animation, but the sound must use the Sun.AU format. No other sound formats are supported yet.

Implementing the applet requires a set of GIF or JPG files containing the images that form the animation.

> **TIP**
>
> Try to keep the size of the images as small as possible. Each image must be downloaded to the client machine, adding significantly to the time required for the applet to load and run.

A wide variety of parameters control the operation of Animator. Here's the breakdown and syntax:

`<APPLET CODE="Animator.class" WIDTH=`*number*` HEIGHT=`*number*`>`: Width should be at least the width in pixels of the widest frame, whereas height should reflect the size of the tallest frame. Smaller values result in the image getting clipped.

`<PARAM NAME=IMAGESOURCE VALUE="`*pathInfo*`">` points to the directory that contains the animation frames. The default directory is the same as the HTML document. By default, the files get named `T1.gif`, `T2.gif`, and so on.

`<PARAM NAME=STARTUP VALUE="`*filename*`">`: An image that gets displayed while the applet loads and prepares to run.

`<PARAM NAME=BACKGROUND VALUE="`*filename*`">`: An image file for use as a background for the animation.

`<PARAM NAME=BACKGROUNDCOLOR VALUE="`*color,color,color*`">`: The color for the animation background, represented as an RGB value with a number from 0 to 255 for each of the settings.

`<PARAM NAME=STARTIMAGE VALUE=`*number*`>`: The first frame in the animation—by default, 1.

`<PARAM NAME=ENDIMAGE VALUE=`*number*`>`: The last frame in the animation.

`<PARAM NAME="NAMEPATTERN" VALUE="`*dir/prefix%N.suffix*`">`: A pattern to use for generating names based on `STARTIMAGE`, `ENDIMAGE`, or `IMAGES`.

`<PARAM NAME="PAUSE" VALUE=`*number*`>`: Number of milliseconds to pause between images—default can be overridden by `PAUSES`.

`<PARAM NAME="PAUSES" VALUE="`*number¦number¦...*`">`: Millisecond delay per frame with each value separated by a vertical bar. Blank uses a default `PAUSE` value.

`<PARAM NAME="REPEAT" VALUE=true>`: If true, the animation continues as a loop.

`<PARAM NAME="POSITIONS" VALUE="`x@y¦x@y...`">`: Screen positions (x@y) for each frame, represented in pixels and separated by vertical bars. A blank value uses the previous frame's position.

`<PARAM NAME="IMAGES" VALUE="`*number¦number¦...*`">`: Used to define an explicit order for frames, which becomes useful if your frames are out of order or you want to reverse the sequence (such as "1¦2¦3¦2¦1").

`<PARAM NAME="SOUNDSOURCE" VALUE="aDirectory">`: Indicates the directory with the audio files. The default is the same directory as the class.

`<PARAM NAME="SOUNDTRACK" VALUE="aFile">`: An audio file to play throughout the animation as background music.

`<PARAM NAME="SOUNDS" VALUE="aFile.au|||||bFile.au">`: Plays audio files keyed to individual frames.

`<PARAM NAME="HREF" VALUE="aURL">`: The URL of the page to visit when the user clicks the animation (if not set, a mouse click pauses or resumes the animation).

Clock

The Clock applet displays an analog clock on-screen, complete with a sweeping second hand. (See Figure 28.7.) Right now, the clock offers no way to control its appearance. It would, however, be a relatively simple matter to add a parameter to control the size of the clock, whether the second hand appears, and the display of the date and time underneath.

FIGURE 28.7.

The Clock applet, a small and simple local-time clock to include on a Web page.

The time is determined by the host machine. It occupies little computer space for a computer implementation of an analog clock—just more than 3K. The following line incorporates the Clock applet:

```
<applet code="Clock2.class" width=170 height=150>
</applet>
```

Nervous Text

Nervous text works like combining the basic HTML heading with a strong dose of really strong coffee and a slab of double-chocolate cake. (See Figure 28.8.) The letters jitter and jump around like Mexican jumping beans on a hot pan.

FIGURE 28.8.

The Nervous Text applet moves each letter around in a frantic, haphazard fashion.

Nervous text takes a string of text as its lone parameter. If not included, the default text is "HotJava." You can also modify the applet's source code to achieve more flexibility, including controlling the size and color of the font. Include the applet with the following code:

```
<PARAM NAME=text VALUE="string">
```

Ticker (`http://www.uni-kassel.de/fb16/ipm/mt/java/ticker.htm`)

The Ticker applet provides one example of the many "ticker tape" applets available (see Figure 28.9). It is one of the improved versions that has made the extra effort to reduce flicker and provide additional control over the text.

FIGURE 28.9.

The Ticker applet provides a flexible way to display scrolling messages on the browser screen.

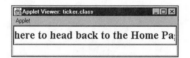

The Ticker applet takes a variety of parameters:

> `<PARAM NAME=msg VALUE="string">`: The message to display.

> `<PARAM NAME=speed VALUE=number>`: The animation speed, expressed as the number of pixels per 100 milliseconds. The default is 10.

> `<PARAM NAME=txtco VALUE="r,g,b">`: The color of the message, expressed as an RGB value with numbers from 0 to 255. If omitted, the default is black.

> `<PARAM NAME=bgco VALUE="r,g,b">`: The color of the background. If omitted, the default appears as light gray.

> `<PARAM NAME=shco VALUE="r,g,b">`: The color of the message shadow. If omitted, no shadow appears.

> `<PARAM NAME=href VALUE="URL">`: The ticker can also serve as a hyperlink if the user clicks the ticker. A relative or complete URL is legal.

> `<PARAM NAME=hrefco VALUE="r,g,b">`: The color of the URL frame. If omitted, the default is blue.

> `<PARAM NAME=start VALUE="yy, mm, dd">`, `<PARAM NAME=exp VALUE="yy, mm, dd">`: Dates to start and stop displaying the applet. If the page gets viewed outside of these dates, as determined by the host machine, the ticker does not display its message. It still occupies space on the screen, however. You can use either date parameter by itself.

> `<PARAM NAME=exfill VALUE="r,g,b">`: If the local date falls outside the start and stop parameters, the box is filled with this color.

Nuclear Power Plant

The Nuclear Power Plant simulation really doesn't seem useful unless you plan to run power plants in Russia. (See Figure 28.10.) It does, however, show a good example of a user interface, object interaction, and animation. After the applet is initialized, you can select one of three powerplant crises—from pump failures to blown turbines. To prevent a meltdown, open and close valves and start pumps as necessary. If you don't work quickly enough, the core turns to mush and releases enough radioactivity to ruin everyone's day.

Figure 28.10.

The Nuclear Plant applet, a creative use of Java as a learning tool and game implementation.

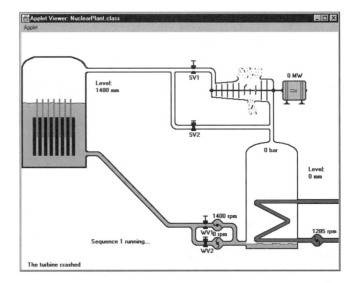

Applet Sources on the Web

The Web offers many sources for applets that you can use. Make sure to check the licensing on the applet. Just because an applet appears on a page doesn't mean you can freely use it.

JavaSoft (`http://java.sun.com/`)

JavaSoft, a subsidiary of Sun Microsystems, handles the Java products. Go to its Web site first when looking for information, documentation, updates, downloads, and other feedback. (See Figure 28.11.)

Originally part of the Sun Web site, JavaSoft received its own space to handle the dramatic increase in attention Java has received since its release.

FIGURE 28.11.

The JavaSoft home page includes links to the Java Developers Kit, HotJava, and other information for Java users and developers.

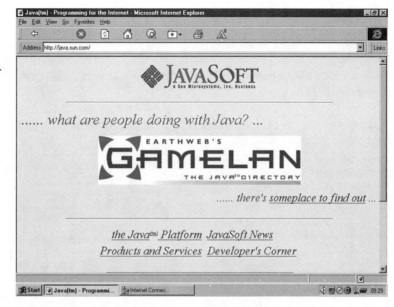

JavaWorld (http://www.javaworld.com/)

The first online publication devoted entirely to Java, JavaWorld comes out monthly and includes news and views about Java developments, along with hands-on tips and tricks. (See Figure 28.12.) Programming contests are a regular feature, and many articles include links to Java-powered sites, source code, and other helpful items.

FIGURE 28.12.

JavaWorld includes interviews with the movers and shakers in the Java realm, along with hands-on examples, tutorials, and contests.

28

BUILDING JAVA
APPLETS

Gamelan (`http://www.gamelan.com/`)

The Gamelan site shows you what the rest of the world is doing with Java. (See Figure 28.13.) Links appear here to some of the best applets to date for the viewing, and you can download some for use on your pages. It also includes a page devoted to JavaScript for links devoted to pages utilizing Java's cousin.

FIGURE 28.13.

Gamelan was developed specifically for the development and advancement of Java. As such, it maintains a comprehensive list of links to applications and applets available on the Web.

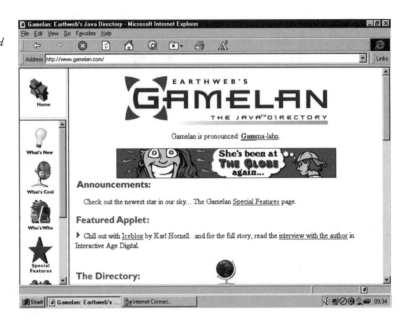

Some of the innovative productions found here include animators, tickers, network utilities, and a "Learn to Dance" applet.

alt.lang.java

Although not technically a source for applets, the `alt.lang.java` newsgroup provides a great source of information about Java and its uses. Following the threads can also lead to Java applets and applications, where you can learn from people already making the most of this new language.

Summary

Java use keeps spreading quickly as more and more hardware and software manufacturers pledge support to the language and concepts. Even if you never have the chance to delve deep into the intricacies of building an applet or application from scratch, an understanding of the basics helps you take full advantage of the powerful capabilities available.

CHAPTER 29

Integrating JavaScript with Java

by Heather Downs

IN THIS CHAPTER

One of JavaScript's most powerful features is its capability to interact with Java. JavaScript scripts may invoke Java methods, examine and modify Java variables, and control Java applets. Java applets, in turn, may access JavaScript methods, properties, and data structures. Applications also can use JavaScript and Java to create dynamic content. HTML can be generated "on the fly" within JavaScript scripts and Java applets, and displayed in browser windows by constructing `javascript:` URLs.

Running Java Applets

JavaScript scripts communicate with Java applets running in an HTML page by accessing members (methods and fields) of the Java objects associated with those applets. Any Java method declared with the `public` modifier is available to be called from JavaScript, and any Java field declared as `public` is available to be examined or modified. The first step in communicating with a Java applet from JavaScript is to obtain a reference to the applet. Once that's accomplished, it's possible to directly access any of the applet's public members.

Referencing Applets

Applets running in a document are reflected in JavaScript within the document's `applets` array. For example, the first applet defined in the current document could be referenced from JavaScript as `document.applets[0]`. The same applet also could be referenced by name as `document.applets["appletName"]`, or simply `document.appletName`, if its name were specified in the applet tag. An applet's name can be specified in the applet tag by giving a value to the `name` attribute, so the following tag

```
<applet name="myApplet" code="testApplet.class" width=100 height=100 MAYSCRIPT></
applet>
```

would create an applet of class `testApplet` named `myApplet`. If that applet also happened to be the first applet on the page, it could be referenced by any of `document.applets[0]`, `document.applets["myApplet"]`, `document.myApplet`.

JavaScript scripts may also reference Java applets running in other frames in the same browser window. For example, if a Java applet were running in a frame called `frame1`, it could be referenced from a sibling frame as `parent.frame1.document.myApplet`.

Controlling Applets

Once a reference to an applet has been obtained, the next step is to communicate with it by invoking one of its methods. For example, if the applet had a public method called `hello()` that took no arguments, that method could be called like

```
document.myApplet.hello();
```

Making that call from within JavaScript has precisely the same effect as calling the applet object's `hello()` method from within Java. As another example, suppose you have a Java applet with an audio soundtrack, and you want to turn the sound on and off from JavaScript. If the applet provided methods like the following, you could call those methods from JavaScript to control the applet's soundtrack:

```
public void soundtrackOn();
public void soundtrackOff();
```

If you wanted to make toggling the soundtrack on and off as simple as clicking a mouse button, you could use JavaScript as "wiring" to hook up radio buttons in an HTML form to the Java applet. The following example shows how a form element's `onclick` method can be used to communicate with the applet:

```
<form>
<input type="radio" checked="true" name="sound"
onclick="document.myApplet.soundtrackOn()">On<br>
<input type="radio" name="sound"
onclick="document.myApplet.soundtrackOff()">Off<br>
</form>
```

The values for the `onclick` event handlers specify that the `soundtrackOn()` or `soundtrackOff()` method of the applet named `myApplet` are called whenever the corresponding radio button is clicked with the mouse. As a slightly more complicated example, which illustrates passing arguments to Java methods, suppose the applet also has a method with the prototype

```
public void changeText(String s);
```

which, when called, changes the text displayed by the applet to the value specified by string `s`. If the following elements were added to the form

```
<input type="text" name="newtext">
<input type="button" value="Change Text"
onclick="document.myApplet.changeText(form.newtext.value)">
```

users could enter new strings into the text input field and have them reflected in the applet. When the Change Text button is clicked, the text field's value is extracted, converted to a Java String, and passed as the argument to the applet's `changeText()` method. This is a powerful paradigm. The ability to pass JavaScript objects to Java methods makes it possible to quickly and easily build attractive GUIs out of standard HTML forms augmented with JavaScript event handlers, and use them to control Java applets.

JavaScript Objects in Java

One of the most difficult and confusing aspects of calling Java methods from JavaScript can be getting the types of the arguments you pass to Java to match up with the types of the arguments for which the Java method is looking. If the two sets of arguments don't match exactly, the attempted function call fails, and you get an error message saying that JavaScript couldn't find a Java method that was expecting the arguments you tried to pass.

Java is a strongly typed language (meaning that every variable has a specific, declared type), and all Java methods must declare, in advance, how many arguments they are expecting, and of what type and in what order. Within a Java program, any attempt to invoke a method with an argument sequence that doesn't exactly match, type for type, the method's declared argument sequence, results in a compile-time error.

JavaScript, in contrast, has much more relaxed typing, and, as an interpreted language, has to do all its checking at runtime anyway. JavaScript variables don't have a declared type; in fact, they don't have to be declared at all, because they can simply come into existence by being referenced. The same JavaScript variable can be assigned a string in one statement, an integer in the next statement, and an array in the next. How, then, are JavaScript objects converted into Java objects when they're passed to Java methods? How does Java know how to find a Java type that exactly matches the JavaScript object's structure? The short answer is that, in general, it doesn't. There probably is no such object. Unless the object happens to fall into one of the following exceptional cases, Java won't necessarily have a class that exactly mirrors the object's JavaScript type, so it simply assigns it a default type, `JSObject`, specifically designed to represent JavaScript objects in Java.

Fortunately, the aforementioned exceptional cases encompass some of the most common and useful data types, including JavaScript's three basic datatypes: strings, numbers, and booleans. JavaScript strings (that is, string constants and variables that have most recently been assigned strings) appear in Java as instances of the Java `String` type; JavaScript numbers (numeric constants and variables most recently assigned integer or real numeric values) are converted to Java `Double` objects, and JavaScript booleans (the Boolean constants `true` and `false`, and variables most recently assigned one of those values) become Java `Boolean` objects. One other special case concerns JavaScript objects that are *wrappers* around Java objects. Such objects are simply "unwrapped" and converted to their original Java types.

Although this fact is currently undocumented, there is additional flexibility in passing JavaScript numbers directly to Java methods. An attempt to make a call like

```
document.myApplet.setNumber(3.7);
```

would succeed if the `myApplet` applet had a method with signature

```
public void setNumber(type x);
```

where *type* is one of the following: `Double`, `double`, `float`, `long`, `int`, `short`, `char`, or `byte`, even though the documentation implies that only `Double` ought to be acceptable. Sources at Netscape say the documentation will be changed to reflect the actual behavior, and not the other way around. In cases where the applet has more than one overloaded method expecting a type from the list above, the first such method (the method closest to the top of the Java source file) is chosen. Tie-breaking by lexicographic location is probably not the best way to resolve conflicts between overloaded methods, and it is very likely that some other mechanism will be devised.

> **TIP**
>
> As this book goes to press, the rules that govern the translation of JavaScript numbers into Java objects are being revised. Be sure to check current JavaScript documentation for the latest rules.

Working With JSObjects

Because complex JavaScript objects like arrays and `window` objects are reflected in Java as objects of type `JSObject`, its important to know how to manipulate those objects and extract information from them. When a `JSObject` represents a JavaScript array, it is useful to be able to examine the individual array elements, and when a `JSObject` represents a JavaScript `window`, `document`, `history`, or similar object, it is useful to be able to examine its properties.

It might at first seem tempting to avoid the whole issue by dissecting objects on the JavaScript side and breaking them into sets of simpler objects. Once broken apart, the elements could be sent to Java as sets of simple objects that would be translated into Java `Strings`, `Doubles`, and `Booleans`. The major drawback to that approach, besides it being a lot of extra work, is that it leaves no way to handle objects of variable size. If it wasn't known, in advance, how many elements an array might have, there would be no way to pass each individual element to a Java method, for Java methods take a number of arguments that is fixed at compile time. It's probably a better idea to simply pass complex JavaScript objects into Java "as is," and learn how to deal with them there.

> **NOTE**
>
> Be sure to include the `MAYSCRIPT` attribute in the applet tag of any applet you want to operate on `JSObject` objects. Without it, an applet doesn't have access to JavaScript objects and properties. This safeguard was designed to let HTML authors include untrusted Java applets on their pages without having to worry that those applets might have access to potentially sensitive information available only in JavaScript.

To make a concrete example out of the situation sketched above, suppose that you wanted to use JavaScript as a GUI for a Java point-plotting applet. With the following variable and function declarations:

```
<script language="JavaScript">
var xvals = new Array();
var yvals = new Array();
```

```
function addPoint(x, y)
{
    xvals[xvals.length] = x;
    yvals[yvals.length] = y;
}

function plotPoints()
{
    document.myApplet.plotPoints(xvals, yvals);
}
</script>
```

and the following HTML form augmented with event handlers

```
<form>
<input type=text name="xval">
<input type=text name="yval"><br>
<input type=button value="Add Point"
onclick="addPoint(form.xval.value, form.yval.value)"><br>
<input type=button value="Plot Points" onclick="plotPoints()">
</form>
```

you could collect (x,y) coordinate pairs using the two text input fields and the addPoint() function and then send them to the applet in one big batch using the plotPoints() function.

Doing things that way would allow you to send an arbitrary number of points to the applet to be plotted, but would require dissection of the point arrays from within Java. This example's plotPoints() Java method is a good representation of things it is possible to do with JSObjects. It might look something like the following:

```
public void plotPoints(JSObject xvals, JSObject yvals)
{
    Double length = (Double) xvals.getMember("length");
    int n = Math.round(length.doubleValue());
    for (int i = 0; i < n; i++)
        try
        {
            String sx = (String) xvals.getSlot(i);
            String sy = (String) yvals.getSlot(i);
Double x = new Double(sx);
            Double y = new Double(sy);
            doPlot(x, y);
        }
        catch (NumberFormatException e)
            System.err.println("Illegal point specification");
}
```

Let's take a closer look at the relevant parts of that program, line by line.

```
public void plotPoints(JSObject xvals, JSObject yvals)
```

This method is expecting two JSObjects, an array of x-coordinates, and an array of y-coordinates. Note that the JavaScript arrays, even numeric ones, don't show up in Java as arrays of one of Java's built-in numeric types. If the function had instead been written with the signature

```
public void plotPoints(double[] xvals, double[] yvals)
```

or something similar, any attempt to call it from JavaScript would have failed. You're stuck with the JSObjects, then, instead of the numeric arrays you might have preferred.

```
Double length = (Double) xvals.getMember("length");
```

This call to getMember() is the first step in converting the arguments from the form in which they were passed into a more useable form. The getMember() method is used to obtain the length property of one of the array objects (the two arrays have the same length). getMember() returns a generic Java Object (the base class for all Java objects), so you need to cast it to a more appropriate and useful type. You know that the length property of JavaScript arrays is a numeric property, and you should recall that JavaScript numbers are reflected in Java as Doubles, so the object returned by getMember() is cast to a Double object. Note that there is no flexibility in the type chosen here; numbers obtained from JSObjects *must* be cast to Double. It is only when JavaScript numeric values are passed directly to Java as function arguments that they can initially appear as Java types other than Double.

```
int n = Math.round(length.doubleValue());
```

Although this statement does not directly involve any JSObjects, it does demonstrate a useful idiom for converting JavaScript numbers into useful Java numeric types. Programmers often find themselves in possession of Double objects when they're more interested in other types, so it can become necessary to convert them. In this case, the Double object's doubleValue() method is used to extract the actual numeric value, and the Math package's round() method to obtain the integer closest to that value.

```
String sx = (String) x.getSlot(i);
String sy = (String) y.getSlot(i);
```

Inside the loop, you need a way to obtain the numeric value of each element of the JSObject objects representing the xvals and yvals arrays. Here the getSlot() method is used to extract the individual element at a given array index. getSlot() takes an integer argument and returns the JavaScript object located at that index. getSlot(), like getMember(), returns a generic Java Object, so again it needs to be cast to a more useful type. You know that the xvals and yvals arrays are populated with JavaScript strings, so Java Strings are the correct type to use in this case. It may seem counter-intuitive at first, because you've been thinking of the array elements as numbers, but String really is the correct cast to make. Remember that the values with which the arrays are populated were originally obtained from text input fields in an HTML form. In JavaScript, just because a string happens to look like a number (consists entirely of digits), doesn't automatically mean that it is a number.

```
Double x = new Double(sx);
Double y = new Double(sy);
```

You need a way to convert strings that look like numbers into actual numbers, and this Double constructor fits the bill nicely. It takes a String as an argument, and returns a Double object corresponding to the double-precision floating-point value represented by the String. If the

String doesn't represent a numeric value, a NumberFormatException is thrown, which is why these statements are wrapped in a try block. If an exception is thrown, the attempt to plot this point is aborted, and the next iteration of the loop begins.

```
doPlot(x, y);
```

This is where, having extracted the useful (x,y) coordinate values from the JSObjects, the call is made to the hypothetical low-level, point-plotting method.

Although an exhaustive explanation of the JSObject class is beyond the scope of this book, one more example should help show off a few more of its methods. Suppose that you wanted to add a method to the applet that plots all the points the user had typed into the form so far, without waiting for the user to explicitly click the Plot Points button. A method like the following would allow the applet to venture out into the JavaScript world and inspect the relevant JavaScript objects whenever it wanted:

```
private void getPoints()
{
    // Get the window and the document.
    JSObject window = JSObject.getWindow(this);
    JSObject document = (JSObject) window.getMember("document");

    // Get the point arrays.
JSObject xvals = (JSObject) document.getMember("xvals");
    JSObject yvals = (JSObject) document.getMember("yvals");

    // Now, just call plotPoints()
    plotPoints(xvals, yvals);
}
```

Take a closer look at the lines in that program that introduce new methods or concepts not found in the preceding example.

```
private void getPoints()
```

Notice that this method is private; it is not intended to be called from JavaScript. Notice also that it takes no arguments, because all the information necessary to complete its task is contained within JavaScript. The whole point, so to speak, of this exercise, is that Java applets are free to seek objects and properties from JavaScript without waiting for some user action on the JavaScript side to start the ball rolling.

```
JSObject window = JSObject.getWindow(this);
```

The JSObject class has a static method called getWindow() which can be used by an applet to obtain the JavaScript window object corresponding to the window that contains the applet. The object returned is simply the same object denoted by window in JavaScript. getWindow() is a particularly important and useful method, because it is the only way a Java applet can obtain a new JSObject (that is, a JSObject not derived from another, pre-existing JSObject) without being passed one explicitly from JavaScript; the JSObject class has no public constructors. The argument to getWindow() is the applet object itself.

```
JSObject document = (JSObject) window.getMember("document");
```

Once the window object is obtained, the `getMember()` method is used to extract a property by name. In this case that property is the window's `document` object, the object denoted by `window.document` in JavaScript. The reason for this is that the variables `xvals` and `yvals`, like all variables defined at top-level scope in a JavaScript script, are properties of the `document` object. Complex JavaScript objects like the `document` object are reflected in Java as `JSObjects`, so the `Object` returned by `getMember()` is cast to that type.

```
JSObject xvals = (JSObject) document.getMember("xvals");
JSObject yvals = (JSObject) document.getMember("yvals");
```

Once you have the `document` object, you can begin to extract the variables you're looking for. The `getMember()` method can once again be used for this purpose. The `xvals` and `yvals` objects are JavaScript arrays, which are reflected in Java as `JSObjects`, so the `Objects` returned by `getMember()` are again cast to that type.

```
plotPoints(xvals, yvals);
```

Now that you've obtained the `JSObjects` representing the `xvals` and `yvals` arrays, you can call the `plotPoints()` method from within Java, exactly as you would have called it from JavaScript.

Two other noteworthy methods of the `JSObject` class are `call()` and `eval()`, which have the following prototypes:

```
public Object call(String methodName, Object args[]);
public Object eval(String s);
```

`call()` calls its object's *methodName* method with arguments given by the args array. It is equivalent to calling

```
this.methodName(arg[0], arg[1], ...);
```

from within JavaScript. For example, the following within an applet

```
JSObject window = JSObject.getWindow(this);
Object args[] = { "Hello, world!" };

window.call("alert", args);
```

is equivalent to the following JavaScript:

```
alert("Hello, world! ");
```

An object's `eval()` method evaluates its argument string as a JavaScript expression. Evaluation occurs within the context of the object. Replacing the last line in the above example with

```
window.eval("alert('Hello, world! ')");
```

yields the same result. Note the use of single quotes inside the double quotes.

Setting Java Properties

Although it is usually not good programming style for Java classes to expose their data members (also called properties or fields) to direct outside access by declaring them public, occasionally situations arise when it can be useful to do so. When Java applets have public fields, JavaScript scripts have the power to directly modify them, just as they have the power to invoke public Java methods. For example, consider the following fragment of a Java applet:

```java
public String theText;

public void setText(String s)
{
    theText = s;
}
```

It is probably better programming practice to set the text like the following:

```java
document.myApplet.setText("Hello world!");
```

It would be equally possible to just write:

```java
document.myApplet.theText = "Hello world!";
```

The same rules that govern translation of JavaScript objects into Java objects during function calls also apply here. This implies, by the way, that only Java Strings, Doubles, Booleans, JSObjects and primitive numeric types can be directly set in this way, because all JavaScript variables are initially reflected in Java as one of those types.

Java Objects in JavaScript

Up until now, this chapter has only discussed the problem of sending objects from JavaScript into Java. It is equally possible, however, to send objects the other way. Suppose you rewrote the setText() method to be a little more picky about acceptable values for theText, and you wanted a way to find out whether a given call to setText() had resulted in theText being successfully set. If you designed the new function to return a boolean flag indicating success or failure, it might look something like the following:

```java
public boolean setText(String s)
{
    if (s.equals("Hello world!"))
    {
        // I'm sick of that string; don't accept it.
        return false;
    }
    else
    {
        theText = s;
        return true;
    }
}
```

If you wrote a JavaScript script that included the following line

```
var changed = document.myApplet.setText("Hello world!")
```

the value returned by `setText()` would be stored in `changed`. The question remains, though; exactly how will the Java `boolean` object returned by `setText()` be converted into a JavaScript object? In this particular case, the answer is simple and intuitive: Java `boolean` objects become JavaScript Boolean objects when they're returned to JavaScript. Passing Java objects to JavaScript is not always quite so simple—there are a number of rules that govern the exact translation for a given object—but the good news is that things often work out just the way one might hope and expect. Java arrays become JavaScript arrays, Java numeric types become JavaScript numbers, Java `booleans` become JavaScript booleans, and Java `Strings` become JavaScript strings. For completeness, the entire set of rules used to govern the conversion follows:

- Java numeric types (`byte`, `char`, `double`, `float`, `int`, `long`, `short`) become JavaScript numbers.
- Java `boolean` becomes JavaScript Boolean.
- Java `JSObjects` are converted back to their original JavaScript objects.
- Java arrays become JavaScript array objects.
- All other Java objects are converted to JavaScript "wrapper" objects that can be used to access the original Java members.

When an attempt is made to convert a JavaScript wrapper into a JavaScript string, number, or Boolean, the original Java object's `toString()`, `doubleValue()`, or `booleanValue()` method, if it exists, is called, and the value of the converted object is the value returned by the corresponding method. If the corresponding method doesn't exist, the conversion fails. Note that Java Strings work as expected in JavaScript, even though they are technically passed to JavaScript as wrapper objects. Any attempt to use one in a context where a JavaScript string is expected causes the correct conversion to be applied.

Using Java Packages

JavaScript's ability to interact with Java isn't limited to applets. JavaScript scripts also have direct access to static methods and fields of core Java packages, and they may even construct new Java objects. Java packages are available in JavaScript within the containing document's `Packages` array. For example, Java's `java.lang.System` package, which can be used for console I/O, can be referenced in JavaScript as `Packages.java.lang.System`, and Java's `java.lang.Math` package can be referenced as `Packages.java.lang.Math`. As a result, to write the value of PI to the Java console, you could use the following:

```
var pi = Packages.java.lang.Math.PI;
Packages.java.lang.System.out.println("pi is: " + pi);
```

As a special shorthand, references to three of the most common packages—java, sun, and netscape—may safely omit the Packages keyword. That is, within a JavaScript document object, java, sun, and netscape are aliases for Packages.java, Packages.sun, and Packages.netscape respectively. Using those aliases, it is possible to re-write the PI-printing example as the following:

```
var pi = java.lang.Math.PI;
java.lang.System.out.println("pi is: " + pi);
```

It also is possible to dynamically construct new Java objects, using the new operator. This is a handy way to access some of Java's powerful built-in utility classes—hash tables, stacks, vectors, dates, and more—without having to write an entire Java applet. In the following JavaScript example, two Java Date objects are constructed, and they are compared using the after method of the Date class to see if the current date is after the deadline.

```
var theDate = new java.util.Date(); // the current date
var deadline = new java.util.Date(96, 6, 26); // July 26, 1996

if (theDate.after(deadline))
    alert("I missed my deadline!");
else
    alert("Made it!");
```

javascript: URLs

javascript: URLs provide a way for Java and JavaScript programmers to create dynamic web content. Simple examples of javascript: URLs include

```
javascript:alert('hello world')
```

which causes an alert dialog to be displayed, and

```
javascript:"<h1>Hello World</h1> JavaScript is fun."
```

which interprets the string as HTML and displays it (properly formatted) in the browser window. javascript: URLs can be used in any context where a URL is allowed. They can be typed directly into a browser's location field, they can be the targets of HTML hyperlinks, and they can be used as arguments to JavaScript's window.open() method and Java's AppletContext.showDocument() method.

> **CAUTION**
>
> Microsoft Internet Explorer has only limited support for javascript: URLs. They are supported when used within HTML documents, but not when used within Java in conjunction with ShowDocument().

A `javascript:` URL consists of the string "`javascript:`" followed by one or more JavaScript statements. Multiple statement are separated by semi-colons. When the URL is executed, the statements are evaluated in sequence, and the "value" of the URL is the value of the last statement.

In JavaScript, any legal expression also can be a statement, so a string constant by itself is a perfectly good statement. This fact is of particular interest, since it is precisely through the use of string constants (and string variables) that HTML-valued JavaScript is passed to the browser to be interpreted.

> **TIP**
>
> If the first character of a string constant or string-valued variable is a <, the browser interprets the contents of the string as HTML. If the string starts with any other character, it is interpreted as plain text.

To use a `javascript:` URL as the target of a hyperlink, simply include it within an HTML document anywhere you would use an HTTP or other URL. For example, clicking

```
<a href="javascript:alert('You clicked me! ') ">Click me</a>
```

causes an alert box to appear, and

```
<a href="javascript: '<b>You clicked me at: </b>' + new Date()">Click me</a>
```

causes a new page displaying the current date to be loaded. Note the use of single quotes inside the double-quoted URL. Using single quotes, or escaped double quotes, is necessary to avoid prematurely ending the string containing the URL.

> **TIP**
>
> The HTML " entity can be used to specify an escaped quote within a `javascript:` URL. Using " is sometimes less confusing than using escaped quotes.

Integrating Java Applets with ActiveX Controls

The ActiveX technology from Microsoft provides a means of embedding Microsoft OLE controls within HTML documents. An OLE control thus embedded is referred to as an ActiveX control. These controls are recognized by Microsoft Internet Explorer 3.0, or by Netscape Navigator equipped with an ActiveX plug-in, such as that provided by NCompass Labs. If such a browser loads an HTML document with an ActiveX control that isn't already present on the browser's host machine, the browser loads that control from the server as well. Naturally, as these controls are really OLE objects, they can only execute in a browser on an OLE-capable platform like Microsoft Windows. This creates a portability issue for browser users who want to access such a document.

The following is an example of the HTML code for embedding an OLE control (in this case an OLE ButtonCtrl object) in an HTML document.

```
<OBJECT ID="MyButton" WIDTH=83 HEIGHT=27
 CLASSID="CLSID:3472D900-5A27-11CF-8B11-00AA00C00903">
    <PARAM NAME="_ExtentX" VALUE="2196">
    <PARAM NAME="_ExtentY" VALUE="714">
</OBJECT>
```

The string given for the CLASSID attribute is the value of the CLSID entry of the ButtonCtrl OLE control type as it appears in the Windows System Registry. Fortunately, it isn't necessary to generate this code by hand. The code in this example was created by the ActiveX Control Pad application from Microsoft. The ActiveX Control Pad, in addition to enabling manual text-editing of HTML documents, provides semi-automated placement and scripting of ActiveX controls. When using the ActiveX Control Pad application to place an ActiveX control within an HTML document, a list of all OLE controls currently known to the System Registry can be summoned. All such OLE controls are available for use by HTML document authors.

An ActiveX control has a set of events, each of which can be associated with a piece of JavaScript code. For example the ButtonCtrl control has an onClick event, similar to that of a button-type input in an HTML form. ActiveX controls can be arbitrarily complex however; for example the Calendar control has the following events that can be scripted: AfterUpdate, BeforeUpdate, Click, DblClick, KeyDown, KeyPress, KeyUp, NewMonth, and NewYear. The following is an example of the code for scripting an event for an ActiveX control:

```
<SCRIPT LANGUAGE="JavaScript" FOR="MyButton" EVENT="onClick()">
alert('hello universe')
</SCRIPT>
```

The ActiveX Control Pad application provides a point-and-click interface for associating actions with events for ActiveX controls, and assists in creating scripts such as the preceding one.

The JavaScript code for one ActiveX control can access event handlers and attributes of other ActiveX controls in the HTML document. For example, suppose the HTML document containing MyButton also contains the NCompass Labs Cube Control, which is a rotating cube that interacts with the user's mouse clicks and drags. The HTML to include this control, as generated by the ActiveX Control Pad application, looks something like the following:

```
<OBJECT ID="MyCube" WIDTH=83 HEIGHT=83
 CLASSID="CLSID:A7048320-D56F-11CE-9046-00AA005CDAE1">
    <PARAM NAME="_Version" VALUE="65536">
    <PARAM NAME="_ExtentX" VALUE="2187">
    <PARAM NAME="_ExtentY" VALUE="2187">
```

```
        <PARAM NAME="_StockProps" VALUE="0">
        <PARAM NAME="Picture1" VALUE="">
        <PARAM NAME="Picture2" VALUE="">
        <PARAM NAME="Picture3" VALUE="">
        <PARAM NAME="Picture4" VALUE="">
        <PARAM NAME="Picture5" VALUE="">
        <PARAM NAME="Picture6" VALUE="">
        <PARAM NAME="BackgroundImage" VALUE="">
        <PARAM NAME="CubeStyle" VALUE="1">
        <PARAM NAME="PictureNo" VALUE="12488">
</OBJECT>
```

Suppose you include the following script in the HTML document:

```
<SCRIPT LANGUAGE="JavaScript" FOR="MyButton" EVENT="onClick()">
Cube1.AboutBox()
</SCRIPT>
```

When the HTML document is loaded, it displays a button and a rotating cube control. When the button is pressed, the AboutBox() method of the cube control is invoked, and the cube control's About Box appears.

If you consider the mechanisms discussed so far, you should see that if a document includes both Java applets and ActiveX controls, its possible to script ActiveX control events so that they access Java applet members and methods. Suppose you have a Java applet called myApplet embedded in an HTML document with the following code:

```
<applet name="myApplet" width=20 height=20 code="testApplet.class" MAYSCRIPT></
applet>
```

A member or method of this Java applet can be accessed from the script for an ActiveX control event in just the same manner as it would be from any other piece of JavaScript code. Suppose the Java code for testApplet looks like the following:

```
class testApplet extends java.applet.Applet
{
    private String itsString = "hello";

    public void myMethod()
    {
        itsString = "world";
    }
}
```

The code to invoke myMethod() by clicking the button MyButton looks like this:

```
<SCRIPT LANGUAGE="JavaScript" FOR="MyButton" EVENT="onClick()">
document.myApplet.myMethod()
</SCRIPT>
```

This section has shown how OLE controls can be embedded in HTML documents (assuming a suitable browser and browser-platform) using the ActiveX technology, and how JavaScript interacts with these controls. It is a simple matter to integrate Java Applets with ActiveX controls—access the Java applet members and methods from the scripts associated with the ActiveX control events.

Certainly the easiest way to author documents of the type described here is with the Microsoft ActiveX Control Pad application. There are numerous books available that document the behavior of the huge variety of OLE controls. A discussion of those controls would be beyond the scope of this book.

Summary

This chapter included a description of some of the ways JavaScript can communicate with Java. It enumerated the rules for translating JavaScript objects into Java and for translating Java objects into JavaScript, and included a discussion of some of the most useful methods in the `JSObject` class.

JavaScript scripts can call methods in Java applets, access static members of core Java packages, and construct new Java objects. Java applets can obtain the JavaScript object associated with the window containing the applet, and use it to access the rest of JavaScript.

`javascript:` URLs are useful for causing JavaScript scripts to be executed in situations when a URL would normally be loaded, such as when an HTML hyperlink is clicked, and for creating and displaying HTML on-the-fly.

JavaScript event handler scripts can be used as wiring to connect ActiveX controls to Java applets.

IN THIS PART

- Using Client-Side Tables in JavaScript

- Database Connectivity Using Server-Side JavaScript

JavaScript Database Applications

Using Client-Side Tables in JavaScript

by Richard Wagner

IN THIS CHAPTER

CHAPTER 30

The Web offers a revolutionary approach to database applications with the capability to access remote data via a Web browser and return the results back to you in HTML format. Although this is now common practice with CGI scripts today, you can also use JavaScript to access data as well.

When you think of Web database access, you typically think exclusively of letting the data reside on the server. In Chapter 31, "Database Connectivity Using Server-Side JavaScript," I look at how you can use server-side JavaScript to access databases. However, JavaScript also allows you to work with data on the client side. In this chapter, I look at how you can work with client-side tables using JavaScript and when and how these can be alternatives to CGI and server-based solutions.

Data Source: Client or Server?

Before looking at how to work with client-side databases in JavaScript, it is essential to discuss when a client-side table makes sense. A *client-side table* is a read-only set of data that can be stored in an HTML file on the client computer. For example, you might want to take data from a relational database and convert it to a structured JavaScript dataset.

Client-side tables have two major limitations. First, the database must be read only. Because the data is actually embedded in your HTML source, you cannot have users add or modify this data and save it on the client side. You could theoretically develop a process to update the same data on the server as needed, reloading the client database when a change occurs. Generally speaking, unless you run through a lot of hoops, a client-side table is read only.

Second, the database must be relatively small. Because the data is stored in the HTML file, it is downloaded in its entirety when the user accesses the Web page. You would obviously never want to embed a 100,000 record database in your file (or a size anywhere close to that); even for users with direct Internet connections, the download time would be very annoying every time they wanted to access your page.

The maximum size of a dataset really depends on the context. If you create a client-side table that will be accessed over a 14.4 to 28.8Kbps modem, you might want to limit the size of the table to no more than 1,000 records. However, if you are creating an intranet solution in which all users have high-speed connections, you might want to bend the envelope and allow many more than that.

Given these limitations, why would you ever want to use a client-side table? There are two reasons. First, for some purposes in which a dataset is relatively small and relatively static, a client-side table can provide a much simpler solution than dealing with CGI scripts or other processes on the Web server. Second, because everything resides on the client—data, searching mechanism, and user interface—you avoid the need to access the server at all. The result is that the search process is much quicker; you avoid the added load on the server to process a search and eliminate two transmissions between the client and server.

You might argue that even though the data is moved to the client for processing, the data still has to pass through the server when the page is downloaded. Of course, that's true, but the server is not required to process a CGI search; send only an HTML file to a client who requests it.

As corporations roll out intranets, many small LAN-based applications will be ported to the Web. Because many of these are database-centric, it is likely that corporate Web servers' traffic will increase just to support these applications. In some cases, client-side tables could help minimize the load on the server. One such example is a company phone list application. What company does not have such a list, at least on paper? In this chapter, I use the phone list application as a practical and useful example for using client-side data to meet a business need.

What Is a Client-Side Table?

As a database application developer, I hear the term "table" and immediately envision a table of columns and rows in a relational database format. For example, Figure 30.1 shows a Paradox table. You can manipulate or search on this data in a variety of ways, depending on the capabilities of the database management software itself.

FIGURE 30.1.

A relational database table.

Unfortunately, although you can work with relational tables on the server side by accessing a database, you cannot do the same using the capabilities of client-side JavaScript. You are forced to convert a database table into a structured format that your JavaScript code can use. In JavaScript, the basic organizing structure you want to use is an array. You can access each element of a JavaScript array and evaluate it—just as a relational database evaluates each record in a table during a query. Figure 30.2 shows this parallel between data in a relational table and that in an array.

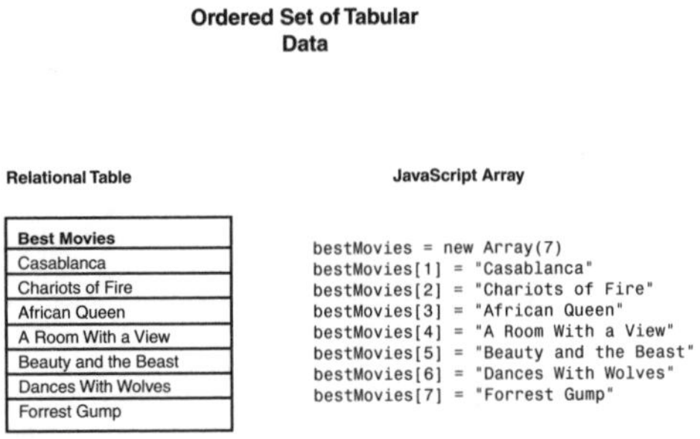

FIGURE 30.2.

You can work with tabular sets of data differently depending on the context.

Ordered Set of Tabular Data

Relational Table

Best Movies
Casablanca
Chariots of Fire
African Queen
A Room With a View
Beauty and the Beast
Dances With Wolves
Forrest Gump

JavaScript Array

```
bestMovies = new Array(7)
bestMovies[1] = "Casablanca"
bestMovies[2] = "Chariots of Fire"
bestMovies[3] = "African Queen"
bestMovies[4] = "A Room With a View"
bestMovies[5] = "Beauty and the Beast"
bestMovies[6] = "Dances With Wolves"
bestMovies[7] = "Forrest Gump"
```

Creating a Lookup Table

The first step to using a client-side table in JavaScript is creating the table itself. A client-side table cannot be an external file, so all the data must be embedded in the HTML file. However, for that information to be useful, you need to structure it so the data can be searched and retrieved as desired.

As shown previously, one option for structuring client-side data is to use a single-dimensioned array. For example, if you wanted to put the entire list of employee names in an array, it would look something like the following:

```
var employees = new Array(10)
employees[1] = "Richard"
employees[2] = "David"
employees[3] = "Rachel"
employees[4] = "Mark"
employees[5] = "Mellon"
employees[6] = "Margo"
employees[7] = "Darius"
employees[8] = "Dan"
employees[9] = "Dave"
employees[10] = "Pepe"
```

You could then use this array and search for individual elements within it based upon what you learned in the array discussion in Chapter 15, "Creating Custom JavaScript Objects." However, a single-dimensional array is not too helpful in this context because most lookup tables have multiple columns of data to track. In the phone list example, suppose you want to track an employee's name, title, department, phone extension, and e-mail address.

A second and more useful option is to create a custom object called `employee` and then group these employee "records" together in a single-dimensional array. Doing this lets you store multiple columns of data in an object but also work with the employee objects as a collective group.

To define the   object, you must first create a constructor method as shown here:

```
function employee(FirstName, LastName, Title, Department, PhoneExt,
        EmailAddress) {
    this.FirstName = FirstName;
    this.LastName = LastName;
```

```
            this.Title = Title;
            this.Department = Department;
            this.PhoneExt = PhoneExt;
            this.EmailAddress = EmailAddress;
}
```

The next steps after creating the object constructor method are creating the employee objects themselves and placing them into the container array called empList. You can perform these two steps using a single line of code for each employee. The first 5 employees in our complete list of 105 are shown here:

```
empList[1] = new employee("Richard", "Wagner", "Chief Technology Officer",
  "R&D", "400",
                    "rwagner@acadians.com")
empList[2] = new employee("Grady", "Anderson", "Programmer", "R&D", "198",
                    "grady@acadians.com")
empList[3] = new employee("Thomas", "Sprat", "Marketing Manager", "Marketing",
    "656",
"tspratt@acadians.com ")
empList[4] = new employee("William", "Cleyball", "Marketing Manager",
    "Marketing", "651",
                    "wcal@acadians.com ")
empList[5] = new employee("Fred", "Tortallini", "Marketing Manager",
    "Marketing", "404",
                    "tort@acadians.com ")
```

You now have the employee data captured in a structured format that is useful for you in client-side JavaScript.

NOTE

Do not get discouraged yet as you think of the manual work that is required to migrate data stored in relational databases to a JavaScript array or object. You have many options in creating this information apart from actually typing the text every time you want to use the data. If the data changes often, you could create a CGI script or other back-end process that generates this code automatically upon exporting a database table.

Creating the Search User Interface

The manner in which you want the users of the application to work with the client-side table will, of course, depend on the exact context of your application. This example calls for a user interface in which the users can search for employees based on text they enter. Because you have several fields in the table, you might want to also give the user the flexibility to search on the four primary searchable fields of the table: FirstName, LastName, Title, and Department.

Suppose you want the results to be presented in an HTML document upon searching. To display both the search definition and results at the same time, you could use a multiframe window. With that in mind, the phone list example uses the following files:

- `employeeInfo.htm` is the parent frameset window that contains the employee database and other global information.
- `searchfrm.htm` is the top-most frame that provides a user interface for entering a search request.
- `results.htm` is the bottom frame that displays the search results. It is blank by default.

Figure 30.3 shows the multiframe window setup for the application.

Figure 30.3.

Database search user interface.

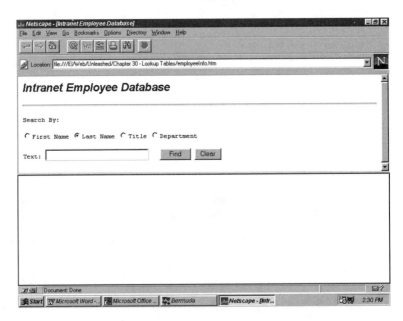

The only part of the user interface that the users will interact with is the search window ( ). The following segment shows the HTML source for the search definition form inside the window:

```
<body>
<form method="POST" name="form">
<pre>Search By: </pre>
<pre><input
     type=radio
     name="searchBy"
     value="FirstName">First Name <input
     type=radio
     checked
     name="searchBy"
     value="LastName">Last Name <input
```

```
      type=radio
      name="searchBy"
      value="Title">Title <input
      type=radio
      name="searchBy"
      value="Department">Department</pre>
<pre>Text: <input
      type=text
      size=30
      maxlength=30
      name="searchByText">    <input
      type=button
      size=20
      name="findButton"
      value="    Find    "
      onClick="doSearch()"> <input
      type=reset
      name="Clear"
      value=" Clear "
      onClick="clearForm()"></pre>
</form>
</body>
```

Processing the Search Request

The heart of an application based on a client-side table is the capability to search on the data. In the employee phone list example, you need to determine the field on which the search should be conducted and then pass that information along with the actual search request to the search processing method.

Search processing is done in two locations in this example. The doSearch() method in the searchForm frame prepares the search and then passes the information to the findEmployee() method of the parent window.

To do this, assign the doSearch() method to the event handler for the Find button. In this function, check to see which of the radio buttons is checked and assign the searchField variable a string value based on the result. Next, after checking to ensure that a value has been entered in the searchByText field, call the parent window's findEmployee() method using the searchField variable and value of the searchByText field as its parameters:

```
function doSearch() {
    var searchField = ""

    if (document.form.searchBy[0].checked) {
        searchField = "FirstName" }
    else {
        if (document.form.searchBy[1].checked) {
            searchField = "LastName" }
        else { if (document.form.searchBy[2].checked) {
                searchField = "Title" }
            else { if (document.form.searchBy[3].checked) {
                searchField = "Department" }
                }
        }
```

```
        }

    if (document.form.searchByText.value == null ||
        document.form.searchByText.value == "") {
          alert("Please enter your search criteria before continuing.") }
    else {
          parent.findEmployee(searchField, document.form.searchByText.value)
    }
}
```

In the parent window (`employeeInfo.htm`), the `findEmployee()` method takes these two parameters and uses them to evaluate the array of employee objects. A `for` loop is used to traverse the array of employee objects, checking the value of the search request (`searchWord` parameter) with the specified property (`searchField` parameter) using the string object's `indexOf()` method.

Before you get into the actual code, it is helpful to look at a more basic but equivalent example. If you wanted to search for the value of `"Richard"` in the `FirstName` property of all the employee objects, your code would look like the following:

```
for (var i=1; i<empList.length; i++) {
    if (empList[i].FirstName.indexOf('Richard') != -1) {
        empList[I].show() }
```

The `for` loop evaluates each object and returns a value greater than or equal to zero if the text is contained within the value of an employee object's `FirstName` property. If a match is found, the employee object's `show()` method is performed. Do not concern yourself with this method yet; it is covered in the section "Displaying Search Results," later in the chapter.

Following the same logic, look again at the phone list application. You have to take care of a problem first; because you want to use the `searchField` parameter to represent an object property name and not a string value, you need to use the built-in `eval()` method. The `eval()` method interprets a string value and evaluates it as a JavaScript expression. If you convert the JavaScript code into a single string, it can be evaluated using the `eval()` method. This code follows:

```
function findEmployee(searchField, searchWord) {
    var str = ""

    // formatting code will go here

    for (var i=1; i<empList.length; i++) {
        str = "if (empList[" + i + "]." + searchField +
            ".indexOf('" + searchWord +
        "') != -1) { empList[" + i + "].show() }"
        eval(str)
    }

    // formatting code will go here
}
```

Displaying the Search Results

The final step in the search process is to present the results of the search to the user. Use the bottom frame (`resultForm`) to display this information. You can enhance the `findEmployee()` method you looked at in the previous section to perform this process.

Because you want to generate HTML on the fly, you want to use the `resultForm`'s document object as a "canvas" to write on. You first need to prepare the document canvas to accept input by using the document `open()` method. Next, to display results in a table format, you can create an HTML table using the `<table>` tag and set up the table header:

```
window.resultForm.document.open()
window.resultForm.document.write("<h2>Matches:</h2>")
window.resultForm.document.write("<table border=1>")
window.resultForm.document.write("<tr><td width=10%><strong>First Name</strong></
td>")
window.resultForm.document.write("<td width=15%><strong>Last Name
  </strong></td>")
window.resultForm.document.write("<td width=20%><strong>Title</strong></td>")
window.resultForm.document.write("<td width=15%><strong>Department
  </strong></td>")
window.resultForm.document.write("<td width=5%><strong>Ext.</strong></td>")
window.resultForm.document.write("<td width=15%><strong>Email</strong>
  </td></tr>")
```

Now that the initial preparation of the `resultForm` is complete, you are ready to process the search as specified earlier. As you recall, each matching employee is called to execute a `show()` method. This method is used to display the employee information as a single record in the table. You therefore need to add a `show()` method to the `employee` object constructor:

```
function employee(FirstName, LastName, Title, Department, PhoneExt,
  EmailAddress) {
    this.FirstName = FirstName;
    this.LastName = LastName;
    this.Title = Title;
    this.Department = Department;
    this.PhoneExt = PhoneExt;
    this.EmailAddress = EmailAddress;
    this.show = emp_show;
}
```

When an employee object's `show()` method is called, the `emp_show()` method is triggered. This method provides the location in which to place code for formatting and displaying the current employee's information. Using the `write()` method, you can place the values of each of the object's properties in separate table cells. The code follows:

```
function emp_show() {
    window.resultForm.document.write("<tr><td width=10%>" +
      this.FirstName + "</td>")
    window.resultForm.document.write("<td width=15%>" +
      this.LastName + "</td>")
```

```
window.resultForm.document.write("<td width=20%>" + this.Title + "</td>")
window.resultForm.document.write("<td width=15%>" + this.Department +
    "</td>")
window.resultForm.document.write("<td width=5%>" + this.PhoneExt +
    "</td>")
window.resultForm.document.write("<td width=15%>" + "<a href='mailto:" +
    this.EmailAddress + "'>" + this.EmailAddress + "</td></tr>")
}
```

Notice that a link is defined for the employee's e-mail address. A user can then click the employee's e-mail address in the table to send a message to him or her.

The final formatting code you need to write is back in the findEmployee() method. After each of the employee records are processed, a write() method ends the table definition by sending a </TABLE> tag. Finally, the canvas is closed to additional input when a close() method is issued. The complete findEmployee() method is shown here:

```
function findEmployee(searchField, searchWord) {
    var str = ""

    window.resultForm.document.open()
    window.resultForm.document.write("<h2>Matches:</h2>")
    window.resultForm.document.write("<table border=1>")
    window.resultForm.document.write("<tr><td width=10%><strong>First Name
        </strong></td>")
    window.resultForm.document.write("<td width=15%><strong>Last Name
        </strong></td>")
    window.resultForm.document.write("<td width=20%><strong>Title
        </strong></td>")
    window.resultForm.document.write("<td width=15%><strong>Department
        </strong></td>")
    window.resultForm.document.write("<td width=5%><strong>Ext.</strong></td>")
    window.resultForm.document.write("<td width=15%><strong>Email</strong></td></
tr>")

    for (var i=1; i<=empList.length-1; i++) {
        str = "if (empList[" + i + "]." + searchField + ".indexOf('"
        + searchWord +
        "') != -1) { empList[" + i + "].show() }"
        eval(str)
    }
    window.resultForm.document.write("</table>")
    window.resultForm.document.close()
}
```

Running the Application

You are now ready to test the application by opening the employeeInfo.htm file in your browser. Suppose you want to search for Grady Anderson. Enter Anderson in the text field, keep the Last Name radio button selected, and click the Find button. Figure 30.4 shows the results. You can clear both the search form and results frame by clicking the Clear button.

FIGURE 30.4.

Search results displayed in a table.

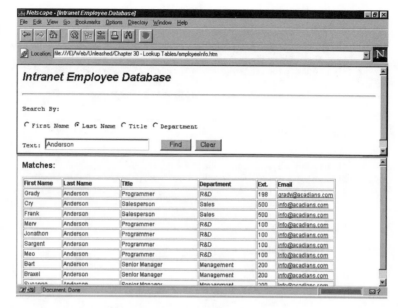

Listing 30.1 provides the complete source code for the employeeINfo.htm parent window, and Listing 30.2 contains the JavaScript source for the searchfrm.htm window.

Listing 30.1. EmployeeInfo.htm.

```
<HTML>
<HEAD>
<TITLE>Intranet Employee Database</TITLE>
<SCRIPT LANGUAGE="JavaScript">

    // Intranet Employee Database
    // JavaScript Unleashed (Sams.net Publishing)
    // Created by Richard J. Wagner (rwagner@acadians.com)

    // Global variables
    var i = 1
    var n = 1

    // Create Array objects
    var empList = new Array()

    // show() - employee object method
    function emp_show() {
        window.resultForm.document.write("<tr><td width=10%>" + this.FirstName
            + "</td>")
        window.resultForm.document.write("<td width=15%>" + this.LastName
```

continues

PART VIII

Listing 30.1. continued

```
                + "</td>")
        window.resultForm.document.write("<td width=20%>" + this.Title
                + "</td>")
        window.resultForm.document.write("<td width=15%>" + this.Department
                + "</td>")
        window.resultForm.document.write("<td width=5%>" + this.PhoneExt
                + "</td>")
        window.resultForm.document.write("<td width=15%>" + "<a href='mailto:"
                + this.EmailAddress + "'>" + this.EmailAddress + "</td></tr>")
    }

    // Employee object constructor
    function employee(FirstName, LastName, Title, Department,
        PhoneExt, EmailAddress) {
        this.FirstName = FirstName;
        this.LastName = LastName;
        this.Title = Title;
        this.Department = Department;
        this.PhoneExt = PhoneExt;
        this.EmailAddress = EmailAddress;
        this.show = emp_show;
    }

    // Search for employee based on field and word
    function findEmployee(searchField, searchWord) {
        var str = ""

        window.resultForm.document.open()
        window.resultForm.document.write("<h2>Matches:</h2>")
        window.resultForm.document.write("<table border=1>")
        window.resultForm.document.write("<tr><td width=10%>
          <strong>First Name</strong></td>")
        window.resultForm.document.write("<td width=15%>
          <strong>Last Name</strong></td>")
        window.resultForm.document.write("<td width=20%><strong>
          Title</strong></td>")
        window.resultForm.document.write("<td width=15%><strong>
          Department</strong></td>")
        window.resultForm.document.write("<td width=5%>
          <strong>Ext.</strong></td>")
        window.resultForm.document.write("<td width=15%><strong>
          Email</strong></td></tr>")

        for (var i=1; i<=empList.length-1; i++) {
            str = "if (empList[" + i + "]." + searchField + ".indexOf('"
            + searchWord +
            "') != -1) { empList[" + i + "].show() }"
            eval(str)
        }
        window.resultForm.document.write("</table>")
        window.resultForm.document.close()
    }


// Create employee objects on start up
empList[1] = new employee(
"Richard", "Wagner", "Chief Technology Officer", "R&D", "400",
```

```
"rwagner@acadians.com")
empList[2] = new employee(
"Grady", "Anderson", "Programmer", "R&D", "198", "grady@acadians.com")
empList[3] = new employee(
"Thomas", "Sprat", "Marketing Manager", "Marketing", "656", "tspratt@acadians.com
")
empList[4] = new employee(
"William", "Cleyball", "Marketing Manager", "Marketing", "651", "wcal@acadians.com
")
empList[5] = new employee(
"Fred", "Tortallini", "Marketing Manager", "Marketing", "404", "tort@acadians.com
")
empList[6] = new employee(
"Smack", "Hopkins", "Marketing Manager", "Marketing", "606", "smack@acadians.com ")
empList[7] = new employee(
"Luey", "Gentry", "Marketing Manager", "Marketing", "450", "luey@acadians.com ")
empList[8] = new employee(
"Erwin", "Waltham", "Marketing Manager", "Marketing", "545", "ew@acadians.com")
empList[9] = new employee(
"Dallas", "Spanner", "Marketing Manager", "Marketing", "656",
"dallas@acadians.com")
empList[10] = new employee(
"Spill", "Hopkins", "Marketing Manager", "Marketing", "120", "spill@acadians.com ")
empList[11] = new employee(
"Huey", "Wagner", "Marketing Asst", "Marketing", "854", "huey@acadians.com ")
empList[12] = new employee(
"Tom", "Longly", "Marketing Asst", "Marketing", "512", "info@acadians.com ")
empList[13] = new employee(
"Huck", "Starback", "Marketing Asst","Marketing", "212", "info@acadians.com ")
empList[14] = new employee(
"Crazy", "Lags", "Marketing Asst","Marketing", "122", "info@acadians.com ")
empList[15] = new employee(
"Bart", "Simpson", "Salesperson", "Sales", "500", "info@acadians.com")
empList[16] = new employee(
"Bill", "O'Reilly", "Salesperson", "Sales", "500", "info@acadians.com")
empList[17] = new employee(
"Sally", "Smatterhorn", "Salesperson", "Sales", "500", "info@acadians.com")
empList[18] = new employee(
"Kim", "Pakki", "Salesperson", "Sales", "500", "info@acadians.com")
empList[19] = new employee(
"Jacob", "Ladder", "Salesperson", "Sales", "500", "info@acadians.com")
empList[20] = new employee(
"Jared", "Gaspe", "Salesperson", "Sales", "500", "info@acadians.com")
empList[21] = new employee(
"Justus", "Argon", "Salesperson", "Sales", "500", "info@acadians.com")
empList[22] = new employee(
"Jordan", "Basker", "Salesperson", "Sales", "500", "info@acadians.com")
empList[23] = new employee(
"Lisa", "Smith", "Salesperson", "Sales", "500", "info@acadians.com")
empList[24] = new employee(
"Cry", "Anderson", "Salesperson", "Sales", "500", "info@acadians.com")
empList[25] = new employee(
"Ollie", "Ryder", "Salesperson", "Sales", "500", "info@acadians.com")
empList[26] = new employee(
"Polly", "Potts", "Salesperson", "Sales", "500", "info@acadians.com")
empList[27] = new employee(
```

continues

Listing 30.1. continued

```
"Xerxes", "Smith", "Salesperson", "Sales", "500", "info@acadians.com")
empList[28] = new employee(
"Sally Rae", "Smith", "Salesperson", "Sales", "500", "info@acadians.com")
empList[29] = new employee(
"Golden", "Driscoll", "Salesperson", "Sales", "500", "info@acadians.com")
empList[30] = new employee(
"Frank", "Anderson", "Salesperson", "Sales", "500", "info@acadians.com")
empList[31] = new employee(
"Merv", "Anderson", "Programmer", "R&D", "100", "info@acadians.com")
empList[32] = new employee(
"Manu", "Waver", "Programmer", "R&D", "100", "info@acadians.com")
empList[33] = new employee(
"Jason", "Driscoll", "Programmer", "R&D", "100", "info@acadians.com")
empList[34] = new employee(
"Ardent", "Matthews", "Programmer", "R&D", "100", "info@acadians.com")
empList[35] = new employee(
"Ortho", "Dontal", "Programmer", "R&D", "100", "info@acadians.com")
empList[36] = new employee(
"Troy", "Smith", "Programmer", "R&D", "100", "info@acadians.com")
empList[37] = new employee(
"Fred", "Barker", "Programmer", "R&D", "100", "info@acadians.com")
empList[38] = new employee(
"Richini", "Barker", "Programmer", "R&D", "100", "info@acadians.com")
empList[39] = new employee(
"Ricardo", "Bollinger", "Programmer", "R&D", "100", "info@acadians.com")
empList[40] = new employee(
"Ron", "Bollinger", "Programmer", "R&D", "100", "info@acadians.com")
empList[41] = new employee(
"Ronald", "Barker", "Programmer", "R&D", "100", "info@acadians.com")
empList[42] = new employee(
"Browser", "Tyler", "Programmer", "R&D", "100", "info@acadians.com")
empList[43] = new employee(
"Serf", "Tyler", "Programmer", "R&D", "100", "info@acadians.com")
empList[44] = new employee(
"Bill", "Tyler", "Programmer", "R&D", "100", "info@acadians.com")
empList[45] = new employee(
"William", "Smith", "Programmer", "R&D", "100", "info@acadians.com")
empList[46] = new employee(
"Billy", "Barker", "Programmer", "R&D", "100", "info@acadians.com")
empList[47] = new employee(
"Kurt", "Barker", "Programmer", "R&D", "100", "info@acadians.com")
empList[48] = new employee(
"John", "Barker", "Programmer", "R&D", "100", "info@acadians.com")
empList[49] = new employee(
"Jonathon", "Anderson", "Programmer", "R&D", "100", "info@acadians.com")
empList[50] = new employee(
"Frederick", "Barker", "Programmer", "R&D", "100", "info@acadians.com")
empList[51] = new employee(
"Smitty", "Tyler", "Programmer", "R&D", "100", "info@acadians.com")
empList[52] = new employee(
"Sargent", "Anderson", "Programmer", "R&D", "100", "info@acadians.com")
empList[53] = new employee(
"Pepe", "Potts", "Programmer", "R&D", "100", "info@acadians.com")
empList[54] = new employee(
"Leo", "Godfrey", "Programmer", "R&D", "100", "info@acadians.com")
empList[55] = new employee(
```

```
"Geo", "Stewart", "Programmer", "R&D", "100", "info@acadians.com")
empList[56] = new employee(
"Meo", "Anderson", "Programmer", "R&D", "100", "info@acadians.com")
empList[57] = new employee(
"Oeo", "Orefo", "Programmer", "R&D", "100", "info@acadians.com")
empList[58] = new employee
"Jack", "Wagner", "Chief Entertainment Officer", "Exec", "300",
"jwagner@acadians.com")
empList[59] = new employee(
"Brady", "Smith", "Programmer", "R&D", "100", "info@acadians.com")
empList[60] = new employee(
"Tristin", "Ryder", "Programmer", "R&D", "100", "info@acadians.com")
empList[61] = new employee(
"James", "Tyler", "Programmer", "R&D", "100", "info@acadians.com")
empList[62] = new employee(
"Charles", "Potts", "Programmer", "R&D", "100", "info@acadians.com")
empList[63] = new employee(
"Bill", "Potts", "Senior Manager", "Management", "200", "info@acadians.com")
empList[64] = new employee(
"Bart", "Anderson", "Senior Manager", "Management", "200", "info@acadians.com")
empList[65] = new employee(
"Ian", "Potts", "Senior Manager", "Management", "200", "info@acadians.com")
empList[66] = new employee(
"Woody", "Smith", "Senior Manager", "Management", "200", "info@acadians.com")
empList[67] = new employee(
"Mark", "Tyler", "Senior Manager", "Management", "200", "info@acadians.com")
empList[68] = new employee(
"Andrew", "Driscoll", "Senior Manager", "Management", "200", "info@acadians.com")
empList[69] = new employee(
"Andy", "Potts", "Senior Manager", "Management", "200", "info@acadians.com")
empList[70] = new employee(
"Dandy", "Driscoll", "Senior Manager", "Management", "200", "info@acadians.com")
empList[71] = new employee(
"Candy", "Potts", "Senior Manager", "Management", "200", "info@acadians.com")
empList[72] = new employee(
"Spander", "Smith", "Senior Manager", "Management", "200", "info@acadians.com")
empList[73] = new employee(
"Landry", "Potts", "Senior Manager", "Management", "200", "info@acadians.com")
empList[74] = new employee(
"Permy", "Smith", "Senior Manager", "Management", "200", "info@acadians.com")
empList[75] = new employee(
"Jostin", "Driscoll", "Senior Manager", "Management", "200", "info@acadians.com")
empList[76] = new employee(
"Justin", "Ryder", "Senior Manager", "Management", "200", "info@acadians.com")
empList[77] = new employee(
"Braxel", "Anderson", "Senior Manager", "Management", "200", "info@acadians.com")
empList[78] = new employee(
"Opene", "Smith", "Senior Manager", "Management", "200", "info@acadians.com")
empList[79] = new employee(
"Juan", "Barker", "Senior Manager", "Management", "200", "info@acadians.com")
empList[80] = new employee(
"Julios", "Driscoll", "Senior Manager", "Management", "200", "info@acadians.com")
empList[81] = new employee(
"Andre", "Barker", "Senior Manager", "Management", "200", "info@acadians.com")
empList[82] = new employee(
"Bernard", "Smith", "Senior Manager", "Management", "200", "info@acadians.com")
```

continues

Listing 30.1. continued

```
empList[83] = new employee(
"Susan", "Ryder", "Senior Manager", "Management", "200", "info@acadians.com")
empList[84] = new employee(
"Susanne", "Anderson", "Senior Manager", "Management", "200", "info@acadians.com")
empList[85] = new employee(
"Chelsey", "Barker", "Senior Manager", "Management", "200", "info@acadians.com")
empList[86] = new employee(
"Cosmo", "Krammer", "Senior Manager", "Management", "200", "info@acadians.com")
empList[87] = new employee(
"Kirby", "Tipple", "Senior Manager", "Management", "200", "info@acadians.com")
empList[88] = new employee(
"George", "Allen", "Senior Manager", "Management", "200", "info@acadians.com")
empList[89] = new employee(
"Boy", "Goeria", "Senior Manager", "Management", "200", "info@acadians.com")
empList[90] = new employee(
"Teddy", "Washington", "Senior Manager", "Management", "200", "info@acadians.com")
empList[91] = new employee(
"Tut", "Kingman", "Senior Manager", "Management", "200", "info@acadians.com")
empList[92] = new employee(
"Oil", "Larenzo", "Secretary", "Company", "800", "info@acadians.com")
empList[93] = new employee(
"Susie", "Que", "Secretary", "Company", "800", "info@acadians.com")
empList[94] = new employee(
"Trista", "Wagner", "Secretary", "Company", "800", "info@acadians.com")
empList[95] = new employee(
"Kimberly", "Smith", "Secretary", "Company", "800", "info@acadians.com")
empList[96] = new employee(
"Rachel", "McDonald", "Secretary", "Company", "800", "info@acadians.com")
empList[97] = new employee(
"Reena", "Smiles", "Secretary", "Company", "800", "info@acadians.com")
empList[98] = new employee(
"Treena", "Miles", "Secretary", "Company", "800", "info@acadians.com")
empList[99] = new employee(
"Corrina", "Triles", "Secretary", "Company", "800", "info@acadians.com")
empList[100] = new employee(
"Rosemarie", "Barlington", "Secretary", "Company", "800", "info@acadians.com")
empList[101] = new employee(
"Il", "Plage", "HR Manager", "Recruiting", "900", "info@acadians.com")
empList[102] = new employee(
"Url", "Page", "HR Manager", "Recruiting", "900", "info@acadians.com")
empList[103] = new employee(
"Youri", "Basto", "HR Manager", "Recruiting", "900", "info@acadians.com")
empList[104] = new employee(
"Pri", "Opeo", "HR Manager", "Recruiting", "900", "info@acadians.com")
empList[105] = new employee(
"Tikki", "Rodrequez", "HR Manager", "Recruiting", "900", "info@acadians.com")
</SCRIPT>

</HEAD>
<FRAMESET ROWS="35%,65%">
  <FRAME SRC="searchfrm.htm" NAME="searchForm" MARGINWIDTH="10"
MARGINHEIGHT="10">
  <FRAME SRC="result.htm" NAME="resultForm" MARGINWIDTH="10" MARGINHEIGHT="10">
<NOFRAMES>
```

```
Sorry, your browser does not support frames.
</NOFRAMES>
</FRAMESET>
<BODY>
</BODY>
</HTML>
```

Listing 30.2. searchfrm.htm.

```
<html>
<head>
<title>Search Form</title>
<SCRIPT LANGUAGE="JavaScript">

    // Intranet Employee Database
    // JavaScript Unleashed (Sams.net Publishing)
    // Created by Richard J. Wagner (rwagner@acadians.com)

    function doSearch() {
        var searchField = ""

        if (document.form.searchBy[0].checked) {
            searchField = "FirstName" }
        else {
            if (document.form.searchBy[1].checked) {
                searchField = "LastName" }
            else { if (document.form.searchBy[2].checked) {
                    searchField = "Title" }
                else { if (document.form.searchBy[3].checked) {
                    searchField = "Department" }

                }
            }
        }

        if (document.form.searchByText.value == null ||
            document.form.searchByText.value == "") {
            alert("Please enter your search criteria before continuing.") }
        else {
            parent.findEmployee(searchField,
             document.form.searchByText.value)
        }
    }

    function clearForm() {
        parent.resultForm.document.open()
        parent.resultForm.document.close()


    }
</SCRIPT><h1><font color="#000000"><em>Intranet Employee Database</em></font>
</h1>
</head>
```

continues

Listing 30.2. continued

```
<hr>
<body bgcolor="#FFFFFF">
<form method="POST" name="form">
<pre>Search By: </pre>
<pre><input
     type=radio
     name="searchBy"
     value="FirstName">First Name <input
     type=radio
     checked
     name="searchBy"
     value="LastName">Last Name <input
     type=radio
     name="searchBy"
     value="Title">Title <input
     type=radio
     name="searchBy"
     value="Department">Department</pre>
<pre>Text: <input
     type=text
     size=30
     maxlength=30
     name="searchByText">    <input
     type=button
     size=20
     name="findButton"
     value="    Find      "
     onClick="doSearch()"> <input
     type=reset
     name="Clear"
     value=" Clear "
     onClick="clearForm()"></pre>
</form>
</body>
</html>
```

Summary

Client-side databases are neither a replacement for larger scale SQL servers nor a means for data entry. However, although limited in their scope, databases embedded in JavaScript code offer an innovative means of offloading some database processing that would usually take place on the server. A client can then be responsible for the entire database search and presentation process.

This chapter looked at client-side databases and explained when they should be used. It also discussed how to use JavaScript arrays as database containers that can be searched using JavaScript's built-in language constructs. A key part of the chapter was detailing a practical example of where a client-side table would be ideal. In the next chapter, I go a level deeper to look at databases that cannot be moved to the client side. I look at how to use JavaScript on the server side to access relational databases.

Database Connectivity Using Server-Side JavaScript

by Richard Wagner

IN THIS CHAPTER

CHAPTER 31

One of the compelling factors in companies moving to the Web as a development platform is the notion that it gives its users easier access to corporate data. Since the advent of the Web, CGI has been the typical means of connecting to databases and generating results in HTML format. Although client-side JavaScript does not have the capability to access data on a database server, you can use its server-based counterpart to perform this process.

This chapter looks at how you can use server-side JavaScript to connect to your back-end data. For this discussion, I highlight Netscape LiveWire, which provides built-in database access within its object framework. If you recall from the discussion in Chapter 20, LiveWire is Netscape's server-side application development environment for Netscape servers.

> **NOTE**
>
> If you have not already done so, you will find it helpful to read Chapter 20, "Server-Side JavaScript," before working with databases and LiveWire. This chapter is intended to build upon what you learned in Chapter 20.

LiveWire Database Connectivity

LiveWire provides the server extensions you need to access external data in a relational database. Figure 31.1 shows the architecture of a LiveWire database application. When a client submits a request that is associated with the database, that information is routed through the Web server to your LiveWire application. It accesses the database and returns a result to the client in HTML format.

> **NOTE**
>
> Before you can connect to a database through JavaScript, you need to have the necessary software installed and configured to provide access to the database server.

FIGURE 31.1.
LiveWire database architecture.

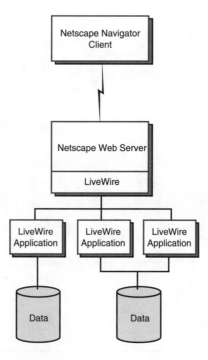

LiveWire Database Object

In addition to LiveWire's state maintenance objects (request, client, project, and server), server JavaScript also boasts a database object. The database object encapsulates all functionality related to interacting with a relational database. Containing no properties, all of its utility stems from its methods, which are shown in Table 31.1. If you have worked with databases using other programming languages, you can see that JavaScript has almost everything you would expect for interacting with SQL databases.

Table 31.1. Database object methods.

Method	Description
connect("*databaseType*", "*serverName*", "*username*", "*password*", "*databaseName*")	Connects LiveWire application to specified database and creates database object.
connected()	Returns true if application is connected to a database.
disconnect()	Closes database connection.

continues

Table 31.1. continued

Method	Description
cursor("*SQLSELECTStatement*", *updateable*)	Creates a database cursor for the specified SQL SELECT statement.
execute("*SQLStatement*")	Executes the specified SQL statement. Use for SQL statements that do not return a cursor.
SQLTable("*SQLSELECTStatement*")	Generates an HTML table to display the results of the SELECT query.
beginTransaction()	Starts a SQL transaction.
commitTransaction()	Commits the current SQL transaction.
rollbackTransaction()	Rolls back the current SQL transaction.
majorErrorCode()	Major error code returned by the database server or ODBC.
majorErrorMessage()	Major error message returned by database server or ODBC.
minorErrorCode()	Secondary error code returned by vendor library.
minorErrorMessage()	Secondary message returned by vendor library.

NOTE

The manner in which LiveWire objects are instantiated is anything but consistent. The set of request, client, project, and server objects are all created implicitly (when they are referenced), whereas the file object (discussed in Chapter 20) uses the conventional new operator.

The database object is created in yet another way. When you connect to a database using the connect() method, a database object is implicitly created.

Connecting to a Database

The first step in working with a database is to connect to it using the connect() method. The parameters of the connect() method include all the pieces of information LiveWire needs to attach itself to an external database:

■ Database type—LiveWire currently supports the following database types: INFORMIX, ODBC, ORACLE, and SYBASE.

- Server name—Use the server name on which the database resides. If you are using ODBC, use the ODBC service name defined in Control Panel's ODBC administration utility.

- Username—Use a valid username defined on the database server.

- Password—Use the password associated with the specified username.

- Database name—For SQL databases that allow multiple databases per server, use the name of the database.

> **TIP**
>
> Not all relational database management systems require or even support all the parameters specified in the connect() method. If your database software does not use one of the parameters, use an empty string ("") as the parameter.

For example, suppose you want to connect to a Microsoft SQL Server database named BEANS that is on a server called STARBUCK. Using the system administrator username (sa) with a password of frap, the statement looks like the following:

```
database.connect("ODBC", "STARBUCK", "sa", "frap", "BEANS")
```

Before trying to perform an operation on the database, you should first check to see if connect() was successful by using the connected() method. For example, the following code attempts to connect to the BEANS database. If the process is not successful, then a message is displayed to the user:

```
database.connect("ODBC", "STARBUCK", "sa", "frap", "BEANS")
if (!database.connected()) {
   write("Unable to connect to the database.") }
```

As you design your LiveWire application, you should give careful thought to the method by which the application connects to the database. Probably the most common approach is to open a connection in the application's initial startup page and keep it open. Other HTML pages within the application can then use this connection when it needs access to the database. Using this method, multiple clients can access the database concurrently using this shared connection. You also have a performance benefit as well because there is less overhead involved with each database transaction.

A second approach is to explicitly connect to a server only when you are going to perform a database operation and then disconnect when you are finished. This is often called the "serial approach" because only a single client can connect to the database at a time. You might also find it helpful to think of it as the "commando approach," because the mission of the code is to get into the database, do business quickly, and leave as soon as you are finished.

Part of the serial methodology is to place an explicit lock on the database before attempting to connect to it. Just as a file object can call the project (or server) `lock()` method to prevent concurrent file access, the database object locks the project (or server) as well. Consider the following example:

```
project.lock()
database.connect("ODBC", "STARBUCK", "sa", "frap", "BEANS")
if (database.connected()) {
    database.execute('UPDATE coffee SET source = "Ethiopia" WHERE type =
    ➥"Sidamo"')
    database.disconnect()
}
project.unlock()
```

Working with SQL SELECT Queries

One of the most common tasks of Web database applications is to perform a SQL SELECT query and return a result set to the user in HTML format. LiveWire gives you two approaches to performing this task, either using the `SQLTable()` method or using a database cursor.

NOTE

Your SQL statements should be ANSI 89 compliant SQL.

Using the `SQLTable()` Method

The easiest, but least flexible, approach is to use the database object's `SQLTable()` method. Using a SELECT statement as its parameter, `SQLTable()` submits a query to the database and transforms the result set into an HTML table. For example, to return a listing of all book records in a table, you could use the following code:

```
var queryString = "SELECT * FROM BOOKS"
database.SQLTable(queryString)
```

Working with Cursor Objects

The `SQLTable()` method provides a quick-and-dirty way to view result sets, but it does not have any mechanism to alter the presentation format of the HTML table. You can use a database cursor to have more control of the output of the result set. A database cursor is essentially a "virtual table" or a pointer to a result set of a query. A cursor maintains a current position (row) within it, enabling you to perform actions on the set of records associated with the cursor.

In LiveWire, a cursor object is contained by a database object and is instantiated when the `cursor()` method is called. The cursor object contains one property and several methods, as shown in Table 31.2.

Database Connectivity Using Server-Side JavaScript

CHAPTER 31

701

31

USING
SERVER-SIDE
JAVASCRIPT

Table 31.2. Properties and methods of the cursor object.

Property/Method	Description
`cursorColumn`	Array of objects corresponding to each column of the cursor.
`close()`	Closes the cursor.
`columns()`	Returns the number of columns in the cursor.
`columnName(columnIndex)`	Returns the name of the column specified by the `columnIndex` parameter.
`next()`	Moves the cursor to the next record in the table.
`insertRow("tableName")`	Inserts a record into the specified table after the current record.
`updateRow("tableName")`	Updates current record of the specified table.
`deleteRow("tableName")`	Deletes the current record of the specified table.

To create a cursor, use the database object's `cursor()` method based on the following:

```
cursorName = database.cursor("SELECTStatement", updateable)
```

The *updateable* parameter is a Boolean (true/false) value that specifies whether you want to allow updates within the cursor.

For example, the following code creates a read-only cursor named books:

```
books = database.cursor("SELECT * FROM BOOKS", false)
```

You can then use the cursor object's methods to navigate through the table. If you want to return the result set to the user as a series of records, you use the following code:

```
books = database.cursor("SELECT * FROM BOOKS", false)
while (books.next()) {
      write("<b>Author: </b>" + books.author + "<p>")
      write("<b>Title: </b><i>" + books.title + "</i><p>)
      write("<b>Edition: </b>" + books.edition + "<p>")
      write("<b>Year: </b>" + books.date + "<p>")
      write("<b>ISBN: </b>" + books.isbn + "<p>")
      write("<b>Publisher: </b>" + books.publisher + "<p>")
}
books.close()
```

The `while` loop uses the `next()` method to traverse through the entire cursor. The statements within the loop are performed on the current record within the cursor.

Notice that you can access the columns (also called fields) as a property of the cursor. When a cursor object is instantiated, an array of columns is created. You can access them by name, as shown in the preceding example, or by number (the column's position within the cursor).

> **NOTE**
>
> One of the few examples where JavaScript is not case sensitive is in referencing columns in a cursor.

For a second example, suppose you want to display the results of the same query in a tabular format. You could embed the HTML table definition tags within the code:

```
Books = database.cursor("SELECT * FROM BOOKS", false)
write("<TABLE>")
write("<TR>")
write("<TH>Author</TH>")
write("<TH>Title</TH>")
write("<TH>Edition</TH>")
write("<TH>Year</TH>")
write("<TH>ISBN</TH>")
write("<TH>Publisher</TH>")
write("</TR>")
while (books.next()) {
     write("<TR>")
     write("<TD>" + books.author + "</TD>")
     write("<TD>" + books.title + "</TD>")
     write("<TD>" + books.edition + "</TD>")
     write("<TD>" + books.year + "</TD>")
     write("<TD>" + books.isbn + "</TD>")
     write("<TD>" + books.publisher + "</TD>")
     write("</TR>")
}
write("</TABLE>")
books.close()
```

Alternatively, you could reference the columns by number rather than by name. Using the `columnName()` and `columns()` methods, you could build a more flexible piece of code:

```
books = database.cursor("SELECT * FROM BOOKS", false)
write("<TABLE>")
write("<TR>")
for (var i=0; i<books.columns(); i++) {
     write("<TH>" + books.columnName(i) + "</TH>")
}
write("</TR>")
while (books.next()) {
     write("<TR>")
     for (var i=0; i<books.columns(); i++) {
          write("<TD>" + books[i] + "</TD>")
     }
     write("</TR>")
}
write("</TABLE>")
books.close()
```

The first `for` loop iterates through each column of the table. Using `columnName()`, the name of the column is embedded within a `<TH>` and `</TH>` tag pair. The second `for` loop uses the

Database Connectivity Using Server-Side JavaScript

CHAPTER **31**

703

31

USING
SERVER-SIDE
JAVASCRIPT

`cursorColumn` array to return the value of the specified column and place it within the `<TD>` and `</TD>` tag pair.

> **NOTE**
>
> A cursor is limited in scope to the current HTML page of an application. As a result, you cannot use it to span an entire multi-page application.

Working with Updateable Cursors

You can create an updateable cursor to let your application modify the current record of the cursor. For a cursor to be updateable, the following conditions must be true for the query statement:

- The SELECT statement must be limited to a single table. You cannot create an updateable cursor on a query containing table joins.
- You must include key values as part of the result set of the SELECT statement.
- Specialized queries such as GROUP BY queries are not updateable.

You can create an updateable cursor by using true as the second parameter of a `cursor()` method. For example, the following code creates an updateable cursor called students:

```
students = database.cursor("SELECT * FROM S_ROOSTER", true)
```

Once you create an updateable cursor, you can make changes to the result set. For example, suppose you want to change all the records with an `Area_Code` column value of 402 to a new value of 949. You could use the following code:

```
var sqlStr = 'SELECT * FROM S_ROOSTER WHERE Area_Code = "402"'
students = database.cursor(sqlStr, true)
while (students.next()) {
    students.Area_Code = "949"
    students.updateRow("S_ROOSTER")
}
students.close()
```

The initial `next()` call puts the pointer on the first record of the cursor, so be sure you call `next()` before trying to update a table using `updateRow()`.

To add a record to a cursor, you need to perform a two-step process:

1. Assign values to the columns of the cursor.
2. Call the cursor's `insertRow()` method.

For example, suppose you want to add a new student to the student roster database based on information from an HTML form. You could use the following code:

```
students = database.cursor("SELECT * FROM S_ROOSTER", true)
students.studentID = client.newID
students.lastName = request.lastName
students.firstName = request.firstName
students.address = request.address
students.city = request.city
students.state = request.state
students.zip = request.zip
students.homePhone = request.homePhone
students.email = request.email
students.insertRow("S_ROOSTER")
students.close()
```

Sending Passthrough SQL Statements

In addition to using cursors, you can send passthrough SQL to the database using the database object's execute() method. *Passthrough SQL* is a SQL statement sent directly to the database server that does not return any data back to your application. The primary advantage to using passthrough SQL is that it enables you to use a SQL database's native SQL dialect to perform data manipulation operations that otherwise might not be supported by other databases.

To perform passthrough SQL, use a valid SQL statement as the parameter for the execute() method:

```
var sqlStr = 'INSERT INTO CUSTOMER (FIRST_NAME, LAST_NAME, PHONE)
              VALUES ("' + client.firstName + '", "' + client.lastName
              + '", "' + client.phone + '")'
database.execute(sqlStr)
```

Performing Transactions

One of the central reasons that companies rely on SQL databases is their capability to maintain data integrity. Transaction control is a key reason for this database power. A transaction is a set of SQL commands that are executed together. When a transaction is *committed* to the database, the actions stick together as a team: Either they all succeed or they all fail. Before a transaction is committed, you can choose to *roll back* (cancel) the changes that were made.

Unless you manage transactions explicitly, LiveWire treats each update to a database as a separate transaction. This functionality is called *auto commit* because transactions are committed automatically. However, you can use the database object's beginTransaction(), commitTransaction(), and rollbackTransaction() methods to bring transaction processing under your control in your application. For example, revisit the example earlier in the chapter that updated all 402 area codes to 949. To ensure data integrity of the S_ROOSTER table, you want to treat the entire process as a single transaction. By providing explicit transaction control, you can ensure that all the records are updated or else none of them are updated. You can then place a beginTransaction() method at the start of the process and a commitTransaction() method at the end:

```
database.beginTransaction()
  var sqlStr = 'SELECT * FROM S_ROOSTER WHERE Area_Code = "402"'
  students = database.cursor(sqlStr, true)
  while (students.next()) {
      students.Area_Code = "949"
      students.updateRow("S_ROOSTER")
  }
  students.close()
database.commitTransaction()
```

Keep in mind the scope of transactions. A transaction is limited to the current HTML page of an application and cannot be spread across an entire multi-page application. Moreover, if a stray `beginTransaction()` method issued at the start of an HTML page is not accompanied by a `rollbackTransaction()` or `commitTransaction()`, LiveWire automatically commits the transaction when you leave the page.

> **NOTE**
>
> LiveWire does not support nested transactions.

Working with Binary Data

LiveWire provides support for working with binary large objects (BLOBs) in your database. You can take one of two approaches to working with BLOBs:

- Store the filename of the binary file in the database and then reference the file when binary data is retrieved. When the file is requested, you can reference it using the value of the column name:
  ```
  <SERVER>
  write("<IMG SRC=" + employee.photoFile + ">")
  </SERVER>
  ```
- Store the binary data within the database itself. If you do store the data within the database, you can use the `cursorColumn` methods `blobImage()` and `blobLink()` to retrieve the data or the `blob()` function to write binary data to the database.

Displaying Images

Using the following syntax, the `blobImage()` method displays an image stored in a database:

```
cursorObject.colName.blobImage("imageFormat" [, "text"] [, "align"],
[, "widthPixels"] [, "heightPixels"] [, "borderPixels"] [, isMap])
```

`blobImage()` creates an HTML image tag (`<IMG>`) based on these parameters, referencing a temporary file that is created in memory. The temporary file is deleted when the page is generated and sent to the client.

The only required parameter is `"imageFormat"`, which is the type of image you are displaying. The most common formats are GIF and JPEG. For example, suppose you want to display an online catalog of apparel. Within an HTML table, you could display a GIF image of the piece of clothing using the following code:

```
sClothes = database.cursor("SELECT * FROM SPRING_APPAREL", false)
write("<TABLE>")
write("<TR>")
write("<TH>Item #</TH>")
write("<TH>Item</TH>")
write("<TH>Styles</TH>")
write("<TH>Sizes</TH>")
write("<TH>Colors </TH>")
write("<TH>Description</TH>")
write("<TH>Image</TH>")
write("</TR>")
while (sClothes.next()) {
     write("<TR>")
     write("<TD>" + sClothes.itemNum + "</TD>")
     write("<TD>" + sClothes.item + "</TD>")
     write("<TD>" + sClothes.styles + "</TD>")
     write("<TD>" + sClothes.sizes + "</TD>")
     write("<TD>" + sClothes.colors + "</TD>")
     write("<TD>" + sClothes.description + "</TD>")
     write("<TD>" + sClothes.image.blobImage("gif") + "</TD>")
     write("</TR>")
}
write("</TABLE>")
sClothes.close()
```

Creating Links to Binary Data

Because of the size of binary data, displaying BLOBs comes at a definite performance cost. You might want to display images only when they are requested by the client. Also, there may be times when you cannot display the data anyway, such as if you are working with audio files. You can use the `blobLink()` method to retrieve binary data from the database and create an HTML link that references the temporary file. The syntax for `blobLink()` follows:

```
cursorObject.colName.blobLink("mimeType" , "linkText")
```

The *mimeType* parameter is any valid MIME type, such as the following:

> image/gif
>
> image/jpeg
>
> image/x-bitmap
>
> audio/x-wav

To illustrate the use of `blobLink()`, modify the previous example so that the image is displayed only if the user requests it. Using `blobLink()`, the following code creates a link using the name of the clothing item (the value of `sClothes.item`):

Database Connectivity Using Server-Side JavaScript

CHAPTER 31

707

31

USING
SERVER-SIDE
JAVASCRIPT

```
sClothes = database.cursor("SELECT * FROM SPRING_APPAREL", false)
write("<TABLE>")
write("<TR>")
write("<TH>Item #</TH>")
write("<TH>Item</TH>")
write("<TH>Styles</TH>")
write("<TH>Sizes</TH>")
write("<TH>Colors </TH>")
write("<TH>Description</TH>")
write("<TH>Image</TH>")
write("</TR>")
while (sClothes.next()) {
    write("<TR>")
    write("<TD>" + sClothes.itemNum + "</TD>")
    write("<TD>" + sClothes.image.blobLink("image/gif", sClothes.item) + "</TD>")
    write("<TD>" + sClothes.styles + "</TD>")
    write("<TD>" + sClothes.sizes + "</TD>")
    write("<TD>" + sClothes.colors + "</TD>")
    write("<TD>" + sClothes.description + "</TD>")
    write("</TR>")
}
write("</TABLE>")
write("<i>Click the item name to view an image of the piece of clothing.</i>")
sClothes.close()
```

It is worth noting the lifetime of a temporary binary file created by the `blobLink()` method. When `blobLink()` is called, a temporary file is created in memory. It is removed either when the client accesses the file by activating the link or sixty seconds after the request was processed—whichever comes first.

Inserting Binary Data into a Database

Another powerful feature of LiveWire is the capability to enter BLOBs into the database. You can use the built-in `blob()` function to assign binary data to a cursor column:

```
sClothes = database.cursor("SELECT * FROM SPRING_APPAREL", true)
sClothes.itemNum = project.newItemNum
sClothes.item = request.item
sClothes.styles = request.styles
sClothes.sizes = request.sizes
sClothes.colors = request.colors
sClothes.description = request.description
sClothes.image = blob(request.filename)
sClothes.insertRow("SPRING_APPAREL")
sClothes.close()
```

Handling Database Errors

When you're programming database applications, an important part of the coding effort should be accounting for database errors as you work with server data. When you send a SQL statement that fails, the database server responds by issuing an error message that specifies the reason for the failure. You can either access that information by its status code or request a more verbose description of the problem.

Most of the methods you use to interact with a database return a status code. A status code is an integer with a range of 0-27. A code of 0 indicates that the command completed success-fully, whereas the other values (shown in Table 31.3) indicate specific errors from the server.

Table 31.3. LiveWire database status codes.

Status Code	Explanation
0	No error
1	Out of memory
2	Object not initialized
3	Type conversion error
4	Database not registered
5	Error reported by server
6	Message from server
7	Error from vendor library
8	Lost connection
9	End of fetch
10	Invalid use of object
11	Column does not exist
12	Invalid positioning within object (bounds error)
13	Unsupported feature
14	Null reference parameter
15	Database object not found
16	Required information is missing
17	Object cannot support multiple readers
18	Object cannot support deletions
19	Object cannot support insertions
20, 21	Object cannot support updates
22	Object cannot support indices
23	Object cannot be dropped
24	Incorrect connection supplied
25	Object cannot support privileges
26	Object cannot support cursors
27	Unable to open

The database object includes four error-handling methods that return error codes and messages from the database server. The values of what is returned depend greatly on the back-end database server. Tables 31.4 through 31.7 list the return values for each of the SQL databases supported by LiveWire.

Table 31.4. Informix database error methods for status code 7 (vendor library error).

Method	Returns
`majorErrorMessage()`	`Vendor Library Error:` *errorMsg* (*errorMsg* is text from Informix.)
`minorErrorMessage()`	`ISAM Error:` *errorMsg* (*errorMsg* is text of the ISAM error code from Informix or an empty string (`""`) if no ISAM error occurred.)
`majorErrorCode()`	Informix error code.
`minorErrorCode()`	ISAM error code (or zero if there is no ISAM error).

Table 31.5. Oracle database error methods for status code 5 (server error).

Method	Returns
`majorErrorMessage()`	`Server Error:` *errorMsg* (where *errorMsg* is translation of Oracle return code).
`minorErrorMessage()`	Oracle server name.
`majorErrorCode()`	Return code as reported by Oracle Call-level Interface (OCI).
`minorErrorCode()`	Operating system error code as reported by OCI.

Table 31.6. Sybase database error methods for status code 7 (vendor library error).

Method	Returns
`majorErrorMessage()`	`Vendor Library Error:` *errorMsg* (where *errorMsg* is error text from DB-Library).
`minorErrorMessage()`	Operating system error text (as specified by DB-Library).
`majorErrorCode()`	DB-Library error number.
`minorErrorCode()`	Severity level (as specified by DB-Library).

Table 31.7. Sybase database error methods for status code 5 (server error).

Method	Returns
majorErrorMessage()	Server Error *errorMsg*, where *errorMsg* is text from SQL server. If severity and message number are both zero, then just the message text is returned.
minorErrorMessage()	SQL server name.
majorErrorCode()	SQL server message number.
minorErrorCode()	Severity level (as specified by SQL server).

To demonstrate the use of these error-handling methods, I return to an example shown earlier in the chapter. In the example shown in the section "Working with Updateable Cursors," I did not add any code to handle possible errors that could arise during an insertRow() operation. You can make the code bulletproof with the following code:

```
students = database.cursor("SELECT * FROM S_ROOSTER", true)
database.beginTransaction()
students.studentID = client.newID
students.lastName = request.lastName
students.firstName = request.firstName
students.address = request.address
students.city = request.city
students.state = request.state
students.zip = request.zip
students.homePhone = request.homePhone
students.email = request.email
status = students.insertRow("S_ROOSTER")
if (status != 0) {
     database.rollbackTransaction()
     if (status == 5 || status == 7) {
        write("An the following error was encountered when the record
was attempted to be inserted into the table: <p>")
        write(database.MajorErrorMessage())
     else {
          handleError(status)
     }
else {
     database.commitTransaction()
     write(request.firstName + " " + request.lastName + " is now on record
          at Web University. <p>")
}
students.close()
```

Putting It All Together

To demonstrate many of the subjects I covered in this chapter, I provide a more extended example of a database application. In this scenario, you are building a Web application for a imaginary school called Virtual University. The application has a threefold purpose:

■ Allow persons to enroll in the university.

■ Allow students to register for classes.

■ Allow students to get a schedule of classes.

Figure 31.2 shows the structure of the application.

FIGURE 31.2.

*Structure of the Virtual
University application.*

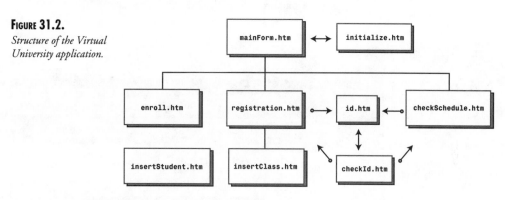

Initializing the Application

When users access the application, it requests `mainPage.htm`. The first responsibility of `mainPage.htm` is to check for a live connection to the database. If it has one, the home page is loaded, but if not, the client is sent to the `initialize.htm` file first:

```
if(!database.connected()) {
    redirect("initialize.htm")
}
```

If the user is accessing the page for the first time, it does not have a connection, so the `initialize.htm` file is requested. The first step of this page is to connect to the database:

```
if (!database.connected()) {
    database.connect("ODBC", "VSERVER", "guest", "lardgut", "SCHOOL")
}
```

If a connection is established, the first task to perform is getting a value for the `lastID` property for the project object. You use this property to determine a unique `StudentID` value (the key field of the `VSTUDENTS` table) for each new student entered in the database. To get this value, a cursor is opened on the `VSTUDENTS` table. Then, the code moves to the last record in the table and retrieves its `StudentID` value. (Because `StudentID` is the key, you can assume that they are sorted by `StudentID`.) This code executes after a `lock()` is placed on the project to ensure that no one else can access the table at the same time. After this process, the client is then redirected back to the home page. This code is shown here:

```
if (database.connected()) {
    project.lock()
        project.lastID = 0
        vCursor = database.cursor("SELECT * FROM VSTUDENTS")
```

```
        while (cursor.next()) {
             project.lastID = vCursor.studentID
        }
        vCursor.close();
    project.unlock()
    redirect("mainpage.htm") }
else {
    write("We are vSorry, but we cannot serve you at this time.
Please try at a later time.")
}
```

Figure 31.3 shows the home page.

FIGURE 31.3.

Virtual University home page.

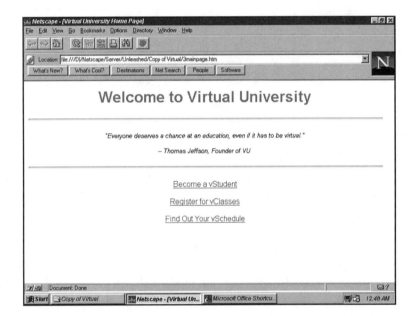

Enrolling as a Student

The first option for a user is to enroll as a student. If the user clicks the Become a vStudent link, the client is sent to the enroll.htm page. This form is a standard HTML form that specifies insertStudent.htm as the ACTION= parameter.

When the user clicks the Submit button, the insertStudent.htm is called. Its first task is to get the StudentID for this new student. To do so, it puts a lock() on the project, increments the project.lastID parameter by 1, and then assigns that value to the client object's studentID parameter:

```
project.lock()
project.lastID = parseInt(project.lastID) + 1
client.studentID = project.lastID
project.unlock()
```

Database Connectivity Using Server-Side JavaScript

CHAPTER 31

713

31

USING
SERVER-SIDE
JAVASCRIPT

Next, the form opens an updateable cursor on the VSTUDENTS table to assign the values from the enrollment form to the columns. After this is done for each column, the insertRow() method inserts the record into the table:

```
// Open up an updateable cursor on the VSTUDENTS table
// Assign form element values to the columns and
// insert the row into the table.
vStudent = database.cursor("SELECT * FROM VSTUDENTS", true)
vStudent.studentID = client.studentID
vStudent.lastName = request.LastName
vStudent.firstName = request.FirstName
vStudent.mi = request.MI
vStudent.address = request.StreetAddress
vStudent.address2 = request.Address2
vStudent.city = request.City
vStudent.state = request.State
vStudent.zip = request.ZipCode
vStudent.country = request.Country
vStudent.homePhone = request.HomePhone
vStudent.workPhone = request.WorkPhone
vStudent.fax = request.FAX
vStudent.email = request.Email
vStudent.url = request.URL
vStudent.dob = request.DateOfBirth
vStudent.sex = request.Personal_Sex
vStudent.major = request.major
status = vStudent.insertRow("VSTUDENTS")
vStudent.close()
if (status != 0) {
        write("Unable to add information at this time. <p>")}
else {
    write("<h1>We welcome you as a vStudent.</h1><p>")
    write("Keep this information for your records. Your StudentID number is " +
            client.studentID + ".<p><p>")
    write('You can now <A HREF="register.htm">click here</A>
to register for classes.')
}
```

Notice that the status code is checked on the insertRow() operation. If an error occurred, the user is notified of the problem. If the operation was successful, the user receives his StudentID number.

Registering for Classes

The second avenue for the application user is registering for classes. A user can get to the Class Registration form either from a link on the home page or after she has enrolled as a new student. Either way, the registration.htm page is called. This page first checks to ensure that the client has a StudentID. If it doesn't, the program redirects the client to an id.htm page after it assigns a value of "registration" to the gotoForm property of the client object:

```
if (client.studentID == null) {
    client.gotoForm = "registration"
    redirect("id.htm")
}
```

The id.htm is a standard HTML form (shown in Figure 31.4) that prompts the user for her StudentID. When the user clicks the Submit button, the checkId.htm file is called by the form's ACTION= parameter.

FIGURE 31.4.

StudentID *prompt for user.*

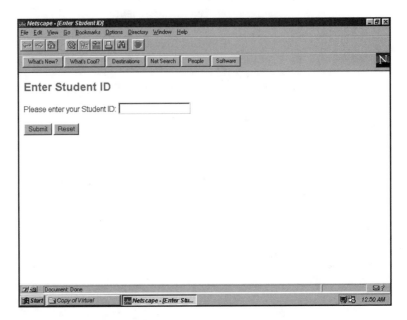

The checkId.htm page is charged with validating the StudentID value entered by the user. Although a real-world application would surely use a password, this program is simply going to check for the existence of a record that has a StudentID equal to the value entered by the user. The cursor opened on the VSTUDENTS table returns a record if the StudentID number is valid. If nothing is returned, the user is asked to return to the id.htm form. If a value was returned, the StudentID is assumed to be valid. The studentID property of the client object is assigned the value of request.StudentID. Finally, the page determines who called the id.htm initially by checking the gotoForm property of the client. If it is the Class Registration page, the client is returned to that page. This code follows:

```
checkid = database.cursor('SELECT * FROM VSTUDENTS WHERE StudentID="' +
          request.StudentID + '"', false)
var i = 0
while (checkid.next()) {
     i++
}
checkid.close()
if (i == 0) {
    write('Invalid StudentID. <A HREF="id.htm">Please reenter</A>.')
else  {
    client.studentID = request.StudentID
    if (client.gotoForm == "registration") {
        client.gotoForm = null
        redirect("registration.htm") }
```

```
else {
    client.gotoForm = null
    redirect("checkSchedule.htm")
}
}
```

After the client has a valid `StudentID`, the Class Registration form is presented to the user, as shown in Figure 31.5. Obviously oversimplified for this example, this page allows the user to register for a single class by filling out the form and clicking Register.

FIGURE 31.5.

Class registration form.

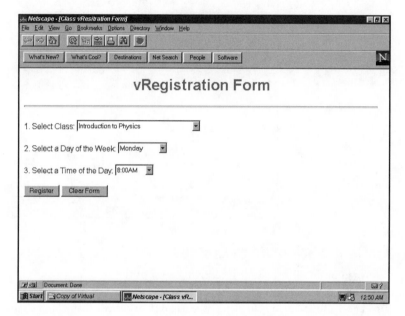

When the Registration form is submitted, the `insertClass.htm` page is called. The process of inserting a class record into the `VCLASSES` table parallels the `insertStudent.htm` process shown earlier in the chapter:

```
vClass = database.cursor("SELECT * FROM VCLASSES", true)
vClass.studentID = client.studentID
vClass.className = request.ClassName
vClass.weekday = request.Weekday
vClass.time = request.Time
status = vClass.insertRow("VCLASSES")
if (status != 0) {
        write("Unable to add information at this time. <p>")}
else {
    write("You will receive email notification confirming
        ➥ your schedule.<p><p>")
    write('<A HREF="register.htm">Click here</A> to register
        ➥for additional classes.')
write('<A HREF="mainpage.htm">Click here</A> to return to the home page.')
}
vClass.close()
```

The user sees a page that confirms the class entry and provides the opportunity to register for more classes or return to the home page. (See Figure 31.6.)

FIGURE 31.6.

Page appears after user registers for a class.

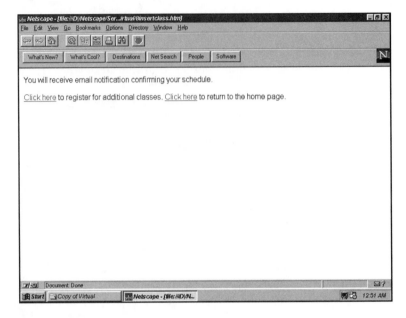

Getting a Schedule of Classes

The final option for the user is receiving a list of the classes that she chose. Clicking the Find Out Your Schedule link requests the checkSchedule.htm page. The checkSchedule.htm page first checks to see if the client has a studentID assigned. If not, the client is redirected to the id.htm page:

```
if (client.studentID == null) {
    client.gotoForm = "checkSchedule"
    redirect("id.htm")
}
```

The next step for the page is to perform a query to return the classes that the user scheduled. Because you already have the StudentID of the user at this point, you need no further information from the user to perform the query.

A cursor is opened on the VCLASSES table using a SELECT statement that returns all records with a StudentID value equal to the client.studentID value. The next step is to put the result set of the cursor into an HTML table. Using the same methodology used earlier in the chapter in building an HTML table on the fly, the class records are presented to the user:

```
vsched = database.cursor('SELECT * FROM VCLASSES WHERE StudentID = "' +
                         client.studentID + '" ORDER BY CLASSNAME', false)

write("<h1>Your Current Class Schedule</h1><p><p>")
write("<TABLE border=2 cellpadding=2 cellspacing=3 width=90%>")
write("<TR>")
for (var i=0; i<vsched.columns(); i++) {
    write("<TH>" + vsched.columnName(i) + "</TH>")
}
write("</TR>")
while (vsched.next()) {
    write("<TR>")
    for (var i=0; i<vsched.columns(); i++) {
        write("<TD>" + vsched[i] + "</TD>")
    }
    write("</TR>")
}
write("</TABLE>")
vsched.close()

write('<A HREF="mainpage.htm">Click here</A> to return to the home page.')
```

Figure 31.7 shows the results of a query.

FIGURE 31.7.

Schedule of classes.

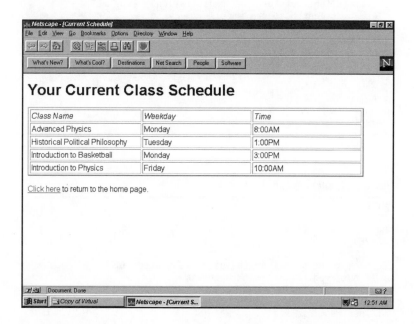

As you dissect this sample application, it is helpful to look at the entire source code for each of the pages of the application. Listings 31.1 through 31.9 provide this for you.

Listing 31.1. checkId.htm.

```
<HTML>
<BODY>
<SERVER>

// Check to see if the record exists in the table.
//
// If so, assign the value of the request.StudentID to the
// Client object parameter studentID. Then go to Registration form.
//
// If not, return to the ID form.
checkid = database.cursor('SELECT * FROM VSTUDENTS WHERE StudentID="' +
          request.StudentID + '"', false)
var i = 0
while (checkid.next()) {
     i++
}
checkid.close()
if (i == 0) {
    write('Invalid StudentID. <A HREF="id.htm">Please reenter</A>.')
else  {
    client.studentID = request.StudentID
    if (client.gotoForm == "registration") {
         client.gotoForm = null
         redirect("registration.htm") }
    else {
         client.gotoForm = null
         redirect("checkSchedule.htm")
    }
}
</SERVER>
</BODY>
</HTML>
```

Listing 31.2. checkSchedule.htm.

```
<HTML>
<HEAD>
<BODY>
<SERVER>

// Check to be sure that the user has a StudentID
// If not, redirect client to id.htm
if (client.studentID == null) {
    client.gotoForm = "checkSchedule"
    redirect("id.htm")
}

// Retrieve the classes of the current studentID
// and place them into a table.
vsched = database.cursor(,SELECT * FROM VCLASSES WHERE StudentID = "' +
                     client.studentID + '" ORDER BY CLASSNAME', false)

write("<h1>Your Current Class Schedule</h1><p><p>")
```

```
write("<TABLE border=2 cellpadding=2 cellspacing=3 width=90%>")
write("<TR>")
for (var i=0; i<vsched.columns(); i++) {
    write("<TH>" + vsched.columnName(i) + "</TH>")
}
write("</TR>")
while (vsched.next()) {
    write("<TR>")
    for (var i=0; i<vsched.columns(); i++) {
        write("<TD>" + vsched[i] + "</TD>")
    }
    write("</TR>")
}
write("</TABLE>")
vsched.close()

write('<A HREF="mainpage.htm">Click here</A> to return to the home page.')
</SERVER>
</BODY>
</HTML>
```

Listing 31.3. enroll.htm.

```
<html>
<head>
<title>Enroll at VU</title>
</head>

<body bgcolor="#FFFFFF">
<h1 align=center><font color="#FF0080">Enroll at VU</font></h1>
<hr>
<form action="insertstudent.htm" method="POST">
<p>Please provide the following contact information:</p>
<blockquote>
<pre><em>      First name </em><input type=text size=25 maxlength=256
name="FirstName">
<em>       Last name </em><input type=text size=25 maxlength=256
name="LastName">
<em>  Middle initial </em><input type=text size=4 maxlength=1 name="MI">
<em>           Title </em><input type=text size=35 maxlength=256
name="Title">
<em>  Street address </em><input type=text size=35 maxlength=256
name="StreetAddress">
<em> Address (cont.) </em><input type=text size=35 maxlength=256
name="Address2">
<em>            City </em><input type=text size=35 maxlength=256
name="City">
<em>  State/Province </em><input type=text size=35 maxlength=256
name="State">
<em> Zip/Postal code </em><input type=text size=12 maxlength=12
name="ZipCode">
<em>         Country </em><input type=text size=25 maxlength=256
name="Country">
```

continues

Listing 31.3. continued

```
<em>      Work Phone </em><input type=text size=25 maxlength=25
name="WorkPhone">
<em>      Home Phone </em><input type=text size=25 maxlength=25
name="HomePhone">
<em>            FAX </em><input type=text size=25 maxlength=25
name="FAX">
<em>          E-mail </em><input type=text size=25 maxlength=256
name="Email">
<em>            URL </em><input type=text size=25 maxlength=25
name="URL">
</pre>
<pre><em>   Date of birth </em><input type=text size=8 maxlength=256
name="DateOfBirth">
<em>            Sex </em><input type=radio checked name="Personal_Sex"
value="Male">Male <input type=radio name="Personal_Sex"
value="Female">Female</pre>
<pre><em>Expected major:</em> <select name="major" size=1>
<option selected>Software Development</option>
<option>Political Philosophy</option>
<option>Music</option>
<option>Art</option>
<option>Physics</option>
<option>Environmental Science</option>
<option>Writing</option>
<option>English Literature</option>
<option>French Studies</option>
<option>Sports and Physical Education</option>
<option>Biochemical Ergodynamics</option>
</select>
</pre>
</blockquote>
<p><input type=submit value="Submit Form"> <input type=reset
value="Reset Form"> </p>
</form>
<p> </h5>
</body>
</html>
```

Listing 31.4. id.htm.

```
<html>
<head>
<title>Enter Student ID</title>
</head>
<body bgcolor="#FFFFFF">
<h2><font color="#FF0080">Enter Student ID</font></h2>
<form action="checkid.htm" method="POST">
<p>Please enter your Student ID: <input type=text size=20
maxlength=256 name="StudentID"></p>
<p><input type=submit value="Submit"> <input type=reset value="Reset"></p>
</form>
</body>
</html>
```

Listing 31.5. `initialize.htm`.

```
<html>
<server>

// Attempt to connect to the database
if (!database.connected()) {
    database.connect("ODBC", "VSERVER", "guest", "lardgut", "SCHOOL")
}

// If connected, lock the project and get the last StudentID
// from the VSTUDENTS table. Assign it to the project property
// called lastID. You can then reference this property when
// the application is running instead of accessing the database
// directly.
//
// When this process is done, redirect client to mainpage
if (database.connected()) {
    project.lock()
        project.lastID = 0
        vCursor = database.cursor("SELECT * FROM VSTUDENTS")
        while (cursor.next()) {
            project.lastID = vCursor.studentID
        }
        vCursor.close();
    project.unlock()
    redirect("mainpage.htm") }
else {
    write("We are vSorry, but we cannot serve you at this time.
Please try at a later time.")
}
</server>
<html>
```

Listing 31.6. `insertClass.htm`.

```
<html>
<body>
<server>

// Insert class record into the database by opening
// an updateable cursor.
vClass = database.cursor("SELECT * FROM VCLASSES", true)
vClass.studentID = client.studentID
vClass.className = request.ClassName
vClass.weekday = request.Weekday
vClass.time = request.Time
status = vClass.insertRow("VCLASSES")
if (status != 0) {
        write("Unable to add information at this time. <p>")}
else {
    write("You will receive email notification confirming your
            schedule.<p><p>")
```

continues

Listing 31.6. continued

```
        write('<A HREF="register.htm">Click here</A> to register for
            additional classes.')
        write('<A HREF="mainpage.htm">Click here</A> to return to
            the home page.')
}
vClass.close()
</server>
</body>
</html>
```

Listing 31.7. insertStudent.htm.

```
<html>
<body>
<server>

// Get a unique studentID from the project lastID property
project.lock()
project.lastID = parseInt(project.lastID) + 1
client.studentID = project.lastID
project.unlock()

// Open up an updateable cursor on the VSTUDENTS table
// Assign form element values to the columns and
// insert the row into the table.
vStudent = database.cursor("SELECT * FROM VSTUDENTS", true)
vStudent.studentID = client.studentID
vStudent.lastName = request.LastName
vStudent.firstName = request.FirstName
vStudent.mi = request.MI
vStudent.address = request.StreetAddress
vStudent.address2 = request.Address2
vStudent.city = request.City
vStudent.state = request.State
vStudent.zip = request.ZipCode
vStudent.country = request.Country
vStudent.homePhone = request.HomePhone
vStudent.workPhone = request.WorkPhone
vStudent.fax = request.FAX
vStudent.email = request.Email
vStudent.url = request.URL
vStudent.dob = request.DateOfBirth
vStudent.sex = request.Personal_Sex
vStudent.major = request.major
status = vStudent.insertRow("VSTUDENTS")
vStudent.close()
if (status != 0) {
        write("Unable to add information at this time. <p>")}
else {
    write("<h1>We welcome you as a vStudent.</h1><p>")
    write("Keep this information for your records.
            Your StudentID number is " + client.studentID + ".<p><p>")
    write('You can now <A HREF="register.htm">click here</A>
            to register for classes.')
```

Database Connectivity Using Server-Side JavaScript

CHAPTER 31

723

31

USING
SERVER-SIDE
JAVASCRIPT

```
}
</server>
</body>
</html>
```

Listing 31.8. `mainPage.htm`.

```
<html>
<head>
<title>Virtual University Home Page</title>
<server>
// If database is not connected, redirect client to the initialize page
if(!database.connected()) {
    redirect("initialize.htm")
}
</server>
</head>

<body bgcolor="#FFFFFF">
<h1 align=center><font color="#FF0080">Welcome to Virtual University
</font></h1>
<hr>
<p align=center><font size=2><em>&quot;Everyone deserves a chance at
an education, even if it has to be virtual.&quot;</em></font></p>
<p align=center><font size=2><em>-- Thomas Jeffson, Founder of VU </em>
</font></p>
<hr>
<p align=center><a href="enroll.htm">Become a vStudent</a></p>
<p align=center><a href="registration.htm">Register for vClasses</a></p>
<p align=center><a href="checkSchedule.htm">Find Out Your vSchedule</a></p>
<p> </p>
</body>
</html>
```

Listing 31.9. `registration.htm`.

```
<html>

<head>
<title>Class vResitration Form</title>
</head>

<body bgcolor="#FFFFFF">
<server>
// Check to be sure that the user has a StudentID
// If not, redirect client to id.htm
if (client.studentID == null) {
    client.gotoForm = "registration"
    redirect("id.htm")
}
</server>
```

continues

Listing 31.9. continued

```
<h1 align=center><font color="#FF0080">vRegistration Form</font></h1>
<hr>
<form action="insertclass.htm" method="POST">
<p>1. Select Class: <select name="ClassName" size=1>
<option selected>Introduction to Physics</option>
<option>Advanced Physics</option>
<option>Historical Political Philosophy</option>
<option>Object-Oriented Design Methodologies</option>
<option>Introduction to Basketball</option>
</select></p>
<p>2. Select a Day of the Week: <select name="Weekday" size=1>
<option>Monday</option>
<option>Tuesday</option>
<option>Wednesday</option>
<option>Thursday</option>
<option>Friday</option>
</select></p>
<p>3. Select a Time of the Day: <select name="Time" size=1>
<option>8:00AM</option>
<option>10:00AM</option>
<option>1:00PM</option>
<option>3:00PM</option>
<option>7:00PM</option>
</select></p>
<p><input type=submit value="Register"> <input type=reset
value="Clear Form"></p>
</form>
</body>
</html>
```

Summary

LiveWire helps bridge the gap between relational databases and the Web by providing tools to create data-enabled Web applications. This chapter discussed these capabilities by focusing on the LiveWire database and cursor objects. Using these techniques, you can create compelling database applications that any Web client can access.

IX

PART

IN THIS PART

- JavaScript Language Summary

- Fundamentals of HTML

- Comparing JavaScript with Microsoft's VBScript

- JavaScript Resources on the Internet

Appendixes

JavaScript Language Summary

by Arman Danesh and
Stephen Le Hunte

IN THIS APPENDIX

APPENDIX A

While Sun was developing the much-lauded Java programming language, Netscape was busy developing a lightweight scripting language called LiveScript. This language was then redefined and renamed JavaScript. With JavaScript, you can provide almost limitless interactivity in your Web pages. The scripting language lets you access events such as startups, document loads, exits, and user mouse clicks. You can also use JavaScript to directly control objects, such as the browser status bar, frames, and even the browser display window. JavaScript also provides interactivity between plug-in modules and Java applets.

After providing a brief overview of creating dynamic documents with JavaScript, this appendix provides a reference section organized by object with properties and methods listed with the object they apply to. A final reference section covers independent functions in JavaScript not connected with a particular object, as well as operators in JavaScript.

NOTE

JavaScript is currently only fully supported by the Netscape Navigator (version 2 and above). Certain scripts might be supported by the Internet Explorer. For more information on JavaScript (including the entire script language documentation), visit the Netscape Web site (`http://home.netscape.com/`). The information provided here details how to include JavaScript scripts within HTML documents, not how to author actual scripts. Such information is well beyond the scope of this appendix.

Dynamic Documents with JavaScript

As mentioned earlier, JavaScript represents a heavily stripped-down and redefined version of the Java programming language. You can use it to control almost any part of the browser (as defined in the JavaScript object model) and to respond to various user actions such as form input and page navigation. JavaScript is particularly valuable because all processing duties are written in the script (embedded into the HTML document), so the entire process defined by the script is carried out on the client side without referring back to a server.

For example, you can write a JavaScript script to verify that the user entered numeric information in a form requesting a telephone number or Zip code. Without any network transmission, an HTML script with embedded JavaScript can interpret the entered text and alert the user with an appropriate message dialog.

A script is embedded in HTML within a `<SCRIPT>` element:

```
<SCRIPT>...</SCRIPT>
```

The text of a script is inserted between `<SCRIPT>` and its end element. Attributes within the `<SCRIPT>` element are specified as follows:

```
<SCRIPT LANGUAGE="JavaScript">
  Script functions go here
</SCRIPT>
```

The LANGUAGE attribute is required unless the SRC attribute is present to specify the scripting language. You can use the optional SRC attribute to specify a URL that loads the text of a script:

```
<SCRIPT LANGUAGE="language" SRC=url>
```

When a JavaScript-enabled HTML document is retrieved by a browser that supports JavaScript, the script functions are evaluated and stored. The functions defined within the script are executed only upon certain events within the page (for example, when the user moves the mouse over an object or enters text in a text box and so on).

So that non–JavaScript-capable browsers do not display the text of the script (browsers display anything they don't recognize as HTML as text on the page), you should enclose the script within comment elements:

```
<SCRIPT LANGUAGE="JavaScript">
<!-- Begin to hide script contents from old browsers.
  Script contents go here.
  End the hiding here.-->
</SCRIPT>
```

JavaScript Objects and Their Properties

This section describes JavaScript objects and their properties. Objects are presented in alphabetical order for easy reference.

The anchor Object

See the anchor property of the document object.

The button Object

The button object reflects a push button from an HTML form in JavaScript.

Properties

name	A string value containing the name of the button element.
value	A string value containing the value of the button element.

Methods

click()	Emulates the action of clicking the button.

Event Handlers

onClick   Specifies JavaScript code to execute when the button is clicked.

The checkbox Object

The checkbox object makes a checkbox from an HTML form available in JavaScript.

Properties

checked   A Boolean value indicating whether the checkbox element is
                  checked.

defaultChecked   A Boolean value indicating whether the checkbox element was
                  checked by default (that is, it reflects the checked attribute).

name   A string value containing the name of the checkbox element.

value   A string value containing the value of the checkbox element.

Methods

click()   Emulates the action of clicking the checkbox.

Event Handlers

onClick   Specifies JavaScript code to execute when the checkbox is clicked.

The Date Object

The Date object provides mechanisms for working with dates and times in JavaScript. You can
create instances of the object with the following syntax:

```
newObjectName = new Date(dateInfo)
```

In this example, *dateInfo* is an optional specification of a particular date and can be one of the
following, where the latter two options represent integer values:

```
"month day, year hours:minutes:seconds"
year, month, day
year, month, day, hours, minutes, seconds
```

If no *dateInfo* is specified, the new object represents the current date and time.

Methods

getDate()	Returns the day of the month for the current Date object as an integer from 1 to 31.
getDay()	Returns the day of the week for the current Date object as an integer from 0 to 6 (where 0 is Sunday, 1 is Monday, and so on).
getHours()	Returns the hour from the time in the current Date object as an integer from 0 to 23.
getMinutes()	Returns the minutes from the time in the current Date object as an integer from 0 to 59.
getMonth()	Returns the month for the current Date object as an integer from 0 to 11 (where 0 is January, 1 is February, and so on).
getSeconds()	Returns the seconds from the time in the current Date object as an integer from 0 to 59.
getTime()	Returns the time of the current Date object as an integer representing the number of milliseconds since January 1, 1970, at 00:00:00.
getTimezoneOffset()	Returns the difference between the local time and GMT as an integer representing the number of minutes.
getYear()	Returns the year of the week for the current Date object as a two-digit integer representing the year without the 1900.

parse(*dateString*)	Returns the number of milliseconds between January 1, 1970, at 00:00:00 and the date specified in *dateString*. *dateString* should take the following format:
	
	`Day, DD Mon YYYY HH:MM:SS TZN`
	`Mon DD, YYYY`

setDate(*dateValue*)	Sets the day of the month for the current Date object. *dateValue* is an integer from 1 to 31.
setHours(*hoursValue*)	Sets the hours for the time for the current Date object. *hoursValue* is an integer from 0 to 23.
setMinutes(*minutesValue*)	Sets the minutes for the time for the current Date object. *minutesValue* is an integer from 0 to 59.
setMonth(*monthValue*)	Sets the month for the current Date object. *monthValue* is an integer from 0 to 11 (where 0 is January, 1 is February, and so on).
setSeconds(*secondsValue*)	Sets the seconds for the time for the current Date object. *secondsValue* is an integer from 0 to 59.

setTime(*timeValue*)	Sets the value for the current Date object. *timeValue* is an integer representing the number of milliseconds since January 1, 1970, at 00:00:00.
setYear(*yearValue*)	Sets the year for the current Date object. *yearValue* is an integer greater than 1900.
toGMTString()	Returns the value of the current Date object in GMT as a string using Internet conventions in the following form: Day, DD Mon YYYY HH:MM:SS GMT
toLocaleString()	Returns the value of the current Date object in the local time using local conventions.
UTC(*yearValue*, *monthValue*, *dateValue*, *hoursValue*, *minutesValue*, *secondsValue*)	Returns the number of milliseconds since January 1, 1970, at 00:00:00 GMT. *yearValue* is an integer greater than 1900. *monthValue* is an integer from 0 to 11. *dateValue* is an integer from 1 to 31. *hoursValue* is an integer from 0 to 23. *minutesValue* and *secondsValue* are integers from 0 to 59. *hoursValue*, *minutesValue*, and *secondsValue* are optional.

The document Object

The document object reflects attributes of an HTML document in JavaScript.

Properties

alinkColor	The color of active links as a string or a hexadecimal triplet.
anchors	Array of anchor objects in the order they appear in the HTML document. Use anchors.length to get the number of anchors in a document.
bgColor	The color of the document's background.
cookie	A string value containing cookie values for the current document.
fgColor	The color of the document's foreground.
forms	Array of form objects in the order the forms appear in the HTML file. Use forms.length to get the number of forms in a document.
lastModified	String value containing the last date of modification of the document.
linkColor	The color of links as a string or a hexadecimal triplet.

links	Array of link objects in the order the hypertext links appear in the HTML document. Use links.length to get the number of links in a document.
location	A string containing the URL of the current document.
referrer	A string value containing the URL of the calling document when the user follows a link.
title	A string containing the title of the current document.
vlinkColor	The color of followed links as a string or a hexadecimal triplet.

Methods

clear()	Clears the document window.
close()	Closes the current output stream.
open(*mimeType*)	Opens a stream that allows write() and writeln() methods to write to the document window. *mimeType* is an optional string that specifies a document type supported by Navigator or a plug-in (for example, text/html, image/gif, and so on).
write()	Writes text and HTML to the specified document.
writeln()	Writes text and HTML to the specified document followed by a newline character.

The form Object

The form object reflects an HTML form in JavaScript. Each HTML form in a document is reflected by a distinct instance of the form object.

Properties

action	A string value specifying the URL where the form data is submitted.
elements	Array of objects for each form element in the order in which they appear in the form.
encoding	String containing the MIME encoding of the form as specified in the ENCTYPE attribute.
method	A string value containing the method of submission of form data to the server.
target	A string value containing the name of the window where responses to form submissions are directed.

Methods

submit()   Submits the form.

Event Handlers

onSubmit   Specifies JavaScript code to execute when the form is submitted. The code should return a true value to let the form be submitted. A false value prevents the form from being submitted.

The frame Object

The frame object reflects a frame window in JavaScript.

Properties

frames   An array of objects for each frame in a window. Frames appear in the array in the order in which they appear in the HTML source code.

parent   A string indicating the name of the window containing the frameset.

self   An alternative for the name of the current window.

top   An alternative for the name of the topmost window.

window   An alternative for the name of the current window.

Methods

alert(*message*)   Displays *message* in a dialog box.

close()   Closes the window.

confirm(*message*)   Displays *message* in a dialog box with OK and Cancel buttons. Returns true or false based on the button clicked by the user.

open(*url*,*name*,*features*) Opens *url* in a window named *name*. If *name* doesn't exist, a new window is created with that name. *features* is an optional string argument containing a list of features for the new window. The feature list contains any of the following name/value pairs separated by commas without additional spaces:

	`toolbar=[yes,no,1,0]`	Indicates if the window should have a toolbar.
	`location=[yes,no,1,0]`	Indicates if the window should have a location field.
	`directories=[yes,no,1,0]`	Indicates if the window should have directory buttons.
	`status=[yes,no,1,0]`	Indicates if the window should have a status bar.
	`menubar=[yes,no,1,0]`	Indicates if the window should have menus.
	`scrollbars=[yes,no,1,0]`	Indicates if the window should have scrollbars.
	`resizable=[yes,no,1,0]`	Indicates if the window should be resizable.
	`width=`*pixels*	Indicates the width of the window in pixels.
	`height=`*pixels*	Indicates the height of the window in pixels.
`prompt(`*message*`,`*response*`)`		Displays *message* in a dialog box with a text entry field with the default value of *response*. The user's response in the text entry field is returned as a string.
`setTimeout(`*expression*`,`*time*`)`		Evaluates *expression* after *time* where *time* is a value in milliseconds. You can name the time-out with the following structure:
		`name = setTimeOut(`*expression*`,`*time*`)`
`clearTimeout(`*name*`)`		Cancels the time-out with the name *name*.

The hidden Object

The `hidden` object reflects a hidden field from an HTML form in JavaScript.

Properties

`name`	A string value containing the name of the hidden element.
`value`	A string value containing the value of hidden text element.

The history Object

The history object allows a script to work with the Navigator browser's history list in JavaScript. For security and privacy reasons, the actual content of the list is not reflected in JavaScript.

Properties

length   An integer representing the number of items on the history list.

Methods

back()   Goes back to the previous document in the history list.

forward()   Goes forward to the next document in the history list.

go(*location*)   Goes to the document in the history list specified by *location*. *location* can be a string or integer value. If it is a string, it represents all or part of a URL in the history list. If it is an integer, *location* represents the relative position of the document on the history list. As an integer, *location* can be positive or negative.

The link Object

The link object reflects a hypertext link in the body of a document.

Properties

target   A string value containing the name of the window or frame specified in the target attribute.

Event Handlers

onClick   Specifies JavaScript code to execute when the link is clicked.

onMouseOver   Specifies JavaScript code to execute when the mouse is over the hypertext link.

The location Object

The location object reflects information about the current URL.

Properties

hash	A string value containing the anchor name in the URL.
host	A string value containing the hostname and port number from the URL.
hostname	A string value containing the domain name (or numerical IP address) from the URL.
href	A string value containing the entire URL.
pathname	A string value specifying the path portion of the URL.
port	A string value containing the port number from the URL.
protocol	A string value containing the protocol from the URL (including the colon but not the slashes).
search	A string value containing any information passed to a GET CGI-bin call (that is, any information after the question mark).

The Math Object

The Math object provides properties and methods for advanced mathematical calculations.

Properties

E	The value of Euler's constant (roughly 2.718), used as the base for natural logarithms.
LN10	The value of the natural logarithm of 10 (roughly 2.302).
LN2	The value of the natural logarithm of 2 (roughly 0.693).
PI	The value of pi, used in calculating the circumference and area of circles (roughly 3.1415).
SQRT1_2	The value of the square root of one half (roughly 0.707).
SQRT2	The value of the square root of two (roughly 1.414).

Methods

abs(*number*)	Returns the absolute value of *number*. The absolute value is the value of a number with its sign ignored, so abs(4) and abs(-4) both return 4.
acos(*number*)	Returns the arc cosine of *number* in radians.
asin(*number*)	Returns the arc sine of *number* in radians.
atan(*number*)	Returns the arc tangent of *number* in radians.

ceil(*number*)	Returns the next integer greater than *number*—in other words, rounds up to the next integer.
cos(*number*)	Returns the cosine of *number* where *number* represents an angle in radians.
exp(*number*)	Returns the value of E to the power of *number*.
floor(*number*)	Returns the next integer less than *number*—in other words, rounds down to the nearest integer.
log(*number*)	Returns the natural logarithm of *number*.
max(*number1*,*number2*)	Returns the greater of *number1* and *number2*.
min(*number1*,*number2*)	Returns the smaller of *number1* and *number2*.
pow(*number1*,*number2*)	Returns the value of *number1* to the power of *number2*.
random()	Returns a random number between zero and one. (At press time, this method was only available on UNIX versions of Navigator 2.0.)
round(*number*)	Returns the closest integer to *number*—in other words, rounds to the closest integer.
sin(*number*)	Returns the sine of *number* where *number* represents an angle in radians.
sqrt(*number*)	Returns the square root of number.
tan(*number*)	Returns the tangent of *number* where *number* represents an angle in radians.

The navigator Object

The navigator object reflects information about the version of Navigator being used.

Properties

appCodeName	A string value containing the code name of the client (for example, "Mozilla" for Netscape Navigator).
appName	A string value containing the name of the client (for example, "Netscape" for Netscape Navigator).
appVersion	A string value containing the version information for the client in the following form: *versionNumber (platform; country)* For instance, Navigator 2.0, beta 6 for Windows 95 (international version), would have an appVersion property with the value 2.0b6 (Win32; I).

userAgent	A string containing the complete value of the user-agent header sent in the HTTP request. This contains all the information in appCodeName and appVersion:

```
Mozilla/2.0b6 (Win32; I)
```

The password Object

The password object reflects a password text field from an HTML form in JavaScript.

Properties

defaultValue	A string value containing the default value of the password element (that is, the value of the value attribute).
name	A string value containing the name of the password element.
value	A string value containing the value of the password element.

Methods

focus()	Emulates the action of focusing on the password field.
blur()	Emulates the action of removing focus from the password field.
select()	Emulates the action of selecting the text in the password field.

The radio Object

The radio object reflects a set of radio buttons from an HTML form in JavaScript. To access individual radio buttons, use numeric indexes starting at zero. For instance, individual buttons in a set of radio buttons named testRadio could be referenced by testRadio[0], testRadio[1], and so on.

Properties

checked	A Boolean value indicating whether a specific button is checked. Can be used to select or deselect a button.
defaultChecked	A Boolean value indicating whether a specific button was checked by default (that is, reflects the checked attribute).
length	An integer value indicating the number of radio buttons in the set.
name	A string value containing the name of the set of radio buttons.
value	A string value containing the value of a specific radio button in a set.

Methods

click()   Emulates the action of clicking a radio button.

Event Handlers

onClick   Specifies JavaScript code to execute when a radio button is clicked.

The reset Object

The reset object reflects a reset button from an HTML form in JavaScript.

Properties

name   A string value containing the name of the reset element.

value   A string value containing the value of the reset element.

Methods

click()   Emulates the action of clicking the reset button.

Event Handlers

onClick   Specifies JavaScript code to execute when the reset button is clicked.

The select Object

The select object reflects a selection list from an HTML form in JavaScript.

Properties

length   An integer value containing the number of options in the selection list.

name   A string value containing the name of the selection list.

options   An array reflecting each of the options in the selection list in the order they appear. The options property has its own properties:

	`defaultSelected`	A Boolean value indicating whether an option was selected by default (that is, reflects the `selected` attribute).
	`index`	An integer value reflecting the index of an option.
	`length`	An integer value reflecting the number of options in the selection list.
	`name`	A string value containing the name of the selection list.
	`options`	A string value containing the full HTML code for the selection list.
	`selected`	A Boolean value indicating whether the option is selected. Can be used to select or deselect an option.
	`selectedIndex`	An integer value containing the index of the currently selected option.
	`text`	A string value containing the text displayed in the selection list for a particular option.
	`value`	A string value indicating the value for the specified option.
`selectedIndex`		Reflects the index of the currently selected option in the selection list.

Event Handlers

`onBlur`	Specifies JavaScript code to execute when the selection list loses focus.
`onFocus`	Specifies JavaScript code to execute when focus is given to the selection list.
`onChange`	Specifies JavaScript code to execute when the selected option in the list changes.

The `string` Object

The `string` object provides properties and methods for working with string literals and variables.

Properties

length   An integer value containing the length of the string expressed as the number of characters in the string.

Methods

anchor(*name*)   Returns a string containing the value of the string object surrounded by an A container tag with the name attribute set to *name*.

big()   Returns a string containing the value of the string object surrounded by a BIG container tag.

blink()   Returns a string containing the value of the string object surrounded by a BLINK container tag.

bold()   Returns a string containing the value of the string object surrounded by a B container tag.

charAt(*index*)   Returns the character at the location specified by *index*.

fixed()   Returns a string containing the value of the string object surrounded by a FIXED container tag.

fontColor(*color*)   Returns a string containing the value of the string object surrounded by a FONT container tag with the COLOR attribute set to *color* where *color* is a color name or an RGB triplet.

fontSize(*size*)   Returns a string containing the value of the string object surrounded by a FONTSIZE container tag with the size set to *size*.

indexOf(*findString*,*startingIndex*)   Returns the index of the first occurrence of *findString*, starting the search at *startingIndex* where *startingIndex* is optional. If *startingIndex* is not provided, the search starts at the beginning of the string.

italics()   Returns a string containing the value of the string object surrounded by an I container tag.

`lastIndexOf(findString,startingIndex)`	Returns the index of the last occurrence of `findString`. This is done by searching backwards from `startingIndex`. `startingIndex` is optional, so the search begins at the last character in the string if no value is provided.
`link(href)`	Returns a string containing the value of the `string` object surrounded by an A container tag with the HREF attribute set to `href`.
`small()`	Returns a string containing the value of the `string` object surrounded by a SMALL container tag.
`strike()`	Returns a string containing the value of the `string` object surrounded by a STRIKE container tag.
`sub()`	Returns a string containing the value of the `string` object surrounded by a SUB container tag.
`substring(firstIndex,lastIndex)`	Returns a string equivalent to the substring starting at `firstIndex` and ending at the character before `lastIndex`. If `firstIndex` is greater than `lastIndex`, the string starts at `lastIndex` and ends at the character before `firstIndex`.
`sup()`	Returns a string containing the value of the `string` object surrounded by a SUP container tag.
`toLowerCase()`	Returns a string containing the value of the `string` object with all characters converted to lowercase.
`toUpperCase()`	Returns a string containing the value of the `string` object with all characters converted to uppercase.

The submit Object

The submit object reflects a submit button from an HTML form in JavaScript.

Properties

| name | A string value containing the name of the submit button element. |
| value | A string value containing the value of the submit button element. |

Methods

| click() | Emulates the action of clicking the submit button. |

Event Handlers

| onClick | Specifies JavaScript code to execute when the submit button is clicked. |

The text Object

The text object reflects a text field from an HTML form in JavaScript.

Properties

defaultValue	A string value containing the default value of the text element (that is, the value of the value attribute).
name	A string value containing the name of the text element.
value	A string value containing the value of the text element.

Methods

focus()	Emulates the action of focusing in the text field.
blur()	Emulates the action of removing focus from the text field.
select()	Emulates the action of selecting the text in the text field.

Event Handlers

onBlur	Specifies JavaScript code to execute when focus is removed from the field.
onChange	Specifies JavaScript code to execute when the content of the field is changed.
onFocus	Specifies JavaScript code to execute when focus is given to the field.
onSelect	Specifies JavaScript code to execute when the user selects some or all of the text in the field.

The `textarea` Object

The `textarea` object reflects a multiline text field from an HTML form in JavaScript.

Properties

`defaultValue`	A string value containing the default value of the `textarea` element (that is, the value of the `value` attribute).
`name`	A string value containing the name of the `textarea` element.
`value`	A string value containing the value of the `textarea` element.

Methods

`focus()`	Emulates the action of focusing on the `textarea` field.
`blur()`	Emulates the action of removing focus from the `textarea` field.
`select()`	Emulates the action of selecting the text in the `textarea` field.

Event Handlers

`onBlur`	Specifies JavaScript code to execute when focus is removed from the field.
`onChange`	Specifies JavaScript code to execute when the content of the field is changed.
`onFocus`	Specifies JavaScript code to execute when focus is given to the field.
`onSelect`	Specifies JavaScript code to execute when the user selects some or all of the text in the field.

The `window` Object

The `window` object is the top-level object for each window or frame and the parent object for the `document`, `location`, and `history` objects.

Properties

`defaultStatus`	A string value containing the default value displayed in the status bar.
`frames`	An array of objects for each frame in a window. Frames appear in the array in the order in which they appear in the HTML source code.

length	An integer value indicating the number of frames in a parent window.
name	A string value containing the name of the window or frame.
parent	A string indicating the name of the window containing the frameset.
self	An alternative for the name of the current window.
status	Used to display a message in the status bar by assigning values to this property.
top	An alternative for the name of the topmost window.
window	An alternative for the name of the current window.

Methods

alert(*message*)	Displays *message* in a dialog box.
close()	Closes the window.
confirm(*message*)	Displays *message* in a dialog box with OK and Cancel buttons. Returns true or false based on the button clicked by the user.
open(*url*,*name*,*features*)	Opens *url* in a window named *name*. If *name* doesn't exist, a new window is created with that name. *features* is an optional string argument containing a list of features for the new window. The feature list contains any of the following name/value pairs separated by commas without additional spaces:

toolbar=[yes,no,1,0]	Indicates if the window should have a toolbar.
location=[yes,no,1,0]	Indicates if the window should have a location field.
directories=[yes,no,1,0]	Indicates if the window should have directory buttons.
status=[yes,no,1,0]	Indicates if the window should have a status bar.
menubar=[yes,no,1,0]	Indicates if the window should have menus.
scrollbars=[yes,no,1,0]	Indicates if the window should have scrollbars.

	`resizable=[yes,no,1,0]`	Indicates if the window should be resizable.
	`width=pixels`	Indicates the width of the window in pixels.
	`height=pixels`	Indicates the height of the window in pixels.
`prompt(message,response)`		Displays *message* in a dialog box with a text entry field with the default value of *response*. The user's response in the text entry field is returned as a string.
`setTimeout(expression,time)`		Evaluates *expression* after *time* where *time* is a value in milliseconds. You can name the time-out with the following structure:
		`name = setTimeOut(expression,time)`
`clearTimeout(name)`		Cancels the time-out with the name *name*.

Event Handlers

`onLoad`	Specifies JavaScript code to execute when the window or frame finishes loading.
`onUnload`	Specifies JavaScript code to execute when the document in the window or frame is exited.

Independent Functions, Operators, Variables, and Literals

This section describes JavaScript's independent functions, operators, variables, and literals.

Independent Functions

`escape(character)`	Returns a string containing the ASCII encoding of *character* in the form %*xx* where *xx* is the numeric encoding of the character.
`eval(expression)`	Returns the result of evaluating *expression* where *expression* is an arithmetic expression.
`isNaN(value)`	Evaluates value to see if it is NaN. Returns a Boolean value. This function is only available on UNIX platforms where certain functions return NaN if their argument is not a number.

A

parseFloat(*string*)	Converts *string* to a floating-point number and returns the value. It continues to convert until it hits a non-numeric character and then returns the result. If the first character cannot be converted to a number, the function returns NaN (zero on Windows platforms).
parseInt(*string*,*base*)	Converts *string* to an integer of base *base* and returns the value. It continues to convert until it hits a non-numeric character and then returns the result. If the first character cannot be converted to a number, the function returns NaN (zero on Windows platforms).
unescape(*string*)	Returns a character based on the ASCII encoding contained in *string*. The ASCII encoding should take the form "%integer" or "hexadecimalValue".

Operators

JavaScript provides the following categories of operators:

- Assignment operators
- Arithmetic operators
- Bitwise operators
- Logical operators
- Logical comparison operators
- Conditional operators
- String operators

After the following sections discuss each type of operator, the section "Operator Precedence" outlines the operator precedence in JavaScript.

Assignment Operators

=	Assigns value of right operand to the left operand.
+=	Adds the left and right operands and assigns the result to the left operand.
-=	Subtracts the right operand from the left operand and assigns the result to the left operand.
*=	Multiplies the two operands and assigns the result to the left operand.
/=	Divides the left operand by the right operand and assigns the value to the left operand.
%=	Divides the left operand by the right operand and assigns the remainder to the left operand.

Arithmetic Operators

+	Adds the left and right operands.
-	Subtracts the right operand from the left operand.
*	Multiplies the two operands.
/	Divides the left operand by the right operand.
%	Divides the left operand by the right operand and evaluates to the remainder.
++	Increments the operand by one (can be used before or after the operand).
- -	Decreases the operand by one (can be used before or after the operand).
-	Changes the sign of the operand.

Bitwise Operators

Bitwise operators deal with their operands as binary numbers but return JavaScript numerical values.

AND (or &)	Converts operands to integers with 32 bits, pairs the corresponding bits, and returns one for each pair of ones. Returns zero for any other combination.
OR (or ¦)	Converts operands to integers with 32 bits, pairs the corresponding bits, and returns one for each pair where one of the two bits is one. Returns zero if both bits are zero.
XOR (or ^)	Converts operands to integer with 32 bits, pairs the corresponding bits, and returns one for each pair where only one bit is one. Returns zero for any other combination.
<<	Converts the left operand to an integer with 32 bits and shifts bits to the left the number of bits indicated by the right operand. Bits shifted off to the left are discarded, and zeros are shifted in from the right.
>>>	Converts the left operand to an integer with 32 bits and shifts bits to the right the number of bits indicated by the right operand. Bits shifted off to the right are discarded, and zeros are shifted in from the left.
>>	Converts the left operand to an integer with 32 bits and shifts bits to the right the number of bits indicated by the right operand. Bits shifted off to the right are discarded, and copies of the leftmost bit are shifted in from the left.

Logical Operators

&&   Logical and returns true when both operands are true; otherwise, it returns false.

¦¦   Logical or returns true if either operand is true. It only returns false when both operands are false.

!   Logical not returns true if the operand is false and false if the operand is true. This is a unary operator and precedes the operand.

Comparison Operators

==   Returns true if the operands are equal.

!=   Returns true if the operands are not equal.

>   Returns true if the left operand is greater than the right operand.

<   Returns true if the left operand is less than the right operand.

>=   Returns true if the left operand is greater than or equal to the right operand.

<=   Returns true if the left operand is less than or equal to the right operand.

Conditional Operators

Conditional expressions take one form:

```
(condition) ? val1 : val2
```

If `condition` is true, the expression evaluates to `val1`; otherwise, it evaluates to `val2`.

String Operators

JavaScript provides two string-concatenation operators:

+   This operator evaluates to a string combining the left and right operands.

+=   This operator is a shortcut for combining two strings.

Operator Precedence

JavaScript applies the rules of operator precedence as follows (from lowest to highest precedence):

Comma   ,

Assignment operators   = += -= *= /= %=

Conditional	? :
Logical or	¦ ¦
Logical and	&&
Bitwise or	¦
Bitwise xor	^
Bitwise and	&
Equality	== !=
Relational	< <= > >=
Shift	<< >> >>>
Addition/subtraction	+ -
Multiply/divide/modulus	* / %
Negation/increment	! - ++ --
Call, member	() []

Fundamentals of HTML

by Kim Daniels

IN THIS APPENDIX

By developing a solid base of HTML knowledge, the developer can more fully implement JavaScript and other interactive and high-level HTML functionality. The fundamental design of HTML documents and the tags that are used are seemingly basic and harmless.

While it's easy to develop simple HTML documents, simple tags, and basic form design, the advantage of HTML is that you also can create more complex documents by building on the simple ones. By using the more complex tags and the attributes associated with them, your documents will grow in complexity and usability with only minor research and trial and error.

It's important to remember that the standards of HTML are changing constantly. The current standards document under development is for HTML 3.2. This document is still evolving with new elements as well as new and refined attributes for these elements.

NOTE

Netscape and Internet Explorer also are continually improving their browsers and HTML capabilities. Remember that there will be tags available for use in these browsers that have not been defined in the standards document. There also will be tags and capabilities that are implemented in one of these browsers but not the other.

By keeping up to date on the latest version releases of the most popular browsers you, as the HTML designer, can keep abreast of the enhancements and implement them as they become available for use to the general public. Luckily, for the most part, enhancements included in HTML 3.2 and the newest browser releases aren't dangerous when displayed in HTML 2.0 browsers. You should always test the usage of your document in older browsers to ensure that the new tags and custom tags that you design with won't negatively affect users of older browsers.

An example of a tag that doesn't work correctly in multiple browsers is the <MARQUEE> tag available for the Microsoft Internet Explorer. In older browsers and in Netscape it displays as straight document text.

This example is an important reason to write a well-defined and segmented document and to account for multiple browsers as you design.

RESOURCE

Sites to watch for information about HTML changes for Netscape, Internet Explorer, and the overall HTML 3.2 standards include the following:

HTML standards—http://www.w3.org

Netscape—http://www.netscape.com

Internet Explorer—http://www.microsoft.com

HTML Basics

JavaScript works so closely with HTML that before writing JavaScript scripts you must first know the basics of HTML document structure and document tags. Writing Web pages is fairly straightforward if you know the HTML basics. A Web page is made up of page text, tags, and sometimes comments.

Text is easy to comprehend. You write text and it appears on the Web page. The part of Web page design that needs more description is the use of tags to surround and enhance the text. Tags tell your page how to behave, tell your text how to display, and enable you to write complex documents for a Web browser.

An HTML tag always begins with the < and ends with the >.

Tags can be just a single marker, as in <P> for a new paragraph. Single markers are either defined as empty tags, or they are non-empty tags that have the capability of being terminated other than with their normal termination tag.

<BASE> is an empty tag. It doesn't apply formatting to text surrounding it. It just defines the document.

The <TD> tag is not an empty tag. It's used to specify that the text following that tag is text to display in a table cell. The </TD> tag is not required in this case, because the <TD> elements are terminated by subsequent <TD> tags and also by the </TR>.

Some tags require an end tag to tell them where to terminate. These tags are called container tags, because they always contain information (normally text) between the start and end tags. In the example,

```
<B>Make this text bold</B>,
```

note that the end tags always have a / before the tag name. Terminator tags are identical to the begin tags except that they contain the additional character.

More complex tags may also have attributes to tell the tag how to behave. If a tag has attributes associated with it, then some (or maybe none) of those attributes may be required for the tag to perform as requested. <TABLE WIDTH=3> defines a table with a width of 3.

Tag location within a document is sometimes very important. Certain tags must be inside of other tags (the <INPUT> tag must be inside the <FORM> tags). Some tags may or may not contain other tags (<HEAD> tags, for instance).

Basic HTML Document Structure

Structure is sometimes very important. In the basic HTML document in Listing B.1, you can see, in Figure B.1, that the document always starts and ends with <HTML></HTML>. The two main tags inside of this are <HEAD> and <BODY>. Each of these two container tags has tags that can be included inside of it.

B

FUNDAMENTALS OF HTML

Listing B.1. Basic HTML page.

```html
<!DOCTYPE HTML PUBLIC "-//W3C//DTD HTML 3.2//EN">
<HTML>
<HEAD>
<TITLE>Basic HTML document</TITLE>
<SCRIPT LANGUAGE="JavaScript">
</SCRIPT>
</HEAD>
<BODY >
<FRAMESET>
<FRAME></FRAME>
<NOFRAMES></NOFRAMES>
</FRAMESET>
<H1>Heading of Basic Document</H1>
<FORM>
<INPUT NAME="EnterBtn" TYPE="SUBMIT">
</FORM>
<OL TYPE=1>
<LI>One
<LI>Two
<LI>Three
<LI>Four
</OL>
<A HREF="HTTP://www.acadians.com"></A>
<BR><BR>
<TABLE WIDTH=3 HEIGHT=3 BORDER>
<TH>Table</TH>
<TR>
<TD>cell1<TD>cell2<TD>cell3
</TR>
<TR>
<TD>cell4<TD>cell5<TD>cell6
</TR>
</TABLE>
<P>
This is a Basic HTML document structure.
</BODY>
</HTML>
```

HTML Tags

<! — —>

These are your HTML comment tags. Comment tags normally begin with `<!--` and end with `-->`. Anything between these two tags is interpreted by the browsers as a comment. Comments can span multiple lines in your document. Any text enclosed in the comment tags is not displayed by the browser.

Comment tags also are used to hide `<SCRIPT>` element information from older browsers. The JavaScript interpreter ignores the `<!-- -->` markings as it reads your document, so you can in a sense comment out the <SCRIPT> information from the browser and let the browser choose to interpret it, if it can.

Attributes: none

FIGURE B.1.

Basic HTML document generated from code Listing B.1.

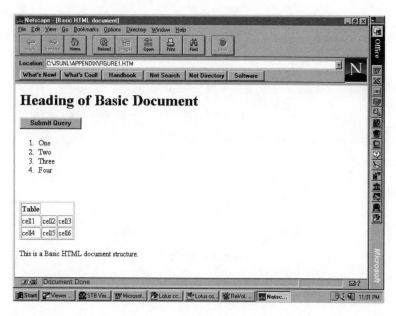

<A> (End Tag Required)

<A> (or anchor) defines a hypertext link in the document. The information between the <A> and </A> may be text or an image. The anchor has one required attribute. You must have either the href attribute, which points to a hypertext link (URL), or the name attribute, which points to a location for use as a target for hypertext links within the same document.

```
<A HREF="http://www.w3.org" >Get newest HTML standards</A>
```

The block of text within the anchor is displayed differently by the browser than normal text or images. The browser normally highlights or underlines the text.

Most browsers also track links that you explored previously and display those link differently, normally by changing the color of the text.

<A> elements may contain the usual text formatting tags but may not contain another <A> element.

Attributes:

href = specifies the location target of the hypertext link.

name = defines the destination of a hypertext link within a document.

target = defines the target frame or window in which to load the selected URL. Without this attribute, the browser loads the link into the current active browser. title = defines the assumed title of the linked document. The actual title of the document can't be guaranteed until the link is actually accessed, but this does give you the ability to title and untitle the document.

<ADDRESS> (End Tag Required)

<ADDRESS> defines the author information for the document; it will include electronic signatures, lists of authors, and other address information. As such it is usually included near the end of the document for reference information.

<ADDRESS> can contain the normal text formatting tags as well as <A>.

Attributes: none

<APPLET> (End Tag Required)

<APPLET> specifies the applet (currently JAVA is the only supported applet) to be loaded and run from this location in the document. The parameters for an applet must be defined by the <PARAM> tag, which can be included inside the <APPLET> tags.

<APPLET> run and load parameters aren't defined in the <APPLET> tag itself because these elements can vary widely depending on the <APPLET>. As a result, the ability to define independent name/value parameter statements was implemented using the <PARAM> element. Listing B.2 shows the definition of the StrangeMarquee applet that required the ScrollValue parameter to run.

Listing B.2. Basic applet.

```
<HTML>
<HEAD></HEAD>
<BODY>
<APPLET CODE="StrangeMarquee.class" HEIGHT="100" WIDTH="100">
<PARAM NAME="ScrollValue" VALUE="25">
</APPLET>
</BODY>
</HTML>
```

<APPLET> is a container element, so it may contain text and the normal text formatting tags.

Attributes:

align = defines the <APPLET> alignment on the page.

code = the required element that specifies the relative URL where the applet is located.

codebase = references the base URL for the code URL. If the attribute isn't used, then the document URL is the base.

`height` = required element to specify the height needed by the element in the document.

`Hspace` = horizontal distance that between the applet and surrounding text.

`Vspace` = vertical distance that between the applet and surrounding text.

`width` = the required element to specify the width needed by the element in the document.

<AREA>

`<AREA>` elements must be contained in `<MAP>` tags. `<AREA>` defines the specific area in a map region that the user can select. There may be multiple areas specified on a specific map. The selection of the area accesses the URL defined by the `href` attribute. (See Listing B.4 for an example of the use of `<AREA>` with the `<MAP>` element.)

Attributes:

`coords` = defines the coordinates of the shape. Rectangles obviously have 4 coordinates to specify the corners, circles have 3 (horizontal and vertical coordinates of the center and radius), and polygons may have many coordinate points.

`href` = hypertext link (URL) that will be accessed when the area of the map is selected.

`nohref` = specifies that the browser should "do nothing" if the area is selected. If no `<AREA>` is supplied for a map, then the default value is `nohref`.

`shape` = shape of the area. Default shape is rectangle (`rect`), but circle (`circ`) and polygon (`poly`) are also valid.

<B> (End Tag Required)

The `<B>` element encloses document text that will be displayed in bold.

Attributes: none

<BASE>

`<BASE>` specifies the base address for all URL references relative to this document. The attribute for `<BASE>` is required.

Attributes:

`href` = URL that is the base URL for all others in the document.

<BASEFONT>

`<BASEFONT>` defines the base font to use in a document. The font is used to override the default font of the browser. This tag should be used before any text in the `<BODY>` to ensure that all text is displayed in the same font.

Attributes:

size = specifies the font size to be used (valid numbers are 1 to 7).

<BGSOUND> (Internet Explorer Only)

<BGSOUND> defines the background sound to be used when your document is displayed in the browser.

Attributes:

loop = number of times sound clip is played (default is 1).

src = location of the file (audio) to be played.

<BIG> (End Tag Required)

<BIG> encloses text that is displayed in a bigger font than the normal font of text.

Attributes: none

<BLINK> (End Tag Required)

The <BLINK> element does exactly as you would expect, making any text enclosed in it blink.

Attributes: none

<BLOCKQUOTE> (End Tag Required)

<BLOCKQUOTE> defines the contained text as a quotation and directs the browser to display it as such. Browsers render <BLOCKQUOTE> differently.

Attributes: none

<BODY> (End Tag Required)

The <BODY> defines the body or the visible section of the HTML document. The <BODY> element and <HEAD> element comprise the document and are contained inside the HTML element. The majority of your HTML text and tags are contained in these tags.

Attributes:

background = defines the location of an image file to be displayed as the background for the document.

bgcolor = specifies the color for the background.

bgproperties = only the allowed value is fixed. Specifies that the background is fixed and not scrolling.

link = specifies the color of unvisited links.

text = specifies the color of document text.

vlink = specifies color of visited links.

 tag is an empty element used to force a line break in the document.

Attributes:

clear = value informs the browser of how far down to go before displaying any more information. Clear can take values of left, right, and all.

<CAPTION>

The <CAPTION> tag defines the caption to give the table object in the document. the <CAPTION> tag is contained in the table tags and may contain the normal text formatting tags.

Attributes:

align = specifies to the browser how to align the text in relation to the table.

<CENTER> (End Tag Required)

<CENTER> horizontally centers the enclosed text on the document page.

Attributes: none

<CITE> (End Tag Required)

The <CITE> element specifies that the enclosed text is a citation and should be displayed as such by the browser.

Attributes: none

<CODE>

The <CODE> element specifies that the enclosed text is code (such as in computer code) and should be displayed as such by the browser.

Most browsers will display the <CODE> element in a fixed-width typewriter link font.

Attributes: none

<CREDIT> (End Tag Required)

<CREDIT> is used to define the credits or acknowledgments for a <BLOCKQUOTE> or <FIG> and it is thus only applicable for use with these elements.

Browsers that aren't capable of using this tag display enclosed text as normal document text.

Attributes: none

<DD>

<DD> specifies a corresponding definition description for a <DT> tag in a list. <DT> and <DD> elements normally occur in pairs in a <DL> list.

Attributes: none

<DIR>

<DIR> defines a list of short items, such as a directory. Elements of the list are defined by <LI> elements.

Attributes:

compact = takes no values but specifies to the browser to display the list in a compact format.

<DIV> (End Tag Required)

<DIV> defines a logical division of information in an HTML document. This element doesn't have significant formatting ability, but does help define sections of the document. The <DIV> tag terminates the previous <P>.

Attributes:

align = specifies how to align the block of document contained within.

<DL> (End Tag Required)

<DL> defines a list of definitions. The definition terms and description are defined by the <DT> and <DD> elements enclosed in the <DL> tags.

Attributes:

compact = takes no values, but specifies to the browser to display the list in a compact format.

<!DOCTYPE>

<!DOCTYPE> is the first tag in your document and it specifies the version of the HTML language supported by this document. The standard string that follows the tag is the public text identifier.

```
<!DOCTYPE HTML PUBLIC "-//W3C//DTD HTML 3.2//EN">
```

Attributes:

The only attribute is the public text identifier string.

<DT>

<DT> specifies a definition term to be displayed in the <DL> list. <DT> is normally paired with <DD> elements, but not always. A list may be defined to have many <DT> elements correspond to one <DD> element.

Attributes: none

<EM>

<EM> specifies that the enclosed tag should be marked emphatically. Most browsers display this in an italicized font.

Attributes: none

<FIG> (HTML 3.0 Only)

The <FIG> elements better define the use of figures or images in HTML 3.x documents. <FIG> defines a formal figure in a document. Figures are defined as floating objects anchored in the document by the align attribute. Text flows around the figures unless specified by the noflow attribute.

Attributes:

align = specifies how to align the figure in the document.

imageMap = active figure for use with this element.

noflow = informs the browser to not let text flow around the figure.

<FN> (HTML 3.0 Only)

<FN> defines a footnote for a document. Footnotes are normally presented as hidden elements and only displayed when requested and referenced through the id tag.

Attributes:

id = reference name to be used to link to the footnote from elsewhere in the document.

<FONT> (End Tag Required)

<FONT> defines the font size to be used for the enclosed text. Tag may either be used as a relative or absolute font size.

Attributes:

color = color for normal text enclosed in these tags.

size = defines font size to use. Absolute fonts are specified by a number. Relative fonts use the + or - and a number to specify the increase or decrease amount from the <BASEFONT>.

<FORM> (End Tag Required)

Form tags enclose the <INPUT> tags of the document that accept user input for use by either CGI, JavaScript, or other interactive processing. <FORM> may not include other <FORM> tags, and must include one of the following user input elements: <INPUT>, <SELECT>, <TEXTAREA>.

Attributes:

action = defines the URL to which all form content is sent. Action is normally directed to a program to run, but also may be a mailto: address.

enctype = specifies the MIME type of data to be sent.

method = specifies the manner, get (default) or post, in which the data is sent to the server.

script = defines the script to run from the <FORM>.

<FRAME>

<FRAME> defines the properties of a frame to be displayed in your frameset. Frames are basically a subset or divided portion of your browser. The important attribute of <FRAME> is src. src defines the URL to be displayed as the frame document. Without this attribute the frame is empty or blank.

Attributes:

marginheight = defines the height of the top and bottom margins of the <FRAME>. The margin height cannot be 0 (to ensure that the margin has some space. If left blank, the browser determines the appropriate spacing.

marginwidth = defines the width of the left and right margins of the <FRAME>. The margin width cannot be 0 (to ensure that the margin has some space). If left blank, the browser determines the appropriate spacing.

name = specifies the name to be given to this frame. By naming your frame you are giving your browser a reference and the frame can now be referenced from the <TARGET> of some other tag.

noresize = specifies to the browser that the user cannot resize this frame. By default this means that bordering frames may also not be resized. The default is to allow resizing.

scrolling = specifies to the browser how scrollbars should be used in the frame. The default is auto, which lets the browser decide whether the scrollbars are necessary. Yes always displays scrollbars, and no never displays scrollbars.

src = specifies the URL for the document that will be loaded into this frame. If src is not specified, the frame is empty by default.

<FRAMESET> (End Tag Required)

<FRAMESET> encloses the set of frame definitions for the document. This tag defines the setup of how the frames are displayed in the document (as demonstrated in Listing B.3). The two allowable attributes of the <FRAMESET> are cols and rows. One of these two, but not both, attributes must be include.

Listing B.3. <FRAMESET> and <FRAME> definition example.

```
<FRAMESET ROWS="10%,80%,10%">
<FRAME NAME="IntroFrame" SCROLLING="NO" NORESIZE>
<FRAME NAME="BodyFrame" SCROLLING="AUTO">
<FRAME NAME="FOOTFrame" SCROLLING="NO" NORESIZE>
<NOFRAMES>
<BODY>
You are viewing a document that best suited for a frames capable browser.
➡ You may continue on from here or download Netscape for a more complete document
</BODY>
</NOFRAMES>
</FRAMESET>
```

Attributes:

cols and rows = are a comma-separated list of widths or heights of the frames. The number of values in the attribute corresponds to the number of <FRAME> definitions within the <FRAMESET>. Values can be defined in three forms: a number representing fixed pixel width or height, a percentage (number and percent sign) to represent the percentage of the document that each <FRAME> will occupy, or a relative value. The relative values are assigned in relation to other fixed numbers or percentages and are allocated until the document has been 100 percent completed.

<Hx> (End Tag Required)

<Hx> tags are heading tags, where x represents a number from 1 to 6. Headings grow progressively less prominent (font size) as the numbers decrease. H1 are main document headings; H6 are much smaller subheadings.

Either the src or dingbat attribute can be used, but not both.

Attributes:

align = specifies the horizontal alignment of the heading.

dingbat = defines the entity name of a symbol file to be used with the heading. The symbol is placed in front of the heading test.

Seqnum = defines a sequence number of the heading relative to other headings in the browser and allows reference to these headings if a stylesheet is used.

skip = defines the number to skip in the sequence numbering scheme. This enables you to keep a consistent number scheme while still being able to skip numbers if required.

src = specifies the URL of an image file to be used as a symbol to go before the heading.

<HEAD> (End Tag Required)

<HEAD> specifies the definition section of your document. Because information included in the <HEAD> section isn't displayed in the browser, only certain information is appropriate to include in the <HEAD> section. Normally these tags contain the <TITLE>, <BASE>, <ISINDEX>, <LINK>, <META>, <NEXTID>, <RANGE>, <STYLE>, and <SCRIPT>. Other elements are located in the <BODY> section.

Attributes: none

<HR>

The <HR> tag displays a horizontal rule (or line) across the document page.

Attributes:

align = specifies the alignment of the line on the page.

noshade = overrides the default display (shaded bar/chiseled look) to show a solid black line.

size = specifies the thickness of the line.

width = specifies the width (or length) of the line. This value may be reflected as the number of pixels, or a percentage relative to the width of the document page itself.

<HTML> (End Tag Required)

<HTML> encloses your entire document. These tags tell the browser that everything included inside of these tags is an <HTML> document. The <HEAD> and <BODY> sections are contained with the <HTML> tags, and normally one or both of these tags are included.

Attributes:

class = defines the <HTML> class for the entire document.

version = used in the same manner as the version definition in the <!DOCTYPE> element, so this element is not needed if <!DOCTYPE> tags have been included.

<I> (End Tag Required)

<I> defines the enclosed text so that it is displayed in an italicized font.

Attributes: none

<IMG>

<IMG> defines an inline image to be displayed in the document text. Currently, the .GIF format of images is the only universally understood image format. Other commonly used formats are X-bitmaps (.xbm), X-Pixelmaps (.xpm), and JPEG (.jpeg or .jpg) formats. Use these formats with caution because all browsers may not be capable of displaying them correctly. Listing B.4 shows the use of a balloon image and also the alternative text if the image is not supported.

Images may be placed anywhere in your document and in this respect are just as easy to place inline as text is.

The image may be defined as an image map, allowing the image in clickable areas on the document.

Listing B.4. Image with mapped areas example.

```
<A HREF="/anchor/testmap">
<IMG SRC="ballon.gif" ALT="Balloon Picture" HSPACE=10 VSPACE=10 USEMAP="#TestMap"
➥ISMAP>
</A>
<MAP NAME="TestMap">
<AREA  SHAPE="circ" COORD="5,10,30,35" HREF="TestArea.html">
</MAP>
```

Attributes:

align = specifies the alignment for the image on the page.

alt = used to specify alternative text for the browser to display instead of the image. The information is important in text-only browsers and very useful overall, enabling a smooth flowing document if the user chooses not to load images.

border = (Netscape Navigator only) specifies the width of the border that will be rendered surrounding the image.

controls = (Internet Explorer only) specifies that viewer controls should be displayed for the AVI clip.

dynsrc = (Internet Explorer only) defines the URL of an AVI-formatted video clip. With this control, the control, loop, loopdelay, and start attributes are also applicable.

height = specifies the actual height of the image to be displayed.

hspace (Netscape Navigator only) = defines the horizontal space, in pixels, to be left between floating images and the surrounding text.

ismap = specifies that the image is a server-side image map and the server determines, based on the <A> given, the URL to access upon selection of the image in the browser.

B

`loop` = (Internet Explorer only) specifies how many times a video clip is played. Default is 1 and the value of `"infinite"` is a valid loop parameter. Infinite will cause the clip to play continuously while the document is loaded.

`loopdelay` = (Internet Explorer only) specifies the delay between replays of the video clip. Value in milliseconds.

`lowsrc` = (Netscape Navigator only) specifies the low-resolution image to be displayed when the main `src` image is loading.

`start` = (Internet Explorer only) defines when the video clip should begin playing. Valid values are `start` and `mouseover`. Both can be used in a comma delimited format.

`src` = specifies the URL to locate the source file for the image. This is a required attribute.

`units` = defines the type of units to be used for height and width. The default is pixels. Also available as a unit of measure is en, which indicates to the browser that this text should be displayed in one-half the point size of normal text in the document.

`usemap` = specifies that the image is a client-side image map by including `<MAP>` and `<AREA>` tag references inside the `<IMG>` definition.

`vspace` = (Netscape Navigator only) defines the vertical space, in pixels, to be left between floating images and the surrounding text.

`width` = specifies the actual width of the image to be displayed. If the image itself is a different size, the browser scales the image to fit the height and width that have been defined.

`<INPUT>`

Input tags define fields on your document where users can enter input. `<INPUT>` elements, by definition, must be contained inside `<FORM>` elements. The user input gathered from `<INPUT>` can be used in CGI applications as well as JavaScript and other methods of HTML processing. The important mandatory attributes for `<INPUT>` are `name` and `type`.

Attributes:

`align` = defines the alignment for the `<INPUT>` element on the page.

`checked` = specifies the checked state of radio buttons and checkboxes.

`max` = defines the upper limit of the range slider.

`maxlength` = specifies the maximum length of text to be accepted in text and password inputs.

`min` = defines the lower limit of the range slider.

`name` = defines the name of the field. Multiple radio buttons with the same name are mutually exclusive.

`size` = defines the physical size of the field. When used in association with text and password `<INPUT>`, `size` defines the number of characters to be accepted before the text begins to scroll.

`src` = specifies the URL of image to be used.

`type` = specifies the type of input field to display in the document. Valid types are as follows:

> `Text` accepts a single line of text input from the user.

> `Password` behaves the same as `text`, except that the text entered is not displayed to the user.

> `CheckBox` displays a single checkbox (Boolean of on/off). Results are only sent to the server when the box is checked.

> `Radio` fields are similar to the `CheckBox` in that they are either selected or not selected. Unlike a `CheckBox`, you can define multiple mutually exclusive radio fields by giving them the same name.

> `Image` fields display a clickable image for the user. The results sent to the server are the coordinates of the selection on the image.

> `Hidden` fields are input fields that are never displayed to the user. Hidden fields are always sent back to the server and are generally used for hard-coded data.

> `Submit` fields are displayed as a button and are used to send all information in the contained `<FORM>` back to the server. Action (JavaScript action) can be taken upon the click of the submit button. If an image is specified in the `src` attribute, then the button is displayed as an image with the same functionality.

> `Reset` fields are also buttons, but have a different action than `Submit`. The reset buttons reset all input fields contained within the form. If an image is specified in the `src` attribute, then the button is displayed as an image with the same functionality.

> `Range` fields are displayed as a slider bar and enable the user to select a number to be sent to the server. The left and right values of the range are specified by the `min` and `max` attributes.

> `File` fields automatically associate a browse button and enable the user to select a local file to send to the server.

> `Scribble` fields are defined as graphical images (defined in the `src` attribute) onto which the user can scribble or draw.

`value` = specifies different things depending on `<INPUT>` type. For buttons (submit and reset) it's the label on the button itself, for text, password, and hidden input, it's the default value, for checkboxes and radio buttons, it's the value returned to the server.

`<ISINDEX>`

`<ISINDEX>` defines this document as searchable. This means that the document can be queried using a keyword search and the browser should prompt the user for a search string. The search string is gathered on the client side and sent back to the server using keywords appended to the URL. The search is performed on the server.

Attributes:

`href` = defines a URL to direct the query if the URL is different from the URL of the document itself.

`prompt` = defines the prompt string that the user sees when a search is requested.

<KBD> (End Tag Required)

<KBD> enclosed text that should be displayed as keyboard input to the user. The browser typically displays this text in a fixed-width typewriter-like font.

Attributes: none

<LH> (HTML 3.0 Only; End Tag Required)

<LH> defines a header for a list. This tag is contained inside any of the list tags (<DL>, <OL>, <UL>) and should be the first tag immediately following the first list tag.

Browsers that can't interpret this tag display the text at the beginning of the list with no special formatting applied. All normal text tags can be used inside this tag.

Attributes: none

<LI> (End Tag Required)

<LI> defines items that make up a list. <LI> tags are contained in either list type of either <UL>, <OL>, <MENU>, or <DIR> and enclose the lines of text for these lists.

<LI> tags may contain text and any of the text markup tags.

Attributes:

`type` = defines the type of bullet display to be used for the list. <UL> acceptable values are `disc` (solid circle), `circle` (open circle), and `square` (square). <OL> acceptable values are `I` (uppercase Roman numerals), `i` (lowercase Roman numerals), `A` (uppercase alphabetized), `a` (lowercase alphabetized), and `1` (numeric).

`value` = defines the start of a numeric counting sequence for a list. List numbering will start at `value` and continue sequentially for remaining items in the list.

<LINK>

<LINK> defines this document's association or relationship with another document. It is used similarly to and has attributes like the <A> tag. <LINK> can be used to maintain a chain of documents, or preload documents with a page.

Attributes:

href = URL of document to which to link.

rel= (or rev) defines what the actual relationship is of this document to another (that is, next, previous).

title = defines the title for this document link in the current document.

<MAP> (End Tag Required)

<MAP> specifies the set of areas (it must contain <AREA> tags) to be used on client-side image maps. (See Listing B.4 for an example of the use <AREA> with the <MAP> element.) The <MAP> element is used as a container to hold the information on all areas (coordinate defined regions) that are grouped together to form the mapping plan for an element.

There may be many <MAP> tags used in a document. A <MAP> tag doesn't necessarily have to be in the current document. It is permissible to define a <MAP> in a document and use the <MAP> (that is, the usemap attribute of an <IMG>) in another document. In this instance it is necessary to include the entire URL path in the usemap statement, instead of just the map name.

Attributes:

name = distinct name for this map area in this document.

<MARQUEE> (Internet Explorer Only; End Tag Required)

<MARQUEE> is a container tag that behaves exactly as one would expect from its name. It displays a scrolling text string in the document like an advertisement marquee. The text contained between the <MARQUEE> tags is used to scroll.

<MARQUEE> displays as normal text in browsers not capable of supporting this element.

Attributes:

align = specifies how to align the surrounding text with the marquee.

behavior = defines the behavior of the text in the marquee box. The default is scroll, whereby the text starts at one side of the box and scrolls completely off the screen on the other side. Slide slides the text across the screen and stops it at the margin on the other side. Alternate bounces the text back and forth across the screen

bgcolor = specifies the color of the marquee box behind the text.

direction = specifies the direction for the text to scroll.

height = specifies height of the marquee. Can be in two formats: pixels, or percentage of document screen.

hspace = defines the margin that will be on the left and right sides of the marquee.

B

FUNDAMENTALS OF HTML

loop = specifies the number of times the marquee will process before it stops.

scrollamount = specifies the space (number of pixels) to allow between redisplaying of the marquee.

scrolldelay = specifies the amount of time to delay the next start of the marquee scroll.

vspace = specifies the width of the marquee. The narrower the marquee, the more difficult the text is to read.

<MATH> (End Tag Required)

<MATH> tags are container tags used to enclose mathematical expressions in a document. These additional tags are needed to account for some of the symbols that are difficult to display, as well as letters that are associated with mathematical and scientific expressions.

Attributes:

box = specifies that the mathematical expression should be framed by a box (or outlines) when it is displayed in the browser.

class = defines the class of the mathematical expression, giving the browser further definition on the correct display formats.

<MENU> (End Tag Required)

<MENU> defines a list of menu items. This is another list definition element designed to include short "menu-like" items. The items in this list are displayed in a compact manner.

This element has the same basic functionality as an unordered list <UL> element.

Attributes:

compact = specifies that the list should be displayed in a more compact format than default.

<META>

<META> specifies information about this document that is not included in other tags. <META> is basically a place to store very detailed specification information regarding the document and its setup and composition.

Attributes:

content = (required) specifies the content associated with the HTTP-equiv or name attributes.

http-equiv = defines information to be used in the response header that is generated in association with the content information and the <META> information.

name = Specifies the name for the meta-information file. The browser is assumed to be able to understand and interpret this name.

\<NEXTID\>

\<NEXTID\> is used in the document to assign a unique identifier to the document. This identifier is used by browsers to determine the identity of the document. \<NEXTID\> has a required attribute of n.

Attributes:

n = specifies the sequence number to assign to the document.

\<NOBR\>

\<NOBR\> (no line break) gives you, the HTML designer, more direct control over text formatting in a browser by specifying to the browser where it may not break a line of text when displaying in the browser.

This element is used to override the browser's default assumptions of how to break lines of text when displaying them in the browsers.

Attributes: none

\<NOFRAMES\> (End Tag Required)

\<NOFRAMES\> is a container tag. Between the tags is text that is displayed if the browser doesn't support frames. \<NOFRAMES\> is important to use so the document won't be unreadable if a browser isn't frame-capable.

The text that is enclosed in the \<NOFRAMES\> tag will not display if a browser if frames are enabled.

Because this information is displayed as the entire body of a document in non-frame enabled browsers, the \<NOFRAMES\> container should include a fairly complete \<BODY\> document to display in the browser. All text formatting tags as well as tags normally used in the \<BODY\> section of the document can be used inside the \<NOFRAMES\> container.

```
<NOFRAMES>
<BODY>
You are viewing a document that best suited for a frames capable browser.
➥ You may continue on from here or download Netscape for a more complete document
</BODY>
</NOFRAMES>
```

Attributes: none

\<NOTE\> (End Tag Required)

\<NOTE\> specifies that the contained text is a comment block for the document. There are three main types, or classes, of notes: note, caution, and warning.

Browsers capable of supporting notes display the note along with a graphic related to the defined class.

Because not all browsers support <NOTE>, its important to include formatting (such as <P> tags) inside the <NOTE> container to distinguish the note from other text in these unsupporting browsers.

Attributes:

class = specifies the type of note. Warning, caution, and note are the three most common classes, but others may be defined.

src = defines a graphic that the browser should use as the icon associated with the <NOTE>.

<OL> (End Tag Required)

<OL> defines an ordered list. An ordered list means that the browser displays the list with alphabetic or sequentially numbered marking preceding the actual list items.

<LI> tags are enclosed in this container tag to define the list items. <LI> are the only tags allowed inside the <OL> container, and are ordered according to the browser's numbering scheme.

```
<OL COMPACT TYPE=A START=C>
<LH>Ordered List Sample
<LI>Internet
<LI>Browser
<LI>HTML
<LI>JavaScript
</OL>
```

As with <UL> (unordered lists), <LI> items should always be kept brief and concise. The purpose of a list is to create short meaningful statements that stand out in the browser. If the information in list items becomes too involved, the list isn't as meaningful.

Attributes:

compact = specifies to the browser to display the list in a more compact manner than it would with the normal-sized font.

continue = specifies to the browser not to start numbering at the beginning, and to instead begin numbering where the ordered list stopped.

start = specifies the value to use to begin numbering the first item in the list.

seqNum = specifies the value to use to begin numbering the first item in the list.

type = defines the type of numbering scheme that the browser should use when displaying the list. Acceptable types are A, a, I, i, and 1. 1 is the default for lists without a TYPE attribute. The other types follow the alphabetic or Roman numeral scheme as specified.

<OPTION>

<OPTION> defines the text string choices that are available in the <SELECT> statement. Multiple <OPTION> tags are allowed for a <SELECT> container element and must be contained within the <SELECT> tags.

Because <OPTION> may be a container element or may be terminated by other means, the normal set of text formatting tags aren't allowable with the <OPTION> element. <OPTION> can be terminated by </OPTION>, the beginning of another <OPTION>, or by </SELECT> (end of the <SELECT> container).

Attributes:

disabled = specifies to the browser to display this <OPTION> as disabled (or grayed-out) in the <SELECT> group. The <OPTION> isn't hidden in the document, but displays in a grayed or dimmer font color.

selected = tells the browser to display this <OPTION> as selected. Selected <OPTION> items aren't mutually exclusive, and therefore more than one <OPTION> in a <SELECT> container may be selected. <SELECT> is a good way to define the default selection for the <SELECT> group

shape = defines the <OPTION> as a geographic shape within the <SELECT>, if the <SELECT> has been defined as an image. As with the <AREA> element, this attribute is defined using coordinates on the document to map out the region of the <OPTION> within the <SELECT> image.

value = specifies what the value (or text string) of the <OPTION> is. The value is optional and the actual content of the <OPTION> string is used as the value if the value attribute isn't explicitly set.

<OVERLAY>

The <OVERLAY> element is used only in conjunction with the <FIG> element and is contained in the <FIG> container to define the image to load as an overlay for the <FIG> image.

Attributes:

src = defines the URL for the location of the <OVERLAY> image.

imagemap = defines the URL link where the click is sent on the server.

units = defines the size (height and width) of the <OVERLAY> image.

x = defines the x coordinate on the <FIG> image where the overlay starts. This coordinate starts from the left side of the <FIG>.

y = along with the x coordinate, the y coordinate further defines the relation of the <OVERLAY> image on the <FIG> image. This coordinate starts from the top of the <FIG>.

B

FUNDAMENTALS OF HTML

<P>

<P> is used to define logical paragraphs or groups of text in a document. The actual outcome is similar to the <BR> tag, but <P> is used to better define blocks of text and, depending on the browser, it is possible to also see first line indentation.

The end </P> is not necessary because a <P> is automatically terminated by the next <P>, but for consistency it's appropriate to use <P> as a container tag, thus explicitly marking the end of one paragraph before beginning another.

Unlike <BR>, multiple <P> tags don't produce multiple breaks in the document. <P> isn't an empty element, and thus successive <P> tags aren't allowed.

Attributes:

align = specifies the alignment of the <P> relative to the margins of the document.

<PARAM>

<PARAM> defines a parameter attribute for the <APPLET> in which the <PARAM> tag is contained. The <PARAM> tag is the method by which <APPLET>-specific parameters are defined for the browser. This element is needed because attributes of an <APPLET> are completely dependent on the nature and type of the applet. PARAM has two attributes that are used in a distinct pair relationship.

Attributes:

name = defines the name of the parameter attribute.

value = defines the value for that attribute.

<PRE> (End Tag Required)

<PRE> tells the browser to display the contained text in the browser exactly as written. This container of information is extremely useful when the text has been preformatted outside of the browser.

<PRE> maintains all tabs, line returns, and other text markings and displays the information in a fixed-width font, with no line spacing adjustments.

Because <PRE> is used to display already formatted text, using HTML text-formatting tags within the <PRE> container isn't recommended.

Attributes:

width = defines the maximum width of the text line for display.

<RANGE>

<RANGE> defines sections of a document as logical groups of information. The purpose of <RANGE> is to define markings that can be used for developers or other events to distinguish groups of information.

<RANGE> has two mandatory attributes of from and to. These attributes hold the information for id tags in the document that mark the beginning and end of this specified range.

These document flags, or markings, are denoted by using the spot tag in the <BODY> of a document or the name attribute of the <A> tag.

Attributes:

class = defines the class to which this range belongs. This attribute helps to distinguish the reason for marking this section of document as a specific range.

from = defines the beginning <ID> tag for this range in the document.

id = defines the <ID> tag (or location name) of this particular range element. This enables the range to become a part of another range in the document.

to = defines the ending <ID> tag for this range in the document.

<S> (End Tag Required)

<S> encloses text that's displayed in the document using the normal text format and the addition of a strike-through line running the length of the text in the container.

Attributes: none

<SAMP> (End Tag Required)

<SAMP> displays enclosed text as sample output from another source. A browser normally displays this in a fixed width typewriter-like font.

<SCRIPT> (End Tag Required)

The <SCRIPT> tag is used to enclose all scripting language statements. <SCRIPT> statements are normally used in the <HEAD> section of the document, but also can be placed in the <BODY> section.

Multiple <SCRIPT> containers are allowed in a document to enable flexibility in defining interactive documents.

Normally <SCRIPT> containers in the <HEAD> section are comprised of JavaScript functions that are called from methods within the <BODY>. <SCRIPT> containers in the <BODY> can be placed directly into the document flow and used in place of method function calls.

B

FUNDAMENTALS OF HTML

Attributes:

language = defines the type of scripting language (that is, JavaScript) in which the statements are written. Currently, if no language attribute is assigned, JavaScript is assumed to be the language.

```
<HEAD>
<SCRIPT LANGUAGE="JavaScript">
<!--
function displayinformation()
{
alert("You have written JavaScript code")
}
//-->
</SCRIPT>
</HEAD>
```

src = specifies the name of the file to locate the script statements. If script statements are not written inline, src informs the browser where the script file is located. The correct file extension for JavaScript files is .js.

```
<HEAD>
<SCRIPT SRC="seperate.js">
</SCRIPT>
</HEAD>
```

<SELECT> (End Tag Required)

The <SELECT> container tag encloses a set of <OPTION> tags (a set may in fact be only one <OPTION>) that the document displays to select from. <SELECT> contains <OPTION> tags to define the options it will include. An example of <SELECT> with options is shown in Figure B.2, with the code displayed in Listing B.5.

<SELECT> must be included inside a <FORM> container and can't be inside the <TEXTAREA> container or another <SELECT> container.

Listing B.5. Select example with multi and single.

```
<HTML>
<HEAD></HEAD>
<BODY ><FORM>
<SELECT NAME="Select Box" SIZE=5 MULTIPLE>
<OPTION>First Option
<OPTION>Second Option
<OPTION SELECTED>Default Option
<OPTION>Third Option
<OPTION DISABLED>Disabled Option
<OPTION>Last Option
</SELECT>

<SELECT NAME="Select Box" SIZE=1 >
<OPTION>First Option
<OPTION>Second Option
<OPTION SELECTED>Default Option
```

```
<OPTION>Third Option
<OPTION DISABLED>Disabled Option
<OPTION>Last Option
</SELECT>
</FORM></BODY>
</HTML>
```

If the `<IMG>` attribute for `<SELECT>` is defined, then the `<SELECT>` container no longer displays as a list of elements (as defined in the `<OPTION>` tags) but inside it is an image in the document with regions that can be selected. These regions are defined by the `shape` attribute of the `<OPTION>` elements that make up the `<SELECT>` container.

Browsers not capable of displaying the `<SELECT>` as an image (and thus the `<OPTIONS>` in that image) display the `<SELECT>` container as normal `<SELECT>` of `<OPTION>`.

Attributes:

`align` = specifies how to align the `<SELECT>` element in relation to surrounding document text.

`img` = defines the URL for the image to be displayed as the `<SELECT>` element.

`multiple` = specifies to the browser that the user may select multiple options from the list. If `multiple` isn't used, then the list is mutually exclusive.

`name` = defines the name of this object.

`size` = specifies that number of options (items) that are displayed at any one time. The normal display time is a drop-down type list or multi-select box. If `multiple` is used, then the browser defines the size attribute internally.

FIGURE B.2.

Use of `<Select>` *and* `<Option>` *with multiple and single selection options.*

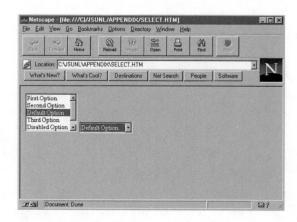

<SMALL> (End Tag Required)

The <SMALL> container tags are used to enclose text that should be displayed in a smaller font than the normal font of text of the document.

Attributes: none

<SPOT>

<SPOT> marks a spot in the document to be used as a label reference, such as with the to and from attributes of the <RANGE> element.

<SPOT> is ignored by browsers that don't support location marking in documents.

Attributes:

id = mandatory element that specifies the name value to be assigned with this marking.

<STRONG> (End Tag Required)

<STRONG> tells the browser to give a strong emphasis to this text. Normally this is displayed as a bold font, but in some browsers it may be underlined and is sometimes displayed identically to the <EM> marking.

This container also can contain other text formatting tags.

Attributes: none

<STRIKE> (End Tag Required)

See the definition of the <S> element.

Attributes: none

<STYLE>

<STYLE> defines the inline style sheet of the document to be used by the browser when displaying the document. Style sheets are used to apply default font and marking styles to certain specified tags used by the document.

Defining style sheets within the <STYLE> container has the same result as loading a separate style sheet file using the <LINK> tag.

The <STYLE> element is handy for defining consistency in the document as well as simplifying the markup in a document. Text formatting tags can be applied in the <STYLE> container to define the style of the document.

Attributes: none

<SUB> (End Tag Required)

The <SUB> container encloses text that is displayed in subscript. Subscript text is displayed in a small font and is slightly below center of the mid-line of normal text.

Attributes: none

<SUP> (End Tag Required)

The <SUP> container encloses text that will be displayed in a superscript to text surrounding it. Superscript text is displayed in a small font and is above center of the mid-line of normal text.

Attributes: none

<TABLE> (End Tag Required)

<TABLE> container tags are used to enclose the definition tags that constitute a table object in the document.

The <TABLE> element itself is basically just the holding container for the other table definition tags. No actual document can be contained within the <TABLE> element unless it's contained by the other <TABLE> definition tags, which include <CAPTION> and <TR> (which contains the <TH> and <TD> tags), an example of which is shown in Figure B.3. (Code Listing B.6 defines the HTML for Figure B.3.) Optional elements that can be contained with the <TABLE> container are <THEAD>, <TBODY>, and <TFOOT>. These optional elements give the table further containership of elements, resulting in better document structure.

B

Listing B.6. Defining a table.

```
<HTML>
<HEAD></HEAD>
<BODY>
<TABLE WIDTH=50% HEIGHT=25% BORDER=2>
<CAPTION>Time Table</CAPTION>
<THEAD>
<TR>
<TH>Train time and prices</TH>
</TR>
</THEAD>
<TBODY>
<TR ALIGN=CENTER VALIGN=MIDDLE>
<TD>10:00</TD>
<TD>20</TD>
<TD>40</TD>
<TD>60</TD>
</TR>
<TR ALIGN=CENTER VALIGN=MIDDLE>
<TD>12:00</TD>
<TD>10</TD>
<TD>30</TD>
```

continues

Listing B.6. continued

```
<TD>50</TD>
</TR>
<TRALIGN=RIGHT VALIGN=MIDDLE>
<TD>2:00</TD>
<TD>5</TD>
<TD>10</TD>
<TD>15</TD>
</TR>
</TBODY>
</TABLE>
</BODY>
</HTML>
```

FIGURE B.3.

Table frame with variable alignments.

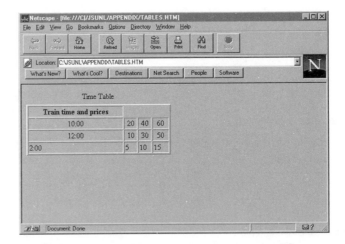

Attributes:

border = specifies the thickness of the border displayed around the table frame. A table frame border defaults to the thinnest border of 1.

Cellpadding = specifies the space that should be left between the walls of the table cell and the contents of that cell.

Cellspacing = specifies the spacing between cells in the table grid and thus the thickness of the grid lines.

<TBODY>

<TBODY> defines the body section of the table element; specifically, <TR> and <TD>. This tag is unnecessary in the absence of <THEAD> and <TFOOT> tags but provides better continuity in table definition.

Attributes: none

`<TD>`

The `<TD>`, or table data element, defines the information to be displayed in the table cell in the table frame. `<TD>` tags are contained with `<TR>` (Table row) tags. Termination of a `<TD>` element is assumed by the start of another `<TD>` element or by the `</TR>`. As a result, `</TD>` tags aren't required. Multiple `<TD>` elements can be defined with the `<TR>` container to display multiple rows in a table.

`<TD>` can contain any data type, but string or text information must first be enclosed in a `<P>` container.

Attributes:

`align` = defines the alignment of the `<TD>` element within the table cell.

`bgcolor` = defines the color of the document background behind this particular cell element in the table.

`colspan` = specifies the number of table cells in the current column that that this cell should span. Setting `Colspan="0"` sets the cell to span the entire length of the table column.

`nowrap` = specifies that the word is not allowed in the table cell.

`rowspan` = specifies the number of table cells in the current row that this cell should span. Setting `rowspan="0"` sets the cell to span the entire length of the table row.

`valign` = defines the vertical placement the `<TD>` element within the cell.

`<TEXTAREA>` (End Tag Required)

The `<TEXTAREA>` element is always contained in the `<FORM>` element of the `<BODY>`. A `<TEXTAREA>` element defines an area (or blob-type input field) where multiple lines of input can be accepted in the document. Listing B.7 shows the example of a `<TEXTAREA>`.

Like `<INPUT>` and `<SELECT>` elements, `<TEXTAREA>` is a `<FORM>` level element used to collect information from the user for processing.

Listing B.7. <Textarea> example.

```
<FORM>
<TEXTAREA NAME="BlobInfo" WRAP=VIRTUAL ROWS=10 COLS=30></TEXTAREA>
</FORM>
```

Attributes:

`align` = defines the alignment of the text area in relation to surrounding text. This attribute is available for use in this environment because browsers treat the `<TEXTAREA>` element as an `<IMG>`-type element, thus allowing alignment to surrounding text.

cols = specifies the number of document columns that the field spans in the document.

name = defines the name of the <TEXTAREA> to be used when referencing the <TEXTAREA> in from other places in the HTML document.

rows = specifies the number of document rows that the field spans in the document.

wrap = specifies that word wrap is allowed in the <TEXTAREA>.

<TFOOT> (End Tag Required)

<TFOOT> defines a footer section to a table frame, similar to the <THEAD> element. The <TFOOT> text is displayed as the last row in a table frame and continues to display even if table data rows scroll out of the viewable area.

<TFOOT> must always be defined as the final element in the <TABLE> container.

Attributes:

align = specifies the horizontal alignment of the footer text within the cell.

valign = specifies the vertical alignment of the footer text within the cell.

<TH> (End Tag Required)

The <TH> element defines the header content for the table element. The content of this tag can be any acceptable HTML content, but straight text must first be enclosed in a text formatting tag container.

Attributes:

align = defines the alignment of the <TD> element within the table cell.

bgcolor = defines the color of the document background behind this particular cell element in the table.

Colspan = specifies the number of table cells in the current column that this cell should span. Setting Colspan="0" defines the cell to span the entire length of the table column.

nowrap = specifies that the word isn't allowed in the table cell.

rowspan = specifies the number of table cells in the current row that this cell should span. Setting rowspan="0" defines the cell to span the entire length of the table row.

valign = defines the vertical placement the <TD> element within the cell.

<THEAD>

The <THEAD> element is used to provide more flexibility to the <TH> tag, by allowing multiple <TH> tags to be enclosed in it.

<THEAD> also provides the ability to keep the table header consistent if the table scrolls.

<THEAD> elements (if implemented) are required to be the initial element of the <TABLE> container. <THEAD> must always precede the <TFOOT> element.

Attributes:

align = specifies the horizontal alignment of the footer text within the cell.

valign = specifies the vertical alignment of the footer text within the cell.

<TITLE>

<TITLE> is a container tag in the <HEAD> section, and defines the text of the title for the document that displays in the title bar of the browser. Every document must have one and only one title element.

Because <TITLE> isn't displayed in the document itself, it can't include any other HTML formatting or reference tags.

<TITLE> elements are important to define correctly because they aren't solely used to display as document titles in the browser title bar. The <TITLE> text also is the link name saved when a user creates an HTML bookmark to your page. Additionally, <TITLE> is used as search criteria when your document is indexed. So, as a rule of thumb, title your documents accurately—it's important!

Attributes: none

<TR>

<TR> elements are used to contain the row attributes for tables. <TR> doesn't contain any content itself, containing instead the <TH> and <TR> elements that define the table cells.

Attributes:

align = specifies the horizontal alignment of the footer text within the cell.

valign = specifies the vertical alignment of the footer text within the cell.

<TT> (End Tag Required)

The <TT> container element encloses text that's displayed in teletype (or fixed-width typewriter-like) text format.

Attributes: none

<U> (End Tag Required)

The <U> element encloses text that is displayed underlined by the browser.

Attributes: none

<UL> (End Tag Required)

The <UL> container element, a listing example of which is shown in Listing B.8, is used to define an unordered list. Unordered lists aren't marked by numbers or sequenced letters, and are marked instead with bullets, or depending on your browser, another small symbol.

Listing B.8. Unordered list example.

```
<UL TYPE=CIRCLE>
<LI>Circle
<LI>Square
<LI>Rectangle
<LI>Polygon
<LI>Triangle
</UL>
```

Items of the UL are defined by the LI tags enclosed in this container. Again, you should probably keep the list text concise so as not to lose the purpose of HTML lists.

Attributes:

compact = tells the browser to display the list in a more compact manner than it would with the normal-sized font.

dingbat = defines an alternate entity to be used as the symbol preceding the list.

plain = specifies that the list should be displayed plain and that no bullet should be used.

src = specifies the URL file to be used as the image for the bullet.

type = defines the type of bullet to use as a symbol preceding the list items. Type options are square (displays a small square), circle (displays a small open circle), and disc (displays a small closed circle).

wrap = defines a list that can wrap either vertically or horizontally, giving the ability to define multi-column lists.

<VAR> (End Tag Required)

The <VAR> element container defines the enclosed text as being a variable name (as in code) and thus the browser should display in the font that the browser normally used for variable references. The normal default is italicized text.

Attributes: none

<WBR>

The <WBR> element, or word break, specifies to the browser that a word break is allowable if one is needed.

<WBR> is used in conjunction with the <NBR> element to define for the browser how to break up text in a document when no line breaks are called for.

Attributes: none

Comparing JavaScript with Microsoft's VBScript

by Richard Wagner

IN THIS APPENDIX

JavaScript is not the lone Web scripting language available. The server side has languages such as PERL that have been around for many years. However, scripting on the client side is a new phenomenon. This arena has two players at the moment—JavaScript and VBScript—that are contending to become the scripting language standard for the Web. Although that battle will rage for some time, it is helpful to look at VBScript and compare its strengths and weaknesses with JavaScript. In this appendix, I discuss what VBScript is, contrast it with JavaScript, and provide a sample VBScript application for you to examine.

> **NOTE**
>
> Look for the latest VBScript information online on Microsoft's site at `http://www.`
> `microsoft.com /vbscript/`.

What Is VBScript?

VBScript is a Web scripting language developed by Microsoft that directly parallels JavaScript. VBScript's legacy is much different from that of JavaScript. Whereas JavaScript was essentially created from scratch loosely based on C++ and Java, VBScript is a part of the Visual Basic family of languages, as shown in Figure C.1. Other family members include Visual Basic—the ubiquitous Windows programming language—and Visual Basic for Applications—a macro language for Microsoft Office and other applications. If you have ever developed software using Visual Basic, you will be able to pick up VBScript much more quickly than you would otherwise.

FIGURE C.1.
Visual Basic family of languages.

Visual Basic	Visual Basic for Applications	VBScript Script
General Windows programs. Client/server database applications.	Scripting language for Microsoft Office and other Windows applications.	Scripting language for the World Wide Web.

If you have digested this book and have a solid understanding of JavaScript, you can think of VBScript as "JavaScript in a Visual Basic wrapper." In other words, you can apply what you've already learned about the JavaScript object model and coding techniques to begin to develop VBScript code in a rather rapid time frame.

Comparing and Contrasting JavaScript and VBScript

Although JavaScript and VBScript have many similarities, they also have several differences. This section outlines these similarities and differences.

Both Are Embedded HTML Languages

Like JavaScript, VBScript is a scripting language embedded in an HTML file. VBScript uses the <SCRIPT> tag in the same way as JavaScript, using "VBScript" or simply "VBS" as the language parameter. For example, the following script shows an alert dialog box when the page is loaded:

```
<HTML>
<HEAD>
<SCRIPT LANGUAGE = "VBS">

    alert("Is this JavaScript or VBScript?")

</SCRIPT>
</HEAD>
</HTML>
```

Interestingly, for an example as basic as an alert dialog box, the syntax of the two languages is the same. If you changed the LANGUAGE parameter to "JavaScript", the same process would be performed.

Both Have an Identical Object Model

Perhaps the single most important factor when comparing JavaScript and VBScript is that they use the same basic object hierarchy. To a Web developer who might need to use both languages on occasion, this is a major coup; it is much easier to deal with language syntax differences than it is to work with two completely different programming paradigms. If you ever need to convert JavaScript code to VBScript or vice versa, your conversion will typically be a 1:1 process.

C

JAVASCRIPT AND MICROSOFT'S VBSCRIPT

NOTE

You can find an excellent resource on the Microsoft Internet Explorer scripting object model on Microsoft's site at http://www.microsoft.com/intdev/sdk/docs/local000.htm. This object model is essentially the same (but not necessarily) as Netscape's JavaScript object model.

Not only is the language object model identical for both scripting languages, but the way in which you work with HTML objects is the same as well. Just as JavaScript can react to events triggered by an event handler of an HTML object, so can VBScript. For example, in the following JavaScript code sample, the text entered in the myText field is converted to uppercase when the user clicks the Convert button:

```
<HTML>
<HEAD>
<SCRIPT LANGUAGE = "JavaScript">
<!--
    function convertText() {
       document.SampleForm.myText.value = document.
       ➥SampleForm.myText.value.toUpperCase()
    }
-->
</SCRIPT>
</HEAD>

<BODY>
<FORM Name="SampleForm">
<INPUT Type=text Name="myText" </INPUT>
<INPUT Type="button" Value="Convert" OnClick="convertText()"</INPUT>
</FORM>
</BODY>
</HTML>
```

If you performed the same process using VBScript, the code would resemble the following:

```
<HTML>
<HEAD>
<SCRIPT LANGUAGE = "VBS">
<!--
    Sub convertText()
       document.SampleForm.myText.value =
       ➥UCase(document.SampleForm.myText.value)
    End Sub
-->
</SCRIPT>
</HEAD>

<BODY>
<H1></H1>
<FORM Name="SampleForm">
<INPUT Type=text Name="myText" </INPUT>
<INPUT Type="button" Value="Convert" OnClick="convertText()"</INPUT>
</FORM>
</BODY>
</HTML>
```

JavaScript Currently Has Wider Industry Support

VBScript's principle asset is its Visual Basic legacy. VBScript provides the millions of Visual Basic programmers an easy segue to Web scripting. However, its biggest liability is that it is currently supported in a single Web browser—Microsoft Internet Explorer 3.0—and in two operating environments—Windows and Macintosh. Microsoft is working with third-party vendors to provide UNIX support, but at the time of writing, this effort has not resulted in a release.

JavaScript, on the other hand, is supported in both Netscape Navigator and Microsoft Internet Explorer and is compatible with any operating environment under which those browsers run. Additionally, JavaScript has been selected by many vendors—such as Borland—as their scripting language in forthcoming Web products. As a result, JavaScript currently has the edge in industry support, but with the muscle of Microsoft behind it, do not count VBScript out.

VBScript Has More Complex Data Types

On the surface, it looks like VBScript is very limited in its capability to work with data types. That is because VBScript has only one data type, `variant`. However, on closer inspection, you will notice that VBScript actually has more power in handling data types than JavaScript does. The `variant` type contains information about the value it is working with at the time and can determine the data type it is being asked to handle in a variety of situations. In other words, if you are using a `variant` variable in the context of a string:

```
myVar = "String1" + "String2"
```

VBScript will treat `myVar` as a string value. In the same way, if you are working with numbers:

```
myVar = 1 + 2
```

VBScript will treat the variable as a numeric value.

Strings and numbers are treated as subtypes within the `variant` type. Table C.1 shows VBScript's numerous subtypes.

Table C.1. Subtypes of VBScript's `variant` type.

Subtype	Description
String	A variable-length string (maximum length of some 2 billion characters).
Byte	Integer between 0 and 255.
Integer	Integer between -32,768 and 32,767.
Long	Integer between -2,147,483,648 and 2,147,483,647.
Single	Single-precision, floating-point number between -3.402823E38 and -1.401298E-45 for negative values and between 1.401298E-45 and 3.402823E38 for positive values.

continues

Table C.1. continued

Subtype	Description
Double	Double-precision, floating-point number between -1.79769313486232E308 and -4.94065645841247E-324 for negative values and between 4.94065645841247E-324 and 1.79769313486232E308 for positive values.
Date (Time)	Number that represents a date between 1/1/100 and 12/31/9999.
Boolean	Logical value (True or False).
Empty	Uninitialized variable. Value is 0 for numeric variables or an empty string ("") for string variables.
Null	Variant contains no valid data (different from Empty.)
Object	ActiveX object.
Error	VBScript error number.

VBScript has a set of conversion functions that go beyond JavaScript's parseFloat and parseInt built-in methods.

NOTE

VBScript is a loosely typed language like JavaScript.

VBScript and JavaScript Offer Varied Strengths

In addition to the data type issue, both VBScript and JavaScript have different strengths and weaknesses from a programming language standpoint.

VBScript is stronger than JavaScript in the following areas:

- **Error handling**. VBScript has greater error-handling capabilities than JavaScript. It has an Err object to capture information about a runtime error as well as an OnError control structure to maintain error-handling routines in your code.

- **Looping**. Both VBScript and JavaScript have a while looping capability, which will repeat a code block while a condition is true. However, VBScript adds a additional capability with its Do..Loop, which repeats a code block while or until a condition is true. For example, the following loop executes until the i variable is equal to 100:

```
<SCRIPT LANGUAGE = "VBS">

    Dim i
    i = 0
    Do Until i = 100
        document.write("I will not chew gum.<p>")
        i = i + 1
    Loop

</SCRIPT>
```

■ **Message boxes**. VBScript's MsgBox (see Figure C.2) and InputBox (see Figure C.3) are similar to alert() and prompt(), respectively, but provide greater customization capabilities, such as title and icon settings, and do not have the same annoying "JavaScript Alert" or "JavaScript Prompt" flags appearing in them.

FIGURE C.2.

MsgBox *message box.*

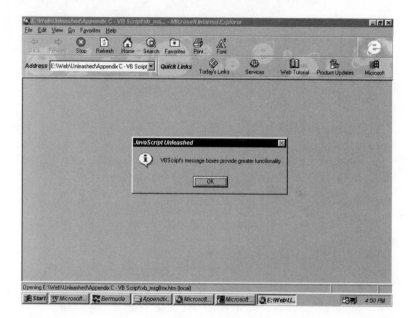

Figure C.3.

InputBox.

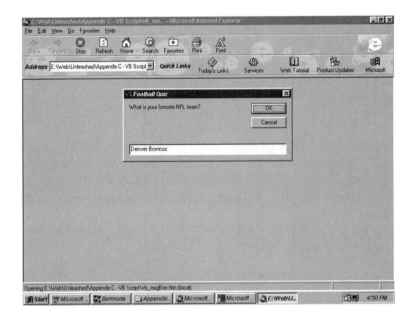

■ **Enhanced <SCRIPT> tag**. VBScript expands the <SCRIPT> tag to enable you to define a script to be directed to a specific object using the FOR parameter or to handle a specific event from this object using the EVENT parameter. For example, the following code defines the event handler for the OkButton object:

```
<form name="TestForm">
    <input type="button" name="OkButton" value="OK">
    <SCRIPT FOR="OkButton" EVENT="onClick" LANGUAGE="VBS">
        msgBox("Thanks for your input.")
    </SCRIPT>
```

JavaScript is stronger than VBScript in the following areas:

■ **Custom objects**. Currently, VBScript has no capability to create custom objects, something that is fundamental to the JavaScript language. This is perhaps VBScript's greatest weakness and forces you to use procedural-style programming methodologies instead of object-oriented ones.

■ **Object referencing**. JavaScript has some powerful keywords to reference objects, such as the this, with, and for..in constructs. VBScript does not have functional equivalents to these.

■ **Math**. Although VBScript allows you to handle commonly used math functions, such as Tan and Cos, JavaScript has a set of math-related methods for even more complex mathematical equations.

VBScript Has Different Procedure Types

VBScript has two different types of procedures: subroutines and functions. A subroutine—denoted using `Sub..End Sub`—is a procedure that does not return a value, whereas a function—denoted with `Function..End Function`—is a procedure that does return a value. For example, the following subroutine, when called, assigns the string literal `"See Spot Run"` to the `TextField` text object but does not return a value to the calling procedure:

```
<SCRIPT LANGUAGE = "VBS">
    Sub convertText()
        document.MyForm.TextField.value = "See Spot Run."
    End Sub
</SCRIPT>
```

For an example of a VBScript function, look at the following code sample. The `showText()` subroutine calls the `getText()` function, which returns the value of the `TextField` text object:

```
<SCRIPT LANGUAGE = "VBS">

    Function getText()
        getText = document.MyForm.TextField.value
    End Function

    Sub showText()
        alert(getText())
    EndSub

</SCRIPT>
```

In contrast, JavaScript has a single procedure type—`method` (also called `function`)—that uses the `function` keyword regardless of whether a value is returned to the calling procedure.

Programming in VBScript

To give you a glimpse of programming in VBScript, I will show you a rudimentary example. In the following sample code, VBScript multiplies two values entered by the user and displays the result in an alert message box:

```
<html>
<head>
<title>Wizard</title>
<SCRIPT LANGUAGE="VBS">
    Sub calculateValues()
        Dim num1, num2, greaterNum, totalVal
        num1 = document.form1.Number1.value
        num2 = document.form1.Number2.value

        totalVal = num1*num2
        alert(totalVal)
    End Sub
</SCRIPT>
</head>
```

```
<h1>Stump the Wizard</font></h1>
<p>Without connecting to a backend server or using a Java applet,
➥the Browser Wizard will multiply the two numbers...</p>

<form name="form1" method="POST">
<pre>First Number:  <input type=text size=5 maxlength=5 name="Number1"></pre>
<pre>Second Number: <input type=text size=5 maxlength=5 name="Number2"></pre>
<p><input type=button name="WizButton" value="Multiply"
➥onClick="calculateValues()"></p>
</form>
</body>
</html>
```

Figure C.4 shows the result.

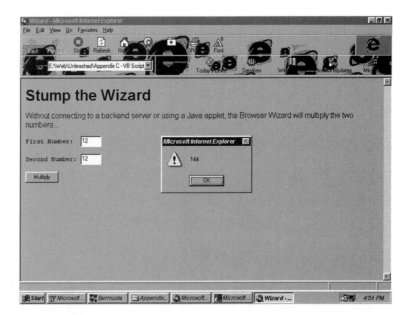

The equivalent JavaScript code is shown here to provide a source of comparison:

```
<html>
<head>
<title>Wizard</title>
<SCRIPT LANGUAGE="JavaScript">

    function calculateValues() {
        num1 = parseFloat(document.forms[0].Number1.value)
        num2 = parseFloat(document.forms[0].Number2.value)
        result = num1 * num2
        alert(result);
    }

</SCRIPT>
</head>
```

```
<body>
<h1>Stump the Wizard</h1>
<p>Without connecting to a backend server or using a Java applet, the Browser
➥Wizard will multiply the two numbers..</p>

<form name="form1" method="POST">

<pre>First Number:  <input type=text size=5 maxlength=5 name="Number1"></pre>
<pre>Second Number: <input type=text size=5 maxlength=5 name="Number2"></pre>
<p><input type=button name="WizButton" value="Multiply"
➥onClick="calculateValues()"></p>
</form>
</body>
</html>
```

Summary

This appendix looked at VBScript and compared its similarities and differences with JavaScript. It also looked at the basics of developing client-side scripts using VBScript.

Microsoft provides a capable alternative to JavaScript in VBScript. If you are accustomed to programming in Visual Basic and your users will primarily use Microsoft Internet Explorer, then VBScript may be the best choice for a scripting language for Web development. Until VBScript gains greater support throughout the industry, it will remain a language that is limited to specific contexts.

JavaScript Resources on the Internet

by Richard Wagner

IN THIS APPENDIX

Because JavaScript is a Web-based technology, I am sure it comes as no surprise that a wealth of information on JavaScript is available on the Internet. This appendix outlines the resources that you will find helpful as you develop JavaScript applications. I include information on the Web, Usenet newsgroups, CompuServe, and Listserv mailing lists.

World Wide Web

The Web offers a plethora of JavaScript sites. Sifting through the bounty, I list here some of the best JavaScript pages I've seen.

> **NOTE**
>
> Obviously, due to the nature of the Web, links change often. Regardless, some of these sites contain maintained JavaScript indexes, so these locations should get you headed in the right direction for JavaScript application development.

Netscape

URL: `http://home.netscape.com/`

Best of Site: Information on future releases of JavaScript, official JavaScript Authoring Guide.

Because Netscape developed the JavaScript language, you would expect its home page to be filled with JavaScript information. The Netscape site is an excellent resource for JavaScript language documentation and other basic JavaScript information. It is also the best place to turn for obtaining information on future versions of JavaScript. At the time of writing, its weak point lies in navigation clues; it is difficult to actually find the JavaScript information on the site even when you know what you are looking for.

For the JavaScript Authoring Guide, visit `http://home.netscape.com/eng/mozilla/3.0/handbook/javascript/index.html`.

> **TIP**
>
> As future betas of Netscape Navigator become available, be sure to check the developer information related to the beta. You will often find information on the latest JavaScript features covered there.

Microsoft

URL: `http://www.microsoft.com/`

Best of Site: ActiveX controls, information on Microsoft's implementation of JavaScript.

Microsoft has a great deal of JavaScript and Web scripting information available on its Web site for developers. You can find details about Microsoft Internet Explorer's scripting object model, VBScript, ActiveX controls, and much more. You will also find the ActiveX Control Pad, which allows you to work with ActiveX controls and JavaScript.

> **TIP**
>
> Watch the Microsoft site for free Web tools to download. Because Microsoft is committed to gaining market share in the Web industry, it is giving away a great deal of its Internet software. Look for the ActiveX Control Pad and other Web developer tools.

JavaScript Explorer Page

URL: `http://www.acadians.com/javascript/jshome.htm`

Best of Site: Business-oriented JavaScript applications, JavaScript editor.

The Acadia Software JavaScript Page contains a wealth of information on JavaScript including examples from *JavaScript Unleashed*, sample business JavaScript applications, JavaScript tools, and an extensive list of JavaScript links.

> **TIP**
>
> Several of the authors of this book are part of Acadia Software. We invite you to visit us on our Web site and hope you find the JavaScript page useful.

Gamelan

URL: `http://www.gamelan.com/`

Best of Site: JavaScript samples, links.

Known for hosting one of the best sites for Java resources, Gamelan also has a vast library of JavaScript information, samples, and tools available.

JavaScript Index

URL: `http://www.c2.org/~andreww/javascript/`

Best of Site: JavaScript samples, programming ideas.

The JavaScript Index is a solid resource for JavaScript applets, programming techniques, and links to examples of JavaScript in action on the Web.

hIdaho Design

URL: `http://www.hidaho.com`

Best of Site: ColorCenter (a JavaScript application), hIdaho Frameset.

hIdaho Design is the home of two well-known resources in the JavaScript community. First, the ColorCenter is one of the best examples of the power of JavaScript as an application development programming language. Second, the hIdaho Frameset is a library of JavaScript functions that simplify the development of multiframe applications.

Live Software's JavaScript Resource Center

URL: `http://jrc.livesoftware.com/`

Best of Site: JavaScript applet samples.

This site contains some good JavaScript examples from Sams.net's *Java Unleashed* book as well as some links to other JavaScript sites.

Netscape World

URL: `http://www.netscapeworld.com/`

Best of Site: Good example of JavaScript-enabled frames.

Netscape World is an online electronic magazine (eZine) that focuses on the Netscape software product line. The site effectively uses JavaScript as a presentation tool.

Web Informant

URL: `http://www.informant.com/`

Best of Site: Articles and downloads from the *Web Informant* magazine.

Web Informant is a new periodical devoted to Web developers. You can find information on JavaScript, Java, ActiveX, and other Web technologies covered in its pages. *Web Informant* is published by Informant Communications Group, which also publishes *Delphi Informant, Oracle Informant,* and *Web Publisher.*

JavaWorld

URL: `http://www.javaworld.com/`

Best of Site: Online articles on JavaScript.

JavaWorld is a periodical devoted to Java programming issues. It also includes a regular technical column on JavaScript. You can read past issues on this site. *JavaWorld* is published by IDG Communications, which publishes *PC World* and *ComputerWorld.*

Borland International

URL: `http://www.borland.com`

Best of Site: IntraBuilder and Latte support and documentation.

Borland is the developer of IntraBuilder, a Web database development tool that uses JavaScript as its native programming language. The company also is the developer of Latte, a state-of-the-art visual Java development environment.

Macmillan Publishing Home Page

URL: `http://www.mcp.com/`

Best of Site: Information on JavaScript books, sample chapters.

The Macmillan Computer Publishing (MCP) site is the home of Sams.net and other MCP imprints, such as Que and New Riders. It is a good resource to find out about upcoming JavaScript and related books. The site often has sample chapters from JavaScript books for you to peruse.

Danny Goodman's JavaScript Pages

URL: `http://www.dannyg.com/javascript`

Best of site: String JavaScript resource with both beginning and advanced topics.

Presented by author Danny Goodman, this site provides an excellent JavaScript resource for beginner JavaScript developers, particularly if you come from an HTML background. The site contains advanced examples and techniques as well.

Ask the JavaScript Pro

URL: `http://www.inquiry.com/techtips/js_pro/`

Best of Site: Tips and techniques.

This site, presented by inquiry.com, provides tips and techniques on using JavaScript.

JavaScript Tip of the Week

URL: `http://www.gis.net/~carter/therest/tip_week.html`

Best of Site: Weekly tips.

As its name suggests, you can stop at this site weekly for a new JavaScript tip.

Gordon McComb's JavaScript Pages

URL: `http://gmccomb.com/javascript/`

Best of site: JavaScript experiments.

This JavaScript resource presented by author Gordon McComb provides JavaScript sample code and experiments.

JavaScript Voodoo Page

URL: `http://rummelplatz.uni-mannheim.de/~skoch/js/script.htm`

Best of Site: Introduction to JavaScript.

This site provides a good tutorial for learning JavaScript.

JavaScript FAQ

URL: `http://www.freqgrafx.com/411/jsfaq.html`

Best of Site: "Just the facts."

This site offers a list of frequently asked questions (FAQ) on JavaScript.

Yahoo!'s JavaScript Page

URL: `http://www.yahoo.com/Computers_and_Internet/Languages/JavaScript/`

Best of Site: Hey, it's Yahoo!

Yahoo!, one of the best known catalogued indexes on the Web, has a section on JavaScript links. It is well worth a visit.

Sun Microsystems

URL: `http://java.sun.com`

Best of Site: Home of Java.

For the latest news and available betas of Java, visit Java's home at Sun Microsystems.

Usenet Newsgroups

A growing number of Usenet newsgroups are devoted to JavaScript and related technologies.

- `comp.lang.javascript`

  This newsgroup focuses on JavaScript development.

- `news.livesoftware.com/livesoftware.javascript.developer`

  Live Software presents this second newsgroup that focuses on JavaScript development.

- `news.livesoftware.com/livesoftware.javascript.examples`

  This JavaScript newsgroup is intended to highlight JavaScript sample applications, applets, or code.

- `comp.lang.java`

  This newsgroup is devoted to Java programming techniques. You can also find other newsgroups in the comp.lang.java hierarchy, most notably comp.lang.java.announce for product release announcements, libraries, and so on.

CompuServe

Although CompuServe is one of the best resources for standard programming languages, it offers only a minor amount of information on JavaScript. The Java Forum has a section devoted to JavaScript. From my experience, the message board traffic has been relatively light.

Listserv Mailing Lists

You might want to join a Listserv mailing list about JavaScript and related information; the following sections outline a couple of your choices.

- `javascript-list@inquiry.com`

  This mailing list features a wide range of JavaScript issues—some beginner, some advanced. To subscribe, send a message to

      listmaster@inquiry.com

  In the text body of your message, enter the following:

      subscribe javascript *firstname lastname*

D

JAVASCRIPT RESOURCES ON THE INTERNET

■ java@borland.com

This mailing list features general information on Java as well as Borland's Java product Latte. It might also contain information on Intra, Borland's JavaScript-based development tool. To subscribe, send a message to

```
listserv@borland.com
```

In the text body of your message, enter the following:

```
subscribe java firstname lastname
```

I

INDEX

Symbols

A

E

T

X-Y-Z

Laura Lemay's Web Workshop: JavaScript

Laura Lemay

Readers will explore various aspects of Web publishing—whether CGI scripting and interactivity, graphics design, or Netscape Gold—in greater depth than the Teach Yourself books.

CD-ROM includes the complete book in HTML format, publishing tools, templates, graphics, backgrounds, and more.

Provides a clear, hands-on guide to creating sophisticated Web pages.

Covers CGI.

Price: $39.99 USA/$56.95 CDN   User Level: Casual–Accomplished
ISBN: 1-57521-141-6   400 pages   7 3/8×9 1/8   09/01/96

Communications/Online–Internet

Teach Yourself JavaScript in a Week, Second Edition

Arman Danesh

Teach Yourself JavaScript in a Week, Second Edition is a new edition of the bestselling JavaScript tutorial. It has been revised and updated for the latest version of JavaScript from Netscape and includes detailed coverage of new features such as how to work with Java applets with LiveConnect, writing JavaScript for Microsoft's Internet Explorer, and more!

CD-ROM includes full version of Netscape Navigator Gold, additional tools, and ready-to-use sample scripts.

Includes in-depth instructions on how to use Netscape Navigator Gold.

Learn the new and advanced features of JavaScript.

Price: $39.99 USA/$56.95 CDN   User Level: Beginning–Intermediate
ISBN: 1-57521-195-5   600 pages   7 3/8×9 1/8   11/01/96

Internet/Programming

Java Professional Developer's Reference

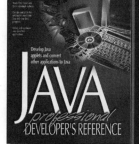

Mike Cohn, et al.

This is the informational, resource-packed development package for professional developers. It explains the components of the Java Development Kit (JDK) and the Java programming language. Everything needed to program Java is included within this comprehensive reference, making it the tool developers will turn to over and over again for timely, accurate information on Java and the JDK.

CD-ROM contains source code from the book and powerful utilities.

Includes tips and tricks for getting the most from Java and your Java programs.

Contains complete descriptions of all the package classes and their individual methods.

Price: $69.99 USA/$98.95 CDN   User Level: Accomplished–Expert
ISBN: 1-57521-129-7   1,400 pages   7 3/8×9 1/8   10/01/96

Internet/Programming

Java Unleashed

Michael Morrison, et al.

Java Unleashed is the ultimate guide to the year's hottest new Internet technologies, the Java language. and the HotJava browser from Sun Microsystems. Java Unleashed is a complete programmer's reference and guide to the hundreds of exciting ways Java is being used to add interactivity to the World Wide Web.

Includes a helpful and informative CD-ROM.

Describes how to use Java to add interactivity to Web presentations.

Shows readers how Java and HotJava are being used across the Internet.

Price: $49.99 USA/$67.99 CDN   User Level: Casual–Accomplished–Expert
ISBN: 1-57521-049-5   1,008 pages   7 3/8×9 1/8   03/01/96

Internet/Programming

Teach Yourself Java in 21 Days

Laura Lemay, et al.

Introducing the first, best, and most detailed guide to developing applications with the hot new Java language from Sun Microsystems.

CD-ROM includes the Java Developer's Kit.

Provides detailed coverage of the hottest new technology on the World Wide Web.

Shows readers how to develop applications using the Java language.

Includes coverage of browsing Java applications with Netscape and other popular Web browsers.

Price: $39.99 USA/$53.99 CDN   User Level: Casual–Accomplished–Expert
ISBN: 1-57521-030-4   500 pages   7 3/8×9 1/8   01/01/96

Internet/Programming

Teach Yourself Web Publishing with HTML 3.2 in 14 Days, Professional Reference Edition

Laura Lemay

This is the updated edition of Lemay's previous bestseller, *Teach Yourself Web Publishing with HTML in 14 Days, Premier Edition.* In it readers will find all the advanced topics and updates including adding audio, video, and animation to Web pages.

CD-ROM included.

Explores the use of CGI scripts, tables, HTML 3.0, Netscape and Internet Explorer extensions, Java applets and JavaScript, and VRML.

Covers HTML 3.0

Price: $59.99 USA/$81.95 CDN   User Level: New–Casual–Accomplished
ISBN: 1-57521-096-7   1,104 pages   7 3/8×9 1/8   06/01/96

Internet/Web Publishing

Presenting ActiveX

Warren Ernst and John J. Kottler

Presenting Active X provides a hands-on glimpse of Microsoft's new ActiveX technologies and describes the roles existing Microsoft technologies play in this new architecture.

CD-ROM contains source code from the book and powerful ActiveX utilities.

Teaches how ActiveX will let Web publishers and developers add "active" elements to their Web pages and Web applications.

Teaches how to use existing technologies to start creating ActiveX-powered Web pages today.

Price: $29.99 USA/$42.95 CDN   User Level: Casual–Accomplished
ISBN: 1-57521-156-4   336 pages   7 3/8×9 1/8   07/01/96

Internet/Programming

Web Programming with Java

Harris & Jones

This book gets readers on the road to developing robust, real-world Java applications. Various cutting-edge applications are presented, allowing the reader to quickly learn all aspects of programming Java for the Internet.

CD-ROM contains source code and powerful utilities.

Readers will be able to create live, interactive Web pages.

Price: $39.99 USA/$56.95 CDN   User Level: Accomplished–Expert
ISBN: 1-57521-113-0   500 pages   7 3/8×9 1/8   09/01/96

Internet/Programming

Add to Your Sams.net Library Today
with the Best Books for Internet Technologies

ISBN	Quantity	Description of Item	Unit Cost	Total Cost
1-57521-141-6		Laura Lemay's Web Workshop: JavaScript (Book/CD-ROM)	$39.99	
1-57521-195-5		Teach Yourself JavaScript in a Week, Second Edition (Book/CD-ROM)	$39.99	
1-57521-129-7		Java Developer's Reference (Book/CD-ROM)	$69.99	
1-57521-049-5		Java Unleashed (Book/CD-ROM)	$49.99	
1-57521-030-4		Teach Yourself Java in 21 Days (Book/CD-ROM)	$39.99	
1-57521-096-7		Teach Yourself Web Publishing with HTML 3.2 in 14 Days, Professional Reference Edition (Book/CD-ROM)	$59.99	
1-57521-156-4		Presenting ActiveX (Book/CD-ROM)	$29.99	
1-57521-113-0		Web Programming with Java (Book/CD-ROM)	$39.99	
		Shipping and Handling: See information below.		
		TOTAL		

Shipping and Handling: $4.00 for the first book, and $1.75 for each additional book. If you need to have it NOW, we can ship product to you in 24 hours for an additional charge of approximately $18.00, and you will receive your item overnight or in two days. Overseas shipping and handling adds $2.00. Prices subject to change. Call between 9:00 a.m. and 5:00 p.m. EST for availability and pricing information on latest editions.

201 W. 103rd Street, Indianapolis, Indiana 46290

1-800-428-5331 — Orders   1-800-835-3202 — FAX   1-800-858-7674 — Customer Service

Book ISBN 1-57521-118-1

What's on the Disc

The companion CD-ROM contains the Java™ Developers Kit from Sun Microsystems, many useful third-party tools and utilities, plus the source code and Java examples from the book.

Windows 95 Installation Instructions

1. Insert the CD-ROM disc into your CD-ROM drive.
2. From the Windows 95 desktop, double-click the My Computer icon.
3. Double-click the icon representing your CD-ROM drive.
4. Double-click the icon titled CDSETUP.EXE to run the installation program.
5. Installation creates a program group named JavaScript Unleashed. This group contains icons to browse the CD-ROM.

NOTE

If Windows 95 is installed on your computer and you have the AutoPlay feature enabled, the CDSETUP.EXE program starts automatically whenever you insert the disc into your CD-ROM drive.

Windows NT Installation Instructions

1. Insert the CD-ROM disc into your CD-ROM drive.

2. From File Manager or Program Manager, choose Run from the File menu.
3. Type drive\CDSETUP.EXE and press Enter, where drive corresponds to the drive letter of your CD-ROM. For example, if your CD-ROM is drive D:, type D:\CDSETUP.EXE and press Enter.

   Installation creates a program group named JavaScript Unleashed. This group contains icons to browse the CD-ROM.

Macintosh Installation Instructions

1. Insert the CD-ROM disc into your CD-ROM drive.
2. When an icon for the CD appears on your desktop, open the disc by double-clicking its icon.
3. Double-click the icon named Guide to the CD-ROM and follow the directions.

Technical Support from Macmillan

We can't help you with Windows or Macintosh problems, or software from third parties, but we can assist you if a problem arises with the CD-ROM itself.

E-mail support: support@mcp.com.

CompuServe: Type GO SAMS to reach the Macmillan Computer Publishing forum. Leave us a message, addressed to SYSOP. If you want the message to be private, address it to *SYSOP.

Telephone: (317) 581-3833

Fax: (317) 581-4773

Mail: Macmillan Computer Publishing
Attention: Support Department
201 West 103rd Street
Indianapolis, IN 46290-1093

Here's how to reach us on the Internet:

World Wide Web (The Macmillan Information SuperLibrary):
http://www.mcp.com/samsnet